THE PLAYS OF
GEORGE CHAPMAN

THE COMEDIES
VOLUME 2

THE PLAYS OF

GEORGE CHAPMAN

EDITED WITH INTRODUCTIONS
AND NOTES BY

THOMAS MARC PARROTT, Ph. D.

Professor of English Literature at Princeton University

THE COMEDIES
VOLUME 2

NEW YORK

RUSSELL & RUSSELL · INC

1961

PUBLISHED 1961 BY RUSSELL & RUSSELL, INC.
BY ARRANGEMENT WITH ROUTLEDGE & KEGAN PAUL LTD.

L. C. CATALOG CARD NO.: 61-13787

PRINTED IN THE UNITED STATES OF AMERICA

THE MASQUE OF THE MIDDLE TEMPLE AND LINCOLN'S INN

THE MOST NOBLE AND CONSTANT COMBINER OF HONOUR AND VIRTUE,
SIR EDWARD PHILIPS, KNIGHT,
MASTER OF THE ROLLS

THIS noble and magnificent performance, renewing the ancient spirit and honour of the Inns of Court, being especially furthered and followed by your most laborious and honoured endeavours (for his Majesty's service, and honour of the all-grace-deserving nuptials of the thrice gracious Princess Elizabeth, his Highness' daughter) deserves especially to be in this sort consecrate to your worthy memory and honour. Honour having never her fair hand more freely and nobly given to Riches (being a fit particle of this invention) than by yours at this nuptial solemnity. To which assisted and memorable ceremony the joined hand and industry of the worthily honoured Knight, Sir H. Hobart, his Majesty's Attorney General, deserving in good part a joint memory with yours, I have submitted it freely to his noble acceptance. The poor pains I added to this royal service being wholly chosen and commanded by your most constant and free favour, I hope will now appear nothing neglective of their expected duties. Hearty will and care enough, I am assured, was employed in me, and the only ingenuous will being first and principal step to virtue, I beseech you let it stand for the performing virtue itself. In which addition of your ever-honoured favours you shall ever bind all my future service to your most wished commandment.

God send you long health, and your virtues will indue you with honour enough,

By your free merits' ever-vowed honourer,

and most unfeignedly affectionate observant,

GEO. CHAPMAN.

The Masque of the Gentlemen of the two combined houses, or Inns of Court, the Middle Temple and Lincoln's Inn.

At the house of the most worthily honoured preferrer and gracer of all honourable actions and virtues, Sir Edward Philips, Knight, Master of the Rolls, all the performers and their assistants made their rendezvous, prepared to their performance, and thus set forth.

Fifty gentlemen, richly attired, and as gallantly mounted, with footmen particularly attending, made the noble vantguard of these nuptial forces. Next (a fit distance observed between them) marched a mock-masque of baboons, attired like fantastical travellers in Neapolitan suits and great ruffs, all horsed with asses and dwarf palfreys, with yellow foot-cloths, and casting cockle-demois about, in courtesy, by way of largess ; torches borne on either hand of them, lighting their state as ridiculously as the rest nobly. After them were sorted two cars triumphal, adorned with great mask-heads, festoons, scrolls, and antic leaves, every part inriched with silver and gold. These were through-varied with different invention, and in them advanced the choice musicians of our kingdom, six in each, attired like Virginian priests, by whom the sun is there adored, and therefore called the Phœbades. Their robes were tucked up before ; strange hoods of feathers and scallops about their necks, and on their heads turbans, stuck with several coloured feathers, spotted with wings of flies of extraordinary bigness, like those of their country ; and about them marched two ranks of torches. Then rode the chief masquers in Indian habits all of a resemblance : the ground-cloth of silver richly embroidered with golden suns, and about every sun ran a trail of gold imitating Indian work ; their bases of the same stuff and work, but betwixt every pane of embroidery went a row of white estridge feathers, mingled with sprigs of gold plate ; under their breasts they wore bawdricks of gold, embroidered high with purl, and about their necks ruffs of feathers spangled with pearl and silver. On their heads high sprigged feathers, compassed in coronets, like the Virginian princes they presented. Betwixt every set of feathers, and about their brows, in the under-part of their coronets shined suns of gold plate, sprinkled with pearl ; from whence sprung rays of the like plate, that mixing with the motion of the feathers, showed exceedingly delightful and gracious. Their legs were adorned with close long white silk stockings, curiously embroidered with gold to the mid-leg.

And over these (being on horseback) they drew greaves, or buskins, embroidered with gold and interlaced with rows of feathers, altogether estrangeful and Indian-like.

In their hands (set in several postures as they rode) they brandished cane darts of the finest gold. Their vizards of olive colour, but pleasingly visaged ; their hair black and large, waving down to their shoulders.

Their horse, for rich show, equalled the masquers themselves, all their caparisons being enchased with suns of gold and ornamental jewels ; to every one of which was tacked a scarfing of silver, that ran sinuously in works over the whole caparison, even to the dazzling of the admiring spectators : their heads, no less gracefully and properly decked with the like light scarfing that hung about their ears, wantonly dangling.

Every one of these horse had two Moors, attired like Indian slaves, that for state sided them, with swelling wreaths of gold and watchet on their heads, which arose in all to the number of a hundred.

The torch-bearers' habits were likewise of the Indian garb, but more stravagant than those of the masquers, all showfully garnished with several-hued feathers. The humble variety whereof stuck off the more amply the masquers' high beauties, shining in the habits of themselves ; and reflected in their kind a new and delightfully-varied radiance on the beholders.

All these sustained torches of virgin wax, whose staves were great canes all over gilded ; and these, as the rest, had every man his Moor attending his horse.

The masquers, riding single, had every masquer his torch-bearer mounted before him.

The last chariot, which was most of all adorned, had his whole frame filled with moulded work, mixed all with paintings and glittering scarfings of silver, over which was cast a canopy of gold borne up with antic figures, and all composed *à la grotes[c]a.*

Before this, in the seat of it as the charioteer, was advanced a strange person, and as strangely habited, half French, half Swiss, his name Capriccio ; wearing on his head a pair of golden bellows, a gilt spur in one hand, and with the other managing the reins of the four horses that drew it.

On a seat of the same chariot, a little more elevate, sate Eunomia, the virgin priest of the goddess Honour, together with Phemis, her herald. The habit of her priest was a robe of white silk gathered about the neck ; a pentacle of silvered stuff about her shoulders, hanging foldedly down, both before and behind ; a vestal veil on her head, of tiffany striped with silver, hanging with a train to the earth.

The Herald was attired in an antique cuirass of silver stuff, with labels at the wings and bases ; a short gown of gold stuff, with wide sleeves, cut in panes ; a wreath of gold on his head, and a rod of gold in his hand.

Highest of all, in the most eminent seat of the triumphal [car], sat, side to side, the celestial goddess Honour, and the earthy deity, Plutus, or Riches. His attire, a short robe of gold, fringed ; his wide sleeves turned up, and out-showed his naked arms ; his head and beard sprinkled with showers of gold ; his buskins clinquant as his other attire. The ornaments of Honour were these : a rich full robe of blue silk girt about her, a mantle of silver worn overthwart, full-gathered, and descending in folds behind, a veil of net lawn embroidered with O's and spangled, her tresses in tucks, braided with silver, the hinder part shadowing in waves her shoulders.

These, thus particularly and with propriety adorned, were strongly attended with a full guard of two hundred halberdiers ; two Marshals (being choice gentlemen of either House) commander-like attired, to and fro coursing to keep all in their orders.

A show at all parts so novel, conceitful, and glorious as hath not in this land (to the proper use and object it had proposed) been ever before beheld. Nor did those honourable Inns of Court at any time in that kind such acceptable service to the sacred Majesty of this kingdom, nor were returned by many degrees with so thrice gracious and royal entertainment and honour. But (as above said) all these so marching to the Court at Whitehall, the King, bride, and bridegroom, with all the Lords of the most honoured Privy Council, and our chief nobility, stood in the gallery before the Tilt-yard to behold their arrival ; who, for the more full satisfaction of his Majesty's view, made one turn about the yard, and dismounted ; being then honourably attended through the gallery to a chamber appointed, where they were to make ready for their performance in the hall, etc.

The King being come forth, the masquers ascended, unseen, to their scene. Then for the works.

First, there appeared at the lower end of the hall an artificial rock, whose top was near as high as the hall itself. This rock was in the undermost part craggy and full of hollow places, in whose concaves were contrived two winding pair of stairs, by whose greces the persons above might make their descents, and all the way be seen. All this rock grew by degrees up into a gold-colour, and was run quite through with veins of gold. On the one side whereof, eminently raised on a fair hill, was erected a silver temple of an octangle figure, whose pillars were of a composed order, and bore up an architrave, frieze, and cornish, over which stood a continued plinth, whereon were advanced statues of silver ; above this was placed a bastard order of architecture, wherein were carved compartments, in one of which was written in great gold capitals, *HONORIS FANUM*. Above all was a *Coupolo* or type, which seemed to be scaled with silver plates.

For finishing of all upon a pedestal was fixed a round stone of silver, from which grew a pair of golden wings, both feigned to be Fortune's. The round stone (when her feet trod it) ever affirmed to be rolling, figuring her inconstancy ; the golden wings denoting those nimble powers that pompously bear her about the world ; on that temple (erected to her daughter, Honour, and figuring this kingdom) put off by her and fixed, for assured sign she would never forsake it.

About this temple hung festoons, wreathed with silver from one pillar's head to another. Besides, the frieze was enriched with carvings, all showing greatness and magnificence.

On the other side of the rock grew a grove, in whose utmost part appeared a vast, withered, and hollow tree, being the bare receptacle of the baboonery.

These following, should in duty have had their proper places after every fitted speech of the actors ; but being prevented, by the unexpected haste of the printer, which he never let me know, and never sending me a proof till he had passed those speeches, I had no reason to imagine he could have been so forward. His fault is, therefore, to be supplied by the observation and reference of the reader, who will easily perceive where they were to be inserted.

After the speech of Plutus (who, as you may see after, first entered) the middle part of the rock began to move, and being

come some five paces up towards the King, it split in pieces with
a great crack, and out brake Capriccio, as before described.
The pieces of the rock vanished, and he spake, as in his place.

At the singing of the first song, full, which was sung by the
Virginian priests, called the Phœbades, to six lutes (being used
as an Orphean virtue for the state of the mines opening) the
upper part of the rock was suddenly turned to a cloud, discovering
a rich and refulgent mine of gold, in which the twelve masquers
were triumphantly seated, their torch-bearers attending before
them ; all the lights being so ordered, that though none were seen,
yet had their lustre such virtue, that by it the least spangle or
spark of the masquers' rich habits might with ease and clearness
be discerned as far off as the s[t]ate.

Over this golden mine in an evening sky the ruddy sun was
seen ready to set ; and behind the tops of certain white cliffs
by degrees descended, casting up a bank of clouds ; in which
awhile he was hidden ; but then gloriously shining, gave that
usually observed good omen of succeeding fair weather.

Before he was fully set, the Phœbades (showing the custom
of the Indians to adore the sun setting) began their observance
with the song, to whose place we must refer you for the manner
and words. All the time they were singing, the torch-bearers
holding up their torches to the sun ; to whom the priests themselves and the rest did, as they sung, obeisance ; which was
answered by other music and voices, at the commandment of
Honour, with all observances used to the King, etc. As in the
following places.

To answer certain insolent objections made against the length
of my speeches and narrations, being (for the probability of all
accidents, rising from the invention of this Masque, and their application to the persons and places for whom and by whom it was presented)
not convenient, but necessary, I am enforced to affirm this : that
as there is no poem nor oration so general, but hath his one particular
proposition ; nor no river so extravagantly ample, but hath his never-
so-narrow fountain, worthy to be named ; so all these courtly and
honouring inventions (having poesy and oration in them, and a
fountain to be expressed, from whence their rivers flow) should
expressively arise out of the places and persons for and by whom
they are presented ; without which limits they are luxurious and vain.
But what rules soever are set down to any art or act (though without
their observation no art, nor act, is true and worthy) yet they are nothing the more followed ; or those few that follow them credited.   Every
vulgarly-esteemed upstart dares break the dreadful dignity of ancient
and autentical Poesy ; and presume luciferously to proclaim in place
thereof repugnant precepts of their own spawn.   Truth and worth
have no faces to enamour the licentious ; but vain-glory and humour.
The same body, the same beauty, a thousand men seeing, only the
man whose blood is fitted hath that which he calls his soul enamoured.
And this out of infallible cause, for men understand not these of
Menander :

> —est morbus opportunitas
> Animæ, quod ictus, vulnus accipit grave.

But the cause of [some] men's being enamoured with Truth, and
of her slight respect in others, is the divine Freedom ; one touching
with his apprehensive finger, the other passing.   The Hill of the
Muses (which all men must climb in the regular way to Truth) is
said of old to be forked.   And the two points of it, parting at
the top, are insania and divinus furor.   Insania is that which
every rank-brained writer and judge of poetical writing is rapt
withal, when he presumes either to write or censure the height of
Poesy, and that transports him with humour, vain glory, and pride,
most profane and sacrilegious ; when divinus furor makes gentle
and noble the never-so-truly inspired writer :

Emollit mores, nec sinit esse feros.

And the mild beams of the most holy inflamer easily and sweetly enter, with all understanding sharpness, the soft and sincerely humane ; but with no time, no study, no means under heaven, any arrogant all-occupation devourer (that will, chandler-like, set up with all wares, selling Poesy's nectar and ambrosia, as well as mustard and vinegar) the chaste and restrained beams of humble truth will ever enter, but only graze and glance at them, and the further fly them.

THE APPLICABLE ARGUMENT OF THE MASQUE

Honour is so much respected and adored that she hath a
temple erected to her like a goddess ; a virgin priest consecrated
to her (which is Eunomia, or Law, since none should dare access
to Honour but by virtue, of which Law, being the rule, must needs
be a chief), and a Herald (called Phemis, or Fame) to proclaim
her institutions and commandments.   To amplify yet more the
divine graces of this goddess, Plutus (or Riches) being by Aristophanes, Lucian, etc., presented naturally blind, deformed, and
dull-witted, is here, by his love of Honour, made see, made sightly,
made ingenious, made liberal,   And all this converted and consecrate to the most worthy celebration of these sacred nuptials ;
all issuing (to conclude the necessary application) from an honourable temple, etc.

> Non est certa fides, quam non injuria versat.
> —— Fallit portus et ipse fidem.

THE NAMES OF THE SPEAKERS

Honour, *a Goddess*
Plutus (*or* Riches), *a God*
Eunomia (*or* Law), *Priest of*
Honour

Phemis, Honour's *Herald*
Capriccio, *a man of wit, etc.*

THE PRESENTMENT

Plutus appeared, surveying the work with this speech

Plu. Rocks ? Nothing but rocks in these masquing
devices ? Is Invention so poor she must needs ever dwell
amongst rocks ?   But it may worthily have chanced (being
so often presented) that their vain custom is now become
the necessary hand of heaven, transforming into rocks some   5
stony-hearted ladies courted in former masques, for whose
loves some of their repulsed servants have perished ; or perhaps some of my flinty-hearted usurers have been here metamorphosed, betwixt whom and ladies there is resemblance
enough ; ladies using to take interest, besides their principal,   10
as much as usurers.   See, it is so ; and now is the time of

restoring them to their natural shapes. It moves, opens,
excellent! This metamorphosis I intend to overhear.

A rock moving and breaking with a crack about Capriccio, *he
enters with a pair of bellows on his head, a spur in one
hand, and a piece of gold ore in the other, etc. He speaks,
ut sequitur*

Cap. How hard this world is to a man of wit! He must
eat through main rocks for his food, or fast. A restless and
tormenting stone his wit is to him; the very stone of Sisyphus
in hell, nay, the Philosopher's Stone, makes not a man
more wretched. A man must be a second Proteus, and turn
himself into all shapes, like Ulysses, to wind through the
straits of this pinching vale of misery. I have turned myself
into a tailor, a man, a gentleman, a nobleman, a worthy man;
but had never the wit to turn myself into an alderman. There
are many shapes to perish in, but one to live in, and that's an
alderman's. 'Tis not for a man of wit to take any rich figure
upon him. Your bold, proud, ignorant, that's brave and clinquant, that finds crowns put into his shoes every morning by
the fairies and will never tell; whose wit is humour, whose
judgment is fashion, whose pride is emptiness, birth his full
man, that is in all things something, in sum total nothing;
he shall live in the land of Spruce, milk and honey flowing
into his mouth sleeping.

Plu. [*aside*] This is no transformation, but an intrusion
into my golden mines: I will hear him further.

Cap. This breach of rocks I have made in needy
pursuit of the blind deity, Riches, who is miraculously arrived
here. For (according to our rare men of wit) heaven standing
and earth moving, her motion (being circular) hath brought
one of the most remote parts of the world to touch at this all-
exceeding island; which a man of wit would imagine must
needs move circularly with the rest of the world, and so ever
maintain an equal distance. But poets (our chief men of wit)
answer that point directly, most ingeniously affirming that
this isle is (for the excellency of it) divided from the world
(*divisus ab orbe Britannus*) and that, though the whole
world besides moves, yet this isle stands fixed on her own feet
and defies the world's mutability, which this rare accident
of the arrival of Riches in one of his furthest-off-situate
dominions most demonstratively proves.

Plu. [*aside*] This is a man of wit indeed, and knows of
all our arrivals.

Cap. With this dull deity Riches, a rich island lying in the South-sea, called Pæana (of the Pæans, or songs, sung to the Sun, whom there they adore), being for strength and riches called the navel of that South-sea, is by Earth's round motion moved near this Britain shore. In which island (being 55 yet in command of the Virginian continent) a troop of the noblest Virginians inhabiting, attended hither the god of Riches, all triumphantly shining in a mine of gold. For hearing of the most royal solemnity of these sacred nuptials, they crossed the ocean in their honour, and 60 are here arrived. A poor snatch at some of the golden ore, that the feet of Riches have turned up as he trod here, my poor hand hath purchased ; and hope the remainder of a greater work will be shortly extant.

Plu. [*advancing*] You, sir, that are miching about my 65 golden mines here !

Cap. What, can you see, sir ? You have heretofore been presented blind, like your mother Fortune and your brother Love.

Plu. But now, sir, you see I see. 70

Cap. By what good means, I beseech you, sir ?

Plu. That means I may vouchsafe you hereafter ; mean space, what are you ?

Cap. I am, sir, a kind of man, a man of wit ; with whom your worship has nothing to do, I think. 75

Plu. No, sir, nor will have anything to do with him. A man of wit—what's that ? A beggar !

Cap. And yet no devil, sir.

Plu. As I am, you mean.

Cap. Indeed, sir, your kingdom is under the earth. 80

Plu. That's true ; for Riches is the Atlas that holds it up ; it would sink else.

Cap. 'Tis rather a wonder it sinks not with you, sir ; y'are so sinfully and damnably heavy.

Plu. Sinful and damnable ? What, a Puritan ? These 85 bellows you wear on your head show with what matter your brain is puffed up, sir : a religion-forger I see you are, and presume of inspiration from these bellows, with which ye study to blow up the settled governments of kingdoms.

Cap. Your worship knocks at a wrong door, sir. I dwell 90 far from the person you speak of.

Plu. What may you be, then, being a man of wit ? A buffoon, a jester ? Before I would take upon me the title

of a man of wit, and be baffled by every man of wisdom for a
buffoon, I would turn bankrout, or set up a tobacco shop,   95
change cloaks with an alchemist, or serve an usurer, be a
watering-post for every groom, stand the push of every
rascal wit, enter lists of jests with trencher-fools and be
fooled down by them, or (which is worse) put them down in
fooling. Are these the qualities a man of wit should run 100
proud of ?

Cap. Your worship, I see, has obtained wit with sight,
which I hope yet my poor wit will well be able to answer ; for
touching my jesting, I have heard of some courtiers that
have run themselves out of their states with jousting ; and why 105
may not I then raise myself in the state with jesting ?   An
honest shoemaker (in a liberal king's time) was knighted for
making a clean boot, and is it impossible that I, for breaking a
clean jest, should be advanced in Court or Council, or at least
served out for an ambassador to a dull climate ?   Jests and 110
merriments are but wild weeds in a rank soil, which, being
well manured, yield the wholesome crop of wisdom and discretion at time o'th' year.

Plu. Nay, nay, I commend thy judgment for cutting
thy coat so just to the breadth of thy shoulders ; he that can- 115
not be a courser in the field let him learn to play the jackanapes
in the chamber ; he that cannot personate the wise man well
amongst wizards, let him learn to play the fool amongst
dizzards.

Cap. 'Tis passing miraculous that your dull and blind 120
worship should so suddenly turn both sightful and witful.

Plu. The riddle of that miracle I may chance dissolve to
you in sequel ; meantime what name sustain'st thou, and
what toys are these thou bear'st so fantastically about thee ?

Cap. These toys, sir, are the ensigns that discover my 125
name and quality, my name being Capriccio ; and I wear
these bellows on my head to show I can puff up with glory all
those that affect me ; and, besides, bear this spur to show
I can spur-gall even the best that contemn me.

Plu. A dangerous fellow ! But what makest thou, poor 130
man of wit, at these pompous nuptials ?

Cap. Sir, I come hither with a charge to do these nuptials,
I hope, very acceptable service ; and my charge is a company of accomplished travellers, that are excellent at anti-
masques, and will tender a taste of their quality, if your wor- 135
ship please.

Plu. Excellent well pleased ! Of what virtue are they besides ?

Cap. Passing grave, sir, yet exceeding acute ; witty, yet not ridiculous ; never laugh at their own jests ; laborious, 140 yet not base ; having cut out the skirts of the whole world in amorous quest of your gold and silver.

Plu. They shall have enough ; call them, I beseech thee call them ; how far hence abide they ?

Cap. Sir (being by another eminent quality the admired 145 soldiers of the world) in contempt of softness and delicacy they lie on the naturally hard boards of that naked tree ; and will your worship assure them rewards fit for persons of their freight ?

Plu. Dost thou doubt my reward, being pleased ?   150

Cap. I know, sir, a man may sooner win your reward for pleasing you than deserving you.   But you great wise persons have a fetch of state, to employ with countenance and encouragement, but reward with austerity and disgrace, save your purses and lose your honours.   155

Plu. To assure thee of reward I will now satisfy thee touching the miraculous cause both of my sight and wit, and which consequently moves me to humanity and bounty ; and all is only this, my late being in love with the lovely goddess Honour.

Cap. If your worship love Honour, indeed, sir, you must 160 needs be bountiful.   But where is the rare goddess you speak of to be seen ?

Plu. In that rich temple, where Fortune fixed those her golden wings, thou seest, and that rolling stone she used to tread upon for sign she would never forsake this kingdom. 165 There is adored the worthy goddess Honour, the sweetness of whose voice, when I first heard her persuasions both to myself and the Virginian princes arrived here to do honour and homage to these heavenly nuptials, so most powerfully enamoured me, that the fire of my love flew up to the sight of mine eyes that 170 have lighted within me a whole firmament of bounty, which may securely assure thee thy reward is certain : and therefore call thy accomplished company to their antimasque.

Cap. See, sir, the time set for their appearance being expired, they appear to their service of themselves.   175

*Enter the Baboons, after whose dance, being antic and delightful,
   they returned to their tree, when* Plutus *spake to* Capriccius

Plu. Gramercy, now Capriccio, take thy men of complement, and travel with them to other marriages. My riches to thy wit, they will get something somewhere.

Cap. What's this?

Plu. A strain of wit beyond a man of wit. I have em- 180 ployed you, and the grace of that is reward enough ; hence, pack, with your complemental fardel. The sight of an attendant for reward is abominable in the eyes of a turn-served politician, and I fear will strike me blind again. I cannot abide these bellows of thy head ; they and thy men of wit have melted 185 my mines with them, and consumed me ; yet take thy life and begone. Neptune let thy predecessor, Ulysses, live after all his slain companions, but, to make him die more miserably living, gave him up to shipwrecks, enchantments ; men of wit are but enchanted, there is no such thing as wit in this 190 world. So take a tree, inure thy soldiers to hardness, 'tis honourable, though not clinquant.

Cap. Can this be possible?

Plu. Alas, poor man of wit, how want of reward daunts thy virtue ! But because I must send none away discon- 195 tented from these all-pleasing nuptials, take this wedge of gold and wedge thyself into the world with it, renouncing that loose wit of thine ; 'twill spoil thy complexion.

Cap. Honour and all Argus' eyes to earth's all-commanding Riches ! *Pluto etiam cedit Jupiter.* *Exit* Capriccio 200

After this low induction by these succeeding degrees the chief masquers were advanced to their discovery

Plu. These humble objects can no high eyes draw. *Plutus calls to Eunomia*
Eunomia (or the sacred power of Law)
Daughter of Jove and goddess Honour's priest,
Appear to Plutus, and his love assist !
Eun. What would the god of Riches? 205 *Eunomia in the Temple gates*
Plu.   Join with Honour ;
In purpos'd grace of those great nuptials ;
And since to Honour none should dare access,
But help'd by Virtue's hand (thyself, chaste [Law],
Being Virtue's rule, and her directful light)
Help me to th' honour of her speech and sight. 210
Eun. Thy will shall straight be honour'd ; all that seek
Access to Honour by clear virtue's beam,
Her grace prevents their pains, and comes to them.

Loud music, and Honour *appears, descending with her herald*
    Phemis, *and* Eunomia (*her priest*) *before her. The music
    ceasing,* Plutus *spake*

  Plu. Crown of all merit, goddess and my love,
'Tis now high time that th'end for which we come   215
Should be endeavour'd in our utmost rite
Done to the sweetness of this nuptial night.
  Hon. Plutus, the princes of the Virgin land,
Whom I made cross the Briton ocean
To this most famed isle of all the world,   220
To do due homage to the sacred nuptials
Of Love and Beauty, celebrated here,
By this hour of the holy even, I know,
Are ready to perform the rites they owe
To setting Phœbus, which (for greater state   225
To their appearance) their first act advances,
And with songs ushers their succeeding dances.
Herald, give summons to the Virgin knights
No longer to delay their purposed rites.
  Her. Knights of the Virgin land, whom Beauty's lights 230
Would glorify with their inflaming sights,
Keep now obscur'd no more your fair intent
To add your beams to this night's ornament ;
The golden-winged Hour strikes now a plain,
And calls out all the pomp ye entertain ;   235
The princely bridegroom and the bride's bright eyes
Sparkle with grace to your discoveries.

At these words the Phœbades (*or Priests* of the Sun) *appeared
    first with six lutes and six voices, and sung to the opening
    of the mine and masquers' discovery this full song :*
                  THE FIRST SONG
        Ope, Earth, thy womb of gold,
          Show, Heaven, thy cope of stars.
        All glad aspects unfold,   240
          Shine out and clear our cares ;
        Kiss, Heaven and Earth, and so combine
        In all mix'd joy our nuptial twine.

*This song ended, a mount opened and spread like a sky, in
    which appeared a sun setting, beneath which sat the twelve
    masquers in a mine of gold, twelve torch-bearers holding
    their torches before them, after which* Honour, *etc.*
  Hon. See now the setting sun casts up his bank,

And shows his bright head at his sea's repair, 245
For sign that all days future shall be fair.
Plu. May He that rules all nights and days confirm it.
Hon. Behold the Sun's fair priests, the Phœbades,
Their evening service in an hymn address
To Phœbus setting, which we now shall hear, 250
And see the forms of their devotions there.

The Phœbades *sing the first stance of the second song ut sequitur :*

One alone

I.

Descend, fair Sun, and sweetly rest
    In Tethys' crystal arms thy toil ;
Fall burning on her marble breast,
    And make with love her billows boil. 255

Another alone

2.

Blow, blow, sweet winds, O blow away
    All vapours from the fined air,
That to his golden head no ray
    May languish with the least impair.

CHORUS

Dance, Tethys, and thy love's red beams 260
    Embrace with joy ; he now descends,
Burns, burns with love to drink thy streams,
    And on him endless youth attends.

After this stance, Honour, etc.

Hon. This superstitious hymn, sung to the Sun,
Let us encounter with fit duties done 265
To our clear Phœbus, whose true piety
Enjoys from heaven an earthly deity.

*Other music and voices, and this second stance was
    sung; directing their observance to the King*

One alone

I.

Rise, rise, O Phœbus, ever rise,
    Descend not to th' inconstant stream ;
But grace with endless light our skies, 270
    To thee that Sun is but a beam.

Another

2.

Dance, ladies, in our Sun's bright rays,
   In which the bride and bridegroom shine ;
Clear sable night with your eyes' days,
   And set firm lights on Hymen's shrine.   275

CHORUS

O may our Sun not set before
   He sees his endless seed arise
And deck his triple-crowned shore
   With springs of human deities.

This ended, the Phœbades *sung the third stance :*

I.

Set, set, great Sun ; our rising love   280
   Shall ever celebrate thy grace ;
Whom, entering the high court of Jove,
   Each god greets rising from his place.

2.

When thou thy silver bow dost bend
   All start aside and dread thy draughts ;   285
How can we thee enough commend,
   Commanding all worlds with thy shafts ?

CHORUS

Blest was thy mother bearing thee
   And Phœbe, that delights in darts ;
Thou artful songs dost set, and she   290
   Winds horns, loves hounds and high-palm'd harts.

After this Honour

Hon. Again our music and conclude this song
To him to whom all Phœbus' beams belong.

The other voices sung to other music the [*fourth*] *stance :*

I.

Rise still, clear Sun, and never set,
   But be to earth her only light ;   295
All other kings, in thy beams met,
   Are clouds and dark effects of night.

2.

As when the rosy morn doth rise,
  Like mists, all give thy wisdom way;
A learned king is, as in skies   300
  To poor dim stars the flaming day.

CHORUS

Blest was thy mother, bearing thee,
  Thee, only relic of her race,
Made by thy virtue's beams a tree
  Whose arms shall all the earth embrace.   305

This done, Eunomia *spake to the masquers set yet above*

Eun. Virginian princes, you must now renounce
Your superstitious worship of these Suns,
Subject to cloudy dark'nings and descents;
And of your fit devotions turn the events
To this our Briton Phœbus, whose bright sky   310
(Enlighten'd with a Christian piety)
Is never subject to black Error's night,
And hath already offer'd heaven's true light
To your dark region, which acknowledge now,
Descend, and to him all your homage vow.   315

> *With this the torch-bearers descended and performed
> another antimasque, dancing with torches lighted
> at both ends, which done the Masquers descended
> and fell into their dances, two of which being past,
> and others with the ladies,* Honour *spake*

[*Hon.*] Music! Your voices now tune sweet and high,
And sing the nuptial hymn of Love and Beauty.
Twins, as of one age, so to one desire,
May both their bloods give an unparted fire.
And as those twins that Fame gives all her prize   320
Combined their life's power in such sympathies,
That one being merry, mirth the other grac'd;
If one felt sorrow, th' other grief embrac'd;
If one were healthful, health the other pleas'd;
If one were sick, the other was diseas'd   325
And always join'd in such a constant troth
That one like cause had like effect in both:
So may these nuptial twins their whole lives' store
Spend in such even parts, never grieving more
Than may the more set off their joys divine,   330
As after clouds the sun doth clearest shine.

The side notes:

The bride
and bride-
groom were
figured in
Love and
Beauty.
Twins of
which
Hippocrates
speaks.

Called
twins,
being both
of an age.

This said, this song of Love and Beauty *was sung, single :*

Bright Panthæa, born to Pan
Of the noblest race of man,
    Her white hand to Eros giving,
With a kiss join'd heaven to earth   335
And begot so fair a birth
    As yet never grac'd the living.

CHORUS

A twin that all worlds did adorn,
For so were Love and Beauty born.

2.

Both so lov'd they did contend   340
Which the other should transcend,
    Doing either grace and kindness ;
Love from Beauty did remove
Lightness, call'd her stain in love,
    Beauty took from Love his blindness.   345

CHORUS

Love sparks made flames in Beauty's sky,
And Beauty blew up Love as high.

3.

Virtue then commix'd her fire,
To which Bounty did aspire,
    Innocence a crown conferring ;   350
Mine and thine were then unus'd,
All things common, nought abus'd,
    Freely earth her fruitage bearing.

CHORUS

Nought then was car'd for that could fade,
And thus the golden world was made.   355

*This sung, the masquers danced again with the ladies, after
which* Honour

Hon. Now may the blessings of the golden age
Swim in these nuptials, even to holy rage ;
A hymn to Sleep prefer, and all the joys
That in his empire are of dearest choice
Betwixt his golden slumbers ever flow   360
In these ; and theirs in springs as endless grow.

This said, the last song was sung, full :

THE LAST SONG

Now, Sleep, bind fast the flood of air,
　　Strike all things dumb and deaf,
And to disturb our nuptial pair
　　Let stir no aspen leaf.　　　　　　　　　365
Send flocks of golden dreams
　　That all true joys presage,
Bring in thy oily streams
　　The milk-and-honey age.
Now close the world-round sphere of bliss,　　370
And fill it with a heavenly kiss.

After this Plutus *to the masquers*

Plu. Come, Virgin knights, the homage ye have done
To Love and Beauty and our Briton Sun,
Kind Honour will requite with holy feasts
In her fair temple ; and her loved guests　　375
Gives me the grace t' invite, when she and I
(Honour and Riches) will eternally
A league in favour of this night combine,
In which Love's second hallow'd tapers shine,
Whose joys may Heaven and Earth as highly please　　380
As those two nights that got great Hercules.

*The speech ended, they concluded with a dance that brought
them off ;* Plutus, *with* Honour *and the rest, conducting
them up to the Temple of* Honour

FINIS

A HYMN TO HYMEN

FOR THE MOST TIME-FITTED NUPTIALS OF OUR THRICE GRACIOUS PRINCESS ELIZABETH, ETC.

Sing, sing a rapture to all nuptial ears,
Bright Hymen's torches drunk up Parcae's tears :
Sweet Hymen, Hymen, mightiest of gods,
Atoning of all-taming blood the odds,
Two into one contracting, one to two   5
Dilating, which no other god can do,
Mak'st sure with change, and let'st the married try
Simil. Of man and woman the variety.
And as a flower, half scorch'd with day's long heat,
Thirsts for refreshing with night's cooling sweat,   10
The wings of Zephyr, fanning still her face,
No cheer can add to her heart-thirsty grace,
Yet wears she gainst those fires that make her fade
Her thick hair's proof, all hid in midnight's shade,
Her health is all in dews, hope all in showers,   15
Whose want bewail'd, she pines in all her powers ;
So love-scorch'd virgins nourish quenchless fires ;
The father's cares, the mother's kind desires,
Their gold, and garments of the newest guise,
Can nothing comfort their scorch'd phantasies ;   20
But taken ravish'd up in Hymen's arms,
His circle holds for all their anguish charms.
Simil. ad Then as a glad graft in the spring sun shines,
eandem That all the helps of earth and heaven combines
explicat. In her sweet growth, puts in the morning on   25
Her cheerful airs, the sun's rich fires at noon,
At even the sweet dews, and at night with stars
In all their virtuous influences shares :
So in the Bridegroom's sweet embrace the Bride
All varied joys tastes in their naked pride,   30
To which the richest weeds are weeds to flowers.
Come, Hymen, then, come, close these nuptial hours

With all years' comforts. Come, each virgin keeps
Her odorous kisses for thee ; golden sleeps
Will in their humours never steep an eye,   35
Till thou invit'st them with thy harmony.
Why stayest thou ? See, each virgin doth prepare
Embraces for thee, her white breasts lays bare
To tempt thy soft hand, lets such glances fly
As make stars shoot to imitate her eye,   40
Puts Art's attires on, that put Nature's down,
Sings, dances, sets on every foot a crown,
Sighs in her songs and dances, kisseth air,
Till, rites and words past, thou in deeds repair.
The whole Court *Io* sings, *Io* the air,   45
Io the floods and fields, *Io*, most fair,
Most sweet, most happy Hymen ; come, away,
With all thy comforts come ; old matrons pray
With young maids' languours ; birds bill, build, and breed,
To teach thee thy kind ; every flower and weed   50
Looks up to gratulate thy long'd-for fruits :
Thrice given are free and timely-granted suits.
There is a seed by thee now to be sown,
In whose fruit Earth shall see her glories shown
At all parts perfect, and must therefore lose   55
No minute's time—from time's use all fruit flows.
Simil And as the tender hyacinth that grows
Where Phoebus most his golden beams bestows,
Is propp'd with care, is water'd every hour,
The sweet winds adding their increasing power,   60
The scattered drops of night's refreshing dew
Hasting the full grace of his glorious hue,
Which, once disclosing, must be gather'd straight,
Or hue and odour both will lose their height ;
So of a virgin, high, and richly kept,   65
The grace and sweetness full-grown must be reap'd,
Or forth her spirits fly in empty air,
The sooner fading the more sweet and fair.
   Gentle, O gentle Hymen, be not then
Cruel, that kindest art to maids and men ;   70
These two one twin are, and their mutual bliss
Not in thy beams, but in thy bosom is ;
Nor can their hands fast their hearts' joys make sweet ;
Their hearts in breasts are, and their breasts must meet.
Let there be peace, yet murmur, and that noise   75

Beget of peace the nuptial battle's joys.
Let peace grow cruel and take wreak of all
The war's delay brought thy full festival.
  Hark, hark, oh now the sweet twin murmur sounds;
Hymen is come, and all his heat abounds;   80
Shut all doors, none but Hymen's lights advance,
Nor sound stir, let dumb joy enjoy a trance.
Sing, sing a rapture to all nuptial ears,
Bright Hymen's torches drunk up Parcae's tears.

FINIS

EASTWARD HO

PROLOGUS

Not out of envy, for there's no effect
Where there's no cause; nor out of imitation,
For we have evermore been imitated;
Nor out of our contention to do better
Than that which is oppos'd to ours in title,   5
For that was good; and better cannot be:
And for the title, if it seem affected,
We might as well have call'd it, 'God you good even,'
Only that Eastward Westwards still exceeds—
Honour the sun's fair rising, not his setting.   10
Nor is our title utterly enforc'd,
As by the points we touch at you shall see.
Bear with our willing pains, if dull or witty;
We only dedicate it to the City.

DRAMATIS PERSONAE

Touchstone, *a goldsmith*
Quicksilver } *apprentices to*
Golding } *Touchstone*
Sir Petronel Flash
Security, *an old usurer*
Bramble, *a lawyer*
Sea-gull, *a sea-captain*
Scapethrift } *adventurers*
Spendall } *bound for* Virginia
Slitgut, *a butcher's apprentice*
Poldavy, *a tailor*
Holdfast } *officers of the*
Wolf } Counter
Hamlet, *a footman*

Potkin, *a tankard-bearer*
A Messenger, A Scrivener
A Drawer, A Coachman, A
  Page, A Constable, Prisoners.
A Friend of the Prisoners

Mistress Touchstone
Gertrude }
Mildred } *her daughters*
Winifred, *wife of Security*
Sindefy, *mistress to* Quicksilver
Bettrice, *a waiting-woman*
Mrs. Fond
Mrs. Gazer

Eastward Ho

ACTUS PRIMI SCENA PRIMA

[Goldsmith's Row]

Enter Master Touchstone *and* Quicksilver *at several doors ;* Quicksilver *with his hat, pumps, short sword and dagger, and a racket trussed up under his cloak. At the middle door, enter* Golding, *discovering a goldsmith's shop, and walking short turns before it*

Touch. And whither with you now ? What loose action are you bound for ? Come, what comrades are you to meet withal ? Where's the supper ? Where's the rendezvous ?

Quick. Indeed, and in very good sober truth, sir——

Touch. 'Indeed, and in very good sober truth, sir ' ! Behind 5 my back thou wilt swear faster than a French footboy, and talk more bawdily than a common midwife ; and now 'indeed and in very good sober truth, sir ' ! But if a privy search should be made, with what furniture are you rigged now ? Sirrah, I tell thee, I am thy master, William Touch- 10 stone, goldsmith, and thou my prentice, Francis Quicksilver ; and I will see whither you are running. Work upon that now !

Quick. Why, sir, I hope a man may use his recreation with his master's profit.

Touch. Prentices' recreations are seldom with their mas- 15 ters' profit. Work upon that now ! You shall give up your cloak, though you be no alderman. Heyday, Ruffians'-hall ! Sword, pumps, here's a racket indeed !

Touchstone *uncloaks* Quicksilver

Quick. Work upon that now !

Touch. Thou shameless varlet, dost thou jest at thy lawful 20 master contrary to thy indentures ?

Quick. Why, 'sblood, sir, my mother's a gentlewoman, and my father a Justice of Peace and of Quorum ! And though I am a younger brother and a prentice, yet I hope I am my

father's son ; and, by God's lid, 'tis for your worship and for   25
your commodity that I keep company.   I am entertained
among gallants, true !   They call me cousin Frank, right !
I lend them moneys, good !   They spend it, well !   But when
they are spent, must not they strive to get more, must not their
land fly ?   And to whom ?   Shall not your worship ha' the   30
refusal ?   Well, I am a good member of the City, if I were
well considered.   How would merchants thrive, if gentlemen
would not be unthrifts ?   How could gentlemen be unthrifts, if
their humours were not fed ?   How should their humours be
fed but by white meat and cunning secondings ?   Well, the   35
City might consider us.   I am going to an ordinary now : the
gallants fall to play ; I carry light gold with me ; the gallants
call, ' Cousin Frank, some gold for silver ! '; I change, gain
by it ; the gallants lose the gold, and then call, ' Cousin Frank,
lend me some silver ! '   Why——   40

    Touch. Why ?   I cannot tell. Seven-score pound art thou
out in the cash ; but look to it, I will not be gallanted out of
my monies.   And as for my rising by other men's fall, God
shield me !   Did I gain my wealth by ordinaries ?   No !   By
exchanging of gold ?   No !   By keeping of gallants' company ?   45
No ! I hired me a little shop, fought low, took small gain, kept
no debt-book, garnished my shop, for want of plate, with good
wholesome thrifty sentences, as, ' Touchstone, keep thy shop,
and thy shop will keep thee.'   ' Light gains makes heavy purses.'   ' 'Tis good to be merry and wise.'   And when I was   50
wived, having something to stick to, I had the horn of surety-
ship ever before my eyes.   You all know the device of the
horn, where the young fellow slips in at the butt-end, and
comes squeezed out at the buccal : and I grew up, and, I
praise Providence, I bear my brows now as high as the best   55
of my neighbours : but thou—well, look to the accounts ;
your father's bond lies for you ; seven-score pound is yet in
the rear.

    Quick. Why, 'slid, sir, I have as good, as proper gallants'
words for it as any are in London, gentlemen of good phrase,   60
perfect language, passingly behaved, gallants that wear socks
and clean linen, and call me ' kind cousin Frank,' ' good cousin
Frank,' for they know my father : and, by God's lid, shall
I not trust 'em ?—not trust ?

    Enter a Page, *as inquiring for* Touchstone's *shop*

    Gold.   What do ye lack, sir ?   What is't you'll buy, sir ?   65

Touch. Ay, marry, sir ; there's a youth of another piece.
There's thy fellow-prentice, as good a gentleman born as thou
art ; nay, and better meaned.   But does he pump it, or racket
it ?   Well, if he thrive not, if he outlast not a hundred such
crackling bavins as thou art, God and men neglect industry.   70

Gold.   (*To the* page)   It is his shop, and here my master
walks.

Touch.   With me, boy ?

Page.   My master, Sir Petronel Flash, recommends his
love to you, and will instantly visit you.   75

Touch.   To make up the match with my eldest daughter,
my wife's dilling, whom she longs to call madam.   He shall
find me unwillingly ready, boy. (*Exit* Page.) There's another
affliction too.   As I have two prentices, the one of a boundless
prodigality, the other of a most hopeful industry, so have I   80
only two daughters : the eldest of a proud ambition and nice
wantonness, the other of a modest humility and comely sober-
ness.   The one must be ladyfied, forsooth, and be attired
just to the court-cut and long tail.   So far is she ill natured to
the place and means of my preferment and fortune, that she   85
throws all the contempt and despite hatred itself can cast
upon it.   Well, a piece of land she has, 'twas her grand-
mother's gift, let her, and her Sir Petronel, flash out that !
But as for my substance, she that scorns me as I am a citizen
and tradesman, shall never pamper her pride with my indus-   90
try, shall never use me as men do foxes, keep themselves
warm in the skin, and throw the body that bare it to the
dunghill.   I must go entertain this Sir Petronel.   Golding,
my utmost care's for thee, and only trust in thee ; look to the
shop.   As for you, Master Quicksilver, think of husks, for thy   95
course is running directly to the Prodigal's hog's-trough ;
husks, sirrah !   Work upon that now !

Exit Touchstone

Quick.   Marry faugh, goodman flat-cap ! 'Sfoot ! though
I am a prentice, I can give arms ; and my father's a Justice-o'-
Peace by descent, and 'sblood——   100

Gold.   Fie, how you swear !

Quick.   'Sfoot, man, I am a gentleman, and may swear by
my pedigree, God's my life !   Sirrah Golding, wilt be ruled
by a fool ?   Turn good fellow, turn swaggering gallant, and
let the welkin roar, and Erebus also.   Look not westward 105
to the fall of D[a]n Phœbus, but to the East—Eastward Ho !

Where radiant beams of lusty Sol appear,
And bright Eoüs makes the welkin clear.

We are both gentlemen, and therefore should be no coxcombs;
let's be no longer fools to this flat-cap, Touchstone. East- 110
ward, bully! This satin belly and canvas-backed Touchstone—'slife, man, his father was a malt-man, and his
mother sold ginger-bread in Christ-church!

Gold. What would ye ha' me do?

Quick. Why, do nothing, be like a gentleman, be idle; 115
the curse of man is labour. Wipe thy bum with testons,
and make ducks and drakes with shillings. What, Eastward
Ho! Wilt thou cry, ' what is't ye lack? ', stand with a bare
pate and a dropping nose under a wooden pent-house, and
art a gentleman? Wilt thou bear tankards, and may'st 120
bear arms? Be ruled, turn gallant, Eastward Ho! Ta, lirra,
lirra, ro! *Who calls Jeronimo? Speak, here I am.* God's
so, how like a sheep thou lookst! O' my conscience some cowherd begot thee, thou Golding of Golding Hall! Ha, boy?

Gold. Go, ye are a prodigal coxcomb! I a cowherd's son, 125
because I turn not a drunken whore-hunting rake-hell like thyself!

Quick. Rake-hell! Rake-hell!

Offers to draw, and Golding *trips up his heels and holds him*

Gold. Pish, in soft terms ye are a cowardly bragging boy!
I'll ha' you whipped.   130

Quick. Whipped? That's good, i'faith! Untruss me?

Gold. No, thou wilt undo thyself. Alas, I behold thee
with pity, not with anger, thou common shot-clog, gull of
all companies; methinks I see thee already walking in Moorfields without a cloak, with half a hat, without a band, a 135
doublet with three buttons, without a girdle, a hose with one
point and no garter, with a cudgel under thine arm, borrowing and begging three-pence.

Quick. Nay, 'slife, take this and take all! As I am a
gentleman born, I'll be drunk, grow valiant, and beat thee. 140
                                                          Exit

Gold. Go, thou most madly vain, whom nothing can recover
but that which reclaims atheists, and makes great persons
sometimes religious—calamity. As for my place and life,
thus I have read :—

> *Whate'er some vainer youth may term disgrace,*   145
> *The gain of honest pains is never base;*

From trades, from arts, from valour, honour springs;
These three are founts of gentry, yea, of kings.   [*Exit*]

[SCENA SECUNDA

A Room in Touchstone's *House*]

Enter Gertrude, Mildred, Bettrice, *and* Poldavy *a tailor;*
Poldavy *with a fair gown, Scotch farthingale, and French fall*
  in his arms; Gertrude *in a French head-attire and citizen's*
  gown; Mildred *sewing, and* Bettrice *leading a monkey*
  after her.

Ger. For the passion of patience, look if Sir Petronel
approach, that sweet, that fine, that delicate, that—for
love's sake, tell me if he come. O sister Mil., though my father
be a low-capped tradesman, yet I must be a lady ;   and, I
praise God, my mother must call me madam. Does he come ?   5
Off with this gown, for shame's sake, off with this gown ;
let not my knight take me in the city-cut in any hand ;   tear't,
pax on't—does he come ?—tear't off. *Thus whilst she*
sleeps, I sorrow for her sake, etc.   [*sings*]
Mil. Lord, sister, with what an immodest impatiency and   10
disgraceful scorn do you put off your city tire ;   I am sorry to
think you imagine to right yourself in wronging that which
hath made both you and us.
Ger. I tell you I cannot endure it, I must be a lady : do
you wear your coif with a London licket, your stammel petti-   15
coat with two guards, the buffin gown with the tuf[t]-taffety
cape, and the velvet lace. I must be a lady, and I will be
a lady. I like some humours of the City dames well : to eat
cherries only at an angel a pound, good ! To dye rich scarlet
black, pretty ! To line a grogram gown clean thorough with   20
velvet, tolerable ! Their pure linen, their smocks of three
pounds a smock, are to be borne withal ! But your mincing
niceries, taffata pipkins, durance petticoats, and silver bod-
kins—God's my life, as I shall be a lady, I cannot endure it !   25
Is he come yet ? Lord, what a long knight 'tis !—*And ever*
she cried, Sho[o]*t home !*—and yet I knew one longer. *And*
ever she cried, Sho[o]*t home.   Fa, la, ly, re, lo, la !* [*sings*]
Mil. Well, sister, those that scorn their nest, oft fly with
a sick wing.   30
Ger. Bow-bell !
Mil. Where titles presume to thrust before fit means

to second them, wealth and respect often grow sullen, and
will not follow. For sure in this I would for your sake I
spake not truth : *Where ambition of place goes before fitness of*   35
birth, contempt and disgrace follow. I heard a scholar once
say that Ulysses, when he counterfeited himself mad, yoked
cats and foxes and dogs together to draw his plough, whilst he
followed and sowed salt ; but sure I judge them truly mad
that yoke citizens and courtiers, tradesmen and soldiers, a   40
goldsmith's daughter and a knight. Well, sister, pray God
my father sow not salt too.

Ger. Alas ! poor Mil., when I am a lady, I'll pray for thee
yet, i'faith ; nay, and I'll vouchsafe to call thee Sister Mil.
still ; for though thou art not like to be a lady as I am, yet sure   45
thou art a creature of God's making, and mayest peradventure
to be saved as soon as I—does he come ?— *And ever and*
anon she doubled in her song. Now, lady's my comfort,
what a profane ape's here ! Tailor, Poldavy, prithee, fit it,
fit it : is this a right Scot ? Does it clip close, and bear up   50
round ?

Pol. Fine and stiffly, i'faith ! 'Twill keep your thighs
so cool, and make your waist so small ; here was a fault in
your body, but I have supplied the defect with the effect of
my steel instrument, which, though it have but one eye,   55
can see to rectify the imperfection of the proportion.

Ger. Most edifying tailor ! I protest you tailors are most
sanctified members, and make many crooked thing go upright.
How must I bear my hands ? Light, light ?

Pol. O, ay, now you are in the lady-fashion, you must do   60
all things light. Tread light, light. Ay, and fall so : that's
the Court amble.   *She trips about the stage*

Ger. Has the Court ne'er a trot ?

Pol. No, but a false gallop, lady.

Ger. *And if she will not go to bed—*   *Cantat*   65

Bet. The knight's come, forsooth.

Enter Sir Petronel, Master Touchstone, *and* Mistress Touchstone

Ger. Is my knight come ? O the Lord, my band ! Sister,
do my cheeks look well ? Give me a little box o' the ear
that I may seem to blush ; now, now ! So, there, there,
there ! Here he is. O my dearest delight ! Lord, Lord,   70
and how does my knight ?

Touch. Fie, with more modesty !

Ger. Modesty! Why, I am no citizen now—modesty!
Am I not to be married? Y'are best to keep me modest,
now I am to be a lady.　　　　　　　　　　　　　75

Sir Pet. Boldness is good fashion and courtlike.

Ger. Ay, in a country lady I hope it is, as I shall be.
And how chance ye came no sooner, knight?

Sir Pet. 'Faith, I was so entertained in the progress with
one Count Epernoum, a Welsh knight; we had a match at　80
balloon too with my Lord Whachum for four crowns.

Ger. At baboon? Jesu! You and I will play at
baboon in the country, knight.

Sir Pet. O, sweet lady, 'tis a strong play with the arm.

Ger. With arm or leg or any other member, if it be　85
a Court sport. And when shall's be married, my knight?

Sir Pet. I come now to consummate it, and your father
may call a poor knight son-in-law.

Touch. Sir, ye are come. What is not mine to keep, I must
not be sorry to forego. A hundred pounds land her grand-　90
mother left her, 'tis yours; herself (as her mother's gift) is
yours. But if you expect aught from me, know my hand
and mine eyes open together; I do not give blindly. Work
upon that now!

Sir Pet. Sir, you mistrust not my means? I am a knight.　95

Touch. Sir, sir, what I know not, you will give me leave
to say I am ignorant of.

Mist. Touch. Yes, that he is, a knight; I know where he
had money to pay the gentlemen-ushers and heralds their fees.
Ay, that he is, a knight; and so might you have been too, if　100
you had been ought else than an ass, as well as some of your
neighbours. And I thought you would not ha' been knighted
(as I am an honest woman) I would ha' dubbed you myself.
I praise God I have wherewithal. But as for your daughter—

Ger. Ay, mother, I must be a lady to-morrow; and by　105
your leave, mother (I speak it not without my duty, but only
in the right of my husband) I must take place of you, mother.

Mist. Touch. That you shall, lady-daughter, and have a
coach as well as I too.

Ger. Yes, mother. But by your leave, mother (I speak　110
it not without my duty, but only in my husband's right)
my coach-horses must take the wall of your coach-horses.

Touch. Come, come, the day grows low; 'tis supper-
time; use my house; the wedding solemnity is at my wife's
cost; thank me for nothing but my willing blessing, for, I can-　120

not feign, my hopes are faint.   And, sir, respect my daughter ;
she has refused for you wealthy and honest matches, known
good men, well-moneyed, better traded, best reputed.

Ger.   Body o'truth !   Chittizens,   chittizens !   Sweet
knight, as soon as ever we are married, take me to thy 125
mercy out of this miserable chitty ; presently carry me out
of the scent of Newcastle coal, and the hearing of Bow-bell ;
I beseech thee down with me, for God's sake !

Touch.   Well, daughter, I have read that old wit sings :

> *The greatest rivers flow from little springs.*   130
> *Though thou art full, scorn not thy means at first ;*
> *He that's most drunk may soonest be athirst.*

Work upon that now !

All but Touchstone, Mildred, *and* Golding *depart*

No, no !   Yond' stand my hopes—Mildred, come hither,
daughter !   And how approve you your sister's fashion ? 135
How do you fancy her choice ?   What dost thou think ?

Mil.   I hope, as a sister, well.

Touch.   Nay but, nay but, how dost thou like her behaviour and humour ?   Speak freely.

Mil.   I am loath to speak ill ; and yet I am sorry of this, 140
I cannot speak well.

Touch.   Well ; very good, as I would wish, a modest answer !   Golding, come hither, hither, Golding !   How dost
thou like the knight, Sir Flash ?   Does he not look big ?
How lik'st thou the elephant ?   He says he has a castle 145
in the country.

Gold.   Pray heaven, the elephant carry not his castle
on his back.

Touch.   'Fore heaven, very well !   But, seriously, how
dost repute him ?   150

Gold.   The best I can say of him is, I know him not.

Touch.   Ha, Golding !   I commend thee, I approve thee,
and will make it appear my affection is strong to thee.
My wife has her humour, and I will ha' mine.   Dost thou
see my daughter here ?   She is not fair, well-favoured or 155
so, indifferent, which modest measure of beauty shall not
make it thy only work to watch her, nor sufficient mischance
to suspect her.   Thou art towardly, she is modest ; thou
art provident, she is careful.   She's now mine ; give me
thy hand, she's now thine,   Work upon that now !   160

Gold. Sir, as your son, I honour you ; and as your servant, obey you.

Touch. Sayest thou so ? Come hither, Mildred. Do
you see yond' fellow ? He is a gentleman, though my
prentice, and has somewhat to take too ; a youth of good 165
hope, well friended, well parted. Are you mine ? You are
his. Work you upon that now !

Mil. Sir, I am all yours ; your body gave me life ; your
care and love, happiness of life ; let your virtue still direct
it, for to your wisdom I wholly dispose myself.　　　170

Touch. Sayst thou so ? Be you two better acquainted.
Lip her, lip her, knave ! So, shut up shop, in ! We must
make holiday.　　　*Exeunt* Golding *and* Mildred
　　　This match shall on, for I intend to prove
　　　Which thrives the best, the mean or lofty love.　　175
　　　Whether fit wedlock vow'd 'twixt like and like,
　　　Or prouder hopes, which daringly o'erstrike
　　　Their place and means. 'Tis honest time's expense,
　　　When seeming lightness bears a moral sense.
　　　Work upon that now !　　　*Exit* 180

ACTUS SECUNDI SCENA PRIMA

[*Goldsmith's Row*]

Touchstone, Golding, *and* Mildred, *sitting on either side
of the stall*

Touch. Quicksilver ! Master Francis Quicksilver ! Master
Quicksilver !

Enter Quicksilver

Quick. Here, sir—Ump !

Touch. So, sir ; nothing but flat Master Quicksilver
(without any familiar addition) will fetch you ! Will you　5
truss my points, sir ?

Quick. Ay, forsooth —Ump !

Touch. How now, sir ? The drunken hiccup so soon
this morning ?

Quick. 'Tis but the coldness of my stomach, forsooth !　10

Touch. What, have you the cause natural for it ?
Y'are a very learned drunkard ; I believe I shall miss some
of my silver spoons with your learning. The nuptial night
will not moisten your throat sufficiently, but the morning
likewise must rain her dews into your gluttonous weasand.　15

Quick. An't please you, sir, we did but drink—Ump !—to the coming off of the knightly bridegroom.

Touch. To the coming off on him ?

Quick. Ay, forsooth ! We drunk to his coming on— Ump !— when we went to bed ; and now we are up, we must 20 drink to his coming off ; for that's the chief honour of a soldier, sir ; and therefore we must drink so much the more to it, forsooth—ump !

Touch. A very capital reason ! So that you go to bed late, and rise early to commit drunkenness ; you fulfil the 25 scripture very sufficient wickedly, forsooth !

Quick. The knight's men, forsooth, be still o' their knees at it—Ump—and because 'tis for your credit, sir, I would be loath to flinch.

Touch. I pray, sir, e'en to 'em again then ; y' are one 30 of the separated crew, one of my wife's faction, and my young lady's, with whom, and with their great match, I will have nothing to do.

Quick. So, sir, now I will go keep my—Ump !—credit with 'em, an't please you, sir !   35

Touch. In any case, sir, lay one cup of sack more o' your cold stomach, I beseech you !

Quick. Yes, forsooth !   *Exit* Quicksilver

Touch. This is for my credit ; servants ever maintain drunkenness in their master's house for their master's credit ; 40 a good idle serving-man's reason. I thank Time the night is past ; I ne'er waked to such cost ; I think we have stowed more sorts of flesh in our bellies than ever Noah's ark received ; and for wine, why, my house turns giddy with it, and more noise in it than at a conduit. Ay me, even beasts 45 condemn our gluttony ! Well, 'tis our city's fault, which, because we commit seldom, we commit the more sinfully ; we lose no time in our sensuality, but we make amends for it. O that we would do so in virtue and religious negligences ! But see, here are all the sober parcels my house 50 can show ; I'll eavesdrop, hear what thoughts they utter this morning.   [*He retires*]

Golding [*and* Mildred *come forward*]

Gold. But is it possible that you, seeing your sister preferred to the bed of a knight, should contain your affections in the arms of a prentice ?   55

Mil. I had rather make up the garment of my affections

in some of the same piece, than, like a fool, wear gowns of
two colours, or mix sackcloth with satin.

Gold. And do the costly garments—the title and fame
of a lady, the fashion, observation, and reverence proper   60
to such preferment—no more inflame you than such con-
venience as my poor means and industry can offer to your
virtues ?

Mil. I have observed that the bridle given to those
violent flatteries of fortune is seldom recovered ; they bear   65
one headlong in desire from one novelty to another, and
where those ranging appetites reign, there is ever more passion than reason ; no stay, and so no happiness. These
hasty advancements are not natural. Nature hath given
us legs to go to our objects, not wings to fly to them.   70

Gold. How dear an object you are to my desires I cannot express ; whose fruition would my master's absolute
consent and yours vouchsafe me, I should be absolutely
happy. And though it were a grace so far beyond my merit
that I should blush with unworthiness to receive it, yet thus   75
far both my love and my means shall assure your requital :
you shall want nothing fit for your birth and education ;
what increase of wealth and advancement the honest and
orderly industry and skill of our trade will afford in any, I
doubt not will be aspired by me ; I will ever make your   80
contentment the end of my endeavours ; I will love you
above all ; and only your grief shall be my misery, and
your delight my felicity.

Touch. Work upon that now ! By my hopes, he wooes
honestly and orderly ; he shall be anchor of my hopes !   85
Look, see the ill-yoked monster, his fellow !

Enter Quicksilver *unlaced, a towel about his neck, in his
flat-cap, drunk*

Quick. Eastward Ho ! *Holla, ye pampered jades of Asia !*
Touch. Drunk now downright, o' my fidelity !
Quick. Ump ! Pull eo, pull eo ! Showse, quoth the caliver.
Gold. Fie, fellow Quicksilver, what a pickle are you in !   90
Quick. Pickle ? Pickle in thy throat ; zounds,
pickle ! Wa, ha, ho ! Good-morrow, knight Petronel ;
morrow, lady Goldsmith ; come off, knight, with a counter-
buff, for the honour of knighthood.
Gold. Why, how now, sir ? Do ye know where you are ?   95

Quick. Where I am? Why, 'sblood, you jolthead, where I am!

Gold. Go to, go to, for shame! Go to bed and sleep out this immodesty : thou sham'st both my master and his house.   100

Quick. Shame? What shame? I thought thou wouldst show thy bringing-up ; and thou wert a gentleman as I am, thou wouldst think it no shame to be drunk. Lend me some money, save my credit ; I must dine with the serving-men and their wives—and their wives, sirrah!   105

Gold. E'en who you will ; I'll not lend thee threepence.

Quick. 'Sfoot, lend me some money! *Hast thou not Hiren here?*

Touch. Why, how now, sirrah? What vein's this, ha?

Quick. Who cries on murther? Lady, was it you? 110 How does our master? Pray thee cry Eastward Ho!

Touch. Sirrah, sirrah, y'are past your hiccup now ; I see y'are drunk—

Quick. 'Tis for your credit, master.

Touch. And hear you keep a whore in town—   115

Quick. 'Tis for your credit, master.

Touch. And what you are out in cash, I know.

Quick. So do I ; my father's a gentleman. Work upon that now! Eastward Ho!

Touch. Sir, Eastward Ho will make you go Westward 120 Ho. I will no longer dishonest my house, nor endanger my stock with your licence. There, sir, there's your indenture ; all your apparel (that I must know) is on your back, and from this time my door is shut to you : from me be free ; but for other freedom, and the moneys you have wasted, 125 Eastward Ho shall not serve you.

Quick. Am I free o' my fetters? Rent, fly with a duck in thy mouth, and now I tell thee, Touchstone—

Touch. Good sir—

Quick. When this eternal substance of my soul—   130

Touch. Well said ; change your gold-ends for your play-ends.

Quick. Did live imprison'd in my wanton flesh—

Touch. What then, sir?

Quick. I was a courtier in the Spanish Court,   135 *And Don Andrea was my name.*

Touch. Good Master Don Andrea, will you march?

Quick. Sweet Touchstone, will you lend me two shillings?

Touch.　Not a penny!　　　　　　　　　　　　　140
Quick.　Not a penny? I have friends, and I have acquaintance; I will piss at thy shop-posts, and throw rotten eggs at thy sign. Work upon that now!

Exit staggering

Touch.　Now, sirrah, you, hear you? You shall serve me no more neither—not an hour longer!　　　　　145
Gold.　What mean you, sir?
Touch.　I mean to give thee thy freedom, and with thy freedom my daughter, and with my daughter a father's love. And with all these such a portion as shall make Knight Petronel himself envy thee! Y'are both agreed, 150 are ye not?
Ambo.　With all submission, both of thanks and duty.
Touch.　Well, then, the great Power of heaven bless and confirm you. And, Golding, that my love to thee may not show less than my wife's love to my eldest daughter, thy 155 marriage-feast shall equal the knight's and hers.
Gold.　Let me beseech you, no, sir; the superfluity and cold meat left at their nuptials will with bounty furnish ours. The grossest prodigality is superfluous cost of the belly; nor would I wish any invitement of states or friends, 160 only your reverent presence and witness shall sufficiently grace and confirm us.
Touch.　Son to my own bosom, take her and my blessing. The nice fondling, my lady, sir-reverence, that I must not now presume to call daughter, is so ravished with desire to 165 hansel her new coach, and see her knight's Eastward Castle, that the next morning will sweat with her busy setting forth. Away will she and her mother, and while their preparation is making, ourselves, with some two or three other friends, will consummate the humble match we have in 170 God's name concluded.

'Tis to my wish; for I have often read
Fit birth, fit age, keeps long a quiet bed.
'Tis to my wish; for tradesmen (well 'tis known)
Get with more ease than gentry keeps his own.　　　175

Exit [with Golding *and* Mildred]

[SCENA SECUNDA

A Room in the House of Security]

Security *solus*

[*Sec.*]　My privy guest, lusty Quicksilver, has drunk too

deep of the bride-bowl; but with a little sleep, he is much
recovered; and, I think, is making himself ready to be
drunk in a gallanter likeness. My house is, as 'twere, the
cave where the young outlaw hoards the stolen vails of his   5
occupation; and here, when he will revel it in his prodigal
similitude, he retires to his trunks, and (I may say softly)
his punks: he dares trust me with the keeping of both;
for I am Security itself; my name is Security, the famous
usurer.   10

Enter Quicksilver *in his prentice's coat and cap, his gallant
breeches and stockings, gartering himself,* Security *following*

Quick. Come, old Security, thou father of destruction!
Th' indented sheepskin is burned wherein I was wrapped;
and I am now loose to get more children of perdition into
thy usurous bonds. Thou feed'st my lechery, and I thy
covetousness; thou art pander to me for my wench, and I   15
to thee for thy cozenages. Ka me, ka thee, runs through
court and country.

Sec. Well said, my subtle Quicksilver! These ka's ope
the doors to all this world's felicity; the dullest forehead
sees it. Let not master courtier think he carries all the   20
knavery on his shoulders: I have known poor Hob in the
country, that has worn hob-nails on's shoes, have as much
villany in's head as he that wears gold buttons in's cap.

Quick. Why, man, 'tis the London highway to thrift;
if virtue be used, 'tis but as a scrap to the net of villany.   25
They that use it simply, thrive simply, I warrant. Weight
and fashion makes goldsmiths cuckolds.

Enter Sindefy, *with* Quicksilver's *doublet, cloak, rapier,
and dagger*

Sin. Here, sir, put off the other half of your prenticeship.
Quick. Well said, sweet Sin.! Bring forth my bravery.
Now let my trunks shoot forth their silks conceal'd.   30
I now am free, and now will justify
My trunks and punks. Avaunt, dull flatcap, then!
Via the curtain that shadow'd Borgia!
There lie, thou husk of my envassall'd state,
I, Sampson, now have burst the Philistines' bands,   35
And in thy lap, my lovely Dali[l]a,
I'll lie, and snore out my enfranchis'd state.

When Sampson was a tall young man,
His power and strength increased than ;
He sold no more nor cup nor can ;   40
But did them all despise.
Old Touchstone, now write to thy friends
For one to sell thy base gold-ends ;
Quicksilver now no more attends
Thee, Touchstone.   45

But, dad, hast thou seen my running gelding dressed to-
day ?

Sec. That I have, Frank. The ostler o'th' Cock dressed
him for a breakfast.

Quick. What, did he eat him ?   50

Sec. No, but he eat his breakfast for dressing him ; and
so dressed him for breakfast

Quick. O witty age, where age is young in wit,
And all youth's words have gray beards full of it !

Sin. But alas, Frank, how will all this be maintained   55
now ? Your place maintained it before.

Quick. Why, and I maintained my place. I'll to the
Court, another manner of place for maintenance, I hope,
than the silly City ! I heard my father say, I heard my
mother sing an old song and a true : *Thou art a she-fool, and*   60
know'st not what belongs to our male wisdom. I shall be a
merchant, forsooth, trust my estate in a wooden trough as
he does ! What are these ships but tennis-balls for the
winds to play withal ? Tossed from one wave to another ;
now under line, now over the house ; sometimes brick-   65
walled against a rock, so that the guts fly out again ; sometimes strook under the wide hazard, and farewell, master
merchant !

Sin. Well, Frank, well : the seas you say, are uncertain ;
but he that sails in your Court seas shall find 'em ten times   70
fuller of hazard ; wherein to see what is to be seen is torment
more than a free spirit can endure ; but when you come
to suffer, how many injuries swallow you ! What care and
devotion must you use to humour an imperious lord, proportion your looks to his looks, smiles to his smiles, fit   75
your sails to the wind of his breath !

Quick. Tush, he's no journeyman in his craft that
cannot do that !

Sin. But he's worse than a prentice that does it ; not

only humouring the lord, but every trencher-bearer, every   80
groom, that by indulgence and intelligence crept into his
favour, and by panderism into his chamber ; he rules the
roast ; and when my honourable lord says it shall be thus,
my worshipful rascal, the groom of his close-stool, says it
shall not be thus, claps the door after him, and who dares   85
enter ?   A prentice, quoth you ?   'Tis but to learn to
live ; and does that disgrace a man ?   He that rises hardly
stands firmly ;   but he that rises with ease, alas, falls as
easily !

Quick.   A pox on you !   Who taught you this morality ?   90

Sec.   'Tis 'long of this witty age, Master Francis.   But,
indeed, Mistress Sindefy, all trades complain of inconveni-
ence, and therefore 'tis best to have none.   The merchant,
he complains and says, ' Traffic is subject to much uncer-
tainty and loss.'   Let 'em keep their goods on dry land,   95
with a vengeance, and not expose other men's substances
to the mercy of the winds, under protection of a wooden
wall (as Master Francis says) ;   and all for greedy desire to
enrich themselves with unconscionable gain, two for one,
or so ;   where I, and such other honest men as live by lending   100
money, are content with moderate profit ;   thirty or forty
i'th'hundred, so we may have it with quietness, and out of
peril of wind and weather, rather than run those dangerous
courses of trading, as they do.

Quick.   Ay, dad, thou mayst well be called Security, for   105
thou takest the safest course.   [*Exit* Sindefy]

Sec.   Faith, the quieter, and the more contented, and,
out of doubt, the more godly ;   for merchants, in their
courses, are never pleased, but ever repining against heaven :
one prays for a westerly wind to carry his ship forth ;   110
another for an easterly to bring his ship home ; and at every
shaking of a leaf he falls into an agony to think what danger
his ship is in on such a coast, and so forth.   The farmer,
he is ever at odds with the weather : sometimes the clouds
have been too barren ; sometimes the heavens forget them-   115
selves ; their harvests answer not their hopes ; sometimes
the season falls out too fruitful, corn will bear no price, and
so forth.   The artificer, he's all for a stirring world ; if his
trade be too full, and fall short of his expectation, then
falls he out of joint.   Where we that trade nothing but   120
money are free from all this ; we are pleased with all
weathers, let it rain or hold up, be calm or windy ; let the

season be whatsoever, let trade go how it will, we take all
in good part, e'en what please the heavens to send us, so
the sun stand not still, and the moon keep her usual returns, 125
and make up days, months, and years.

Quick. And you have good security !

Sec. Ay, marry, Frank, that's the special point.

Quick. And yet, forsooth, we must have trades to live
withal ; for we cannot stand without legs, nor fly without 130
wings, and a number of such scurvy phrases. No, I say
still, he that has wit, let him live by his wit ; he that has
none, let him be a tradesman.

Sec. Witty Master Francis, 'tis pity any trade should
dull that quick brain of yours ! Do but bring Knight 135
Petronel into my parchment toils once, and you shall never
need to toil in any trade, o'my credit. You know his wife's
land ?

Quick. Even to a foot, sir ; I have been often there ;
a pretty fine seat, good land, all entire within itself.　　140

Sec. Well wooded ?

Quick. Two hundred pounds' worth of wood ready to
fell, and a fine sweet house, that stands just in the midst
on't, like a prick in the midst of a circle ; would I were
your farmer, for a hundred pound a year !　　145

Sec. Excellent Master Francis, how I do long to do
thee good ! How I do hunger and thirst to have the honour
to enrich thee ! Ay, even to die that thou mightest inherit
my living ; even hunger and thirst ! For o' my religion,
Master Francis—and so tell Knight Petronel—I do it to do 150
him a pleasure.

Quick. Marry, dad, his horses are now coming up to
bear down his lady ; wilt thou lend him thy stable to set
'em in ?

Sec. Faith, Master Francis, I would be loath to lend 155
my stable out of doors ; in a greater matter I will pleasure
him, but not in this.

Quick. A pox of your hunger and thirst ! Well, dad,
let him have money ; all he could any way get is bestowed
on a ship now bound for Virginia ; the frame of which voyage 160
is so closely conveyed that his new lady nor any of her friends
know it. Notwithstanding, as soon as his lady's hand is
gotten to the sale of her inheritance, and you have furnished
him with money, he will instantly hoist sail and away.

Sec. Now, a frank gale of wind go with him, Master 165

Frank! We have too few such knight adventurers. Who
would not sell away competent certainties to purchase,
with any danger, excellent uncertainties? Your true knight
venturer ever does it. Let his wife seal to-day; he shall
have his money to-day.   170

Quick. To-morrow she shall, dad, before she goes into
the country; to work her to which action with the more
engines, I purpose presently to prefer my sweet Sin. here to
the place of her gentlewoman; whom you (for the more
credit) shall present as your friend's daughter, a gentle- 175
woman of the country, new come up with a will for awhile
to learn fashions, forsooth, and be toward some lady; and
she shall buzz pretty devices into her lady's ear, feeding
her humours so serviceable, as the manner of such as she
is, you know—   180

Sec. True, good Master Francis!

Enter Sindefy

Quick. That she shall keep her port open to anything
she commends to her.

Sec. O' my religion, a most fashionable project; as
good she spoil the lady, as the lady spoil her, for 'tis three 185
to one of one side. Sweet Mistress Sin., how are you bound
to Master Francis! I do not doubt to see you shortly wed
one of the head men of our city.

Sin. But, sweet Frank, when shall my father Security
present me?   190

Quick. With all festination; I have broken the ice to
it already; and will presently to the knight's house, whither,
my good old dad, let me pray thee with all formality to man
her.

Sec. Command me, Master Francis, I do hunger and 195
thirst to do thee service. Come, sweet Mistress Sin., take
leave of my Winifred, and we will instantly meet frank
Master Francis at your lady's.

Enter Winifred *above*

Win. Where is my Cu. there? Cu.?
Sec. Ay, Winnie!   200
Win. Wilt thou come in, sweet Cu.?
Sec. Ay, Winnie, presently!

                    Exeunt [Winifred, Security, *and* Sindefie]
Quick. Ay, Winnie, quod he! That's all he can do, poor

man, he may well cut off her name at Winnie. O 'tis an
egregious pander ! What will not an usurous knave be, so he 205
may be rich ? O 'tis a notable Jew's trump ! I hope to live
to see dogs' meat made of the old usurer's flesh, dice of his
bones, and indentures of his skin ; and yet his skin is too thick
to make parchment, 'twould make good boots for a peterman
to catch salmon in. Your only smooth skin to make fine 210
vellum is your Puritan's skin ; they be the smoothest and
slickest knaves in a country.   [*Exit*]

[SCENA TERTIA

Before Sir Petronel's *Lodging*]

Enter Sir Petronel *in boots, with a riding wan*[d] [*followed
by* Quicksilver]

Sir Pet. I'll out of this wicked town as fast as my horse
can trot. Here's now no good action for a man to spend
his time in. Taverns grow dead ; ordinaries are blown up ;
plays are at a stand ; houses of hospitality at a fall ; not a
feather waving, nor a spur jingling anywhere. I'll away   5
instantly.

Quick. Y'ad best take some crowns in your purse, knight,
or else your Eastward Castle will smoke but miserably.

Sir Pet. O, Frank, my castle ! Alas, all the castles I
have are built with air, thou know'st !   10

Quick. I know it, knight, and therefore wonder whither
your lady is going.

Sir Pet. Faith, to seek her fortune, I think. I said I had
a castle and land eastward, and eastward she will, without
contradiction ; her coach and the coach of the sun must meet   15
full butt. And the sun being out-shined with her ladyship's
glory, she fears he goes westward to hang himself.

Quick. And I fear, when her enchanted castle becomes
invisible, her ladyship will return and follow his example.

Sir Pet. O that she would have the grace, for I shall   20
never be able to pacify her, when she sees herself deceived so.

Quick. As easily as can be. Tell her she mistook your
directions, and that shortly yourself will down with her to
approve it ; and then clothe but her crupper in a new gown,
and you may drive her any way you list. For these women,   25
sir, are like Essex calves, you must wriggle 'em on by the tail
still, or they will never drive orderly.

Sir Pet. But, alas, sweet Frank, thou know'st my hability will not furnish her blood with those costly humours.

Quick. Cast that cost on me, sir. I have spoken to my old 30 pander, Security, for money or commodity; and commodity (if you will) I know he will procure you.

Sir Pet. Commodity! Alas, what commodity?

Quick. Why, sir, what say you to figs and raisins?

Sir Pet. A plague of figs and raisins, and all such frail 35 commodities! We shall make nothing of 'em.

Quick. Why then, sir, what say you to forty pound in roasted beef?

Sir Pet. Out upon 't! I have less stomach to that than to the figs and raisins; I'll out of town, though I sojourn with 40 a friend of mine; for stay here I must not; my creditors have laid to arrest me, and I have no friend under heaven but my sword to bail me.

Quick. God's me, knight, put 'em in sufficient sureties, rather than let your sword bail you! Let 'em take their 45 choice, either the King's Bench or the Fleet, or which of the two Counters they like best, for, by the Lord, I like none of 'em.

Sir Pet. Well, Frank, there is no jesting with my earnest necessity; thou know'st if I make not present money to 50 further my voyage begun, all's lost, and all I have laid out about it.

Quick. Why, then, sir, in earnest, if you can get your wise lady to set her hand to the sale of her inheritance, the blood-hound, Security, will smell out ready money for you in- 55 stantly.

Sir Pet. There spake an angel! To bring her to which conformity, I must feign myself extremely amorous; and alleging urgent excuses for my stay behind, part with her as passionately as she would from her foisting hound.   60

Quick. You have the sow by the right ear, sir. I warrant there was never child longed more to ride a cock-horse or wear his new coat, then she longs to ride in her new coach. She would long for everything when she was a maid. and now she will run mad for 'em. I lay my life, she will 65 have every year four children; and what charge and change of humour you must endure while she is with child, and how she will tie you to your tackling till she be with child, a dog would not endure. Nay, there is no turnspit dog bound to his wheel more servilely than you shall be to her wheel; for 70

as that dog can never climb the top of his wheel but when
the top comes under him, so shall you never climb the top
of her contentment but when she is under you.

Sir Pet. 'Slight, how thou terrifiest me !

Quick. Nay, hark you, sir ; what nurses, what mid- 75
wives, what fools, what physicians, what cunning women
must be sought for (fearing sometimes she is bewitched, sometimes in a consumption) to tell her tales, to talk bawdy to
her, to make her laugh, to give her glisters, to let her blood
under the tongue and betwixt the toes ; how she will revile 80
and kiss you, spit in your face, and lick it off again ; how she
will vaunt you are her creature, she made you of nothing ;
how she could have had thousand mark jointures ; she could
have been made a lady by a Scotch knight, and never ha'
married him ; she could have had [panadas] in her bed 85
every morning ; how she set you up, and how she will pull
you down : you'll never be able to stand of your legs to
endure it.

Sir Pet. Out of my fortune, what a death is my life
bound face to face to ! The best is, a large time-fitted 90
conscience is bound to nothing ; marriage is but a form in
the school of policy, to which scholars sit fastened only with
painted chains. Old Security's young wife is ne'er the further
off with me.

Quick. Thereby lies a tale, sir. The old usurer will be here 95
instantly with my punk Sindefy, whom you know your
lady has promisèd me to entertain for her gentlewoman ;
and he (with a purpose to feed on you) invites you most
solemnly by me to supper.

Sir Pet. It falls out excellently fitly ; I see desire of gain 100
makes jealousy venturous.

Enter Gertrude

See, Frank, here comes my lady. Lord, how she views thee !
She knows thee not, I think, in this bravery.

Ger. How now ? Who be you, I pray ?

Quick. One Master Francis Quicksilver, an't please your 105
ladyship.

Ger. God's my dignity ! As I am a lady, if he did not
make me blush so that mine eyes stood a-water, would
I were unmarried again ! Where's my woman, I pray ?

Enter Security *and* Sindefy

Quick. See, madam, she now comes to attend you. 110

Sec. God save my honourable knight and his worshipful lady !

Ger. Y'are very welcome ; you must not put on your hat yet.

Sec. No, madam ; till I know your ladyship's further 115 pleasure, I will not presume.

Ger. And is this a gentleman's daughter new come out of the country ?

Sec. She is, madam ; and one that her father hath a special care to bestow in some honourable lady's service, to put her 120 out of her honest humours, forsooth ; for she had a great desire to be a nun, an't please you.

Ger. A nun ? What nun ? A nun substantive, or a nun adjective ?

Sec. A nun substantive, madam, I hope, if a nun be a noun. 125 But I mean, lady, a vowed maid of that order.

Ger. I'll teach her to be a maid of the order, I warrant you ! And can you do any work belongs to a lady's chamber ?

Sin. What I cannot do, madam, I would be glad to learn.

Ger. Well said, hold up, then ; hold up your head, I say ! 130 Come hither a little.

Sin. I thank your ladyship.

Ger. And hark you—good man, you may put on your hat now ; I do not look on you—I must have you of my faction now ; not of my knight's, maid !   135

Sin. No, forsooth, madam, of yours.

Ger. And draw all my servants in my bow, and keep my counsel, and tell me tales, and put me riddles, and read on a book sometimes when I am busy, and laugh at country gentlewomen, and command anything in the house for my 140 retainers ; and care not what you spend, for it is all mine ; and in any case be still a maid, whatsoever you do, or whatsoever any man can do unto you.

Sec. I warrant your ladyship for that.

Ger. Very well ; you shall ride in my coach with me into 145 the country to-morrow morning. Come, knight, I pray thee let's make a short supper, and to bed presently.

Sec. Nay, good madam, this night I have a short supper at home waits on his worship's acceptation.

Ger. By my faith, but he shall not go, sir ; I shall swoun 150 and he sup from me.

Sir Pet. Pray thee, forbear ; shall he lose his provision ?

Ger. Ay, by[r]lady, sir, rather than I lose my longing.
Come in, I say ; as I am a lady, you shall not go.   155
Quick. [*aside to* Security] I told him what a burr he
had gotten.
Sec. If you will not sup from your knight, madam, let
me entreat your ladyship to sup at my house with him.
Ger. No, by my faith, sir ; then we cannot be abed soon 160
enough after supper.
Sir Pet. What a med'cine is this ! Well, Master Security,
you are new married as well as I ; I hope you are bound as
well. We must honour our young wives, you know.
Quick. [*aside to* Security] In policy, dad, till to-morrow 165
she has sealed.
Sec. I hope in the morning, yet, your knighthood will
breakfast with me ?
Sir Pet. As early as you will, sir.
Sec Thank your good worship ; I do hunger and thirst 170
to do you good, sir.
Ger. Come, sweet knight, come ; I do hunger and thirst to
be abed with thee.   *Exeunt*

ACTUS TERTII SCENA PRIMA

[*A Room in* Security's *House*]

Enter Sir Petronel, Quicksilver, Security, Bramble, *and* Winifred

Sir Pet. Thanks for our feast-like breakfast, good Master
Security ; I am sorry (by reason of my instant haste to so
long a voyage as Virginia) I am without means by any kind
amends to show how affectionately I take your kindness, and
to confirm by some worthy ceremony a perpetual league   5
of friendship betwixt us.
Sec. Excellent knight, let this be a token betwixt us of
inviolable friendship : I am new married to this fair gentlewoman, you know, and by my hope to make her fruitful,
though I be something in years, I vow faithfully unto you to 10
make you godfather (though in your absence) to the first
child I am blest withal ; and henceforth call me gossip, I
beseech you, if you please to accept it.
Sir Pet. In the highest degree of gratitude, my most
worthy gossip ; for confirmation of which friendly title, let 15
me entreat my fair gossip, your wife here, to accept this dia-

mond, and keep it as my gift to her first child, wheresoever my
fortune, in event of my voyage, shall bestow me.

Sec. How now, my coy wedlock, make you strange of so
noble a favour ? Take it, I charge you, with all affection, and,   20
by way of taking your leave, present boldly your lips to
our honourable gossip.

Quick. [*aside*] How venturous he is to him, and how
jealous to others !

Sir Pet. Long may this kind touch of our lips print in our   25
hearts all the forms of affection. And now, my good gossip,
if the writings be ready to which my wife should seal, let
them be brought this morning before she takes coach into the
country, and my kindness shall work her to dispatch it.

Sec. The writings are ready, sir. My learned counsel   30
here, Master Bramble the lawyer, hath perused them ; and
within this hour I will bring the scrivener with them to your
worshipful lady.

Sir Pet. Good Master Bramble, I will here take my leave
of you then. God send you fortunate pleas, sir, and con-   35
tentious clients !

Bram. And you foreright winds, sir, and a fortunate
voyage !   *Exit*

Enter a Messenger

Mes. Sir Petronel, here are three or four gentlemen
desire to speak with you.   40

Sir Pet. What are they ?

Quick. They are your followers in this voyage, knight,
Captain Seagull and his associates ; I met them this morning,
and told them you would be here.

Sir Pet. Let them enter, I pray you ; I know they long to   45
be gone, for their stay is dangerous.

Enter Seagull, Scapethrift, *and* Spendall

Sea. God save my honourable Colonel !

Sir Pet. Welcome, good Captain Seagull and worthy
gentlemen. If you will meet my friend Frank here and me, at
the Blue Anchor Tavern by Billingsgate this evening, we   50
will there drink to our happy voyage, be merry, and take
boat to our ship with all expedition.

Spen. Defer it no longer, I beseech you, sir ; but as your
voyage is hitherto carried closely, and in another knight's
name, so for your own safety and ours, let it be continued,   55

our meeting and speedy purpose of departing known to as few as is possible, lest your ship and goods be attached.

Quick. Well advised, Captain ! Our colonel shall have money this morning to dispatch all our departures ; bring those gentlemen at night to the place appointed, and with 60 our skins full of vintage we'll take occasion by the vantage, and away.

Spen. We will not fail but be there, sir.

Sir Pet. Good morrow, good Captain and my worthy associates. Health and all sovereignty to my beautiful 65 gossip ; for you, sir, we shall see you presently with the writings.

Sec. With writings and crowns to my honourable gossip. I do hunger and thirst to do you good, sir !　　　*Exeunt*

SCENA SECUNDA

[*An inn-yard*]

Enter a Coachman *in haste, in's frock, feeding*

Coach. Here's a stir when citizens ride out of town, indeed, as if all the house were afire ! 'Slight, they will not give a man leave to eat's breakfast afore he rises !

Enter Hamlet, *a footman, in haste*

Ham. What, coachman ! My lady's coach, for shame ! Her ladyship's ready to come down.　　　　　　　　5

Enter Potkin, *a tankard-bearer*

Pot. 'Sfoot, Hamlet, are you mad ? Whither run you now ? You should brush up my old mistress !

　　　　　　　　　　　　　　　　　　[*Exit* Hamlet]

Enter Sindefy

Sin. What, Potkin ? You must put off your tankard, and put on your blue coat and wait upon Mistress Touch-stone into the country.　　　　　　　　　　*Exit* 10

Pot. I will, forsooth, presently.　　　　　　　　*Exit*

Enter Mistress Fond *and Mistress* Gazer

Fond. Come, sweet Mistress Gazer, let's watch here, and see my Lady Flash take coach.

Gaz. O' my word here's a most fine place to stand in. Did you see the new ship launched last day, Mistress Fond ? 15

Fond. O God, and we citizens should lose such a sight !

Gaz. I warrant here will be double as many people to
see her take coach as there were to see it take water.

Fond. O she's married to a most fine castle i'th' country,
they say.   20

Gaz. But there are no giants in the castle, are there ?

Fond. O no ; they say her knight killed 'em all, and therefore he was knighted.

Gaz. Would to God her ladyship would come away !

Enter Gertrude, Mistress Touchstone, Sindefy, Hamlet,
Potkin

Fond. She comes, she comes, she comes !   25

Gaz. } Pray heaven bless your ladyship !
Fond }

Ger. Thank you, good people ! My coach, for the love
of heaven, my coach ! In good truth I shall swoun else.

Ham. Coach, coach, my lady's coach !   *Exit*

Ger. As I am a lady, I think I am with child already, I long 30
for a coach so. May one be with child afore they are married,
mother ?

Mist. Touch. Ay, by'r lady, madam ; a little thing does
that ; I have seen a little prick no bigger than a pin's head
swell bigger and bigger till it has come to an ancome ; and e'en 35
so 'tis in these cases.

Enter Hamlet

Ham. Your coach is coming, madam.

Ger. That's well said. Now, heaven, methinks I am
e'en up to the knees in preferment !

[*sings*]

But a little higher, but a little higher, but a little higher,   40
There, there, there lies Cupid's fire !

Mist. Touch. But must this young man, an't please you,
madam, run by your coach all the way a-foot ?

Ger. Ay, by my faith, I warrant him ! He gives no other
milk, as I have another servant does.   45

Mist. Touch. Alas, 'tis e'en pity, methinks ! For God's
sake, madam, buy him but a hobby-horse ; let the poor
youth have something betwixt his legs to ease 'em. Alas,
we must do as we would be done to !

Get. Go to, hold your peace, dame ; you talk like an old 50
fool, I tell you !

Enter Sir Petronel *and* Quicksilver

Sir Pet. Wilt thou be gone, sweet honeysuckle, before I
can go with thee ?

Ger. I pray thee, sweet knight, let me ; I do so long to
dress up thy castle afore thou com'st. But I marle how　55
my modest sister occupies herself this morning, that she
cannot wait on me to my coach, as well as her mother.

Quick. Marry, madam, she's married by this time to prentice Golding. Your father, and some one more, stole to
church with 'em in all the haste, that the cold meat left at　60
your wedding might serve to furnish their nuptial table.

Ger. There's no base fellow, my father, now ! But he's
e'en fit to father such a daughter : he must call me daughter
no more now ; but ' madam,' and ' please you, madam,' and
' please your worship, madam,' indeed. Out upon him, marry　65
his daughter to a base prentice !

Mist. Touch. What should one do ? Is there no law for
one that marries a woman's daughter against her will ? How
shall we punish him, madam ?

Ger. As I am a lady, an't would snow, we'd so pebble　70
'em with snow-balls as they come from church ; but, sirrah
Frank Quicksilver !

Quick. Ay, madam.

Ger. Dost remember since thou and I clapped what-d'ye-
call'ts in the garret ?　　　　　　　　　　　　　　　75

Quick. I know not what you mean, madam.

Ger. [*sings*] *His head as white as milk, all flaxen was his*
　　　　　　hair ;
　　　　But now he is dead, and laid in his bed,
　　　　And never will come again.

God be at your labour !　　　　　　　　　　　　　80

Enter Touchstone, Golding, Mildred, *with rosemary*

Sir Pet. [*aside*] Was there ever such a lady ?

Quick. See, madam, the bride and bridegroom !

Ger. God's my precious ! God give you joy, Mistress
What-lack-you ! Now out upon thee, baggage ! My sister
married in a taffeta hat ! Marry, hang you ! Westward with　85
a wanion t'ye ! Nay, I have done wi' ye, minion, then, i'faith ;
never look to have my count'nance any more, nor anything
I can do for thee. Thou ride in my coach, or come down to
my castle ! Fie upon thee ! I charge thee in my ladyship's
name, call me sister no more.　　　　　　　　　　　　90

Touch. An't please your worship, this is not your sister ; this is my daughter, and she calls me father, and so does not your ladyship, an't please your worship, madam.

Mist. Touch. No, nor she must not call thee father by heraldry, because thou mak'st thy prentice thy son as well as 95 she. Ah, thou misproud prentice, dar'st thou presume to marry a lady's sister ?

Gold. It pleased my master, forsooth, to embolden me with his favour ; and though I confess myself far unworthy so worthy a wife (being in part her servant, as I am your 100 prentice) yet since (I may say it without boasting) I am born a gentleman, and by the trade I have learned of my master (which I trust taints not my blood) able with mine own industry and portion to maintain your daughter, my hope is heaven will so bless our humble beginning that in the 105 end I shall be no disgrace to the grace with which my master hath bound me his double prentice.

Touch. Master me no more, son, if thou think'st me worthy to be thy father.

Ger. Son ? Now, good Lord, how he shines, and you 110 mark him ! He's a gentleman !

Gold. Ay, indeed, madam, a gentleman born.

Sir Pet. Never stand o' your gentry, Master Bridegroom ; if your legs be no better than your arms, you'll be able to stand upright on neither shortly. 115

Touch. An't please your good worship, sir, there are two sorts of gentlemen.

Sir Pet. What mean you, sir ?

Touch. Bold to put off my hat to your worship—

Sir Pet. Nay, pray forbear, sir, and then forth with your 120 two sorts of gentlemen.

Touch. If your worship will have it so, I say there are two sorts of gentlemen. There is a gentleman artificial, and a gentleman natural. Now though your worship be a gentleman natural—work upon that now ! 125

Quick. Well said, old Touchstone ; I am proud to hear thee enter a set speech, i'faith ! Forth, I beseech thee !

Touch. Cry you mercy, sir, your worship's a gentleman I do not know. If you be one of my acquaintance, y'are very much disguised, sir. 130

Quick. Go to, old quipper ! Forth with thy speech, I say !

Touch. What, sir, my speeches were ever in vain to your gracious worship ; and therefore, till I speak to you—gallan-

try indeed—I will save my breath for my broth anon.
Come, my poor son and daughter, let us hide ourselves in our 135
poor humility, and live safe. Ambition consumes itself
with the very show. Work upon that now!

[*Exeunt* Touchstone, Golding, *and* Mildred]

Ger. Let him go, let him go, for God's sake! Let him
make his prentice his son, for God's sake! Give away his
daughter, for God's sake! And when they come a-begging to 140
us for God's sake, let's laugh at their good husbandry, for
God's sake! Farewell, sweet knight, pray thee make haste
after.

Sir Pet. What shall I say? I would not have thee go.

Quick. Now, O now, I must depart; 145
   Parting though it absence move—
This ditty, knight, do I see in thy looks in capital letters.

*What a grief 'tis to depart, and leave the flower that has
   my heart!*
My sweet lady, and alack for woe, why should we part so?

Tell truth, knight, and shame all dissembling lovers; does 150
not your pain lie on that side?

Sir Pet. If it do, canst thou tell me how I may cure it?

Quick. Excellent easily! Divide yourself in two halves,
just by the girdlestead; send one half with your lady, and
keep the tother yourself; or else do as all true lovers do— 155
part with your heart, and leave your body behind. I have
seen't done a hundred times: 'tis as easy a matter for a
lover to part without a heart from his sweetheart, and he
ne'er the worse, as for a mouse to get from a trap and leave 160
her tail behind him. See, here comes the writings.

Enter Security *with a* Scrivener

Sec. Good morrow to my worshipful lady! I present
your ladyship with this writing, to which if you please to
set your hand with your knight's, a velvet gown shall attend
your journey, o' my credit. 165

Ger. What writing is it, knight?

Sir Pet. The sale, sweetheart, of the poor tenement I
told thee of, only to make a little money to send thee down
furniture for my castle, to which my hand shall lead thee.

Ger. Very well! Now give me your pen, I pray. 170

Quick. [*aside*] It goes down without chewing, i'faith!

Scriv. Your worships deliver this as your deed?

Ambo. We do.

Ger. So now, knight, farewell till I see thee !

Sir Pet. All farewell to my sweetheart !   175

Mist. Touch. God-b'w'y', son knight !

Sir Pet. Farewell, my good mother !

Ger. Farewell, Frank ; I would fain take thee down if
I could.

Quick. I thank your good ladyship ; farewell, Mistress 180
Sindefy.   *Exeunt* [Gertrude *and her party*]

Sir Pet. O tedious voyage whereof there is no end !
What will they think of me ?

Quick. Think what they list. They longed for a vagary
into the country and now they are fitted. So a woman 185
marry to ride in a coach, she cares not if she ride to her ruin.
'Tis the great end of many of their marriages. This is not
[the] first time a lady has rid a false journey in her coach,
I hope.

Sir Pet. Nay, 'tis no matter, I care little what they think ; 190
he that weighs men's thoughts has his hands full of nothing.
A man, in the course of this world, should be like a surgeon's
instrument—work in the wounds of others, and feel nothing
himself. The sharper and subtler, the better.

Quick. As it falls out now, knight, you shall not need 195
to devise excuses, or endure her outcries, when she returns ;
we shall now be gone before, where they cannot reach us.

Sir Pet. Well, my kind compeer, you have now the assurance we both can make you ; let me now entreat you, the
money we agreed on may be brought to the Blue Anchor, 200
near to Billingsgate, by six o'clock ; where I and my chief
friends, bound for this voyage, will with feasts attend you.

Sec. The money, my most honourable compere, shall
without fail observe your appointed hour.

Sir Pet. Thanks, my dear gossip. I must now impart 205
To your approved love a loving secret,
As one on whom my life doth more rely
In friendly trust than any man alive.
Nor shall you be the chosen secretary
Of my affections for affection only :   210
For I protest (if God bless my return)
To make you partner in my actions' gain
As deeply as if you had ventur'd with me
Half my expences. Know then, honest gossip,
I have enjoy'd with such divine contentment   215
A gentlewoman's bed, whom you well know,

That I shall ne'er enjoy this tedious voyage,
Nor live the least part of the time it asketh,
Without her presence ; so I thirst and hunger
To taste the dear feast of her company.　　　　　220
And if the hunger and the thirst you vow,
As my sworn gossip, to my wished good
Be (as I know it is) unfeign'd and firm,
Do me an easy favour in your power.

　　Ser.　Be sure, brave gossip, all that I can do,　　225
To my best nerve, is wholly at your service :
Who is the woman, first, that is your friend ?

　　Sir Pet.　The woman is your learned counsel's wife,
The lawyer, Master Bramble ; whom would you
Bring out this even in honest neighbourhood,　　230
To take his leave with you of me your gossip,
I, in the meantime, will send this my friend
Home to his house, to bring his wife disguis'd,
Before his face, into our company ;
For love hath made her look for such a wile　　235
To free her from his tyrannous jealousy.
And I would take this course before another,
In stealing her away to make us sport
And gull his circumspection the more grossly.
And I am sure that no man like yourself　　240
Hath credit with him to entice his jealousy
To so long stay abroad as may give time
To her enlargement in such safe disguise.

　　Sec.　A pretty, pithy, and most pleasant project !
Who would not strain a point of neighbourhood　　245
For such a point-device, that, as the ship
Of famous Draco went about the world,
Will wind about the lawyer, compassing
The world himself ; he hath it in his arms,
And that's enough for him without his wife.　　250
A lawyer is ambitious, and his head
Cannot be prais'd nor rais'd too high,
With any fork of highest knavery.
I'll go fetch her straight.　　　　　*Exit* Security

　　Sir Pet.　So, so.　Now, Frank, go thou home to his house, 255
Stead of his lawyer's, and bring his wife hither,
Who, just like to the lawyer's wife, is prison'd
With his stern usurous jealousy, which could never
Be over-reach'd thus but with over-reaching.

Enter Security

Sec. And, Master Francis, watch you th' instant time 260
To enter with his exit : 'twill be rare,
Two fine horn'd beasts—a camel and a lawyer !   [*Exit*]
  Quick. How the old villain joys in villany !

Enter Security

Sec. And hark you, gossip, when you have her here,
Have your boat ready, ship her to your ship   265
With utmost haste, lest Master Bramble stay you.
To o'er-reach that head that out-reacheth all heads,
'Tis a trick rampant ! 'Tis a very quiblin !
I hope this harvest to pitch cart with lawyers,
Their heads will be so forked. This sly touch   270
Will get apes to invent a number such.   *Exit*
  Quick. Was ever rascal honey'd so with poison ?
He that delights in slavish avarice,
Is apt to joy in every sort of vice.
Well, I'll go fetch his wife, whilst he the lawyer's.   275
  Sir Pet. But stay, Frank, let's think how we may dis-
guise her upon this sudden.
  Quick. God's me, there's the mischief ! But hark you,
here's an excellent device ; 'fore God, a rare one ! I will
carry her a sailor's gown and cap, and cover her, and a 280
player's beard.
  Sir Pet. And what upon her head ?
  Quick. I tell you, a sailor's cap ! 'Slight, God forgive
me, what kind of figent memory have you ?
  Sir Pet. Nay, then, what kind of figent wit hast thou ? 285
A sailor's cap ? How shall she put it off
When thou present'st her to our company ?
  Quick. Tush, man, for that, make her a saucy sailor.
  Sir Pet. Tush, tush, 'tis no fit sauce for such sweet
    mutton !
I know not what t' advise.   290

Enter Security, *with his wife's gown*

Sec.   Knight, knight, a rare device !
Sir Pet. 'Swounds, yet again !
Quick.   What stratagem have you now ?
Sec. The best that ever ! You talk'd of disguising ?
Sir Pet. Ay, marry, gossip, that's our present care.
Sec. Cast care away then ; here's the best device

For plain security (for I am no better)   295
I think, that ever liv'd : here's my wife's gown,
Which you may put upon the lawyer's wife,
And which I brought you, sir, for two great reasons ;
One is, that Master Bramble may take hold
Of some suspicion that it is my wife,   300
And gird me so, perhaps, with his law-wit ;
The other (which is policy indeed)
Is that my wife may now be tied at home,
Having no more but her old gown abroad,
And not show me a quirk, while I firk others.   305
Is not this rare ?
    Ambo.   The best that ever was.
    Sec. Am I not born to furnish gentlemen ?
    Sir Pet. O my dear gossip !
    Sec. Well, hold, Master Francis ! Watch when the law-
yer's out, and put it in. And now I will go fetch him. 310

                          Exit[urus]

    Quick. [*aside*] O my dad ! He goes, as 'twere the devil,
to fetch the lawyer ; and devil shall he be, if horns will
make him.
    Sir Pet. Why, how now, gossip ? Why stay you there
musing ?   315
    Sec. A toy, a toy runs in my head, i'faith !
    Quick. A pox of that head ! Is there more toys yet ?
    Sir Pet. What is it, pray thee, gossip ?
    Sec. Why, sir, what if you should slip away now with
my wife's best gown, I having no security for it ?   320
    Quick. For that, I hope, dad, you will take our words.
    Sec. Ay, by th' mass, your word ! That's a proper
      staff
For wise Security to lean upon !
But 'tis no matter, once I'll trust my name
On your crack'd credits ; let it take no shame.   325
Fetch the wench, Frank.   *Exit*
    Quick.   I'll wait upon you, sir,
And fetch you over, you were ne'er so fetch'd.
Go to the tavern, knight ; your followers
Dare not be drunk, I think, before their captain. *Exit*
    Sir Pet. Would I might lead them to no hotter service 330
Till our Virginian gold were in our purses !   *Exit*

[SCENA TERTIA]

Enter Seagull, Spendall, *and* Scapethrift, *in the Tavern,*
with a Drawer `

Sea. Come, drawer, pierce your neatest hogsheads, and
let's have cheer, not fit for your Billingsgate tavern, but
for our Virginian colonel ; he will be here instantly.

Draw. You shall have all things fit, sir ; please you have
any more wine ?   5

Spen. More wine, slave ? Whether we drink it or no,
spill it, and draw more.

Scape. Fill all the pots in your house with all sorts of
liquor, and let 'em wait on us here like soldiers in their
pewter coats ; and though we do not employ them now, yet   10
we will maintain 'em till we do.

Draw. Said like an honourable captain ; you shall have
all you can command, sir.   *Exit* Drawer

Sea. Come, boys, Virginia longs till we share the rest of
her maidenhead.   15

Spen. Why, is she inhabited already with any English ?

Sea. A whole country of English is there, man, bred of
those that were left there in '79. They have married with
the Indians, and make 'em bring forth as beautiful faces as
any we have in England ; and therefore the Indians are so   20
in love with 'em, that all the treasure they have they lay at
their feet.

Scape. But is there such treasure there, captain, as I
have heard ?

Sea. I tell thee, gold is more plentiful there than copper   25
is with us ; and for as much red copper as I can bring, I'll
have thrice the weight in gold. Why, man, all their drip-
ping-pans and their chamber-pots are pure gold ; and all
the chains with which they chain up their streets are massy
gold ; all the prisoners they take are fettered in gold ; and   30
for rubies and diamonds, they go forth on holidays and
gather 'em by the sea-shore to hang on their children's
coats and stick in their caps, as commonly as our children
wear saffron-gilt brooches and groats with holes in 'em.

Scape. And is it a pleasant country withal ?   35

Sea. As ever the sun shined on ; temperate and full of
all sorts of excellent viands : wild boar is as common there
as our tamest bacon is here ; venison as mutton. And

then you shall live freely there, without sergeants, or courtiers, or lawyers, or intelligencers, only a few industrious　40
Scots, perhaps, who, indeed, are dispersed over the face of
the whole earth.　But as for them, there are no greater
friends to Englishmen and England, when they are out on't,
in the world than they are.　And for my own part, I would
a hundred thousand of 'em were there, for we are all one　45
countrymen now, ye know, and we should find ten times
more comfort of them there than we do here.　Then for your
means to advancement there, it is simple, and not pre-
posterously mixed.　You may be an alderman there, and
never be scavenger : you may be a nobleman, and never　5c
be a slave.　You may come to preferment enough, and
never be a pander ; to riches and for[t]une enough, and have
never the more villany nor the less wit.

Spen.　God's me !　And how far is it thither ?

Sea.　Some six weeks' sail, no more, with any indifferent　55
good wind.　And if I get to any part of the coast of Africa,
I'll sail thither with any wind ; or when I come to Cape
Finisterre, there's a foreright wind continual wafts us
till we come at Virginia.　See, our colonel's come.

Enter Sir Petronel, *with his followers*

Sir Pet.　Well met, good Captain Seagull, and my noble　60
gentlemen !　Now the sweet hour of our freedom is at hand.
Come, drawer, fill us some carouses, and prepare us for the
mirth that will be occasioned presently.　Here will be a
pretty wench, gentlemen, that will bear us company all our
voyage.　65

Sea.　Whatsoever she be, here's to her health, noble
Colonel, both with cap and knee.

Sir Pet.　Thanks, kind Captain Seagull !　She's one I love
dearly, and must not be known till we be free from all that
know us.　And so, gentlemen, here's to her health !　70

Ambo.　Let it come, worthy Colonel, We do hunger
and thirst for it.

Sir Pet.　Afore heaven, you have hit the phrase of one
that her presence will touch from the foot to the forehead,
if ye knew it.　75

Spen.　Why, then, we will join his forehead with her
health, sir ; and, Captain Scapethrift, here's to 'em both !

[*All kneel and drink*]

Enter Security *and* Bramble

Sec. See, see, Master Bramble, 'fore heaven, their voyage
cannot but prosper ! They are o' their knees for success
to it.   80

Bram. And they pray to god Bacchus.

Sec. God save my brave colonel, with all his tall captains and corporals. See, sir, my worshipful learned counsel,
Master Bramble, is come to take his leave of you.

Sir Pet. Worshipful Master Bramble, how far do you   85
draw us into the sweet-brier of your kindness ! Come, Captain Seagull, another health to this rare Bramble, that hath
never a prick about him.

Sea. I pledge his most smooth disposition, sir. Come,
Master Security, bend your supporters, and pledge this   90
notorious health here.

Sec. Bend you yours likewise, Master Bramble ; for it
is you shall pledge me.

Sea. Not so, Master Security ; he must not pledge his
own health.   95

Sec. No, Master Captain ?

Enter Quicksilver, *with* Winny *disguised*

Why, then, here's one is fitly come to do him that honour.

Quick. Here's the gentlewoman your cousin, sir, whom,
with much entreaty, I have brought to take her leave of
you in a tavern ; ashamed whereof, you must pardon her 100
if she put not off her mask.

Sir Pet. Pardon me, sweet cousin ; my kind desire to
see you before I went, made me so importunate to entreat
your presence here.

Sec. How now, Master Francis, have you honoured 105
this presence with a fair gentlewoman ?

Quick. Pray, sir, take you no notice of her, for she will
not be known to you.

Sec. But my learned counsel, Master Bramble here, I
hope may know her.   110

Quick. No more than you, sir, at this time ; his learning
must pardon her.

Sec. Well, God pardon her for my part, and I do, I'll be
sworn ; and so, Master Francis, here's to all that are going
eastward to-night towards Cuckold's Haven ; and so to the 115
health of Master Bramble.

Quick. I pledge it, sir. [*kneels*] Hath it gone round,
Captains ?

Sea. It has, sweet Frank ; and the round closes with
thee.   120

Quick. Well, sir, here's to all eastward and toward
cuckolds, and so to famous Cuckold's Haven, so fatally
remembered.   *Surgit*

Sir Pet. [*To* Winifred] Nay, pray thee, coz, weep not.
Gossip Security !   125

Sec. Ay, my brave gossip!

Sir Pet. A word, I beseech you, sir ! Our friend, Mistress
Bramble here, is so dissolved in tears that she drowns
the whole mirth of our meeting. Sweet gossip, take her
aside and comfort her.   130

Sec. [*aside to* Winifred] Pity of all true love, Mistress
Bramble ! What, weep you to enjoy your love ? What's the
cause, lady ? Is't because your husband is so near, and your
heart earns to have a little abused him ? Alas, alas, the
offence is too common to be respected ! So great a grace 135
hath seldom chanced to so unthankful a woman, to be rid
of an old jealous dotard, to enjoy the arms of a loving young
knight, that, when your prickless Bramble is withered with grief
of your loss, will make you flourish afresh in the bed of a lady.

Enter Drawer

Draw. Sir Petronel, here's one of your watermen come 140
to tell you it will be flood these three hours ; and that 'twill
be dangerous going against the tide, for the sky is overcast,
and there was a porcpisce even now seen at London Bridge,
which is always the messenger of tempests, he says.

Sir Pet. A porcpisce ! What's that to th' purpose ? 145
Charge him, if he love his life, to attend us ; can we not
reach Blackwall (where my ship lies) against the tide, and
in spite of tempests ? Captains and gentlemen, we'll begin
a new ceremony at the beginning of our voyage, which I
believe will be followed of all future adventurers.   150

Sea. What's that, good Colonel ?

Sir Pet. This, Captain Seagull. We'll have our provided supper brought aboard Sir Francis Drake's ship, that
hath compassed the world ; where, with full cups and banquets, we will do sacrifice for a prosperous voyage. My 155
mind gives me that some good spirits of the waters should
haunt the desert ribs of her, and be auspicious to all that
honour her memory, and will with like orgies enter their
voyages.

Sea.   Rarely conceited !   One health more to this motion, 160
and aboard to perform it.   He that will not this night be
drunk, may he never be sober.

> *They compass in* Winifred, *dance the drunken round, and
> drink carouses*

Bram.   Sir Petronel and his honourable Captains, in these
young services we old servitors may be spared.   We only
came to take our leaves, and with one health to you all, I'll 165
be bold to do so.   Here, neighbour Security, to the health
of Sir Petronel and all his captains.

Sec.   You must bend then, Master Bramble ; [*they kneel*]
so, now I am for you.   I have one corner of my brain, I
hope, fit to bear one carouse more.   Here, lady, to you that 170
are encompassed there, and are ashamed of our company.
Ha ha, ha !   By my troth, my learned counsel, Master
Bramble, my mind runs so of Cuckold's Haven to-night, that
my head runs over with admiration.

Bram. [*aside*]   But is not that your wife, neighbour ?   175

Sec. [*aside*]   No, by my troth, Master Bramble.   Ha,
ha, ha !   A pox of all Cuckold's Havens, I say !

Bram. [*aside*]   O' my faith, her garments are exceeding
like your wife's.

Sec. [*aside*]   *Cucullus non facit monachum*, my learned 180
counsel ; all are not cuckolds that seem so, nor all seem not
that are so.   Give me your hand, my learned counsel ; you
and I will sup somewhere else than at Sir Francis Drake's
ship to-night.—Adieu, my noble gossip !

Bram.   Good fortune, brave Captains ;   fair skies God 185
send ye !

Omnes.   Farewell, my hearts, farewell !

Sir Pet.   Gossip, laugh no more at Cuckold's Haven,
gossip.

Sec.   I have done, I have done, sir ; will you lead, Master 190
Bramble ?   Ha, ha, ha !   *Exit* [*with* Bramble]

Sir Pet.   Captain Seagull, charge a boat !

Omnes.   A boat, a boat, a boat !   *Exeunt*

Draw.   Y'are in a proper taking, indeed, to take a boat,
especially at this time of night, and against tide and tem- 195
pest.   They say yet, ' drunken men never take harm.'   This
night will try the truth of that proverb.   *Exit*

[SCENA QUARTA

Outside Security's *House*]

Enter Security

Sec. What, Winny! Wife, I say! Out of doors at this time! Where should I seek the gad-fly? Billingsgate, Billingsgate, Billingsgate! She's gone with the knight, she's gone with the knight! Woe be to thee, Billingsgate! A boat, a boat, a boat! A full hundred marks for a boat!   5

Exit

ACTUS QUARTUS. SCENA PRIMA

Enter Slitgut, *with a pair of ox-horns, discovering Cuckold's Haven above*

Slit. All hail, fair haven of married men only, for there are none but married men cuckolds! For my part, I presume not to arrive here, but in my master's behalf (a poor butcher of East-cheap) who sends me to set up (in honour of Saint Luke) these necessary ensigns of his homage. And   5
up I got this morning, thus early, to get up to the top of this famous tree, that is all fruit and no leaves, to advance this crest of my master's occupation. Up then; heaven and Saint Luke bless me, that I be not blown into the Thames as I climb, with this furious tempest. 'Slight, I think the   10
devil be abroad, in likeness of a storm, to rob me of my horns! Hark how he roars! Lord, what a coil the Thames keeps! She bears some unjust burthen, I believe, that she kicks and curvets thus to cast it. Heaven bless all honest passengers that are upon her back now; for the bit   15
is out of her mouth, I see, and she will run away with 'em! So, so, I think I have made it look the right way; it runs against London Bridge, as it were, even full butt. And now let me discover from this lofty prospect, what pranks the rude Thames plays in her desperate lunacy. O me,   20
here's a boat has been cast away hard by! Alas, alas, see one of her passengers labouring for his life to land at this haven here! Pray heaven he may recover it! His next land is even just under me; hold out yet a little, whatsoever thou art; pray, and take a good heart to thee. 'Tis a man;   25
take a man's heart to thee; yet a little further, get up o' thy legs, man; now 'tis shallow enough. So, so, so! Alas, he's down again! Hold thy wind, father; 'tis a man in a night-cap. So! Now he's got up again; now he's past

the worst ; yet, thanks be to heaven, he comes toward me 30
pretty and strongly.

Enter Security *without his hat, in a night-cap, wet band, etc.*

Sec. Heaven, I beseech thee, how have I offended thee !
Where am I cast ashore now, that I may go a righter way
home by land ? Let me see. O I am scarce able to look
about me ! Where is there any sea-mark that I am acquainted 35
withal ?

Slit. Look up, father ; are you acquainted with this
mark ?

Sec. What ! Landed at Cuckold's Haven ! Hell and
damnation ! I will run back and drown myself.   40

                              He falls down

Slit. Poor man, how weak he is ! The weak water has
washed away his strength.

Sec. Landed at Cuckold's Haven ! If it had not been
to die twenty times alive, I should never have scaped death !
I will never arise more ; I will grovel here and eat dirt till 45
I be choked ; I will make the gentle earth do that which
the cruel water has denied me !

Slit. Alas, good father, be not so desperate ! Rise, man ;
if you will, I'll come presently and lead you home.

Sec. Home ! Shall I make any know my home, that 50
has known me thus abroad ? How low shall I crouch away,
that no eye may see me ? I will creep on the earth while
I live, and never look heaven in the face more. *Exit creeping*

Slit. What young planet reigns now, trow, that old men
are so foolish ? What desperate young swaggerer would 55
have been abroad such a weather as this upon the water ?
Ay me, see another remnant of this unfortunate shipwrack,
or some other ! A woman, i'faith, a woman ! Though
it be almost at St. Katherine's, I discern it to be a woman,
for all her body is above the water, and her clothes swim 60
about her most handsomely. O, they bear her up most
bravely ! Has not a woman reason to love the taking up
of her clothes the better while she lives, for this ? Alas,
how busy the rude Thames is about her ! A pox o' that wave !
It will drown her, i'faith, 'twill drown her ! Cry God mercy, 65
she has scaped it, I thank heaven she has scaped it ! O
how she swims like a mermaid ! Some vigilant body look
out and save her. That's well said ; just where the priest
fell in, there's one sets down a ladder, and goes to take her

up. God's blessing o' thy heart, boy ! Now take her up 70
in thy arms and to bed with her. She's up, she's up ! She's
a beautiful woman, I warrant her ; the billows durst not
devour her.

Enter the Drawer *in the* Tavern *before, with* Winifred

Draw. How fare you now, lady ?

Win. Much better, my good friend, than I wish ; as 75
one desperate of her fame, now my life is preserved.

Draw. Comfort yourself : that Power that preserved you
from death can likewise defend you from infamy, howsoever you deserve it. Were not you one that took boat
late this night with a knight and other gentlemen at Billings- 80
gate ?

Win. Unhappy that I am, I was.

Draw. I am glad it was my good hap to come down thus
far after you, to a house of my friend's here in St. Katherine's,
since I am now happily made a mean to your rescue from 85
the ruthless tempest, which (when you took boat) was so
extreme, and the gentleman that brought you forth so
desperate and unsober, that I feared long ere this I should
hear of your shipwrack, and therefore (with little other
reason) made thus far this way. And this I must tell you, 90
since perhaps you may make use of it, there was left behind
you at our tavern, brought by a porter (hired by the young
gentleman that brought you) a gentlewoman's gown, hat,
stockings, and shoes ; which, if they be yours, and you
please to shift you, taking a hard bed here in this house of 95
my friend, I will presently go fetch you.

Win. Thanks, my good friend, for your more than good
news. The gown with all things bound with it are mine ;
which if you please to fetch as you have promised, I will
boldly receive the kind favour you have offered till your 100
return ; entreating you, by all the good you have done in
preserving me hitherto, to let none take knowledge of what
favour you do me, or where such a one as I am bestowed,
lest you incur me much more damage in my fame than you
have done me pleasure in preserving my life. 105

Draw. Come in, lady, and shift yourself ; resolve that
nothing but your own pleasure shall be used in your discovery.

Win. Thank you, good friend ; the time may come, I
shall requite you.   *Exeunt* 110

Slit. See, see, see ! I hold my life, there's some other
a taking up at Wapping now ! Look, what a sort of people
cluster about the gallows there ! In good troth it is so. O
me, a fine young gentleman ! What, and taken up at the
gallows ! Heaven grant he be not one day taken down 115
there ! O' my life, it is ominous ! Well, he is delivered
for the time. I see the people have all left him ; yet will
I keep my prospect awhile, to see if any more have been
shipwracked.

Enter Quicksilver, *bare head*

Quick. Accurs'd that ever I was sav'd or born !   120
How fatal is my sad arrival here !
As if the stars and Providence spake to me,
And said, ' The drift of all unlawful courses
(Whatever end they dare propose themselves
In frame of their licentious policies)   125
In the firm order of just Destiny
They are the ready highways to our ruins.'
I know not what to do ; my wicked hopes
Are, with this tempest, torn up by the roots.
O which way shall I bend my desperate steps,   130
In which unsufferable shame and misery
Will not attend them ? I will walk this bank,
And see if I can meet the other relics
Of our poor shipwrack'd crew, or hear of them.
The knight—alas !—was so far gone with wine,   135
And th' other three, that I refus'd their boat,
And took the hapless woman in another,
Who cannot but be sunk, whatever Fortune
Hath wrought upon the others' desperate lives.   [*Exit*]

Enter Petronel, *and* Seagull, *bareheaded*

Sir Pet. Zounds, Captain, I tell thee, we are cast up 140
o' the coast of France ! 'Sfoot, I am not drunk still, I hope !
Dost remember where we were last night ?

Sea. No, by my troth, knight, not I ; but methinks we
have been a horrible while upon the water and in the water.

Sir Pet. Ay me, we are undone for ever ! Hast any 145
money about thee ?

Sea. Not a penny, by heaven !

Sir Pet. Not a penny betwixt us, and cast ashore in
France !

Sea. Faith, I cannot tell that; my brains nor mine 150
eyes are not mine own yet.

Enter two Gentlemen

Sir Pet. 'Sfoot, wilt not believe me? I know't by th'
elevation of the pole, and by the ltitude and alatitude of
the climate. See, here comes a couple of French gentlemen;
I knew we were in France; dost thou think our Englishmen 155
are so Frenchified that a man knows not whether he be in
France or in England, when he sees 'em? What shall we
do? We must e'en to 'em, and entreat some relief of 'em.
Life is sweet, and we have no other means to relieve our lives
now but their charities.   160

Sea. Pray you, do you beg on 'em then; you can speak
French.

Sir Pet. *Monsieur, plaist-il d'avoir pitié de nostre grande
infortune. Je suis un povre chevalier d'Angleterre qui
a souffri l'infortune de naufrage.*   165

1st Gent. *Un povre chevalier d'Angleterre?*

Sir Pet. *Oui, monsieur, il est trop vray; mais vous scavés
bien nous sommes toutes subject à fortune.*

2nd Gent. A poor knight of England? A poor knight
of Windsor, are you not? Why speak you this broken 170
French, when y'are a whole Englishman? On what coast
are you, think you?

Sir Pet. On the coast of France, sir.

1st Gent. On the coast of Dogs, sir; y'are i'th' Isle o'
Dogs, I tell you. I see y'ave been washed in the Thames 175
here, and I believe ye were drowned in a tavern before, or
else you would never have took boat in such a dawning as
this was. Farewell, farewell; we will not know you for
shaming of you.—I ken the man weel; he's one of my
thirty pound knights.   180

2nd Gent. No, no, this is he that stole his knighthood
o' the grand day for four pound, giving to a page all the
money in's purse, I wot well.   *Exeunt [Gentlemen]*

Sea. Death, Colonel, I knew you were overshot!

Sir Pet. Sure I think now, indeed, Captain Seagull, we 185
were something overshot.

Enter Quicksilver

What, my sweet Frank Quicksilver! Dost thou survive
to rejoice me? But what! Nobody at thy heels, Frank?
Ay me, what is become of poor Mistress Security?

Quick. Faith, gone quite from her name, as she is from 190
her fame, I think ; I left her to the mercy of the water.

Sea. Let her go, let her go ! Let us go to our ship at
Blackwall, and shift us.

Sir Pet. Nay, by my troth, let our clothes rot upon us,
and let us rot in them ; twenty to one our ship is attached 195
by this time ! If we set her not under sail this last tide, I
never looked for any other. Woe, woe is me, what shall
become of us ? The last money we could make, the greedy
Thames has devoured ; and if our ship be attached, there
is no hope can relieve us. 200

Quick. 'Sfoot, knight, what an unknightly faintness
transports thee ! Let our ship sink, and all the world that's
without us be taken from us, I hope I have some tricks in
this brain of mine shall not let us perish.

Sea. Well said, Frank, i'faith ! O my nimble-spirited 205
Quicksilver ! 'Fore God, would thou hadst been our
colonel !

Sir Pet. I like his spirit rarely ; but I see no means he
has to support that spirit.

Quick. Go to, knight ! I have more means than thou 210
art aware of. I have not lived amongst goldsmiths and gold-
makers all this while, but I have learned something worthy
of my time with 'em. And not to let thee stink where thou
stand'st, knight, I'll let thee know some of my skill presently. 215

Sea. Do, good Frank, I beseech thee !

Quick. I will blanch copper so cunningly that it shall
endure all proofs but the test : it shall endure malleation,
it shall have the ponderosity of Luna, and the tenacity of
Luna, by no means friable. 220

Sir Pet. 'Slight, where learn'st thou these terms, trow ?

Quick. Tush, knight, the terms of this art every ignorant
quack-salver is perfect in ! But I'll tell you how yourself
shall blanch copper thus cunningly. Take arsenic, otherwise called realga (which, indeed, is plain ratsbane) ; sublime 225
'em three or four times, then take the sublimate of this
realga, and put 'em into a glass, into chymia, and let 'em
have a convenient decoction natural, four-and-twenty
hours, and he will become perfectly fixed ; then take this
fixed powder, and project him upon well-purged copper, *et* 230
habebis magisterium.

Ambo. Excellent Frank, let us hug thee !

Quick. Nay, this I will do besides: I'll take you off
twelvepence from every angel, with a kind of aqua-fortis,
and never deface any part of the image.   235
Sir Pet. But then it will want weight?
Quick. You shall restore that thus: take your sal
achyme prepared and your distilled urine, and let your
angels lie in it but four-and-twenty hours, and they shall
have their perfect weight again. Come on, now; I hope 240
this is enough to put some spirit into the livers of you; I'll
infuse more another time. We have saluted the proud air
long enough with our bare sconces. Now will I have you
to a wench's house of mine at London, there make shift to
shift us, and after, take such fortunes as the stars shall assign 245
us.
Ambo. Notable Frank, we will ever adore thee!
                                                    Exeunt

Enter Drawer, *with* Winifred *new-attired*

Win. Now, sweet friend, you have brought me near
enough your tavern, which I desired I might with some
colour be seen near, inquiring for my husband, who, I must 250
tell you, stale thither the last night with my wet gown we
have left at your friend's,—which, to continue your former
honest kindness, let me pray you to keep close from the
knowledge of any; and so, with all vow of your requital,
let me now entreat you to leave me to my woman's wit and 255
fortune.
Draw. All shall be done you desire; and so all the fortune you can wish for attend you.   *Exit* Drawer

Enter Security

Sec. I will once more to this unhappy tavern before I
shift one rag of me more; that I may there know what is 260
left behind, and what news of their passengers. I have
bought me a hat and band with the little money I had about
me, and made the streets a little leave staring at my night-
cap.
Win. O my dear husband! Where have you been 265
to-night? All night abroad at taverns! Rob me of my
garments, and fare as one run away from me! Alas, is this
seemly for a man of your credit, of your age, and affection
to your wife?
Sec. What should I say? How miraculously sorts 270
this! Was not I at home, and called thee last night?

Win. Yes, sir, the harmless sleep you broke ; and my
answer to you would have witnessed it, if you had had the
patience to have stayed and answered me : but your so
sudden retreat made me imagine you were gone to Master 275
Bramble's, and so rested patient and hopeful of your coming
again, till this your unbelieved absence brought me abroad
with no less than wonder, to seek you where the false knight
had carried you.

Sec. Villain and monster that I was, how have I 280
abused thee ! I was suddenly gone indeed ; for my sudden
jealousy transferred me. I will say no more but this :
dear wife, I suspected thee.

Win. Did you suspect me ?

Sec. Talk not of it, I beseech thee ; I am ashamed to 285
imagine it. I will home, I will home ; and every morning
on my knees ask thee heartily forgiveness.   *Exeunt*

[*Slit.*] Now will I descend my honourable prospect, the
farthest seeing sea-mark of the world ; no marvel, then, if
I could see two miles about me. I hope the red tempest's 290
anger be now over-blown, which sure, I think, Heaven sent
as a punishment for profaning holy Saint Luke's memory
with so ridiculous a custom. Thou dishonest satire, farewell to honest married men ; farewell to all sorts and degrees
of thee ! Farewell, thou horn of hunger, that call'st th' Inns 295
o' Court to their manger ! Farewell, thou horn of abundance, that adornest the headsmen of the commonwealth !
Farewell, thou horn of direction, that is the city lanthorn !
Farewell, thou horn of pleasure, the ensign of the huntsman !
Farewell, thou horn of destiny, th' ensign of the married 300
man ! Farewell, thou horn tree, that bearest nothing but
stone-fruit !   *Exit*

[SCENA SECUNDA

A Room in Touchstone's *House*]

Enter Touchstone

Touch. Ha, sirrah ! Thinks my knight adventurer we
can no point of our compass ? Do we not know north-
north-east, north-east-and-by-east, east-and-by-north, nor
plain eastward ? Ha ! Have we never heard of Virginia ? Nor the Cavallaria ? Nor the Colonoria ? Can 5
we discover no discoveries ? Well, mine errant Sir Flash,
and my runagate Quicksilver, you may drink drunk, crack
cans, hurl away a brown dozen of Monmouth caps or so, in

sea ceremony to your *bon voyage ;* but for reaching any
coast, save the coast of Kent or Essex, with this tide, or　10
with this fleet, I'll be your warrant for a Gravesend toast.
There's that gone afore will stay your admiral and vice-
admiral and rear-admiral, were they all (as they are) but
one pinnace and under sail, as well as a remora, doubt it
not, and from this sconce, without either powder or shot.　15
Work upon that now ! Nay, and you'll show tricks, we'll
vie with you a little. My daughter, his lady, was sent eastward by land, to a castle of his i' the air (in what region I
know not) and, as I hear, was glad to take up her lodging in
her coach, she and her two waiting-women, her maid and　20
her mother, like three snails in a shell, and the coachman
a-top on 'em, I think. Since they have all found the way
back again by Weeping Cross ; but I'll not see 'em. And
for two on 'em, madam and her malkin, they are like to
bite o' the bridle for William, as the poor horses have done　25
all this while that hurried 'em, or else go graze o' the common.
So should my Dame Touchstone too ; but she has been my
cross these thirty years, and I'll now keep her to fright
away sprites, i'faith. I wonder I hear no news of my son
Golding. He was sent for to the Guildhall this morning　30
betimes, and I marvel at the matter ; if I had not laid up
comfort and hope in him, I should grow desperate of all.
See, he is come i' my thought ! How now, son ? What
news at the Court of Aldermen ?

Enter Golding

Gold. Troth, sir, an accident somewhat strange, else it　35
hath little in it worth the reporting.
Touch. What ? It is not borrowing of money, then ?
Gold. No, sir ; it hath pleased the worshipful commoners
of the city to take me one i' their number at presentation
of the inquest——　40
Touch. Ha !
Gold. And the alderman of the ward wherein I dwell to
appoint me his deputy——
Touch. How ?
Gold. In which place I have had an oath ministered　45
me, since I went.
Touch. Now, my dear and happy son, let me kiss thy new
worship, and a little boast mine own happiness in thee.
What a fortune was it (cr rather my judgment, indeed) for

me, first, to see that in his disposition which a whole city   50
so conspires to second ! Ta'en into the livery of his company the first day of his freedom ! Now (not a week married)
chosen commoner and alderman's deputy in a day ! Note
but the reward of a thrifty course. The wonder of his
time ! Well, I will honour Master Alderman for this act   55
(as becomes me) and shall think the better of the Common
Council's wisdom and worship while I live, for thus meeting,
or but coming after me, in the opinion of his desert. Forward, my sufficient son, and as this is the first, so esteem
it the least step to that high and prime honour that expects   60
thee.

Gold. Sir, as I was not ambitious of this, so I covet no
higher place ; it hath dignity enough, if it will but save me
from contempt ; and I had rather my bearing in this or
any other office should add worth to it, than the place give   65
the least opinion to me.

Touch. Excellently spoken ! This modest answer of
thine blushes, as if it said, I will wear scarlet shortly. Worshipful son ! I cannot contain myself, I must tell thee ; I
hope to see thee one o' the monuments of our city, and   70
reckoned among her worthies to be remembered the same
day with the Lady Ramsey and grave Gresham, when the
famous fable of Whittington and his puss shall be forgotten,
and thou and thy acts become the posies for hospitals ; when
thy name shall be written upon conduits, and thy deeds   75
played i' thy lifetime by the best companies of actors, and
be called their get-penny. This I divine ; this I prophesy.

Gold. Sir, engage not your expectation farther than my
abilities will answer ; I, that know mine own strengths,
fear 'em ; and there is so seldom a loss in promising the   80
least, that commonly it brings with it a welcome deceit.
I have other news for you, sir.

Touch. None more welcome, I am sure !

Gold. They have their degree of welcome, I dare affirm.
The Colonel and all his company, this morning putting forth   85
drunk from Billingsgate, had like to have been cast away
o' this side Greenwich ; and (as I have intelligence by a
false brother) are come dropping to town like so many
masterless men, i' their doublets and hose, without hat, or
cloak, or any other——   90

Touch. A miracle ! The justice of Heaven ! Where
are they ? Let's go presently and lay for 'em,

Gold. I have done that already, sir, both by constables
and other officers, who shall take 'em at their old Anchor,
and with less tumult or suspicion than if yourself were seen   95
in't, under colour of a great press that is now abroad, and
they shall here be brought afore me.

Touch. Prudent and politic son ! Disgrace 'em all that
ever thou canst ; their ship I have already arrested. How
to my wish it falls out, that thou hast the place of a justicer 100
upon 'em ! I am partly glad of the injury done to me, that
thou mayst punish it. Be severe i' thy place, like a new
officer o' the first quarter, unreflected. You hear how our
lady is come back with her train from the invisible castle ?

Gold. No ; where is she ?   105

Touch. Within ; but I ha' not seen her yet, nor her
mother, who now begins to wish her daughter undubbed,
they say, and that she had walked a foot-pace with her
sister. Here they come ; stand back.

[Enter] Mistress Touchstone, Gertrude, Mildred, Sindefy

God save your ladyship, save your good ladyship ! Your   110
ladyship is welcome from your enchanted castle, so are your
beauteous retinue. I hear your knight errant is travelled
on strange adventures. Surely, in my mind, your ladyship
hath fished fair and caught a frog, as the saying is.

Mist. Touch. Speak to your father, madam, and kneel   115
down.

Ger. Kneel ? I hope I am not brought so low yet ;
though my knight be run away, and has sold my land, I am
a lady still.

Touch. Your ladyship says true, madam ; and it is   120
fitter and a greater decorum, that I should curtsey to you
that are a knight's wife, and a lady, than you be brought o'
your knees to me, who am a poor cullion and your father.

Ger. Law ! My father knows his duty.

Mist. Touch. O child !   125

Touch. And therefore I do desire your ladyship, my
good Lady Flash, in all humility, to depart my obscure cot-
tage, and return in quest of your bright and most transparent castle, however presently concealed to mortal eyes.
And as for one poor woman of your train here, I will take   130
that order, she shall no longer be a charge unto you, nor
help to spend your ladyship ; she shall stay at home with
me, and not go abroad, not put you to the pawning of an

odd coach-horse or three wheels, but take part with the
Touchstone. If we lack, we will not complain to your lady- 135
ship. And so, good madam, with your damosel here, please
you to let us see your straight backs in equipage ; for truly
here is no roost for such chickens as you are, or birds o'
your feather, if it like your ladyship.

Ger. Marry, fist o' your kindness ! I thought as much. 140
Come away, Sin., we shall as soon get a fart from a dead
man, as a farthing of courtesy here.

Mil. O good sister !

Ger. Sister, sir reverence ! Come away, I say, hunger
drops out at his nose.   145

Gold. O madam, fair words nèver hurt the tongue.

Ger. How say you by that ? You come out with your
gold ends now !

Mist. Touch. Stay, lady-daughter ! Good husband !

Touch. Wife, no man loves his fetters, be they made of 150
gold. I list not ha' my head fastened under my child's
girdle ; as she has brewed, so let her drink, o' God's name !
She went witless to wedding, now she may go wisely a-begging. It's but honeymoon yet with her ladyship ; she has
coach-horses, apparel, jewels, yet left ; she needs care for 155
no friends, nor take knowledge of father, mother, brother,
sister, or anybody. When those are pawned or spent, perhaps we shall return into the list of her acquaintance.

Ger. I scorn it, i'faith ! Come, Sin.

Mist. Touch. O madam, why do you provoke your 160
father thus ?

Exit Gertrude [*with* Sindefy]

Touch. Nay, nay ; e'en let pride go afore, shame will
follow after, I warrant you. Come, why dost thou weep
now ? Thou art not the first good cow hast had an ill calf,
I trust. [*Exit* Mistress Touchstone] What's the news 165
with that fellow ?

Enter Constable

Gold. Sir, the knight and your man Quicksilver are
without ; will you ha' 'em brought in ?

Touch. O by any means ! [*Exit* Constable] And, son,
here's a chair ; appear terrible unto 'em on the first inter- 170
view. Let them behold the melancholy of a magistrate,
and taste the fury of a citizen in office.

Gold. Why, sir, I can do nothing to 'em, except you
charge 'em with somewhat.

Touch. I will charge 'em and recharge 'em, rather than 175
authority should want foil to set it off. [*Offers* Golding *a
chair*]

Gold. No, good sir, I will not.

Touch. Son, it is your place ; by any means——

Gold. Believe it, I will not, sir.

Enter Knight Petronel, Quicksilver, Constable, Officers

Sir Pet. How misfortune pursues us still in our misery ! 180

Quick. Would it had been my fortune to have been
trussed up at Wapping, rather than ever ha' come here !

Sir Pet. Or mine to have famished in the island !

Quick. Must Golding sit upon us ?

Con. You might carry an M. under your girdle to Master 185
Deputy's worship.

Gold. What are those, Master Constable ?

Con. An't please your worship, a couple of masterless
men I pressed for the Low Countries, sir.

Gold. Why do you not carry 'em to Bridewell, accord- 190
ing to your order, they may be shipped away ?

Con. An't please your worship, one of 'em says he is a
knight ; and we thought good to shew him to your worship,
for our discharge.

Gold. Which is he ?   195

Con. This, sir !

Gold. And what's the other ?

Con. A knight's fellow, sir, an't please you.

Gold. What ! A knight and his fellow thus accoutred ?
Where are their hats and feathers, their rapiers and their 200
cloaks ?

Quick. O they mock us !

Con. Nay, truly, sir, they had cast both their feathers
and hats too, before we see 'em. Here's all their furniture,
an't please you, that we found. They say knights are now 205
to be known without feathers, like cockerels by their spurs,
sir.

Gold. What are their names, say they ?

Touch. [*aside*] Very well this ! He should not take knowledge of 'em in his place, indeed.   210

Con. This is Sir Petronel Flash.

Touch. How !

Con. And this, Francis Quicksilver. ,

Touch. Is't possible ? I thought your worship had

been gone for Virginia, sir; you are welcome home, sir. 215
Your worship has made a quick return, it seems, and no
doubt a good voyage. Nay, pray you be covered, sir. How
did your biscuit hold out, sir? Methought I had seen
this gentleman afore. Good Master Quicksilver, how a
degree to the southward has changed you!   220

Gold. Do you know 'em, father?—Forbear your offers
a little, you shall be heard anon.

Touch. Yes, Master Deputy; I had a small venture
with them in the voyage—a thing called a son-in-law, or so.
Officers, you may let 'em stand alone, they will not run 225
away; I'll give my word for them. A couple of very honest
gentlemen. One of 'em was my prentice, Master Quicksilver here; and when he had two year to serve, kept his
whore and his hunting nag, would play his hundred pound
at gresco, or primero, as familiarly (and all o' my purse) as 230
any bright piece of crimson on 'em all; had his changeable
trunks of apparel standing at livery, with his mare, his
chest of perfumed linen, and his bathing-tubs, which when
I told him of, why he—he was a gentleman, and I a poor
Cheapside groom! The remedy was, we must part. Since 235
when, he hath had the gift of gathering up some small
parcels of mine, to the value of five hundred pound, dispersed among my customers, to furnish this his Virginian
venture; wherein this knight was the chief, Sir Flash—one
that married a daughter of mine, ladyfied her, turned two 240
thousand pounds' worth of good land of hers into cash within
the first week, bought her a new gown and a coach, sent
her to seek her fortune by land, whilst himself prepared for
his fortune by sea; took in fresh flesh at Billingsgate, for
his own diet, to serve him the whole voyage—the wife of a 245
certain usurer called Security, who hath been the broker
for 'em in all this business. Please, Master Deputy, work
upon that now!

Gold. If my worshipful father have ended.

Touch. I have, it shall please Master Deputy.   250

Gold. Well then, under correction——

Touch. [*aside to* Golding] Now, son, come over 'em with
some fine gird, as thus, 'Knight, you shall be encountered,
that is, had to the Counter,' or, 'Quicksilver, I will put
you into a crucible,' or so.   255

Gold. Sir Petronel Flash, I am sorry to see such flashes
as these proceed from a gentleman of your quality and rank;

for mine own part, I could wish I could say I could not see
them; but such is the misery of magistrates and men in
place, that they must not wink at offenders. Take him 260
aside—I will hear you anon, sir.

Touch. I like this well, yet; there's some grace i' the
knight left—he cries.

Gold. Francis Quicksilver, would God thou hadst turned
quacksalver, rather than run into these dissolute and lewd
courses! It is great pity; thou art a proper young man, 265
of an honest and clean face, somewhat near a good one;
God hath done his part in thee; but thou hast made too
much and been too proud of that face, with the rest of thy
body; for maintenance of which in neat and garish attire
(only to be looked upon by some light housewives) thou hast 270
prodigally consumed much of thy master's estate; and
being by him gently admonished at several times, hast returned thyself haughty and rebellious in thine answers,
thund'ring out uncivil comparisons, requiting all his kindness with a coarse and harsh behaviour, never returning 275
thanks for any one benefit, but receiving all as if they had
been debts to thee and no courtesies. I must tell thee,
Francis, these are manifest signs of an ill-nature; and God
doth often punish such pride and outrecuidance with scorn
and infamy, which is the worst of misfortune. My worship- 280
ful father, what do you please to charge them withal?
From the press I will free 'em, Master Constable.

Con. Then I'll leave your worship, sir.

Gold. No, you may stay; there will be other matters
against 'em. 285

Touch. Sir, I do charge this gallant, Master Quicksilver, on suspicion of felony; and the knight as being acces-
sary in the receipt of my goods.

Quick. O God, sir!

Touch. Hold thy peace, impudent varlet, hold thy 290
peace! With what forehead or face dost thou offer to
chop logic with me, having run such a race of riot as thou
hast done? Does not the sight of this worshipful man's
fortune and temper confound thee, that was thy younger
fellow in household, and now come to have the place of a 295
judge upon thee? Dost not observe this? Which of all
thy gallants and gamesters, thy swearers and thy swaggerers,
will come now to moan thy misfortune, or pity thy penury?
They'll look out at a window, as thou rid'st in triumph to

Tyburn, and cry, ' Yonder goes honest Frank, mad Quick- 300
silver ! ' ' He was a free boon companion, when he had
money,' says one ; ' Hang him, fool ! ' says another, ' he
could not keep it when he had it ! ' ' A pox o'the cullion,
his master,' says a third, ' he has brought him to this ' ;
when their pox of pleasure and their piles of perdition 305
would have been better bestowed upon thee, that hast ventured for 'em with the best, and by the clue of thy knavery
brought thyself weeping to the cart of calamity.

Quick. Worshipful master !

Touch. Offer not to speak, crocodile ; I will not hear a 310
sound come from thee. Thou hast learnt to whine at the
play yonder. Master Deputy, pray you commit 'em both
to safe custody, till I be able farther to charge 'em.

Quick. O me, what an unfortunate thing am I !

Sir Pet. Will you not take security, sir ? 315

Touch. Yes, marry, will I, Sir Flash, if I can find him,
and charge him as deep as the best on you. He has been
the plotter of all this ; he is your enginer, I hear. Master
Deputy, you'll dispose of these. In the meantime, I'll to
my Lord Mayor, and get his warrant to seize that serpent 320
Security into my hands, and seal up both house and goods
to the King's use or my satisfaction.

Gold. Officers, take 'em to the Counter.

Quick. } O God !
Sir Pet. }

Touch. Nay, on, on ! You see the issue of your sloth. 325
Of sloth cometh pleasure, of pleasure cometh riot, of riot
comes whoring, of whoring comes spending, of spending
comes want, of want comes theft, of theft comes hanging ;
and there is my Quicksilver fixed.   *Exeunt*

ACTUS QUINTUS. SCENA PRIMA

[Gertrude's *Lodging*]

Gertrude [*and*] Sindefy

Ger. Ah, Sin., hast thou ever read i' the chronicle of any
lady and her waiting-woman driven to that extremity that
we are, Sin. ?

Sin. Not I, truly, madam ; and if I had, it were but
cold comfort should come out of books now.   5

Ger. Why, good faith, Sin., I could dine with a lament-

able story now. *O hone, hone, o no nera, etc. !* Canst thou
tell ne'er a one, Sin. ?

Sin. None but mine own, madam, which is lamentable
enough : first to be stolen from my friends, which were   10
worshipful and of good accompt, by a prentice in the habit
and disguise of a gentleman, and here brought up to London
and promised marriage, and now likely to be forsaken, for
he is in possibility to be hanged !

Ger. Nay, weep not, good Sin. ; my Petronel is in as   15
good possibility as he. Thy miseries are nothing to mine,
Sin. : I was more than promised marriage, Sin. ; I had it,
Sin., and was made a lady, and by a knight, Sin. ; which
is now as good as no knight, Sin. And I was born in London,
which is more than brought up, Sin. ; and already forsaken,   20
which is past likelihood, Sin. ; and instead of land i' the
country, all my knight's living lies i' the Counter, Sin. ;
there's his castle now !

Sin. Which he cannot be forced out of, madam.

Ger. Yes, if he would live hungry a week or two. ' Hun-   25
ger ', they say, ' breaks stone walls.' But he is e'en well
enough served, Sin., that so soon as ever he had got my hand
to the sale of my inheritance, run away from me, and I had
been his punk, God bless us ! Would the Knight o' the
Sun, or Palmerin of England, have used their ladies so, Sin. ?   30
Or Sir Lancelot, or Sir Tristram ?

Sin. I do not know, madam.

Ger. Then thou know'st nothing, Sin. Thou art a fool,
Sin. The knighthood nowadays are nothing like the knighthood of old time. They rid a-horseback ; ours go a-foot.   35
They were attended by their squires ; ours by their lackeys.
They went buckled in their armour ; ours muffled in their
cloaks. They travelled wildernesses and deserts ; ours
dare scarce walk the streets. They were still prest to engage
their honour ; ours still ready to pawn their clothes. They   40
would gallop on at sight of a monster ; ours run away at
sight of a sergeant. They would help poor ladies ; ours
make poor ladies.

Sin. Ay, madam, they were knights of the Round Table
at Winchester, that sought adventures ; but these of the   45
Square Table at ordinaries, that sit at hazard.

Ger. True, Sin., let him vanish. And tell me, what shall
we pawn next ?

Sin. Ay, marry, madam, a timely consideration ; for

our hostess (profane woman!) has sworn by bread and 50
salt, she will not trust us another meal.

Ger. Let it stink in her hand then. I'll not be beholding to her. Let me see, my jewels be gone, and my gowns,
and my red velvet petticoat that I was married in, and my
wedding silk stockings, and all thy best apparel, poor Sin.! 55
Good faith, rather than thou shouldest pawn a rag more,
I'd lay my ladyship in lavender—if I knew where.

Sin. Alas, madam, your ladyship?

Ger. Ay, why? You do not scorn my ladyship, though
it is in a waistcoat? God's my life, you are a peat indeed! 60
Do I offer to mortgage my ladyship for you and for your
avail, and do you turn the lip and the alas to my ladyship?

Sin. No, madam; but I make question who will lend
anything upon it?

Ger. Who? Marry, enow, I warrant you, if you'll seek 65
'em out. I'm sure I remember the time when I would ha'
given one thousand pounds (if I had had it) to have been
a lady; and I hope I was not bred and born with that appetite alone : some other gentle-born o' the City have the same
longing, I trust. And for my part, I would afford 'em a 70
penn'orth; my ladyship is little the worse for the wearing,
and yet I would bate a good deal of the sum. I would lend
it (let me see) for forty pound in hand, Sin.—that would
apparel us—and ten pound a year—that would keep me and
you, Sin. (with our needles)—and we should never need to 75
be beholding to our scurvy parents. Good Lord, that
there are no fairies nowadays, Sin.!

Sin. Why, madam?

Ger. To do miracles, and bring ladies money. Sure,
if we lay in a cleanly house, they would haunt it, Sin. I'll 80
try. I'll sweep the chamber soon at night, and set a dish
of water o' the hearth. A fairy may come, and bring a
pearl or a diamond. We do not know, Sin. Or, there may
be a pot of gold hid o' the backside, if we had tools to dig
for't? Why may not we two rise early i' the morning, Sin., 85
afore anybody is up, and find a jewel i' the streets worth a
hundred pound? May not some great court-lady, as she
comes from revels at midnight, look out of her coach as 'tis
running, and lose such a jewel, and we find it? Ha?

Sin. They are pretty waking dreams, these. 90

Ger. Or may not some old usurer be drunk overnight,
with a bag of money, and leave it behind him on a stall?

For God's sake, Sin., let's rise to-morrow by break of day,
and see.　I protest, law, if I had as much money as an alderman, I would scatter some on't i'th' streets for poor ladies　95
to find, when their knights were laid up.　And, now I remember my song o' the Golden Shower, why may not I
have such a fortune ?　I'll sing it, and try what luck I shall
have after it.

> *Fond fables tell of old*　　　　　　　100
> 　*How Jove in Danäe's lap*
> *Fell in a shower of gold,*
> 　*By which she caught a clap ;*
> 　　*O had it been my hap*
> *(How ere the blow doth threaten)*　　105
> 　*So well I like the play,*
> 　*That I could wish all day*
> *And night to be so beaten.*

Enter Mistress Touchstone

O here's my mother !　Good luck, I hope.　Ha' you brought
any money, mother ?　Pray you, mother, your blessing. 110
Nay, sweet mother, do not weep.

Mist. Touch.　God bless you !　I would I were in my
grave !

Ger.　Nay, dear mother, can you steal no more money
from my father ?　Dry your eyes, and comfort me.　Alas, 115
it is my knight's fault, and not mine, that I am in a waistcoat, and attired thus simply.

Mist. Touch.　Simply ? 'Tis better than thou deserv'st.
Never whimper for the matter.　Thou shouldst have looked
before thou hadst leaped.　Thou wert afire to be a lady, 120
and now your ladyship and you may both blow at the coal,
for ought I know.　Self do, self have.　' The hasty person
never wants woe,' they say.

Ger.　Nay, then, mother, you should ha' looked to it.
A body would think you were the older ; I did but my kind, 125
I.　He was a knight, and I was fit to be a lady.　'Tis not
lack of liking, but lack of living, that severs us.　And you
talk like yourself and a cittiner in this, i'faith.　You show
what husband you come on, I wis.　You smell the Touchstone—he that will do more for his daughter that he has 130
married a scurvy gold-end man and his prentice, than
he will for his tother daughter, that has wedded a knight

and his customer. By this light, I think he is not my
legitimate father.

Sin. O good madam, do not take up your mother so ! 135

Mist. Touch. Nay, nay, let her e'en alone ! Let her
ladyship grieve me still, with her bitter taunts and terms.
I have not dole enough to see her in this miserable case, I,
without her velvet gowns, without ribands, without jewels,
without French wires, or cheat-bread, or quails, or a little 140
dog, or a gentleman-usher, or anything, indeed, that's fit
for a lady——

Sin. [aside] Except her tongue.

Mist. Touch. And I not able to relieve her, neither, being
kept so short by my husband. Well, God knows my heart. 145
I did little think that ever she should have had need of her
sister Golding.

Ger. Why, mother, I ha' not yet. Alas, good mother,
be not intoxicate for me ! I am well enough ; I would not
change husbands with my sister, I. The leg of a lark is 150
better than the body of a kite.

Mist. Touch. I know that, but—

Ger. What, sweet mother, what ?

Mist. Touch. It's but ill food when nothing's left but
the claw.
　　　　　　　　　　　　　　　　　　　　　　　155

Ger. That's true, mother. Ay me !

Mist. Touch. Nay, sweet lady-bird, sigh not. Child,
madam, why do you weep thus ? Be of good cheer ; I shall
die, if you cry and mar your complexion thus.

Ger. Alas, mother, what should I do ?　　　　　　160

Mist. Touch. Go to thy sister's, child ; she'll be proud thy
ladyship will come under her roof. She'll win thy father
to release thy knight, and redeem thy gowns and thy coach
and thy horses, and set thee up again.

Ger. But will she get him to set my knight up too ? 165

Mist. Touch. That she will, or anything else thou'lt ask
her.

Ger. I will begin to love her if I thought she would do
this.

Mist. Touch. Try her, good chuck, I warrant thee.　170

Ger. Dost thou think she'll do't ?

Sin. Ay, madam, and be glad you will receive it.

Mist. Touch. That's a good maiden ; she tells you true.
Come, I'll take order for your debts i' the ale-house.

Ger. Go, Sin., and pray for thy Frank, as I will for my 175
Pet.
　　　　　　　　　　　　　　　　　　[Exeunt]

[SCENA SECUNDA

Goldsmith's Row]

Enter Touchstone, Golding, Wolf

Touch. I will receive no letters, Master Wolf; you shall
pardon me.

Gold. Good father, let me entreat you.

Touch. Son Golding, I will not be tempted; I find mine
own easy nature, and I know not what a well-penned subtle   5
letter may work upon it; there may be tricks, packing, do
you see? Return with your packet, sir.

Wolf. Believe it, sir, you need fear no packing here;
these are but letters of submission all.

Touch. Sir, I do look for no submission. I will bear   10
myself in this like blind Justice. Work upon that now!
When the Sessions come, they shall hear from me.

Gold. From whom come your letters, Master Wolf?

Wolf. And't please you, sir, one from Sir Petronel, another from Francis Quicksilver, and a third from old Se-   15
curity, who is almost mad in prison. There are two to
your worship, one from Master Francis, sir, another from
the knight.

Touch. I do wonder, Master Wolf, why you should
travail thus in a business so contrary to kind or the nature   20
o' your place, that you, being the keeper of a prison, should
labour the release of your prisoners! Whereas, methinks,
it were far more natural and kindly in you to be ranging
about for more, and not let these scape you have already
under the tooth. But they say you wolves, when you ha'   25
sucked the blood once, that they are dry, you ha' done.

Wolf. Sir, your worship may descant as you please o'
my name; but I protest I was never so mortified with any
men's discourse or behaviour in prison; yet I have had of
all sorts of men i' the kingdom under my keys, and almost   30
of all religions i' the land, as Papist, Protestant, Puritan.
Brownist, Anabaptist, Millenary, Family-o'-Love, Jew,
Turk, Infidel, Atheist, Good-Fellow, etc.

Gold. And which of all these, thinks Master Wolf, was
the best religion?   35

Wolf. Troth, Master Deputy, they that pay fees best;
we never examine their consciences farder.

Gold. I believe you, Master Wolf. Good faith, sir, here's
a great deal of humility i' these letters.

Wolf. Humility, sir ? Ay, were your worship an eye-   40
witness of it, you would say so. The knight will i' the
Knight's Ward, do what we can, sir ; and Master Quicksilver would be i' the Hole, if we would let him. I never
knew or saw prisoners more penitent, or more devout. They
will sit you up all night singing of psalms and edifying the   45
whole prison ; only Security sings a note too high sometimes,
because he lies i' the twopenny ward, far off, and cannot
take his tune. The neighbours cannot rest for him, but
come every morning to ask what godly prisoners we have.

Touch. Which on 'em is't is so devout—the knight or the   50
tother ?

Wolf. Both, sir ; but the young man especially. I
never heard his like. He has cut his hair too. He is so well
given, and has such good gifts. He can tell you almost all the
stories of the *Book of Martyrs*, and speak you all *The Sick*   55
Man's Salve without book.

Touch. Ay, if he had had grace—he was brought up
where it grew, I wis. On, Master Wolf !

Wolf. And he has converted one Fangs, a sergeant, a
fellow could neither write nor read, he was called the   60
Bandog o' the Counter ; and he has brought him already
to pare his nails and say his prayers ; and 'tis hoped he will
sell his place shortly, and become an intelligencer.

Touch. No more ; I am coming already. If I should
give any farder ear I were taken. Adieu, good Master   65
Wolf ! Son, I do feel mine own weaknesses ; do not impo-
tune me. Pity is a rheum that I am subject to ; but I will
resist it. Master Wolf, fish is cast away that is cast in dry
pools. Tell hypocrisy it will not do ; I have touched and
tried too often ; I am yet proof, and I will remain so ; when   70
the Sessions come they shall hear from me. In the meantime, to all suits, to all entreaties, to all letters, to all tricks,
I will be deaf as an adder, and blind as a beetle, lay mine
ear to the ground, and lock mine eyes i' my hand against
all temptations.   *Exit*   75

Gold. You see, Master Wolf, how inexorable he is.
There is no hope to recover him. Pray you commend me
to my brother knight, and to my fellow Francis ; present
'em with this small token of my love [*giving money*] ; tell
'em, I wish I could do 'em any worthier office ; but in this,   80
'tis desperate ; yet I will not fail to try the uttermost of
my power for 'em. And, sir, as far as I have any credit

with you, pray you let 'em want nothing ; though I am not
ambitious they should know so much.

Wolf. Sir, both your actions and words speak you to be　85
a true gentleman. They shall know only what is fit, and no
more. *Exeunt*

[SCENA TERTIA

The Counter]

Holdfast, Bramble ; Security [*apart*]

Hold. Who would you speak with, sir ?

Bram. I would speak with one Security, that is prisoner
here.

Hold. You are welcome, sir ! Stay there, I'll call him to
you. Master Security !　　　　　5

Sec. Who calls ?

Hold. Here's a gentleman would speak with you.

Sec. What is he ? Is't one that grafts my forehead now
I am in prison, and comes to see how the horns shoot up and
prosper ?　　　　　10

Hold. You must pardon him, sir ; the old man is a
little crazed with his imprisonment.

Sec. What say you to me, sir ? Look you here, my
learned counsel, Master Bramble ! Cry you mercy, sir !
When saw you my wife ?　　　　　15

Bram. She is now at my house, sir ; and desired me that
I would come to visit you, and inquire of you your case,
that we might work some means to get you forth.

Sec. My case, Master Bramble, is stone walls and iron
grates ; you see it, this is the weakest part on 't. And for　20
getting me forth, no means but hang myself, and so to be
carried forth, from which they have here bound me in intolerable bands.

Bram. Why, but what is't you are in for, sir ?

Sec. For my sins, for my sins, sir, whereof marriage is　25
the greatest ! O had I never married, I had never known
this purgatory, to which hell is a kind of cool bath in respect ;
my wife's confederacy, sir, with old Touchstone, that she
might keep her jubilee and the feast of her new moon. Do
you understand me, sir ?　　　　　30

Enter Quicksilver

Quick. Good sir, go in and talk with him. The light
does him harm, and his example will be hurtful to the weak

prisoners. Fie, Father Security, that you'll be still so
profane ! Will nothing humble you ?

[Exeunt Security, Bramble, Holdfast, and Quicksilver]

Enter two Prisoners *with a friend*

Friend. What's he ?   35

1st *Pris.* O he is a rare young man ! Do you not know
him ?

Friend. Not I ! I never saw him, I can remember.

2nd *Pris.* Why, it is he that was the gallant prentice of
London—Master Touchstone's man.   40

Friend. Who ? Quicksilver ?

1st *Pris.* Ay, this is he.

Friend. Is this he ? They say he has been a gallant
indeed.

[1st] *Pris.* O the royallest fellow that ever was bred up   45
i' the City ! He would play you his thousand pound a-
night at dice ; keep knights and lords company ; go with
them to bawdy-houses ; had his six men in a livery ; kept
a stable of hunting-horses, and his wench in her velvet gown
and her cloth of silver. Here's one knight with him here 50
in prison.

Friend. And how miserably he is changed !

1st *Pris.* O that's voluntary in him : he gave away all
his rich clothes as soon as ever he came in here among the
prisoners ; and will eat o' the basket, for humility.   55

Friend. Why will he do so ?

[1st] *Pris.* Alas, he has no hope of life ! He mortifies
himself. He does but linger on till the Sessions.

2nd *Pris.* O he has penned the best thing, that he calls
his *Repentance* or his *Last Farewell*, that ever you heard. 60
He is a pretty poet, and for prose—you would wonder how
many prisoners he has helped out, with penning petitions
for 'em, and not take a penny. Look ! This is the knight,
in the rug gown. Stand by !

Enter Sir Petronel, Bramble, Quicksilver

Bram. Sir, for Security's case, I have told him. Say he 65
should be condemned to be carted or whipped for a bawd,
or so, why, I'll lay an execution on him o' two hundred
pound ; let him acknowledge a judgment, he shall do it in
half an hour ; they shall not all fetch him out without paying
the execution, o' my word.   70

Sir Pet. But can we not be bailed, Master Bramble ?

Bram. Hardly; there are none of the judges in town, else you should remove yourself (in spite of him) with a *habeas corpus.* But if you have a friend to deliver your tale sensibly to some justice o' the town, that he may have feeling of it (do you see) you may be bailed; for as I understand the case, 'tis only done *in terrorem;* and you shall have an action of false imprisonment against him when you come out, and perhaps a thousand pound costs.

Enter Master Wolf

Quick. How now, Master Wolf? What news? What return?

Wolf. Faith, bad all! Yonder will be no letters received. He says the Sessions shall determine it. Only Master Deputy Golding commends him to you, and with this token wishes he could do you other good. [*giving money*]

Quick. I thank him. Good Master Bramble, trouble our quiet no more; do not molest us in prison thus with your winding devices; pray you depart. For my part, I commit my cause to Him that can succour me; let God work His will. Master Wolf, I pray you let this be distributed among the prisoners, and desire 'em to pray for us. [*Exit*]

Wolf. It shall be done, Master Francis.

1st Pris. An excellent temper!

2nd Pris. Now God send him good luck!

Exeunt [Bramble, *two* Prisoners *and* Friend]

Sir Pet. But what said my father-in law, Master Wolf?

Enter Holdfast

Hold. Here's one would speak with you, sir.

Wolf. I'll tell you anon, Sir Petronel. Who is't?

Hold. A gentleman, sir, that will not be seen.

Enter Golding

Wolf. Where is he? Master Deputy! Your worship is welcome—

Gold. Peace!

Wolf. Away, sirrah! [*Exit* Holdfast *with* Sir Petronel]

Gold. Good faith, Master Wolf, the estate of these gentlemen, for whom you were so late and willing a suitor, doth much affect me; and because I am desirous to do them some fair office, and find there is no means to make my father relent so likely as to bring him to be a spectator of their miseries, I have ventured on a device, which is, to

make myself your prisoner, entreating you will presently
go report it to my father, and (feigning an action at suit of 110
some third person) pray him by this token [*giving a ring*]
that he will presently, and with all`secrecy, come hither
for my bail ; which train, if any, I know will bring him
abroad ; and then, having him here, I doubt not but we shall
be all fortunate in the event.   115

Wolf.   Sir, I will put on my best speed to effect it. Please
you come in.

Gold.   Yes ; and let me rest concealed, I pray you.   [*Exit*]

Wolf.   See here a benefit truly done, when it is done
timely, freely, and to no ambition.   *Exit* 120

[SCENA QUARTA

A Room in Touchstone's *House*]

Enter Touchstone, Wife, Daughters, Sindefy, Winifred

Touch.   I will sail by you and not hear you, like the wise
Ulysses.

Mil.   Dear father !

Mist. Touch.   Husband !

Ger.   Father !

Win. and Sin.   Master Touchstone !   5

Touch.   Away, sirens, I will immure myself against your
cries, and lock myself up to [y]our lamentations.

Mist. Touch.   Gentle husband, hear me !

Ger.   Father, it is I, father, my Lady Flash. My sister 10
and I am friends.

Mil.   Good father !

Win.   Be not hardened, good Master Touchstone !

Sin.   I pray you, sir, be merciful !

Touch.   I am deaf, I do not hear you ; I have stopped 15
mine ears with shoemakers' wax, and drunk Lethe and
mandragora to forget you. All you speak to me I commit
to the air.

Enter Wolf

Mil.   How now, Master Wolf ?

Wolf.   Where's Master Touchstone ? I must speak 20
with him presently ; I have lost my breath for haste.

Mil.   What's the matter, sir ? Pray all be well !

Wolf.   Master Deputy Golding is arrested upon an execution, and desires him presently to come to him, forthwith.

Mil. Ay me! Do you hear, father?   25

Touch. Tricks, tricks, confederacy, tricks! I have 'em
in my nose—I scent 'em!

Wolf. Who's that? Master Touchstone?

Mist. Touch. Why, it is Master Wolf himself, husband.

Mil. Father!   30

Touch. I am deaf still, I say. I will neither yield to the
song of the siren, nor the voice of the hyena, the tears of the
crocodile, nor the howling o' the wolf. Avoid my habita-
tion, monsters!

Wolf. Why, you are not mad, sir? I pray you look   35
forth, and see the token I have brought you, sir.

Touch. Ha! What token is it?

Wolf. Do you know it, sir?

Touch. My son Golding's ring! Are you in earnest,
Master Wolf?   40

Wolf. Ay, by my faith, sir! He is in prison, and required me to use all speed and secrecy to you.

Touch. My cloak, there—pray you be patient. I am
plagued for my austerity. My cloak! At whose suit,
Master Wolf?   45

Wolf. I'll tell you as we go, sir.   *Exeunt*

[SCENA QUINTA

The Counter]

Enter Friend, Prisoners

Friend. Why, but is his offence such as he cannot hope
of life?

1st Pris. Troth, it should seem so; and 'tis great pity,
for he is exceeding penitent.

Friend. They say he is charged but on suspicion of   5
felony yet.

2nd Pris. Ay, but his master is a shrewd fellow; he'll
prove great matter against him.

Friend. I'd as lief as anything I could see his *Farewell.*

1st Pris. O 'tis rarely written; why, Toby may get   10
him to sing it to you; he's not curious to anybody.

2nd Pris. O no! He would that all the world should
take knowledge of his repentance, and thinks he merits
in't, the more shame he suffers.

1st Pris. Pray thee, try what thou canst do.   15

2nd Pris.   I warrant you he will not deny it, if he be not hoarse with the often repeating of it.   *Exit*

1st Pris.   You never saw a more courteous creature than he is, and the knight too ; the poorest prisoner of the house may command 'em.   You shall hear a thing admirably   20 penned.

Friend.   Is the knight any scholar too ?

1st Pris.   No, but he will speak very well, and discourse admirably of running horses and White-Friars, and against bawds, and of cocks ; and talk as loud as a hunter, but is   25 none.

Enter Wolf *and* Touchstone

Wolf.   Please you, stay here, sir ; I'll call his worship down to you.   [*Exit*]

Enter [2nd Prisoner *with*] Quicksilver, Petronel *and* [Security ; Golding *with* Wolf, *who stand aside*]

1st Pris.   See, he has brought him, and the knight too. Salute him, I pray.   Sir, this gentleman, upon our report,   30 is very desirous to hear some piece of your *Repentance*.

Quick.   Sir, with all my heart ;   and, as I told Master Toby, I shall be glad to have any man a witness of it.   And the more openly I profess it, I hope it will appear the heartier and the more unfeigned.   35

Touch.   [*aside*] Who is this ?   My man Francis, and my son-in-law ?

Quick.   Sir, it is all the testimony I shall leave behind me to the world and my master that I have so offended.

Friend.   Good sir !   40

Quick.   I writ it when my spirits were oppressed.

Sir Pet.   Ay, I'll be sworn for you, Francis !

Quick.   It is in imitation of Mannington's, he that was hanged at Cambridge, that cut off the horse's head at a blow.

Friend.   So, sir !   45

Quick.   To the tune of ' I wail in woe, I plunge in pain.'

Sir Pet.   An excellent ditty it is, and worthy of a new tune.

> *Quick.*   *In Cheapside, famous for gold and plate,*
> *Quicksilver, I did dwell of late ;*   50
> *I had a master good and kind,*
> *That would have wrought me to his mind.*

> *He bade me still, Work upon that,*
> *But, alas, I wrought I knew not what !*
> *He was a Touchstone black, but true,*   55
> *And told me still what would ensue ;*
> *Yet woe is me ! I would not learn ;*
> *I saw, alas, but could not discern !*

Friend.   Excellent, excellent well !
Gold. [*aside to* Wolf]   O let him alone ; he is taken already.   60

> *Quick.   I cast my coat and cap away,*
> *I went in silks and satins gay ;*
> *False metal of good manners I*
> *Did daily coin unlawfully.*
> *I scorn'd my master, being drunk ;*   65
> *I kept my gelding and my punk ;*
> *And with a knight, Sir Flash by name,*
> *Who now is sorry for the same—*

Sir Pet.   I thank you, Francis.

> [*Quick.*]   *I thought by sea to run away,*   70
> *But Thames and tempest did me stay.*

Touch.   [*aside*] This cannot be feigned, sure. Heaven pardon my severity ! The ragged colt may prove a good horse.

Gold.   [*aside*] How he listens, and is transported ! He has   75
forgot me.

> *Quick.   Still Eastward Ho was all my word ;*
> *But westward I had no regard,*
> *Nor never thought what would come after,*
> *As did, alas, his youngest daughter !*   80
> *At last the black ox trod o' my foot,*
> *And I saw then what long'd unto 't ;*
> *Now cry I, ' Touchstone, touch me still,*
> *And make me current by thy skill.'*

Touch.   [*aside*]   And I will do it, Francis.   85
Wolf. [*aside to* Golding]   Stay him, Master Deputy ; now
is the time ; we shall lose the song else.
Friend.   I protest it is the best that ever I heard.
Quick.   How like you it, gentlemen ?
All.   O admirable, sir !   90
Quick.   This stanze now following alludes to the story

of Mannington, from whence I took my project for my
invention.

Friend. Pray you go on, sir.

> *Quick.*   *O Mannington, thy stories show*   95
> *Thou cut'st a horse-head off at a blow !*
> *But I confess, I have not the force*
> *For to cut off the head of a horse ;*
> *Yet I desire this grace to win,*
> *That I may cut off the horse-head of Sin,*   100
> *And leave his body in the dust*
> *Of sin's highway and bogs of lust,*
> *Whereby I may take Virtue's purse,*
> *And live with her for better, for worse.*

Friend. Admirable, sir, and excellently conceited !   105
Quick. Alas, sir !

Touch. [*coming to* Golding *and* Wolf] Son Golding and
Master Wolf, I thank you ; the deceit is welcome, especially
from thee, whose charitable soul in this hath shown a high
point of wisdom and honesty. Listen, I am ravished with   110
his repentance, and could stand here a whole prenticeship
to hear him.

Friend. Forth, good sir !

> *Quick.*   This is the last, and the *Farewell.*
> *Farewell, Cheapside, farewell, sweet trade*   115
> *Of Goldsmiths all, that never shall fade ;*
> *Farewell, dear fellow prentices all,*
> *And be you warned by my fall :*
> *Shun usurers, bawds, and dice, and drabs ;*
> *Avoid them as you would French scabs.*   120
> *Seek not to go beyond your tether,*
> *But cut your thongs unto your leather ;*
> *So shall you thrive by little and little,*
> *Scape Tyburn, Counters, and the Spital !*

Touch. And scape them shalt thou, my penitent and   125
dear Francis !

Quick. Master !

Sir Pet. Father !

Touch. I can no longer forbear to do your humility
right. Arise, and let me honour your repentance with the   130
hearty and joyful embraces of a father and friend's love.
Quicksilver, thou hast eat into my breast, Quicksilver,

with the drops of thy sorrow, and killed the desperate opinion
I had of thy reclaim.

Quick. O sir, I am not worthy to see your worshipful 135
face !

Sir Pet. Forgive me, father !

Touch. Speak no more ; all former passages are forgotten, and here my word shall release you. Thank this
worthy brother and kind friend, Francis.—Master Wolf, 140
I am their bail.   *A shout in the prison*

Sec. Master Touchstone ! Master Touchstone !

Touch. Who's that ?

Wolf. Security, sir.

Sec. Pray you, sir, if you'll be won with a song, hear 145
my lamentable tune too :

SONG

O Master Touchstone,
* My heart is full of woe ;*
Alas, I am a cuckold !
* And why should it be so ?*   150
Because I was a usurer
* And bawd, as all you know,*
For which, again I tell you,
* My heart is full of woe.*

Touch. Bring him forth, Master Wolf, and release his 155
bands. This day shall be sacred to mercy and the mirth
of this encounter in the Counter. See, we are encountered
with more suitors !

Enter Mistress Touchstone, Gertrude, Mildred, Sindefy, Winifred
Save your breath, save your breath ! All things have
succeeded to your wishes ; and we are heartily satisfied in 160
their events.

Ger. Ah, runaway, runaway ! Have I caught you ?
And how has my poor knight done all this while ?

Sir Pet. Dear lady wife, forgive me !

Ger. As heartily as I would be forgiven, knight. Dear 165
father, give me your blessing, and forgive me too ; I ha'
been proud and lascivious, father, and a fool, father ; and
being raised to the state of a wanton coy thing, called a
lady, father, have scorned you, father, and my sister, and
my sister's velvet cap too ; and would make a mouth at 170
the City as I rid through it ; and stop mine ears at Bow-bell.

I have said your beard was a base one, father ; and that
you looked like Twierpipe the taberer ; and that my mother
was but my midwife.

Mist. Touch.   Now God forgi' you, child madam !   175

Touch.   No more repetitions ! What is else wanting to
make our harmony full ?

Gold.   Only this, sir, that my fellow Francis make amends
to Mistress Sindefy with marriage.

Quick.   With all my heart !   180

Gold.   And Security give her a dower, which shall be
all the restitution he shall make of that huge mass he hath
so unlawfully gotten.

Touch.   Excellently devised ! A good motion ! What
says Master Security ?   185

Sec.   I say anything, sir, what you'll ha' me say. Would
I were no cuckold !

Win.   Cuckold, husband ? Why, I think this wearing
of yellow has infected you.

Touch.   Why, Master Security, that should rather be a   190
comfort to you than a corasive. If you be a cuckold, it's
an argument you have a beautiful woman to your wife ;
then you shall be much made of ; you shall have store of
friends, never want money ; you shall be eased of much o'
your wedlock pain, others will take it for you. Besides,   195
you being a usurer and likely to go to hell, the devils will
never torment you, they'll take you for one o' their own
race. Again, if you be a cuckold, and know it not, you are
an innocent ; if you know it and endure it, a true martyr.

Sec.   I am resolved, sir. Come hither, Winny !   200

Touch.   Well, then, all are pleased, or shall be anon.
Master Wolf, you look hungry, methinks ; have you no
apparel to lend Francis to shift him ?

Quick.   No, sir, nor I desire none ; but here make it my
suit, that I may go home through the streets in these, as a   205
spectacle, or rather an example, to the children of Cheapside.

Touch.   Thou hast thy wish. Now, London, look about,
And in this moral see thy glass run out :
Behold the careful father, thrifty son,
The solemn deeds which each of us have done ;   210
The usurer punish'd, and from fall so steep
The prodigal child reclaim'd, and the lost sheep.

EPILOGUS

[*Quick.*]   Stay, sir, I perceive the multitude are gathered
together to view our coming out at the Counter. See, if
the streets and the fronts of the houses be not stuck with
people, and the windows filled with ladies, as on the solemn
day of the Pageant !   5
O may you find in this our pageant, here,
    The same contentment which you came to seek ;
And as that show but draws you once a year,
    May this attract you hither once a week.   *Exeunt*

FINIS

THE BALL

THE PERSONS OF THE COMEDY

Lord Rainbow
Sir Ambrose Lamount
Sir Marmaduke Travers
Colonel Winfield
Mr. Bostock
Mr. Freshwater [*a traveller*]
Mr. Barker
Monsieur Le Frisk [*a dancer*]
Gudgeon [*servant of Freshwater*]
Solomon [*servant of Lucina*]
Confectioner

Servants

Lady Lucina [*a rich widow*]
Lady Rosamond
Lady Honoria
Mistress Scutilla [*attendant on Lucina*]

[*Characters in the Masque*]
Venus
Diana
[Cupid]

The Ball

ACTUS PRIMUS

[SCENE I

A Street in London]

Enter Sir Marmaduke Travers *and* Mr. Bostock

Bos. Whither so fast, Sir Marmaduke ? A word !
Mar. My honourable blood ? Would I could stay
To give thee twenty ! I am now engag'd
To meet a noble gentleman.
Bos.   Or rather
A gentlewoman ; let her alone, and go   5
With me.
Mar.   Whither ?
Bos.   I'll show thee a lady of fire.
Mar. A Lady of the Lake were not so dangerous.
Bos. I mean a spirit. In few words, because
I love thee, I'll be open ; I am going
To see my mistress.   10
Mar.   I'll dispense with my
Occasion, to see a handsome lady ;
I know you'll choose a rare one.
Bos.   She is a creature
Worth admiration, such a beauty, wit,
And an estate besides ; thou canst not choose
But know her name, the Lady Lucina.   15
Mar. Is she your mistress ?
Bos.   Mine ! Whose but mine ?
Am I not nobly born ? Does not my blood deserve her ?
Mar. To tell you truth, I was now going thither,
Though I pretended an excuse, and with
A compliment from one that is your rival.
Bos. Does she love anybody else ?   20
Mar.   I know not ;

But she has half-a-score, upon my knowledge,
Are suitors for her favour.
  Bos.   Name but one,
And if he cannot show as many coats—
  Mar. He thinks he has good cards for her, and likes   25
His game well.
  Bos.   Be an understanding knight,
And take my meaning; if he cannot shew
As much in heraldry—
  Mar. I do not know how rich he is in fields;
But he is a gentleman.   30
  Bos. Is he a branch of the nobility?
How many lords can he call cousin? Else
He must be taught to know he has presum'd
To stand in competition with me.
  Mar. You wo' not kill him?   35
  Bos.   You shall pardon me,
I have that within me must not be provok'd;
There be some living now that ha' been kill'd
For lesser matters.
  Mar.   Some living that ha' been kill'd!
  Bos. I mean, some living that ha' seen examples
Not to confront nobility; and I   40
Am sensible of my honour.
  Mar.   His name is
Sir Ambrose—
  Bos.   Lamount, a knight of yesterday!
And he shall die to-morrow; name another,
  Mar. Not so fast, sir, you must take some breath.
  Bos. I care no more for killing half a dozen   45
Knights of the lower house, I mean that are not
Descended from nobility, than I do
To kick [my] footman; and Sir Ambrose were
Knight of the Sun, King Oberon should not save him,
Nor his Queen Mab.   50
            Enter Sir Ambrose Lamount
  Mar.   Unluckily, he's here, sir.
  Bos. Sir Ambrose! How does thy knighthood, ha?
  Amb. My [imp] of honour, well! I joy to see thee.
  Bos. Sir Marmaduke tells me thou art suitor to
Lady Lucina.
  Amb.   I have ambition
To be her servant,   55

Bos.   Hast ?

Th'art a brave knight, and I commend thy judgment.

   Amb.   Sir Marmaduke himself leans that way too.

   Bos.   Why didst conceal it ?   Come, the more the merrier !

But I could never see you there.

   Mar.   I hope,

Sir, we may live ?   60

   Bos.   I'll tell you, gentlemen,

Cupid has given us all one livery ;

I serve that lady too, you understand me ;

But who shall carry her, the Fates determine ;

I could be knighted too.

   Amb.   That would be no addition to your blood.   65

   Bos.   I think it would not ; so my lord told me.

Thou know'st my lord, not the earl, my tother

Cousin ?   There's a spark !   His predecessors

Have match'd into the blood ; you understand.

He put me upon this lady ; I proclaim   70

No hopes ; pray let's together, gentlemen ;

If she be wise—I say no more ; she sha' not

Cost me a sigh, nor shall her love engage me

To draw a sword ; I ha' vow'd that.

   Mar.   You did

But jest before.   75

   Amb.   'Twere pity that one drop

Of your heroic blood should fall to th' ground.

Who knows but all your cousin lords may die ?

   Mar.   As I believe them not immortal, sir.

   Amb.   Then you are gulf of honour, swallow all ;

May marry some queen yourself, and get princes   80

To furnish the barren parts of Christendom.

Enter a servant, Solomon

   Sol.   Sir Marmaduke, in private !

   [*aside to Marmaduke*]   My lady would

Speak with you.

   Amb. [*aside*]   'Tis her servant, what's the matter ?

   Bos. [*aside*]   I hope he is not sent for.

   Sol.   But come alone ;

I shall be troubled with their inquiries ;   85

But I'll answer 'em.

   Amb.   Solomon !

   Sol.   [*aside to* Ambrose] My lady would speak with you, sir.

Amb.   Me ?

Sol.   Not too loud ; I was troubled with Sir Marmaduke.

Mar. [*aside*] This is good news.

Bos. [*aside*]   I do not like this whispering.

Sol.   Forget not the time, and to come alone.   90

Amb.   This is excellent.

Bos.   Solomon, dost not know me ?

Sol.   [*aside to Bostock*]   My business is to you, sir ;
These kept me off ; my Lady Lucina
Has a great mind to speak with you ;
Little do these imagine how she honours [you]   95

Bos.   If I fail, may the surgeon, when he opens
The next vein, let out all my honourable blood !
There's for thy pains—what thou shalt be hereafter
Time shall declare ; but this must be conceal'd.

                                        Exit [Solomon]

Amb.   You look pleasant.   100

Mar.   No, no ; I have no cause ; you smile, Sir Ambrose.

Amb.   Who, I ?—The Colonel !

Enter the Colonel [Winfield]

Mar.   But of our file, another of her suitors.

Amb.   Noble Colonel !

Win.   My honour'd knights, and men of lusty kindred ! 105

Bos.   Good morrow !

Win.   Morrow to all ! Gentlemen, I'll tell you
Who is returned.

Amb.   From whence ?

Win.   A friend of ours,
That went to travel.

Mar.   Who, who ?

Win.   I saw him within these three minutes, and know not 110
how I lost him again ; he's not far off : d'ye keep a catalogue
of your debts ?

Bos.   What debts ?

Win.   Such dulness in your memory ! There was,
About six months ago, a gentleman   115
That was persuaded to sell all his land,
And to put the money out most wisely,
To have [five] for one, at his return from Venice.
The shotten herring is hard by.

Amb.   Jack Freshwater !
I'll not see him yet.   120

Bos.   Must we pay him ?

Win. It will be for your honour ; marry, we,
Without much stain, may happily compound,
And pay him nothing.

Enter Freshwater *and* Monsieur Le Frisk [*and* Gudgeon|
                    Here comes the thing.
With what formality he treads, and talks,
And manageth a toothpick like a statesman !   125
  Amb. How he's transform'd !
  Mar.   Is not his soul Italian ?
  Bos. I'll not bid him welcome home.
  Amb.   Nor I !
  Mar. What's the tother rat that's with him ?
  Win. D'ye not know him ? 'Tis the Court dancing weasel.
  Mar. A dancer, and so gay ?   130
  Win. A mere French footman, sir ; does he not look
Like a thing come off o' th' salt-cellar ?
  Mar.   A dancer !
I would allow him gay about the legs ;
But why his body should exceed decorum,
Is a sin o' th' state.   135
  Fresh. [*To* Le Frisk]   That's all
I can inform you of their dance in Italy.
Marry, that very morning I left Venice,
I had intelligence of a new device.
  Le Frisk. For the dance, monsieur ?
  Fresh.   *Si, signor.* I know not
What countryman invented ['em], but they say   140
There be chopinos made with such rare art,
That, worn by a lady when she means to dance,
Shall, with their very motion, sound forth music,
And, by a secret sympathy, with their tread
Strike any tune, that, without other instrument,   145
Their feet both dance and play.
  Le Frisk.   Your lodging, monsieur,
That, when I have leisure, I may dare
Present an humble servitor ?
  Fresh. I do lie at the sign of *Donna Margaretta de Pia*, in the
Strand.   150
  Gud. At the Maggot-a-Pie in the Strand, sir.
  Le Frisk. At *de Magdepie ; bon ! Adieu, serviteur !* *Exit*
  Amb. He wo' not know us.
  Gud.   D'ye see those gentlemen ?
  Fresh. Thou Pa[n]talone, be silent !

Win.   I'll speak to him.
Y'are welcome home, sir.   155
   Fresh.   Signor ! *Exit* [*with* Gudgeon]
   Win. He wo' not know me ; this is excellent ;
He shall be acquainted better ere I part
With any sums.
   Amb.   Next time we'll not know him.
   Bos. Would all my creditors had this blessed ignorance !
   Mar. Now, Colonel, I'll take my leave.   160
         Exeunt [Marmaduke *and* Ambrose]
   Bos. I am engag'd too.
   Win.   Well !
   Bos.   I shall meet you anon ;
I am to wait upon a cousin of mine.
   Win. A countess ?

Enter Lord Rainbow *and* Barker

   Bos. My lord !
   Lord R. Cousin !   165
   Bos. Your lordship honours me in this acknowledgment.
   Lord R. Colonel !
   Bos. [*to* Barker]   D'ye not know me, sir ?
   Bar. Y'are not a proclamation
That every man is bound to take notice on,
And I cannot tell who you are by instinct.   170
   Lord R. A kinsman of mine, Frank !
   Win.   Good morrow to your lordship !
   Lord R. Colonel, your humble servant ! Hark you, Frank !

    [*Exeunt* Lord Rainbow *and* Barker]

   Bos. You are acquainted with my lord, then ?
Is he not a complete gentleman ? His family
Came in with the Conqueror.   175
   Win. You had not else been kin to him.
   Bos.   A poor slip,
A scion from that honourable tree.
   Win. He is the ladies' idol, they ha' not leisure
To say their prayers for him ; a great advancer
Of the new Ball.   180
   Bos. Nay, he's right, right as my leg, Colonel !
   Win. But tother gentleman, you do not know his inside ?
   Bos. I ha' seen him ; he looks philosophical.
   Win. Who ? He's the wit, whom your nobility
Are much oblig'd to for his company ;   185

He has a railing genius, and they cherish it?
Fling[s] dirt in every face when he's i' th' humour,
And they must laugh, and thank him; he is dead else.
　Bos. Will the lords suffer him?
　Win. Or lose their mirth; he's known in every science, 190
And can abuse 'em all; some ha' supposed
He has a worm in's brain, which at some time
O' th' moon doth ravish him into perfect madness,
And then he prophesies, and will depose
The Emperor, and set up Bethlem Gabor.　　　195
　Bos. He's dead; I hope he wo' not conjure for him.
　Win. His father sha' not scape him, nor his ghost,
Nor heaven, nor hell; his jest must ha' free passage.
He's gone, and I lose time to talk on him;
Farewell, your Countess may expect too long.　200
　[*Bos.*] Farewell, colonel.　　　　　　*Exeunt*

[SCENE II

A Room in Lady Honoria's House]

Enter Lady Rosamond and Lady Honoria

　Ros. Why do you so commend him?
　Hon.　　　　　　　　　　　　Does he not
Deserve it? Name a gentleman in the kingdom
So affable, so moving in his language,
So pleasant, witty, indeed everything
A lady can desire.　　　　　　　　　　5
　Ros.　　　　　　Sure thou dost love him;
I'll tell his lordship, when I see him again,
How zealous you are in his commendation.
　Hon. If I be not mistaken, I have heard
Your tongue reach higher in his praises, madam,
Howe'er you now seem cold; but, if you tell him　10
My opinion, as you shall do him no pleasure,
You can do me no injury: I know
His lordship has the constitution
Of other courtiers; they can endure
To be commended.　　　　　　　　　15
　Ros.　　　　　But, I prithee, tell me,
Is [it] not love whence this proceeds? I have,
I must confess, discours'd of his good parts,
Desir'd his company—
　Hon.　　　　　　　And had it?

Ros.   Yes,
And had it.
 Hon.   All night ?
 Ros.   You are not, I hope, jealous ?
If I should say all night, I need not blush.   20
It was but at a ball ; but what of this ?
 Hon. E'en what you will.
 Ros.   I hope you ha' no patent
To dance alone with him ? If he ha' privilege
To kiss another lady, she may say
He does salute her, and return a cursie   25
To show her breeding, but I'll now be plainer,
Although you love this lord, it may [be] possible
He may dispose his thoughts another way.
 Hon. He may so.
 Ros.   Who can help it ? He has eyes
To look on more than one, and understand[s],   30
Perhaps, to guide and place his love upon
The most deserving object.
 Hon.   Most deserving !
This language is not level with that friendship
You have profess'd ; this touches a comparison.
 Ros. Why, do you think all excellence is throng'd 35
Within your beauty ?
 Hon.   You are angry, lady ;
How much does this concern you, to be thus
Officious in his cause ! If you be not
Engag'd by more than ordinary affection,
I must interpret this no kind respect   40
To me.
 Ros.   Angry ! Ha, ha !
 Hon. You then transgress against civility.
 Ros. Good madam, why ? Because
I think, and tell you, that another lady
May be as handsome in some man's opinion ?   45
Admit I lov'd him too, may not I hold
Proportion with you, on some entreaty.
     Enter Lord [Rainbow *behind*]
 Lord R. [*aside*] They're loud, I'll not be seen yet.
 Ros. What is it that exalts you above all
Comparison ? My father was as good   50
A gentleman, and my mother has as great
A spirit.

Hon.   Then you love him too ?
Ros.   'Twill appear
No greater miracle in me, I take it ;
Yet difference will be ; perhaps I may
Affect him with a better consequence.   55
    Hon. Your consequence, perhaps, may be denied too.
Why, there are no such wonders in your eye,
Which other composition[s] do not boast of ;
My lord, no doubt, hath in his travels clapp'd
As modest cheeks, and kiss'd as melting lips.   60
    Ros. And yet mine are not pale.
    Hon.   It may be they
Blush for the teeth behind them.
    Ros.   I have read
No sonnets on the sweetness of your breath.
    Hon. 'Tis not perfum'd.
    Ros. But I have heard of your tongue exalted much,   65
Highly commended.
    Hon.   Not above your forehead,
When you have brush'd away the hairy pent[house],
And made it visible.
    Lord R.   I'll now interrupt 'em.
They'll fall by the ears else presently.   [*He comes forward*]
    Hon.   My lord !
    Lord R. What, in contention, ladies ?   70
    Ros.   Oh, my lord, you're welcome.
    Lord R. Express it in discovery of that
Made you so earnest ; I am confident
You were not practising a dialogue
To entertain me.
    Hon.   Yet it did concern you.
    Ros. Do not you blush ? Fie, madam !   75
    Lord R. Nay, an you come to ' blush ' once, and ' fie,
        madam ',
I'll know the secret, by this kiss I will,
And this.   *Kisses them*
    Hon.   You were kiss'd first, discover now,
At your discretion.
    Ros.   My lord, we were in jest.
    Hon. It might have turned to earnest, if your lordship   80
Had not interpos'd
    Lord R.   Come, out with it.
    Ros. We had a difference—

Lord R.   Well said!

Ros.   About a man i' the world—you are best name him.

Hon.   You have the better gift at telling secrets.

Lord R.   Yet again! Come, I'll help it out: there is   85
A gentleman i' th' world, some call a lord—

Ros.   Did your lordship overhear us?

Lord R.   Nay, nay, you must stand to't—one whom you
>   love.

It will appear no greater miracle
In you, I take it; one, no doubt, that hath   90
Travell'd, and clapp'd as modest cheeks, and kiss'd
As melting lips:—thus far I'm right; but what
Name this most happy man doth answer to,
Is not within my circle.

Hon.   Yet you know him.

Ros.   Not to retain your lordship i' th' dark,   95
Confident you'll not accuse my modesty
For giving you a truth, you shall not travel
Beyond yourself to find his name; but do not
Triumph, my lord.

Lord R.   Am I so fortunate?
Then, Love, I do forgive thee, and will cherish   100
The flame I did suspect would ruin me.
You two divide my love, only you two;
Be gentle in your empire, heavenly ladies.
No enemy abroad can threaten you;
Be careful, then, that you maintain at home   105
No civil wars.

Hon.   How d'ye mean, my lord?

Lord R.   [*to* Rosamond] You are pleased to smile upon
>   me, gentle lady,

And I have took it in my heart more than
Imaginary blessings. With what pleasure
Could I behold this beauty, and consume   110
My understanding to know nothing else!
My memory to preserve no other figure!

Ros.   My lord, I am not worth your flattery.

Lord R.   I flatter you! Venus herself be judge,
To whom you are so like in all that's fair,   115
'Twere sin but to be modest—

Ros.   How, my lord?

Lord R.   Do not mistake me, 'twere
A sin but to be modest in your praises;

Here's a hand! Nature, show me such another,
A brow, a cheek, a lip, and everything;   120
Happy am I that Cupid's blind!
   Ros.   Why happy?
   Lord R. If he could see, he would forsake his mistress
To be my rival, and for your embraces
Be banish'd heaven.
   Hon.   My lord, I'll take my leave.
   Lord R. [*to* Honoria] If you did know how great a part 125
    of me
Will wither in your absence, you would have
More charity; one accent of unkind
Language from you doth wound me more than all
The malice of my destinies. Oh, dear madam,
You say you'll take your leave of your poor servant;   130
Say rather, you will dwell for ever here,
And let me stay and gaze upon your heavenly form
   Hon. I can be patient
To hear your lordship mock me; these are but
A coarse reward for my good thoughts.   135
   Lord R.   This 'tis
To use plain dealing, and betray the inside
Of our hearts to women! Did you think well of me
So late, and am I forfeited already?
Am I a Christian?
   Hon.   Yes, I hope, my lord!
   Lord R. Make me not miserable, then, dear madam,   140
With your suspicion I dissemble with you;
But you know too well what command your beauty
Has upon me.
   Hon. Give me leave, my lord, to wonder you can love me,
With such a flame you have express'd, yet she   145
Your mistress.
   Lord R.   You are both my mistresses.
   Ros. I like not this so well.
   Lord R. There is no way but one to make me happy.
   Hon. I wish, my lord, I had the art to effect
What you desire.   150
   Ros.   Or I!
   Lord R.   It is within
Your powers.
   Hon.   Speak it, my lord.

Lord R.   Since it is so,
That I'm not able to determine which
My heart, so equal unto both, would choose,
My suit is to your virtues, to agree
Between yourselves whose creature I shall be ;   155
You can judge better of your worths than I.
My allegiance shall be ready if you can
Conclude which shall ha' the supremacy ;
Take pity on your servant, gentle ladies,
And reconcile a heart too much divided :   160
So with the promise of my obedience
To her that shall be fairest, wisest, sweetest,
Of you two, when I next present a lover,
I take distracted leave.   *Exit*

Hon. Why, this is worse than all the rest.   165
Ros.   He's gone,
And has referr'd himself to us.
Hon.   This will
Ask counsel.
Ros.   And some time ; I would be loath
To yield.
Hon.   And I ; Cupid instruct us both !   *Exeunt*

ACTUS SECUNDUS

[SCENE I

A Street]

Enter Barker, Freshwater, *and* Gudgeon

Bar. And what made you to undertake this voyage,
Sweet Signor Freshwater ?
Fresh.   An affection
I had to be acquainted with some countries.
Gud. [*aside to* Freshwater] Give him good words.
Bar. And you return fraught home with the rich devices,   5
Fashions of steeples, and the situations
Of gallowses, and wit, no doubt, a bushel.
What price are oats in Venice ?
Fresh.   Signor,
I kept no horses there ; my man and I——
Bar. Were asses.   10
Fresh.   How, signor ?
Gud. [*aside*] Give him good words ; a pox take him !
Bar. Had not you land once ?

Fresh.　　　　　　　　I had some dirty acres.

Gud.　I am his witness.

Fresh.　Which I reduc'd into a narrow compass,
Some call it selling.　　　　　　　　　　　　　15

Gud.　He would sell bargains of a child.

Fresh.　And 'twas a thriving policy.

Bar.　　　　　　　　　　　As how?

Fresh.　It was but two hundred pound per annum, sir,
A lean revenue.

Bar.　　　And did you sell it all?

Fresh.　I did not leave an acre, rod, or perch;　　20
That had been no discretion; when I was selling,
I would sell to purpose; do you see this roll?
I have good security for my money, sir;
Not an egg here but has five chickens in't.
I did most politicly disburse my sums,　　　　25
To have five for one at my return from Venice;
And now, I thank my stars, I am at home.

Bar.　And so,
By consequence, in three months your estate
Will be five times as much, or quintupled!　　30

Fresh.　Yes, signor, quintupled.
I wo'not purchase yet; I mean to use
This trick seven years together; first,
I'll still put out, and quintuple, as you call't,
And when I can in my exchequer tell　　　　35
Two or three millions, I will fall a-purchasing.

Bar.　Kingdoms, I warrant!

Fresh.　　　　　　　　　I have a mind to buy
Constantinople from the Turk, and give it
The Emperor.

Bar.　　　　What think you of Jerusalem?
If you would purchase that, and bring it nearer,　　40
The Christian pilgrims would be much obliged to ye.
When did you wash your socks?

Fresh.　　　　　　　　　I wear none, signor.

Bar.　Then 'tis your breath; to your lodging, and per-
　　fume it;
You'll tell the sweeter lies to them that will
Lose so much time to ask about your travel.　　45
You wo' not sell your debts?

Fresh.　　　　　　　Sell 'em? No, signor.

Bar.　Have you as much left, in ready cash, as will

Keep you and this old troll a fortnight longer ?
Die, and forgive the world ; thou mayst be buried,
And ha' the church-cloth, if you can put in   50
Security, the parish shall be put
To no more charge. Dost thou hope to have a penny
Of thy own money back ? Is this an age
Of five for one ? Die, ere the town takes notice.
There is a hideous woman carries ballets,   55
And has a singing in her head ; take heed
And hang thyself, thou mayst not hear the [tune] ;
You remember Coryate ?
    Fresh.   Honest Tom Odcombe.
    Bar. We'll ha' more verses of thy travels, coxcomb ;
Books shall be sold in bushels in Cheapside,   60
And come in like the peascods, wain-loads full,
Of thee and thy man Apple-John, that looks
As he had been a se'nnight in the straw,
A ripening for the market. Farewell, russeting,
Thou art not worth my spleen ; do not forget   65
My counsel, hang thyself, and thou go'st off
Without a Sessions.   *Exit*
    Fresh.   Fine ! I'm glad he's gone.
Gudgeon, what dost thou think ?
    Gud. I think y'are well rid of [a] railing madcap.
    Fresh. Nay, nay, he'll not spare a lord ;   70
But were not I best call in my moneys, Gudgeon ?
My estate wo' not hold out ; I must be more
Familiar with my gentlemen.

                Enter Lord [Rainbow]

    Lord R. Jack Freshwater, welcome from Venice !
    Fresh. I thank your honour.   75
    Lord R.   Was it not Frank Barker
That parted from you ?
    Fresh.   Yes, my lord.
    Lord R.   What's the matter ?
    Fresh. There is a sum, my lord.
    Lord R.   Where is it, signor ?
    Fresh. There was a sum, my lord, delivered
From your poor servant, Freshwater.
    Lord R.   I remember,
But I have business now ; come home to me,   80
The money's safe ; you were to give me five
For one, at your return.

Fresh. I five ?   Your lordship has forgot the cinquepace.

Lord R. Something it is ; but when I am at leisure,
We will discourse of that, and of your travel.   85
Farewell, signor.   *Exit*

Fresh. Is't come to this ?   If lords play fast and loose,
What shall poor knights and gentleman ?   Hum !   'Tis he.

Enter Colonel [Winfield]

Win. A pox upon him !   What makes he in my way ?

Fresh. Noble colonel !   90

Win. *Que dites-vous, monsieur ?*

Fresh. *Que dites-vous ?*

Win. *Ah, oui !—je ne parle pas Anglais.*

[*Fresh.*] There were five English pieces.

Win. *Je ne parle* [*pas*] *Anglais.*   Me speak no word Eng- 95
lish ; *votre serviteur !*   *Exit*

Fresh. Adieu, five pieces !   Gudgeon, gape ; is't not he ?
They wo' not use me o' this fashion.   Did he not
Speak to me in the morning ?

Gud.   Yes, sir.

Fresh.   I think so.

[*Gud.*] But then you would not know him in Italian, and 100
now he will not know you in French.

Fresh. Call you this selling of land, and putting out
money to multiply estate ?

Gud. To quintuply five for one !   Large interest !

Fresh. Five for one !   'Tis ten to one, if I get my principal. 105

Gud. Your roll is not at the bottom yet ; try the rest.

Fresh. I ha', signor, farewell.   *Exeunt*

[SCENE II

A Room in Lucina's *House*]

Enter Scutilla *and* Solomon

Scut. Didst speak with the Colonel ?

Sol. I met him opportunely after all the rest, and told
him how much it would concern his livelihood to make haste.

Scut. He must not be seen yet; you know where to
attend for him ; give him access by the garden to my   5
chamber, and bring me nimbly knowledge when he is there.

Sol. I shall, forsooth.   *Exit*

Enter the Dancer [Le Frisk], Lady Rosamond, Lady Lucina,
and Lady Honoria

Le Frisk. Very well ! A[h], dat be skirvy ! You run,
trot, trot, trot ; pshaw, follow me ! *Foutre, madame !*
Can you not tell, so often learning. Madam, you foot it now,   10
plaît-il ? (*Another lady dances.*) Excellent ! Better den
excellent ; pshaw !—You be laughed when you come to de
ball ; I teach tree hundred never forgot so much, me sweat
taking pain, and fiddling, ladies.

Luc. Fiddling ladies, you molecatcher !   [*Strikes him*]   15
Le Frisk. Pourquoy ? For telling you dance not well ?
You commit *fat*, and beat me for my diligence ; begar, you
dance your pleasure !

Hon. No, Monsieur Le Frisk, put not up your pipe ;
my lady was but in jest, and you must take it for a favour.   20
Le Frisk. I vear no favours in dat place ; should any
gentleman of England give me blow, *diable,* me teach him
French passage !

Ros. Nay, you sha' not be so angry ; I must have a coranto.
Pray, madam, be reconcil'd.   25
Luc. Come, monsieur, I am sorry.
Le Frisk. Sorry ! Tat is too much, *par ma foy !* I kiss
tat white hand, give me one, two, tree buffets. *Allez, allez ;*
look up your countenance, your English man spoil you, he no
teach you look up ; pshaw ! Carry your body in the swim-   30
ming fashion, and—*Dieu ! allez, mademoiselle,* ha, ha, ha !
So, *fort bon !* Excellent, begar !   *Dance*
Luc. Nay, a country dance ! Scutilla, you are idle.
You know we must be at the ball anon ; come.
Le Frisk. Where is the ball this night ?   35
Luc. At my Lord Rainbow's.
Le Frisk. Oh, he dance finely, begar ! He deserve the ball
of de world ; fine, fine, gentleman ! Your oder men dance
lop, lop, with de lame leg as they want crushes, begar, and
look for *argent* in the ground, pshaw !   40

They dance a new country dance.
Ha, ha, *fort bon !*
Ros. Now, madam, we take our leave.
Luc. I'll recompense this kind visit : does your coach
stay ?
Hon. Yes, madam ;
Your ladyship will be too much troubled.   45

Luc.   I owe more service.

Scut.   Monsieur, you'll be gone too ?

Le Frisk.   I have more lady, my scholars.

                    [Hiding his kit under his coat]

Scut.   Is that the way of your instrument ?

Le Frisk.   *A la mode de France. Vite, vite ! Adieu, madame,*
votre serviteur !   50

   [Luc.]   Adieu, demi-monsieur !

                       Exeunt [all but Scutilla]

       Enter Solomon *and* Colonel [Winfield]

Scut.   Sir, you are welcome.

Win.   I thank you, lady.   *[Exit* Solomon]

Scut.   The time's too narrow to discourse at large,
But I intend you a service ; you have deserv'd it   55
In your own nobleness to one I call a kinsman,
Whose life, without your charity, had been
Forfeit to his general's anger, 'twas not
Without his cause you after quit your regiment.

Win.   He was my friend ; forget it.   60

Scut.   You were sent for
By the Lady Lucina.

Win.   Whose command I wait.

Scut.   'Twas my desire to prepare you for
The entertainment ; be but pleas'd to obscure
Yourself behind these hangings a few minutes ;
I hear her, you may trust me.   65

Win.   Without dispute, I obey you, lady.

                     [Exit Winfield]

         Enter Lady Lucina

Luc.   Now, Scutilla, we are ripe, and ready
To entertain my gamesters ; my man said
They promised all to come.   I was afraid
These ladies, in their kind departure, would not   70
Bequeathe me opportunity, and the mirth
Doth in the imagination so tickle me,
I would not willingly have lost it for
A jewel of some value.

Scut.   Then your purchase holds.

Luc.   If they hold their affections, and keep touch,   75
We'll ha' some sport.

          Enter Solomon

Sol.   Sir Marmaduke Travers !   *[Exit* Solomon]

Luc.   Away, Scutilla,

And laugh not loud between our acts; we'll meet
Again like music, and make ourselves merry.

    Scut. I wait near you.   *Exit* Scutilla]

Enter Sir Marmaduke

    Luc. Sir Marmaduke, I thought I should have had   80
Your visit without a summons.

    Mar.   Lady, you gave
One feather to the wings I had before;
Can there be at last a service to employ
Your creature?

    Luc. Something hath pleaded for you in your absence. 85

    Mar. Oh, let me dwell upon your hand! My stars
Have then remember'd me again.

    Luc.   How do the fens?
Goes the draining forward, and your iron mills?

    Mar. Draining, and iron mills? I know not, madam.

    Luc. Come, you conceal your industry and care   90
To thrive; you need not be so close to me.

    Mar. By this hand, lady, have I any iron mills?

    Luc. I am abus'd else; nay, I do love
One that has windmills in his head—

    Mar.   How, madam?

    Luc. Projects and proclamations; did not you   95
Travel to Yarmouth to learn how to cast
Brass buttons? Nay, I like it, it is an age
For men to look about 'em; shall I trust
My estate to one that has no thrift, a fellow
But with one face? My husband shall be a Janus.   100
He cannot look too many ways. And is
Your patent for making vinegar confirm'd?
What a face you put upon't! Nay, ne'er dissemble;
Come, I know all; you'll thank that friend of yours,
That satisfied my inquiry of your worth   105
With such a welcome character; but why
Do I betray myself so fast? Beshrew
His commendations!

    Mar. [*aside*]   How is this? Somebody,
That meant me well, and knew her appetite
To wealth, hath told this of me. I'll make use on't.—   110
Well, madam, I desir'd these things more private,
Till something worth o' mine, which I am now
Promoving, had been perfect to salute you;

But I perceive you hold intelligence
In my affairs, which I interpret love,　　　　　　　115
And I'll requite it ; will you be content
Be a countess for the present ?
   Luc.　　　　　　　　　　I shall want
No honour in your love.
   Mar.　　　　　　　　When shall we marry ?
   Luc.　Something must be prepar'd.
   Mar.　　　　　　　A licence, and say no more.
How blest am I !　Do not blush,　　　　　　　120
I wo' not kiss your lip till I ha' brought it.　　　*Exit*
   Luc.　Ha, ha !—Scutilla.

          [*Enter* Scutilla]

   Scut.　[*aside to* Winfield]　Be secret still.
   Luc.　　　　　　　Canst thou not laugh ?
   Scut.　　　　　　　　　Yes, madam.
You have kept your word ; the knight's transported, gone
To prepare things for the wedding.　　　　　　125
   Luc.　How didst thou like the iron mills ?
   Scut.　And the brass buttons !　Rarely ; have you devices
To jeer the rest ?
   Luc.　All the regiment on 'em, or I'll break my bow-strings.

          [*Enter* Solomon]

   Sol.　Sir Ambrose Lamount !　　　　　　130
   Luc.　Away, and let the swallow enter.
              [*Exit* Solomon]

    Enter Sir Ambrose *and* Solomon

              Why, sirrah,
Did I command you give access to none
But Sir Ambrose Lamount, whom you know I sent for ?
Audacious groom !
   Sol.　　　　It is Sir [Ambrose], madam.
   Luc.　It is Sir Ambrose Coxcomb, is it not ?　　135
[*to* Ambrose]　Cry mercy, noble sir, I took you muffled,
For one that every day solicits me
To bestow my little dog upon him ; but you're welcome :
I think I sent for you.　[*Exit* Solomon]
   Amb.　　　　　It is my happiness
To wait your service, lady.　　　　　　　140
   Luc.　　　　　　　I hear say

You have vow'd to die a bachelor ; I hope
It is not true, sir ?

    Amb.   I die a bachelor ?

    Luc. And that you'll turn religious knight.

    Amb. I turn religious knight ? Who has abus'd me ?

    Luc. I would only know the truth ; it were great pity.   145
For my own part I ever wish'd you well,
Although, in modesty, I have been silent.
Pray what's o'clock ?

    Amb.   How's this ?

    Luc. I had a dream last night; methought I saw you
Dance so exceedingly rarely, that I fell   150
In love.

    Amb.   In love with me ?

    Luc.   With your legs, sir.

    Amb. My leg is at your service to come over.

    Luc. I wonder'd at myself, but I considered,
That many have been caught with handsome faces ;
So my love grew—   155

    Amb.   Upwards ?

    Luc.   What followed in my dream
I ha' forgot.

    Amb.   Leave that to finish waking.

    Luc. Since the morning
I find some alteration ; you know
I have told you twenty times I would not love you,
But whether 'twere your wisdom or your fate,   160
You would not be satisfied ; now I know not,
If something were procur'd, what I should answer.

    Amb. A licence ! Say no more.

    Luc. Would my estate were doubled !

    Amb.   For my sake ?

    Luc. You have not purchas'd since you fell in love ?   165

    Amb. Not much land.

    Luc. Revels have been some charge to you ; you were
      ever
A friend to ladies ! Pity but he should rise
By one, has fallen with so many ! Had you not
A head once ?   170

    Amb. A head ? I have one still.

    Luc.   Of hair, I mean ;
Favours ha' glean'd too much : pray pardon me,
If it were mine, they should go lo[c]k their bracelets,

Or stay till the next crop ; but I blush, sir,
To hold you in this discourse : you will, perhaps,
Conster me in a wrong sense ; but you may use   175
Your own discretion till you know me better,
Which is my soul's ambition.
   Amb.   I am blest.
   Win. [*within*] Cunning gipsy, she'll use me thus, too,
When I come to't.
   Amb.   Lady, I know your mind ; when I see you next— 180
                                  Exit
   Luc.   You will see me again. Ha, ha, ha !—Scutilla.

[*Enter* Scutilla]

   Scut.   Here, madam, almost dead with stifling my laughter.
Why, he's gone for a licence ; you did enjoin him no silence.
   Luc.   I would have 'em all meet, and brag o' their several
hopes, they wo' not else be sensible, and quit me of their 185
tedious visitation.—Who's next ? I would the Colonel
were come, I long to have a bout with him.

[*Enter* Solomon]

   Sol.   Mr. Bostock, madam.
   Luc.   Retire, and give the jay admittance.
                    [*Exit* Solomon *and* Scutilla]

Enter Bostock

   Bos.   Madam, I kiss your fair hand.   190
   Luc.   Oh, Mr. Bostock !
   Bos.   The humblest of your servants.
   Luc.   'Two'not become your birth and blood to stoop
To such a title.
   Bos.   I must confess, dear lady,
I carry in my veins more precious honour
Than other men, blood of a deeper crimson ;   195
But you shall call me anything.
   Luc.   Not I, sir ;
It would not become me to change your title,
Although I must confess I could desire
You were less honourable.
   Bos.   Why, I prithee,
Is it a fault to spring from the nobility ?   200
There be some men have sold well-favour'd lordships
To be ill-favoured noblemen, and though

I wear no title of the state, I can
Adorn a lady.
    Luc.   That is my misfortune ;
I would you could not, sir.   205
    Bos.   Are you the worse
For that ? Consider, lady.
    Luc.   I have considered,
And I could wish, with all my heart, you were
Not half so noble, nay, indeed, no gentleman.
    Bos. How, lady ?
    Luc. Nay, if you give me leave to speak my thoughts, 210
I would you were a fellow of two degrees
Beneath a footman, one that had no kindred
But knights o' th' post ; nay, worse, pardon me, sir,
In the humour I am in, I wish, and heartily,
You were a son o' the people, rather than—   215
    Bos. Good madam, give me your reason.
    Luc.   Because I love you.
    Bos. Few women wish so ill to whom they love.
    Luc. They do not love like me then.
    Bos.   Say you so ?
    Luc. My wealth's a beggar ; nay, the title of
A lady, which my husband left, is a shadow,   220
Compar'd to what you bring to ennoble me,
And all the children you will get ; but I,
Out of my love, desire you such a one
That I might add to you, that you might be
Created by my wealth, made great by me ;   225
Then should my love appear ; but, as you are,
I must receive addition from you.
    Bos. [*aside*] Nobody hears.—Why, hark you, lady, could
You love me, if I were less honourable ?
    Luc. Honourable ? Why, you cannot be so base   230
As I would have you, that the world might say
My marriage gave you somewhat.
    Bos.   Say you so ?
Under the rose, if that will do you a pleasure,
The lords do call me cousin, but I am—
    Luc. What ?   235
    Bos. Suspected.
    Luc. How ?
    Bos. Not to be lawful ; I came in at the wicket,
Some call it the window.

Luc.   Can you prove it ?
Bos. Say no more.   240
Luc. Then I prefer you before all my suitors :
Sir Ambrose Lamount and Sir Marmaduke Travers
Are all mountebanks.
   Bos.   What say to the colonel ?
   Luc. A lance-prisado ! How my joy transports me !
But shall I trust to this ? Do not you flatter ?   245
Will not you fly from that and be legitimate,
When we are married ? You men are too cunning.
With simple ladies.
   Bos.   Do but marry me,
I'll bring the midwife.
   Luc.   Say no more ; provide
What you think necessary, and all shall be   250
Dispatch'd.
   Bos.   I guess your meaning, and thus seal
My best devotion.   *Exit*

[*Enter* Scutilla]

   Scut. [*aside to* Winfield]   Away now, and present yourself.
   Luc. Oh, Scutilla !
Hold me, I shall fall in pieces else. Ha, ha, ha !
   Scut. Beshrew me, madam, but I wonder at you ;   255
You wound him rarely up !
   Luc. Have not I choice of precious husbands ? Now,
And the Colonel were here, the task were over.
   Scut. Then you might go play—

Enter Colonel [Winfield]

                   Madam, the Colonel !
   Luc. Is he come once more ? Withdraw ; bid him 260
  march hither.
   Win. Now is my turn.—Madam !
   Luc. Y' are welcome, sir ; I thought you would have
  gone,
And not grac'd me so much as with a poor
Salute at parting.
   Win.   Gone whither ?
   Luc.   To the wars.
   Win. [*aside*] She jeers me already.—No, lady, I'm 265
  already

Engag'd to a siege at home, and till that service
Be over, I enquire no new employments.

   Luc. For honour's sake, what siege ?

   Win.   A citadel,
That several forces are set down before,
And all is entrench'd.   270

   Luc.   What citadel ?

   Win.   A woman.

   Luc. She cannot hold out long.

   Win. Ostend was sooner taken than her fort
Is like to be, for anything I perceive.

   Luc. Is she so well provided ?

   Win.   Her provision
May fail her, but she is devilish obstinate ;   275
She fears nor fire, nor famine.

   Luc.   What's her name ?

   Win. Lucina.

   Luc.   Ha, ha, ha ! Alas, poor Colonel !
If you'll take my advice, remove your siege ;
A province will be sooner won in the
Low Countries. Ha, ha, ha !   280

   Win.   Lady, you sent for me.

   Luc. 'Twas but
To tell you my opinion in this business.
You'll sooner circumcise the Turk's dominions,
Than take this toy you talk of, I do know it ;
Farewell, good soldier ! Ha, ha, ha ! And yet 'tis pity. 285
Is there no stratagem, no trick, no undermine ?
If she be given so desperate, your body
Had need to be well victuall'd ; there's a city
And suburbs in your belly, and you must
Lay in betimes, to prevent mutiny   290
Among the small guts, which, with wind of venge[ance] else,
Will break your guard of buttons. Ha, ha, ha !
Come, we'll laugh, and lie down in the next room, Scutilla.

                          Exit [*with* Scutilla]

   Win. So, so ! I did expect no good.
Why did not I strike her ? But I'll do something,   295
And be with you to bring before you think on't.
Malice and Mercury assist me !   *Exit*

ACTUS TERTIUS

[SCENE I

A Room in Lord Rainbow's *House*]

Enter Lord [Rainbow] *and* Barker

Bar. So, so ; y'ave a precious time on't.

Lord R. Who can help it, Frank ? If ladies will
Be wild, repentance tame 'em ! For my part
I court not them, till they provoke me to't.

Bar. And do they both affect you ?   5

Lord R.   So they say,
And did justify it to my face.

Bar.   And you
Did praise their modesty ?

Lord R.   I confess I prais'd 'em
Both, when I saw no remedy.

Bar.   You did ;
And they believ'd ?

Lord R.   Religiously !

Bar.   Do not,
Do not believe it, my young lord ; they'll make   10
Fools of a thousand such ; they do not love you.

Lord R. Why, and shall please your wisdom ?

Bar.   They are women ;
That 's a reason, and may satisfy you ;
They cannot love a man.

Lord R.   What then ?

Bar.   Themselves,
And all little enough ; they have a trick   15
To conture with their eyes, and perhaps raise
A masculine spirit, but lay none.

Lord R.   Good Cato,
Be not over-wise now : what is the reason
That women are not sainted in your calendar ?
You have no frosty constitution.   20

Bar. Would you were half so honest !

Lord R.   Why, a woman
May love thee one day.

Bar.   Yes, when I make legs
And faces, like such fellows as you are.

Enter Monsieur Le Frisk

Lord R. Monsieur Le Frisk !

Le Frisk. Serviteur !   25
Lord R. Nay, Frank, thou sha't not go.
Bar. I'll come again, when you ha' done your jig.
Le Frisk. Ah, *monsieur !*
Lord R. Come, you shall sit down ; this fellow will make
thee laugh.   30
Bar. I shall laugh at you both, and I stay.
Lord R. Hark you, monsieur, this gentleman has a
great mind to dance.
Le Frisk. He command my service ; please your lord-
ship begin, tat he may see your profit. *Allez !* Ha !   35
                          [Lord Rainbow *dances*]
Lord R. How like you this, Frank ?
Bar. Well enough for the dog-days ; but have you no
other dancing for the winter ? A man may freeze, and walk
thus.
Le Frisk. It be all your grace, monsieur ; your dance   40
be horse-play, begar, for de stable, not de chamber ; your
ground passage—ha !—never hurt de back, monsieur, nor
trouble de leg mush ; ha ! *Platt-il,* you learn, monsieur ?
Lord R. For mirth's sake, and thou lovest me.
Le Frisk. Begar, I teach you presently dance with all de   45
grace of de body for your good, and my profit.
Bar. Pardon me, my lord.
Le Frisk. Oh, not *pardonnez-moi !*
Lord R. Do but observe his method.
Bar. I shall never endure it ; pox upon him !   50
Le Frisk. 'Tis but dis in de beginning, one, two, tree,
four, five, the cinquepace ; *allez, monsieur.* Stand upright,
a[h], begar !
Lord R. Let him set you into th' posture.
Le Frisk. My broder, my lord, know well for de litle kit—   55
he fiddle—and me for de posture of de body. Begar, de king
has no two such subjects ; ha ! Dere be one foot, two
foot—have you tree foot ? Begar, you have more den I
have den.
Bar. I shall break his fiddle.   60
Lord R. Thou art so humorous.
Le Frisk. One—*bien !*—two—ha, you go too fast ! You
be at Dover, begar, and me be at Greenwish ; tree—toder
leg ; pshaw !
Bar. A pox upon your legs ! I'll no more.   65
Le Frisk. *Pourquoy ?*

Lord R. Ha, ha, ha! I would some ladies were here
to laugh at thee now. You wo' not be so rude to meddle
with the monsieur in my lodging?

Bar. I'll kick him to death, and bury him in a bass-viol,   70
Jack-a-Lent!

Le Frisk. Jack-a-Lent! Begar, you be jackanape! If
I had my weapon you durst no affront me; I be as good
gentleman, an for all my fiddle, as you: call me a Jack-a-de-
Lent!   75

Lord R. Rail upon him, monsieur; I'll secure thee; ha,
ha, ha! [*Holding* Barker]

Le Frisk. Because your leg have de pock, or something
dat make 'em no vell, and frisk, you make a fool of a monsieur. My lord use me like gentleman, an I care no rush   80
for you; be desperate, kill me, and me complain to de king,
and teach new dance, galliard to de gibbet; you be hanged
in English fashion.

Bar. Go, y'are an impertinent lord, and I will be
revenged.   *Exit*   85

Lord R. Ha, ha, good Diogenes!—Come, monsieur, you
and I wo' not part yet.

Le Frisk. My lord, if you had not been here, me wod
have broken his head with my fiddle.

Lord R. You might sooner have broke your fiddle; but   90
strike up.

Le Frisk. *Allez, ha! Bon!*   *They dance in*

[SCENE II

A Street]

Enter Bostock

Bos. I spy Sir Marmaduke coming after me.
This way I'll take to avoid his tedious questions,
He'll interrupt me, and I ha' not finish'd
Things fit for my design.

Enter Sir Ambrose

Amb. [*aside*] 'Tis Master Bostock; little does he think   5
What I am going upon; I fear I sha' not
Contain my joys.

Bos.   Good fortune to Sir Ambrose!

Amb. Sir, you must pardon [me], I cannot wait
Upon you now, I ha' business of much consequence.

Bos.   I thought to have made the same excuse to you,   10
For, at this present, I am so engag'd—
Amb.   We shall meet shortly.
Both.   Ha, ha, ha !
Bos. [*aside*]   Poor gentleman, how is he beguil'd !
Amb. [*aside*]   Your nose is wip'd.   Hum, 'tis Sir Marma-   15
duke ;

Enter Sir Marmaduke

I must salute him.
Bos.   The Colonel ?   There's no going back.

[*Enter* Colonel Winfield]

Mar. [*aside*]   What misfortune's this ?   But 'tis no
matter—
[*To* Sir Ambrose]   Noble sir, how is't ?
Amb.   As you see, sir.
Win.   As I could wish ; noble Master Bostock !   20
Bos.   Your humble servant, Colonel !
                              [*attempting to depart*]
Win.   Nay, nay, a word !
Mar. [*aside*]   I sha' not forbear jeering these poor things.
They shall be mirth.
Win.   What, all met so happily !
And how, my sparks of honour ?
Amb. [*aside*]   Things so tickle me,
I shall break out.   25
Win.   When saw you our mistress, Lady Lucina ?
Amb.   My suit is cold there ; Master Bostock carries
The lady clean before him.
Bos.   No, no, not [I] ; it is Sir Marmaduke.
Mar.   I glean by-smiles after Sir Ambrose.   30
Win.   None of you see her to-day ?   I may as soon marry
the moon, and get children on her ; I see her not this three
days ; 'tis very strange, I was to present my service this
morning.
Mar.   You'll march away with all.   35
Win.   I cannot tell, but there's small sign of victory ;
And yet methinks you should not be neglected,
If the fens go forward, and your iron mills.
Mar.   Has she betray'd me ?
Win.   Some are industrious,
And have the excellent skill to cast brass buttons.   40
Mar.   Colonel, softly !

Win. How will you sell your vinegar a pint ?
The patent['s] something saucy.
    Amb. The Colonel jeers him.
    Bos.   Excellent, ha, ha !
    Win. [*to* Sir Ambrose] Had not you a head once ?—   45
Of hair, I mean—favours ha' glean'd too much ;
If ladies will have bracelets, let 'em stay
Till the next crop.
    Amb.   Hum ! The very language
She us'd to me !
    Bos. Does he jeer him too ? Nay, nay, prithee spare him ! 50
    Ha, ha !
    Win. [*to* Bostock] You may do much, and yet I could
    desire
You were less honourable, for though you have
Blood of a deeper crimson, the good lady,
Out of her love, could wish you were a thing
Beneath a footman, and that you had no kindred   55
But knights o' th' post.
    Bos.   Good Colonel—
    Win.   Nay, pardon me ;
In the humour I am in, I wish, and heartily,
You were a son o' th' people.
    Bos.   Colonel !
How the devil came he by this ?
    Win. Under the rose, there was a gentleman   60
Came in at the wicket. These are tales of which
The Greeks have store. Fair hopes, gentlemen !
    Mar. How came you by this intelligence ?
    Win. Nay, I'll no whispering ; what I say to one
Will concern every man ; she has made you coxcombs.   65
    Amb. It does appear.
    Win.   And more than does appear yet ;
I had my share.
    Bos.   That's some comfort ; I was afraid—
    Win. But you shall pardon me, I'll conceal
The particulars of her bountiful abuses
To me ; let it suffice, I know we are all   70
Jeer'd most abominably : I stood behind
The hangings, when she sign'd your several passes,
And had my own at last, worse than the constable's ;
That this is true you shall have more than oath,
I'll join wi' ye in revenge, and if you wo' not.   75
I will do't alone.

Mar.   She is a devil.

Amb.   Damn her then !   Till we think on something else,
Let's all go back, and rail upon her.

Bos.   Agreed ; a pox upon her !

Mar.   We cannot be too bitter ; she's a hell-cat.   80

Amb.   D'ye hear ?   Listen to me : our shames are equal,
Yet if we all discharge at once upon her,
We shall but make confusion, and perhaps
Give her more cause to laugh ; let us choose one
To curse her for us all.   85

Win.   'Tis the best way ;
And if you love me, gentlemen, engage me.
I deserve this favour for my discovery ;
I'll swear her into hell.

Mar.   Troth, I ha' no good vein, I'm content.

Bos.   Gentlemen, noble Colonel, as you respect   90
A wounded branch of the nobility,
Make it my office ; she abus'd me most ;
And if the devil do not furnish me
With language, I'll say he has no malice.

Win.   If they consent.   95

Mar. ⎫
Amb. ⎬   With all our hearts.

Bos.   I thank you, gentlemen.

Win.   But let's all together, I'll not be
Barr'd, now and then, to interpose an oath,
As I shall find occasion.

Bos.   You'll relieve me,
When I take breath, then you may help, or you,   100
Or any, to confound her.

Win.   Let's away !

Bos.   Never was witch so tortur'd.   *Exeunt*

[SCENE III

A Room in Lady Lucina's *House*]

Enter Freshwater, Gudgeon, *and* Solomon

Sol.   Noble Master Freshwater, welcome from travel !

Fresh.   Where be the ladies ?

Sol.   In the next room, sir.
My Lady Rosamond is sitting for her picture ;
I presume you will be welcome.

Fresh.   An English painter ?

Sol.   Yes, sir.   5

Fresh.   Prithee let me see him.

   He gives Freshwater *access to the chamber, and returns*

Sol.   This way, honest Gudgeon :

How [are] the matters abroad ?   A touch of thy travel, what

  news ?

Gud.   First, let me understand the state of things at home.

Sol.   We have little alteration since thou went'st ; the

same news are in fashion, only gentlemen are fain to ramble   10

and stumble 'for their flesh since the breach o' th' Bank-side.

Gud.   Is my aunt defunct ?

Sol.   Yet the viragoes ha' not lost their spirit ; some on

'em have challenged the field every day, where gentlemen

have met 'em ; oh, the dog-days bit shrewdly, 'twas a vil-   15

lanous dead vacation.

Gud.   Is Paul's alive still ?

Sol.   Yes, yes ; a little sick o' th' stone ; she voids some

every day, but she is now in physic, and may in time recover.

Gud.   The Exchange stands ?   20

Sol.   Longer than a church ; there is no fear, while the

merchants have faith.   A little of thy travels, for the time

is precious ; what things have you seen or done, since you

left England ?

Gud.   I have not leisure to discourse of particulars ; but,   25

first, my master and I have run France through and through.

Sol.   Through and through !   How is that, man ?

Gud.   Why, once forward, and once backward, that's

through and through.

Sol.   'Twas but a cowardly part to run a kingdom through   30

backward.

Gud.   Not with our horses, Solomon, not with our horses.

   Enter Freshwater *and* Lady Rosamond

Fresh.   Madam, I did not think your ladyship

Had so little judgment.

[*R*]*os.*   As how, signor ?

Fresh.   As to let an Englishman draw your picture,   35

And such rare monsieurs in town.

Ros.   Why not English ?

Fresh.   Oh, by no means, madam ;

They ha' not active pencils.

Ros.   Think you so ?

Fresh. You must encourage strangers, while you live ;
It is the character of our nation, we are famous   40
For dejecting our own countrymen.
  Ros.   Is that a principle ?
  Fresh. Who teaches you to dance ?
  Ros.   A Frenchman, signor.
  Fresh. Why, so, 'tis necessary.
Trust, while you live, the Frenchman with your legs,
Your faces with the Dutch. If you mislike   45
Your face, I mean if it be not sufficiently
Painted, let me commend, upon my credit,
A precious workman to your ladyship.
  Ros. What is he ?
  Fresh. Not an Englishman, I warrant you !   50
One that can please the ladies every way ;
You sha' not sit with him all day for shadows.
He has regalos, and can present you with
Suckets of fourteen-pence a pound, Canary,
Prunellas, Venice glasses, Parmesan,   55
Sugars, Bologna sausages, all from Antwerp ;
But he will make olla podridas most incomparably.
  Ros. I have heard of him by a noble lady,
Told me the tother day, that sitting for
Her picture, she was stifled with a strange   60
Perfume of horns.
  Fresh. A butcher told me of 'em ; very likely.
  Ros. When I have need
Of this rare artist, I will trouble you
For my directions. Leaving this discourse,   .   65
How thrives your catalogue of debtors, signor ?
  Fresh. All have paid me, but—
  Ros. You sha' not name me in the list of any
That are behind ; beside my debt, a purse
For clearing the account. [*giving him a purse.*]   70
  Fresh.   You are just, madam,
And bountiful, though I came hither with
Simple intention to present my service.
It shall be cross'd.—Gudgeon, remember too
Her ladyship's name.
  [*Ros.*] My cousin has the same provision for you.   75

                  Enter Barker *and* Lady Honoria

  Gud. Sir, Master Barker !

Fresh. Madam, I'll take my leave. I'll find another
Time to attend my lady ; there's no light.—
I cannot abide this fellow.   *Exit with* Gudgeon

Hon. Madam, Master Barker hath some design,   80
Which he pretends concerns us both.

Ros.   He's welcome.
What is't ?

Bar.   My lord commends him to ye.

Ros. Which lord, sir ?

Bar. The lord, the fine, the wanton, dancing lord ;
The lord that plays upon the gittern, and sings,   85
Leaps upon tables, and does pretty things,
Would have himself commended.

Ros. So, sir !

Bar.   He loves you both, he told me so,
And laughs behind a vizard at your frailty ;
He cannot love that way you imagine,   90
And ladies of the game are now no miracles,

Hon. [*aside to* Lady Rosamond] Although he use to rail
    thus, yet we have
Some argument to suspect his lordship's tongue
Has been too liberal.

Ros. [*aside to* Lady Honoria] I find it too, and blush 95
    within to think
How much we are deceived. I may be even
With this May-lord.   *Exit*

Hon.   But does his lordship think
We were so taken with his person ?

Bar. You would not, and you knew as much as I.

Hon. How, sir ?   100

Bar. I ha' been acquainted with his body,
Ha' known his baths and physic.

Hon. Is't possible ? I am sorry now at heart
I had a good thought on him ; he shall see't,
For I will love some other in revenge,   105
And presently, if any gentleman
Ha' but the grace to smile, and court me up to't.

Bar. Hum !

Hon. A bubble of nobility ! A giddy,
Fantastic lord ! I want none of his titles.   110
Now, in my imaginations he appears
Ill-favoured, and not any part about him
Worth half a commendation ; would he were here !

[*Bar.*]   You'd make more on him.

Hon.   That I might examine,
And do my judgment right between you two now.   115
How much he would come short ; you have an eye
Worth forty of his, nose of another making :
I saw your teeth e'en now, compared to which,
His are of the complexion of his comb,
I mean his box, and will in time be yellower,   120
And ask more making clean ; you have a show
Of something on your upper lip, a witch
Has a philosopher's beard to him ; his chin
Has just as many hounds as hairs, that ever
My eyes distinguish'd yet ; you have a body   125

    *   *   *   *   *   *

And unpromising in his slashes, one
May see through him ; and for his legs, they both
Would but make stuffing for one handsome stocking ;
They're a lord's, I will be sworn.   I dote upon him !
I could wish somewhat—but I'm sorry, sir,   130
To trouble you so much ; all happy thoughts
Possess you !   *Exit*

Bar.   How is this ? If I have wit
To apprehend, this lady does not hate me.
I have profess'd a cynic openly ;
This language melts, I'll visit her again.   135

Enter Honoria

Hon.   Sir, I have a small request to you.
Bar.   Lady, command.
Hon.   If you think I have power
Or will to deserve from you any courtesy,
Pray learn to dance.   140
Bar.   To dance ?
Hon.   At my entreaty, sir, to dance.
It was the first thing took me with his lordship ;
You know not what may follow ; fare you well !   *Exit*
Bar.   What pretends this ?   To dance !   There's some-
    thing in't.
I've reveng'd myself already upon my lord ;
Yet deeper with my lady is the sweeter :   145
Something must be resolv'd.   *Exit*

[SCENE IV

Another Room in Lady Lucina's *House*]

Enter Lady Lucina *and* Scutilla [*laughing*]

Luc. Enough, enough, of conscience ! Let's reserve
Part of the mirth to another time ; I shall
Meet some [o' their] hot worships at the ball,
Unless their apprehension prompt 'em earlier
To know their folly in pursuing me.   5

Enter Solomon

Sol. Madam, the gentlemen that were here this morning
In single visits, are come all together,
And pray to speak with you.
  Luc.   They've met already.
Give 'em access.   [*Exit* Solomon]
  Scut.   I wonder what they'll say.

Enter Bostock, [Sir Ambrose] Lamount, Colonel [Winfield]
and [Sir Marmaduke] Travers

Win. Be confident, she shall endure it.   10
[*Luc.*]   So, so ;
How d'ye, gentlemen ? Y'are very welcome.
  Amb. 'Tis no matter for that ; we do not come to be
Welcome, neither will we be welcome. Speak, Master Bos-
    tock.
  Bos. We come to mortify you.
  Luc.   You will use no violence ?
  Bos. But of our tongues ; and in the names of these   15
Abused gentlemen, and myself, I spit
Defiance. Stand further off, and be attentive ;
Weep, or do worse ; repentance wet thy linen,
And leave no vein for the doctor !
  Luc.   They're mad.
  Scut. There is no danger, madam ; let us hear 'em ;   20
If they scold, we two shall be hard enough for 'em,
And they were twenty.
  Bos.   Thou basilisk !
  Luc.   At first sight ?
  Bos. Whose eyes sh[oo]t fire and poison !
Malicious as a witch, and much more cunning ;
Thou that dost ride men—   25

Luc.   I ride men ?

Bos.   Worse than the nightmare ! Let thy tongue be
   silent,
And take our scourges patiently ; thou hast,
In thy own self, all the ingredients
Of wickedness in thy sex, able to furnish
Hell, if't were insufficiently provided,   30
With falsehood and she-fiend[s] of thy own making !
Circe, that charm'd men into swine, was not
So much a Jew as thou art ; thou hast made
Us asses, dost thou hear ?

Amb.   He speaks for us all.

Bos.   But it is better we be all made such,   35
Than any one of us be monster'd worse,
To be an ox, thy husband.

Scut.⎫
Luc. ⎭   Ha, ha, ha !

Bos. · Dost thou laugh, crocodile ?

Win.   That was well said !

Bos.   Spirit of flesh and blood, I'll conjure thee,
And let the devil lay thee on thy back,   40
I care not.

Mar.   Admirable Bostock !

Win.   That spirit of flesh and blood was well enforc'd.

Bos.   You thought us animals, insensible
Of all your jugglings, did you, Proserpine ?

Amb.   Ay, come to that !   45

Bos.   And that we lov'd—lov'd, with a pox !—your phys-
   nomy.
Know we but tried thee, beldam, and thou art
Thyself a son o' th' earth.

Amb.   How ! She a son ?

Bos.   'Twas a mistake ; but she knows my meaning.
I begin to be aweary, gentlemen,   50
I'll breathe awhile.

Win.   'Tis time ; and that you may
Not want encouragement, take that. [*Strikes him*]

Bos.   Gentlem[a]n, Colonel, what d'ye mean ?

Win.   You shall know presently ; dare but lift thy voice
To fright this lady, or but ask thy pardon,   55
My sword shall rip thy body for thy [heart]
And nail it on her threshold ; or if you,
The proudest, offer but in looks to justify

The baseness of this wretch, your souls shall answer 't.

Mar. How's this ? 60

Win. Oh, impudence unheard !— Pardon, madam,
My tedious silence ; the affront grew up
So fast, I durst not trust my understanding
That any gentleman could attempt so much
Dishonour to a lady of your goodness.— 65
Was this your project, to make me appear
Guilty of that I hate beyond all sacrilege ?
Was it for this you pray'd my company,
You tadpoles ?—'Tis your presence charms my sword,
Or they shall quickly pay their forfeit lives ; 70
No altar could protect 'em.

Amb. We are betray'd.

Mar. Was it not his plot to have us rail ?

Win. Say, shall I yet be active ?

Luc. By no means ;
This is no place for blood, nor shall [my] cause
Engage to such a danger.

Win. Live to be 75
Your own vexations, then, till you be mad,
And then remove yourself with your own garters.
You sha'not go, before I know from whose
Brain this proceeded ;—you are the mirth.
Was ever civil lady so abus'd 80
In her own house by ingrateful horse-leeches ?
Could your corrupted natures find no way
But this to recompense her noble favours,
Her courteous entertainments ? Would any heathens
[Have] done like to you ? Admit she was 85
So just to say she could see nothing in you
Worthy her dearer thoughts (as, to say truth,
How could a creature of her wit and judgment
Not see how poor and miserable things
You are at best ?) must you, impudent, 90
In such a loud and peremptory manner,
Disturb the quiet of her thoughts and dwelling ?
Gentlemen ? Rather hinds, scarce fit to mix,
Unless you mend [your] manners, with her drudges.

Luc. This shows a nobleness, does't not, Scutilla ? 95

Bos. Why, sir, did not you tell us ?

Win. [*threatening him*] What did I tell you ?

Bos. Nothing !

Win.   Begone, lest I forget myself!

Bos.   I have a token to remember you.

A palsy upon your fingers, noble Colonel!

Mar.   Was this his stratagem! We must be gone.   100

Exit [*with* Sir Ambrose *and* Bostock]

Luc.   Sir, I must thank ye, and desire your pardon

For what has pass'd to your particular.

Win.   Y'ave more than satisfied my service in

Th' acknowledgment; disdain cannot provoke me

To be so insolent.   105

Luc.   Again I thank you.

Win.   I can forget your last neglect, if you

Think me not too unworthy to expect

Some favour from you.

Luc.   How d'ye mean?

Win.   Why, as

A servant should, that is ambitious

To call you mistress, till the happier title   110

Of wife crown his desires.

Luc.   I must confess,

This has won much upon me; but two words

To such a bargain; y'are a gentleman,

I'm confident, would adventure for me.

Win.   As far as a poor life could speak my service. 115

Luc.   That's fair, and far enough: I make not any

Exception to your person.

Win.   Body enough,

I hope, to please a lady.

Luc.   But—

Win.   To my fortune?

Luc.   To that the least; I have estate for both.

Win.   Though i[t] hold no comparison with yours,   120

It keeps me like a gentleman.

Luc.   I have a scruple.

Win.   You honour me in this;

There's hope, if I can take away that care,

You may be mine.

Luc.   Sir, can you put me in security   125

That you have been honest?

Win.   Honest! How d'ye mean?

Luc.   Been honest of your body; you are gentlemen,

Out of the wars live lazy and feed high,

Drink the rich grape, and in Canary may

Do strange things, when the wine has wash'd away   130
Discretion.
    Win.   What is your meaning, lady ?
    Luc. I do not urge you for the time to come,
Pray understand ; have you been honest hitherto ?
And yet, because you sha' not trouble friends
To be compurgators, I'll be satisfied,   135
If you will take your own oath that you are.
    Win. Honest of my body ?
    Luc. Yes, sir ; it will become me to be careful
Of my health ; I'll take your own assurance ;
If you can clear your body by an oath,   140
I'll marry none but you, before this gentlewoman.
    Win. Your reason why you use me thus ?
    Luc. I wonder you will ask ; do not I hear
How desperate some ha' been, what pain, what physic !
    Win. This is a tale of a tub, lady.   145
    Luc. You rid no match without a shirt, to shew
The complexion of your body. I ha' done, sir ;
When you resolve to swear y' are honest, I
Vow to [b]e yours, your wife ; I am not hasty,
Think on't, and tell me, when we meet again,   150
Anon, to-night, to-morrow, when you please ;
So farewell, noble Colonel. Come, Scutilla.   *Exeunt*
    Win. Is't come to this ? I am jeer'd again
Is't possible to be honest at these years ?
A man of my complexion, and acquaintance !   155
Was ever a gentleman put to this oath before
O' this fashion ?
If I ha' the grace now to forswear myself,
Something may be done, and yet 'tis doubtful,
She'll have more tricks ; if widows be thus coltish,   160
The devil will have a task that goes a-wooing.   *Exit*

ACTUS QUARTUS

[SCENE I

A Room in Lord Rainbow's *House*]

Enter Lord [Rainbow] *and* Bostock

    Bos. Such an affront, my lord, I was asham'd on't !
A mere conspiracy to betray our fames ;
But had you seen how poorly they behav'd
Themselves, such carven knights, a pair of drone bees !

I' th' midst of my vexation if I could   5
Forbear to laugh, I ha' no blood in me.
They were so far from striking, that they stood
Like images, things without life and motion,
Fear could not make so much as their tongue tremble ;
Left all to me.   10
    Lord R.   So, so ; what then did you ?
    Bos. The lady laugh'd too, and the Colonel
Increas'd his noise to see how she derided
The poor knights.
    Lord R.   Leave their character, and proceed
To what you did.
    Bos.   You shall pardon me, my lord,
I am not willing to report myself ;   15
They, and the lady, and the Colonel,
Can witness I came on.
    Lord R. But how came you off, cousin ? That must
      commend you.
    Bos. I ha' my limbs, my lord, no sign of loss
Of blood, you see ; but this was fortune. How   20
The Colonel came off's uncertain.
    Lord R.   Do not you know ?
    Bos. No, I left him ; I think ['twas] time,
    Lord R.   You did not kill him ?
    Bos. Upon my faith, my lord, I meant it not ;
But wounds fall out sometime when the sword's in.
These are poor things to brag on ; I ha' sav'd   25
Myself, you see.
    Lord R. If it be so, I'll call you cousin still !
My sati[r]ist !
                Enter Barker
            Hark, you shall beat this fellow.
    Bos. Shall I, my lord ? Without cause ?
    Lord R.   He shall give you
Cause presently.—How now, gumm'd taffeta ?   30
    Bar. I pay for what I wear, my satin lord ;
Your wardrobe does not keep me warm ; I do not
Run o' th' ticket with the mercer's wife,
And lecher out my debts at country-houses.
    Lord R. There's something else you do not.   35
    Bar. I do not use to flatter such as you are,
Whose bodies are so rotten they'll scarce keep
Their souls from breaking out ; I write no odes

Upon your mistress, to commend her postures,
And tumbling in a coach towards Paddington ;   40
Whither you hurry her to see the pheasants,
And try what operation the eggs have
At your return. I am not taken with
Your mighty nonsense, glean'd from heathenish plays,
Which leave a curse upon the author for 'em ;   45
Though I have studied to redeem you from
The infection of such books, which martyr sense
Worse than an almanack.
    Lord R.   Excellent satire !
But lash not on ; stop here, or I shall kick
Your learned worship.   50
    Bar. But do not, I advise you, do not.
    Lord R.   Why do not ?
    Bar. It will fall heavy o' somebody ; if your lordship
Kick me, I shall not spare your cousin there.
    Lord R. On that condition, what do you think o' that ?
                                    [*Kicks* Barker]
    Bar. What do you think ?   [*Kicks* Bostock] 55
    Bos. Excellently well followed, by my troth, la !
He'll pitch the bar well, I warrant, he does so
Follow his kick.
    Bar. Let it go round.   [*Kicks him again*]
    Bos.   Good ! Right as my leg again !
    Lord R. Your leg ! 'Twas he that kick'd you.   60
    Bos. D'ye think I do not feel it ?
    Lord R. Why d'ye not use your toes, then ?
    Bos. What, for a merry touch,
A trick, a turn upon the toe ?—D'ye hear, sir ?—
Y'are good company but if thou lovest me—   65
    Bar. Love you ? Why, d'ye hear, sir ?—
    [*Bos.*]   Ay, ay !
    Bar. What a pox should any man see in you,
Once to think on you ? Love a squirt !—
Shall I tell thee what thou art good for ?
    Bos.   Ay !
    Bar. For nothing !   70
    Bos. Good again ! My lord, observe him, ' for nothing ' !
    Bar. Yes, thou wo't stop a breach in a mud wall,
Or serve for a Priapus in the garden,
To fright away crows, and keep the [cornbin shutter],
Thou wo't.   75

Bos. Ha, ha ha !

Bar. Or thou wo't serve at Shrovetide to ha' thy legs
Broken with penny truncheons in the street ;
'Tis pity any cock should stand the pelting,
And such a capon unpreferr'd.   80

Bos.   Ha, ha, ha !

Bar. Cry mercy, y'are a kinsman to the lord,
A gentleman of high and mighty blood.

Lord R. But cold enough ; wo' not all this provoke him ?

Bar. Dost hear ? For all this, I will undertake
To thrash a better man out of a wench   85
That travels with her buttermilk to market
Between two dorsers, any day o' th' week,
My twice-sod tail of green fish ! I will do't,
Or lose my inheritance ; tell me, and do not stammer,
When wert thou cudgell'd last ? What woman beat thee ?   90

Bos. Excellent Barker !

Bar.   Thou art the town-top ;
A boy will set thee up, and make thee spin
Home with an eel-skin ; do not marry, do not ;
Thy wife will coddle thee, and serve thee up
In plates with sugar and rose-water to   95
Him that had the grace to cuckold thee :
And if Pythagoras' transmigration
Of souls were true, thy spirit should be tenant
To a horse.

Bos.   Why to a horse ?

Bar. A switch and spur would do some good upon you ; 100
Why dost thou interfere ? Get the grincomes, go,
And straddle, like a gentleman that would
Not shame his kindred : but what do I
Lose time with such a puppy ?

Bos. Well, go thy ways, I'll justify thy wit   105
At my own peril.

Bar. [*to* Lord Rainbow] I would speak with you ;
Be not too busy with your lordship's legs,
I'll tell you somewhat.

Lord R.   Speak to th' purpose, then.

Bar. I bestow'd
A visit on the ladies which you wot on ;   110
They have their wits still, and resolve to keep 'em,
They wo' not hang themselves for a young lord,
Nor grow into consumption ; other men

Have eyes, and nose, and lips, and handsome legs too ;
So fare you well, my lord ; I left your kick   115
With your cousin.—Bye, bye, otter !   *Exit*
   Lord R.   Very well !
But hark you, cousin Bostock, you have a [mild]
And modest constitution ; I expected
You would have lifted up your leg.
   Bos.   To kick him ?
Why, and you would ha' given a thousand pound,   120
I could not do't for laughing ; beside,
He was your friend, my lord.
   Lord R.   Did you spare him
For that consideration ?
   Bos.   Howsoever,
What honour had it been for me to quarrel,
Or wit, indeed ? If every man should take   125
All the abuses that are meant, great men
Would be laughed at ; some fools must ha' their jests.
Had he been any man of blood or valour,
One that profess'd the sword, such as the Colonel,
Less provocation would ha' made me active.   130

      Enter Sir Ambrose *and* Sir Marmaduke

   Lord R.   The eagles takes no flies ; is that it ?—How now,
Sir Ambrose, and my honour'd friend, Sir Marmaduke !
You are strangers.
   Mar.   Your lordship's pardon.—Master Bostock !
   Bos. [*aside*] Now I shall be put to't ;
This ta[l]king will undo me.   135
   Lord R.   Prithee tell me ?
Is the Colonel alive still ?
   Amb. Alive, my lord ! Yes, yes he's alive.
   Bos. Did your lordship think absolutely he was dead ?
   Lord R. But he is shrewdly wounded ?
   Amb.   No, my lord,
He is very well ; but 'twas your kinsman's fortune—   140
   Bos. Prithee, ne'er speak on't.
   Lord R.   What ?
   Mar.   To have a blow,
A box o' the ear.
   Lord R. How ?
   Mar.   With his fist, and an indifferent round one.

Bos.   Yes, yes, he did strike me, I could ha' told you that ;
But wherefore did he strike ?   Ask 'em that.   145
   Mar.   If you would know, my lord, he was our orator,
To rail upon the lady for abusing us,
Which, I confess, he did with lung and spirit ;
[For] which, in the conclusion, the Colonel
Stroke him to th' ground.   150
   Bos.   He did so, 'tis a truth.
   Lord R.   And did you take it ?
   Bos.   Take it ?
He gave it me, my lord, I asked not for it ;
But 'tis not yet reveng'd.
   Amb.   'Tis truth, we suffer'd
A little, but the place protected him.
   Bos.   It was no place indeed—
   Mar.   Now since you had   155
The greatest burden in the affront—
   Bos.   The blow ?
   Mar.   Right ! We would know whether your resolution
Be first to question him ; for our cause appears
Subordinate, and may take breath, till you
Ha' call'd him to account.   160
   Bos.   I proclaim nothing,
And make no doubt the Colonel will give me
Satisfaction, like a gentleman.
   Amb.   We are answer'd,
And take our leave, my lord.
   Lord R.   We shall meet at the Ball anon, gentlemen.
   Mar.   Your lordship's servants !—Now to our design.   165
                                                 Exeunt

   Bos.   My lord, I take my leave too.
   Lord R.   Not yet, cousin ; you and I ha' not done.
   Bos.   What you please, cousin !
   Lord R.   You have cozen'd me too much.
   Bos.   I, my good lord ?
   Lord R.   Thou most unheard-of coward !
How dare you boast relation to me ?   170
Be so impudent as to name, or think upon me ?
Thou stain to honour ! Honour ? Th'art beneath
All the degrees of baseness : quit thy father,
Thy suppos'd one, and with sufficient testimony
Some serving-man leap'd thy mother, or some juggler   175
That conjures with old bones, some woman's tailor,

When he brought home her petticoat and took measure
Of her loose body, or I'll cullis thee
With a bottom.
    Bos.   Good my lord !
    Lord R.   Be so baffled,
In presence of your mistress ! 'Tis enough   180
To make the blood of all thou knowest suspected ;
And I'll ha' satisfaction—
    Bos.   My lord !
    Lord R.   For using of my name in ordinaries,
I' th' list of other whom you make your privilege
To domineer, and win applause sometimes   185
With tapsters, and threadbare tobacco merchants,
That worship your gold-lace and ignorance,
Stand bare, and bend their hams, when you belch out
'My lord,' and 'tother cousin,' in a bawdy-house,
Whom, with a noise, you curse by Jack and Tom,   190
For failing you at Fish-street, or the Steel-yard. [*draws*]
    Bos.   My very good lord !
    Lord R.   Will you not draw ?
    Bos.   Not against your honour ; but you shall see—
    Lord R.   And vex my eyes, to look on such a land-rat.
Were all these shames forgotten, how shall I   195
Be safe in honour with that noble lady,
To whom I sinfully commended thee,
Though 'twere not much, enough to make her think
I am as base as thou art ; and the Colonel,
And all that have but heard thee call me cousin ?   200
What cure for this, you malt-worm ? Oh, my soul,
How it does blush to know thee, bragging puppy !
D'ye hear me—thunder and lightning !—what
Nobility my predecessors boasted,
Or any man from honour's stock descended ;   205
How many marquises and earls are number'd
In their great family ; what coats they quarter ;
How many battles our forefathers fought—
'Tis poor, and not becoming perfect gentry
To build their glories at their fathers' cost,   210
But at their own expense of blood or virtue
To raise them living monuments : our birth
Is not our own act ; honour upon trust
Our ill deeds forfeit ; and the wealthy sums
Purchased by others' fame or sweat, will be   215

Our stain, for we inherit nothing truly
But what our actions make us worthy of.
And are you not a precious gentleman ?
Thou art not worth my steel ; redeem this love
Some generous way of undertaking, or   220
Thou shalt be given up to boys and ballets,
The scorn of footmen, a disgrace more black
Than bastard. Go to the Colonel—
    Bos.   I will, my lord.
    Lord R. But, now I think on't, 'twill be necessary
That first you right my honour with the lady.   225
You shall carry a letter ; you will do't ?
    Bos. I'll carry anything.
    Lord R.   Expect it presently. *Exit*
    Bos. Such another conjuring will make me
Believe I am illegitimate indeed.
This came first keeping company with the blades,   230
From whom I learnt to roar and run away ;
I know 'tis a base thing to be a coward,
But every man is not born to be a Hercules ;
Some must be beat, that others may be valiant.   *Exit*

[SCENE II

A Room in Lady Honoria's *House*]

Enter Rosamond *and* Honoria *whispering ;* Sir Marmaduke
and Sir Ambrose *following*

    Ros. [*aside to* Honoria] Let it be so, they will else be
      troublesome.
    Mar. This cannot, I hope, displease you, lady, 'tis
No new affection, I protest, although
This be the first occasion I took
To express it.   5
    Ros.   You did ill in the impression ;
Although your bashfulness would not permit you
To speak in your own cause, you might have sent
Your meaning ; I can make a shift to read
A scurvy hand ; but I shall tell you, sir—
    Mar. Prithee do.   [*They whisper*] 10
    Hon. Is't possible
Your heart hath been tormented in love's flame,
And I the cause ?

Amb.   Your beauty hath the power
To melt a Scythian's bosom ; those divine
Beams would make soft the earth, when rugged winter   15
Hath seal'd the crannies up with frost ; your eye
Will make the frigid region temperate,
Should you but smile upon't : account it then
No wonder if it turn my breast to ashes.
   Ros. [*aside to* Sir Marmaduke] I see you are in love, by   20
      your [invention],
And cause I pity a gentleman should lose
His passion, I'll acquaint you with a secret.
   Mar.   The Lady Honoria ?
   Ros.   What misfortune 'twas
You did not first apply yourself to her,
That can reward your love, and hath a heart   25
Spacious to entertain you ! She does love you,
Upon my knowledge, strangely, and so
Commends you in your absence !
   Mar.   Say you so, lady ?
Pardon, I beseech you, the affection
I profess'd to your ladyship, 'twas but   30
A compliment ; I am sorry, I protest.
   Ros.   Oh, 'tis excus'd, sir ; but I must tell you,
Perhaps you wo' not find her now so tractable,
Upon the apprehension she was slighted ;
But to prescribe you confidence were to   35
Suspect your art and bold discretion.
   Hon. [*aside to* Sir Ambrose] 'Tis as I tell you, sir ; no
      lady in
The world can speak more praises of your body ;
She knows not yet your mind.
   Amb.   Is't possible ?
   Hon.   And yet, because she saw your compliments   40
Directed so unhappily to me,
I know not how you'll find her on the sudden ;
But 'tis not half an hour since you possess'd
The first place in her thoughts.
   Amb.   Shall I presume,
You will excuse the love I did present   45
Your ladyship ? It was not from my heart,
I hope you will conceive so.
   Hon.   A slight error.
   Amb.   I am ashamed on't.

Hon.   'Tis sufficient
That you recant; no more neglect.
   Ros. [*to* Sir Ambrose]   You are pleasant.
   Amb. Be you so too; I'll justify thou shalt   50
Have cause.
   Ros. To wonder at you; what's your meaning, sir?
   Amb. Sweet lady,
What thoughts make sad your brow? I have observ'd
Your eyes shoot clearer light.   55
   Ros.   You are deceiv'd,
I am not melancholy.
   Amb.   Be for ever banish'd
The imagination of what can happen
To cloud so rare a beauty; y'are in love.
   Ros. In love? Who told you so?
   Amb.   But that's no wonder,
We all may love, but you have only power   60
To conquer where you place affection.
And triumph o'er your wishes.
   Hon. [*To* Sir Marmaduke I love you?
Y'are strangely, sir, mistaken;
Put your devices on some other lady;
I ha' been so far from [any] affection to you,   65
That I ha' labour'd, I confess, to unsettle
The opinion of my Lady Rosamond,
Who, I confess, loves you, and that extremely.
   Mar. How! She love me? Then I ha' made fine work.
   Hon. What cunning she is mistress of, to hide   70
Her strange affections, or what power she has,
She does [not] fly into your arms, I know not.
   Ros. [*to Sir* Ambrose] Are you so dull?
Why, this was but to try your constancy;
I have heard her swear you are the prop'rest knight,   75
The very Adonis! Why, she has got your picture,
And made it the only saint within her closet;
I blush at your credulity.
   Amb.   Is't e'en so?
I have undone myself with her already.
Pardon me, gentle madam, I must leave you.   80
   Ros. With all my heart.
                Enter Monsieur [Le Frisk]
Hon.   We are reliev'd.
Monsieur Le Frisk!

Le Frisk.   Très humble serviteur, madame ! Me sweat with
de hast to wait upon your ladyships ; I pray give me de leave,
dispatch presently, for I must figaries to be done.   85

Ros.   Gentlemen, let your passions breathe awhile ;
A little music may correct the error,
And you may find yourselves.

Le Frisk. Allez !

Amb.   With all my heart ! Sir Marmaduke, let's help   90
To exercise the ladies.

Mar.   A good motion !

Le Frisk.   And, begar, noting in de world more profit your
body den de motion *à la mode de France.*

Mar.   I am for any frisk.

Frisk.   Ha, de frisk ! You jump upon my name, and,   95
begar, you have my nature to de right, hey ! And all de
world is but frisk.

Hon.   A country dance, then.

Le Frisk.   Ha, *monsieur, madame, allez !*
                    They dance.

Fort bon ! Très excellent ! Begar, so ! I crave your patience, 100
madam, gentlemen, you be at de Ball—*ma foi !*—you see
dat was never in dis world.

Ros.   What, monsieur ?

Le Frisk.   What do you think dat is ?   Me tell you ;
begar, you see me play de part of de Cupid.   105

Hon.   A French Cupid ?

Le Frisk.   Begar, French Cupid, why ? Dere is no love
like de French love, dat is Cupid ; love is hot, and de French
is hot.

Ros.   How comes it to pass that you are to play Cupid, 110
monsieur ?

Le Frisk.   My lord give me command me have device and
de masque for de ladies, and me no trust little jacknape to
play young Cupid, but myself.

Hon.   Cupid is a child ; you have a beard, monsieur.   115

Le Frisk.   Me care not de hair for dat ; begar, de little god
may have de little beard : Venus, his moder, have de mole,
and Cupid, her shild, may have the black mussel.

Hon.   But, monsieur, we read Cupid was fair, and you are
black ; how will that agree ?   120

Le Frisk.   Cupid is fair, and monsieur is black ; why,
monsieur is black den, and Cupid is fair, what is dat ? A
fair lady love de servant of the black complexion—*de bonne*

heure ! The colour is not de mush ; Vulcan was de black-
smith, and Cupid may be de black gentleman, his son legi- 125
timate.

Amb. 'Tis the way to make Cupid the boy no bastard.

Le Frisk. But do you no publish this invention ; me meet
you at de Ball armed with quiver and de bow.

Hon. You wo' not shoot us, I hope ; you'll spare our 130
hearts.

Le Frisk. Begar, me shit you, if me can, and your 'arts
shall bleed one, two, tree gallon ; *adieu, madame, serviteur,*
gentlemen, *très-humble !*   [*Exit.*]

Amb. *Adieu, monsieur !*—Now, madam, with your favour 135
I must renew my suit.

Hon.   Y'ad better buy a new one ;
Nay, then, we shall be troubled.   *Exit*

Amb.   You'll withdraw,
I'll follow you.   [*Exit*]

Mar.   Come, come, I know you love me.

Ros. You may enlarge your folly, my dear knight ;
But I have pardon'd you for love already.   [*Exit*] 140

Mar. This sha' not serve your turn ; I came hither
Not to be jeered, and one of you shall love me.   *Exit*

[SCENE III

A Room in Lady Lucina's House]

Enter Bostock, Lady Lucina, *and* Scutilla

Luc. Oh, impudence ! Dares he return ?

Scut.   It seems so.

Bos. Most gracious madam, my cousin, your Lord [Rain-
bow,]

Commends himself in black and white. [*gives her a letter*]

Luc.   To me ?

Bos. D'ye think 'tis from myself ?

Scut. You might ha' done't in black and blue.   5

Bos. Scutilla, how does thy poor soul ? Thou hast no
husband nor children to commend me to.

Scut. The poor soul's well ; I hope your body is
Recover'd ; does not your left cheek burn still ?
We ha' so talked of you.   10

Luc. [*reads*] *I am sorry any gentleman that has relation*

to me should be so forgetful of your honour and his own ; but
though he have forfeited opinion, let me continue innocent in
your thoughts. I have sent you a small jewel to expiate my
offence for commending him. I expect your ladyship at the　15
Ball, where you shall make many happy to kiss your hand ;
and in their number the true admirer of your virtue,

　　　　　　　　　　　　　　　　　[RAINBOW]

My lord is honourable.

　　Bos.　A slight jewel, madam.　　　　[*gives her the jewel*]
　　Luc.　　　　　　　　　　I am his servant.
　　Bos.　Nay, faith, my lord is right ; I ha' not met　　20
The Colonel since you know when.
　　Scut.　You ha' more reason to remember.
　　Bos.　I would be so bold to ask you a question.
　　Luc.　In the meantime give me leave—we are none but
　　　　friends—
I know y'are valiant—　　　　　　　　　　　　　　25
　　Bos.　No, no, you do not know't, but I know myself.
　　Scut.　That's more.
　　Luc.　But will you answer me ? Why did not you
Strike him again ?
　　Scut.　　　　　　　That might ha' caus'd blood.
　　Bos.　You're i' th' right.　　　　　　　　　　30
　　Luc.　　　　　　　You did not fear him ?
　　Bos.　But blood[s] are not alike, terms were not even ;
If I had kill'd him there had been an end—
　　Luc.　Of him !
　　Bos.　Right, madam !—but if he had wounded me,
He might ha' kill'd heaven knows how many.　　　　35
　　Scut.　Strange !
　　Bos.　D'ye not conceive it ? So many drops of mine,
So many gentlemen ; nay more, who knows
Which of these might ha' been a knight, a lord—
　　Luc.　Perhaps a prince ?　　　　　　　　　40
　　Bos.　　　　　　　Princes came from the blood,
And should I hazard such a severation
Against a single life ? 'Tis not I fear
To fight with him, by these hilts ! But what wise gamester
Will venture a hundred pound to a flaw'd sixpence ?
　　Scut.　Madam, the Colonel !　　　　　　　45
　　Bos.　　　　　　　And he were ten Colonels,
I'll not endure his company. [*To* Scutilla] Sweet lady,
You and I'll retire.

Scut.   And [you] were less honourable—

Bos. He should not seek me then.

Scut. He should rather hardly find you ; I'm your servant.

Exit [Scutilla *with* Bostock]

Enter Colonel [Winfield]

Luc. I was wishing for you, sir ;   50
Your judgment of these diamonds ?

Win.   The stones are pretty.

Luc. They were a lord's, sent me for a token,
You cannot choose but know him, the Lord [Rainbow]

Win. So, so, so ! I am like to speed.

Luc.   Is not he
A pretty gentleman ?   55

Win.   And you are sure he's honest ?

Luc. As lords go now-a-days, that are in fashion ;
But cry you mercy, you ha' put me in mind ;
I did propound a business to you, sir.

Win. And I came prepar'd to answer you.

Luc. 'Tis very well, I'll call one to be a witness.   60

Win. That was not, I remember, in our covenant,
You sha' not need.

Luc.   I'll fetch you a book to swear by.

Win. Let it be *Venus and Adonis*, then,
Or Ovid's wanton *Elegies*, Aristotle's
Problems, *Guy of Warwick*, or *Sir Bevis ;*   65
Or if there be a play-book you love better,
I'll take my oath upon your Epilogue.

Luc. Y'are very merry ; well, swear how you please.

Win. In good time !
You do expect now I should swear I'm honest ?   70

Luc. Yes, sir, and 'tis no hard condition,
If you reflect upon my promise.

Win.   What ?

Luc. To marry you, which act must make you lord
Of me and my estate, a round possession ;
Some men have gone to hell for a less matter.   75

Win. But I wo' not be damn'd for twenty thousand
Such as you are, [had] every one a million,
And I the authority of a Parliament
To marry wi' ye all ; I would not, by
This flesh ! [*taking her hand*] Now I ha' sworn.   80

Luc.   I think so, Colonel ;

Bless me ! Twenty thousand wives ? 'Twould ne'er
Come to my turn ; and you'd not live to give
The tithe benevolence.
   Win.   They would find pages, fools,
Or gentlemen-ushers.
   Luc.   Then, upon the matter,
You being not willing, sir, to take your oath,   85
I may be confident you are not honest.
   Win. Why, look upon me, lady, and consider,
With some discretion, what part about me
Does look so tame you should suspect me honest ?
How old d'ye think I am ?   90
   Luc.   I guess at thirty.
   Win. Some i' th' world doubted me not so much ;
At thirteen I was ever plump and forward ;
My dry-nurse swore at seven I kiss'd like one
Of five-and-twenty ; setting that aside,
What's my profession ?   95
   Luc.   A soldier
   Win.   So ;
Examine a whole army, and find one soldier
That hates a handsome woman ; we cannot march
Without our bag and baggages ; and is it possible
When we come home, where women's pride and all
Temptation to wantonness abounds,   100
We should lose our activity ?
   Luc.   You soldiers
Are brave fellows.
   Win.   When we have our pay.
We vow no chastity till we marry, lady ;
'Tis out of fashion, indeed, with gentlemen
To be honest and of age together ; 'tis sufficient   105
We can provide to take our pleasures, too,
Without infection ; a sound body is
A treasure, I can tell you ; yet if that
Would satisfy you, I should make no scruple
To swear ; but otherwise you must pardon us,   110
As we must pardon you.
   Luc.   Us, sir !
   Win.   Yes, you ;
As if you ladies had not your figaries,
And martial discipline, as well as we,
Your outworks and redoubts, your court of guard,

Your sentries, and perdus, sallies, retreats,   115
[Parleys], and stratagems ; women are all honest,
Yes, yes, exceeding honest ! Let me ask you
One question—I'll not put you to your oath ;
I do allow you Hyde Park and Spring Garden—
You have a recreation call'd THE BALL,   120
A device transported hither by some ladies
That affect tennis ; what d'ye play a set ?
There's a foul racket kept under the line,
Strange words are bandied, and strange revels, madam.
    Luc.   The world imagines so.   125
    Win.   Nay, y' are all talk'd of.
    Luc.   But if men had more wit and honesty,
They would let fall their stings on something else ;
This is discours'd but when corantos fail,
Or news at ordinaries ; when the phlegmatic Dutch
Ha' ta'en no fisher-boats, or our coal-ships land   130
Safe at Newcastle ; y' are fine gentlemen !
But to conclude of that we met for, your honesty,
Not justified by an oath, as I expected,
Is now suspended : will you swear yet ?
    Win.   Why, I thought you had been a Christian, widow ! 135
Have I not told you enough ?   You may meet one
Will forfeit his conscience, and please you better,
Some silkworm o' the City, or the Court ;
There be enough will swear away their soul
For your estate, but I have no such purpose ;   140
The wars will last, I hope.
    Luc.   So, so.—Scutilla !
          Enter Scutilla
You were present when I promis'd the Colonel
To be his wife, upon condition
He could secure my opinion by his oath,
That he was honest ; I am bound in honour   145
Not to go back.—Y'ave done it, I am yours, sir.
Be you a witness to this solemn contract.
    Win.   Are you in earnest, lady ?
I ha' not sworn.
    Luc.   You have given better truth ;
He that can make this conscience of an oath,   150
Assures his honesty.
    Win.   In mind !
    Luc.   What's past

I question not ; if, for the time to come,
Your love be virtuous to me.

Win.   Most religious,
Or let me live the soldier's dishonour,
And die the scorn of gentlemen. I ha' not   155
Space enough in my heart to entertain thee.

Luc. Is not this better than swearing ?

Win.   I confess it.

Luc. Now I may call you husband ?

Win. No title can more honour me.

Luc.   If please you,
I'll show you then my children.   160

Win.   How ! Your children ?

Luc. I ha' six that call me mother.

Win.   Hast, faith ?

Luc. The elder may want softness to acknowledge you ;
But some are young enough, and may be counsell'd
To ask your blessing ; does this trouble you ?

Win. Trouble me ? No ! But it is the first news, lady, 165
Of any children.

Luc.   Nay, they are not like
To be a burden to us ; they must trust
To their own portions, left 'em by their father—

Win. Where ?

Luc.   But of my estate ; I can not keep
Anything from 'em, and I know you are   170
So honest, you'd not wish me wrong the orphans.
'Tis but six thousand pound in money, Colonel,
Among them all, beside some trifling plate
And jewels, worth a thousand more.

Win.   No more ?

Luc. My jointure will be firm to us ; two hundred   175
Per annum.

Win.   Is it so ? And that will keep
A country house, some half a dozen cows,
We shall ha' cheese and butter-milk ; one horse
Will serve me and your man to ride to markets.

Luc. Canst be content to live i' th' country, Colonel ? 180

Win. And watch the peas, look to the hay, and talk
Of oats and stubble ; I ha' been brought up to't,
And, for a need, can thrash.

Luc.   That will save somewhat.

Win. I' th' year ; beside my skill in farrowing pigs :

Oh, 'tis a wholesome thing to hold the plough,   185
And wade up to the calf i' th' dirty furrows—
Worse than sleeping in a trench or quagmire !
You ha' not heard me whistle yet ?
   Luc.   No, indeed !
   Win. Why, there's it ! [*aside*] She does counterfeit.—
   Well, lady,
Be you in jest or earnest, this is my resolution,   190
I'll marry you, and y'ad forty children,
And not a foot of land to your jointure. Heaven
Will provide for's, and we do our endeavours.
Where be the children ? Come, how many boys ?
   Luc. As many as you can get, sir.   195
   Win.   How ?
   Luc.   No more.
Since y'are so noble, know I tried your patience ;
And now I am confirm'd : my estate is yours,
Without the weight of children or of debts ;
Love me, and I repent not.
   Win.   Say'st thou so ?   200
I would we had a priest here !
   Luc.   There remains,
To take away one scruple.
   Win.   Another gi[m]crack ?
   Luc. I have none, 'tis your doubt, sir ;
And, ere we marry, you shall be convinc'd
Some malice has corrupted your opinion
Of that we call the Ball.   205
   Win.   Your dancing business ?
   Luc. I will entreat your company to-night,
Where your own eyes shall lead you to accuse,
Or vindicate our fames.
   Win.   With all my heart.
   Scut. Madam, Master Bostock
Expects within.   210
   Luc.   You shall be reconcil'd to him.
   Win. With Bostock willingly ; then to th' Ball,
Which, for your sake, I dare not now suspect.
Where union of hearts such empire brings,
Subjects, methinks, are crown'd as well as kings. *Exeunt*

ACTUS QUINTUS
[SCENE I
The Ball Room]

Enter Monsieur [Le Frisk] *and* Servants *with perfume*

Le Frisk. Bon ! Fort bon ! Here a little, dere a little
more ; my lord hire dis house of the city merchant ; begar,
it smell musty, and he will have all sweet for de ladies ;
perfume, perfume every corner presently, for dere is purpose
to make all smoke anon, begar—   5

Enter Lady Rosamond *and* Honoria

Très humble serviteur, mesdames !

Hon. Where is my lord ?

Le Frisk. He wait on you presently.   [*Enter* Freshwater]
Monsieur de Freshwater !

Fresh. Monsieur le Frisk, these ladies were pleased to   10
command my attendance hither.

Le Frisk. Welcome to de Ball, *par ma foi !* You pardon,
monsieur, I have much trouble in my little head, I can no stay
to compliment ; *à vostre service !*   *Exit*

Fresh. In all my travels, I have not seen a more con-   15
venient structure.

Ros. Now you talk of your travels, signor, till my lord
come, you shall do us a special favour to discourse what
passages you ha' seen abroad.

Hon. Were you ever abroad before, signor ?   20

Fresh. I hardly ever was at home, and yet
All countries [to a] wise man are his own.
Did you never travel, ladies ?

Ros. We are no ladies errant, 'tis enough
For such as you, that look for state employment.   25

Fresh. Yet there be ladies ha' your languages,
And, married to great men, prove the better statesmen.

Ros. We have heard talk of many countries.

Fresh. And you may hear talk ; but give me the man
That has measured 'em ; talk's but talk——   30

Hon. Have you seen a fairer city than London ?

Fresh. London is nothing—

Ros. How ! Nothing ?

Fresh. To what it will be a hundred years hence.

Ros. I have heard much talk of Paris.   35

Hon. You have been there, I'm sure.

Enter Lord [Rainbow]

Fresh. I tell you, madam; I took shipping at Gravesend, and had no sooner passed the Cantons and Grisons, making some stay in the Valtelline, but I came to Paris, a pretty hamlet, and much in the situation like Dunstable; 'tis in the 40 province of Alcantara, some three leagues distant from Seville, from whence we have our oranges.

Lord R. [*aside*] Is the fellow mad?

Ros. I have heard Seville is in Spain.

Fresh. You may hear many things. The people are civil 45 that live in Spain, or there may be one town like another; but if Seville be not in France, I was never at Seville in my life.

Hon. Proceed, sir.

Fresh. Do not I know Paris? It was built by the young- 50 est son of King Priam, and was called by his name; yet some call it Lutetia, because the gentlewomen there play so well upon the lute.

Lord R. [*aside*] What a rascal is this!

Fresh. Here I observed many remarkable buildings, as 55 the University, which some call the Louvre; where the students made very much of me, and carried me to the Bear-garden, where I saw a play on the Bank-side, a very pretty comedy, called *Martheme*, in London.

Ros. Is't possible? 60

Fresh. But there be no such comedians as we have here; yet the women are the best actors, they play their own parts, a thing much desired in England by some ladies, Inns-o'-Court gentlemen, and others; but that by the way—

Hon. See, sir! 65

Fresh. I had stayed longer there, but I was offended with a villanous scent of onions, which the wind brought from St. Omer's.

Ros. Onions would make you sleep well.

Fresh. But the scent, 'tis not to be endured, I smelt on 'em 70 when I came to Rome; and hardly scaped the Inquisition for't.

Hon. Were you at Rome, too, signor?

Fresh. 'Tis in my way to Venice. I'll tell you, madam, I was very loath to leave their country. 75

Ros. Which country

Fresh. Where was I last?

Hon. In France.

Fresh. Right, for I had a very good inn, where mine host was a notable good fellow, and a cardinal.   80

Ros. [*aside*] How, a cardinal ? Oh, impudence !

Fresh. Oh, the catches we sang ! And his wife, a pretty woman, and one that warms a bed one o' th' best in Europe.

Hon. [*aside*] Did you ever hear the like ?

Ros. [*aside*] I did before suspect him.   85

Fresh. But mine host—

Hon. The cardinal ?

Fresh. Right !—Had a shrewd pate, and his ears were something o' th' longest ; for one, upon the oath of a w——Walloon that—from Spain to the Low Countries, and the other 90 from Lapland into Germany.

Ros. Say you so ?

Fresh. A parlous head, and yet loving to his guests, as mine host Banks, as red in the gills, and as merry a—; but anger him, and he sets all Christendom together by the ears. Well, 95 shortly after, I left France, and sailing along the Alps, I came to Lombardy, where I left my cloak, for it was very hot travelling, and went a pilgrim to Rome, where I saw the tombs, and a play in Pompey's theatre ; here I was kindly entertained by an anchorite, in whose chamber I lay, and 100 dr[an]k cider.

Lord R. [*aside*] Nay, now he is desperate.

Hon. [*aside*] Do not interrupt him.

Fresh. What should I trouble you with many stories ? From hence I went to Naples, a soft kind of people, and clothed 105 in silk ; from thence I went to Florence, from whence we have the art of working custards, which we call Florentines ; Milan, a rich state of haberdashers ; P[ied]mont, where I had excellent venison ; and Padua, famous for the pads, or easy saddles, which our physicians ride upon, and first brought 110 from thence, when they commenced doctor.

Ros. Very good !

Fresh. I see little in Mantua, beside dancing upon the ropes ; only their strong beer, better than any I ever drunk at the Trumpet ; but Venice—of all the champion countries— 115 do not mistake, they are the valiantest gentlemen, under the sun—

Ros. Is that it ?

Fresh. O the Catazaners we turned there !

Hon. Who was wi' ye ?   120

Fresh. Two or three Magnificcs, grandees of the state ; we tickled 'em in the very [R]ialto ; by the same token, two or three English spies told us they had lain leger three months to steal away the Piazza, and ship it for Covent Garden, a pretty fabric and building upon the—; but I was compelled 125 to make short stay here, by reason [one] of the Duke's concubines fell in love wi' me, gave me a ring of his, out of a solid diamond, which afterwards I lost, washing my hands in the salt water.

Hon. You should ha' fished for't, and as good luck as 130 she that found her wedding-ring in the haddock's belly.

Fresh. No, there was no staying ; I took post-horse presently for Genoa, and from thence to Madri[d], and so to the Netherlands.

Ros. And how sped you among the Dutch ? 135

Fresh. Why, we were drunk every day together ; they get their living by it.

Hon. By drinking ?

Fresh. And making bargains in their tippling ; the Jews are innocent, nay, the devil himself is but a dunce to 'em, of 140 whose trade they are.

Hon. What's that ?

Fresh. They fish, they fish still ; who can help it ? They have nets enough, and may catch the Province in time ; then let the kingdoms look about 'em : they can't be idle, 145 and they have one advantage of all the world, they'll ha' no conscience to trouble 'em. I heard it whispered they want butter ; they have a design to [churn] the Indies, and remove their dairy ; but that, as a secret, shall go no further. I caught a surfeit of boar in Holland ; upon my recovery I 150 went to Flushing, where I met with a handsome froe, with whom I went to Middleborough, by the—, and left her drunk at Rotterdam ; there I took shipping again for France, from thence to Dover, from Dover to Gravesend, from Gravesend to Queenhi[th]e, and from thence to what I am 155 come to.

   Lord R. [*advancing*] And, noble signor, you are very welcome.

Fresh. [*aside*] I hope he did not overhear me.

   Lord R. I am much honour'd, ladies, in your presence.

Fresh. Absence had been a sin, my lord, where you 160 Were pleas'd to invite.

Enter Monsieur [Le Frisk]

Le Frisk. Fie, fie ! My lord, give me one ear.

                      He whispers with my lord

Lord R. Interrupt me no more, good monsieur.

Fresh. Monsieur Le Frisk, a word, a word, I beseech you ;
no *excusez-moi,*   165

              Exit Freshwater *and* Monsieur [Le Frisk]

Lord R. Have you thought, ladies, of your absent servant,
Within whose heart the civil war of love—

Ros. May end in a soft peace.

Lord R.   Excellent, lady !

Hon. We had armies too, my lord, of wounded thoughts.

Lord R. And are you agreed to which I must devote 170
My loving service, and which is wisest, fairest ?
Is it concluded yet ?

Hon.   You did propound
A hard province, and we could not determine
As you expected ; but if your flame be not extinct,
We have devis'd another way.   175

Lord R.   You make my ambition happy ;
And, indeed, I was thinking 'twas impossible
That two such beauties should give place to either,
And I am still that humble [v]otary
To both your loves.   180

Ros.   Then this : we have made lots,
That what we cannot, Fate may soon [decide,]
And we are fix'd to obey our destiny ;
There is but two. [*showing the lots*] One, and your wishes
    guide you !

Lord R. And will you satisfy my chance ?

Hon.   We should
Be else unjust.   185

Lord R.   What method shall we use ?

Ros. Your hat, my lord, if you vouchsafe the favour ?

Hon. Dare you expose your head to the air so long ?

Lord R. Most willingly ; put in.

Ros.   There is Fortune.

Hon. That draw which quickly tell how much I love you.

Lord R. So, so !   190
Now let me see ; I commend your device,
Since I am uncapable of both ;
This is a way indeed ; but, your favour—

    Ros. Let's have fair play, my lord.

    Lord R.   What fool is he,

That, having the choice of mistresses, will be   195

Confin'd to one, and rob himself ? I am yet

The favourite of both ; [this] is no policy.

I could make shift with both abed.

    Ros.   You are merry !

    Lord R. In troth, and so I am, and in the mind

I am in will give myself no cause to th' contrary.   200

D'ye see ? I'll draw you both.

    Hon.   How ? Both !

    [*Lord R.*] You cannot otherwise be reconcil'd ;

I'll be content to marry one, and do

Service to th' other's petticoat ; I must tell you,

I am not without precedent.   205

    Hon.   There you triumph.

    Lord R. Within, the name of Venus. [*drawing*]

                        Ha ! A blank ?

By this light, nothing, neither name nor mark !

    Both. Ha, ha, ha !

    Lord R.   This is a riddle yet.

    Ros. 'Tis quickly solv'd : your lordship was too confi-
       dent ;

We never were at such a loss, my lord,   210

As with the hazard of our wit or honour

To court you with so desperate affection.

    Hon. By our example know some ladies may

Commend, nay, love a gentleman, and yet

Be safe in their own thoughts : and see, [*tearing the lots*] as far 215

As modesty and honour will allow us,

We are still servants to your lordship.

    Lord R.   Say so ?

Why, look you, ladies, that you may perceive

How I can be temperate too ; first, I thank you

Heartily, and to recompense your wit,   220

Present another lottery ; you sha' not

Suspect I have a thought that will betray

Your innocence to scandal : let me entreat

You take your chance too. This for you, madam,

And this is left your fortune : do me honour   225

To wear these pair of jewels for my sake ;

So, with a confidence of your happy pardon

For what is past, hereafter I shall pay

To your true virtues better service than
So unnecessary trials.   230
    Ros.   And to show
We are not coy, my lord, we'll wear your jewel[s].
    Lord R. And be their ornament.

        Enter [Lady Lucina], Colonel [Winfield], Bostock

    Win.   All happiness to your lordship.
Your [revels] are not full [yet,] noble ladies.
    Lord R. Your presence will soon make us active. [*to*
    Lucina] Madam,
I was bold—   235
    Bos.   She has your diamond, my lord.
    Lord R. And can you pardon?
    Bos.   Nay, nay, we are friends;
Are we not, madam?
    Luc.   I were else unmerciful.
    Bos. The Colonel, too, has given me satisfaction.
    Win. I think you had enough,
    Bos. As much as I desir'd, and here's my hand,   240
While I can draw a sword command me.
    Win.   What?
    Bos. To put it up again. All friends, all friends;
A pox o' quarrelling!
    Win.   I kiss your hand, sir.
    Bos. Kiss my hand! kiss my—— noble ladies, here.
    Win. Why is the music silent all this while?   245
Has it no voice to bid these ladies welcome?

    A golden Ball descends, enter Venus *and* Cupid

    Ven. Come, boy, now draw thy powerful bow,
        Here are ladies' hearts enough
        To be transfix'd; this meeting is
        To ruffle ladies, and to kiss.   250
        These are my orgies: from each eye
        A thousand wanton glances fly;
        Lords and ladies of the game,
        Each breast be full of my own flame!
        Why shoots not Cupid? These are all   255
        Met in honour of my Ball,
        Which Paris gave [on] Ida hill;
        I'll maintain these revels still.
        Why stays Cupid all this while?

[Enter Diana]

Dian. Venus doth herself beguile.   260
Ven. Diana here ! Go back again.
Dian. These are none of Venus' train.
       No spark of this lascivious fire
       Dwells in their bosoms ; no desire,
       But what doth fill Diana's breast,   265
       In their modest thoughts do rest.
       Venus, this new festival
       Shall be still Diana's Ball ;
       A chaste meeting ever here ;
       Seek thy votaries otherwhere.   270
Ven. You're chaste indeed ! Do not we know,
       You to your sweetheart nightly go ?
       [Endymion] is not kiss'd ! No, you
       On his face but let fall dew !
       Some may wonder what doth ail   275
       Your lips, but kisses made them pale ;
       Methinks the Moon should blush.
Dian.   I do
       Sometimes, but 'tis for such as you ;
       Then hide myself within a mist
       For shame to see thee clipp'd and kiss'd.   280
Ven. Draw, Cupid ; shall thy mother be
       Bra[v]d by a huntress ? Let me see
       I want one shaft. [*offers to take his bow*]
Cup.   Mo[th]er, not so,
       You may quickly break my bow ;
       Here Diana doth command ;   285
       My bow is frozen to my hand ;
       Beside, the ladies' breasts are here,
       Such proofs against my shafts, I fear,
       Each arrow would, to our disgrace,
       Break, or rebound in my own face ;   290
       Mo[th]er, fly hence, or you will be,
       If you'll stay, made as chaste as she.
Ven. Can her magic charm them so ?
       Then 'tis time that Venus go
       To seek her own more choice delight :   295
       Against my will, enjoy this night. [*Exit*]
Dian. Cupid, if you mean to stay,
       Throw your licentious shafts away ;
       Then you are Love, then be embrac'd,

    Love is welcome while he's chaste.   300
    Now, some other strain to show
    What pleasures to this night we owe.

                          A Dance

   Enter [Freshwater *and*] Barker, *like a* Satyr *dancing*

Fresh. My lord, my ladies, will you see a monster?
I have not met such another in all my travels.
   Luc. What have we here, a satyr?   305
   Bos. No, 'tis a dancing bear.
   Lord R.   What is the device?
   Bar. Wonder that a satyr can
    Put off wildness and turn man.
    Love such miracles can do;
    But this owes itself to you,   310
    Bright lady. [*to* Honoria]
   [*Hon.*]   Keep the goblin from me, gentlemen.
   Bar. You'll know me. [*unmasking*]
   Omnes. Barker!
   Bar.   No more the cynic; I protest
You have converted me.
   [*Hon.*]   Your meaning, sir?
   Bar. I am the man you did encourage, madam,   315
To learn to dance; I shall do better shortly;
Your love will perfect me, and make me soft
And smooth as any reveller.
   [*Hon.*]   Ha, ha, ha!
My love! I am not mad to love a satyr,
For that's thy best condition. Judgment all!   320
How scurvily this civility shows in him.
Faith, rail, and keep your humour still; it shows excellent.
Does he not become the beast? [Do] the lords
Allow you pension?
   Omnes.   Ha, ha, ha!
   Bar. You are a witch, I'll justify it; and there is not 325
One honest thought among the whole sex of you.
D'ye laugh, loose-witted ladies? There are not
In hell such furies: that's a comfort yet
To him that shall go thither; he shall have
Less torment after death, than he finds here.   330
   Lord R. Why, Barker!
   Bar. Your wit has got the squirt too; I'll traduce
Your Ball for this, and if there be a post

That dares write mischief, look to be worse
Than executed.   *Exit* 335
    Lord R. He will come to himself again when he hath
      purg'd.
Freshwater !

Enter Sir [Marmaduke] *and* Sir [Ambrose]

    [*Mar.*] Madam, your servants beg this favour from you.
    Ros. What is't ?
    [*Mar.*] That since your resolutions will admit   340
No change of hearts, you will not publish how
We ha' been jeer'd.
    Ros.   Not jeer'd ; but you came on
So desperate.
    Hon.   We love our own, when we preserve
Gentlemen's honour.
    Win.   Then let's toss the ball.
    Lord R. Signor Freshwater !   345
    Fresh. Mercy and silence, as you are honourable.
    Lord R. [N]ay, it concern[s] these gentlemen.
    Fresh. Why, if I must ! Gentlemen, you imagine I ha'
been at Venice ; but I stayed at Gravesend all this summer,
expecting a wind, and finding it so uncertain, will defer the 350
voyage till the spring. I am not the first whom the winds
and seas have crossed.
    [*Mar.*] Then you have crossed no sea ?
    Fresh. If you please, I'll require but my principal ; and
for your good company, I'll stay at home for good and all 355
to be merry.
    Lord R. Nay, nay ; you shall go your voyage ;
We would not have you lose the benefit
Of travel ; when you come home, you may summon
Your debtors by a drum, and showing your bag   360
Of certificates——
    Bos. Receive your money when you can get it, and be
knighted.
    Fresh I thank you, gentlemen : I am in a way, now I
have sold my land and put out my money, to live, I see ! 365
My heart wo' not dance to-night ; I may to Gravesend in the
morning : I can be but pickled in salt-water, and I'll venture
one drowning to be revenged.
    [*Lord R.*] Again again ; set, set !

A Dance

Luc.   What think you of all this ?

Win.   To my wishes ; 370

An innocent and generous recreation.

Lord R.   Ladies and gentlemen, now a banquet waits
        you ;

Be pleased to accept, 'twill give you breath, and then

Renew our revels, and to th' Ball again.   *Exeunt omnes*

FINIS.

SIR GILES GOOSECAP, KNIGHT

[DRAMATIS PERSONAE]

Eugenia, *a widow and a noble lady*

Hippolyta
Penelope } *lady virgins and companions to Eugenia*

Winifred, *gentlewoman to Eugenia*

[Anabell, *attendant on Eugenia*]

Momford, *a nobleman, uncle to Eugenia*

Clarence, [a] *gentleman, friend to Momford*

Foulweather, *a French-affected traveller and a captain*

Sir Giles Goosecap, *a foolish knight*

Sir Cuthbert Rudesby, a *blunt knight*

Sir Clement Kingcob, *a knight*

Lord Tales

Lord Furnifall

Bullaker, *a French page*

Jack
Will } *pages*

[Doctor Versey]

[Horatio, *a singer*

[A Messenger]

[Musicians]

Sir Giles Goosecap, Knight

ACTUS PRIMUS

SCENA PRIMA

[Before the House of Eugenia]
Enter Bullaker *with a torch*

Bull. This is the Countess Eugenia's house, I think. I
can never hit off these same English city houses, though I
were born here ; if I were in any city in France, I could
find any house there at midnight.

Enter Jack *and* Will

Jack. These two strange hungry knights, Will, make   5
the leanest trenchers that ever I waited on.

Will. A plague on them, Jack ; they leave us no fees at
all for our attendance. I think they use to set their bones
in silver, they pick them so clean. See, see, see, Jack,
what's that ?   10

Jack. O' my word, Will, 'tis the great baboon, that was
to be seen in Southwark.

Will. Is this he ? Gods my life, what beasts were we,
that we would not see him all this while ; never trust me if
he look not somewhat like a man ; see how prettily he holds 15
the torch in one of his fore-feet. Where's his keeper, trow ;
is he broke loose ?

Jack. Hast ever an apple about thee, Will ? We'll
take him up sure ; we shall get a monstrous deal of money
with him.   20

Will. That we shall, i'faith, boy ! And look thou here,
here's a red cheeked apple to take him up with.

Jack. Excellent fit, o' my credit ! Let's lay down our
provant and to him.

Bull. [aside] I'll let them alone awhile.   25

Jack. Give me the apple to take up Jack, because my
name is Jack.

Will.   Hold thee, Jack, take it.

Jack.   Come Jack, come Jack, come Jack!

Bull.   I will come to you, sir. I'll Jack ye o' my word,   30
I'll Jack ye!

Will.   Gods me, he speaks, Jack! O pray pardon us,
sir!

Bull.   Out, ye moped monkies! Can ye not know a
man from a marmoset in these Frenchified days of ours?   35
Nay, I'll Jackefie you a little better yet.

Both.   Nay good sir, good sir, pardon us!

Bull.   Pardon us! Out ye home-bred peasants! Plain
English, 'pardon us'? If you had parled, and not spoken,
but said *Pardonne-moi,* I would have pardoned you, but   40
since you speak and not parley, I will cudgel ye better yet.

Ambo.   O *pardonne-moi, monsieur.*

Bull.   *Bien, je vous remercie;* there's *pardonne pour vous,*
sir, now.

Will.   Why, I thank ye for it, sir; you seem to be a   45
squire of our order, sir.

Jack.   Whose page might you be, sir?

Bull.   I am now the great French travellers page—

Will.   Or rather the French travellers great page, sir;
on, on!   50

Bull.   Hight Captain Foulweather, alias Commendations; whose valour's within here at supper with the Countess Eugenia, whose proper eaters I take you two to be.

Will.   You mistake us not, sir.

Jack.   This Captain Foulweather, alias Commendations,   55
Will, is the gallant that will needs be a suitor to our Countess.

Will.   Faith, and if Foulweather be a welcome suitor to
a fair lady, has good luck.

Jack.   O sir, beware of one that can shower into the laps
of ladies. Captain Foulweather! Why he's a Captinado,   60
or Captain of Captains, and will lie in their joints, that give
him cause to work upon them, so heavily that he will make
their hearts ache, I warrant him. Captain Foulweather!
Why he will make the cold stones sweat for fear of him a
day or two before he come at them. Captain Foulweather!   65
Why he does so domineer, and reign over women.

Will.   A plague of Captain Foulweather! I remember
him now, Jack, and know him to be a dull moist-brained ass.

Jack.   A Southern man, I think.

Will.   As fearful as a hare, and 'a will lie like a lapwing,   70

and I know how he came to be a captain, and to have his
surname of Commendations.

Jack.   How, I prithee, Will ?

Will.   Why, sir, he served the great Lady Kingcob and
was yeoman of her wardrobe, and because 'a could brush up   75
her silks lustily, she thought he would curry the enemies'
coats as soundly, and so by her commendations he was
made Captain in the Low Countries.

Jack.   Then being made captain only by his lady's commendations, without any worth also of his own, he was   80
ever after surnamed Captain Commendations ?

Will.   Right !

Bull.   Ay, sir, right ; but if he had not said right, my Captain should have taken no wrong at his hands, nor yours
neither, I can tell ye.   85

Jack.   What are those two knights' names, that are thy
Captain's comrades, and within at supper with our lady ?

Bull.   One of their names, sir, is Sir Giles Goosecap ;
the other's, Sir Cut. Rudesby.

Will.   Sir Giles Goosecap ! What's he ? A gentleman ?   90

Bull.   Ay, that he is, at least if he be not a nobleman ;
and his chief house is in Essex.

Jack.   In Essex ? Did not his ancestors come out of
London ?

Bull.   Yes, that they did, sir ! The best Goosecaps in   95
England comes out of London, I assure you.

Will.   Ay, but, sir, these must come into it before they
come out on't, I hope ; but what countryman is Sir Cut.
Rudesby ?

Bull.   A Northern man, or a Western man, I take him ;   100
but my Captain is the emphatical man ; and by that pretty
word 'emphatical' you shall partly know him ; for 'tis a
very forcible word, in troth, and yet he forces it too much,
by his favour ; marry, no more than he does all the rest
of his words ; with whose multiplicity often times he tra-   105
vails himself out of all good company.

Jack.   Like enough ; he travelled for nothing else.

Will.   But what qualities haunt Sir Giles Goosecap now,
sir ?

Bull.   Sir Giles Goosecap has always a death's head (as   110
it were) in his mouth, for his only one reason for everything
is, ' because we are all mortal ' ; and therefore he is generally called the mortal knight ; then hath he another pretty

phrase too, and that is, he will ' tickle the vanity on't ' still
in everything ; and this is your *summa totalis* of both their   115
virtues.

Jack. 'Tis enough, 'tis enough, as long as they have
land enough ; but now muster your third person afore us, I
beseech you.

Bull. The third person and second knight, blunt Sir   120
Cut. Rudesby, is indeed blunt at a sharp wit, and sharp at
a blunt wit ; a good bustling gallant, talks well at rovers ;
he is two parts soldie ; as slovenly as a Switzer, and somewhat like one in face too ; for he wears a bush beard will
dead a cannon-shot better than a wool-pack ; he will come   125
into the presence like your Frenchman in foul boots, and
dares eat garlic as a prep[a]rative to his courtship. You
shall know more of him hereafter ; but, good wags, let me
win you now for the geographical parts of your ladies in
requital.   130

Will. That you shall, sir, and the hydrographical, too, and
you will ; first my lady, the widow and Countess Eugenia,
is, in earnest, a most worthy lady, and, indeed, can do more
than a thousand other ladies can do, I can tell ye.

Bull. What's that, I pray thee ?   135

Jack. Marry, sir, he means she can do more than sleep,
and eat, and drink, and play at noddy, and help to make
herself ready.

Bull. Can she so ?

Will. She is the best scholar of any woman, but one,   140
in England ; she is wise and virtuous.

Jack. Nay, she has one strange quality for a woman
besides, though these be strange enough that he has reckoned.

Bull. For God's sake, what's that ?

Jack. She can love reasonable constantly, for she loved   145
her husband only, almost a whole year together.

Bull. That's strange indeed ; but what is your fair lady,
sir ?

Jack. My lady, sir, the Lady Hippolyta—

Will. That is as chaste as ever was Hippolytus.   150

Jack. True, my pretty Parenthesis !—is half a maid, half
a wife, and half a widow.

Bull. Strange tale to tell ! How canst thou make
this good, my good *Assumpsit* ?

Jack. Thus, sir : she was betrothed to a gallant young   155
gentleman that loved her with such passion and admira-

tion that he never thought he could be so blessed as to enjoy
her in full marriage, till the minister was marrying them ;
and even then, when he was saying ' I, Charles, take thee,
Hippolyta,' with extreme joy he began to look pale, then 160
going forwards saying ' to my wedded wife,' he looked paler,
and then pronouncing ' for richer, for poorer, as long as
we both shall live,' he looked extreme pale. Now, sir,
when she comes to speak her part, and said ' I, Hippolyta,
take thee, Charles,' he began to faint for joy, then saying 165
' to my wedded husband,' he began to sink, but then going
forth to ' for better, for worse,' he could stand no longer,
but with very conceit, it seemed, that she, whom he tendered
as the best of all things, should pronounce the worst, and
for his sake, too, he sunk downright, and died suddenly. And 170
thus being half married, and her half husband wholly dead,
I hope I may with discretion affirm her half a maid, half a
wife, and half a widow ; do ye conceive me, sir ?

Bull. O Lord, sir, I devour you quick ! And now, sir, I
beseech you open unto me your tother lady, what is she ? 175

Will. I'll answer for her, because I know her ladyship
to be a perfect maid indeed.

Bull. How canst thou know that ?

Will. Passing perfectly, I warrant ye !

Jack. By measuring her neck twice, and trying if it 180
will come about her forehead and slip over her nose ?

Will. No, sir, no ; by a rule that will not slip so, I warrant
you, which for her honour's sake I will let slip unto you.
God's so, Jack, I think they have supped !

Jack. By'r Lady, we have waited well the while !   185

Will. Well, though they have lost their attendance, let
us not lose our suppers, Jack.

Jack. I do not mean it ; come, sir, you shall go in and
drink with us, i'faith !

Bull. *Pardonne-moi, monsieur !*   190

Both. No pardoning, in truth, sir !

Bull. *Je vous remercie de bon cœur.*   *Exeunt*

[SCENA II

A Room in Eugenia's *House*]

Enter Goosecap, Rudesby, Foulweather, Eugenia, Hippolyta,
Penelope, Winifred

Rud. A plague on you, sweet ladies ! 'Tis not so late ;
what needed you to have made so short a supper ?

Goose. In truth, Sir Cut., we might have tickled the vanity on't an hour longer, if my watch be trustible.

Foul. Ay, but how should these beauties know that, Sir Giles ? Your watch is mortal, and may err.

Goose. That's sooth, Captain ; but do you hear, honest friend, pray take a light and see if the moon shine, I have a sun-dial will resolve presently.

Foul. Howsoever, believe it, ladies, 'tis unwholesome, uncourtly, unpleasant, to eat hastily and rise suddenly ; a man can shew no discourse, no wit, no stirring, no variety, no pretty conceits, to make the meat go down emphatically.

Eug. Winifred !

Win. Madam !

Eug. I prithee go to my uncle the Lord Momford, and entreat him to come quicken our ears with some of his pleasant spirit ; this same Foulweather has made me so melancholy ; prithee make haste.

Win. I will, madam.   *Exit*

Hip. We will bid our guests good night, madam ; this same Foulweather makes me so sleepy.

Pen. Fie upon it, for God's sake, shut the casements, here's such a fulsome air comes into this chamber ! In good faith, madam, you must keep your house in better reparations, this same Foulweather beats in so filthily.

Eug. I'll take order with the porter for it, lady.   Good night, gentlemen.

Rud. Why, good night, and be hanged, and you'll needs be gone !

Goose. God give you good night, madams, thank you for my good cheer ; we'll tickle the vanity on't no longer with you at this time, but I'll indite your ladyship to supper at my lodging one of these mornings ; and that ere long too, because we are all mortal, you know.

Eug. Light the Lady Penelope and the Lady Hippolyta to their chambers ! Good night, fair ladies !

Hip. Good night, madam ; I wish you may sleep well after your light supper.

Eug. I warrant you, lady, I shall never be troubled with dreaming of my French suitor.   *Exeunt* [*the* ladies]

Rud. Why, how now, my Frenchified Captain Foulweather ? By God's lud, thy surname is never thought upon here ; I perceive here's nobody gives thee any commendations.

Foul. Why, this is the untravelled rudeness of our gross English ladies now; would any French lady use a man thus, think ye ? Be they any way so uncivil and fulsome ? They say they wear foul smocks and coarse smocks; I say they lie, and I will die in't.   50

Rud. Ay, do so, pray thee, thou shalt die in a very honorable cause, thy country's general quarrel, right !

Foul. Their smocks, quoth you ? O' my word you shall take them up so white, and so pure, so sweet, so emphatical, so moving.   55

Rud. Ay marry, sir, I think they be continually moving.

Foul. But if their smocks were coarse or foul—

Rud. Nay, I warrant thee, thou carest not, so thou wert at them.

Foul. 'Sdeath, they put not all their virtues in their   60
smocks, or in their mocks, or in their stewd cocks, as our ladies do.

Rud. But in their stewed pox, there's all their gentility.

Goose. Nay, good Sir Cut., do not aggravate him no   65
more.

Foul. Then they are so kind, so wise, so familiar, so noble, so sweet in entertainment, that when you shall have cause to discourse or sometimes to come nearer them, if your breath be ill, your teeth ill, or anything about you ill,   70
why, they will presently break with ye in kind sort, good terms, pretty experiments, and tell you plain this : ' thus it is with your breath, sir ; thus it is with your teeth, sir ; this is your disease ; and this is your medicine.'

Goose. As I am true mortal knight, it is most super-   75
latively good, this !

Foul. Why this is courtly now, this is sweet, this [is] plain, this is familiar ; but, by the Court of France, our peevish dames are so proud, so precise, so coy, so disdainful, and so subtle, as the Pomonian Serpent. *Mort Dieu*, the Punk of   80
Babylon was never so subtle !

Rud. Nay, do not chafe so, Captain.

Foul. Your Frenchman would ever chafe, Sir Cut., being thus moved.

Rud. What, and play with his beard so ?   85

Foul. Ay, and bristle ; it doth express that passion of anger very full, and emphatical.

Goose. Nay, good knight, if your French would bristle,

let him alone; in troth, our ladies are a little too coy and
subtle, Captain, indeed.   90

Foul. Subtle, Sir Giles Goosecap? I assure your soul,
they are as subtle with their suitors, or loves, as the Latin
dialect, where the nominative case and the verb, the substantive and the adjective, the verb and the [ad]verb, stand
as far asunder, as if they were perfect strangers one to an-   95
other, and you shall hardly find them out; but then learn
to construe and parse them, and you shall find them prepared and acquainted, and agree together in case, gender,
and number.

Goose. I detest, Sir Cut., I did not think he had been   100
half the quintessence of a scholar he is.

Foul. 'Slid, there's not one of them truly emphatical!

Goose. Yes, I'll ensure you, Captain, there are many of
them truly emphatical: but all your French ladies are not
fat, are they, sir?   105

Foul. Fat, sir? Why do ye think emphatical is fat,
Sir Giles?

Rud. God's my life, brother knight, didst thou think
so? Heart, I know not what it is myself, but yet I never
thought it was fat, I'll be sworn to thee.   110

Foul. Why, if any true courtly dame had had but this
new-fashioned suit to entertain anything indifferently
stuffed, why, you should have had her more respective by
far.

Rud. Nay, there's some reason for that, Captain; me-   115
thinks a true woman should perpetually doat upon a new
fashion.

Foul. Why y'are i'th' right, Sir Cut. *In nova fert animus
mutatas dicere formas.* 'Tis the mind of man and woman to
affect new fashions; but to our minceatives, forsooth, if   120
he come like to your *Bisogno*, or your boor, so he be rich, or
emphatical, they care not; would I might never excel a
Dutch skipper in courtship, if I did not put distaste into
my carriage of purpose; I knew I should not please them.
Laquays, allume la torche.   125

Rud. 'Slid, here's neither torch, nor lackey, methinks.

Foul. O mon Dieu!

Rust. O do not swear, Captain.

Foul. Your Frenchman ever swears, Sir Cut., upon the
lack of his lackey, I assure you.   130

Goose. See, here he comes, and my lady's two pages;
they have been tickling the vanity on't, yfaith!

SCENA TERTIA

Enter to them, Jack, Bullaker, Will

Jack. Captain Foulweather, my lady the Countess
Eugenia commends her most kindly to you, and is determined to-morrow morning early, if it be a frost, to take
her coach to Barnet to be nipped ; where if it please you to
meet her, and accompany her homeward, joining your wit   5
with the frost and help to nip her, she does not doubt but
though you had a sad supper, you will have a joyful breakfast.

Foul. I shall, indeed, my dear youth.

Rud. Why, Captain, I abused thee, I see ; I said the   10
ladies respected thee not, and now I perceive the widow is
in love with thee.

Foul. 'Sblood, knight, I knew I had struck her to the
quick ! I wondered she departed in that extravagant fashion ;
I am sure I passed one *passado* of courtship upon her that   15
has heretofore made a lane amongst the French ladies like
a culverin shot, I'll be sworn ; and I think, Sir Giles, you
saw how she fell under it.

Goose. O as clear as candlelight, by this daylight !

Rud. O good knight o' the post ! He'll swear anything !   20

Will. The other two ladies commend them no less kindly
to you two knights too ; and desire your worships would
meet them at Barnet i'th' morning with the Captain.

Foul., Goose., Rud. O good sir !

Goose. Our worships shall attend their ladyships thither.   25

Jack. No, Sir Giles, by no means ; they will go privately
thither ; but if you will meet them there—

Rud. Meet them ? We'll die for't, but we'll meet them.

Foul. Let's go thither to-night, knights, and you be true
gallants.   30

Rud. Content.

Jack. [*aside*] How greedily they take it in, sirrah ?

Goose. No, it is too far to go to-night, we'll be up betimes i'th' morning, and not go to bed at all.

Foul. Why it's but ten miles, and a fine clear night, Sir   35
Giles.

Goose. But ten miles ? What do ye talk, Captain ?

Rud. Why ? Dost think it's any more ?

Goose. Ay, I'll lay ten pounds it's more than ten mile,
or twelve either.   40

Rud. What, to Barnet ?

Goose. Ay, to Barnet !

Rud. 'Slid, I'll lay a hundred pound with thee, if thou
wilt.

Goose. I'll lay five hundred to a hundred. 'Slight, I   45
will not be outborne with a wager in that I know ; I am
sure it was four years agone ten miles thither, and I hope
'tis more now. 'Slid do not miles grow, think you, as well
as other animals ?

Jack. O wise knight !   50

Goose. I never inned in the town but once, and then
they lodged me in a chamber so full of these ridiculous fleas
that I was fain to lie standing all night, and yet I made my
man rise and put out the candle too, because they should
not see to bite me.   55

Foul. A pretty project !

Bull. In truth, Captain, if I might advise you, you
should tarry and take the morning afore you.

Foul. How ? *O mon Dieu,* how the villain *poultron*
dishonours his travel ! You buffoonly *moucheron,* are you   60
so mere rude and English to advise your Captain ?

Rud. Nay, I prithee, Foulweather, be not tempestuous
with thy poor lackey.

Foul. Tempestuous, Sir Cut. ? Will your Frenchman, think you, suffer his lackey to advise him ?   65

Goose. O God, you must take heed, lackey, how you advise
your Captain ; your French lackey would not have done it.

Foul. He would have been poxed first. *Allume la
torche* ! Sweet pages, commend us to your ladies, say we
kiss their white hands, and will not fail to meet them. Knights,   70
which of you leads ?

Goose. Not we, sir ; you are a Captain, and a leader.

Rud. Besides, thou art commended for the better man,
for thou art very Commendations itself, and Captain Commendations.   75

Foul. Why, what though I be Captain Commendations ?

Rud. Why, and Captain Commendations is hearty commendations, for captains are hearty, I am sure, or else hang
them !

Foul. Why, what if I be hearty commendations ? Come,   80
come, sweet knights, lead the way.

Rud. O Lord, sir, always after my hearty commendations.

Foul. Nay, then you conquer me with precedent, by the autentical form of all justice letters. *Allons !*   *Exeunt* 85

Jack. Here's a most sweet gudgeon swallowed, is there not ?

Will. Ay, but how will they digest it, thinkest thou, when they shall find our ladies not there ?

Jack. I have a vaunt-couriering devise shall make them 90 digest it most healthfully.   *Exeunt*

SCENA QUARTA

[*A Room in* Momford's *House*]

Enter Clarence, Musicians

Clar. Work on, sweet love ; I am not yet resolv'd
T' exhaust this troubled spring of vanities
And nurse of perturbations, my poor life ;
And therefore, since in every man that holds
This being dear, there must be some desire,   5
Whose power t'enjoy his object may so mask
The judging part, that in her radiant eyes
His estimation of the world may seem
Upright and worthy, I have chosen love
To blind my reason with his misty hands   10
And make my estimative power believe
I have a project worthy to employ
What worth so ever my whole man affords :
Then sit at rest, my soul, thou now hast found
The end of thy infusion ; in the eyes   15
Of thy divine Eugenia look for Heaven.
Thanks, gentle friends !   *A song to the viols*
Is your good lord and mine gone up to bed yet ?

Enter Momford

Mom. I do assure ye not, sir, not yet, nor yet, my deep
and studious friend ; not yet, musical Clarence.   20

Clar. My lord ?

Mom. Nor yet, thou sole divider of my lordship.

Clar. That were a most unfit division,
And far above the pitch of my low plumes ;
I am your bold and constant guest, my lord.   25

Mom. Far, far from bold, for thou hast known me long,
Almost these twenty years, and half those years

Hast been my bed-fellow, long time before
This unseen thing, this thing of naught indeed,
Or atom, called my lordship, shin'd in me ;   30
And yet thou mak'st thyself as little bold
To take such kindness as becomes the age
And truth of our indissoluble love,
As our acquaintance sprung but yesterday ;
Such is thy gentle and too tender spirit.   35
    Clar. My lord, my want of courtship makes me fear
I should be rude, and this my mean estate
Meets with such envy and detraction,
Such misconstructions and resolv'd misdooms
Of my poor worth that, should I be advanc'd   40
Beyond my unseen lowness but one hair,
I should be torn in pieces with the spirits
That fly in ill-lung'd tempests through the world,
Tearing the head of Virtue from her shoulders,
If she but look out of the ground of glory ;   45
'Twixt whom and me, and every worldly fortune,
There fights such sour and curst antipathy,
So waspish and so petulant a star,
That all things tending to my grace or good
Are ravish'd from their object, as I were   50
A thing created for a wilderness,
And must not think of any place with men.
    Mom. O hark you, sir, this wayward mood of yours
Must sifted be, or rather rooted out.
You'll no more music, sir ?   55
    Clar.   Not now, my lord.
    Mom. Begone, my masters, then ; to bed, to bed !
    Clar. I thank you, honest friends. *Exeunt* Musicians
    Mom. Hence with this book ; and now, Monsieur Clarence,
methinks plain and prose friendship would do excellent well
betwixt us : come, thus, sir, or rather thus, come, sir [*embrac-*   60
ing him] ; 'tis time, I trow, that we both lived like one body,
thus, and that both our sides were slit, and concorporate
with organs fit to effect an individual passage even for our
very thoughts ; suppose we were one body now, and I
charge you believe it, whereof I am the heart, and you the   65
liver.
    Clar. Your lordship might well make that division, if
you knew the plain song.
    Mom. O, sir, and why so, I pray ?

Clar. First, because the heart is the more worthy entrail, 70
being the first that is born and moves, and the last that
moves and dies ; and then being the fountain of heat too ;
for wheresoever our heat does not flow directly from the
heart to the other organs, there their action must of necessity
cease ; and so without you I neither would nor could live. 75

Mom. Well, sir, for these reasons I may be the heart ;
why may you be the liver now ?

Clar. I am more than ashamed to tell you that, my lord.

Mom. Nay, nay, be not too suspicious of my judgment
in you, I beseech you. Ashamed, friend ? If your love 80
overcome not that shame, a shame take that love, I say.
Come, sir, why may you be the liver ?

Clar. The plain and short truth is, my lord, because I
am all liver, and turned lover.

Mom. Lover ? 85

Clar. Lover, i'faith, my lord !

Mom. Now, I prithee, let me leap out of my skin for
joy. Why, thou wilt not now revive the sociable mirth of
thy sweet disposition ? Wilt thou shine in the world anew,
and make those that have slighted thy love with the austerity 90
of thy knowledge dote on thee again with thy commanding
shaft of their humours ?

Clar. Alas, my lord, they are all far out of my aim ; and
only to fit myself a little better to your friendship, have
I given these wilful reins to my affections. 95

Mom. And, i'faith, is my sour friend to all worldly desires
o'ertaken with the heart of the world, Love ? I shall be
monstrous proud now to hear she's every way a most rare
woman, that I know thy spirit and judgment hath chosen.
Is she wise ? Is she noble ? Is she capable of thy virtues ? 100
Will she kiss this forehead with judicial lips, where so much
judgment and virtue deserves it ? Come, brother twin, be
short, I charge you, and name me the woman.

Clar. Since your lordship will shorten the length of my
follies' relation, the woman that I so passionately love is no 105
worse lady than your own niece, the too worthy Countess
Eugenia.

Mom. Why so, so, so, you are a worthy friend—are you
not ?—to conceal this love-mine in your head, and would
not open it to your heart ! Now beshrew my heart, if my 110
heart dance not for joy, though my heels do not ; and they
do not, because I will not set that at my heels that my friend

sets at his heart.   What, friend and nephew both ? Nephew
is a far inferior title to friend, I confess, but I will prefer
thee backwards, as many friends do and leave their friends 115
worse than they found them.

Clar. But, my noble lord, it is almost a prodigy, that I,
being only a poor gentleman, and far short of that state
and wealth that a lady of her greatness in both will expect in
her husband—   120

Mom. Hold thy doubt, friend ; never fear any woman,
unless thyself be made of straw or some such dry matter,
and she of lightning. Audacity prospers above probability
in all worldly matters. Dost not thou know that Fortune
governs them without order, and therefore Reason, the 125
mother of order, is none of her counsel ? Why should a man
desiring to aspire an unreasonable creature, which is a
woman, seek her fruition by reasonable means ? Because
thyself builds upon reason, wilt thou look for congruity in a
woman ? Why, there is not one woman amongst one thou- 130
sand, but will speak false Latin and break Priscian's head.
Attempt nothing that you may with great reason doubt of,
and, out of doubt, you shall obtain nothing. I tell thee,
friend, the eminent confidence of strong spirits is the only
witchcraft of this world ; spirits wrastling with spirits, as 135
bodies with bodies ; this were enough to make thee hope well,
if she were one of these painted communities that are ravished
with coaches, and upper hands, and brave men of dirt ; but
thou knowest, friend, she's a good scholar, and like enough
to bite at the rightest reason ; and Reason evermore *ad optima* 140
hortatur, to like that which is best, not that which is bravest,
or richest, or greatest, and so consequently worst. But
prove what she can, we will turn her, and wind her, and
make her so pliant that we will draw her through a wedding-
ring, i'faith !   145

Clar. Would to God we might, my lord !

Mom. I'll warrant thee, friend !

Enter Messenger

Mess. Here is Mistress Winifred from my Lady Eugenia
desires to speak with your lordship.

Mom. Marry, enter, Mistress Winifred ; even here I 150
pray thee.—From the Lady Eugenia, do you hear, friend ?

Clar. Very easily on that side, my lord.

Mom. Let me feel. Does not thy heart pant apace ?

By my heart, well laboured, Cupid ! The field is yours, Sir
God, and upon a very honourable composition. I am sent 155
for now, I am sure, and must even truss, and to her.

Enter Winifred

Witty Mistress Winifred, nay come near, woman ! I am
sure this gentleman thinks his chamber the sweeter for your
sweet presence.

Win. My absence shall thank him, my lord.   160

Mom. What, rude, Mistress Winifred ? Nay, faith,
you shall come to him, and kiss him for his kindness.

Win. Nay, good, my lord, I'll never go to the market
for that ware ; I can have it brought home to my door.

Mom. O, Winifred a man may know by the market- 165
folks how the market goes.

Win. So you may, my lord, but I know few lords that
think scorn to go to that market themselves.

Mom. To go to it, Winifred ? Nay, to ride to it, i'faith !

Win. That's more than I know, my lord.   170

Mom. You'll not believe it, then, till you are a horse-
back, will ye ?

Win. Come, come, I am sent of a message to you ; will
you hear it ?

Mom. Stop, stop, fair Winifred ! Would you have 175
audience so soon ? There were no state in that, i'faith !
This fair gentlewoman, sir——

Win. Now we shall have a fiction, I believe.

Mom. Had three suitors at once.

Win. You'll leave out none my lord.   180

Mom. No more did you, Winifred ; you interfered with
them all in truth.

Win. O monstrous, Lord, by this light !

Mom. Now, sir, to make my tale short I will do that
which she did not, viz. leave out the first two. The third, 185
coming the third night for his turn——

Win. My lord, my lord, my lady does that that no body
else does, desires your company ; and so fare you well !

Mom. O stay a little, sweet Winifred, help me but to
truss my points again, and have with you.   190

Win. Not I, by my truth, my lord ! I had rather see your
hose about your heels, than I would help you to truss a point.

Mom. O witty Winifred ! For that jest take thy
passport, and tell thy lady, thou left'st me with my hose
about my heels.   195

Win. Well, well, my lord, you shall sit till the moss grow
about your heels, ere I come at you again.   *Exit*

Mom. She cannot abide to hear of her three suitors.
But is not this very fit, my sweet Clarence? Thou seest
my rare niece cannot sleep without me; but, for thy com- 200
pany sake, she shall to-night; and in the morning I will
visit her early; when do thou but stand in that place, and
thou mayst chance hear (but art sure to see) in what subtle
and far-fetched manner I'll solicit her about thee.

Clar. Thanks, worthy lord!   *Exeunt* 205

FINIS ACTUS PRIMI

ACTUS SECUNDI SCENA PRIMA

[*A Room in* Eugenia's *House*]

Clarence *solus*

Clar. I, that have studied with world-scorning thoughts
The way of heaven, and how true heaven is reach'd,
To know how mighty and how many are
The strange affections of enchanted number,
How to distinguish all the motions   5
Of the celestial bodies, and what power
Doth separate in such form this massie round,
What is his essence, efficacies, beams,
Footsteps, and shadows; what Eternesse is,
The world, and time, and generation;   10
What soul the world's soul is, what the black springs
And unreveal'd original of things,
What their perseverance, what is life and death,
And what our certain restauration—
Am with the staid heads of this time employ'd   15
To watch with all my nerves a female shade.   [*Retires*]

Enter Winifred, Anabell, *with their sewing works, and sing.*
After their song enter Lord Momford

Mom. Witty Mistress Winifred, where is your Countess,
I pray?

Win. Faith, your lordship is bold enough to seek her
out, if she were at her urinal.   20

Mom. Then sh'as done, it seems, for here she comes to save
me that labour. [*Enter* Eugenia] Away, wenches, get
you hence, wenches!   *Exeunt*

Eug. What, can you not abide my maids, uncle?

Mom. I never could abide a maid in my life, niece ; but 25
either I draw away the maid, or the maidenhead, with a wet
finger.

Eug. You love to make yourself worse than you are still.

Mom. I know few mend in this world, madam ; for
the worse the better thought on, the better the worse spoken 30
on, ever, amongst women.

Eug. I wonder where you have been all this while with
your sentences.

Mom. Faith, where I must be again presently ! I cannot
stay long with you, my dear niece.   35

Eug. By my faith, but you shall, my lord ! God's pity,
what will become of you shortly, that you drive maids
afore you, and offer to leave widows behind you, as mankindly as if you had taken a surfeit of our sex lately, and
our very sight turned your stomach ?   40

Mom. God's my life, she abuses her best uncle ; never
trust me, if it were not a good revenge to help her to the
loss of her widowhead !

Eug. That were a revenge and a half, indeed !

Mom. Nay, 'twere but a whole revenge, niece, but such 45
a revenge as would more than observe the true rule of a
revenger.

Eug. I know your rule before you utter it : *Ulciscere
inimico[s], sed sine tuo incommodo.*

Mom. O rare niece, you may see what 'tis to be a 50
scholar now ; learning in a woman is like weight in gold,
or lustre in diamonds, which in no other stone is so rich or
refulgent.

Eug. But say, dear uncle, how could you find in your
heart to stay so long from me ?   55

Mom. Why, alas, niece, y'are so smeared with this wilful-
widow's-three-years black weed, that I never come to you
but I dream of corses and sepulchres and epitaphs all the
night after, and, therefore, adieu, dear niece !

Eug. Beshrew my heart, my lord, if you go these three 60
hours !

Mom. Three hours ! Nay, niece, if I dance attendance
three hours (alone in her chamber) with any lady so near
allied to me, I am very idle, i'faith !—[*aside*] Marry,
with such another I would dance one, two, three, four, and 65
five, though it cost me ten shillings. And now I am in,
have at it ! My head must devise something while my feet

are piddling thus, that may bring her to some fit consideration of my friend, who, indeed, is only a great scholar, and
all his honours and riches lie in his mind.   70

Eug.   Come, come, pray tell me, uncle, how does my
cousin Momford ?

Mom.   Why, well, very well, niece ; and so is my friend
Clarence well, too ; and then is there a worthy gentleman well,
as any is in England, I can tell ye.   75

He danceth speaking

Eug.   But when did you see my cousin ?

Mom.   And 'tis pity, but he should do well, and he shall
do well, too, if all my wealth will make him well.

Eug. [*aside*]   What means he by this, trow ?—Your
lordship is very dancitive, methinks.   80

Mom.   Ay, and I could tell you a thing would make
your ladyship very dancitive, or else it were very duncitive,
i'faith !—[*aside*] Oh how the skipping of this Christmas block
of ours moves the block-head heart of a woman, and, indeed,
anything that pleaseth the foolish eye, which presently runs   85
with a lying tale of excellence to the mind.

Eug.   But I pray tell me, my lord, could you tell me of
a thing would make me dance, say you ?

Mom.   Well, farewell, sweet niece, I must needs take
my leave, in earnest.   90

Eug.   Lord bless us, here's such a stir with your farewells !

Mom.   I will see you again within these two or three
days, o' my word, niece.

Eug.   God's precious, two or three days ! Why this
lord is in a marvellous strange humour. Sit down, sweet   95
uncle ; i'faith, I have to talk to you about great matters.

Mom.   Say then, dear niece ; be short, utter your mind
quickly now.

Eug.   But I pray tell me first, what's that would make
me dance, i'faith ?   100

Mom.   Dance ! What dance ?   Hitherto your dancer's
legs bow, forsooth, and caper and jerk and firk and dandle
the body above them, as it were their great child ; though
the special jerker be above this place, I hope ; here lies that
should fetch a perfect woman over the coals, i'faith !   105

Eug.   Nay, good uncle, say what's the thing you could
tell me of ?

Mom.   No matter, no matter ! But let me see. [*Study-
ing her face*]   A passing prosperous forehead of an exceed-

ing happy distance betwixt the eye-brows, a clear lightning 110
eye, a temperate and fresh blood in both the cheeks : excellent marks, most excellent marks of good fortune !

Eug.   Why, how now, uncle, did you never see me before ?

Mom.   Yes, niece ; but the state of these things at this
instant must be specially observed, and these outward 115
signs, being now in this clear elevation, show your untroubled
mind is in an excellent power to prefer them to act forth
then a little, dear niece.

Eug.   This is excellent !

Mom.   The crises here are excellent good, the proportion 120
of the chin good, the little aptness of it to stick out good,
and the wart above it most exceeding good.   Never trust
me, if all things be not answerable to the prediction of a
most divine fortune towards her ; now if she have the grace
to apprehend it in the nick, there's all. 125

Eug.   Well, my lord, since you will not tell me your
secret, I'll keep another from you ; with whose discovery
you may much pleasure me, and whose concealment may
hurt my estate.   And if you be no kinder than to see me
so endangered, I'll be very patient of it, I assure you. 130

Mom.   Nay, then, it must instantly forth.   This kind
conjuration even fires it out of me ; and, to be short,
gather all your judgment together, for here it comes.
Niece, Clarence, Clarence, rather my soul than my friend
Clarence, of too substantial a worth to have any figures cast 135
about him (notwithstanding no other woman with empires
could stir his affections) is with your virtues most extremely
in love, and without your requital dead.   And, with it,
Fame shall sound this golden distich through the world of
you both : 140

> *Non illo melior quisquam, nec amantior æqui*
> *Vir fuit, aut illa reverentior ulla Deorum.*

Eug.   Ay me, poor dame !   O you amaze me, uncle !
Is this the wondrous fortune you presage ?
What man may miserable women trust ? 145

Mom.   O peace, good lady !   I come not to ravish you
to anything.   But now I see how you accept my motion, I
perceive how, upon true trial, you esteem me.   Have I rid
all this circuit to levy the powers of your judgment that I
might not prove their strength too suddenly with so violent 150
a charge, and do they fight it out in white blood, and show
me their hearts in the soft christal of tears ?

Eug. O uncle, you have wounded yourself in charging
me, that I should shun judgment as a monster if it would
not weep. I place the poor felicity of this world in a worthy 155
friend, and, to see him so unworthily revolted, I shed not
the tears of my brain, but the tears of my soul. And if
ever Nature made tears th' effects of any worthy cause, I
am sure I now shed them worthily.

Mom. [*aside*] Her sensual powers are up, i'faith! I 160
have thrust her soul quite from her tribunal. This is her
sedes vacans, when her subjects are privileged to libel against
her and her friends.—But weeps my kind niece for the
wounds of my friendship? And I touched in friendship
for wishing my friend doubled in her singular happiness? 165

Eug. How am I doubled, when my honour and good
name, two essential parts of me, would be less and lost.

Mom. In whose judgment?

Eug. In the judgment of the world.

Mom. Which is a fool's bolt? *Nihil a virtute nec a* 170
veritate remotius, quam vulgaris opinio. But, my dear niece,
it is most true that your honour and good name, tendered
as they are the species of truth, are worthily two essential
parts of you. But as they consist only in airy titles and
corruptible blood (whose bitterness *sanitas et non nobilitas* 175
efficit) and care not how many base and execrable acts they
commit, they touch you no more than they touch eternity.
And yet shall no nobility you have in either be impaired
neither.

Eug. Not to marry a poor gentleman?   180

Mom. Respect him not so ; for as he is a gentleman, he
is noble ; as he is wealthily furnished with true knowledge,
he is rich, and therein adorned with the exactest complements
belonging to everlasting nobleness.

Eug. Which, yet, will not maintain him a week. Such 185
kind of nobleness gives no coats of honor, nor can scarce get
a coat for necessity.

Mom. Then is it not substantial knowledge (as it is in
him) but verbal and fantastical, for *Omnia in illa ille com-*
plexu tenet.   190

Eug. Why seeks he me then?

Mom. To make you joint partners with him in all things,
and there is but a little partial difference betwixt you that
hinders that universal jointure. The bigness of this circle
held too near our eye keeps it from the whole sphere of the 195

sun ; but could we sustain it indifferently betwixt us and it, it would then without check of one beam appear in his fulness.

Eug. Good uncle, be content, for now shall I never dream of contentment.   200

Mom. I have more than done, lady, and had rather have suffered an alteration of my being than of your judgment ; but, dear niece, for your own honour's sake repair it instantly.

Enter Hippolyta, Penelope, Jack, Will

See here comes the ladies ; make an April day on['t], dear love, and be suddenly cheerful.—God save you, more 205 than fair ladies ! I am glad you're come, for my business will have me gone presently.

Hip. Why, my Lord Momford, I say ! Will you go before dinner ?

Mom. No remedy, sweet beauties, for which rudeness I 210 lay my hands thus low for your pardons.

Pen. O courteous Lord Momford !

Mom. Niece !—*Mens est quae sola quietos,*
Sola facit claros, mentemque honoribus ornat.   [*Retires*]

Eug. *Verus honos juvat, at mendax infamia terret.*   215

Mom. [*aside to* Clarence] Mine own dear nephew !

Clar.   What success, my lord ?

Mom. Excellent, excellent ! Come I'll tell thee all.

Exeunt

Hip. Do you hear, madam, how our youths here have gulled our three suitors ?   220

Eug. Not I, lady ! I hope our suitors are no fit meat for our pages.

Pen. No, madam, but they are fit sauce for any man's meat, I'll warrant them !

Eug. What's the matter, Hippolyta ?   225

Hip. They have sent the knights to Barnet, madam, this frosty morning to meet us there.

Eug. Is't true, youths ? Are knights fit subjects for your knaveries.

Will. Pray pardon us, madam, we would be glad to please 230 anybody.

Jack. Ay, indeed, madam, and we were sure we pleased them highly to tell them you were desirous of their company.

Hip. O, 'twas good, Eugenia ! Their livers were too hot, you know, and for temper sake they must needs have 235 a cooling card played upon them.

Will. And, besides, madam, we would have them know
that your two little pages, which are less by half than two
leaves, have more learning in them than is in all their three
volumes.   240

Jack. Ay, i'faith, Will, and put their great pagical index
to them, too !

Hip. But how will ye excuse your abuses, wags ?

Will. We doubt not, madam, but if it please your ladyship to put up their abuses—   245

Jack. Trusting they are not so dear to you, but you may.

Will. We shall make them gladly furnish their pockets
with them.

Hip. Well, children and fools, agree as you will, and
let the world know now, women have nothing to do with 250
you.

Pen. Come, madam, I think your dinner be almost
ready.

Enter [Lord] Tales, [Sir Clement] Kingcob

Hip. And see here are two honorable guests for you,
the Lord Tales, and Sir [Clement] Kingcob.   255

Tales. Lack you any guests, madam ?

Eug. Ay, my lord, such guests as you.

Hip. There's as common an answer, as yours was a question, my lord.

King. Why ? All things should be common between 260
lords and ladies, you know.

Pen. Indeed, Sir [Clement] Kingcob, I have heard you
are either of the Family of Love, or of no religion at all.

Eug. He may well be said to be of the Family of Love,
he does so flow in the loves of poor overthrown ladies.   265

King. You speak of that I would do, madam ; but, in
earnest, I am now suing for a new mistress ; look in my hand,
sweet lady, and tell me what fortune I shall have with her.

Eug. Do you think me a witch, Sir [Clement] ?

King. Pardon me, madam, but I know you to be learned 270
in all things.

Eug. Come on, let's see !

Hip. He does you a special favour, lady, to give you his
open hand, for 'tis commonly shut they say.

King. What find you in it, madam ?   275

Eug. Shut it now, and I'll tell ye.

King. What now, lady ?

Eug.   Y'ave the worst hand that ever I saw knight have ;
when 'tis open one can find nothing in it, and when 'tis shut
one can get nothing out on't.   280

King.   The age of letting go is past, madam ; we must
not now let go, but strike up men's heels, and take 'em as they
fall.

Eug.   A good Cornish principle, believe it, Sir [Clement] !

Tales.   But I pray tell me, Lady Penelope, how entertain 285
you the love of my cousin, Sir Giles Goosecap ?

Pen.   Are the Goosecaps akin to you, my lord ?

Tales.   Even in the first degree, madam.   And Sir Giles,
I can tell ye, though he seem something simple is composed
of as many good parts as any knight in England.   290

Hip.   He should be put up for concealment, then, for he
shows none of them.

Pen.   Are you able to reckon his good parts, my lord ?

Tales.   I'll do the best I can, lady.   First, he dances as
comely and lightly as any man, for upon my honour I have 295
seen him dance upon eggs, and 'a has not broken them.

Pen.   Nor cracked them, neither ?

Tales.   That I know not ; indeed I would be loath to lie,
though he be my kinsman, to speak more than I know by
him.   300

Eug.   Well, forth, my lord !

Tales.   He has an excellent skill in all manner of perfumes, and if you bring him gloves from forty pence to forty
shillings a pair, he will tell you the price of them to twopence.

Hip.   A pretty sweet quality, believe me !   305

Tales.   Nay, lady, he will perfume you gloves himself
most delicately, and give them the right Spanish titillation.

Pen.   Titillation !   What's that, my lord ?

Tales.   Why, lady, 'tis a pretty kind of term new come up
in perfuming, which they call a titillation.   310

Hip.   Very well expounded, my lord !   Forth with your
kinsman's parts, I pray.

Tales.   He is the best sempster of any woman in England,
and will work you needle-work edgings and French purls,
from an angel to four angels a yard.   315

Eug.   That's precious ware, indeed !

Tales.   He will work you any flower to the life, as like
it as if it grew in the very place, and being a delicate perfumer,
he will give it you his perfect and natural savour.

Hip.   This is wonderful ; forth, sweet Lord Tales !   320

Tales. He will make you flies and worms, of all sorts, most lively, and is now working a whole bed embroidered with nothing but glow-worms; whose lights 'a has so perfectly done, that you may go to bed in the chamber, do anything in the chamber, without a candle.   325

Pen. Never trust me if it be not incredible! Forth, my good lord!

Tales. He is a most excellent turner, and will turn you wassail bowls and posset cups, carved with libbards' faces and lions' heads, with spouts in their mouths to let out the 330 posset-ale most artificially.

Eug. Forth, good Lord Tales!

Pen. Nay, good my lord, no more! You have spoken for him thoroughly, I warrant you!

Hip. I lay my life Cupid has shot my sister in love with 335 him out of your lips, my lord.

Eug. Well, come in, my lords, and take a bad dinner with me now, and we will all go with you at night to a better supper with the Lord and Lady Furnifall.

King. [*and*] *Tales.* We attend you, honourable ladies. 340
Exeunt

ACTUS TERTII SCENA PRIMA

[*Near Barnet*]

Enter Rudesby, Goosecap.

Rud. Bullaker!

Bull. [*within*] Ay, sir!

Rud. Ride and catch the Captain's horse.

Bull. [*within*] So I do, sir.

Rud. I wonder, Sir Giles, you would let him go so, and 5
not ride after him.

Goose. Would I might never be mortal, sir Cut., if I rid not after him till my horse sweat so that he had ne'er a dry thread on him, and hollo'd and hollo'd to him to stay him till I had thought my fingers' ends would have gone off with 10
holloings, I'll be sworn to ye; and yet he ran his way like a Diogenes, and would never stay for us.

Rud. How shall we do to get the lame captain to London, now his horse is gone?

Goose. Why, he is but a lame jade, neither, Sir [Cut.]; 15
we shall soon o'ertake him, I warrant ye!

Rud. And yet thou say'st thou gallop'st after him as fast as thou couldst, and couldst not catch him; I lay my life

some crabfish has bitten thee by the tongue, thou speakest so
backward still.   20

Goose. But here's all the doubt, Sir Cut. ; if nobody
should catch him now, when he comes at London, some boy
or other would get up on him, and ride him hot into the water
to wash him.   I'll be sworn I followed one that rid my horse
into the Thames, till I was up to th' knees hitherto ; and   25
if it had not been for fear of going over shoes, because I am
troubled with the rheum, I would have taught him to wash
my horse when he was hot, i'faith !

Enter Foulweather

How now, sweet Captain, dost feel any ease in thy pain yet ?

Rud. Ease in his pain, quoth you ! Has good luck if   30
he feel ease in pain, I think ; but would any ass in the world
ride down such a hill as Highgate is, in such a frost as this,
and never light.

Foul. God's precious, Sir Cut., your Frenchman never
lights, I tell ye !   35

Goose. Light, Sir Cut. ! 'Slight, and I had my horse
again, there's ne'er a paltry English frost on them all should
make me light.

Rud. Go to, you French zanies, you !   You will follow
the French steps so long, till you be not able to set one sound   40
step o' th' ground all the days of your life.

Goose. Why, Sir Cut., I care not if I be not sound, so I
be well ; but we were justly plagued by this hill for following
women thus.

Foul. Ay, and English women, too, Sir Giles !   45

Rud. Thou art still prating against English women ; I
have seen none of the French dames, I confess, but your
greatest gallants, for men, in France were here lately, I am
sure ; and, methinks, there should be no more difference
betwixt our ladies and theirs than there is betwixt our lords   50
and theirs ; and our lords are as far beyond them, i' faith,
for person and courtship, as they are beyond ours for fan-
tasticality.

Foul. O Lord, Sir Cut. ! I am sure our ladies hold our
lords tack for courtship, and yet the French lords put them   55
down.   You noted it, Sir Giles.

Goose. O God, sir ! I stood and heard it, as I sat i' th'
presence.

Rud. How did they put them down, I pray thee ?

Foul. Why, for wit and for courtship, Sir [Cut.].   60

[*Rud.*]   As how, good left-handed François ?

Foul. Why, sir, when Monsieur L'Ambois came to your mistress, the Lady Hippolyta, as she sate in the presence—sit down here, good Sir Giles Goosecap—he kneeled me by her thus, sir, and with a most quaint French start in his 65 speech of *ah bellissime*, ' I desire to die now,' says he, ' for your love that I might be buried here.'

Rud. A good pickt-hatch compliment, by my faith ! But, I prithee, what answered she ?

Foul. She ! I scorn to note that, I hope. Then did he 70 vie it again with another ha.

Rud. That was ha, ha. I would have put the third ha to it, if I had been as my mistress, and ha ha ha'd him out of the presence, i'faith !

Foul. ' Ha ! ' says he, ' these fair eyes ! I would not for 75 a million they were in France ; they would renew all our civil wars again.'

Goose. That was not so good, methinks, Captain.

Rud. Well judged, i'faith ! There was a little wit in that, I must confess ; but she put him down far, and answered 80 him with a question, and that was, whether he would seem a lover or a jester ? If a lover, 'a must tell her far more likelier than those, or else she was far from believing them ; if a jester, she could have much more ridiculous jests than his of twenty fools that followed the Court ; and told him 85 she had as lief be courted with a brush faggot as with a Frenchman, that spent itself all in sparks, and would sooner fire one's chimney than warm the house, and that such sparks were good enough yet to set thatched dispositions a-fire, but hers was tiled with sleight and respected them as slightly. 90

Goose. Why, so, Captain ! And yet you talk of your great Frenchman ; [would] to God little England had never known them, I may say !

Foul. What's the matter, Sir Giles ? Are you out of love with Frenchmen now of a sudden ?   95

Goose. 'Slid, Captain, would['t] not make one ? I'll be sworn they took away a mastie dog of mine by commission, now I think on't, makes my tears stand in my eyes with grief ; I had rather lost the dearest friend that ever I lay withal in my life, b[y] this light ! Never stir if he 100 fought not with great Sackerson four hours to one, foremost take up hindmost, and took so many loaves from him that

he starved him presently. So at last the dog could do no
more than a bear could do, and the bear being heavy with
hunger, you know, fell upon the dog, broke his back, and 105
the dog never stirred more.

Rud. Why, thou sayst the Frenchmen took him away!

Goose. Frenchmen! Ay, so they did too, but yet, and
he had not been killed, 'twould ne'er 'a grieved me.

Foul. O excellent unity of speech!   110

Enter Will *and* Jack *at several doors*

Will. Save ye, knights!

Jack. Save you, Captain!

Foul. Pages, welcome, my fine pages!

Rud. Welcome, boys!

Goose. Welcome, sweet Will, good Jack!   115

Foul. But how chance you are so far from London now,
pages? Is it not almost dinner-time?

Will. Yes, indeed, sir; but we left our fellows to wait
for once, and could not choose, in pure love to your worships,
but we must needs come and meet you, before you met our 120
ladies, to tell you a secret.

Omnes. A secret! What secret, I pray thee?

Jack. If ever your worships say anything, we are undone
forever.

Omnes. Not for a world, believe it!   125

Will. Why, then, this it is: we overheard our ladies,
as they were talking in private, say they refused to meet
you at Barnet this morning of purpose, because they would
try which of you were most patient.

Jack. And some said you, Sir Giles; another you, Sir 130
[Cut.]; and the third you, Captain.

Omnes. This was excellent.

Will. Then did they swear one another not to excuse
themselves to you by any means, that they might try you
the better. Now, if they shall see you say nothing in the 135
world to them, what may come of it, when ladies begin to
try their suitors once, I hope your wisdoms can judge a little.

Foul. Oho, my little knave, let us alone now, i'faith!
Would I might be cashiered if I say anything!

Rud. Faith, and I can forbear my tongue as well as 140
another, I hope.

Goose. Would I might be degraded if I speak a word;
I'll tell them I care not for losing my labour.

Foul.   Come, knights, shall we not reward the pages?

Rud.   Yes, I prithee, do. Sir Giles, give the boys some- 145
thing.

Goose.   Never stir, Sir Cut., if I have ever a groat about
me but one three-pence.

Foul.   Well, knights, I'll lay out for's all. Here, my
fine pages!   150

Will.   No indeed, an't it please your worship.

Foul.   O pages, refuse a gentleman's bounty?

Jack.   Cry you mercy, sir! Thank you, sweet Captain!

Foul.   And what other news is stirring, my fine viliacos?

Will.   Marry, sir, they are invited to a great supper to- 155
night to your lord's house, Captain, the Lord Furnifall ; and
there will be your great cousin, Sir Giles Goosecap, the Lord
Tales, and your uncle, Sir Cut. Rudesby, Sir [Clement]
Kingcob.

Foul.   The Lord Tales! What countryman is he?   160

Jack.   A Kentish lord, sir ; his ancestors came forth of
Canterbury.

Foul.   Out of Canterbury?

Will.   Ay, indeed, sir, the best Tales in England are your
Canterbury Tales, I assure ye!   165

Rud.   The boy tells thee true, Captain.

Jack.   He writes his name, sir, Tales, and he being the
tenth son his father had, his father christened him Decem
Tales, and so his whole name is the Lord Decem Tales.

Goose.   O' my mortality, the boy knows more than I do 170
of our house.

Rud.   But is the Lady Furnifall, Captain, still of the
same drinking humour she was wont to be?

Foul.   Still of the same, knight, and is never in any sociable vein till she be tipsy, for in her sobriety she is mad, 175
and fears my good little old lord out of all proportion.

[*Rud.*]   And therefore, as I hear, he will earnestly invite
guests to his house of purpose to make his wife drunk, and
then dotes on her humour most profanely.

Foul.   'Tis very true, knight ; we will sup with them to- 180
night, and you shall see her ; and now I think on't, I'll tell
you a thing, knights, wherein, perhaps, you may exceedingly
pleasure me.

Goose.   What's that, good Captain?

Foul.   I am desirous to help my lord to a good merry 185
fool, and if I could help him to a good merry one, he might
do me very much credit, I assure ye!

Rud. 'Sblood, thou speakest to us as if we could serve thy turn !

Foul. Oh France ! Sir Cut., your Frenchman would 190
not have taken me so for a world, but because fools come
into your companies many times to make you merry.

Rud. As thou dost.

Goose. Nay, good Sir Cut., you know fools do come
into your companies.   195

Rud. Ay, and thou know'st it too, no man better.

Foul. Bear with choler, Sir Giles.

Will. But would you help your lord to a good fool so
fain, sir ?

Foul. Ay, my good page, exceeding fain.   200

Jack. You mean a wench, do you not, sir, a foolish wench?

Foul. Nay, I would have a man fool for his lordship,
page.

Will. Does his lordship love a fool so well, I pray ?

Foul. Assure thyself, page, my lord loves a fool as he 205
loves himself.

Jack. Of what degree would you have your fool, sir ;
for you may have of all manner of degrees ?

Foul. Faith, I would have him a good emphatical fool,
one that would make my lord laugh well, and I cared not. 210

Will. Laugh well, hum ! Then we must know this,
sir ; is your lord costive of laughter, or laxative of laughter ?

Foul. Nay, he is a good merry little lord, and, indeed,
something laxative of laughter.

Will. Why then, sir, the less wit will serve his lordship's 215
turn. Marry, if he had been costive of laughter, he must
have had two or three drams of wit the more in his fool, for
we must minister according to the quantity of his lordship's humour , you know, and if he should have as much
wit in his fool, being laxative of laughter , as if he were 220
costive of laughter, why, he might laugh himself into an
epilepsy and fall down dead suddenly, as many have done
with the extremity of that passion ; and I know your lord
cares for nothing but the health of a fool.

Foul. Th' art i' th' right, my notable good page.   225

Jack. Why, and for that health, sir, we will warrant his
Lordship that if he should have all Bacon *de sanitate tuenda*
read to him, it should not please his Lordship so well as our
fool shall.

Foul. Remercie, my more than English pages !   230

Goose. O' my word, I have not seen pages have so much wit, that have never been in France, Captain.

Foul. 'Tis true, indeed, Sir Giles. Well, then, my almost French elixirs, will you help my lord to a fool so fit for him as you say ?   235

Will. As fit, I'll warrant you, Captain, as if he were made for him ; and he shall come this night to supper, and fool where his lordship sits at table.

Foul. Excellent fit ! Fail not now, my sweet pages.

Jack. Not for a world, sir ; we will go both and seek him 240 presently.

Foul. Do so, my good wags.

Will. Save you, knights !

Jack. Save you, Captain !   *Exeunt* [Pages]

Foul. Farewell, my pretty knaves ! Come, knights, 245 shall we resolve to go to this supper ?

Rud. What else ?

Goose. And let's provide torches for our men to sit at door withal, Captain.

Foul. That we will, I warrant you, Sir Giles !   250

Rud. Torches ? Why, the moon will shine, man !

Goose. The moon, Sir Cut. ! I scorn the moon, i'faith ! 'Slid, sometimes a man shall not get her to shine and if he would give her a couple of capons—and one of them must be white too ! God forgive me, I could never abide her 255 since yesterday, she served me such a trick tother night.

Rud. What trick, Sir Giles ?

Goose. Why, Sir Cut., cause the days be mortal and short now, you know, and I love daylight well, I thought it went away faster than it needed, and run after it into Finsbury 260 fields i' th' calm evening to see the windmills go, and even as I was going over a ditch, the moon, by this light, of purpose runs me behind a cloud, and lets me fall into the ditch, by heaven !

Rud. That was ill done in her, indeed, Sir Giles.   265

Goose. Ill done, Sir Cut. ? 'Slid a man may bear and bear, but, and she have no more good manners but to make every black slovenly cloud a pearl in her eye, I shall ne'er love English moon again while I live, I'll be sworn to ye !

Foul. Come, knights, to London ! Horse, horse, horse ! 270
                [*Exeunt* Foulweather *and* Goosecap]

Rud. In what a case he is with the poor English moon, because the French moons (their torches) will be the less in

fashion, and, I warrant you, the Captain will remember it
too, though he say nothing ; he seconds his resolute chase
so and follows him.   I'll lay my life you shall see them the   275
next cold night shut the moonshine out of their chambers,
and make it lie without doors all night.   I discredit my wit
with their companies, now I think on't.   Plague o' God on
them !   I'll fall a-beating on them presently.   *Exit*

[SCENA SECUNDA

A Room in Momford's *House*]

Enter Lord Momford *and* Clarence, [*and*] Horatio

Clar.   Sing, good Horatio, while I sigh and write.
According to my master Plato's mind
The soul is music, and doth therefore joy
In accents musical, which he that hates
With points of discord is together tied,   5
And barks at Reason consonant in sense.
Divine Eugenia bears the ocular form
Of music and of Reason, and presents
The soul exempt from flesh in flesh inflam'd ;
Who must not love her then that loves his soul ?   10
To her I write ; my friend, the star of friends,
Will needs have my strange lines greet her strange eyes,
And for her sake I'll pour my poor soul forth
In floods of ink ; but did not his kind hand
Bar me with violent grace I would consume   15
In the white flames of her impassionate love,
Ere my harsh lips should vent the odorous blaze.
For I am desperate of all worldly joys,
And there was never man so harsh to men.
When I am fullest of digested life   20
I seem a lifeless Embryon to all,
Each day rack'd-up in night-like funeral,
Sing, good Horatio, whilst I sigh and write.

Canto

The Letter

*Suffer him to love that suffers not loving ; my love is without
passion, and therefore free from alteration.*—   25
Prose is too harsh, and verse is poetry,
Why should I write then ?   Merit clad in ink
Is but a mourner, and as good as naked.

I will not write, my friend shall speak for me.
Sing one stave more, my good Horatio.   30

Canto

I must remember I know whom I love,
A dame of learning, and of life exempt
From all the idle fancies of her sex;
And this, that to another dame would seem
Perplex'd and folded in a r[e]deless veil,   35
Will be more clear than ballads to her eye.
I'll write, if but to satisfy my friend.
Your third stance, sweet Horatio, and no more.

Canto

How vainly do I offer my strange love!
I marry, and bid states, and entertain   40
Ladies with tales and jests, and lords with news,
And keep a house to feed Actæon's hounds
That eat their master, and let idle guests
Draw me from serious search of things divine
To bid them sit and welcome, and take care   45
To sooth their palates with choice kitchen stuff,
As all must do that marry and keep house!
And then look on the left side of my yoke,
Or on the right, perhaps, and see my wife
Draw in a quite repugnant course from me,   50
Busied to starch her French purls and her puffs,
When I am in my *anima reflexa,*
Quid sit felicitas? Quæ origo rerum?
And make these beings that are known to be
The only serious objects of true men   55
Seem shadows with substantial stir she keeps
About her shadows, which, if husbands love,
They must believe; and thus my other self
Brings me another body to dispose,
That have already much too much of one,   60
And must not look for any soul of her
To help to rule two bodies.
      Mom.   Fie for shame!
I never heard of such an antidame.
Do women bring no help of soul to men?
Why, friend, they either are men's souls themselves,   65
Or the most witty imitatrixes of them,

Or prettiest sweet apes of human souls
That ever Nature fram'd ; as I will prove.
For, first, they be *substantiæ lucidæ*,
And purer than men's bodies, like their souls,   70
Which men's harsh hairs, both of their breast and chin,
Occasion'd by their gross and ruder heat,
Plainly demonstrates ; then, like souls, they do
Movere corpora, for no power on earth
Moves a man's body, as a woman does ;   75
Then do they *dare formas corpori*,
Or add fair forms to men, as their souls do,
For, but for women, who would care for forms ?
I vow I never would wash face nor hands,
Nor care how ragg'd or slovenly I went,   80
Were't not for women, who of all men's pomps
Are the true final causes. Then they make
Men in their seeds immortal, like their souls,
That else would perish in a span of time.
Oh, they be soul-like creatures, and my niece   85
The soul of twenty rare souls still'd in one !
   Clar. That, that it is, my lord, that makes me love.
   Mom. Oh, are ye come, sir ? Welcome to my niece,
As I may say, at midnight. Gentle friend,
What have you wrote, I pray.   90
   Clar. [*giving* Momford *the letter*] Strange stuff, my lord.
   Mom. Indeed the way to believe is to love ;
                              He reads and comments
And the right way to love is to believe.
This will I carry now with pen and ink
For her to use in answer ; see, sweet friend,
She shall not stay to call ; but while the steel   95
Of her affection is made soft and hot,
I'll strike, and take Occasion by the brow.
Blest is the wooing that's not long a-doing.   *Exit*
   Clar. Had ever man so true and noble friend,
Or would men think this sharp world's freezing air   100
To all true honour and judicial love
Would suffer such a flourishing pine in both
To overlook the box-trees of this time ?
When the learn'd mind hath by impulsion wrought
Her eyes' clear fire into a knowing flame,   105
No elemental smoke can darken it,
Nor Northern coldness nip her Daphnean flower.

O sacred Friendship, thanks to thy kind power,
That being retir'd from all the faithless world,
Appear'st to me in my unworldly friend ;   110
And for thine own sake let his noble mind
By moving precedent to all his kind
(Like just Deucalion) of Earth's stony bones
Repair the world with human blood and flesh,
And dying Virtue with new life refresh.   *Exit* 115

ACTUS QUARTUS

[SCENA PRIMA

A Room in Eugenia's *House*]

Enter Tales, Kingcob, Eugenia, Hippolyta, Penelope,
Winifred

King. 'Tis time to leave your chests, ladies ; 'tis too
studious an exercise after dinner.

Tales. Why is it called chests ?

Hip. Because they lean upon their chests that play at it.   5

Tales. I would have it called the strife of wits, for 'tis
a game so witty that, with strife for mastery, we hunt it
eagerly.

Eug. Specially where the wit of the Goosecaps are in chase,
my lord.   10

Tales. I am a Goosecap by the mother's side, madam ;
at least my mother was a Goosecap.

Pen. And you were her white son, I warrant, my lord !

Tales. I was the youngest, lady, and therefore must be
her white son, ye know ; the youngest of ten I was.   15

Hip. And the wisest of fifteen.

Tales. And, sweet lady, will ye cast a kind eye now upon
my cousin, Sir Giles Goosecap.

Pen. Pardon, my lord, I have never a spare eye to cast
away, I assure ye !   20

Tales. I wonder you should count it cast away, lady,
upon him ; do you remember those few of his good parts
I rehearsed to you ?

Pen. Very perfectly, my lord ; amongst which one of
them was that he was the best sempster of any woman in 25
England. Pray let's see some of his work.

Hip. Sweet lord, let's see him sew a little.

Tales. You shall, o' my honour, lady !

Eug. He's a goodly great knight, indeed ; and a little
needle in his hand will become him prettily.   30
King. From the Spanish pike to the Spanish needle he
shall play with any knight in England, lady.
Eug. But not *e converso*, from the Spanish needle to the
Spanish pike.
King. I think he be too wise for that indeed, madam,   35
for he has twenty miles length in land lies together, and he
would be loath to bring it all to the length of a pike.
Hip. But no man commends my blunt servant, Sir
Cut. Rudesby, methinks.
King. He is a kind gentleman, lady, though he be blunt,   40
and is of this humour, the more you presume upon him
without ceremony, the more he loves you. If he know you
think him kind once, and will say nothing but still use him,
you may melt him into any kindness you will ; he is right
like a woman and had rather you should bluntly take the   45
greatest favour you can of him than shamefastly entreat it.
Eug. He says well to you, Hippolyta.
Hip. Ay, madam, but they say he will beat one in jest,
and bite in kindness, and tear one's ruffs in courtship.
King. Some that he makes sport withal, perhaps, but   50
none that he respects, I assure ye !
Hip. And what's his living, Sir [Clement] ?
King. Some two thousand a year, lady.
Hip. I pray do not tell him that I asked, for I stand
not upon living.   55
King. O good lady, who can live without living ?

Enter Momford

Mom. Still here, lordings ? Good companions, i' faith !
I see you come not for victuals.
Tales. Victuals, my lord ? I hope we have victuals at
home.   60
Mom. Ay, but, sweet lord, there is a principle in the
politician's physic : ' Eat not your meat upon other men's
trenchers, and beware of surfeits of your own cost.' Many
good companions cannot abide to eat meat at home, ye know.
And how fares my noble niece, now, and her fair lady feres ?   65
Eug. What wind blows you hither, trow ?
Mom. Hark you, madam, the sweet gale of one Clarence's
breath, with this, his paper sail, blows me hither.
                          [*Offering her a letter*]

Eug. Ay me, still in that humour ? Beshrew my heart
if I take any papers from him.   70

Mom. Kind bosom, do thou take it then.

Eug. Nay then, never trust me.

Mom. Let it fall, then, or cast it away, you were best,
that every body may discover your love-suits, do ! There's
somebody near, if you note it !—And how have you spent   75
the time since dinner, nobles ?

King. At chests, my lord.

Mom. [*aside to* Eugenia] Read it, niece.

Eug. [*aside to* Momford] Here, bear it back, I pray.

Mom. [*aside to* Eugenia] I bear you on my back to hear   80
you.—And how play the ladies, Sir [Clement] ; what men
do they play best withal, with knights or rooks.

Tales. With knights, my lord.

Mom. 'Tis pity their board is no broader, and that some
men called gulls are not added to their game.   85

King. Why, my lord ? It needs not ; they make the
knights gulls.

Mom. That's pretty Sir [Clement].—[*Aside to* Eugenia]
You have begun, I know, niece ; forth, I command you !

Eug. [*aside*] O y'are a sweet uncle !   90

Mom. I have brought her a little Greek to help me
out withall, and she's so coy of her learning, forsooth, she
makes it strange. Lords and ladies, I invite you all to supper
to-night and you shall not deny me.

All. We will attend your lordship.   95

Tales. Come, ladies, let's into the gallery a little.

                    Exeunt [*all but* Momford *and* Eugenia]

Mom. And now what says my own dear niece, i'faith ?

Eug. What should she say to the backside of a paper ?

Mom. Come, come ! I know you have been o' the belly
side.   100

Eug. Now was there ever lord so prodigal
Of his own honour'd blood and dignity.

Mom. Away with these same horse-fair allegations !
Will you answer the letter ?

Eug. God's my life, you go like a cunning spokesman ! 105
Answer, uncle ? What, do ye think me desperate of a
husband ?

Mom. Not so, niece ; but careless of your poor uncle.

Eug. I will not write, that's certain.

Mom. What, will you have my friend and I perish? 110
Do you thirst our bloods?

Eug. O y'are in a mighty danger, no doubt on't!

Mom. If you have our bloods, beware our ghosts, I can
tell ye. Come, will ye write?

Eug. I will not write, i'faith! 115

Mom. I'faith, dame, then I must be your secretary, I
see; here's the letter, come, do you dictate, and I'll write.

Eug. If you write no otherwise than I dictate, it will
scare prove a kind answer, I believe.

Mom. But you will be advised, I trust. Secretaries are 120
of counsel with their Countesses. Thus it begins: *Suffer
him to love that suffers not loving.* What answer you to that?

Eug. He loves extremely that suffers not in love!

Mom. He answers you for that presently; his love is
without passion, and therefore free from alteration, for *pati,* 125
you know, is *in alterationem labi;* he loves you in his soul,
he tells you, wherein there is no passion. Say, dame, what
answer you?

Eug. Nay, if I answer anything—

Mom. Why, very well, I'll answer for you. 130

Eug. You answer? Shall I set my hand to your answer?

Mom. Ay, by my faith shall ye!

Eug. By my faith, but you shall answer as I would have
you then.

Mom. Always put in with advice of your secretary, 135
niece; come, what answer you?

Eug. Since you needs will have my answer, I'll answer
briefly to the first and last part of his letter.

Mom. Do so, niece, and leave the midst for himself, o'
God's name! What is your answer? 140

He writes and she dictates

Eug. *I cannot but suffer you to love, if you do love—*

Mom. Why, very good, there it is—*and will requite
your love;* say you so?

Eug. Beshrew my lips then, my lord!

Mom. Beshrew my fingers but you shall! What, you 145
may promise to requite his love, and yet not promise him
marriage, I hope, Well—*and will requite your love.*

Eug. Nay, good my lord, hold your hand, for I'll be
sworn I'll not set my hand to't.

Mom. Well, hold off your hand, good madam till it 150
should come on; I'll be ready for it anon, I warrant ye!

Now forth—*my love is without passion and therefore free from alteration ;* what answer you to that, madam ?

Eug. Even this, my lord : *your love, being mental, needs no bodily requital.* 155

Mom. I am content with that, and here it is—*but in heart*—

Eug. What but in heart ?

Mom. Hold off your hand yet, I say—*I do embrace and repay it.* 160

Eug. You may write, uncle ; but if you get my hand to it—

Mom. Alas, niece, this is nothing ! Is't anything to a bodily marriage to say you love a man in soul, if your hearts agree and your bodies meet not ? Simple marriage rites ! 165 Now let us forth ; he is in the way to felicity and desires your hand.

Eug. *My hand shall always sign the way to felicity*—

Mom. Very good ! May not any woman say this now ? Conclude now, sweet niece. 170

Eug. *And so God prosper your journey !*

Mom. Charitably concluded, though far short of that love I would have shown to any friend of yours, niece, I swear to you ! Your hand, now, and let this little stay his appetite. 175

Eug. Read what you have writ, my lord.

Mom. What needs that, madam ? You remember it, I am sure.

Eug. Well, if it want sense in the composition, let my secretary be blamed for it. There's my hand. [*She signs*] 180

Mom. Thanks, gentle niece ; now I'll read it.

Eug. Why now more than before, I pray ?

Mom. That you shall see straight. [*Reads.*] *I cannot but suffer you to love, if you do love, and will requite your love.*

Eug. Remember that requital was of your own putting 185 in, but it shall be after my fashion, I warrant ye !

Mom. Interrupt me no more—*Your love, being mental, needs no bodily requital, but in heart I embrace and repay it ; my hand shall always sign the way to felicity, and myself, knit with you in the bands of marriage, ever walk with you in it,* 190 *and so God prosper our journey*

                    Eugenia.

Eug. God's m[y] life, 'tis not thus, I hope !

Mom. By my life, but it is, niece !

Eug. By my life, but 'tis none of my deed, then !   195
  Mom. Do you use to set your hand to that which is not
your deed ?   Your hand is at it, niece, and if there be any
law in England, you shall perform it, too.
  Eug. Why, this is plain dishonoured deceit !
Does all your truest kindness end in law ?   200
  Mom. Have patience, niece, for, whatsoe'er I say,
Only the laws of faith and thy free love
Shall join my friend and thee, or naught at all,
By my friend's love, and by this kiss, it shall !
  Eug. Why, thus did false Acontius snare Cydippe.   205
  Mom. Indeed, dear love, his wile was something like,
And then 'tis no unheard of treachery,
That was enacted in a goddess' eye.
Acontius' worthy love fear'd not Diana
Before whom he contriv'd this sweet deceit,   210
  Eug. Well, there you have my hand ; but I'll be sworn
I never did thing so against my will.
  Mom. 'Twill prove the better, madam, doubt it not.
And to allay the billows of your blood,
Rais'd with my motion bold and opposite,   215
Dear niece, sup with me and refresh your spirits.
I have invited your companions,
With the two guests that din'd with you to-day,
And will send for the old Lord Furnifall,
The Captain, and his mates, and (though at night)   220
We will be merry as the morning lark.
  Eug. No, no, my lord ; you will have Clarence there.
  Mom. Alas, poor gentleman ! I must tell you now,
He's extreme sick and was so when he writ,
Though he did charge me not to tell you so,   225
And for the world he cannot come abroad
  Eug. Is this the man that without passion loves ?
  Mom. I do not tell you he is sick with love ;
Or if he be, 'tis wilful passion ;
Which he doth choose to suffer for your sake,   230
And could restrain his sufferance with a thought.
Upon my life he will not trouble you ;
And therefore, worthy niece, fail not to come.
  Eug. I will on that condition.
  Mom.   'Tis perform'd.
For were my friend well, and could comfort me,   235
I would not now entreat your company ;

But one of you I must have or I die ;
Oh such a friend is worth a monarchy.   *Exeunt*

[SCENA SECUNDA

A Room in Lord Furnifall's *House*]

Enter Lord Furnifall, Rudesby, Goosecap, Foulweather, Bullaker

   Furn. Nay, my gallants, I will tell you more.
   All. Forth, good my lord !
   Furn. The evening came and then our waxen stars
Sparkled about the heavenly Court of France,
When I, then young and radiant as the sun,   5
Gave lustre to those lamps, and curling thus
My golden foretop, stepp'd into the presence,
Where, set with other princely dames I found
The Countess of Lancalier and her niece,
Who, as I told you, cast so fix'd an eye   10
On my behaviours, talking with the king.
   All. True, my good lord !
   Furn. They rose when I came in, and all the lights
Burn'd dim for shame, when I stood up and shin'd.
   Foul. O most passionate description, Sir Cut. !   15
   Rud. True, of a candle's end !
   Goose. The passing'st description of a candle that ever
lived, Sir Cut.
   Furn. Yet aim'd I not at them, nor seem'd to note
What grace they did me, but found courtly cause   20
To talk with an accomplish'd gentleman
New come from Italy ; in quest of news
I spake Italian with him.
   Rud.   What, so young ?
   Furn. *O rarissime volte cadono nel parlar nostro familiare.*
   Foul. 'Slid, 'a could speak it, knight, at three year old !   25
   Furn. Nay, gentle Captain, do not set me forth ;
I love it not, in truth, I love it not.
   Foul. 'Slight, my lord, but truth is truth, you know !
   Goose. I dare ensure your lordship truth is truth, and
I have heard in France they speak French as well as their   30
mother tongue, my lord.
   Furn. Why, 'tis their mother tongue, my noble knight.
But (as I tell you) I seem'd not to note
The ladies' notes of me, but held my talk
With that Italianate Frenchman, and took time   35

(Still as our conference serv'd) to show my courtship
In the three quarter leg and settled look,
The quick kiss of the top of the forefinger,
And other such exploits of good accost ;
All which the ladies took into their eyes   40
With such attention that their favours swarm'd
About my bosom, in my heart, mine ears,
In scarves about my thighs, upon mine arms,
Thick on my wrists, and thicker on my hands ;
And still the less I sought, the more I found.   45
All this I tell to this notorious end
That you may use your courtship with less care
To your coy mistresses ; as when we strike
A goodly salmon with a little line,
We do not tug to hale her up by force,   50
For then our line would break, and our hook lost,
But let her careless play alongst the stream,
As you had left her, and she'll drown herself.
  Foul.   O' my life, a most rich comparison !
  Goose.   Never stir if it be not a richer caparison than my 55
lord my cousin wore at tilt, for that was broidered with
nothing but moonshine i' th' water, and this has salmons
in't.   By heaven, a most edible caparison !
  Rud.   Odious, thou wouldst say, for comparisons are
odious.   60
  Foul.   So they are, indeed, Sir Cut. ; all but my lord's.
  Goose.   Be caparisons odious, Sir Cut. ?   What, like
flowers ?
  Rud.   O ass !   They be odorous.
  Goose.   A botts o' that stinking word, ' odorous ' ; I can 65
never hit on't.
  Furn.   And how like you my Court-counsel, gallants, ha ?
  Foul.   Out of all proportion excellent, my lord ; and
believe it, for emphatical courtship your lordship puts down
all the lords of the Court.   70
  Furn.   No, good Captain, no !
  Foul.   By France, you do, my lord, for emphatical court-
ship !
  Furn.   For emphatical courtship, indeed, I can do some-
what.   75
  Foul.   Then does your merry entertainment become
you so festively that you have all the bravery of a St.
George's Day about ye, when you use it.

Furn. Nay, that's too much, in sadness, Captain !

Goose. O good my lord, let him praise you whatsoe'er 80
it costs your lordship.

Foul. I assure your lordship, your merry behaviour does
so festivally show upon you that every high holiday, when
ladies would be most beautiful, every one wishes to God
she were turned into such a little lord as you, when y'are 85
merry.

Goose. By this fire, they do, my lord ; I have heard 'em.

Furn. Marry, God forbid, knight, they should be turned
into me ; I had rather be turned into them, o' mine honor !

Foul. Then for your lordship's quips and quick jests, 90
why, *Gesta Romanorum* were nothing to them, o' my virtue !

Furn. Well, well, well, I will hear thee no more, I will
hear thee no more, good Captain ! Th'ast an excellent wit,
and thou shalt have crowns, o' mine honour ! And now,
knights, and Captain, the fool you told me of, do you all know 95
him.

Goose. I know him best, my lord.

Furn. Do you, Sir Giles ? To him then, good knight,
and be here with him, and here, and here, and here again ;
I mean paint him unto us, Sir Giles, paint him lively, lively 100
now, my good knightly boy !

Goose. Why, my good lord ? He will ne'er be long from
us, because we are all mortal, you know.

Furn. Very true !

Goose. And as soon as ever we go to dinner and supper 105
together—

Rud. Dinner and supper together ! When's that,
trow ?

Goose. 'A will come you in amongst us with his cloak
buttoned, loose under his chin—— 110

Rud. Buttoned loose, my lord ?

Goose. Ay, my lord, buttoned loose still, and both the
flaps cast over before both his shoulders afore him.

Rud. Both shoulders afore him ?

Furn. From before him, he means ; forth, good Sir Giles ! 115

Goose. Like a potentate, my lord !

Rud. Much like a potentate, indeed !

Goose. For all the world like a potentate, Sir Cut., ye
know.

Rud. So, sir ! 120

Goose. All his beard nothing but hair——

[R]ud. Or something else.

Goose. Or something else, as you say.

Foul. Excellent good !

Goose. His melons, or his apricocks, oranges, always in 125
an unclean handkerchief, very cleanly, I warrant you, my
lord !

Furn. A good neat fool, Sir Giles, of my honour !

Goose. Then his fine words that he sets them in, ' concatical,' ' a fine annise-seed-wench fool,' ' upon ticket,' and 130
so forth.

Furn. Passing strange words, believe me !

Goose. Know'th every man at the table, though he never
saw him before, by sight, and then will he fool you so finely,
my lord, that he will make your heart ache till your eyes run 135
over.

Furn. The best that ever I heard ! Gramercy, good
knight, for thy merry description. Captain, I give thee
twenty companies of commendations, never to be cashiered.

Enter Jack *and* Will *on the other side*

Ambo. Save your lordship !   140

Furn. My pretty cast of Merlins, what prophecies with
your little masterships ?

Jack. Things that cannot come to pass, my lord ; the
worse our fortunes.

Foul. Why, what's the matter, pages ?   145

Rud. How now, my lady's foisting hounds !

Goose. Master Jack, Master Jack ; how do ye, Master
William ? Frolic ?

Will. Not so frolic as you left us, Sir Giles.

Furn. Why, wags, what news bring you, o' God's name ?   150

Jack. Heavy news, indeed, my lord ; pray pardon us.

Furn. Heavy news ? Not possible your little bodies
could bring 'em then. Unload those your heavy news, I
beseech ye.

Will. Why, my lord, the fool we took for your lordship 155
is thought too wise for you, and we dare not present him.

Goose. 'Slid, pages, you'll not cheat's of our fool, will ye ?

Jack. Why, Sir Giles, he's too dogged and bitter for you
in truth ; we shall bring you a fool to make you laugh, and
he shall make all the world laugh at us.   160

Will. Ay, indeed, Sir Giles, and he knows you so well,
too.

Goose. Know me ? 'Slight, he knows me no more than the beggar knows his dish !

Jack. Faith, he begs you to be content, Sir Giles, for he 165 will not come.

Goose. Beg me ? 'Slight, I would I had known that ! Tother day I thought I had met him in Paul's ; and he had been anybody else but a pillar, I would have run him through, by heaven ! Beg me ?   170

Foul. He begs you to me content, Sir Giles, that is, he prays you.

Goose. O does he praise me ? Then I commend him.

Furn. Let this unsuitable fool go, Sir Giles ; we will make shift without him.   175

Goose. That we will, o' my word, my lord ; and have him, too, for all this.

Will. Do not you say so, Sir Giles, for to tell you true that fool is dead.

Goose. Dead ? 'Slight, that cannot be, man ! I know 180 he would have writ to me, an't had been so.

Furn. Quick or dead, let him go, Sir Giles.

Jack. Ay, my lord, for we have better news for you to harken after.

Furn. What are they, my good novations ?   185

Jack. My Lord Momford entreats your lordship and these knights and captain to accompany the Countess Eugenia and the other two ladies at his house at supper to-night.

Will. All desiring your lordship to pardon them for not eating your meat to-night.   190

Furn. With all my heart, wags, and there's amends. My hearts, now set your courtship o' the last, o' the tainters, and prick up yourselves for the ladies.

Goose. O brave, Sir Cut. ! Come, let's prick up the ladies.   195

Furn. And will not the knights' two noble kinsmen be there ?

Jack. Both will be there, my lord.

Furn. Why, there's the whole lot us then, and there shall we knock up the whole triplicity of your nuptials.   200

Goose. I'll make my lord my cousin speak for me.

Foul. And your lordship will be for me, I hope.

Furn. With tooth and nail, Captain, o' my lordship !

Rud. Hang 'em, tits ! I'll pummel myself into 'em.

Jack. Your lordship your cousin, Sir Giles, has promised 205 the ladies they shall see you sew.

Goose. God's me, would I might never be mortal if I do
not carry my work with me!
　Furn. Do so, Sir Giles, and withal use means
To taint their high bloods with the shaft of Love.　　　210
Sometimes a finger's motion wounds their minds,
A jest, a gesture, or a pretty laugh,
A voice, a present : ah, things done i' th' nick
Wound deep and sure ; and let fly your gold,
And we shall nuptials have ; hold, belly, hold!　　　215
　Goose. O rare, Sir Cut., we shall eat nut-shells ; hold,
belly, hold!　　　　　　*Exeunt* [Furnifall *and the* Knights]
　Jack. O pitiful knight, that knows not nuptials from nut-
shells!
　Will. And now *comme portez-vous, monsieur* ?　　　220
　Bull. *Porte bien, vous remercie.*
　Jack. We may see it, indeed, sir, and you shall go afore
with us.
　Bull. No, good *monsieurs!*
　Will. Another crash in my lady's cellar, i'faith, *mon-* 225
sieur.
　Bull. *Remercie de bon cœur, monsieurs.*　　　*Exeunt*

[SCENA TERTIA

A Room in Momford's *House*]

Enter Clarence, Momford

　Mom. How now, my friend, does not the knowing beams,
That through thy common sense glance through thy eyes
To read that letter, through thine eyes retire
And warm thy heart with a triumphant fire ?
　[*Clar.*] My lord, I feel a treble happiness　　　　5
Mix in one soul, which proves how eminent
Things endless are above things temporal
That are in bodies needfully confin'd :
I cannot suffer their dimensions pierc'd,
Where my immortal part admits expansure,　　　　10
Even to the comprehension of two more
Commix'd substantially with her mere self.
　Mom. As how, my strange and riddle-speaking friend ?
　Clar. As thus, my lord : I feel my own mind's joy
As it is separate from all other powers ;　　　　15
And then the mixture of another soul
Join'd in direction to one end like it ;

And thirdly the contentment I enjoy,
As we are join'd, that I shall work that good
In such a noble spirit as your niece,   20
Which in myself I feel for absolute ;
Each good mind doubles his own free content
When in another's use they give it vent.
   Mom.   Said like my friend, and that I may not wrong
Thy full perfections with an emptier grace   25
Than that which show presents to thy conceits,
In working thee a wife worse than she seems,
I'll tell thee plain a secret which I know.
My niece doth use to paint herself with white,
Whose cheeks are naturally mix'd with red,   30
Either because she thinks pale looks moves most,
Or of an answerable nice affect
To other of her modest qualities,
Because she would not with the outward blaze
Of tempting beauty tangle wanton eyes,   35
And so be troubled with their tromperies ;
Which construe as thou wilt, I make it known
That thy free comment may examine it,
As willinger to tell truth of my niece
Than in the least degree to wrong my friend.   40
   Clar.   A jealous part of friendship you unfold,
For was it ever seen that any dame
Would change of choice a well-mix'd white and red
For bloodless paleness, if she striv'd to move ?
Her painting then is to shun motion ;   45
But if she mended some defect with it,
Breeds it more hate than other ornaments
Which (to supply bare nature) ladies wear ?
What an absurd thing is it to suppose
(If Nature made us either lame or sick)   50
We would not seek for sound limbs or for health
By Art, the rector of confused Nature ?
So in a face, if Nature be made lame[r]
Than Art can make it, is it more offence
To help her want there than in other limbs ?   55
Who can give instance where dames' faces lost
The privilege their other parts may boast ?
   Mom.   But our most court-received poet says
That painting is pure chastity's abater.
   Clar.   That was to make up a poor rime to Nature,   60

And far from any judgment it conferr'd ;
For lightness comes from hearts, and not from looks ;
And if inchastity possess the heart,
Not painting doth not race it, nor, being clear,
Doth painting spot it :   65
Omne bonum naturaliter pulchrum.
For outward fairness bears the divine form,
And moves beholders to the act of love,
And that which moves to love is to be wish'd,
And each thing simply to be wish'd is good.   70
So I conclude mere painting of the face
A lawful and a commendable grace.
   Mom.   What paradox dost thou defend in this ?
And yet through thy clear arguments I see
Thy speech is far exempt from flattery ;   75
And how illiterate Custom grossly errs
Almost in all traditions she prefers.
Since then the doubt I put thee of my niece
Checks not thy doubtless love, forth, my dear friend ;
And to a[dd] force to those impressions,   80
That now have carv'd her fantasy with love,
I have invited her to supper here,
And told her thou art most extremely sick,
Which thou shalt counterfeit with all thy skill.
   Clar.   Which is exceeding small to counterfeit.   85
   Mom.   Practise a little ; love will teach it thee ;
And then shall Doctor Versey, the physician,
Come to thee while herself is in my house,
With whom as thou confer'st of thy disease,
I'll bring my niece with all the lords and ladies   90
Within your hearing under feign'd pretext
To show the pictures that hang near thy chamber ;
Where when thou hear'st my voice, know she is there,
And therefore speak that which may stir her thoughts,
And make her fly into thy opened arms.   95
Ladies whom true worth cannot move to ruth
True lovers must deceive to show their truth.   *Exeunt*

      FINIS ACTUS QUARTI

ACTUS QUINTI SCENA PRIMA

[*A Room at* Lord Momford's *House*]

Enter Momford, Furnifall, Tales, Kingcob, Rudesby, Goosecap, Foulweather, Eugenia, Hippolyta, Penelope, Winifred

Mom. Where is Sir Giles Goosecap here ?
Goose. Here, my lord !
Mom. Come forward, knight ; 'tis you that the ladies admire at working, o' my honour !
Goose. A little at once, my lord, for idleness' sake.   5
Furn. Sir Cut., I say ! To her, Captain !
Pen. Come, good servant, let's see what you work.
Goose. Why, look you, mistress, I am making a fine dry sea, full of fish playing in the bottom, and here I'll let in the water so lively that you shall hear it roar.   10
Eug. Not hear it, Sir Giles ?
Goose. Yes, in sooth, madam ; with your eyes.
Tales. Ay, lady ; for when a thing is done so exceedingly to the life as my knightly cousin does it, the eye oftentimes takes so strong a heed of it that it cannot contain it alone,   15
and therefore the ear seems to take part with it.
Hip. That's a very good reason, my lord.
Mom. What a jest it is to hear how seriously he strives to make his foolish kinsman's answers wise ones.
Pen. What shall this be, servant ?   20
Goose. This shall be a great whale, mistress, at all his bigness, spouting huge hills of salt water afore him, like a little water squirt ; but you shall not need to fear him, mistress, for he shall be silk and gold, he shall do you no harm, and he be ne'er so lively.   25
Pen. Thank you, good servant !
Tales. Do not think, lady, but he had need tell you this aforehand, for, o' mine honour, he wrought me the monster Caucasus so lively that at the first sight I started at it.
Mom. The monster Caucasus, my lord ? Caucasus is a   30
mountain ; Cacus, you mean.
Tales. Cacus, indeed, my lord, cry you mercy !
Goose. Here I'll take out your eye, and you will, mistress.
Pen. No, by my faith, servant ! 'Tis better in.
Goose. Why, lady, I'll but take it out in jest, in earnest.   35
Pen. No ; something else there, good servant.
Goose. Why, then, here shall be a camel, and he shall

have horns, and he shall look for all the world like a maid
without a husband.

Hip.   O bitter Sir Giles !   40

Tales.   Nay, he has a dry wit, lady, I can tell ye.

Pen.   He bobbed me there, indeed, my lord.

Furn.   Marry him, sweet lady, to answer his bitter bob.

King.   So she may answer him with horns, indeed.

Eug.   See what a pretty work he wears on his boot-hose. 45

Hip.   Did you work them yourself, Sir Giles, or buy them ?

Goose.   I bought 'em for nothing, madam, in th' Exchange.

Eug.   Bought 'em for nothing ?

Tales.   Indeed, madam, in th' Exchange they so honour
him for his work that they will take nothing for anything 50
he buys on 'em.   But where's the rich night-cap you wrought,
cousin ?   If it had not been too little for you, it was the best
piece of work that ever I saw.

Goose.   Why, my lord, 'twas big enough when I wrought
it, for I wore pantables then, you know.   55

Tales.   Indeed the warmer a man keeps his feet the less
he needs wear upon his head.

Eug.   You speak for your kinsman the best that ever I
heard, my lord.

Goose.   But I believe, madam, my lord cousin has not 60
told you all my good parts.

Tales.   I told ['em] so, I warrant you, cousin !

Hip.   What do you think he left out, Sir Giles ?

Goose.   Marry, madam, I can take tobacco now, and I
have bought glow-worms to kindle it withal, better than 65
all the burning-glasses i' th' world.

Eug.   Glow-worms, Sir Giles ?   Will they make it burn ?

Goose.   O good madam, I feed 'em with nothing but fire
o' purpose ; I'll be sworn they eat me five faggots a week in
charcoal.   70

Tales.   Nay, he has the strangest devices, ladies, that
ever you heard, I warrant ye !

Furn.   That's a strange device, indeed, my lord.

Hip.   But your sewing, Sir Giles, is a most gentlewoman-
like quality, I assure you.   75

Pen.   O far away, for now, servant, you need never
marry ; you are both husband and wife yourself.

Goose.   Nay, indeed, mistress, I would fain marry for all
that, and I'll tell you my reason, if you will.

Pen.   Let's hear it, good servant,   80

Goose. Why, madam, we have a great match at football towards, married men against bachelors, and the married men be all my friends, so I would fain marry to take the married men's parts, in truth.

Hip. The best reason for marriage that ever I heard, 85 Sir Giles.

Goose. I pray will you keep my work a little, mistress ; I must needs strain a little courtesy, in truth. *Exit* Sir Giles

Hip. God's my life, I thought he was a little to blame !

Rud. Come, come, you hear not me, dame.   90

Furn. Well said, Sir Cut. ; to her now ; we shall hear fresh courting.

Hip. Alas, Sir Cut., you are not worth the hearing ; everybody says you cannot love, howsoever you talk on't.

Rud. Not love, dame ? 'Slid what argument wouldst 95 have of my love, trow ? Let me look as red as scarlet afore I see thee, and when thou com'st in sight, if the sun of thy beauty do not white me like a [shepherd's] holland, I am a Jew to my Creator.

Hip. O excellent !   100

Rud. Let me burst like a toad, if a frown of thy brow has not turned the very heart in my belly, and made me ready to be hanged by the heels for a fortnight to bring it to the right again.

Hip. You should have hanged longer, Sir Cut. ; 'tis not 105 right yet.

Rud. Zouns, bid me cut off the best limb of my body for thy love, and I'll lay't in thy hand to prove it. Dost think I am no Christian ; have I not a soul to save ?

Hip. Yes, 'tis to save yet, I warrant it ; and will be 110 while 'tis a soul, if you use this.

Furn. Excellent courtship of all hands ; only my Captain's courtship is not heard yet. Good madam, give him favour to court you with his voice.

Eug. What should he court me withal else, my lord ? 115

Mom. Why, I hope, madam, there be other things to court ladies withal, besides voices.

Furn. I mean with an audible sweet song, madam.

Eug. With all my heart, my lord, if I shall be so much indebted to him.   120

Foul. Nay, I will be indebted to your ears, lady, for hearing me sound music.

Furn. Well done, Captain, prove as it will now.

Enter Messenger

Messenger. My lord, Doctor Versey, the physician, is
come to see Master Clarence.   125
  Mom. Light and attend him to him presently.
  Furn. To Master Clarence ?   What, is your friend sick ?
  Mom. Exceeding sick.
  Tales.   I am exceeding sorry.
  King. Never was sorrow worthier bestowed
Than for the ill state of so good a man.   130
  Pen. Alas, poor gentleman ! Good my lord, let's see
    him.
  Mom. Thanks, gentle lady, but my friend is loath
To trouble ladies since he cannot quit them
With anything he hath that they respect.
  Hip. Respect, my lord ! I would hold such a man   135
In more respect than any emperor,
For he could make me empress of myself,
And in mine own rule comprehend the world.
  Mom. How now, young dame ! What, suddenly in-
    spir'd ?
This speech hath silver hairs, and reverence asks,   140
And sooner shall have duty done of me
Than any pomp in temporal empery.
  Hip. Good madam, get my lord to let us greet him.
  Eug. Alas, we shall but wrong and trouble him.
His contemplations greet him with most welcome.   145
  Furn. I never knew a man of so sweet a temper,
So soft and humble, of so high a spirit.
  Mom. Alas, my noble lord, he is not rich,
Nor titles hath, nor in his tender cheeks
The standing lake of impudence corrupts ;   150
Hath nought in all the world, nor nought would have
To grace him in the prostituted light.
But if a man would consort with a soul
Where all man's sea of gall and bitterness
Is quite evaporate with her holy flames,   155
And in whose powers a dove-like innocence
Fosters her own deserts, and life and death
Runs hand in hand before them, all the skies
Clear and transparent to her piercing eyes,
Then would my friend be something, but till then   160
A cipher, nothing, or the worst of men.
  Foul. Sweet lord, let's go visit him.

Enter Goosecap

Goose. Pray, good my lord, what's that you talk on?

Mom. Are you come from your necessary business, Sir
Giles? We talk of the visiting of my sick friend, Clarence. 165

Goose. O good my lord, let's visit him, cause I know his
brother.

Hip. Know his brother! Nay, then, Count, do not
deny him.

Goose. Pray, my lord, whether was eldest, he or his elder 170
brother?

Mom. O the younger brother eldest, while you live, Sir
Giles!

Goose. I say so still, my lord; but I am so borne down
with truth, as never any knight i'th' world was, I think. 175

Tales. A man would think he speaks simply now; but
indeed it is in the will of the parents to make which child
they will youngest or eldest; for often we see the youngest
inherit, wherein he is eldest.

Eug. Your logical wit, my lord, is able to make anything 180
good.

Mom. Well, come, sweet lords and ladies, let us spend
The time till supper-time with some such sights
As my poor house is furnished withal,
Pictures and jewels, of which implements   185
It may be I have some will please you much.

Goose. Sweet lord, let's see them.   *Exeunt*

[SCENA SECUNDA

Another Room in Lord Momford's *House*]

Enter Clarence *and* Doctor

Doct. I think your disease, sir, be rather of the mind
than the body.

Clar. Be there diseases of the mind, Doctor?

Doct. No question, sir; even as there be of the body.

Clar. And cures for them, too?   5

Doct. And cures for them too, but not by physic.

Clar. You will have their diseases griefs, will ye not?

Doct. Yes, oftentimes.

Clar. And do not griefs ever rise out of passions?

Doct. Evermore.   10

Clar. And do not passions proceed from corporal dis-
tempers?

Doct. Not the passions of the mind, for the mind many times is sick when the body is healthful.

Clar. But is not the mind's sickness of power to make   15
the body sick ?

Doct. In time, certain.

Clar. And the body's ill affections able to infect the mind ?

Doct. No question.

Clar. Then if there be such a natural commerce of   20
powers betwixt them that the ill estate of the one offends
the other, why should not the medicines for one cure the
other ?

Doct. Yet it will not, you see.

Hei mihi quod nullis amor est medicabilis herbis !   25

Clar. Nay, then, Doctor, since you cannot make any
reasonable connection of these two contrarieties, the mind
and the body, making both subject to passion, wherein you
confound the substances of both, I must tell you there is
no disease of the mind but one, and that is ignorance.   30

Doct. Why, what is love ? Is not that a disease of the
mind ?

Clar. Nothing so ; for it springs naturally out of the
blood, nor are we subject to any disease or sorrow whose
causes or effects simply and natively concern the body, that   35
the mind by any means partaketh ; nor are there any passions in the soul, for where there are no affections there are no
passions : and *Affectus* your master Galen refers *parti
irascenti*, for *illic est anima sentiens ubi sunt affectus ;* therefore the rational soul cannot be there also.   40

Doct. But you know we use to say ' my mind gives me
this or that,' even in those addictions that concern the body.

Clar. We use to say so, indeed, and from that use comes
the abuse of all knowledge and her practice, for when the
object in question only concerns the state of the body, why   45
should the soul be sorry or glad for it ? If she willingly mix
herself, then she is a fool ; if of necessity and against her
will, a slave ; and so, far from that reason and freedom
that the Empress of Reason and an eternal substance should
comprehend.   50

Doct. Divinely spoken, sir, but very paradoxically.

Enter [*above*] Momford, Tales, Kingcob, Furnifall, Rudesby,
     Goosecap, Foulweather, Eugenia, Penelope, Hippolyta,
     Winifred [*and a* Servant]

   Mom. Who's there ?

[Serv.] I, my lord.

Mom. Bring hither the key of the gallery ; methought
I heard the Doctor and my friend.   55

Furn. I did so, sure.

Mom.   Peace, then, awhile, my lord !
We will be bold to eavesdrop, for I know
My friend is as respective in his chamber,
And by himself, of anything he does,
As in a critic synod's curious eyes,   60
Following therein Pythagoras' golden rule :
Maxime omnium teipsum reverere.

Clar. Know you the Countess Eugenia, sir ?

Doct. Exceeding well, sir ; she's a good learned scholar.

Clar. Then I perceive you know her well indeed.   65

Doct. Methinks you two should use much conference.

Clar. Alas, sir, we do very seldom meet,
For her estate and mine are so unequal,
And then her knowledge passeth mine so far
That I hold much too sacred a respect   70
Of her high virtues to let mine attend them.

Doct. Pardon me, sir, this humbleness cannot flow
Out of your judgment, but from passion.

Clar. Indeed I do account that passion
The very high perfection of my mind,   75
That is excited by her excellence,
And therefore willingly and gladly feel it ;
For what was spoken of the most chaste queen
Of rich P[h]asiaca may be said of her ;
Moribus antevenit sortem, virtutibus annos,   80
Sexum animo, morum nobilitate genus.

Doct. A most excellent distich.

Mom. Come, lords, away ; let's not presume too much
Of a good nature ; not for all I have
Would I have him take knowledge of the wrong   85
I rudely offer him ; come, then, I'll show
A few rare jewels to your honour'd eyes,
And then present you with a common supper.

Goose. Jewels, my lord ? Why, is not this candlestick one of your jewels, pray ?   90

Mom. Yes, marry, is it, Sir Giles, if you will.

Goose. 'Tis a most fine candlestick, in truth ; it wants
nothing but the languages.

Pen. The languages, **servant** ! Why the languages ?

Goose.   Why, mistress, there was a latten candlestick here   95
afore, and that had the languages, I am sure.

Tales.   I thought he had a reason for it, lady.

Pen.   Ay, and a reason of the sun too, my lord ; for his
father would have been ashamed on't.

Exeunt [Momford *and the rest*]

Doct.   Well, Master Clarence, I perceive your mind   100
Hath so incorporate itself with flesh
And therein rarefied that flesh to spirit
That you have need of no physician's help.
But, good sir, even for holy Virtue's health
And grace of perfect knowledge, do not make   105
Those groundworks of eternity you lay
Means to your ruin and short being here ;
For the too strict and rational course you hold
Will eat your body up, and then the world,
Or that small point of it where Virtue lives,   110
Will suffer diminution ; it is now
Brought almost to a simple unity,
Which is (as you well know) *simplicior puncto ;*
And if that point fail once, why, then, alas,
The unity must only be suppos'd.   115
Let it not fail, then ; most men else have sold it ;
Though you neglect yourself, uphold it.
So with my reverend love I leave you, sir.   *Exit*

Clar.   Thanks, worthy Doctor, I do amply quite you.
I prop poor Virtue, that am propp'd myself,   120
And only by one friend in all the world !
For Virtue's only sake I use this wile,
Which otherwise I would despise, and scorn ;
The world should sink, and all the pomp she hugs
Close in her heart in her ambitious gripe,   125
Ere I sustain it, if this slend'rest joint,
Mov'd with the worth that worldlings love so well,
Had power to save it from the throat of hell.

He draws the curtains and sits within them

Enter Eugenia, Penelope, Hippolyta

Eug.   Come on, fair ladies, I must make you both
Familiar witnesses of the most strange part   130
And full of impudence, that e'er I play'd.

Hip.   What's that, good madam ?

Eug.   I, that have been so more than maiden-nice

To my dear lord and uncle not to yield
By his importunate suit to his friend's love   135
In look or almost thought, will of myself,
Far past his expectation or his hope,
In action and in person greet his friend,
And comfort the poor gentleman's sick state.
    Pen. Is this a part of so much impudence ?   140
    Eug. No, but I fear me it will stretch to more.
    Hip. Marry, madam, the more the merrier !
    Eug. Marry, madam ? What, should I marry him ?
    Hip. You take the word, methinks, as though you would,
And if there be a thought of such kind heat   145
In your cold bosom, would to God my breath
Might blow it to the flame of your kind heart !
    Eug. God's precious, lady, know ye what you say,
Respect you what I am and what he is,
What the whole world would say, and what great lords   150
I have refused and might as yet embrace,
And speak you like a friend to wish me him ?
    Hip. Madam, I cast all this, and know your choice
Can cast it quite out of the christal doors
Of your judicial eyes ; I am but young,   155
And be it said, without all pride I take
To be a maid, I am one, and, indeed,
Yet in my mother's womb to all the wiles
Wea[v']d in the looms of greatness and of state ;
And yet, even by that little I have learn'd   160
Out of continual conference with you,
I have cried harvest home of thus much judgment
In my green sowing time that I could place
The constant sweetness of good Clarence' mind,
Fill'd with his inward wealth and nobleness,   165
Look, madam, here ; when others' outward trash
Should be contented to come under here.
    Pen. And so say I, upon my maidenhead !
    Eug. 'Tis well said, ladies ; thus we differ then
I to the truth-wise, you to worldly men.   170
And now, sweet dames, observe an excellent jest
(At least in my poor jesting) ; th' Earl, my uncle,
Will miss me straight, and I know his close drift
Is to make me and his friend Clarence meet
By some device or other he hath plotted.   175
Now when he seeks us round about his house

And cannot find us, for we may be sure
He will not seek me in his sick friend's chamber
(I have at all times made his love so strange)
He straight will think I went away displeas'd,   180
Or heartily careless of his heartiest suit,
And then I know there is no grief on earth
Will touch his heart so much ; which I will suffer
To quite his late good pleasure wrought on me,
For, I'll be sworn, in motion and in progress   185
Of his friend's suit I never in my life
Wrastled so much with passion, or was mov'd
To take his firm love in such jealous part.
    Hip. This is most excellent, madam, and will prove
A niece-like and a noble friend's revenge.   190
    Eug. Bold in a good cause, then, let's greet his friend.
            [*Drawing the curtains and disclosing* Clarence]
Where is this sickly gentleman ?   At his book ?
Now in good truth I would these books were burn'd
That rap men from their friends before their time.
How does my uncle's friend ? No other name   195
I need give him to whom I give myself.
    Clar. O madam, let me rise that I may kneel,
And pay some duty to your sovereign grace.
    Hip. Good Clarence, do not work yourself disease ;
My lady comes to ease and comfort you.   200
    Pen. And we are handmaids to her to that end.
    Clar. Ladies, my heart will break if it be held
Within the verge of this presumptuous chair.
    Eug. Why, Clarence, is your judgment bent to show
A common lover's passion ? Let the world,   205
That lives without a heart and is but show,
Stand on her empty and impoisoned form ;
I know thy kindness and have seen thy heart
Cle[f]t in my uncle's free and kindly lips,
And I am only now to speak and act   210
The rites due to thy love : oh, I could weep
A bitter shower of tears for thy sick state,
I could give passion all her blackest rites,
And make a thousand vows to thy deserts ;
But these are common ; knowledge is the bond,   215
The seal, and crown of our united minds,
And that is rare and constant, and for that
To my late written hand I give thee this.

See, Heaven, the soul thou gav'st is in this hand ;
This is the knot of our eternity,   220
Which Fortune, Death, nor Hell, shall ever loose.

[*She draws the curtains concealing* Clarence, *herself,
and her attendants*]

Enter Bullaker, Jack, Will

Jack. What an unmannerly trick is this of thy Countess
to give the noble Count her uncle the slip thus !

Will. Unmannerly,   you   villain ?   O   that   I   were
worthy to wear a dagger to any purpose for thy sake !   225

Bull. Why, young gentlemen, utter your anger with your
fists.

Will. That cannot be, man, for all fists are shut, you
know, and utter nothing ; and, besides, I do not think my
quarrel just for my lady's protection in this cause, for I   230
protest she does most abominably miscarry herself.

Jack. Protest, you saucy Jack, you ! I should do my
country and courtship good service to beat thy colt's teeth
out of thy head for suffering such a reverend word to pass
their guard. Why, the oldest courtier in the world, man,   235
can do no more than protest.

Bull. Indeed, page, if you were in France, you would
be broken upon a wheel for it ; there is not the best duke's
son in France dares say ' I protest,' till he be one and thirty
year old at least, for the inheritance of that word is not to be   240
possessed before.

Will. Well, I am sorry for my presumption then ; but
more sorry for my lady's ; marry, most sorry for thee, good
Lord Momford, that will make us most of all sorry for our-
selves, if we do not find her out.   245

Jack. Why, alas, what should we do ? All the stars of
our heaven see we seek her as fast as we can ; if she be crept
into a rush, we will seek her out or burn her.

Enter Momford

Mom. Villains, where are your ladies ? Seek them out.
Hence, home, you monsters, and still keep you there,   250
Where Levity keeps in her inconstant sphere.

Exeunt Pages

Away, you precious villains ! What a plague
Of varied tortures is a woman's heart ?
How like a peacock's tail with different lights
They differ from themselves ; the very air   255

Alters the aspen humours of their bloods ;
Now excellent good, now super-excellent bad :
Some excellent good, Some ?   But one of all !
Would any ignorant baby serve her friend
Such an uncivil part ?   'Sblood, what is learning ?   260
An artificial cobweb to catch flies,
And nourish spiders ?   Could she cut my throat
With her departure, I had been her calf
And made a dish at supper for my guests
Of her kind charge ; I am beholding to her.   265
Puff ! Is there not a feather in this air
A man may challenge for her ?   What, a feather,
So easy to be seen, so apt to trace
In the weak flight of her unconstant wings ?
A mote, man, with the most, that with the sun   270
Is only seen, yet with his radiant eye
We cannot single so from other motes
To say this mote is she. Passion of death !
She wrongs me past a death. Come, come, my friend
Is mine, she not her own, and there's an end.   275

> [Eugenia *draws the curtains disclosing* Clarence, *herself*
> *and her attendants*]

   Eug.   Come, uncle, shall we go to supper now ?
   Mom.   Zouns, to supper !   What a dor is this ?
   Eug.   Alas, what ails my uncle ?   Ladies, see !
   Hip.   Is not your lordship well ?
   Pen.   Good, speak, my lord !
   Mom.   A sweet plague on you all, ye witty rogues !   280
Have you no pity in your villainous jests,
But run a man quite from his fifteen wits ?
   Hip.   Will not your lordship see your friend and niece ?
   Mom.   Would I might sink if I shame not to see her !
Tush, 'twas a passion of pure jealousy ;   285
I'll make her now amends with adoration.
Goddess of Learning and of Constancy,
Of Friendship, and every other Virtue
   Eug.   Come, come, you have abus'd me now, I know,
And now you plaster me with flatteries.   290
   Pen.   My lord, the contract is knit fast betwixt them.
   Mom.   Now all heaven's quire of angels sing amen,
And bless these true born nuptials with their bliss ;
And, niece, though you have cozen'd me in this,

I'll uncle you yet in another thing,   295
And quite deceive your expectation ;
For where you think you have contracted hearts
With a poor gentleman, he is sole heir
To all my earldom, which to you and yours
I freely and forever here bequeath.   300
Call forth the lords, sweet ladies, let them see
This sudden and most welcome novelty ;
But cry you mercy, niece ; perhaps your modesty
Will not have them partake this sudden match.
    Eug. O uncle, think you so ? I hope I made   305
My choice with too much judgment to take shame
Of any form I shall perform it with.
    Mom. Said like my niece, and worthy of my friend.

     Enter Furnifall, Tales, Kingcob, Goosecap, Rudesby,
        Foulweather, Jack, Will, Bullaker

    Mom. My lords, take witness of an absolute wonder,
A marriage made for virtue, only virtue ;   310
My friend and my dear niece are man and wife.
    Furn. A wonder, of my honour, and withal
A worthy precedent for all the world.
Heaven bless you for it, lady, and your choice !
    Ambo. Thanks, my good lord !   315
    Tales. An accident that will make policy blush,
And all the complements of wealth and state,
In the successful and unnumber'd race
That shall flow from it, fill'd with fame and grace.
    King. So may it speed, dear Countess, worthy Clarence. 320
    Ambo. Thanks, good Sir [Clement].
    Furn. Captain, be not dismay'd ; I'll marry thee,
For while we live thou shalt my consort be.
    Foul. By France, my lord, I am not griev'd a whit,
Since Clarence hath her ; he hath been in France,   325
And therefore merits her if she were better.
    Mom. Then, knights, I'll knit your happy nuptial knots,
I know the ladies' minds better than you ;
Though my rare niece hath chose for virtue only,
Yet some, more wise than some, they choose for both,   330
Virtue and wealth.
    Eug.   Nay, uncle, then I plead
This goes with my choice—' Some more wise than some '—
For only virtue's choice is truest wisdom.

Mom. Take wealth and virtue both amongst you then ;
They love ye, knights, extremely, and, Sir Cut.,   335
I give the chaste Hippolyta to you ;
Sir Giles, this lady—
　Pen.　　　　　Nay, stay there, my lord !
I have not yet prov'd all his knightly parts ;
I hear he is an excellent poet too.
　Tales. That I forgot, sweet lady. Good Sir Giles,   340
Have you no sonnet of your pen about ye ?
　Goose. Yes, that I have, I hope, my lord my cousin.
　Furn. Why, this is passing fit.
　Goose. I'd be loath to go without paper about me against
my mistress—hold my work again ; a man knows not 345
what need he shall have, perhaps.
　Mom. Well remembered, o' my honour, Sir Giles.
　Goose. Pray read, my lord ; I made this sonnet of my
mistress.
　Rud. Nay, read thyself, man !   350
　Goose. No, in truth, Sir Cut., I cannot read mine own
hand.
　Mom. Well, I will read it.
Three things there be which thou shouldst only crave,
Thou pom'roy, or thou apple of mine eye ;   355
Three things there be which thou shouldst long to have,
And for which three each modest dame would cry ;
Three things there be that should thine anger suage,
An English mastiff and a fine French page.
　Rud. 'Sblood, ass, there's but two things ! Thou sham'st 360
thyself.
　Goose. Why, Sir Cut., that's *poetica licentia* ; the verse
would have been too long, and I had put in the third. 'Slight,
you are no poet, I perceive !
　Pen. 'Tis excellent, servant !   365
　Mom.　　　　　　　Keep it, lady, then ;
And take the only knight of mortal men.
　Goose. Thank you, good my lord, as much as though
you had given me twenty shillings, in truth ; now I may
take the married men's parts at football.
　Mom. All comforts crown you all ; and you, Captain, 370
For merry form's sake let the willow crown.
A wreath of willow bring us hither straight.
　Furn. Not for a world should that have been forgot.
Captain, it is the fashion, take this crown.

Foul.   With all my heart, my lord, and thank you too ; 375
I will thank any man that gives me crowns.

Mom.   Now will we consecrate our ready supper
To honour'd Hymen as his nuptial rite ;
In form whereof first dance, fair lords and ladies,
And after sing ; so we will sing and dance,   380
And to the skies our virtuous joys advance.

The Measure

Now to the song, and do this garland grace.

Canto

> *Willow, willow, willow,*
> *Our Captain goes down :*
> *Willow, willow, willow,*   385
> *His valour doth crown.*
> *The rest with rosemary we grace.*
> *O Hymen, let thy light*
> *With richest rays gild every face,*
> *And feast hearts with delight.*   390
> *Willow, willow, willow,*
> *We chant to the skies ;*
> *And with black and yellow*
> *Give courtship the prize.*

FINIS

NOTES

THE BLIND BEGGAR OF ALEXANDRIA

INTRODUCTION

The Blind Beggar of Alexandria, the first [1] play which we have authentic warrant for ascribing to Chapman, was produced by the Lord Admiral's men at Henslowe's theatre, the Rose. It is mentioned as a new play in Henslowe's *Diary* under the date of February 12, 1595–6: ' R꜀ at the blind beger of elexandrea iii͈ '. It seems to have met with instant and long-continued success, for it was performed again on February 16, 19, 22, and 26, presumably in March, although Henslowe's records are lacking for that month, twice in April, thrice in May, twice in June, and once in July. After the gap in Henslowe's *Diary*, which extends from July 18 to October 27, 1596, the record of its performances begins again on November 6, and eight more are noted, the last falling on April 1, 1596–7, after which it was apparently withdrawn.[2] This gives us twenty-two recorded performances, a number exceeded only by three plays mentioned by Henslowe during this period, one of which was the ever popular *Dr. Faustus*.

Certain later entries in Henslowe show that this play was revived in 1601. Under the dates of May 2, 5, 8, and 22 (or June 4), he notes disbursements amounting to £9. 3s. 4d. for new costumes, including ' fourscore ounce of copper lace for the man's gown and a suit for the blind beggar '.

Some time after the play was first withdrawn from the stage the manuscript came into the hands of a publisher, and was entered in the Stationers' Registers under the date of August 15, 1598 : ' To Wm. Jones upon condition that it belong to no other man '. It was published by Jones in the same year with the following title-page :

> The Blinde Begger of Alexandria, most pleasantly discoursing his variable humours in disguised shapes full of conceite and pleasure. As it hath beene sundry times publickly acted in London by the right honorable the Earle of Nottingham, Lord High Admirall his servantes. By George Chapman : Gentleman. Imprinted at London for William Jones, dwelling at the signe of the Gun, neere Holburne Conduict, 1598.

The manuscript from which Jones printed was presumably a stage copy, as is shown by the careful stage-directions—see, for example, those on pp. 12, 16, 34 and 39. The original version seems to have been heavily cut in this manuscript, for the printed play contains only about 1,600 lines, and the omissions are such as to render the serious

---

[1] The ascription to Chapman of *Two Italian Gentlemen*, entered in the Stationers' Register, November 12, 1584, and of *The Disguises*, a lost play, mentioned by Henslowe under the date of October 2, 1595, will be discussed in the third volume of this edition. Mr. Crawford assigns the first of these to Chapman on the strength of a quotation from the play in Allot's *England's Parnassus*. See *Notes on the Malone Society's Publications*, 1910. Mr. Fleay (*Biog. Chron.*, vol. i, p. 57) takes *The Disguises* to be an early version of Chapman's *May-Day*; Lee (*French Renaissance*, p. 420, *n.*) with more probability a translation of Godard's *Les Desguisez*.

[2] Perhaps to make room for Chapman's next comedy, *An Humourous Day's Mirth*, called by Henslowe *The Comody of Umers*, see below, p. 685.

part of the play almost unintelligible. It is plain, as we may learn from the advertisement of the title-page, that it was the farcical scenes, in which the beggar displayed ' his variable humours in disguised shapes ', and not the romantic story of Aegiale and Cleanthes, which caught the fancy of the public. It is not unlikely that the former scenes have been enlarged beyond their original form ; it is certain that the latter have been cut down. As a consequence the play, as it now stands, totally lacks unity, coherence, and proportion. That the author is to be charged with this lack appears to me more than doubtful.

Nothing is known of any source whence Chapman may have derived the incidents of this play. It is likely enough, as Koeppel[1] says, that the various disguises of the hero may be original with Chapman, although disguises and their consequent misunderstandings were a stock feature of Italian comedy, with which Chapman was familiar ;[2] but it seems likely that some source must have existed for the romantic story of the play. I am inclined to think that the names of the leading characters, Cleanthes, Aegiale, Aspasia, Doricles, and some of the place names,[3] Corrucus, Phasiaca, Bebritia, point to the field of late Greek romance as the original source. Certain incidents of the main plot, the adulterous passion of Aegiale[4] for Cleanthes, her false denunciation of him to the king, the magic of Hella, the sorceress, the transformation of Diones into a tree, the mysterious connexion between a branch of this tree and the life of the king, all seem to me to point in the same direction. It is possible, I believe, to reconstruct the original story, at least in its main outline, and I shall attempt to do so here, with the hope that this may lead some day to the discovery of the source which Chapman used.

Queen Aegiale of Egypt, wedded to the old King Ptolemy, falls madly in love with Cleanthes, the most famous warrior of the kingdom (cf. *sc.* viii, ll. 11–12). To make the way clear to her goal she murders his wife. Cleanthes learns of this and rejects the advances of the Queen, who thereupon denounces him to Ptolemy as having made love to her. Cleanthes is banished, but returns in disguise and persuades the Queen to cut off and burn a branch of the tree into which her son had been transformed by a sorceress. This she does in the hope of bringing about her husband's death and so winning Cleanthes for a husband. Ptolemy, it appears, had been advised by an oracle that if he married his daughter, Aspasia, to Prince Doricles of Arcadia, he would conquer four neighbouring kingdoms. Cleanthes prevents the marriage by slaying Doricles, and, soon after Ptolemy's death in battle against the four kings who have invaded Egypt, weds Aspasia, defeats the invaders, and becomes king. Aegiale in despair puts an end to herself.

Most of this story, as the reader will see, is contained, or implied in the play, but the conclusion is badly marred. Both Aspasia and

---

[1] *Quellen-Studien zu den Dramen Chapmans*, 1897, p. 2.

[2] See below, pp. 732–3.

[3] See the notes on these names, pp. 678, 679 below. Irus, the name assumed by Cleanthes when disguised as the beggar, is, of course, from Homer, *Odyssey*, XVIII ; the Spaniard, Bragadino, is the Miles Gloriosus of Latin and Italian comedy ; but these names give us no clue to the source of the main plot.

[4] Koeppel (*loc. cit.*, p. 2) points out the general likeness between Aegiale and the Phaedra of Euripides.

Aegiale disappear from the action before the close of the play, but we are entitled, I think, to assume from scene ix that Cleanthes slew Doricles in order to win Aspasia and the kingdom, and a death like Phaedra's seems the only fitting termination of Aegiale's career. The original story, if this reconstruction at all fairly represents it, contained striking dramatic possibilities, and one can only regret that Chapman marred it by the introduction of an absurd and coarse farce, the adventures of the disguised Cleanthes, which proved so successful with the audiences of the Rose that it finally crowded the romantic original wholly into the background. One can hardly believe that the present abrupt and unsatisfactory close of the play is due to Chapman, for the veriest tyro of a playwright would have recognized the necessity of disposing in some fashion of Aegiale and Aspasia. That nothing of the sort occurs in the play as it now stands is probably to be attributed to omissions by the actors rather than to Chapman's original neglect.

If this hypothesis, that the printed play rests upon a stage version which was in many respects a perversion of the original, be correct, it is evident that no criticism of the play in its present form can have much value. It is fruitless to denounce it with Swinburne [1] as a ' crude and graceless piece of work ' unless we could recover the source and see how far Chapman was responsible for the clumsy handling of the plot. It may, however, be of some use in determining the characteristics of Chapman as a comic writer to point out, even in this presumably mutilated version of his first remaining play, his recognition of the value of lively and continuous action. Taken simply as farce, there is undeniable value in such a scene as that of Count Hermes' encounter with the valiant Spaniard Bragadino, and in the double intrigue of Cleanthes, in his double rôle of Hermes and Leon, with his pair of wives. The characterization is of the slightest ; whatever traits Chapman may originally have given to the tragic figure of Aegiale have been quite obliterated in the alterations. Most of the figures in the play are mere puppets ; but Cleanthes has something of the energy, ingenuity, and calm disregard of moral scruples, which marks, as a rule, the intriguer in Chapman's comedies, the character who sets the action in motion and moves the others as he pulls the strings, Lemot, for example, in *An Humourous Day's Mirth*, Rinaldo in *All Fools*, and Tharsalio in *The Widow's Tears*. Pego is the first sketch of the buffoon which Chapman elaborated later in Sir Giles Goosecap and in Poggio, a character doubtless more effective on the stage than in the study.

The comic scenes are for the most part written in a lively, vigorous and idiomatic prose. The metrical scenes show Chapman already master of a blank verse infinitely superior as a means of dramatic expression to the rhymed couplets and stanzaic forms in which his earlier poems, *The Shadow of Night*, 1594, *Ovid's Banquet* and *The Amorous Zodiac*, 1595, had been written. Swinburne notes ' a faint echo ' of Marlowe in the better passages, and it is clear, that Marlowe served as Chapman's model for blank verse. It is plain, I think, that the blank verse of this comedy, even at its best, as in the description of the jewels in scene v, represents an earlier and less independent treatment of this metre than we find in his first remaining tragedy,

[1] *George Chapman*, p. 44.

Bussy D'Ambois, and so furnishes a further argument against those [1] who would carry back the date of that tragedy to 1595-6. To me, at least, it is difficult to account for the difference between the weighty, sententious, and involved verse of *Bussy*, and the light, simple, and sometimes flat, style of the *Blind Beggar* except on the hypothesis of a considerable time spent by the poet in the practice of this form of versification. *Bussy* gives us the definitely formed style of Chapman, at least for his tragedies; the *Blind Beggar* presents the work of a follower of Marlowe. The two can hardly have been contemporaneous.

Chapman, however, is no blind imitator of Marlowe. There is plain in this play, I think, an effort on his part to restrain and temper the super-abundant energy and over-elaborate ornamentation of much of his master's verse, and thus to render it a fitter medium for the action and dialogue of comedy. It is one of Chapman's great merits, imperfectly recognized hitherto, that he developed the blank verse of comedy along lines which made it later, in the hands of Middleton, Fletcher, and others, such a perfect medium of expression, rising to heights of lyric beauty and sinking to the level of conversational give-and-take, as the situation demanded. Chapman reaches his highest point in this development, I think, in the verse scenes of *Monsieur D'Olive* and *The Gentleman Usher*, but we may note his first attempt at this remodelling of Marlowe's blank verse in *The Blind Beggar*. And this is only one of several reasons which seem to me to demand for this play, crude, imperfect, and sadly mutilated as it is, a somewhat more respectful consideration than it has hitherto received.

Addendum.—In the thesis of M. Schoell, mentioned in the preface, which came into my hands after these pages were in type, attention is called to Edward Pudsey's MS. book of Shakespearian extracts, reprinted in *Stratford-on-Avon Note-books*, No. 1. In this MS. under the heading of *Irus* there occur six quotations, five of which may be found, in a slightly altered form, in *The Blind Beggar*, viz., sc. i, ll. 337-8; sc. iii, ll. 99-104; sc. v, l. 2; sc. vii., l. 43, and ll. 97-8. The sixth does not appear in the printed play, but was probably |taken from a MS. copy, other and presumably fuller than that sent to the printer. This contemporary book of extracts thus furnishes another proof that the play, as we have it, is only an imperfect copy of Chapman's work.

M. Schoell mentions as parallels to the Cleanthes-Aegiale story two Italian *novelle : Il Pecorone* XXIII, 2, and Straparola, *Notte* IV, Fav. 1. The similarity between the stories and the play is so slight, and the *motif* common to both so ancient and widespread that I do not think either tale can be regarded as a source of the play ; still less can a story from the *Heptameron*, (Nov. 8) for the behaviour of Cleanthes to his wives. M. Schoell further points out some interesting parallels between this play and Day and Chettle's *Blind Beggar of Bednal Green*, 1600, especially in Act IV. of the latter play, where Momford, like Irus, makes use of his double personality to appear as a witness on his own behalf. There can be little doubt that Day or Chettle borrowed this incident from Chapman's play.

---

[1] Schelling, *Elizabethan Drama*, vol. i, p. 414 ; vol. ii, p. 548, is the latest critic to support this view.

THE BLIND BEGGAR OF ALEXANDRIA

i, 8. *Where art thou become :* what is become of thee. For similar forms compare *All Fools*, V, ii, 5, and Greene's *Alphonsus of Aragon, Prologue,* l. 54 :

> *Where be thy scholars now become, I trow ?*

and II, i, 434-5 :

> *Where is the knight become*
> *Which made the blood besprinkle all the place ?*

i, 43. The *Duke*. Ptolemy, the ruler of Egypt, is here called *Duke*, elsewhere *King*. See iii, 29 ; iv, 114 ; vi, 11 ; viii, 3 ; ix, 20 ; and x, 39. Probably the title *Duke* in this line is a mere mistake due to haste on the part of the author, or to a carelessness on that of the printer ; but I have preferred not to alter the original text.

i, 85-6. These lines, with the exception of the first word in l. 85, are quoted under the head of *Wisedome* in R. Allot's compilation, *England's Parnassus*, 1600, and correctly assigned to G. Chapman.

i, 109. With these words Irus throws off his disguise, and appears as Cleanthes.

i, 160. May one not suspect this line to be a good-natured parody of the first line of one of the most famous passages in Marlowe, 1 *Tamburlaine*, V, i, 160 :

> *What is beauty saith my sufferings then ?*

i, 176. *For to know :* this archaic form of the infinitive is found four times in this play, *viz.* in iii, 52, viii, 19, and ix, 119, as well as the present line. When I remarked, in my note on *Alphonsus*, II, ii, 314, that I had not noticed any instances of this form in Chapman, I had forgotten this early comedy.

i, 183-4. *Abraham's asses' catalogue of coxcombs.* There is probably a reference here to the Abraham-men, or discharged bedlamites, with whom England was then infested. A good description of these 'mad rascals' is given by Dekker in *The Bellman of London* (p. 98, Temple Classics edition). The *asses* and *coxcombs* of our text would be those who were imposed upon by these sturdy beggars. See also Text Notes, p. 682.

i, 193. *A [b]one in your belly :* a child in your womb. I owe this emendation and explanation to Mr. Brereton. See Text Notes, p. 682.

i, 232. *So it doth become :* this fashion is becoming to you.

i, 238-40. This speech, as well as ll. 267-69 below, is spoken aside. Cf. ll. 241 and 271.

i, 298. *Without all cry :* beyond all measure. The phrase *out of*, or *without, all cry*, is not uncommon in Elizabethan English. It may mean either beyond all dispute, or, as here, beyond measure. See Nash, *Works*, vol. i, p. 327, McKerrow's edition.

i, 308. *Nuptial rosemary and thyme :* rosemary, the emblem of constancy, was constantly used in garlands at weddings (cf. *Sir Giles Goosecap*, V, ii, 387) ; thyme as a symbol of sweetness was also in request on such occasions.

i, 356. *Recorder.* 'The Recorder was originally a person with legal knowledge appointed by the mayor and aldermen to record or keep in mind the proceedings of their courts and the customs of the city.'—*New English Dictionary.*

ii, 10. *Patch that I am :* fool that I am. Cf. *Comedy of Errors*, III, i, 32 :

> *Mome, malthorse, capon, coxcomb, idiot, patch.*

Chapman uses this term, of course, for the sake of the play on words which is continued in l. 13.

---

[1] As this play is not divided into acts, the references are by scene and line.

ii, 37. *Bonaventure:* an obscure word of which the *New English Dictionary* gives but this single instance, assigning with some hesitation the meaning of ' adventurer ' to it. The same dictionary gives also a single instance of *boneventor*, perhaps the same word, which occurs in *Five Years King James* in *Harleian Misc.*, V, 351, where it occurs in connexion with ' roaring-boys ', ' bravadoes ', and other such terms of reproach.

ii, 51. *Rifle for her:* put her up as a prize to gamble, or raffle for ; cf. like uses of the phrase in Dekker, *Northward Ho* (*Dramatic Works*, vol. iii, p. 74), and *Lanthorn and Candle Light* (*Prose Works*, vol. iii, p. 276).

ii, 62–63. *Great elixir, or golden medicine:* the elixir was the essence sought for by the alchemists which had the property of turning baser metals into gold, hence *golden medicine*. It was often conceived of as taking the form of a stone, hence *Philosopher's* (i.e. alchemist's) *stone*. See below, l. 68.

ii, 91. *Handy dandy:* an old child's game, known at least in the age of Chaucer, in which an object was passed rapidly from one hand to the other of one player, and the other player was bidden to guess in which hand it remained. The words, *prickly prandy*, are a mere rhyming refrain, one of several, as *Jack-a-dandy*, *sugar candy*, etc., often accompanying this game.

ii, 95. *Bite your thumbs:* to bite the thumb *at* any one was considered an insult (see *Romeo and Juliet*, I, i, 41, *sqq.*), but the thumb was also bitten as a mark of vexation and shame. See *Dick of Devonshire*, IV, iii (Bullen, *Old Plays*, vol. ii, p. 80), where a beaten Spaniard leaves the stage, *biting his thumb*.

ii, 105–6. Cf. below, iii, 22–27.

ii, 120. *Corrucus:* this name is possibly a form of Corycos, a town in Cilicai, mentioned by Pliny, V, 22, i. See also Servius on Virgil, *Georgics* IV, 127.

ii, 123. *Without more ado:* a pun on the double *adieu* of the Spaniard in l. 121.

ii, 134. *Noise of musicians:* band of musicians.

ii, 138. *Spagnolo, [pr]esto:* Spaniard, quick. See Text Notes, p. 682.

iii, 12. *Four neighbour kings:* cf. scene viii.

iii, 33. ' Of whom I will feign to have had an unexpected sight '.

iii, 66. *These three things across:* with these words the maid probably lays three things, knives, or sprays of flowers, crosswise on the table for good luck.

iii, 80. *Hoise my gait:* lift up my steps, i.e. walk in an affected high-stepping manner.

iii, 130. *The fig I eat:* perhaps the sense is that the sweet taste of the fig prevents the eater from distinguishing the flavour of the wine.

iv, Stage-direction. *With sound*, i.e. to the sound of music.

iv, 14. After this line Aspasia and her attendants apparently leave the stage.

iv, 28. Evidently something has been lost after this line. See Text Notes, p. 682.

iv, 121. This line is an evident ' gag ' addressed to the audience.

Scene v. There is a distinct likeness between Elimine's behaviour to her sisters in the early part of this scene, and Gertrude's treatment of her sister and mother in *Eastward Ho*, I, ii. Cf. ll. 7 and 30–31 of this scene with *Eastward Ho*, I, ii, 43–4, and Elimine's insistence on taking precedence of her sister, l. 6 with Gertrude's words to her mother, *Eastward Ho*, I, ii, 105–7.

v, 7. *What skill:* what matters it. *Call sisters:* call each other sisters.

v, 37–9. Cf. the pet names addressed by the citizen to his wife in *The Knight of the Burning Pestle: cony* (*Induction*, l. 47) ; *mouse*, I, ii, 20 ; *chicken*, I, ii, 26 ; *lamb*, I, ii, 28 ; etc.

v, 45–51. *Ariadne's crown:* the constellation *Corona Borealis*, also known as *Ariadne's Crown*. *Diana* is one of the names given by Latin authors to the constellation *Virgo*. *Berenice's everburning hair:* the constellation, *Coma Berenices*, named after Berenice, wife of Ptolemy Euergetes. She dedicated a lock of her hair for the safe return of her husband from an expedition. It was stolen from the temple, and a flattering astronomer reported that it had been changed into this constellation.

Andromeda . . . Perseus: the reference in each case is to the constellation, or *asterism,* l. 53, so named.

v, 54–56. The first instance in Chapman's plays of a simile which in varied forms occurs several times. Cf. *Byron's Conspiracy,* III, i, 6–17, and V, ii, 71–78.

v, 65. *I shall be sped:* I shall obtain my desire.

v, 78. *My mistress:* Druso is the servant of Samathis, now the wife of Leon.

vi, 16. *The branch.* Cf. below, ll. 43–5 and 54–7.

vi, 36. *God's angel:* i.e. God's messenger of death. This expression seems to have amused Dekker, who appears to parody it twice, in *Satiromastix* (*Dramatic Works,* vol. i, p. 193), *bv this candle which is none of God's angels,* and in *Northward Ho* (*Ibid.* vol. iii, p. 26), *by this iron which is none o' God's angel.*

vii, 1–3. 'Do you reckon to levy, or seize upon husbands because you are a countess? Have you a royal license to do so?' The *broad seal* is the Great Seal of England such as would be affixed to any special license to seize upon goods. Cf. Jonson's coinage of a verb from this phrase in *Cynthia's Revels,* V, iii :

Thy presence broadseals our delights for pure.

vii, 11. *There you lay:* where you lay.

vii, 21. *Short-heels:* used like the more familiar *light-heels* as a term of reproach for a wanton; cf. *The Widow's Tears,* III, i, 152.

vii, 43. Cf. *Sir Giles Goosecap,* V, ii, 355 :

Thou pom'roy, or thou apple of mine eye.

vii, 64, 65. The same play on words appears in *Bussy D'Ambois,* III, ii, 152–3.

vii, 75. *Shooting a cockhye:* the *New English Dictionary* gives only this one example of the word *cockhye,* and declares that the sense is uncertain. It appears to be some sort of an arrow.

vii, 97–8. *His moveables:* cf. *Sir Giles Goosecap,* III, ii, 73–5

vii, 114. *Count ass:* i.e. countess. This sort of pun found peculiar favour with the older Elizabethan dramatists. In his note on *Satiromastix,* l. 77 (*Materialien zur Kunde,* vol. xx) Dr. Scherer calls attention to similar puns by Jonson and Dekker : *Aristarchus—or stark ass* (*Every Man Out, Induction,* Mermaid edition, vol. i, p. 122) and *Crispinus, that Crispin-ass* (Dekker, *Dramatic Works,* vol. i, p. 212). I cannot agree with Dr. Scherer that *Maecenasses* (*Satiromastix,* l. 1,680) is another example of this pun.

vii, 123–4. *Say black is mine eye:* the phrase means 'to bring a charge of misconduct against me'. The *New English Dictionary* gives examples of this phrase from an early sixteenth century satire down to *Tom Jones* (Book IX, chap. iv). There is an interesting parallel to the present instance in Fletcher's *Love's Cure,* III, i : *I can say black's your eye, though it be grey.*

viii. Stage-direction. The name *Phasiaca* appears to be coined from Phasis, a town in ancient Colchis on the river of the same name, which was regarded in ancient times as the boundary between Asia and Europe. The name *Bebritia* seems to be a distortion, possibly due to a mere misprint, for Bebrycia, an ancient name for Bithynia. It is interesting to note that both these names seem to hark back to the legend-cycle of the Argonauts.

ix, 24–33. These lines are evidently one of the many variations played on Marlowe's theme of *The Passionate Shepherd.* See Bullen's edition of Marlowe, vol. iii, pp. 283–92.

ix, 49. This line reappears in *The Poetaster,* III, i, where it is spouted by one of Tucca's boys who are exhibiting their histrionic powers before the actor to whom Tucca wishes to hire them out. Mr. Boas in his edition of Kyd, p. 400, sees in the *Poetaster* passage a parody of a famous situation in the *Spanish Tragedy* at the beginning of II, v ; but the line in question does not appear in Kyd's play, and as Belimperia is hurried off the stage before the entrance of Hieronimo no such question could have been addressed to her. The situation in *The Blind Beggar* is so different from that in the *Spanish Tragedy* that we need not suppose that Chapman is in any way imitating Kyd. It seems plain that Jonson in the *Poetaster* was having a laugh at one of the early extravagancies of his friend Chapman. The laugh is repeated in *Eastward Ho*, II, i, 110, where the drunken Quicksilver spouts this line, slightly altered, among other tag-ends of old plays. Mr. Bullen and Professor Schelling in their editions of *Eastward Ho* both take it that Quicksilver is quoting from the *Spanish Tragedy*, though admitting that the line in question does not appear in any extant version of that play.

ix, 86. *Caspia :* the context shows that this is the name of an Egyptian city, but none such is known to classical geography.

ix, 102. *Serian groves :* possibly there may be here some reference to the Serapium in Alexandria.

x, 31–2. *Widows of the beggar and the King :* i.e. the deserted wives of him who was Irus the beggar and is now King of Egypt, *both their husbands*, l. 32, Leon and Count Hermes, being metamorphosed into Cleanthes.

x,·43. Schoell points out that this line is an echo of Kyd:

> *The hopeless father of a hapless son.*
> > *Spanish Tragedy*, IV, iv, 83.

x, 66. *The slaughter of the Count :* i.e. the murder of Doricles by the Count.

x, 71. The reader will be at once reminded of Portia's famous plea for mercy, especially of the lines :

> *And earthly power doth then show likest God's*
> *When mercy seasons justice.*

There is, however, a still closer parallel in a play sometimes ascribed to Shakespeare. Queen Philippa, pleading with her husband for the burghers of Calais, says :

> *And kings approach the nearest unto God*
> *By giving life and safety unto men.*
> > *Edward III*, V, i, 41–2.

Professor Sonnenschein (*The Times*, Literary Supplement, September 16, 1904, and elsewhere) has pointed out that Portia's speech is based upon Seneca's *De Clementia*. The only sentence in that treatise which bears any close resemblance to the line in Chapman occurs in I, xix, 9 : *Non proximum eis [deis] locum tenet is qui se ex deorum natura gerit beneficus et largus et in melius potens?* There is a much closer verbal analogy in Cicero, *Pro Ligario*, xii, 38 : *Homines enim ad deos nulla re proprius accedunt quam salutem hominibus dando.* Both Cicero and Seneca draw upon what Professor Sonnenschein has called ' the common stock of Stoic maxims', and Chapman, borrowing the general idea from them, has given it a form of his own.

x, 76. *Ambo :* i.e. both women, Elimine and Samathis.

x, 101. *In this taking :* in this plight, referring to her pregnancy. The phrase occurs again in *All Fools*, V, i, 17, *The Gentleman Usher*, III, ii, 226, and e'sewhere.

x, 123. *Has the sweet of them :* excels them. I do not recall any other use of this phrase, but the meaning is plain from the context.

x, 127. *This :* i.e. Samathis with whom Bion has fallen in love.

x, 130. Cf. *Who ever lov'd, that lov'd not at first sight ?*
> > *Hero and Leander*, I, 176.

x, 161. *The blackest is the fairest :* cf. the proverb ' Black is a pearl in a woman's eye', which appears in *An Humourous Day's Mirth*, viii, 225, and *Sir Giles Goosecap*, III, i, 268.

x, 165. *Horns.* The allusion is to the horns of a cuckold which Pego thinks Elimine will bestow upon black Porus and so complete his resemblance to the devil.

x, 176–7. An echo from Marlowe :

> *With full Natolian bowls*
> *Of Greekish wine now let us celebrate*
> *Our happy conquest.*
> > *2 Tamburlaine*, II, iii, 45–7.

TEXT NOTES

The Blind Beggar of Alexandria was first printed in 1598. There are two copies of this, the first quarto and only old edition, at the Bodleian Library, Malone 240, and Malone 163, and two at the British Museum, C. 12. g. 4 and C. 34. c. 11. The last of these four shows a few trifling differences from the others, which I have pointed out in the notes; but on the whole the copies agree very closely.

It was not reprinted until 1873, when it appeared in *The Comedies and Tragedies of George Chapman*,[1] as the first play in the first volume. This, barring one or two slight errors and a couple of silent corrections of misprints in the original, is an exact reprint of the quarto. I refer to this edition as P.

It was next printed in 1874 in a modernised form with a few emendations in *The Works of Chapman* (vol. i—*Plays*), edited by R. H. Shepherd. I refer to this edition as S. No other edition of the play has appeared, so far as I am aware, until the present.

The text of *The Blind Beggar* is far from satisfactory. The quarto seems to have been printed from a stage copy which had been very considerably abbreviated. In one place at least, sc. iv, l. 28, there is an evident hiatus, and there are numerous places where the text is plainly corrupt. Verse is sometimes printed as prose, and the punctuation is perhaps more confusing than usual in the old texts. There is no division into acts or scenes, and no list of the numerous characters who appear in the play. On the whole it is, quite apart from its aesthetic and ethical deficiencies, a rather unsatisfactory play to read in the old copies, nor does Shepherd's edition do much to help it. I have made an honest effort to render it more intelligible to the reader, not only by modernising the spelling and punctuation, but by dividing it into scenes, giving a list of the *dramatis personae*, and by emending so far as possible the corruptions of the text. All departures from the original, except changes of spelling and punctuation, are recorded in the notes that follow.

Scene i, l. 51. Q. *off.* S. emends *oft.*

55. S. puts a comma after *then*, thus making two questions. But the second *what* may well be equivalent to *that*, in which case no punctuation is needed. I have preferred to keep the old reading.

63–4. The parentheses are mine.

81. Q. *count.* A manuscript note in one of the British Museum copies, C. 34. c. 11, alters to *Court* which is no doubt correct, although S. retains *Count*, apparently believing that the ruler of Egypt is called *Count* here as he is called *Duke* in l. 43 above.

82. Q. *Toples*, printing in italics as if a proper name.

86. The Qq. in the Bodleian have the misprint *eathlye*; the British Museum copies have correctly *earthlye.*

96–97. Q. *To him that succours him, Ile threaten death, But he that doth not threaten him shall die,*

This is evidently corrupt. Deighton (*Old Dramatists*, p. 127) proposes to alter *succours* to *threatens* in l. 96, and *threaten* to *succour* in l. 97. The second of the changes seems necessary, and had already been made by S. The first, however, shows that Deighton misunderstood the passage. The Queen proposes to follow the advice of Irus (cf. l. 70), but says in an aside that she will punish with death those who obey her command. I have indicated this aside by placing ll. 97–8 in parenthesis.

120. Q. *noble men.* S. emends.

126. In the stage-direction after this line Q. has *Samaphis.* The spelling of this name evidently puzzled the old printer; on p. 16, l. 53 we get the form *Psamathis*, a form nearer to the Greek proper name, Psamathe, from which this name is probably derived. I have used throughout the usual form of the Q. *Samathis.*

[1] Published by John Pearson, London, 1873.

137-8. One line in Q.

147. Q. prints *that* as the last word of l. 146.

169. *lea[v]e.* Q. *leane,* a misprint which P. silently corrects.

171-3. Q. prints as two lines ending *on the* and *pray.*

184. Q. *asses, Catalog.* S. corrects.

186. Q. prints *who could have* as the last words of l. 185, putting no punctuation mark between *all* and *who.* S. corrects.

193. Q. *alone in.* Brereton, *Modern Language Review,* October, 1907, emends *a bone in,* calling attention to the phrase to *breed young bones,* i.e. to be pregnant, which occurs in the old *King Leir,* (reprint issued by the Malone Society, l. 844,) and in *The Broken Heart,* II, i, 142.

197-200. Q. prints as prose.

204-207. Q. prints as prose.

211. Q. prints *now* as last word of l. 210.

220-1. Q. prints as one line.

232. Q. has no punctuation in this line. I put a comma after *better,* but it might be placed after *so* with quite as good sense.

247. Q. *hart;* S. *heart.*

256. Q. prints *descend* as last word of l. 255.

257. Q. reads *woe, you choose.*

280. Q. misprints *rihcest.* P. silently corrects.

324-5. Q. prints as one line.

338. Q. reads *humor and this gowne.* Brereton (*loc. cit.*) suggests a period after *humor,* but I think a semi-colon is sufficient.

345-7. Q. prints as prose, and has *Aleantisthenes* in l. 345. S. corrects to *Antisthenes ;* cf. sc. iv. l. 40.

Scene ii, ll. 9-13. Q. prints as four lines ending, *eye, cloth, velvet patch,* and *better.* In l. 11 Q. has *a fustian;* S. alters *a* to *of,* but this does not seem necessary.

15-16. Q. divides into one long and one short line, ending *love,* and *straight.* P. arranges as in the text.

44-5. Q. *solid or firme fayth ;* but *fayth* is evidently an exclamation.

74-5. Q. *in sophistical . . . span-*

iard a borne. Brereton (*loc. cit.*) emends the latter phrase to *a Spaniard born.*

188. Q. *spaniola questo, questo, spaniola questo.* S. follows Q., but the passage is plainly corrupt. The presence of *presto* in l. 133 points to the necessary emendation.

Scene iii, l. 7. Q. *that.* P. misprints *thar.*

11. Q. *fosaken ;* S. corrects.

14-16. Q. prints as two lines of prose. For *pride* in l. 16 we might perhaps read *prime,* but I prefer not to alter the text.

17. Q. *our.* S. emends *your.*

23. Q. *ceaselesse.* P. misprints *cealesse.*

28. Q. *am I.* S. alters to *I am.*

35. After *find* we might perhaps supply *it.*

46. Q. prints *he fled* as the last words of l. 45.

63-4. Q. prints as one line.

65. Q. prints as two lines, ending *true* and *good.*

87. P. omits *be* in this line.

94-5. Q. prints as one line.

103-4. Q. prints as one line.

114. Q. *cuppe.* Perhaps we should read *cups.*

118. Q. reads *What frollicke love mirth.* S. puts a comma after *frolic,* but I think the word is an interjection, and punctuate accordingly.

Scene iv, l. 13. Q. *game ;* possibly we should read *games.*

23. Q. *merites,* which may be either singular or plural. I follow S. in printing *merit's.*

28. There is no break in Q. after this line ; but a verb of which *Love* is the subject is evidently wanting. Perhaps only a line such as

Has bent his bow and shot his fiery darts

or

Shoots darts of hot and passionate desire has dropped out. But this is mere conjecture.

41 44. Q. prints as five lines ending *Leon, Burgomaister, on the, moveables,* and *Leon.*

63-65. Q. ends these lines with *foure, statute,* and *denies.* I am inclined to think that *only* in l. 63 has crept in by mistake, perhaps from l. 65. Possibly we should arrange as four lines ending *him, receive, in,* and *denies.* This would give us one short line, but these are common in this play.

79. Deighton (*loc. cit.*), p. 127, omits *other,* calling attention to the repetition of this line in this shortened form in l. 178 below. This is a plausible conjecture, but the metre is so irregular in much of this play that it seems idle to emend here and there to restore it, and the line is quite intelligible as it stands.

83-89. Q. assigns this speech to *Gen.* i.e. *Gentleman.* This can only be Euribates, the friend of Antisthenes, to whom Q. assigns ll. 137 and 145-8.

87-89. Q. ends these lines with *forhead, wittnesse,* and *woorde.* I follow Brereton's suggestion in printing *A hellish conscience* as a short line.

95. *Well known.* Q. prints as the first words of l. 96.

139-141. Q. prints as prose.

162-3. Q. prints as one line.

185-7. Q. assigns this speech to *Euge.,* apparently a combination of *Eu*[*ribates*] and *Ge*[*ntleman*].

Scene v, ll. 1-4. Q. prints as prose. In l. 4 Q. has no punctuation. S. follows Q.; but *what* seems to be an ejaculation, and *woman* directly addressed to *Martia.*

44. *With.* Q. *Which,* a not uncommon misprint, which S. corrects.

47. Q. *fingers of Diana;* I emend to *figure,* a change which Mr. Daniel informs me he had long ago made in his copy of the play.

55. I am inclined to think we should read *the* for *their.*

71. *My husband makes.* Q. prints as the first words of l. 72.

81. Q. *To have a graces from thy summer darted.* This is unintelligible. I follow Deighton (*loc. cit.*), p. 127, in transposing *graces* and *summer.*

104. Q. *the choice.* So S.; but on the strength of l. 107, I prefer to read *thy choice.*

130. P. omits the second *as* in this line.

146-7. Q. prints as one line.

154. Q. reads *without a health.* S. properly omits *a.*

Scene vi. In the stage-direction at the beginning of the scene Q. misprints *wiuh,* which P. silently corrects to *with.*

l. 31-2. Q. *hate me not for love, and it is not lust hath.* P. inserts *that* after *lust* without any authority, and S. follows P. I suggest placing a semi-colon after *not,* shifting *and* to follow *is,* and placing a comma after *is.* This seems to me to make the passage intelligible with the minimum of change.

78. Perhaps we should read *this branch;* cf. l. 55 above.

Scene vii, l. 7. Q. *woman.* S. corrects.

24. Q. *Heare you Usurers wife stay.* S. alters to *Here, you usurer's wife, stay;* but I think no change is needed except commas after *you* and *wife.*

Scene ix, l. 50. Q. *weedes.* Brereton (*loc. cit.*) emends *meads.*

85-8. Q. assigns this speech to *Cl.,* i.e. *Clearchus,* one of the lords who attends Ptolemy. Cf. the stage-direction at the beginning of sc. iv. His entrance is not noted in the Q., but he must have come in with Ptolemy after l. 55. S. assigns the speech to Euribates.

105. Q. *mimphick.* S. emends *Memphic.*

121-8. Q. prints as prose, and does not indicate the speakers.

133-4. Q. prints as two short lines ending *maister* and *woord.* The passage seems to me to be prose.

Scene x, l. 10. P. misprints *aud* for Q. *and.*

99. In the stage-direction after this line Q. reads *with a child.* It is plain from ll. 105-107 that the child is yet unborn. Cf. the direction after l. 30 above.

113-115. Q. prints as prose.

124. The words *for him* are evidently interpolated, perhaps as a 'gag'. The rhyme shows that the line should end with *grace.*

138. Q. *my loving joy.* This is unintelligible. I suggest *my loves* (i.e. the women whom he has loved) *enjoy.*

AN HUMOUROUS DAY'S MIRTH

INTRODUCTION

ON May 11, 1597, when the Admiral's Men were playing at Henslowe's theatre, The Rose, the old entrepreneur entered in his diary
the receipt of a sum,[1] the exact amount of which we are unable to
determine, from the first performance of a play which he called *The
Comodey of Umers*. This play was formerly[2] identified with Jonson's
Every Man in his Humour; but since we have Jonson's own statement[3] that the latter was 'acted by the Lord Chamberlain's players
in 1598', it cannot be the same as the new play presented by the
Admiral's Men. Chapman is known to have been writing for the
Admiral's Men at this time, and his play, *An Humourous Day's Mirth*,
was in existence, and had been performed by them before March 10,
1598, when a reference is made to it in the 'inventory[4] of goods of My
Lord Admiral's Men' taken by Henslowe on that date. There is,
therefore, a high degree of probability, if not an absolute certainty,
that Chapman's play and *The Umers* are one and the same.

The new comedy seems to have been a fairly successful play. It
was performed a second time on May 19, and again on May 24 and 31;
on June 4, 7, 11, 17, and 21, and on July 7 and 13. After the gap in
Henslowe's *Diary* which extends from July 28 to October 11, two more
performances are recorded, one in October, another in November,
giving us thirteen in all. No further record remains, but another gap
in Henslowe's *Diary* occurs here, and it is by no means impossible that
the play was performed again in the winter season of 1597-8. In the
spring of 1598 Chapman was at work on another play[5] for the company.

---

[1] The entry reads: *ne. tt* [probably *rec'd* or *taken*] *at the comodey of umers*,
02-03-00-13-00.

[2] Malone, *Variorum Shakespeare*, vol. iii, p. 307; Gifford, *Jonson's Works*,
vol. i, p. xxv. It is unfortunate that Mr. Courthope (*History of English
Poetry*, vol. iv, p. 269) should have reproduced this now exploded error.

[3] On the title-page of this play in the Folio edition of his works in 1616.
That Jonson's statement cannot refer to the revised form of his play, which
we know from other sources to have been acted by the Chapel Children, is
shown by the title-page of the first quarto, 1601, which announces the play
'as it hath beene sundry times publickly acted by the right Honorable the
Lord Chamberlaine his servants'.

[4] Henslowe notes among the costumes belonging to the company 'Verones
sonnes hosse [hose],' and later under March 13, 'Labesya's [La Besha's] clocke
with gowlde buttenes'; see Collier, *Henslowe's Diary*, p. 272. Also under 'a
note of all such books as belong to the Stock' *The Umers*; see Collier, p. 276.
Henslowe's latest editor, Mr. Greg (*Henslowe's Diary*, pt. ii, p. 184) accepts
the identification of *The Umers* and Chapman's play as practically certain.

[5] 'Lent unto Mr. Chapmane the 16 of May 1598 in earneste of a boocke for
the companye xxxx[s] wittnes Wm. Birde'—Greg's *Henslowe's Diary*, p. 86.
Greg believes this payment to be for a play now lost, called later the *Isle of*

There is no entry in the Stationers' Registers for this play. Fleay, *London Stage*, p. 107, includes it in a list of plays which Henslowe paid for licensing for the press independently of the Stationers' Company. The inclusion of Chapman's play in this list, however, is purely conjectural, and Greg (*Henslowe's Diary*, pt. ii, pp. 113–6) has shown that the licenses were paid for leave to perform, not to print these plays. *An Humourous Day's Mirth* was first published in 1599 in quarto form with the following title-page :

> A plesant Comedy entituled :   *An Humerous ḍayes Myrth.*   As it hath been sundrie times publikely acted by the right honourable the Earle of Nottingham Lord high Admirall his servants.   By G.C.   At London.   Printed by Valentine Syms : 1599.

The state of the text would seem to show that this quarto was printed from a stage copy, and was not revised by the author.   Possibly the company sold it to Syms shortly after Chapman left [1] them for the Chapel Children.

No source is known for the plot of this play, and it may well be doubted if any exists.   Koeppel (*loc. cit.*, p. 3) has pointed out a certain similarity between the scene in which Lemot persuades Florilla to abandon her solitary life and prove her virtue amid the temptations of the court and a story [2] of Boccaccio's, *Decameron*, III, 5.   Possibly also, as Koeppel suggests, the melancholy humour of Dowsecer may be a reflection of the mood of Hamlet in the pre-Shakespearian play of that name.   But to point out such similarities is not to indicate a source or model for Chapman's play, and when we take into consideration the tenuity of plot and the superabundance of extraneous incident and humourous characterization in this comedy, it seems probable that Koeppel is justified in asserting that Chapman seems to have built it up independently of any source.   A brief analysis of the main action will, I think, make this clear.

The scene is laid in France, and the actors are for the most part courtiers in attendance upon an unnamed king.   Old Count Labervele is jealous of his wife, the young Countess Florilla, in spite of her assumption of a Puritanic strictness of manners.   The old Countess Moren is jealous of her young husband, and flies out at him on every faint suspicion that he is thinking of another woman.   Old Count Foyes is jealously watchful of his daughter, Martia, whom he wishes to marry to the rich fool La Besha, and whom, to that end, he secludes from all other company.   Lemot, the King's minion, who plays the principle part in the comedy, and who like the Vice in the old Moral plays is mischief-maker in general, begins a series of intrigues which lead to a complete entanglement of these various threads.   He easily persuades Florilla that she ought to prove the steadfastness of her virtue by exposing it to the temptations of the court, and induces her to give him an appointment at Verone's tavern, bringing with her Martia to meet

---

a Woman, or *The Fount of New Fashions.*   See entries for June 15 and September 31, 1598, and Greg's comment thereon in his edition of Henslowe, pt. ii, pp. 194 and 198.

[1] Chapman's name does not occur in Henslowe's *Diary* after July 17, 1599, and there is reason to believe that in 1600 or soon after Chapman was writing for the Chapel Children.   See below, p. 702.

[2] The resemblance is very slight.   Jonson's *The Devil is an Ass*, I, iv–vi, presents a much closer rendering of the Italian story.

the King, who has fallen in love with the latter lady. In the meantime the King and his courtiers visit Labervele to see the humour of Dowsecer, the Count's son by a former marriage, who has put on an antic disposition of philosophic melancholy. During this visit Dowsecer and Martia fall in love with each other, and Lemot secures permission from Countess Moren for her husband to dine at Verone's on the strict understanding that no ladies are to be of their party.

At the tavern Lemot induces Moren to take his place in a private room with the King and the two ladies. He then informs La Besha of Martia's presence in the tavern, and slips out to tell Countess Moren and Count Labervele of the behaviour of their respective partners. They appear at the tavern along with Foyes and La Besha, and thunder for admittance. The party of pleasure breaks up in confusion ; the King carries Martia off, Moren disguises himself to escape the wrath of his wife, and Florilla, after appealing in vain to the mocking Lemot for assistance, hurries home to don her Puritan attire, and to pretend that she has never left her private garden.

Not satisfied with the mischief he has wrought so far, Lemot now runs to the Queen and tells her that the King, after having carried Martia off, has been attacked by Dowsecer at the head of a band of ruffians threatening to mutilate him, and that he, Lemot, has been wounded in defending the King. Guided by Lemot, the Queen and her attendants hasten to the tavern to save the King. Here they are surprised first by the appearance of Dowsecer, who has come to rescue Martia from Moren, whom he supposed her ravisher, and then of the King himself with Martia on his arm. There is a general clearing-up of mistakes; Lemot is pardoned for his pranks because of his wit, Florilla appears in Puritan dress and forgives her husband for his suspicions, Dowsecer and Martia are united by the King, and the play ends with a pageant and lottery in the tavern, at which Moren is unmasked as one of the torch-bearers.

Such, in brief, is the main action of the play, complicated enough even in this simplified analysis. In the original it is almost impossible to follow, on account of the multiplicity of figures, the tangled threads of the action, the elaborate wit combats, and the scenes in which the diverse ' humours ' of the play are paraded for the entertainment of the audience. So frequent are these last scenes, that it seems no unfair assumption to suppose that the play was written mainly for their sake, and that action and dialogue were invented to display a series of comic character studies.

Herein lies, I think, the significance of this play of Chapman's in the development of English comedy. Plays of this type, which subordinate everything else to the portrayal of comic character, have received the technical name of the Comedy of Humours. Of this species Jonson is the supreme master. Miss Woodbridge in her interesting *Studies in Jonson's Comedy*, p. 41, contrasts his method with Shakespeare's, and points out that, whereas in Shakespeare the serious interest determines the main plot, and the comic interest is either relegated to the episodes or embodied in the treatment of the serious scenes, in Jonson the comic interest determines the main plot. ' He starts with his group of characters whose comic aspects he wished to bring out. To this end he invents situations for them, and by combining these situations he gets a plot for the comedy '. It has usually been assumed that Jonson was essentially the creator as well as the acknowledged master of the Comedy of Humours ; but in this play of Chapman's we have a work which corresponds almost to the letter with the definition of a typical Jonsonian comedy quoted above. Ward (*English Dramatic Literature*, vol. ii, p. 433) declares that we may see in this play the influence of Jonson ' with whose *Every Man in his Humour* it was nearly contemporaneous '. As a matter of fact, *An Humourous Day's Mirth* was on the stage of the Rose more than a year before Jonson's play was brought out by Shakespeare's [1] company. It is clear, I think, that the influence worked in the opposite direction from that which Dr. Ward suggests, and that it was this faulty but suggestive play of Chapman's which opened Jonson's eyes to his own peculiar vein and so led to the composition of *Every Man in his Humour* and Jonson's other comic masterpieces. Chapman and Jonson were for some years at least intimately associated. They collaborated in at least one play for the Rose,[2] and later in one for the Children [3] at Blackfriars, and possibly on one for the King's [4] men. They had many tastes in common, particularly their love for the classics, and, no doubt, mutually influenced each other. I shall have occasion hereafter to point out Jonson's influence on Chapman, but in this instance it seems clear that Chapman led the way.

This, however, is by no means equivalent to saying that Chapman's early comedy deserves to rank with Jonson's masterpieces. Swinburne [5] speaks of it as ' a crude and coarse sample of workmanship ', and calls the characters ' a confused crowd of rough sketches huddled together on a ragged canvass '. To this severe judgment we may, perhaps, note some exceptions. The workmanship is crude, no doubt, but it is markedly superior to that shown in *The Blind Beggar*. The characters are certainly huddled together. One of Chapman's persistent faults, in comedy as in tragedy, was his habit of cumbering the stage with superfluous figures. There are some twenty characters in *An Humourous Day's Mirth*, and most of these fully deserve Swinburne's strictures. It is one of the permanent excellencies of Jonson's comedy that his minor figures are for the most part as sharply drawn and as individual as the leading characters. But the minor figures of this play are mere puppets. It is impossible to distinguish between Colinet, Catalian, Rowley, and Berger. Blanuel's ' humour ' is elaborately displayed in one scene, and then apparently forgotten. Verone is a poor shadow of the bluff host who figures in so many Elizabethan comedies, or of his immortal prototype, Harry Bailey of *The Canterbury Tales*. Chapman, it is plain, had not that quick eye for eccentricities of character which was one of the greatest gifts of Jonson.

Yet it is easy to underrate Chapman's actual achievement in this

---

[1] Jonson's play was produced by the Lord Chamberlain's Men in 1598. A letter from Tobie Matthew to Dudley Carleton dated September 20, 1598, speaks of it as a new play at that date. See Castelain, *Ben Jonson*, p. 215, *n*.

[2] Henslowe paid Chapman £3 on October 23, 1598, for his ' play-book '—whatever that may mean—and ' two acts of a tragedy on Benjamin's plot'.

[3] *Eastward Ho* by Chapman, Jonson and Marston, produced by this company in 1605.

[4] *Sejanus*, 1603. Jonson's address to the reader, prefixed to the quarto of 1605, informs us that ' a second pen had good share ' in the play as acted, and calls his collaborator ' so happy a genius '. Shakespeare and Chapman have both been named as possible collaborators in *Sejanus*. The latter seems to me the likelier.

[5] *George Chapman*, p. 45.

play. The leading figures in the comedy are by no means rough
sketches. The character of the chief intriguer, Lemot, for example,
is clearly and fully developed. A witty and audacious courtier, fertile
in devices and excuses, he represents a distinct advance in individuality
upon the intriguing slave of Latin comedy, and points the way to the
gentlemanly intriguers of seventeenth century drama. It is interesting to note that Chapman has carefully kept him free from all taint
of self-interest or sensuality. Lemot loves mischief for its own sake,
and takes a purely intellectual pleasure in his intrigues. This is particularly remarkable in his affair with Florilla. One knows only too
well how a comic writer of the Restoration would have treated such
a theme.

La Besha, on the other hand, represents the nadir of intellectual
life. Like Chapman's later and more careful study of the type, Sir
Giles Goosecap, his ' humour ' consists in the utter absence of a sense
of perception, logic, or proportion. He is an overgrown child without
the child's sweetness or charm, and in his action in the play he appears
at every point as the blundering simpleton, the fool positive.

The figure of Dowsecer, the melancholic scholar, seems somewhat
out of place in Chapman's gallery of humorous portraits. Chapman
himself was too good a scholar to make a mock of scholarship or to
caricature the lover of antiquity as a mere pedant. And so the courtly
mob that comes to jest at Dowsecer remains to wonder at him ; the
King pronounces his ' humour ' a ' holy fury not a frenzy ', and Martia
loses her heart to him at first sight. The theme of the scholar converted to a lover is perhaps more fit for romantic than for satiric comedy,
and Chapman, who was later [1] to handle this theme with dignity and
grace, makes but little of it here. The love affair of Dowsecer and
Martia is crowded into the background by the various intrigues
and misunderstandings that centre round Verone's tavern.

The portraits of the unequally matched couples, on the contrary,
are sharply satiric. The old Countess is a virago who dominates her
young husband by sheer force of tongue. Moren is a slight, but distinct sketch of the cowed and hen-pecked husband. Old Labervele,
impotent alike in love and anger, is a full-length portrait of the uxorious
elder. His whole existence centres around his young wife, of whom
he is at once amorous and suspicious. He is busy, officious, and
prompt to outbursts of jealousy, but so completely enslaved that he
subsides into complacent satisfaction again at a mere word from his
wife.

The character of Florilla is Chapman's masterpiece in this play. I
cannot understand Swinburne's comment that her part comes to little
or nothing. It is true that the part is not elaborately developed ; the
action in which she figures is only one of the various threads of the
play, and almost disappears before the close in the motley web woven
by Lemot. But this action, so far as it goes, is well sustained and
satisfactorily concluded, and within its limits the portrait of Florilla
is perfect. Fair, young, and delicate, she professes a Puritan austerity
of morals, dresses more like a milkmaid than a Countess, and shows
the characteristic Puritan dislike of poetry, rich dress, courtly manners
and ancient beliefs. Below this surface severity, however, there lies,
as her husband truly suspects, an irresistible desire for the pleasures of

---

[1] In the story of Clarence and Eugenia in *Sir Giles Goosecap*.

youth and the gaieties of the court. She sees in Lemot a means of obtaining these objects of her desire, and listens to him as she would have listened to any other tempter who could have made her the same offers.   There is no struggle in her mind before yielding, nor any sense of shame when Lemot unmasks her hypocrisy, only an outburst of anger and a quick decision to resume her rôle of the Puritan. Her woman's wit enables her to do this, and to convict her doting husband of the ungrounded nature of his suspicions, for which in the end she forgives him with an air of virtuous superiority.   There is neither repentance nor change of character on her part.   The only lesson that she has learned from her adventure is to be somewhat more careful in her choice of a partner in an escapade from virtue, and one feels that such a choice will not be long in making, nor Labervele long avoid his destiny.   The portrait, which, I fancy, was drawn from the life, is etched in with a pen dipped in gall, and shows more plainly than anything else in his work the detestation with which Chapman the humanist regarded the Puritan assumption of peculiar virtue.

The greater part of the play is written in prose, but there are three scenes entirely in blank verse, and three more in which prose and verse are intermingled. It seems to have been Chapman's intention to employ verse for the high places of the drama, the soliloquy with which the play opens, the rhapsodies of Dowsecer, and the decisive interview between Lemot and Florilla.   Prose is employed in the more familiar passages and in the scenes of lively action.   The prose scenes seem to me, in their frequent use of puns, their lively word-combats, and their straining after point and finish, to betray the influence of Lyly; but there is no trace of the artificial balance, antithesis, and simile which characterize Euphuism proper.   The verse represents a further progress along the line already[1] noted away from the tragic splendours of Marlowe toward the simplicity, lightness, and ease proper for comedy.

All in all *An Humourous Day's Mirth* represents a very great advance over Chapman's first work.   It is pure comedy, unmixed with tragic or romantic elements ; there is a coherent, though not very well proportioned plot, and a power of humourous characterization remarkable in so early a work.   Judged by an absolute standard, the play has little permanent merit ; but it is of real interest to the student, not only as representing a new stage in the development of Chapman's art, but also as an early example of one of the most highly developed types of Elizabethan comedy.

[1] See above, p. 676.

AN HUMOUROUS DAY'S MIRTH

NOTES

Scene i. The scene is laid in the private garden of Florilla, *my wife's close walk*, l. 7.

i, 4. *Rest:* an abbreviated form of 'arrest'; cf. sc. vii, l. 115.

i, 36. *Pathetical:* i.e. sympathetic; cf. *The Gentleman Usher*, I, i, 166.

Scene ii. The place of this scene is undetermined; possibly a street in Paris.

ii, 51-2. The Latin *end* is from Terence, *Adephi*, IV, i, 21. A similar phrase appears in Plautus, *Stichus*, IV, i, 71. It appears to allude to 'some fable in which a wolf appears just as he is being spoken of' (Sloman's note on the passage in Terence) or to the old superstition that a wolf who saw a man before he was seen by him deprived the man of the power of speech. See Otto *Sprichwörter der Römer*, p. 199.

ii, 74. *For his living sake:* on account of his estate. Foyes wishes to marry Martia to the rich gull, Labesha; cf. sc. iii.

ii, 92. *Start mad:* a curious variant of 'stark mad', probably by analogy with the old and correct form 'start naked', i.e. 'tail naked', modern English 'stark naked'. The same form occurs in sc. iv, l. 246.

Scene iii. This scene is laid at the house of Foyes.

iii, 3. *'Tis art:* I do not understand this phrase, unless Foyes means that there is an art of preparing the body. Perhaps the text is corrupt.

iii, 23. *Honeysuckle:* The word has here the rather uncommon sense of 'honey'; cf. *Eastward Ho*, III. ii, 52.

Scene iv. Like scene i, this scene is laid in Florilla's private garden, cf. l. 16.

iv, 18-19. The idea that fairies vanished before the increasing light of religion is an old one. Compare Chaucer's satirical use of this idea in *The Wife of Bath's Tale*, 1-25, and Richard Corbett's poem, *The Fairies' Farewell*:

> But since of late Elizabeth,
> And later James, came in,
> They never danced on any heath
> As when the time hath bin.
>
> By which we note the fairies
> Were of the old profession;
> Their songs were Ave-Maries,
> Their dances were procession.
> But now, alas! they all are dead,
> Or gone beyond the seas,
> Or farther for religion fled,
> Or else they take their ease.

iv, 55-6. This well-known anecdote of Diogenes is found in Plutarch, *De Profectibus in Virtute*, viii: *Diogenes e vola quemdam bibere conspicatus, poculum pera ejecit.*

iv, 94. *Du Bartas*; Guillaume de Salluste du Bartas, 1544-1590, the famous French Huguenot poet, author of *Le Sepmaine*, and other poems. He was well known in England where he was spoken of as the 'divine Du Bartas'. His reputation as a religious poet is made use of in this passage to furnish Catalian, who feigns to be a candidate for the ministry (cf. ll 122-4), with a creditable patron.

iv, 125–6. *Vicar of hell :* possibly with a reference to Skelton, *'whom Harry the 8 nam'd in merriment his Vicar of hell'* (*Areopagitica*—edited by Hales, p. 20) probably with a pun on the name of his parish of Dis, or Diss, in Norfolk.

iv, 137. *Imp of desolation :* cf. *desolate,* i.e. dissolute, sc. vi, ll. 23 and 27.

iv, 139–40. Cf. the words spoken by Lorenzo in the disguise of Snail, the chimney-sweeper, in *May-Day,* III, ii, 6–9.

iv, 243. It is perhaps worth noting that the book of Habakkuk contains but three chapters.

Scene v. The scene is laid in the house of Count Moren, cf. l. 188.

v, 32. *A fair taking :* a pretty pickle. Cf. note on *The Blind Beggar,* sc. x, l. 101.

v, 63. *Mote I thee :* may I thrive. The archaic forms are used, of course, for the sake of the puns.

v, 81–82. Compare the scene in *The Wise Woman of Hogsdon,* where the mock-pedant sets Sir Boniface to decline *Iamano* after the first conjugation.

v, 89–91. The various bird-names in these lines were Elizabethan synonyms for a fool. For *hammer* see note on *The Gentleman Usher,* I, i, 152. A *dizzard* is a jester, a fool.

v, 102. *Thou smellest of the mother :* you are like your mother.

v, 109. Here Catalian and Blanuel shoulder Labesha off, and allow Lemot an opportunity to whisper to Martia.

v, 148. Here Catalian and Blanuel embrace Labesha, and give Moren a chance to speak aside to Martia.

Scene vi. The scene is laid at Count Labervele's house.

vi, 23. *Desolate :* an old form for ' dissolute '. The *New English Dictionary* gives a quotation dating 1579 with this meaning.

Scene vii. This scene like the preceding is laid at Count Labervele's house, cf. l. 34.

vii, 7. *A king of clouts :* the phrase occurs in the first quarto of *Hamlet,* 1603 (l. 1,490, Furness's *Variorum*), but disappears in later editions. Possibly it occurred in the old *Hamlet,* in which case Chapman would be parodying it here.

vii, 65–6. The quotation, apparently made from memory, is drawn from Cicero's *Tusculanae Disputationes,* iv, 17, 37 : *Quid enim videatur ei magnum in rebus humanis cui aeternitas omnis totiusque mundi nota sit magnitudo.* The following lines, 67–9, give a sufficiently close translation.

vii, 82. *Acorns :* according to the old poets, the chief food of mankind in the pure age of Saturn. Cf. Ovid, *Metamorphoses,* I, 103–6, and Juvenal, *Satire VI,* 1–10.

vii, 92. *Her mortal enemy :* Dowsecer himself, as the satirist of the world's customs.

vii, 106. *Written books :* the account books of the tailors, from whom they have got their hose on credit ; cf. *The Widow's Tears,* I, i, 33–5.

vii, 111. *A hand in the margent :* a sign sometimes used in old books to call attention to some important passage in the text.

vii, 116. I fancy that here Dowsecer puts on the hose hind side foremost, or in some such fashion shows his contempt for the *goodly gear.* This seems to be indicated by l. 117.

vii, 125–8. Cf. the character of the *French-affected traveller,* Foulweather, in *Sir Giles Goosecap,* and of his French page, whom the boys pretend to mistake for an ape in the first scene of that play.

vii, 129. *Piannet* is ' a local name for a magpie.'—*New English Dictionary.*

vii, 131–3. With the sentiment cf. *The Revenge of Bussy,* II, i, 192–5 :

> So these painted men,
> All set on out-side, look upon within,
> And not a peasant's entrails shall you find
> More foul and measled, nor more starv'd of mind.

vii, 135. *This rare piece :* i.e. the picture brought in by Lavel, stage-direction after l. 50 above. It is apparently the portrait of a lady.

vii, 159. *Thus must I do :* apparently Dowsecer here bows and pretends to court the picture.

vii, 162. *God's precious coals :* the *New English Dictionary* gives this curious phrase as ' an obsolete interjection ' and cites examples of *precious cole(s)* from Gascoigne and Heywood. I have not met it elsewhere.

vii, 175. *They :* i.e. the earth and my flesh.

vii, 177. For comment on this puzzling line, see Text Notes, p. 697.

vii, 180–187. With this passage cf. one of the additions to *The Spanish Tragedy*, III, xi, 14–28 (Shick's edition), especially ll. 15–19 :

> *Why might not a man love a calf as well,*
> *Or melt in passion o'er a frisking kid,*
> *As for a son ?   Methinks a young bacon,*
> *Or a fine little smooth horse colt,*
> *Should move a man as much as doth a son.*

vii, 210–11. *Digestion :* Chapman uses this word to denote the well-ordered universe, the *cosmos*, as opposed to the *indigesta moles* of chaos.   For a similar coupling of these terms, see Text Notes, p. 698.

vii, 230. *Flattering Fabian :* the *New English Dictionary* cites examples of *flaunting Fabian* from Florio, 1598, who makes it a synonym for a swaggerer, a roisterer, and from Nash, 1599, who makes it equivalent to *Palmerin*, i.e. champion.   Dr. Bradley suggests it may refer to the *licens Fabius* of Propertius, IV, i, 26.   In the present passage *flattering* may be a misprint for *flaunting*, or an intentional alteration of a phrase apparently current at this time.   Either interpretation would make sense.

viii, 10. Valere appears to be another innkeeper.   His name occurs in xi, 19, and in xiv, 116, where it appears to be a mistake for Verone.

viii, 11. The *Boy* is, of course, Verona's son.   He is called *Boy* throughout the play except in the stage-direction at the beginning of this scene, and in that after sc. xiv, 181.

viii, 186. *That same gentleman :* i.e. Rowley.

viii, 192. *Shifts :* note the pun.   *Shifts* means either devices or shirts.

viii, 211. For a similar use of *brittle*, cf. *The Gentleman Usher*, I, i, 23.

viii, 223. A proverb which occurs not infrequently in Elizabethan literature. Cf. *The Widow's Tears*, II, i, 14, and Peele's *Edward* I :

> *An aged saying and a true,*
> *Black will take no other hue.*
>
> Sc. viii, ll. 30–31.

In Bohn's edition of Ray's *Proverbs*, p. 72, we are referred back to Pliny for its origin : *Lanarum nigrae nullum colorem bibunt. Nat. Hist.*, viii, 193.

viii, 223–4. *That same old Justice :* i.e. Foyes.

viii, 225. Another proverb.   Chapman alludes to it again in *Sir Giles Goosecap*, III, i, 268, and apparently in *The Blind Beggar*, sc. x, l. 156.   It appears in Ray's *Proverbs* in the form : A black man's a jewel in a fair woman's eye.   See also Heywood, *Second Part of the Iron Age :*

> *A black complexion*
> *Is always precious in a woman's eye.*
> *Dramatic Works*, vol. iii, p. 364.

viii, 243. *This lord :* i.e. Moren.

viii, 320. Cf. sc. v, l. 12.

Scene ix. This scene is laid at the house of Count Moren.   It was probably played on the balcony while the other actors remained seated on the main stage representing Verone's ordinary, to which Lemot returns in the next scene.

ix, 14. *Her husband :* i.e. Florilla's husband, Labervele.

Scene xi. This scene is laid in the street before the door of Verone's ordinary. After the exit of the actors in the preceding scene, the main stage, cleared of its tables, chairs, etc., is supposed to be the street on which Labervele and the others appear.   Cf. ll. 5 and 41 below.

xi, 12. The hatband was a special mark of the young gallant in Elizabethan days, and was worn in many shapes and colours. Dekker bids his novice ' put off to none, unless his hatband be of a newer fashion than yours, and three degrees quainter' (*The Gull's Hornbook*, p. 35, Temple Classics.

xi, 20. *Uttered this :* divulged the secret of Florilla's visit to the ordinary.

xi, 56. *Beso las manos :* I kiss your hands.

Scene xii. After Lemot leaves the stage Verone and the others issue upon it, and it is once more supposed to be a room in his ordinary.

xii, 35. The quotation seems to have originated with Nigellus, called Wire-kerus, a Canterbury monk of the late twelfth century. In his *Speculum Stultorum* one finds :

> *Est igitur felix aliena pericula cautum*
> *Quem faciunt, formant et ratione regi.*

See Wright's *Anglo-Latin Satirical Poets*, vol. i, p. 145, (Rolls Series, vol. 59). It seems to have become proverbial in the form here quoted. I owe this reference to my colleague, Dr. Root.

Scene xiii. The stage once more becomes the street on which the Queen and the Countess, attended by *all the rest of the Lords*, appear in search of their truant husbands.

Scene xiv. There is no real necessity for a new scene here. Moren appears upon the street where Martia has been taken from him (cf. above, sc. xi, l. 18), Catalian and Berger take up their positions at the two opposite sides of the stage and turn Moren back as he attempts to leave first by one door and then by the other. For the shift of scene, see below, note on l. 181.

xiv, 16. *Hern*: a form now obsolete, except in certain dialects, of ' hers'.

xiv, 19. *Drunken f[r[oes :* the Bacchanals. Cf. Peele's *Arraignment of Paris,* II, i, 24, where *froes* means ' wives'. Chapman, who uses the word twice elsewhere (see Text Notes, p. 699) apparently restricts it to the female followers of Bacchus.

xiv, 27. M. Schoell points out that a lottery was a frequent entertainment at Elizabeth's Court. There is an interesting example of one devised by Lyly, see Bond's *Lyly*, vol. i, p. 499.

xiv, 65. *A curious lady :* a fastidious, or perhaps scrupulous, lady.

xiv, 96. Dowsecer's speech has probably been cut.

xiv, 178–9. With the phrase *debate 'twixt man and wife,* cf. *All Fools,* IV, i, 225.

xiv, 180. *Scripturian :* student of the Scriptures.

xiv, 181. Here the scene shifts and without further notice than that contained in the text we are to suppose it the interior of Verone's tavern. Such changes of place within a scene are not infrequent in Elizabethan drama. See my note on *Bussy D'Ambois,* III, ii, 321.

xiv, 297. Florilla in her character of a Puritan denounces rosary and crucifix as idolatrous.

TEXT NOTES

An Humourous Day's Mirth was first printed in 1599 by Valentine Syms. Of this edition, the first and only quarto, there are two copies in the British Museum,[1] C. 12. g. 4, and C. 34. c. 14. These agree very closely, though there are two or three small differences between them which I point out below.

The play was next reprinted in *The Comedies and Tragedies of George Chapman* (Pearson, London, 1873, vol. i). This is a reprint of the original, but it is not absolutely reliable, as it silently corrects a number of misprints of the quarto and introduces a number of misprints of its own. I have recorded these in the text notes where I refer to this edition as P.

The next and up to the present the latest edition of *An Humourous Day's Mirth* is that of Shepherd in the *Works of Chapman—Plays,* 1874. This is a modernized edition, based upon P. but introducing certain changes and emendations. I refer to it as S.

---

[1] There are also copies in the Bodleian and in Dyce's collection at the Albert and Victoria Museum.

The text of this play is one of the most unsatisfactory of all Chapman's dramas. It is very badly printed, abounds in mistakes and corruptions, and owing to the varying abbreviations used to denote the names of the speakers is often most confusing. Nor has the only former editor done much to clear up this confusion. In fact, there are not a few instances where, owing to a misunderstanding of the situation on his part, the modern text is more perplexing than the old. I have done my utmost to remedy this by standardizing these abbreviations, by introducing in square brackets such stage-directions as seem necessary to make the situation clear, and by modernizing the spelling and punctuation, I have been forced to introduce numerous emendations, some of which may, perhaps, seem rather daring; but the corrupt condition of the text calls for boldness on the part of the editor if it is to be rendered intelligible. These emendations are all recorded in the text notes, and the reader may accept them or restore the original text at his good pleasure; but I believe I may claim to have presented for the first time a readable text of this play.

The Q. shows no division into acts or scenes. I have inserted the latter where they seemed called for, but have made no attempt to group them into acts.

The Q. is printed throughout as prose, even such stanzas as sc. i, ll. 29–32 and sc. xiv, ll. 221–232 being set as prose. Only where a single speech is equivalent to one line of blank verse do we find any correspondence between the setting of the printer and the intention of the author. For it is quite plain that a large portion of this play, especially the long soliloquies such as that with which the first scene opens, were written in blank verse. The previous editor has in part restored this, but I have been able to rearrange many passages as verse which he had either overlooked or regarded as prose.

The list of *Dramatis Personae* is here printed for the first time.

Scene i, l. 1. Q. *throwt.* S. *through.* It is plain, I think, that Chapman intended a monosyllabic pronunciation of ' throughout ', and I have attempted to indicate this by printing *thr'out.*

11–12. Brereton (*Modern Language Review*, vol. iii, No. 1) would read *by the which,* referring to *counterfeit* in l. 10. But the pronoun may be regarded as referring to *the holy green* of l. 7, in which case no change is necessary. Brereton further suggests that the words *rare and* should perhaps be rejected ' for the sake of the verse', but such a rejection would leave us with an abnormally long line, and I have preferred to follow S. in printing the last three words of the sentence as a short line.

16. Swinburne (*George Chapman*, p. 46) long ago called attention to the evident hiatus of sense and metre in this line. Following his suggestion, I have inserted *careful* before *for itself.*

17. Q. *is.* I emend *'Tis*, which seems to me to be demanded by the context.

28. Q. *well in nought,* which is unintelligible. I follow a suggestion of Mr. Daniel in reading *well enough.*

29. *Despair.* Q. *tis spare.* S. prints *'Tis Despair*, but the old printer probably mistook *dispaire* in the MS. for *tis spare.* Cf. sc. iv, l. 32.

Scene ii, l. 6. Q. *humor*; possibly we should read *humours*, which seems to be called for by *them* in l. 8; but I have preferred not to change the old text here.

69. Q. *in love with love, by Martia.* Deighton (*Old Dramatists*, p. 128) emends *lovely Martia.* This seems a capital emendation, especially in view of the recurrence of the epithet in l. 92 below.

72. Q. *Moris.* S. emends *Moren's.* The Q. is very careless in the matter of printing the proper names of this play. Cf. the form *Morene* in Q. in sc. iii, l. 33.

81. Q. *Cat.* Possibly this should be regarded as an intentional and jocular abbreviation; but there are so many evidences of haste and carelessness in the printing of the play that I have preferred with S. to restore the full form of the name.

Scene iv, ll. 1–9. S. prints as prose, but it is evidently blank verse, and I have arranged it as such. The presence of two short lines in quick succession in ll. 3 and 5 might be avoided by printing ll. 3–5 as two lines ending *tells me* and *off*, but this would make l. 3 very rough.

21. One of the British Museum copies, C. 34. c. 14, reads *more* for *much* in this line.

32. Q. *Dispaire.* Cf. text note on sc. i, l. 29.

56. C. 34. c. 14 reads *will* for *would* in this line.

63. Q. *banishment.* S. emends *punishment*, which is no doubt correct.

94. Q. *du Barto.* Below in l. 123 Q. has *du Barte.* S. adopts the latter form in both places, but I have preferred the proper form of the French poet's name. See note on p. 691.

138. Q. *lookes,* an evident misprint which S. corrects.

162. The *t* has dropped out in *to*, the first word of this line, in Q. P. restores it.

164. Q. *thou.* P. prints *thogh.*

189. Q. misprints *yon*, which P. corrects.

199. C. 34. c. 14 reads *most* for *more* in this line.

228. Q. omits *in* in this line. S. supplies it.

230. Q. *unworthily*, which S. follows, but it is plainly wrong. Brereton (*loc. cit.*) emends *worthily*.

Scene v, ll. 1, 5 and **8.** Q. prints *Mar.* as the name of the speaker in these lines, which is the usual abbreviation for *Martia.* P. misprints *Mor.* for *Mar.* in the last instance which probably led S. to print *Mar., Mar.* and *Mo.* respectively. The context shows that the speaker is Lord Moren in all three cases, and I have accordingly printed *M[o]r.*

3. Q. *Pardon a moy.* I emend *pardonnez-moi.*

51. Q. prints *Cat* as the name of the speaker, which S. abbreviates to *Ca.* It is plain, however, from l. 53 that the speaker is a woman, and I therefore print *Count[ess]*, which is sup-

ported by the Q. *Con,* i.e *Countess* in l. 56.

129. Q. *auy,* which P. corrects to *any.*

165. After this line Q. has *Enter Lemot ;* but Lemot has been on the stage since l. 48. The old direction, which should have followed l. 160, probably indicates Lemot's advance to the front of the stage to take part in the conversation from which he has been withdrawn for a time; cf. *The Widow's Tears,* II, ii, 55.

177. Q. prints *Me.* as the name of the speaker, an evident misprint which S. corrects to *Mo.*

195. Q. abbreviates *Lord* to *L.* Cf. sc. vi, l. 131 and elsewhere.

196 and **202.** Q. prints *Co.* and *C.* respectively as the name of the speaker. S. prints *Mo.*, for *Moren*, in both cases ; but I think the speaker is *Colinet.*

Scene vi, ll. 23 and **27.** Q. *desolate.* S. alters to *dissolute* ; but see note on this line, above, p. 692.

29. The word *Reason* is extrametrical, and may originally have been in the margin to denote the speaker in the imaginary colloquy.

66. Q. *see,* which S. follows ; but I think it is plainly a misprint for *sir.* The same misprint occurs in ll. 110 and 130 below.

88. Q. misprints *moret* ; S. corrects.

111. Q. *love is required* ; S. *requited.* The insertion of a comma after *love* makes the text intelligible.

126. Q. *choise,* which S. alters to *choice* ; but it is plainly a misprint for *close*, the adjective used with *walk* in sc. i, l. 7, sc. vii, l. 248, and sc. xiv, l. 140.

Scene vii, l. 2. Q. prints *C.* for the name of the speaker ; S. prints *Ca.*, for *Catalan* ; but cf. note on sc. v, ll. 196, 202.

16. Q. *luuatike.* P. silently corrects.

38. Q. *siniora defoulasa* ; S. *Signor de Foulasa.* I prefer the French form *Seigneur.*

39. Q. *barendrie* ; S. *barrendry* ; but no such word is known. I suggest *barony.*

59. Between *or* and *at* in this line
Q. has the word *that*. It is
plainly intrusive, perhaps suggested by *that* four words before,
and was properly omitted by S.

63. Q. *she may*. Possibly we
should read *they may*, referring to
objects, l. 62. But if we take *she*
as referring to *soul*, l. 61, and
suppose the sentence to be
broken off after *may*, the old
text may be allowed to stand.

65-66. Q. *Quid Dei potes videri
magnum in rebus humanis quae
aeterni omnes* to thy *ousque notas
sic omnibus magna tutor*. This
extraordinarily corrupt passage
was no doubt due to the printer's
ignorance of the Latin which apparently was read aloud to him.
Thus only can we explain such
corruptions as *Quid Dei* for
Quid ei and *magna tutor* for
magnitudo. See note p. 692.

73. Q. *make*. S. corrects *made*.

81. Q. *virtue or honest drifts ;
but he cares, he cares, he cares.*
S. follows Q. ; but the passage
is plainly corrupt. Although
printed as prose, the speech of
which this line is a part is in
regular and musical blank verse.
What is needed instead of *he
cares* is a monosyllable which
shall have a meaning opposed
to *honest drifts*. The only word
I can think of is *snares*, no improper contents, at least in a
satiric speech, of *lawyer's bills*.
I am glad to say that this
emendation has been approved
by Mr. Daniel.

82. Q. *for acorns now are in request*. The line, for any attempt
to reconstruct Dowsecer's speech
will show that this is a line, is
deficient by one foot, and means,
as it stands, exactly the opposite
of what it should. For Dowsecer is plainly, according to the
old convention of satire, praising
the antique times when men
lived on acorns in contrast to
the present age of luxury and de-
generation. I suggest the insertion of *no more* after *now*.
Mr. Daniel proposes *but small*
after *in*. Either will do.

83. Q. *but the okes poore fruit
did nourish men*. I insert *when*
after *but*, an emendation ap-

proved by Mr. Daniel and Mr.
Brereton.

93. Q. *lenity*. So S. It is barely
possible that this word may be
right, if we take it as used as
an ironical equivalent for *tenderness*, or *mercy*. But this seems
far-fetched, and the misprint
for *levity*, i.e. *fickleness*, or *vanity*
is so easy that I have ventured,
following a suggestion of Mr.
Daniel, to substitute the latter
word.

98. Q. *wives*. I am strongly inclined to suspect that here we
have another misprint, and that
the true reading is *wines*, which
would fit in well with *carouses*
and *aqua-vitae*. But as the text
is intelligible, I have allowed it
to stand.

108. Q. *match*, which S. follows.
But this makes nonsense of the
passage. I suggest *much*, which
corresponds well to *more* in the
next phrase.

112-3. Q. *house*, which S. follows. But is plainly a misprint
for *hose*. Cf. *a pair of large hose,
a codpiece* in the stage-direction
after l. 50 above.

114. Q. *your*, which S. follows.
I emend *you*.

117. Q. *And he doth despise our
purposes*. I have ventured to
insert *so* after *And*, not only to
complete the metre, but because
the context seems to require
some such word. Cf. note on
p. 692.

119. Q. prints *La.* as the name of
the speaker. I take it the speech
belongs to *Lavel*, the friend of
Dowsecer.

130. Q. *tailes*, which S. follows.
Following a suggestion of Brereton (*loc. cit.*, p. 57), I read *curls*
to correspond with *locks*. *Tailes*
appears to have been suggested
by *tail* in l. 129.

155. Q. *make*; S. *makes*. The
verb is attracted into the plural
by the phrase *men and women*.

168. Q. *confesse*, which S. follows.
I emend *consent*, a correction
which has been approved by
Mr. Daniel and Mr. Brereton.

177. The line seems corrupt, unless we can take *they* as equivalent to *them*, an objective attracted into the nominative case

by its position. Or we might read *that* for *they*, a suggestion approved by Mr. Daniel. Or finally we may have to do here with a case of transposition and the line originally may have read something like this :

And when these in the spring the grass converts.

As the matter seems so uncertain, I have decided to let the old text stand.

183. Q. *sonne sonnes.* S. emends *son's sons*, which I accept for the sake of making the text more intelligible to the modern reader, although it is by no means unlikely that Chapman wrote *sonne sonnes* for the sake of euphony.

195. Q. *An haplesse man*, which S. follows. I think *An* is probably a mere misprint for *Ah*.

201-2. Q. *and she as I hope wel observed hath uttered many kind conceits of hers.* Following Brereton's suggestion (*loc. cit.* p. 57) I place *as I hope* between commas, print *h'ath*, i.e. *he hath*, and read *her* for *hers*. These slight changes make the speech intelligible.

211. Q. *gestion.* I emend *digestion.* For a like coupling of *chaos*, l. 210, and *digestion*, cf. :

The chaos of eternal night
To which the whole digestion of
the world
Is now returning.

Revenge of Bussy, V, i, 1–3, Cf. also *Bussy D'Ambois*, IV, i 163–4.

222. Q. gives *Lab.* as the name of the speaker, the same abbreviation which it has used in l. 218 for Labervele. But it seems plain that the speaker here is the foolish Labesha. The same abbreviation appears in Q. in l. 245, where also I take Labesha to be the speaker.

237, 241, 243. In all these lines Q. prints *Mar.*, i.e. *Martia* as the name of the speaker. But this is palpably a misprint for *Mor*[en].

Scene viii, l. 10. Q. *Verones*, but the maid is speaking to Verone. S. emends *Valere's.* See note, p.693.

16–17. Q. *name in the of God I*

trowee. S. corrects the transposition and reads *trow ye.* The latter change seems uncalled for.

21. Q. prints *Boy* as the name of the speaker. P. misprints *Foy.*

24, 32. Q. *Sateena*, and *Jacenan.* S. follows Q. ; but both forms appear misprints for the maid's name *Jaquena.*

76. Q. *what.* P. misprints *that*, and is followed by S.

84. Q. prints *Ve.* as the name of the speaker. P. misprints *Ne.*

110. Q. *tittle*, which P. silently corrects to *little.*

148. Q. assigns this speech to *La.* I think the speaker is *Labesha*, although in this passage Q. uses *Be.* as the abbreviation for his name in ll. 135, 140, 144, 150, 154 and 156. In l. 178, however, Q. uses *Lab.* for *Labesha.*

172. Q. prints *Lor.* as the name of the speaker. This is not a misprint, I think, but an abbreviation for Lord Moren. At the close of this scene in ll. 271, 274, 278, 283, 289, 291, and 305, Q. prints *Lord* before Moren's speeches.

195. Q. prints *Lem.* as the name of the speaker. P. misprints *Lea.*

227. Q. *here comes hither Labeshu, Catalian, and I have beene.* S. emends *he comes hither. Labesha, Catalian and I have been.* The word *he* before *comes* is plainly necessary. I incline to think that it has simply dropped out of the text, not that it has been corrupted into *here.* Perhaps we should read *here he comes. Hither, Labesha! Catalian and I, etc.*

245 and 251. Q. *promptus.* I emend *promptos.* Fleay (*Biog. Chron.*, vol. i, p. 55) points out that the same error occurs in the anonymous play *Every Woman in her Humour*, III, i. See Bullen, *Old Plays*, vol. iv, p. 348.

277. Q. *such.* P. misprints *snch.*

308. Q. *go yfaith!* Possibly *I* has dropped out after *go*, but I prefer to read *go I, faith!* taking the *y* of Q. to be a corruption of the original *I.* Cf. sc. ix, l. 14.

313. Q. *see*, a misprint for *sir* as in sc. vi, ll. 66, 110 and 130.

Scene x, ll. 4 and 5. Q. assigns both

these speeches to *Le.* The first is probably Labesha's, the second Lemot's.

Scene xi, l. 10. Q. *silent.* S. corrects to *silence.*

17. Q. *Lor.*, P. *Lord*, for *Mor.* as above, Sc. viii, ll. 271, *ssq.*

19. In Q. the stage-direction *Enter the Puritan, etc.*, follows the speech *What vilain, etc.* It is evident that it is misplaced and that the speech belongs to the entering Florilla.

46. The stage-direction *He bites* is printed in Q. as part of the text.

56. Q. *Besilos manus;* S. *Besilas manos.*

73. Q. *wench*, an impossible word for Florilla to use to Lemot. S. corrects *wretch.*

Scene xii, l. 1. Here and elsewhere in this scene Q. prints *Host* instead of *Ver.* for the name of the speaker.

3. Q. *no heres.* S. corrects *now, here's.*

11. In the stage-direction after this line Q. has *Gentleman*, which S. retains, but it is an evident misprint for *Gentlemen.*

Scene xiii, l. 6. Q. *his right*, which S. retains; but I think it plain that we should read *my right.* Cf. l. 4.

43, 51. The speeches of the Countess in these lines are in Q. assigned to *Cat.* and *Coun.*

46. The word *her*, omitted in Q., is restored by S.

58. Q. *fall.* S. corrects *falls.*

96. The word *it*, omitted in Q., is restored by S.

Scene xiv, l. 10. The word *him*, omitted in Q., is restored by S.

19. Q. *foes*, which S. retains. But the word should be *froes*, i.e. women. Cf. *Monsieur D'Olive*, II, i, 179, and *The Shadow of*

Night (*Poems*, p. 6) in both which cases it is applied to the Bacchanals.

44. Q. *Ca.*, which S. retains. I think the speech belongs to the Countess.

54 and 58. Q. prints *La.* as the speaker's name. It should be *Le*[*mot*]. In l. 58 P. misprints *Lea.*

66. Q. *over*, which S. retains; but I think it plainly a mistake for *offer.*

79–80. For Q. *Le.* and *Qu.* in these lines P. misprints *La.* and *Ru.*

116. Q. *Valeres.* But the Host would not be likely to present his device at his rival's house. S. emends *Verone's.*

117. Q. *Whith.* P. silently corrects.

130. Q. *for.* P. misprints *or.*

192. Here and throughout the scene Q. prints *Host* for *Ver.*

206. Q. *voice.* Following a suggestion of Fleay's communicated to me by Mr. Daniel, I read *verse* to rhyme with *scarce.* The same change is necessary in l. 226.

227–8. Q. *here is Fortune good, but il by the rood.* S. retains, but it seems plain that we should read *not ill.*

229. The word *sir* seems to have dropped out of Q.

253. Q. prints *Labesh.* as the name of the speaker, but it is plain that Labervele is speaking and paying for himself and Florilla.

272–3. Q. *The villaines.* Possibly we should read *thy villanies.*

294. I supply *a*, which seems to have dropped out of Q.

308. Q. *a cats eyes.* I emend *a caduceus* to correspond with *Mercury's rod.*

355. Q. *Why.* P. misprints *Who.*

ALL FOOLS

INTRODUCTION

All Fools was first published in 1605 in quarto form with the following title-page :

> *Al Fooles A Comedy, Presented at the Black Fryers, And lately before his Maiestie. Written by George Chapman. At London, Printed for Thomas Thorpe.* 1605.

It had, however, been composed some years before this date. In Henslowe's *Diary* under the date of January 22, 1598 (i.e. 1598–9) there occurs the entry : *Lent unto thomas dowton . . . to Leand unto Mr. Chapman in earneste of a Boocke called the world Rones a whelles* [1] *the some of iii*[u]. Further advance payments were made by Henslowe, twenty shillings on February 13, the same sum on June 2, forty shillings on June 21, and finally there occurs an entry which identifies [2] this play with *All Fools : Lent unto thomas dowton the 2 of July* 1599 *to pay Mr. Chapman in full payment for his Boocke called the world Rones a whelles and now all foolles but the foolle some of xxx*[s].

Henslowe was at this time in close connexion with the Admiral's Men acting at his theatre, the Rose, and Dowton, or Downton, to whom he advanced the earnest money for Chapman, was a prominent member of this company. Though there is no record of an actual

---

[1] I.e. *The World runs on Wheels*, a proverbial phrase of the day.

[2] This identification has always been regarded as certain. Mr. Greg (*Henslowe's Diary*, pt. ii, pp. 175, 294) has raised the question whether the entry may not refer to two different plays, and the payment of thirty shillings include ' the remainder (say 10s.) due for the *World* and a sum (say 20s.) in earnest for *All Fools* '. In this case, however, Chapman, who, as Greg notes, commanded better prices than most of Henslowe's playwrights, would have accepted less by ten shillings or a pound for the *World* than he had received for his previous comedy *The Isle of Women* (see Greg, as above, pp. 194, 198). There is nothing surprising in the change of name from the *World Runs on Wheels* to *All Fools*, especially when the first title was such an awkward one. As to the objection that there is nothing in the printed play to suggest the latter part of the second title (*but the Fool*) this, as Greg admits, may have been due to a later revision of the play. It is quite possible that the gulling of Rinaldo, which makes the title *All Fools* appropriate, was wanting in the older form which might therefore well be called *All Fooles but the Fool*, i.e. the knavish, intriguing Rinaldo, who corresponds to the Vice or Fool of earlier comedies. Further, if Chapman received twenty shillings or so in advance for *All Fools* on July 2, it seems a little strange that a fortnight later, July 17, he should have received £2 in advance for another unfinished play, a Pastoral Tragedy (see Greg, as above, p. 204). In this case Chapman would have been at work upon and receiving advances for two plays at the same time, a fact which seems inconsistent with what we know of the practice of Elizabethan playwrights. It is not well to be dogmatic in these matters, but it seems simpler to conclude that the *World* and *All Fools* were but two names for one play.

performance of *All Fools* by the Admiral's Men, we are entitled, I
suppose, to assume that it was performed by them at the Rose in the
late summer or autumn of 1599. Chapman's name does not appear
in Henslowe's *Diary* after the entry of July 17, 1599, and there is
reason to believe that soon after this date he transferred his services
to the Children of the Chapel [1] at Blackfriars. It was by this company
that *All Fools* was again performed, according to Professor Wallace,
after the close of the plague [2] of 1603.

The performance at Court, ' before his Majesty ', occurred, according
to a list published by Cunningham (*Extracts from the Accounts of the
Revels at Court. Shakespeare Society*, 1842, p. 202), on New Year's
night, 1604–5. This list is now known to be a forgery, but it was
apparently compiled from authentic documents used by Malone, but
now lost, and the statement regarding *All Fools* is accepted as correct.
This performance was given by the Children of Her Majesty's Revels,
the same company under a new name as the Children of the Chapel.
There is no trace of any later performance, and I doubt whether *All
Fools* appeared on the boards again until its performance at Harvard [3]
in 1909.

The main source of *All Fools* has long [4] been known to be the *Heautontimoroumenos* of Terence. Koeppel redirected attention to this
source (*Quellen und Forschungen*, 1897), and an elaborate study of
Chapman's indebtedness to this play has been made by Dr. Stier in
a dissertation, *Chapman's All Fools*, published at Halle in 1904. Recently attention [5] has been called to the fact that Chapman drew not
only upon this play of Terence, but also upon the *Adelphi*. In fact
All Fools may properly be described as a ' contamination ' of these
two plays, just as Jonson's *The Case is Altered* [6] is of the *Aulularia*
and the *Captivi* of Plautus. And both *All Fools* and *The Case is*

---

[1] Wallace (*Children of the Chapel*, p. 75) dates *Sir Giles Goosecap*, Chapman's first play for this company, as early as the autumn of 1600. This is a
year earlier than the *terminus a quo* given by Fleay (*Biographical Chronicle*,
vol. ii, pp. 322–3). As Professor Wallace reserves the evidence for his assertion, discussion of his statement would be premature. I am pleased, however,
to note that his researches have led him to the opinion which I expressed as
early as 1906 (*The Authorship of Sir Giles Goosecap* in *Modern Philology*, July,
1906) that Chapman began to write at an early date for this company and
was at work for them and their successors during a period 1600 to 1605, when
he is commonly said to have renounced the stage and to have devoted himself
to the translation of Homer, an error which is unfortunately repeated in the
Cambridge History of English Literature, vol. vi, p. 36.

[2] This plague was extremely severe, about one-sixth of the population of
London perishing within the year during which it raged. The theatres were
closed on May 26, 1603, and not re-opened until April 9, 1604 (Murray, *English
Dramatic Companies*, vol. i, pp. 147–8). Unless Blackfriars was allowed to
open before the Globe, the Fortune, and the Curtain, which are mentioned by
name in the proclamation cited by Murray, *All Fools* could not have been
played there before the spring of 1604.

[3] See below, p. 712.

[4] Langbaine, *English Dramatic Poets*, 1691.

[5] By Miss Woodbridge, *Journal of Germanic Philology*, vol. i, p. 338, and
independently by Mr. Kennedy in a paper read at Princeton in 1904.

[6] Jonson's play probably preceded Chapman's. Wallace (*op. cit.*, p. 58)
dates it on evidence as yet unpublished as early as 1597. It is referred to in
Nash's *Lenten Stuff*, entered in the Stationers' Registers, January 11, 1598–9.

Altered contain, in addition to plots drawn from Latin comedy, a large element derived from English [1] life, letters, and stage convention.

A brief account of the two plays on which *All Fools* depends will serve to show what use Chapman made of his sources. In the *Heauton-timoroumenos* we have a pair of fathers and a pair of sons. The first father, Menedemus, whose self-torturing remorse gives its name to the play, has driven his son, Clinia, from home by his vehement reproaches for a love affair with a poor but honest girl, Antiphila. The father bitterly regrets his harshness, and devotes himself to a life of labour in order to acquire a fortune for his son in case the latter should return. His neighbour, Chremes, also has a son, Clitipho, who before the beginning of the play has become entangled in an amour with a courtesan called Bacchis. Just as the play opens Clinia returns, unknown to his father, and with the consent of his old friend, Clitipho, sends a slave to invite Antiphila to meet him at the house of Chremes. To the surprise of both young men Bacchis accompanies Antiphila. Syrus, Clitipho's slave—the typical intriguer of Latin comedy—had persuaded her to visit his master, intending to pass her off on Chremes as the mistress of Clinia, while Antiphila, introduced as an attendant of Bacchis, was to be consigned to the care of Clitipho's mother.

Next morning Chremes informs Menedemus of his son's return, warns him of the extravagance of Bacchis, whom he takes for the young man's mistress, and advises him not to pardon his son at once and receive Bacchis into his house, but rather to postpone a reconciliation till some more suitable arrangement could be made. Shortly after this Chremes discovers that his own son has been taking improper liberties with Bacchis. He rebukes him sharply and orders him off, while he consults with Syrus about a plan to get rid of Clinia and his mistress. Syrus hits on the idea of transferring Bacchis, bag and baggage, to the house of Menedemus, telling him the simple truth that she is the mistress of his neighbour's son, but giving Chremes to understand that this statement is a trick played on Menedemus to induce him to receive the lady. Just before the transfer is accomplished it transpires that Antiphila is the daughter of Chremes himself, exposed in her youth and brought up in ignorance of her parents. Clinia is overjoyed at the prospect of being able to marry the girl he loves. He visits his father, and informs him of the discovery. Menedemus comes straightway to Chremes to beg his daughter's hand for Clinia. Chremes at once informs him that Syrus and the young men have played a trick upon him, that Clinia is only feigning love for Antiphila, and that Bacchis is really his mistress. Menedemus returns to his house deeply distressed at the deceit which he thinks has been practised on him. Here, however, he receives the strongest possible proof of his son's innocence and Clitipho's connexion with Bacchis, and returns to triumph over the deluded Chremes. The latter now consents to give Antiphila to Clinia, and after reducing his own son to despair by the threat of disinheritance, pardons him on condition that he break with Bacchis, marry a neighbour's daughter, and settle down.

The close resemblance between the *Heautontimoroumenos* and *All Fools* will be apparent to every reader of Chapman's play. Setting aside the underplot and the final solution of the main intrigue—of

---

[1] For *The Case is Altered* see Baskerville, *English Elements in Jonson's Early Comedy*, published by the University of Texas, 1911.

which a word hereafter—the underlying structure of *All Fools* is taken
directly from the Latin comedy. The initial deceit practised on Gostanzo, his advice to Marc. Antonio to defer a reconciliation with his
son, the imprudent behaviour of Valerio to Gratiana while she is staying
in his father's house, the transfer of this lady from the house of Gostanzo to that of Marc. Antonio, the device by which this is effected, i.e.
the truth told with intent to deceive, the momentary triumph of Marc.
Antonio and his humiliation when Gostanzo reveals the supposed
trick, the ocular proof which convinces Marc. Antonio of the true state
of affairs, the wrath of Gostanzo when he learns the truth, and
his threat to disinherit his son—all have their exact counterparts in
the *Heautontimoroumenos*. In the conduct of the plot Gostanzo corresponds to Chremes, Marc. Antonio to Menedemus, Valerio to Clitipho,
Fortunio to Clinia, Gratiana to Bacchis, Bellanora to Antiphila, and
Rinaldo to the crafty slave, Syrus.

In addition to these structural resemblances, there are numerous
instances where Chapman follows Terence in details sometimes merely
taking a hint, sometimes directly translating the Latin. Thus the
readiness [1] of Marc. Antonio to pardon his son's supposed offence (*All
Fools*, I, i, 270–274) corresponds exactly to the temper of Menedemus
when informed of Clinia's amour (*Heauton*, ll. 463–6); Antonio's fear
lest his son might ' run into the wars ' (*All Fools*, I, i, 304 *sqq.*) is derived from the statement of Menedemus that Clinia had run away to
enlist as a soldier (*Heauton*, ll. 117, *sqq.*); and the words, ' you ope
him doors to any villany ' (*All Fools*, I, i, 275) are a direct translation
of *huic quantam fenestram ad nequitiem patefeceris* (*Heauton*, l. 481).

So far as plot goes there is little resemblance between *All Fools* and
the *Adelphi*, but there is an unmistakeable likeness between the main
characters of the two plays and their inter-relations.

In the *Adelphi* we have also a pair of fathers, Demea and Micio,
and a pair of sons, Ctesphio and Æschinus.[2] Demea lives in the
country and has brought his son up there with the utmost strictness; Micio, the citizen, has on the contrary treated his son with
every indulgence. Demea, the harsh and miserly father, is very well
satisfied with his system of education, and takes every opportunity
of blaming Micio's indulgence, while holding up his own son as a
model of good conduct and sobriety. As a matter of fact, however,
this son has completely hoodwinked his father, and when the play
opens is involved in an amour with a music-girl. Demea gets

---

[1] These and other resemblances have been pointed out by Dr. Stier. For
further parallels, cf. *A. F.*, I, i, 284 and *Heauton*, l. 463; *A.F.*, I, ii, 111, 117–8,
138–9, and *Heauton*, ll. 332, 328, 376–7. Compare also the satisfaction with
which Gostanzo hears of Rinaldo's device upon Marc. Antonio (*A.F.*, III, i,
90–93) with Chremes' approval of Syrus (*Heauton*, ll. 760–70), and *A.F.*, III,
i, 109–11, with *Heauton*, ll. 591–3. In *A.F.*, IV, i, 24–6, we have as Koeppel
notes (*loc. cit.*, p.7) an elaboration of the Terentian simplicity of *Heauton*, ll. 502–5
into picturesque Elizabethan metaphor. The same might perhaps be said
of *A.F.*, IV, i, 54 and *Heauton*, l. 857. There are further a group of close
parallels in the scenes where Gostanzo and Chremes respectively learn the
truth (cf. *A.F.*, V, ii, 123–44, with *Heauton*, ll. 900–918). Finally it is something more than a coincidence that exactly the same time, one night, elapses
between the second and third acts of both plays (cf. *A.F* , III, i, 28 and
Heauton, l. 410).
[2] The fact that Æschinus is really the son of Demea and only adopted by
his uncle, Micio, is from the present point of view of no importance.

wind of the intrigue, but is deluded [1] by a crafty slave—called
Syrus, as in the *Heautontimoroumenos*—into believing that the other
son, Æschinus, is the guilty party, and that Ctesipho's sole connexion
with the intrigue has been to reproach his brother for his bad conduct.
At the close of the play when Demea learns the truth, he suddenly
resolves to alter his system, outdoes even Micio in generosity, and
brings the action to a happy ending. The likeness between the character and conduct of Demea and Gostanzo, and of Ctesipho and Valerio,
is too pronounced to be accidental, and this likeness is of the first
importance in Chapman's play.   The self-torturing motif of . the
Heautontimoroumenos is, as we have seen, wanting in *All Fools*, and
in its place we have as the mainspring of the action the character of
Gostanzo, for it is his harsh and grudging disposition which drives
Valerio into a secret marriage and makes him unwilling to confess his
act until he has made sure beforehand of his father's forgiveness.
The *dénouement* of the main action, also, seems, as we shall see later
(p. 706), to have been influenced, if not directly suggested, by that
of the *Adelphi*.[2]

In addition to these borrowings from the *Heautontimoroumenos* and
the *Adelphi*, Stier has pointed out a striking resemblance between
two incidents which occur in the last acts of *All Fools* and Terence's
Eunuch respectively.   Like Parmeno in the *Eunuch* (ll. 923, ssq.),
Rinaldo is discovered boasting of the cleverness by which he tricked
others (*A.F.*, V, i, 11, ssq.), he is approached by one of his dupes with
a plausible story, and frightened into betraying the whereabouts of
his friend (his master in the *Eunuch*) to that friend's father in the
hope of saving the friend and himself from dire consequences. The
further similarity that no harm comes of the betrayal and that in both
cases the father is reconciled to his erring son, adds, I think, to the
probability that Chapman borrowed this incident from the *Eunuch*.
Possibly this borrowing was an afterthought introduced when Chapman revised his play (see above, p. 701, n.).   There are, moreover, two
passages in which a certain verbal likeness exists between *All Fools*
and the *Eunuch*, although in both cases Chapman has transformed
rather than translated the original Latin ; cf. *All Fools*, I, ii, 101–3
and II, i, 205 with the *Eunuch*, ll. 372–3 and 1044–6 respectively.[3]

[1] Cf. *A.F.*, I, i, 194–222 and *Adelphi*, ll. 392–413.

[2] There are, moreover, a number of scattered passages in *All Fools* in which
the influence of the *Adelphi* is more or less plainly perceptible.   Thus when
Gostanzo sneers at the poverty of Gratiana (*A.F.*, I, i, 253–6, 263, 289–93)
we are reminded of Demea's objection to Pamphila as a wife for Æschinus
(*Adelphi*, ll. 728–9).   The drunken insolence of Valerio to his father is reminis-
cent of the behaviour of Syrus to Demea (cf. especially *A.F.*, V, ii, 97–8 with
Adelphi, l. 797). Marc. Antonio's comment on Gostanzo's niggardliness toward
his son (*A.F.*, II, i, 184–6) is an expansion of a like remark by Micio (*Adelphi*,
l. 64).   And, finally, the ' old acquaintance and long neighbourhood ' of Gostanzo and Marc. Antonio (*A.F.*, II, i, 20) corresponds rather to the fraternal
relation between Demea and Micio than to the acquaintance barely three
months old (*Heauton*, ll. 53–4, 118, 146) of Chremes and Menedemus.

[3] Stier notes further that the allusion by Rinaldo to Gostanzo's advances to
Gratiana (*A.F.*, IV, i, 98–9) may be derived from Plautus in whose work we
have three instances of a father enamoured of his son's mistress (*Casina*,
Asinaria, and *Mercator*).   This is possible, but as Chapman makes no further
use of this motif, I am inclined to think that he invented it simply to heighten
the hypocrisy of Gostanzo.

One might imagine from the numerous resemblances in plot, characterization, and dialogue between *All Fools* and these Latin comedies, that the work of Chapman was that of a mere adapter, and that *All Fools* was, at best, a clever mosaic of bits borrowed from the classics. The truth, however, is quite the contrary. Chapman has handled his materials with the greatest freedom. In the first place he has made some striking alterations in the *dramatis personae ;* Bacchis, the courtesan, becomes Gratiana, the secret wife ; Antiphila, the exposed daughter, becomes Bellanora who has never left her father's house ; Syrus, the slave, becomes Rinaldo, a younger brother of Bellanora, and a bosom friend of the hero. With these changes[1] the whole world of the New Comedy of Menander and Terence, a world of courtesans, exposed infants, and rascally slaves, disappears from the scene, and we find ourselves at once in modern times. Following a convention of early Elizabethan comedy, as Jonson did in the first version of *Every Man in his Humour,* Chapman lays the scene in Italy, but the whole atmosphere of the play is that of Elizabethan England. This transformation is aided by Chapman's addition to the original plot of a sub-plot dealing with the ' humour ' of a jealous husband, which both in theme and treatment is purely English.

Even in his handling of the main plot Chapman has shown himself quite free. He has re-arranged, altered, and invented scenes and incidents, at will. Thus at the very opening of the action Chapman diverges from his model. The incident which starts the intrigue of the *Heautontimoroumenos* is the unexpected and incredible impudence of Syrus in bringing Bacchis to the house of Chremes. For this Chapman substitutes a surprisal[2] of the lovers by the stern parent, a rally in their defence by the quick-witted Rinaldo, and a lie, told on the spur of the moment, from whose natural consequences springs the whole course of the intrigue.

Chapman has not, I think, been so successful in his alteration of the *dénouement.* A change of some sort was, of course, forced upon him, for the solution of the *Heautontimoroumenos* had become impossible after his transformation of the courtesan into the secret wife. Chapman, who is never very happy in his solutions, seems in this case to have adopted that of the *Adelphi.* But the change of heart in Demea which makes possible the happy ending of this play is carefully motivated by Terence, whereas the conversion of Gostanzo is both unexpected and unconvincing. Good acting and the illusion of the stage would, perhaps, carry it off in the theatre, but to the reader it remains, as Swinburne has noted, the one marked blemish of the play.

The transference of the lady, on the other hand, from one house to the other is more happily motivated in Chapman, I think, than in Terence. Nothing is more likely than that Gostanzo, when he discovers his son dangling about the supposed wife of Fortunio, should

---

[1] Koeppel, (*loc. cit.*, p. 6), was, I believe, the first to point out these changes and their effect upon the play.

[2] Possibly Chapman took a hint for this surprise from two scenes in the *Adelphi* (III, iii, and V, iii) in the first of which Demea learns of Ctesipho's connexion with the seizure of the music-girl, and in the second discovers him revelling with her at the house of Micio. But if so, Chapman has treated his source with even more than his usual freedom, and it is impossible to pronounce positively upon the question.

take immediate steps to remove the dangerously attractive lady from his house. Chremes, on the contrary, though sharply rebuking his son for his improper conduct, seems quite content to allow Bacchis to remain with him. She does indeed leave his house for that of Menedemus shortly afterwards ; but it is on the suggestion of Syrus, and so far as I can see there is no good reason for her shift of quarters. Professor Koeppel, indeed, objects (*loc. cit.*, p. 6) that Chapman, in the haste of adaptation, has made a gross blunder in permitting Gostanzo to indulge in ' the incredible folly ' of believing that Marc. Antonio would receive Gratiana as Valerio's wife. But Chapman's alterations, successful or not, are carefully planned, and the folly of Gostanzo is amply accounted for by his overweening contempt of his neighbour's simplicity. Such an honest fool as Marc. Antonio, he believes, will swallow anything (*All Fools*, III, i, 95–98). Gostanzo, like the other characters in the play, is gulled through his master-passion.

One of the happiest of Chapman's departures from his original is a piece of pure invention, the scene of Valerio's mock repentance and his father's feigned forgiveness (*All Fools*, IV, i). There is not even a suggestion of such a scene in the Latin, yet it springs legitimately from the situation. It is a bit of high comedy ; the frantic protestations of the young scapegrace, the exaggerated anger of his father, the growing alarm of Gratiana as the jest seems to her to be passing into earnest, and the frank amazement of the honest Marc. Antonio for whose supposed benefit the performance is enacted, all combine to form a situation as delightful to the reader of to-day as it must have been on the stage of the Blackfriars. I have said elsewhere [1] that Chapman's comic force lies in incident and situation rather than in character or dialogue, and there is hardly another scene in Chapman's work where his grasp on a comic situation and his ability to develop all its latent springs of mirth appears so fully.

The chief characters of *All Fools* as well as the main plot are, as I have shown, taken over from Terence. At bottom they are the stock figures of New Comedy, the stern father, the indulgent father, the riotous son, and the crafty intriguer. But Chapman's transforming power is revealed even more clearly in his elaboration of the characters than in his adaptation of the plot. Gostanzo is something more than a reproduction of Chremes or Demea. Harsh, miserly, and hypocritical, his dominant characteristic is an overweening self-conceit, which is treated by Chapman after the fashion of one of Jonson's ' humours '. Valerio, too, is not the mere stock type of the prodigal, but a highly individualized Elizabethan gallant. He has all the courtly graces ; he sings, he dances, he touches the theorbo, he knows the languages. And he has other less laudable accomplishments ; he drinks, dices, wenches and swaggers. He is a distinct forerunner of the rakish hero of Restoration comedy, but it is characteristic of Chapman's work, as it is of his time, that while the Restoration rake is, almost without exception, merely repulsive to modern taste, the character of Valerio is instinct with the Elizabethan [2] charm of youth, high spirits, and poetry. Like his father, however, he is dominated by a master-

---

[1] In my introduction to the *Belles-Lettres* edition of *All Fools*, p. xxxiv.
[2] Compare, for example, Valerio's impassioned outburst on love (*All Fools*, I, i, 97–123) with the utterances of any hero of Restoration comedy on the relation of the sexes.

passion, that of parade. He is as vain of his accomplishments and
gentlemanly vices as his father is of his worldly wisdom; and his vanity,
like his father's self-conceit, is treated by Chapman as a ' humour '.
Rinaldo, too, represents a complete transformation of the intriguing
slave of the new comedy. Not only is his social status elevated, but
he is portrayed as a scholar, ' a clerk of Padua ', with a touch of the
scholar's cynicism and contempt for women (*All Fools*, I, i, 44–91).
He has, of course, the ready wit and genius for intrigue of Syrus,
Davus, and the other familiar figures of Plautus and Terence. Chapman had already drawn such a figure in Lemot of *An Humourous
Day's Mirth*. But in Rinaldo the love of intrigue has become almost
a mania. He has a finger in every man's pie, and is never happy unless
he is meddling. It is through this exaggeration of his dominant
quality that Rinaldo, too, becomes a ' humourous ' figure. The character of Marc. Antonio alone among the main figures has remained
substantially unaltered. In Chapman as in Terence he is merely the
stock type of the indulgent father. The women of the play, it may
be said in passing, are mere puppets. Gratiana and Bellanora are
simply the necessary figures in the intrigue ; the fine differentiation
of character between Bacchis and Antiphila which we find in Terence
has been quite obliterated. This was a natural, though not, perhaps,
a necessary consequence of Chapman's alteration of the plot ; but in
his neglect to realize the character of Gazetta Chapman seems to me
to have let slip a valuable dramatic opportunity. But, in general
with only a few exceptions, Chapman seems to have felt little interest
in the characters of women.

It is in the sub-plot of *All Fools* that Chapman's delight in the
comedy of ' humours ' is most apparent. There is little action in this
part of the play ; it depends for its interest almost wholly upon the
' humour ' of its characters, the jealous husband, the amorous courtier,
the pedantic notary and doctor. Chapman's originality in this sub-
plot has been disputed. Professor Koeppel (*loc. cit.*, p. 7) holds that
the theme was suggested by the success of *The Merry Wives of Windsor* ;
Dr. Stier that Cornelio is a counterpart of Kitely in *Every Man in his
Humour*. But the date of *The Merry Wives* is too uncertain to permit
a positive statement that Chapman, who was at work on *All Fools* in
January, 1599, was influenced by Shakespeare's play, and while Kitely
doubtless antedates Cornelio, the treatment of jealousy as a comic
motif is far older than either, and Chapman had already employed it
in *An Humourous Day's Mirth* at a date certainly earlier than either
The Merry Wives or Jonson's play. The characterization of Cornelio,
with one exception to be presently noted, seems to me at once original
and brilliant. It would, of course, be absurd to compare Chapman
with Shakespeare as a character-creator, though I confess I do not
take Master Ford to be one of Shakespeare's supreme creations, but
with Jonson he stands on a more even footing. The character of
Kitely is, no doubt, more profoundly studied and more intense than
that of Cornelio ; but Jonson's very depth and intensity detracts here,
as elsewhere, from his success as a comic writer. Jealousy as a comic
theme must be lightly handled, and treated as an absurdity. If it is
taken seriously, the work begins to drift toward tragedy and the figures
of Leontes and Othello appear ominously on the horizon. One can
hardly ask, however, for a more ridiculous figure of the jealous husband
than Chapman has given us in Cornelio, whose suspicions arise wholly

from his own imagination, lead him on to unreasonable action, and
are finally laid as easily as they have been aroused. The one fault,
and it seems to me serious, in the characterization of Cornelio appears
in the conclusion, when we hear that he has never been really jealous
of his wife, but has only played the part to ' bridle her stout stomach '
(*All Fools*, V, ii, 213). Unless we are to take this as a mere boast of
his—a subtlety of which I hardly can believe Chapman capable—it
is plain that consistency of character has here been sacrificed to a
desire to round out the plot and to show that those who had believed in
Cornelio's jealousy, like the other characters in the play, were all fools.

The minor figures in the sub-plot, the doctor and the notary, are
little more than caricatures, amusing enough on the stage, where each
in turn does his turn and disappears, but having little connexion with
real life. The courtier, Dariotto, on the other hand, is an admirable
study of the philanderer and the fop, a forerunner of such typical
figures of Restoration comedy as Sir Fopling Flutter and Sir Novelty
Fashion. He is evidently drawn from the life, and one has but to
compare his strongly marked individuality with the minor figures of
An Humourous Day's Mirth, the undistinguishable Colinets, Blanuels
and Rowleys, to see how far Chapman had advanced in the art of
character-portrayal.

The fact that *All Fools*, though originally written for the Admiral's
Men and presumably performed by them at the Rose, was later presented by the boys' company at Blackfriars, makes it natural for us
to assume a revision [1] of the play. Its present form would therefore
represent Chapman's fully developed power as a writer of comedy.
A discovery of the hypothetical first form which would permit us to
judge the extent of his development between 1599 and 1603 or 1604
would be of the greatest interest. From internal evidence, which is
all we have, it is impossible, I think, to pronounce with any degree of
precision how far the play was altered in revision. Certainly the outline of the main plot and its chief characters must have been the same
in both versions. I fancy the improvements consisted mainly in
polishing [2] the verse, in sharpening the dialogue, in the introduction
of new incidents, in heightening the ' humours ', and notably in the
addition of a couple [3] of long prose speeches parodying the manner
of Lyly in a way which must have been especially entertaining to the
cultivated audience of Blackfriars. Stier has pointed out in the first
of these some of the typical characteristics of Euphuism, antithesis,
the rhetorical question, alliteration, annomination, and plays on words.
The ludicrous alteration of a well-known passage in Lyly (see below,
p. 718) makes it evident that we are here dealing with a conscious and
deliberate parody of Lyly's style. These characteristics of Euphuism
are not so evident in the second passage, although a careful examina-

---

[1] Fleay, perhaps, goes too far in speaking of ' the absolute certainty ' of
Chapman's refashioning this play (*Biographical Chronicle*, vol. i, p. 57) ; but
there is little reason to doubt that it took place. There is almost a moral
certainty that a play first presented at the Rose would need alteration to
adapt it to the different character of both the stage and the audience of Blackfriars. Chapman's careful revision of *Bussy* occurred, I believe, when this
play was taken over from Paul's Boys by the company acting at Whitefriars.
See my article in *The Modern Language Review* for January, 1908.

[2] Cf. the number of minute changes made in Chapman's revision of *Bussy*.

[3] The Page's speech (III, i, 182 *ssq.*) and Valerio's oration (V, ii, 236 *ssq.*).

tion will easily discover some of them, but the comic theme of the oration combined with the affected gravity of the treatment shows that Chapman is ridiculing the formal and elaborate discourses with which Lyly's work abounds.

The *Prologue* to *All Fools* was certainly composed for the first performance at Blackfriars.[1] Written a year or more after the close of the so-called War of the Theatres, it betrays an uneasy consciousness of the fickle taste of the Elizabethan audience. Plays in which personal satire was predominant—such plays as *Sir Giles Goosecap* and *The Poëtaster*, for example—have been hissed off (*exploded*, l. 16) by some discontented auditors, while, on the other hand, pure comedy of incident has been pronounced flat and tasteless. Nor has it been possible to assure the success of a play by lively dialogue marked by ' quick Venerian jests '. Sometimes these have ravished the audience, sometimes they have left it quite unmoved. Neither author nor actor understands the hidden causes of success or failure, and therefore the playwright puts in an humble plea for a patient hearing, particularly addressed to that part of the audience which sat upon the stage. The bad behaviour of these gallants—described in detail by Dekker[2]—especially their practice of leaving the theatre in the middle of a play, must have been most embarrassing to the actors and a potent cause in bringing about the failure of a play.

It is interesting to compare the tone of this prologue with that which characterizes Jonson's early addresses to his audiences. Chapman lacks Jonson's proud assurance of artistic righteousness; he avoids alike Jonson's bitter denunciation of his critics and his appeal to better natures to support his crusade against ' the ragged follies of the time '. He is something of a fatalist, and, having once done his work, entrusts it to Fortune to survive or perish as the Goddess wills. Yet there is throughout the *Prologue* a vein of sub-acid satire on the fickleness and irresponsibility of the audience which utters the judgments of Fortune. Their talents for criticism, assisted as these are by fair attire and a conspicuous position on the stage, are doubtless great, and their condemnation must make fools of the actors. But after all the question rises whether their judgments may not be merely the judgments of fools :

Auriculas asini quis non habet ?

A fitting quotation to introduce a play which bears the title of *All Fools*.

From many points of view *All Fools* is a most interesting play. It is of interest in the development of Chapman's art. Compared with *All Fools*, *The Blind Beggar* and *An Humourous Day's Mirth* are crude and imperfect sketches. It is of interest in the development of Elizabethan comedy, for, with the possible exception of Shakespeare's *Comedy of Errors*, it represents the most successful attempt of that age to domesticate Latin comedy on the English stage. Jonson attempted the same task about the same time, or possibly a little earlier, in *The Case is Altered* ; but it is no injustice to Jonson to say that in

---

[1] It contains among other things an interesting allusion to the practice of sitting on the stage customary at Blackfriars, if not wholly confined to that theatre. See Wallace, *Children of the Chapel*, chap. xi, and Baskerville's criticism of Wallace's views in *Modern Philology*, April, 1911.

[2] *The Gull's Hornbook*, chapter vi.

this one instance his work is decidedly inferior to Chapman's. *The Case is Altered*, apart from episodical English elements, adheres almost slavishly to its originals, and the two borrowed plots are placed in juxtaposition rather than blended into a harmonious whole. Jonson's play is an interesting experiment, Chapman's, on the whole, a successful achievement in the adaptation of Latin comedy. Apart from the somewhat unsatisfactory conclusion, the faulty features of *All Fools* appear in the original sub-plot rather than in the part which Chapman took over from his sources.

Chapman undoubtedly gained much from his study and imitation of Terence. One of his chief faults as a playwright was his inability to construct a coherent, well-proportioned, and interesting plot. The story of *The Blind Beggar* is a farrago of romantic and farcical incidents; the plot of *An Humourous Day's Mirth*, complicated as it seems on the first perusal, may be reduced, on analysis, to a couple of practical jokes. Even in later plays such as *Sir Giles Goosecap* and *The Widow's Tears* this weakness of plot structure is apparent. But for *All Fools* Terence gave Chapman the solid and well-constructed groundwork of the play as a basis on which the superstructure of incident, situation, and humorous character might be erected.

A comparison of *All Fools* with a play of Jonson's produced in the same year, *Every Man out of his Humour*, throws light upon an interesting difference in dramatic technic between the two playwrights. Both plays are comedies of ' humours ', and in both the motif is the same, the ' humour ' as a master-passion by means of which a man is tricked and, in the end, cured through ridicule. Gostanzo and Cornelio at the close of *All Fools* are striking instances of men ' out of their humour ', to use Jonson's phrase. Jonson, however, the greatest theorist of Elizabethan playwrights, was so far misled by his theory of satirical drama that in *Every Man out of his Humour* he entirely neglected to provide a coherent intrigue. Scene after scene of this play contains only an exhibition of various ' humours ', admirably done, of course, but essentially satire rather than drama. Chapman had already done something of this kind in *An Humourous Day's Mirth*, but in *All Fools* the exploitation of the various ' humours ' springs naturally from the course of the intrigue and enlivens the action without attempting to serve as a substitute for it. As a result Jonson's play is to-day interesting merely to the student of Elizabethan manners, while *All Fools* has the universal interest that naturally attaches to a good story well presented in true dramatic form.

In *All Fools*, contrary to his method in *An Humourous Day's Mirth*, Chapman has employed verse for much the greater part of the play. In fact, only three scenes (III, i, IV, i, and V, ii) contain prose. The prose passages belong without exception to the underplot and present matter of broad farce or satirical parody, for which Chapman rightly judged prose to be the proper vehicle. Chapman had by this time obtained such a mastery of blank verse that he was able to use it fluently in scenes of lively dialogue and bustling action, as well as in more elevated passages. The verse rises and falls with its theme, at times swift, simple, and unadorned, at times soaring to outbursts of true poetic beauty. The play is in structure and background essentially realistic, a comedy of intrigue and manners; but Chapman has imparted to it something of that flavour of romance which is the characteristic charm of Elizabethan comedy. *All Fools* differs markedly in this respect from *Every Man in his Humour*, especially in its final and more realistic form, or from *Eastward Ho*, in which the influence of Jonson is predominant. The ethical earnestness which is so constant a feature of Jonson's comedy is wholly wanting in this play. Yet Chapman does not sink here to the cynicism which mars some of his later work, notably *The Widow's Tears*. The characters in *All Fools* are non-moral, rather immoral; it would be patently absurd to judge them by the standards which we apply to real life or realistic figures. ' Over all the dialogue and action there plays ', says Swinburne,[1] ' a fresh and radiant air of mirth and light swift buoyancy of life '. And nothing contributes so much to this atmosphere as the ease and charm of Chapman's verse.

After all the true test of a play is the stage, and it was with a sense of real satisfaction that I saw *All Fools* sustain this test during a performance by a company of amateur actors—students of Harvard University—in the spring of 1909. For a detailed account of this performance I would refer any reader who may be interested in the revival of Elizabethan drama to my letter in *The Nation* (New York) of April 22, 1909. It is enough to say here that the acting, amateurish and imperfect as it naturally and necessarily was, revealed a vitality of comic power in Chapman's work that I, at least, had never realized before. The various ' humours ', in particular, proved immensely more effective upon the stage than in the closet. The complicated intrigue became in the action as clear as day, and the whole performance manifestly delighted a mixed and highly critical audience. Their spontaneous bursts of applause were to me a convincing testimony to the dramatic and comic genius of an author who has seldom been accorded his just place among the Elizabethan poet-playwrights.

[1] Swinburne, *George Chapman*, p. 49.

Addendum.—Since these pages were put in type, the investigation of Mr. Ernest Law has shown that the list of plays published by Cunningham (see above, p. 702) is correct, the document on which it is based being indisputably genuine, and not, as was long believed, a modern forgery; see Law, *Some Supposed Shakespeare Forgeries*, 1911. This fixes the date *ad quem* of *All Fools*.

ALL FOOLS

NOTES

Prologus.

l. 4. *Hell . . . heaven :* the pit and gallery of the theatre.

ll. 11–12. ' He is more happy who can enter into the contest backed by your favour '.

ll. 14–6. *Eupolis and Cratinus :* contemporaries of Aristophanes, and like him writes of ' Old Comedy ', *the ancient comic vein.* Chapman probably got their names from Horace :

> *Eupolis atque Cratinus Aristophanesque poetae.*
>
> Satires, I, iv, I.

There is doubtless a reference in ll. 14–5 to the bitter satire with its *personal application* prevalent during the War of the Theatres. The word *exploded* has here its etymological sense, ' driven off '; Chapman probably borrows it from a well-known passage in Horace, *Satires*, I, x, 74–77, in which the phrase *explosa Arbuscula* occurs.

l. 24. *Panegyric spleen :* humour of applause. The spleen in the physiology of Chapman's day was supposed to be the seat of various emotions, not of ill-humour alone. Thus in *The Maid's Tragedy*, III, ii, 268, Evadne and the King are spoken as laughing as if ' their spleens would break '.

l. 27. *Mystery* has here its modern sense. Collier's reading, *misery* (see Text Notes, p. 727) destroys the meaning of the passage.

l. 28. *United heads :* the combined wits of the audience.

l. 29. *The stage :* a place on the stage, such as was specially sought after in private theatres by the gallants of the day. See the *Induction* to *Cynthia's Revels*, and *The Gull's Hornbook*, chapter vi.

l. 30. *Our other audience :* the rest of the audience as contrasted with those who sat on the stage itself.

l. 34. ' That the merit of a play has the least possible influence on the satisfaction which the greater part of the audience derive from it '. *Contents* is the plural of the abstract noun ' content ', i.e. ' satisfaction ', or ' pleasure ', and refers to the various degrees of satisfaction felt by the individual members of the audience.

l. 35. From Persius, *Satire* I, 121.

I, i, 1. *One self cause :* one and the same cause.

I, i, 33–4. ' The service of love is like that of our capricious lords where favourites have more influence than true servants '.

I, i, 38. *He :* i.e. Valerio. The nominative case is used instead of the objective for the sake of emphasis.

I, i, 40. Fortunio has to wear the willow as a token of his ill success in love ; Valerio as a married man is predestined to the horn.

I, i, 45–51. These lines present a striking contrast to one of the most famous passages in Marlowe (*1 Tamburlaine*, V, i, 160–173), which may have been in Chapman's mind as he wrote. Chapman's point of view is that of the stoic who reckons beauty as an external phenomenon.

I, i, 47. *A cozening picture :* Collier refers to Tollet's note on *Twelfth Night*, V, i, 244, in Johnson and Steevens' edition of Shakespeare : ' It is a pretty art that in a pleated paper and table furrowed and indented men make one picture to represent several faces—that being viewed from one place or standing did show the head of a Spaniard, and from another the head of an ass '. Chapman makes repeated reference to this ' pretty art '; see *Chabot*, I, i, 68–72, and *Ovid's Banquet of Sense*, stanza 3.

I, i, 55. *Made me happy:* esteemed me fortunate.

I, i, 67. *Men rich in dirt:* wealthy landowners. Cf. *Hamlet*, V, ii, 90 : *spacious in the possession of dirt*, and *Sir Giles Goosecap*, I, iv, 138, *brave men of dirt*.

I, i, 69–76. There are several reminiscences of Juvenal in this outburst. See *Satire VI*, ll. 166–9, 461–6, 474–80. With ll. 69–72, cf. *Monsieur D'Olive*, I, i, 351–4.

I, i, 80–90. Schoell notes that this simile occurs in Nash (*Anatomy of Absurditie; Works*, vol. i., p. 34, McKerrow's edition), and suggests that Chapman borrowed it from him. McKerrow's note on the passage shows that the simile first occurs in Lucian, *Imagines*, 11. In phrasing and application Chapman seems to me nearer to Lucian than to Nash.

I, i, 92. *The poor fox.* The reference is to the well-known fable of Æsop (*Fabulae Æsopicae*, no. 46, Teubner edition).

I, i, 97–104. Collier (*History of English Dramatic Poetry*, vol. iii, p. 257, n. edition of 1831) asserts that ' the whole thought and soul of the expressions are here borrowed from a madrigal by Andrea Navagero, which is inserted in Domenichi's collection, *Rime Diverse*, Venice, 1546, beginning :

> *Leggiadre donne, che quella bellezza*
> *Che natura vi diede'.*

I have examined this poem, which occurs, vol. i, p. 98 of *Rime Diverse*, but can only find a very general resemblance of thought. There is no ground, I believe, for charging Chapman with having imitated the Italian.

I, i, 130. Cf. *The Arcadia*, Book II (p. 108, edition of 1638) : ' Dametas who came whistling and counting upon his fingers how many load of hay seventeen fat oxen eat up in a year '. The rustic Dametas is throughout contrasted with the chivalric and amorous heroes of the romance, much as Rinaldo here contrasts Valerio's earlier occupations with his present condition.

I, i, 148. *Machiavellian.* The name of the great Florentine was in Chapman's day a byword to denote an unscrupulous intriguer. Marlowe in the *Prologue* to *The Jew of Malta* (1598–90) was the first to bring him upon the stage, after which there are numberless references to him in the drama.

I, i, 153. *Canst skill of :* understandest. *Skill* is the now obsolete verb meaning to be ' versed in' ' or practised in the use of '.

I, i, 156–7. *Tobacco-shops.* ' It should be observed ', says Gifford in a note on Jonson's *Alchemist*, I, i, 404–5, ' that the houses of druggists (tobacconists) were not merely furnished with tobacco, but with conveniences for smoking it. Every well-frequented shop was an academy of this " noble art " where professors regularly attended to initiate the country aspirant '. Barnaby Rich in his tract on the abuses of his time, called *The Honestie of this Age*,[1] 1614, introduces a shoemaker in talk with a starving poet, possibly Robert Greene, and puts into his mouth the statement that ' three companies . . . have gotten all the trade into their own hands ; the first is to keep an ale house, the second a tobacco house, and the third to keep a brothel house '.

I, i, 164. *Gentlewoman :* a trisyllable.

I, i, 249. ' I do not know why you should have such an opinion of him '. For this now obsolete meaning of *intend*, see the *New English Dictionary*, sub *intend* IV, 15.

I, i, 260–1. ' 'Tis to be feared that his over-confident conduct is not grounded upon the goodness of his choice which would warrant his action '.

I, i, 264–6. ' If my son has made choice of a woman whose birth and virtues make her his equal '. *Disparagement* has here its original meaning, ' marriage to one of inferior rank ', implying also the disgrace attaching to such a marriage.

I, i, 301. *Want of misery :* i.e. miserable poverty.

I, i, 316. *Padua.* Cf. ' The Citie of Padua renowned . . . for the antiquitie of the famous Universitie ' (Greene's *Mamillia*, 1583). The university, founded in the thirteenth century, appears to have been the best known

---

[1] Reprinted by the Percy Society in 1844, vol. xi, p. 42.

of all Italian universities to Englishmen of Shakespeare's day. The references to it in Elizabethan literature are innumerable. In *May-Day* Chapman introduces a student from Padua as one of the gulls of the play, a figure not found in the Italian original. The pedant in *The Gentleman Usher* has also studied at Padua.

I, i, 355. *Well qualified :* dowered with good qualities.

I, ii, 14. *One I hate :* with this reference to another suitor of Bellanora, cf. III, i, 7–9. No such figure appears in the play as it stands at present.

I, ii, 32. *With his best :* by all possible means.

I, ii, 37. ' Changes from a farmer into an out-and-out gallant '.

I, ii, 46–7. So in *Mother Bombie* (III, iii 17–18), old Stellio, jealous of his daughter's intercourse with Accius, says to her : ' I pray you look homeward, it is a cold air, and you want your muffler '.

I, ii, 51. *Chopping logic :* bandying arguments. There is often an implication of disrespectful action in this phrase, which is applied, as here, to a wife arguing with her husband, in *The Knight of the Burning Pestle*, I, iv, 31, to a son arguing with his mother, or, as in the quotation from Usher given in the *New English Dictionary*, sub *chop*, 8, to a subject arguing with his Prince.

I, ii, 57. *Heifer.* It seems somewhat curious that Gratiana should call Cornelio a heifer, but the reference is not so much to the sex of the animal as to its youth and lack of horns.

I, ii, 67. *Barley-break :* an old game originally played by three couples. There is an elaborate poetical description of it in Lamon's eclogue, *Arcadia*, Book I, and a briefer one in Suckling's little poem, beginning

> *Love, Reason, Hate, did once bespeak*
> *Three mates to play at barley-break.*

I, ii, 75. A bailiff with his staff of office.

I, ii, 78. The subject of *calls* is *Nature* in l. 77.

I, ii, 81. *John Death.* The proper name *John* is sometimes used as a representative proper name for a servant or a messenger. A passage from Jonson seems to show that it was especially applied to constables or bailiffs :

> *All constables are truly Johns for the king,*
> *Whate'er their names are, be they Tony or Roger.*
> *Tale of a Tub*, IV, ii.

I, ii, 87–8. ' What good cause my profound sagacity gives for you all to love me '.

I, ii, 94–5. ' What rage against her would seize her father's mind '.

I, ii, 118. *To lie at rack and manger :* to live in plenty, to want for nothing. The *New English Dictionary* gives quotations from Wyclif to Carlyle to illustrate this use. A closely analogous use to the present appears in *Greene's Mourning Garment* (Grosart's edition, vol. ix, p. 178) in the warning speech of the serving-man to Philador : ' Live not here, master, without doing somewhat ; Mars himself hateth to be ever on Venus' lap, he scorneth to lie at rack and manger '. Cf. the Scottish phrase ' *heck and manger* ' used by Scott in *Waverley*, chapter lxiv.

I, ii, 122–4. Cf. *The Widow's Tears*, II, iii, 69. In both cases the allusion is to the fabled practice of the she-bear's licking her unformed cubs into their natural shape.

I, ii, 141. *Them :* i.e. Fortunio and Gratiana.

II, i, 28. *All your amities :* friendship with all of you.

II, i, 39. *Hear odds :* learn the difference.

II, i, 42. *Come-you-seven :* a gambler, specifically a dice player, probably with reference to the game of hazard in which seven is the best ' main ' for the caster, and would therefore be invoked by him.

II, i, 53. *Through a grate :* through the grating of a door or window, i.e. at a distance, not intimately. Mr. Brereton (*Modern Language Review*, vol. iii, p. 398) suggests that the reference is to ' the well-known grating

of the Counter ', a prison in which debtors were confined. This is possible,
but the use of almost the same phrase above (I, ii, 99) leads me to believe
that the reference is general rather than specific. Professor Wallace
(*Children of the Chapel*, p. 132, n.) takes the same phrase in a satire of
Davies to allude to a grating in front of a box above the stage. It might
possibly be so interpreted here.

II, i, 67. *To shift . . . contentment* : to satisfy and get rid of him. Jonson
(*English Grammar*, chap. vii) states that in ' all nouns trisyllabic ' the
accent falls on the first syllable. If Chapman observed this rule the metre
of the line is perfectly regular.

II, i, 109. ' Were the irresistible instruments by which you were seduced '.

II, i, 152-3. *Invited the Duchess of his house.* Collier's reading, *the dutchess
to his house*, shows how he understood the passage. I can, however, find
no authority for such a use of *of* after *invite* and incline to believe that
the sense is ' invited the Duchess who was the head of his family '.

II, i, 163. *Drinking tobacco :* a common phrase at this time for ' smoking '.
The first certain instance that I find of it is in Jonson, *Every Man in his
Humour*, III, ii, *The most divine tobacco that ever I drunk*, although
Donne's use of the phrase, in *Satire I*, may antedate this. In *Every Man
out of his Humour*, III, iii, Jonson represents a gallant courting his mis-
tress between whiffs of a pipe.

II, i, 171-6. Gostanzo mentions various kinds of verse, some of which perhaps
need a word of explanation. An *Exordium* is the introduction or proem
of a composition, whether in verse or prose ; *Sonnets in dozens* are probably songs or sonnets of twelve lines in length, such as Sidney's *Sonnet
LIV* or Shakespeare's *Sonnet CXXVI ; Quatorzains*, the true sonnet in
fourteen lines. ' When the true sonnet was reintroduced into English,
it was often technically designated by the French word *quatorzain* rather
than by *sonnet*. Watson is congratulated on " scaling the skies in lofty
quatorzains " in verses before his *Passionate Centurie*, 1582. Cf. *crazed
quatorzains* in Thomas Nash's preface to his edition of Sidney's *Astrophel
and Stella*, 1591 ; and *Amours in Quatorzains* on the title-page of the
first edition of Drayton's Sonnets, 1594 '.—Lee (*Elizabethan Sonnets*,
p. xxxiii, n.). *Sdruciolla* are the triple or dactylic rhymes called *sdrucciolo*,
i.e. slippery, in Italian. Harrington, who made frequent use of these
rhymes in his translation of *Orlando Furioso*, 1591, defends himself in his
preface against those who criticized this practice by quoting the example
of Sir Philip Sidney (*An Apologie of Poetrie*, reprinted in Haslewood's
Ancient Critical Essays, Pt. II, pp. 143-5).

II, i, 208. *Th' evening crowns the day :* an old proverb. Hazlitt, *English
Proverbs*, p. 380, cites several more or less close parallels from Latin and
Italian.

II, i, 210. *Fortune in a string.* Cf. :

> *The Scythian Emperor*
> *Leads Fortune tied in a chain of gold.*
> > *Locrine*, II, i, 14-15.

and

> *Thou hast not Fortune tied in a chain.*
> > *Selimus* (Temple edition, l. 2420).

See also somewhat similar expression in Greene's *Alphonsus*, IV, iii,
1481, and *I Tamburlaine*, I, ii.

II, i, 221. With the stage-direction *Enter* Gazetta *sewing*, cf. that after
l. 229 below and *Sir Giles Goosecap*, II, i, stage-direction after l. 16.

II, i, 226. *Swagger.* In his address ' To the Understander ' prefixed to
Achilles Shield, 1598, Chapman says, ' Swaggering is a new word amongst
them [the young and over-captious readers of his work] and round-headed
custom gives it privilege with much imitation, being created as it were
by a natural Prosopopeia without etymology or derivation '. A slightly
earlier use of the word than this in the text appears in *The Case is Altered*,
I, i, where Juniper says to Valentine, *When shall we swagger.*

II, i, 229-31. With this speech of Valerio's cf. a similar bit of swaggering by Quintiliano, *May-Day*, IV, i, 23–27. The word *copesmate* may mean either 'adversary' or 'companion'. It has the first sense here; the second in IV, i, 244 below. *This light*, l. 230, refers to his sword.

II, i, 233–4. Fleay (*Biographical Chronicle*, vol. i, p. 58) sees here 'a palpable allusion to a speech of Ophelia's, *Hamlet*, IV, v, 176–180', and points out that 'the *columbine* does not occur among her flowers in the early version of *Hamlet* [1603]; it is [first] found in the 1604 quarto'. Fleay seems to imply that the presence of this 'palpable allusion' points to a revision of *All Fools* after Shakespeare's revision of *Hamlet*. Personally, I cannot feel the force of the 'palpable allusion'. It consists merely in the fact that two flowers out of the half-dozen in Ophelia's garland are mentioned here with the same meaning assigned or implied. But the language of flowers, in which the pansy refers to *lover's thoughts* and the columbine, the cuckold's flower, to ingratitude, was probably as familiar to Chapman as to Shakespeare, and there is such dramatic propriety in the jealous Cornelio's reference to these flowers that we may well believe that Chapman composed the lines without any thought of the passage in *Hamlet*.

II, i, 240. For a similar play on *adore* and *adhorn*, cf. *The Widow's Tears*, I, i, 108–9.

II, i, 252. The phrase *to dance in a net* seems originally to have meant 'to act with practically no disguise while expecting to escape notice'—*New English Dictionary*, sub *net*. In this sense it is plainly used in Greene's *Pandosto*, 1588 (*Works*, vol. iv, p. 293, and p. 344, where the phrase is explained on the basis of an old story). Cf. the phrases *March in a net* (*Spanish Tragedy*, IV, iv, 118) and *Hide in a net* (*King Henry V*, I, ii, 93). Later, as in Dryden, *Sir Martin Marrall*, IV, i, and *Limberham*, II, i, the phrase evidently means 'to do something undetected'. This passage in Chapman seems an early instance of the later meaning.

II, i, 281. *Play Menelaus:* an allusion to the hospitable reception given by Menelaus to Paris who came to rob him of his wife. See Ovid, *Heroides: Epistola* xvi, 127.

II, i, 282. *Well-taught waiting-woman:* cf. *Monsieur D'Olive*, V, i, 185–195.

II, i, 290–1. 'I will disappoint their aims by taking care myself of the mark they aim at', i.e. Gazetta's honour.

II, i, 303. *Leather jerkins:* the buff-coats of the sergeants who arrested debtors.

II, i, 306. *Forget his day:* pass the day on which payment was due.

II, i, 307. *Sort of corporals:* company of sergeant's under-officers, or yeomen, like Snare in *2 King Henry IV*.

II, i, 334. *Besides their books:* apart from, without, their briefs. Cf. Harvey's phrase: *I take it M. Proctor was beside his book* (*Letter-Book of Gabriel Harvey*, Camden Society, n.s., vol. xxxiii, p. 51).

II, i, 336–8. A reference to the 'War of the Theatres'. Possibly Jonson whose satirical comedies *Cynthia's Revels* and *The Poetaster* had been produced by the Chapel Children, is alluded to as *your best poet*.

II, i, 345–6. *Put a mad spleen into a pigeon:* cf.:

> I am pigeon-livered and lack gall.
>
> *Hamlet*, II, ii, 605.

II, i, 377. *Languages:* to read and speak Italian was an elegant accomplishment of the Elizabethan courtier. Chapman seems to forget here that Italian would be Valerio's mother-tongue, but in Castiglione's *Cortegiano* (*Tudor Translations*, p. 369) Italian, as well as French and Spanish, is mentioned as 'one of the conditions' of a courtier.

II, i, 380. *Against the hair:* usually the phrase means 'against one's natural bent or inclination'. Here it seems to mean 'in spite of a seeming impossibility'.

II, i, 384. See Text Notes, p. 729.

II, i, 394. 'Touch' was the proper technical word for playing upon the theorbo or lute.

II, i, 397. *No husband:* no niggard, perhaps with a pun on Valerio's position as husbandman or farmer to his father. In the stage-direction following this line Valerio *untrusses*, i.e. loosens the points which bound doublet and hose together, to give greater freedom for the capers he cuts. Cf. the stage-direction in *Sir Giles Goosecap*, II, i, 75, *he danceth speaking*.

II, i, 408–9. In the first line *natural* means ' a gift of nature ' probably with an implied pun on the meaning ' foolish ', ' ridiculous '; in the second *natural* means ' legitimate,' not ' bastard ' as we would now understand it. Valerio means that his father would renounce him as no true son if the old man knew his gifts.

III, i, 14–15. According to the Homeric mythology accepted by Virgil, the ivory gate of sleep was that through which deluding visions came to men. ' Twain are the gates of shadowy dreams, the one is fashioned of horn and one of ivory. Such dreams as pass through the portals of sawn ivory are deceitful, and bear tidings that are unfulfilled ' *Odyssey*, XIX, 562, *ssq.* (Butcher and Lang's translation). See also *Æneid*, VI, 893–6.

III, i, 20–22. These lines appear to be a snatch of an old song.

III, i, 30–31. *Head of the right modern fashion :* i.e. adorned with horns. So in l. 53 below the reference is to the horns of the cuckold.

III, i, 91. *In sadness :* seriously, truly.

III, i, 94. A *gudgeon* is a small fish much used for bait. Hence metaphorically for bait, or a trap or device to catch any one. Cf. *Monsieur D'Olive*, IV, ii, 155. It has also, by extension, the meaning, one who will swallow any bait, hence a credulous person. Cf. the modern colloquial use of ' sucker ', and see the quotation given in *The Century Dictionary* under *Sucker*, 7. This latter sense appears in *The Gentleman Usher*, I, ii, 171–2.

III, i, 107. *Tó sing the cuckoo's note :* i.e. to be a cuckold. Cf. *Love's Labour's Lost*, V, ii, 908–12.

III, i, 115. *Out of blind Fortune's hands :* when deprived of the aid of Fortune.

III, i, 119. ' Halliwell : " *Grope* or *tickle*, a kind of fishing by putting one's hand into the water holes where fish lie, and tickling them about the gills, by which means they'll become so quiet that a man may take them in his hand "—*Dict. Rust.* Catching trout in this manner is an old and deadly mode of poaching '. Cited from the note on *Twelfth Night*, II, v, 23, in Furness's *Variorum Shakespeare*.

III, i, 123. ' Even that quantity of common sense which fools usually have '.

III, i, 130. *His :* i.e. Dariotto's.

III, i, 134. *Procure her quiet :* make her peace.

III, i, 139. *Yellow fury :* jealousy.

III, i, 144–5. Cf. below, V, ii, 306–7.

III, i, 147. Cf. Juvenal's phrase :

> *Quis custodiet ipsos custodes.*
>
> *Satire VI*, 347–8.

III, i, 150. *The keeper's fee ;* cf. the old rhyme quoted in *Woodstock*, chap. xxxi :

> *The haunch to thee,*
> *The breast to me,*
> *The hide and the horns for the keeper's fee.*

and also :

> *Here's a deer whose skin's a keeper's fee.*
>
> *3 King Henry VI*, III, i, 22.

III, i, 179. *Mercurio :* here referred to as the god of eloquence.

III, i, 190. *Set to :* impressed.

III, i, 205–7. Stier points out (*loc. cit.*, p. 60) that these lines contain a parody of a well-known passage in Euphues : ' As therefore the sweetest rose hath his prickle, the finest velvet his brack, the fairest flour his bran '. (Lyly—*Works*, edited by Bond, vol. i, p. 184. Cf. also vol. i, p. 179, where the passage re-occurs with the substitution of the leopard and his spots for the flour and bran.) The repetition of this passage almost word for word in *A Merry Knack to know a Knave*, 1594, shows that it was familiar to the stage. As Stier says, Chapman's introduction of the homely cheese and its rind into this high-flown passage shows his purpose of ridiculing Lyly's style.

III, i, 215. *Gardens near the town:* Collier in his note on this passage cites the following from Stubbes, *Anatomy of Abuses*, 1595 : ' In the fields and suburbs of the city they [citizens' wives] have gardens either paled or walled round very high, with their arbours and bowers fit for the purpose. . . . Then to these gardens they repair, when they list with a basket and a boy, where they meeting their sweethearts, receive their wished desires '.

III, i, 233. *The law allows them no wills.* By the Acts of 32 Henry VII, c. 1 and 34, 35 Henry VIII, c. 5, married women were rendered incapable of devising real estate. By common law in England a married woman could not, except in a few exceptional cases, make a will without her husband's consent until the *Married Women's Property Act* of 1882.

III, i, 247. *Men of their hands :* men of prowess, here of course in the wars of love.

III, i, 274. *Lips perfum'd :* the use of perfumes on the person was one of the marks of a courtier. Corin, in *As You Like It*, III, ii, 65, speaks of the courtier's perfumed hands.

III, i, 275. *Playest the stallion :* cf. *Monsieur D'Olive*, I, i, 238.

III, i, 286. Cf. the phrase *a wound shall never bleed*, III, i, 425, below. The phrase is perhaps borrowed from Ovid :

> *Haec est praecipuo victoria digna triumpho,*
> *In qua, quaecumquest, sanguine praeda caret.*
>
> > *Amores*, II, xii, 5–6.

III, i, 302. I have not been able to discover the source of this phrase. Professor Rand of Harvard suggests that Chapman, with memories of certain lines of Ovid (*Amores*, II, xix, 3 ; *Ars Amoris*, ii, 247 and iii, 603) may have himself composed the line after a well-known phrase of Terence :

> *Sine Cerere et Libero friget Venus.*
>
> > *Eunuchus*, 372.

III, i, 297–308. There is a general resemblance between this passage and various lines in Ovid, *Elegies*, II, 19.

III, i, 314. *These two :* Valerio and Claudio.

III, i, 318. Cf. IV, i, 304, and note below.

III, i, 345. With these words, I suppose, Dariotto makes horns at Cornelio. This would account for the latter's outburst.

III, i, 349. *Raise the streets :* call on the passers-by for aid ; cf. *An Humourous Day's Mirth.* sc. xiii, l. 90.

III, i, 363. *Your hat must wear it.* It was a common practice at that time to wear a lady's favour, as a glove, or knot of ribbon, in the hat. Cf. *May-Day*, I, i, 275–6.

III, i, 383. One of the innumerable allusions in Elizabethan literature to the *lues venerea* as of French origin. Cf. *The Widow's Tears*, V, iii, 319.

III, i, 384. *Stood on my arms :* insisted upon my coat-of-arms, boasted of being a gentleman. The phrase is used for the sake of the pun. The same play on words occurs in *Eastward Ho*, III, ii, 113–15.

III, i, 388. *Good cards :* good proofs, perhaps with special reference to genealogical charts. Card and chart meant much the same thing in Chapman's day.

III, i, 396. *Mutton :* a common term for a loose woman : cf. *May-Day*, V., i, 348.

III, i, 411. *Writ of error :* a writ brought to procure the reversal of a judgment on the ground of error.

III, i, 422–3. *Came in at the window :* is a bastard child. Valerio alludes, like Cornelio in ll. 258–9 above, to the report that the Page is a natural son of Dariotto. For the phrase, cf. *The Ball*, II, ii. 238–9 and *King John*, I, i, 171, and see Steevens' note on the latter passage for similar expressions.

III, i, 426. *Rings loud acquittance :* makes, or proclaims, payment in full. See Text Notes, p. 729.

III, i, 428. *Salve your license :* make good the liberty you took of embracing Gratiana.

III, i, 440. *Hearty policy :* thorough-going dissimulation.

IV, i, 29. *White son :* innocent son, probably with a satirical allusion to the phrase *white boy*, a term of endearment which occurs in *The Yorkshire Tragedy*, sc. iv, in Ford's *'Tis Pity*, I, iv, and elsewhere.

IV, i, 31-2. 'Credulity hastens the coming of imbecile decrepitude as the magnet draws iron '.

IV, i, 50. Gostanzo calmly assumes the credit of Rinaldo's plan. Cf. above, III, i, 78-79.

IV, i, 53. *This fount :* Gostanzo touches his head as he speaks.

IV, i, 62. *My circumstance lessening the fact :* the circumstance that Marc. Antonio shortly before had believed himself similarly slighted by his son and yet had not been angry, serves to lessen in his eyes *the fact*, i.e. crime, of Valerio's deceiving his father.

IV, i, 82-3. 'With the thunderbolt of my anger cut off the support which you derive from my living, i.e. estate '. The language is purposely exaggerated.

IV, i, 85-93. An obscure passage. Possibly something has been lost, but I am rather inclined to believe that Chapman intended to give Valerio a speech which should have more sound than sense. The crux of the passage appears to be the word *creator*, l. 90. Collier proposed to read *crater*, but this word in the sense of drinking-cup does not appear in English until more than a hundred years after *All Fools*, and its more familiar meaning would, I think, make nonsense of the passage. As I understand it, Valerio is pretending to appeal to his father by the tie of blood. His tears issue from his inward eyes, and are indeed drops of blood (cf. *With tears trickling down thy cheeks and drops of blood falling from thy heart.—Mother Bombie*, I, iii, 173-4) and this blood comes originally from *the creator* (i.e. begetter) *of his heart*, that is, from his father himself.

IV, i, 115-6. Probably an allusion to Esau's selling his birthright for a mess of pottage.

IV, i, 121. *Of any :* by any one.

IV, i, 132-4. ' I do not think you so old as to be incapable of looking again with eyes of love on such a beauty as Gratiana's '.

IV, i, 140. *It :* love, understood from *affections*, l. 139.

IV, i, 147-8. The *New English Dictionary* sub *leather* gives a quotation from Golding, 1583, which mentions ' the common proverb . . . we cut large thongs of other men's leather '. The proverb appears also in *The Paston Letters*, vol. iii, p. 372, and in Heywood's *Proverbs*, pt. ii, chap. v. Farmer in a note on this passage in his edition of Heywood, p. 402, gives a parallel from a French MS. dating ca. 1300 :

> *D'autrui cuir font large curoie.*

See also Bohn, *Hand-Book of Proverbs*, p. 148.

IV, i, 150. ' Such simple souls as Marc. Antonio will submit to anything '.

IV, i, 158-60. It is not apparent whether Gratiana speaks these words in earnest or merely to second Valerio. Gostanzo evidently believes the latter (see l. 161 and note) ; but he wholly misunderstands the situation, and I incline to believe that Gratiana is so overcome by the excellence of Valerio's acting that, for the moment, she believes he is renouncing her in earnest.

IV, i, 161. *She has her lyripoop :* has her wits about her. The word *lyripoop*, i.e. a scarf or hood (*lyripipium*) worn by one who had taken a university degree, was used figuratively to denote first learning, then wit or common sense. It occurs frequently in Lyly and a passage in *Mother Bombie*, I, iii, 128, probably suggested it to Chapman : *There's a girle that knowes her lerripoope*. See Bond's note on the word in his edition of Lyly, vol. ii, p. 556.

IV, i, 185-6. Cf. *The Winter's Tale*, IV, iv, 605-6 : *What a fool Honesty is ! and Trust, his sworn brother.*

IV, i, 204. *Bear a brain :* hold in mind, remember. The phrase is not uncommon in Elizabethan drama. Cf. *Romeo and Juliet*, I, iii, 29, and the note thereon in Furness's *Variorum*.

IV, i, 214. *The honour'd action :* the marriage.

IV, i, 220. *In her true kind :* as your wife.

IV, i, 225. *Debate twixt man and wife:* cf. *Humourous Day's Mirth,* sc. xiv, 178–9.

IV, i, 247–50. *White sheet . . . capital letters:* the sheet in which adulterers did public penance, and the letters indicative of their sin which were bound upon their foreheads.

IV, i, 262–3. *Keeps the stable:* ' The phrase to *keep one's stables* was a familiar phrase in Shakespeare's day ; and meant to keep a personal watch over one's wife's or one's mistress' chastity '—Ingleby—*Shakespeare Hermeneutics,* p. 77. Ingleby cites the present passage and one from Greene's *James IV,* I, ii, 457–8, as examples of this phrase and in explanation of a debated passage in *The Winter's Tale,* II, i, 134. See also his note on p. 78 in connexion with ll. 266–7.

IV, i, 291. Cf. *The Spanish Curate,* IV, v, 98.

IV, i, 294. *Autentical dashes over the head.* In my previous edition of *All Fools* I explained this as the dashes over words to represent a missing ' m ' or ' n ', whose omission, Cornelio thinks, would invalidate the document. A friend suggests that the reference is to the pen-flourishes with which a document of this kind would be ornamented at the beginning (*over the head*). The suggestion is a plausible one and, at least, worth recording.

IV, i, 297. *Butiro and Caseo:* butter and cheese. Augustine Vincent (*Discovery of Errors,* 1622) speaks of ' Scogan's scholar who read Butyrum et Caseum for Brutum et Cassium '. This story does not appear in *Scoggin's Jests ;* but there were doubtless many stories connected with this possibly fictitious Court Fool, and Chapman put the well-known error into the mouth of the Notary to amuse his audience. The phrase, *Butler and Cason's case,* in l. 298, would then be a supposed translation of the mock Latin.

IV, i, 301–2. *In Florence.* This chance utterance is the only thing in the play which fixes the scene. From V, ii, 16, we might imagine it laid at Venice.

IV, i, 304. *We will all mark you.* There is a play on the word *mark* here. It not only means ' listen to ', but also put ' a mark on '. Cf. the phrase *marker of men's wives,* III, i, 318, above.

IV, i, 319. *Easement's chamber ;* chamber of ease, or water-closet.

IV, i, 331. *Fifteen hundred and so forth.* Fleay (*Biog. Chron.,* vol. i, p. 58) notes this date as one of the proofs that *All Fools* was originally acted in the sixteenth century.

IV, i, 333. *What else:* i.e. of course, what else should I do ?

IV, i, 340. *At large:* in large letters.

IV, i, 342. *Ah, ass:* addressed, I take it, to Gazetta, although possibly it might be taken as an aside, showing the first sign of wavering on Cornelio's part.

IV, i, 343. *My nose bleed:* an omen of ill-luck. Nash (*Terrors of the Night,* Works, vol. i, p. 358) says of the superstitious man ' if his nose bleed, some of his kinsfolks is dead '. In *The Duchess of Malfi,* II, iii, 42, Antonio's nose bleeds just before he loses the paper, the discovery of which by Bosola brings about the catastrophe of the play.

IV, i, 353. *Howlet nor cuckoo.* Cf. *The Case is Altered,* V, iii : *the very owl whom other birds do stare and wonder at.* An owl discovered by other birds in the daytime is frequently attacked by them. The cuckoo deserves, if it does not receive, the same treatment.

IV, i, 363. *With his glory:* by means of his vanity.

IV, i, 374. *Like two parts in me.* Professor Baker suggests that this may mean ' as if I were two different persons, the man who may be gulled, and the man who can gull others '. This does not seem satisfactory, but the passage is obscure and very probably corrupt. A friend suggests *like two harts in May,* with an allusion to the fable of the stag caught by his horns. Mr. Brereton (*Modern Language Review,* vol. iii, p. 398) suggests *like two fast in ice.* Neither of these seem to me convincing.

V, i, 7–10. ' To some Fortune gives pretty faces or some natural qualities which have nothing to do with the mind, by means of which they make a favourable impression on the senses (*live in sensual acceptation*) and make a brave show without having a trace of real worth '.

V, i, 14. *In themselves no piece.* I take it that this means no flaw, or broken bit, in their wits. Possibly *no piece* is a misprint for *one piece*, i.e. an unbroken whole.

V, i, 17. See note on *The Blind Beggar*, sc. x, l. 101.

V, i, 38. *Bear him out :* bring him off.

V, i, 38–39. *Made means to the officers to sequester him :* sent messengers to induce the officers to keep him for a while in private instead of taking him to the debtors' prison. With this sense of *made means*, cf. *The Gentleman Usher*, I, ii, 158.

V, i, 42. *Take present order :* take immediate measures to release him.

V, i, 53-4. These lines seem to me a characteristic instance of Chapman's fondness for metaphorical statement. The figure, suggested, no doubt, by *storm* in l. 52, is of ships beaten by the violence of the wind into a *horrid* harbour, i.e. one bristling with rocks.

V, i, 60-1. *To see through*, or *far into, a mill-stone* is a proverbial expression appearing as early as Heywood's *Proverbs* (p. 21), meaning to have extraordinary acuteness. But Cornelio boasts that his trick (*sleight*) is a mill-stone which will baffle Rinaldo.

V, i, 69. A *red lettice*, i.e. lattice window, was formerly the common sign of a tavern. Cf. the page's quip on Bardolph : '*a calls me e'en now, my lord, through a red lattice, and I could discern no part of his face from the window—* 2 *King Henry IV*, II, ii, 85-7. See also *The Merry Wives of Windsor*, II, ii, 28, and the note thereon in the *Variorum*, and *Antonio and Mellida*, V, i, 22-4 : *I am not as well known by my wit as an ale-house by a red lattice.*

V, i, 75. This phrase occurs three times in the eighteenth epigram of the second book of Martial.

V, ii, 2. *Shift chances :* change the luck. From ll. 86-7 below it would appear that Valerio has been losing, and it is a common superstition among gamblers that a change of seat brings a change of luck.

V, ii, 5. *Where . . . becomes.* Cf. note on *The Blind Beggar*, sc. i, l. 8.

V, ii, 8. *In print :* in exact order. The phrase is common in Elizabethan English occurring in Lyly (*Works*, vol. ii, p. 168), Greene (*Works*—Grosart, vol. ii, p. 219, vol. ix, p. 308), Shakespeare, *Love's Labour's Lost*, III, i, 173, Jonson, *Staple of News*, I, i, and elsewhere.

V, ii, 16. *Rialto :* Chapman transfers to Florence the well-known quarter of Venice whose name had become a synonym for market or exchange.

V, ii, 20. *To a very scute.* The phrase seems to mean to a penny, or some such small sum ; but a *scute* or *scudo* is a coin of varying value, usually worth several shillings.

V, ii, 24. *Wall eye :* a staring eye. Valerio implies that Dariotto's eyes are popping out from his head because of his constant ogling of women.

V, ii, 34. *Unpledg'd.* In order to *overtake* (l. 28) the others who have been already drinking, Dariotto is ordered to drink a *crowned cup*, i.e. a brimming glass without the customary ' pledge ', or answering draught from one of the company.

V, ii, 39. *Noise :* a band of musicians. Cf. *The Blind Beggar*, sc. ii, l. 134.

V, ii, 42. For a similar pun, see *Sir Giles Goosecap*, II, i, 238-9.

V, ii, 43. *Pudding-cane tobacco :* tobacco rolled into a tight stick or cane in the shape of a sausage (*pudding*), which had to be shredded by the knife before smoking. See the reproduction of an old Dutch woodcut in Fairholt's *Tobacco—its History*.

V, ii, 44. *Your linstock.* The page ordered by Valerio to fetch tobacco (l. 37) has approached his master with a stick of *pudding-cane tobacco* in one hand and a pipe-light made of the leaf of a book in the other. He purposely misunderstands Valerio's demand to see the leaf and answers that it is not *leaf* but *cane tobacco*. Whereupon to make his meaning clear Valerio says : *I mean your linstock*, i.e. a forked stick which held the match by which a cannon was fired, here used for the bit of paper which was to fire Valerio's pipe.

V, ii, 48–51. This was apparently a current joke in Chapman's day. Ben Jonson related it to Drummond, who recorded it in an MS. volume of miscellanies (see *Archæologica Scotica*, vol. iv, p. 78) as follows : ' One who had fired a pipe of tobacco with a ballad sware he heard the singing of it in his head thereafter the space of two days '. With the pun on *singing in the head*, cf. *The Ball*, II, i, 55–6.

V, ii, 56. *Without hat or knee :* without taking off his hat or bending his knee. Cf. *Eastward Ho*, III, iii, 66–7, where Seagull drinks a lady's health *both with cap and knee.*

V, ii, 63. *Run all ahead :* run headlong.

V, ii, 65. It was an old belief that the elephant had no joints and so could not kneel. Sir Thomas Browne (*Vulgar Errors*, III, i) calls this ' an old and grey-headed error even in the days of Aristotle '.

V, ii, 77. *Set me :* set a stake, make a bet with me. Valerio proposes to Dariotto to begin dicing at once ; the others may join then *when they have done the ladies right*, i.e. when they have answered the ladies' toasts. The phrase *to do one right*, i.e. to answer his pledge, is very common in Elizabethan drama. See the note in the *Variorum* on *2 King Henry IV*, V, iii, 76 for numerous examples.

V, ii, 85. *Let's set him round :* let all of us bet against him. Valerio accepts the challenge, and cries *At all* (l. 86), meaning that he casts at the total sum of their stakes.

V, ii, 98. *Thrifty sentences :* prudent maxims. Cf. a similar use of *sentences* in *Sir Giles Goosecap*, II, i, 32–3.

V, ii, 99–100. There is an old proverb, quoted in Bohn's *Handbook of Proverbs*, p. 89, to the effect that everything has an end and a pudding (i.e. a blood, or bag, pudding) has two. See also *The Knight of the Burning Pestle*, I, i, 92–3 :

> *Although, as writers say, all things have end*
> *And that we call a pudding hath his two.*

To bring the text into closer conformity with the proverb, Mr. Daniel suggests reading *fine* or *term* for *time* ; but it is not unlikely that the drunken Valerio is mixing up another proverb, *there is a time for everything*, with that quoted above.

V, ii, 100–102. *Satisfaction . . . insinuate.* Valerio is talking deliberate nonsense in ridicule of his father's *sentences.*

V, ii, 103. *A trial :* I understand that Valerio encourages his father, who is inarticulate with rage, to try again. Mr. Daniel suggests that we might read *at all*, the sense being that Valerio turns to the dice again and repeats his exclamation of l. 86 above.

V, ii, 113. *Comes upon :* is attacking, is hitting at.

V, ii, 115. *Your brain's too short :* cf. *Bussy D'Ambois*, I, i, 209–10 : *Has your Worship so short a head ?*

V, ii, 121. *For colour sake :* for the sake of the ·pretence.

V, ii, 141. *A great piece of work :* Gostanzo, of course, is speaking ironically.

V, ii, 145. Fortunio, who has been standing apart, now comes forward and kneels before Gostanzo to thank him for his gift of all his fortune to Bellanora.

V, ii, 153. *Fly out in your wits :* pass away in consideration of your witty tricks.

V, ii, 154. *No indecorum :* there has been no behaviour improper to your characters as young men. The old technical sense of *decorum* is, I think, strongly implied.

V, ii, 158. *Silence, my masters :* Rinaldo addresses these words to the rest of the company who have broken into applause at the end of Gostanzo's speech.

V, ii, 190. *Come cut and long-tail :* a proverbial expression meaning *come one and all.* A *cut* is a curtailed horse. The phrase occurs in *The Merry Wives of Windsor*, III, iv, 47, and in Jonson's *Love's Welcome to Welbeck* :

At Quiniain he,
In honour of this bridaltee,
Hath challeng'd either wide countee
Come Cut and Long-tail.

V, ii, 195.   *Look to her water :* diagnose her case.   Cf. *Monsieur D'Olive*, II, i, 9–10.

V, ii, 205–6.   *Young men, etc. :* quoted by Camden (*Remains*, p. 228, edition of 1605) as the well-known saying of a certain Dr. Metcalfe.

V, ii, 213.   *Bridle her stout stomach :* restrain her high spirit.

V, ii, 214.   *Draw on the colour :* obtain a pretext.

V, ii, 226.   *Within my compass :* into my reach.   Cf. :

And draw within the compass of suspect
The unviolated honour of your wife.
                                       Comedy of Errors, III, i, 87.

V, ii, 228.   *In grain :* an abbreviated form of ' dyed in grain ', ' dyed a fast colour ', hence *in grain* means ' genuine ', ' through and through ', often used, as here, with a contemptuous sense.

V, ii, 235.   *Potable humour :* flowing vein, with reference to Valerio's recent potations.

V, ii, 259.   *What worthier crest :* cf. the song in *As You Like It*, IV, ii.   In *Bussy D'Ambois*, IV, i, 124–5 Monsieur says :

Married men's ensigns are not made with fingers ;
Of divine fabric they are, not men's hands.

V, ii, 293.   *The Saturnian bull :* the bull which was really Jove, the son of Saturn.

V, ii, 296.   *Hold by the horn :* a play on *horn*, perhaps also on *hold by*, in the sense of ' cling to ', as Europa did, and ' retain ' as Europe does.

V, ii, 300–1.   *I have read that the lion :* a fable which occurs in More's *History of Richard III*, and also in Camden's *Remains*.

V, ii, 307.   Cf. III, i, 143–5, above.

V, ii, 316.   *Fine for :* pay a fine in order to escape.   It was not uncommon in England at that time for a rich citizen to evade the duties of a trouble-some office by paying a certain sum into the public chest.   Cf. :

He will be of the clothing of his company,
And next spring called to the scarlet.

But he'll be wise, preserve his youth and fine for't.
                                       The Alchemist, I, iii.

That is, Drugger, of whom these words are spoken, will be one of the liverymen of his company, and next spring elected sheriff ; but he will pay a fine in composition and preserve his youth.   Cf. also Shirley's use of the phrase :

This is old Barnacle,
One that is to fine for alderman.
                                       The Gamester, II, ii.

V, ii, 329.   I suppose Marc. Antonio's words are addressed to Cornelio, urging him to take Valerio's hand.

V, ii, 331.   *Spread like wild-geese :* I confess I do not quite understand the sense of this ; but I fancy it means ' increase and multiply '.

Epilogue, l. 11.   *Welcome :* a substitute for an obvious rhyme.

TEXT NOTES

All Fools was published for the first time in 1605 by Thomas Thorpe in quarto form.   The printer's name is not given, but the devices used show him to have been G. Eld.   There is but one quarto edition of *All Fools*, but the sheets seem to have been corrected as the book was going through the press, and as a result the remaining copies show numerous variations.   I have consulted copies in the Drummond of Hawthornden collection belonging to the University of Edinburgh (D), in the Advocates' Library at Edinburgh (A), the two copies in the British Museum (B.M.), the Malone copy in the Bodleian (M), the Dyce copy in the Victoria and Albert Museum (Dy), one in the Boston Public Library (B.P.L.), and two copies belonging to Mr. T. J. Wise. I have recorded a number of interesting variations in these copies in the following notes, but do not profess to have made a complete collation.

The first reprint of *All Fools* appeared in Dodsley's *Select Collection of Old Plays*, 1780 (Do.). It was next reprinted in Walter Scott's *Ancient British Drama*, 1810. Collier included it in his new edition of Dodsley, *Select Collection of Old Plays*, 1825, printing the Dedication [1] for the first time, and emending the text in various places. I denote this edition by Co. A professedly exact reprint of the quarto is included in *The Comedies and Tragedies of George Chapman*, published by Pearson in 1873 (P). This is unfortunately marred by several omissions and misprints. The editor of this edition, R. H. Shepherd, then presented a modernized text (S) in *The Works of George Chapman—Plays*, published by Chatto and Windus, 1874–5. It was next included in the Mermaid Edition (*George Chapman*, edited by W. L. Phelps, 1895), where the text is based upon P. but is modernized throughout. The latest edition up to the present is that included in *The Belles-Lettres Series* (*All Fooles and The Gentleman Usher*, edited by Thomas Marc Parrott, 1907), where the old text is preserved except for certain necessary changes (see p. xlviii of that edition) and the most important variations, and emendations are recorded in the footnotes. The present text presents in the main a modernized form of my earlier edition. In the following notes I refer to the quarto as Q. when all the copies that I have consulted agree on one reading ; when variants occur I have denoted the copies in question by the symbols attached to them above. Where I have recorded a modern emendation or suggestion I have marked it in the same way, thus Do. is the first Dodsley reprint, Co. Collier's edition, P. the Pearson reprint, and S. Shepherd's edition.

In Q. the play is divided into acts, but not into scenes. These have been supplied in brackets in this edition.

On the whole the text of *All Fools* is far superior to that of the preceding plays of Chapman. It may have been corrected in proof by the author,[2] and the frequency of Latin stage directions seems to me to show that it was probably printed from Chapman's own manuscript. There is no entry of this play in the Stationers' Registers.

THE DEDICATION.

To my long lou'd and Honourable
friend Sir Thomas Walsingham
Knight.

Should I expose to euery common eye,
    The least allow'd birth of my shaken braine ;
And not entitle it perticulerly
    To your acceptance, I were wurse then vaine.
And though I am most loth to passe your sight
    with any such light marke of vanitie,
Being markt with Age for Aimes of greater weight,
    and drownd in darke Death-ushering melancholy,
Yet least by others stealth it be imprest,
    without my pasport, patcht with others wit,
Of two enforst ills I elect the least ;
    and so desire your loue will censure it ;
Though my old fortune keep me still obscure,
The light shall still bewray my ould loue sure.

These lines, apparently a dedicatory sonnet to Chapman's friend and patron,

---

[1] For the authenticity of the Dedication, see below, p. 726.
[2] That Chapman sometimes at least read the proof of his published works is shown by his complaint as to the printer's neglect to send him a proof of *The Masque of The Middle Temple and Lincoln's Inn*, see above, p. 442.

Sir Thomas Walsingham [1] do not appear in any copy of the original quarto that I have been able to consult, with the one exception to be presently noted. Nor did they appear in the first reprint of this play, that in the 1780 Dodsley. The second reprint, however, the 1825 Dodsley, contains them with the following note by the editor, J. P. Collier :

' This dedication by Chapman to his patron is now for the first time inserted, the copies of *All Fools* seen and used by Mr. Reed [the editor of the 1780 Dodsley] being without it. Whether it was inserted in a few impressions in 1605 and afterwards cancelled does not appear, though it seems probable that it was so, because in the dedication of his *Byron's Conspiracy and Tragedy* to the same distinguished individual, Chapman apologizes for previous neglect and seeming ingratitude to his patron " in dispensing with his right in his other impressions ". It was found in a copy in the possession of Mr. Rodd [2] of Great Newport Street '.

Collier's discovery was apparently accepted without any question, although the inconsistency of his later statements [3] might well have raised a doubt as to his accuracy. It was reprinted in all subsequent editions of the play down to that in the *Belles-Lettres Series*, and was quoted by Swinburne [4] as an authentic poem. Fleay (*Biog. Chron.*, vol. i, p. 59) remarked that its genuineness had been suspected, but did not say by whom, and he himself seems inclined to accept it.

While preparing my edition of *All Fools* for the *Belles-Lettres Series*, I was struck with the fact that the Dedication appeared to be wanting in all extant copies of the quarto, and that Collier's own copy had disappeared. Inasmuch as Collier's unsupported statements are notoriously of doubtful authority, I began to suspect that the Dedication might be another of his ' mystifications ', and published my suspicions in *Notes and Queries*, May 6, 1906. Not receiving any further light on the subject, and being unable to trace the Collier quarto at the time of the publication of my edition of *All Fools*, I removed the Dedication to an appendix in which I gave its history, stated the reasons for my suspicions, and declared that a final settlement of the problem would depend upon the rediscovery of Collier's copy.

Shortly after the publication of my edition a copy of *All Fools* was purchased by Mr. J. H. Wrenn of Chicago, which proved to be the Collier quarto and contained the disputed Dedication. This copy was inspected by Mr. T. J. Wise, who reported his conclusions to me, and I in turn communicated them to the *Athenæum*, where they appeared on July 27, 1908. To this article I refer the student for Mr. Wise's detailed statement ; here I shall briefly summarize his conclusion.

[1] Sir Thomas Walsingham, a kinsman of Elizabeth's great minister, was a distinguished patron of literature in the reigns of Elizabeth and James I. Blunt, the publisher of Marlowe's unfinished *Hero and Leander*, dedicated this poem to him in 1598 ; Chapman dedicated his continuation of Marlowe's poem to Lady Walsingham in the same year. In 1608 Chapman dedicated to Walsingham and his son Thomas *The Conspiracy and Tragedy of Charles Duke of Byron*. This prose dedication, printed on pp. 151–2 of my edition of Chapman's *Tragedies*, contains the phrase cited above by Collier. Taken along with the context, Chapman's words do not seem to contain an apology ' for previous neglect and seeming ingratitude ', but rather to imply that, owing to Walsingham's known dislike to having works dedicated to him, Chapman has hitherto refrained from such dedications, but has decided to offer him the dedication of these plays, ' lest the world may repute it a neglect in me of so ancient and worthy a friend '.

[2] Rodd was a well-known bookseller of that day. He is mentioned by Collier in his *History of Dramatic Poetry* (ed. 1831), vol. iii, p. 79, n. Rodd's copy of the quarto was acquired by Collier, for a MS. note in Dyce's hand in the latter's copy, now in the Albert and Victoria Museum, states : ' The Dedication to Walsingham is found only in a single copy of this play which belongs to Mr. Collier. He reprinted twelve copies of that Dedication, and one of them is inserted here '. I have transcribed the Dedication from the printed leaf bound up in Dyce's copy, and printed it above. It differs from the reprint in P. only in the last line, where P. misprints *beway*.

[3] In 1831 he said that the Dedication ' seems to have been cancelled in many copies ' (*History of Dramatic Poetry*, vol. ii, p. 93). In his revised edition of this work in 1879 he speaks of it (vol. iii, p. 74) as ' a sonnet prefixed to only a few copies ' ; later on (p. 196) he says it ' seems to have been cancelled in all extant copies '—a curious remark, indeed, if he possessed a unique copy containing the Dedication.

[4] *George Chapman*, pp. 47–8.

The history of the copy has been traced from its appearance in the hands of Rodd through those of J. P. Collier, Frederic Ouvry, Robson and Kerslake, and W. Stadow to its present owner, Mr. Wrenn. The Dedication Mr. Wise pronounces 'a palpable forgery'. The original blank leaf (Sig. A1) of the copy has been cancelled, and a new leaf on which the Dedication had been printed has been inserted between A2 and A3. This leaf was one 'manufactured at the correct period', apparently one taken from some Elizabethan quarto, but considerably smaller than the other leaves of the book in which it was inserted. To hide this defect its margins have been 'beautifully and skillfully' extended to the required size. The two leaves between which it is placed are 'in every way sound and perfect'. Had this leaf been originally part of the book in which it appears it is 'utterly impossible' for it to have become so reduced in size as to need such extension, while its immediate fellows presented margins 'intact and undoctored'. Taking into consideration Collier's well-known propensity for playing tricks upon the public, there can be little or no doubt but that this tampering with the copy must be charged to him, and, as a consequence, that the Dedication must be regarded as his own composition, to authenticate which as a work of Chapman the tampering with the copy in question was undertaken.

Actors. I reprint the list of *Dramatis Personae* as it appears in the Q., adding the Drawer who speaks one line, V, ii, 40. The name of *Kyte* does not occur in the text where he appears as Notary. See the stage-direction after IV, i, 226, IV, i, 246–7, and elsewhere. The name of the page, *Curio*, occurs only once, in III, i, 220. It is possible that it may here be only an abbreviation for *Mercurio* (see III, i, 179), in which case it has been improperly included among the names of the actors.

Prologus.

l. 7. Q. has an interrogation mark, equivalent to an exclamation, after *it*.

27. All Qq. *mistery*, except B.P.L. which has *misery*, a reading adopted by Co.

I, i, 3. B.P.L. and one of the B.M. Qq. (C. 13. c. 10) read correctly *straines ;* the others have *steaines*.

33. Q. and previous editors *Lords*, but the word is evidently in the possessive plural.

66–7. The punctuation of Q., a semi-colon after *jesters*, a comma after *durt*, and no point after *tytles*, obscures the sense. It has been followed by Co. and S. I have altered it to bring out the meaning.

81. Q. *riches*. Do. emends *richest*.

153. P. misprints *Syn.* for *Ryn.* as the speaker's name.

185. A., D. and B.P.L. read *unusering ;* the other Qq. that I have seen *unnurishing*, which has been accepted by all editors.

224–6. Q. prints as two lines ending *breath* and *wife*, with a comma after *Yet*.

231. P. has *father father*, a misprint not found in Q.

233. Q. *wife*, an obvious misprint retained, however, by Do. and Co. P. prints *wife* and S. *wise*, which is, of course, correct.

238. P. misprints *wlll*.

238–41. Q. prints Rinaldo's speech as three lines ending *Sir, secret*, and *will*.

264. Q. *soone*. Co. *son*.

322–3. Q. prints *If . . . extreame* as one line.

I, ii, 5. Q. *love sportes*. Do. *love-sports*. Cf. *The Gentleman Usher*, IV, iv, 52, where Q. has *loue-sports*.

23. Q. *Extreames heate*. Do. emends.

24. Q. *sacietie*. Do. emends.

42. All Qq. I have seen except M. read *See see wee, wee*. S. was the first to correct.

68–69. The Q. and previous editors assign this speech to *For|tunio*]. But it seems plain from the following speech of Valerio that he is answering a remark by his wife. Hence the speech should belong to Gratiana, in whose mouth the phrase, *we shall break*, i.e. we shall be parted, is much more appropriate than in Fortunio's.

There are several instances of speeches wrongly assigned in Q. Cf. III, i, 426 ; IV, i, 358, and V, ii, 97.

69. Q. *Jelosie Spy-all.* Co. *jealousy Spy-all.* S. *jealous spy-all.* I believe the true reading to be *jealous espial* from which the corruption in the text might easily proceed. It is possible, however, as Dr. Bradley suggests, that the original reading may have been *jealouse spiall.* Dr. Bradley further suggests that *displease* in this line may be a corruption for *disperse.*

90. Q. *Scholards ;* editors *scholar.* I retain the old form *scholard.*

139. Q., Do. and Co. have a question mark after *father.* It is, however, equivalent to an exclamation mark.

144. Q. *conseave ;* editors *conceive.* This seems to me nonsense. Dr. Bradley suggests *conferme* from which *conseave* would be an easy corruption. Dr. Bradley calls attention to a passage in Shirley, *The Doubtful Heir,* V, ii (Dyce's edition, vol. iv, p. 344) :
And I have satisfied these lords so well
They are confirm'd in your just claim and person
where the meaning is the same as in the present passage. Mr. Daniel suggests reading *conserve* (i.e. preserve) for *conseave.*

147. Q. *Actus Prima,* an evident misprint.

II, i, 7. Q. *or friend.* P. misprints *a friend,* and is followed by S.

9. All Qq. that I have seen, except M. and one of Mr. Wise's copies, read *Adsolve.* The *New English Dictionary* gives no other instance of this word, and the alternate reading of *resolve* (in M.) is, no doubt, correct. The mistake seems to have been corrected while the quarto was going through the press, and *adsolve* may hereafter be treated as a ' ghost-word '.

26. Q. *parle.* Co. *parley.* Since the word was pronounced as a dissyllable, I have preferred the modern form.

30. Most Qq. read *veale.* M. *weale.*

37. Q. *Trope,* a misprint which P. silently corrects to *Troye.* Do. *Troy.*

39. In Q. the stage-direction after this line comes after l. 37.

80. Q. *glases.* Co. *glosses.* S. *glozes. Glazes,* is, no doubt, the true reading ; see the *New English Dictionary,* sub *glaze.*

86. Q. prints as two lines ending *and better, Sonne.*

90. Q. *imploy.* Co. *employ.* S. *imply,* which seems to me preferable.

109. Q. *vnresisted organies.* P. misprints *vuresisted.* Do. emends *organies,* a misprint for *orgaines,* to *organs.*

128. Q. prints as two lines ending *complement ?, sheepes-head.*

134. Most Qq. read *courtlie.* D. *courtlier,* which I followed in my first edition.

168. P. wrongly omits *had* in this line.

172-6. Q. prints the words from *Exordion* to *cooplets* in italics.

173. Q. *Epithalamious,* a misprint silently corrected by P.

174. Q. *Quatorzanies* (cf. *organies* in l. 109 above). A. *Quatorzaines.*

176. Q. *Sdrnciolla.* Co. *Sdruciolo .* S. *Sdruciolla.*

198. Q. *make,* followed by previous editors. I have ventured to emend *made,* which is required by the syntax. I have also altered Q. *worke* in l. 201 below to *work'd.* Possibly the original reading represents Chapman's own loose construction.

226-8. Q. prints Rinaldo's speech as two lines ending *meete you, bellie full.*

234-5. Q. prints as three lines ending *Columbine ? Garden, mine.*

235. Q. *Him ?* Do. emends *Hem !*

239-271. In this passage P. assigns all the speeches of Gratiana to *Val.* There is no authority for this in any quarto that I have seen.

273. P. misprints *Gf* for Q. *Of.*

288. Q. *shew,* followed by all editors. I believe it to be a misprint for *crew,* induced by *shew* in the next line. Cf. the phrase *crew of gallants, May-Day,* I, i, 389. Mr. Brereton suggests *sort.*

295. I have inserted the entrance of the Page in the stage-direction after this line to prepare for his exit after l. 395.

325. The second *with* in this line is omitted by Co. probably on the ground that it may be a printer's repetition of the first *with*. The omission improves the metre, but I have preferred to let the text stand.

336. *Became.* Q. prints as the last word of l. 335. Co. suggests *has become.* S. prints *is become.* The metre is improved by shifting the word to its present place.

384. Q. *on lyte.* Co., who retains the old reading, pronounces it unintelligible, and suggests *'em light.* S. reads *on't light.* I take *lyte* as the old adjective ' lite ' meaning ' little ', and *on* as a mere misprint for *um*, i.e. *'em.*

405-6. Q. and previous editors give this speech to Dariotto, but it seems to me quite out of keeping with the situation for Dariotto to abuse Valerio's voice at this moment. On the other hand, the mock modesty of the speech is exactly that which he shows in ll. 382 and 393 above.

406-7. Q. prints Cornelio's speech as one line, including the stage-direction.

419. Q., Do. and Co., *the voice.* S. emends *thy voice.*

421-4. Q. prints as three lines of prose, ending *Dan, jarre,* and *jelousy.* In l. 421 Q. prints *Mast,* indicating, perhaps, the monosyllabic pronunciation of the word in this line.

III, i, 79-80. Q. prints as two lines of prose ending *home* and *house.*

120. For *fat* Do. has *far.* Deighton (*Old Dramatists*) suggests *pat.* Co., who retains the old reading, remarks that it is a hit at the thriving profession.

122. Q. *be miracle.* Do. emends *by.*

246. Co. reads *superannuated ;* but *superannated* occurs in Elizabethan English.

261. Q. *villayne.* Previous editors *villain.* I think the sense requires *villainy*, and the original reading may well have been *villaynie.*

323. Q. *looke.* S. emends *looks.*

385. Q. *other.* Co. *others.*

397. Q. *hazards.* Co. *hazard.*

426.-7 Q. prints these lines as part of Dariotto's speech, and is followed by all editors ; but it seems to me plain that they belong to Valerio, who is rejoicing in having paid back Dariotto for ridiculing him in II, i.

444. Q. *I will.* P. misprints *will I.*

IV, i, 19-21. Q. prints as two lines, ending *Antonio* and *so.*

38. Q. *what.* P. misprints *wht.*

53. Q. *our.* Co. emends *your.* Cf. V, ii, 122.

75-6. Q. prints Marc. Antonio's speech as one line.

77-8. Q. prints the words *Your father* to *knees* as one line.

90. *Creator.* So. Q. Co. suggests *crater*, which was received into the text by S. There is no need of change. See Notes, p.720.

92. Q. *but.* P. misprints *bfit.*

109-16. In M. the whole passage from *Father* to *this* is printed as a speech of Valerio. Other Qq. correctly assign ll. 110-116 to Gostanzo.

160. Q. *tist.* Co. emends *tis.*

162-4. Q. prints Gratiana's speech as two lines ending *world* and *selfe.* In l. 162 P. wrongly omits *me* after *love.*

168. Q. and the earlier editors read *live still my sonne.* S. puts a comma after *still*, which seems to me the proper punctuation.

185-6. Q. prints as one line.

188-9. Q. prints Marc. Antonio's speech as one line.

227. P. wrongly omits *let.*

252.-3 Q. *in minde.* Co. *on mine.* There seems to be no reason for changing *in* to *on*, but I believe *mine* to be the true reading. The suggestion has been made that *minde* is equivalent to ' my [Cornelio's] mind ', but this does not seem idiomatic.

295. Q. *out.* In a footnote to Co. O.G. [Octavius Gilchrist] suggests *on't*, which is clearly correct.

307. P. misprints *Gentlemen*, and S. omits the word.

311. Q. *cuffodie*, a plain misprint, silently corrected by P.

319. Q. *easements chamber.* Co.

easements, chamber; but the first word is in the possessive case.

845. Q. *thi's.* Co. *this is.*

358. Q. gives this speech to Valerio. Co. suggests that it belongs to the Notary, but does not make the change. S. emends.

360. Q. *Balerio,* which misled Do. into printing *Bellanora.* Co. emends.

V, i, 11–12. Q. has a comma after *gulling* and a colon after *Cornelio.* Earlier editors omit the comma. I think the present punctuation brings out the true sense of the text.

24. Q. *bourd,* which Co. retains; but it is only a variant of 'board', 'accost'.

60. Q. *slight a Milstone.* Co. follows Q. printing *mill-stone,* which S. corrupts to *milestone.* The true reading, of course, is *sleight a mill-stone.* I had pointed this out in my notes in the *Belles-Lettres* edition before seeing Mr. Brereton's note (*loc. cit.,* p. 58) on the passage.

V, ii, 42–44. Q. prints the Page's speech and Valerio's reply each as one line.

59–62. Q. prints as three lines of prose ending *our, knees,* and *Taverne.*

63. Q. *chargd,* followed by Do. and Co. S. emends *charge.*

73. Q. and previous editors assign this speech to Claudio; but from the context, especially l. 76, it appears evident that it belongs to Dariotto.

77. Q. and previous editors *let mee rest;* but this is plainly a printer's error; *the rest* is the subject of *come* in l. 78.

97–103. Q. assigns this speech to Gostanzo. S. emends.

111. Co. suggests *o' th' city;* but *come at* may well mean *come to.*

117. Q. *eyes,* followed by Co. S. emends *eye's.*

131–2. Q. prints Marc. Antonio's speech as one line.

134–5. Q. prints Marc. Antonio's speech as one line.

164. Q. prints *good Cornelio* as the last words of l. 163.

179. Q. and previous editors *indiscreete,* but it is evidently two words.

280. Q. *there is Beast.* Co. suggests *where is beast,* which S. adopts. I think *no* has simply fallen out of the text.

295. *Europ[e].* Co.'s emendation for Q. *Europa.*

309–10. Q. *irrevitable,* which is followed by previous editors. Following the suggestion of the *New English Dictionary,* I read *irrenitable,* 'not to be avoided by struggle'. Brereton suggests *inevitable.*

Epilogue. The parenthesis in the last line appears in most copies of Q.; but those in the Drummond and the Dyce collections lack it.

MAY-DAY

INTRODUCTION

May-Day was first published in 1611 with the following title-page :
*May-Day. a witty Comedie, divers times acted at the Blacke Fryers.
Written by George Chapman.   London.   Printed for John Browne
dwelling in Fleetstreete in Saint Dunstones Church-yard.   1611.*
It does not appear to have been entered [1] in the Stationers' Registers.
As in the case of many Elizabethan plays, the date of publication is
considerably later than that of composition. *May-Day*, which we
know to have been acted at Blackfriars, and which was evidently
written for performance by a company [2] of children, must have been
acted, at any rate, before Blackfriars was taken over by the King's
men in 1609.   There is a general consensus of opinion that *May-Day*
belongs to the first years of the seventeenth century.   Fleay dates it
in 1601 (*Biographical Chronicle*, vol. i, p. 57) ; Schelling about 1600
(*Elizabethan Drama*, vol. i, p. 462) ; Wallace [3] in 1601 or 1602.
Schoell (*Chapman as a Comic Writer*) places it as late as 1604 ; but
this seems to me unlikely.   I should incline to date it after *Sir Giles
Goosecap*, late in 1601, or early 1602, probably in the spring of 1602.

This date is fixed mainly by internal evidence, the numerous imitations or parodies of other plays which we know to have been produced
from 1599 to 1601.   Thus we have in IV, i, 18–19 a mock quotation
from *Antonio's Revenge*, registered in 1601, but probably produced a
year or so earlier.   There is an unmistakable likeness between Quintiliano's advice to Innocentio regarding the proper behaviour in an
ordinary (I, i, 378–439) and Carlo's instructions to Sogliardo (*Every
Man out of his Humour*, I, i, and III, i).   Quintiliano himself is closely
akin to Shift [4] of *Every Man Out*, 1599.   There is a patent imitation [5]
of *Twelfth Night*, 1600, in *May-Day*, III, iii ; compare especially the
letter of Innocentio with that of Sir Andrew Aguecheek.   It is altogether likely that we have here echoes of recent plays.   The misquotation from Marston, [6] for example, would have fallen quite flat a

---

[1] Browne, the publisher, may have been called to account for this omission ;
at any rate he was careful to enter in the following year, April 17, 1612, two
plays by Chapman, *The Widow's Tears* and *The Revenge of Bussy*, which were
published in 1612 and 1613 respectively.

[2] See the stage-direction at the very beginning of the play.

[3] Wallace (*Children of the Chapel*) wavers as to the date.   On p. 118 he
dates it *c.* May, 1602 ; on p. 75 he says that it was written late in 1601 and
performed doubtless in the Christmas season of 1601–2.   The first conjecture seems to me to be more probable.

[4] Cf. below, p. 736.

[5] Pointed out by Koeppel (*Quellen-Studien*, 1897, p. 62).

[6] The jest lies in putting a speech of the ranting tyrant of Marston into the
mouth of the swaggering cheater of *May-Day*, and the point of this jest
would be lost as soon as Marston's lines had faded from men's memories.

few years after Marston's play had disappeared from the stage. There are, on the other hand, two passages which would seem to point to a later date than 1602. One of these is the parody (III, iii, 196) of a line from *Hamlet* (I, ii, 114) which appears only in the revised form of that play, the quarto of 1604. The other (I, iii, 379, *ssq.*) contains a parallel to a passage in *The Gull's Hornbook* of Dekker, chap. v. The date of the latter work, 1607, makes it impossible that Dekker could have read [1] *May-Day*. Perhaps the best way to account for these passages is to assume a revision of *May-Day* later than 1607. There is nothing unlikely in this hypothesis, for the comedy may well have been touched up and these passages inserted for a performance by the Revels Company at their new theatre in Whitefriars, *c.* 1610, a performance which would account for the publication of the play in 1611. We know from the title-page that *The Widow's Tears* originally written for performance in Blackfriars before 1608 was revived at Whitefriars and published, a year after *May-Day*, in 1612.

The source [2] of *May-Day* has been shown by Stiefel (*Shakespeare Jahrbuch*, vol. xxxv, p. 180 *ssq.*) to be the *Alessandro* of Alessandro Piccolomini, ca. 1545. Piccolomini, a famous Italian scholar and man of letters (1508–1578), was the author of two or three comedies—the *Hortensio* may not be his—of the regular type of the Italian *commedia erudita*. This school was based upon the plays of Plautus and Terence. Its framework, so to speak, was classical, and it took over many of the stock figures of Latin comedy, the deluded father, sometimes severe, sometimes senilely amorous, the rakish son, the roguish servant, the swaggering soldier, the bawd, the courtesan, and so on. It adopted also some of the stock devices of Latin comedy, especially the solution of the plot by means of a recognition (*anagnorisis*). The scene, however, was regularly laid in contemporary Italy, and the chief value [3] of these plays consists in their pictures of middle-class Italian life in the sixteenth century. The *Alessandro* seems to have been a particularly successful play. Stiefel notes ten editions published before 1600. It was honoured by countless imitations in later Italian comedy, and furnished suggestions for at least two French [4] comedies of the sixteenth century, *Les Esbahis* by Jacques Grévin, and *Les Còntens* by Odet de Tournèbe. Critics of the age spoke of it in the highest terms, and Piccolomini was called the Prince [5] of comic writers.

The *Alessandro* is quite [6] forgotten to-day, but it was at the height

[1] The closeness of the parallel, see below, p. 742, proves, I think, a borrowing by either Chapman or Dekker from a work which lay before the author as he wrote, and unless Dekker had access to the stage copy of *May-Day*, which seems most unlikely, we are forced to believe that he was the original author. No common source, from which the two authors could have drawn independently, is known to me.

[2] Fleay's conjecture (*Biographical Chronicle*, vol. i, p. 57) that *May-Day* was founded upon an old play, *The Disguises* mentioned by Henslowe as acted at the Rose, October 2, 1595, has been put out of court by Stiefel's discovery. For *The Disguises*, see p. 673, n. 1 above.

[3] See Symonds, *The Renaissance in Italy—Italian Literature*, chap. xi, for a discussion of the merits and limitations of the *commedia erudita*.

[4] This has been pointed out by M. Schoell in the thesis above mentioned.

[5] See Stiefel (*loc. cit.*), pp. 182, 192.

[6] Gaspary, *Geschichte der Italienischen Litteratur*, vol. ii, p. 615, mentions this play in passing ; but it is not even named in many histories of Italian literature.

of its fame in Chapman's time. Chapman's familiarity with Italian comedy is shown in his dedication of *The Widow's Tears*, and it is not surprising, therefore, that he should have pitched upon so popular a play for an experiment in adapting the *commedia erudita* to the Elizabethan stage.

Stiefel has given an elaborate analysis of the *Alessandro* and a detailed account of Chapman's borrowings, alterations, and additions. It will be sufficient here to summarize briefly his results.

The Italian play contains three quite distinct plots. There is first the serious love-story of Cornelio's passion for Lucilla, daughter of Gostanzo. Her father has betrothed her to a certain Lonardo, who does not appear in the play, and for this reason she at first repels the suit of Cornelio, while Gostanzo rejects the proposals of his father, Vincentio. Lucilla, however, finally yields, sends a loving letter to Cornelio, admits him, on promise of good behaviour, to her chamber, which he enters by means of a rope ladder, and vows to marry him. The lovers are detected by Gostanzo, who rushes off to call a policeman and punish the intruder, whom he naturally takes to be Cornelio, although he has not seen his face. Cornelio escapes, and his servant substitutes for him a certain Brigida, disguised as a man. She is arrested and avows that she has come there in disguise for the love of Gostanzo himself. The old man now renounces his anger against Cornelio, and finally consents to give him Lucilla in marriage.

There is also a comic underplot dealing with the senile passion of Gostanzo for Brigida, the wife of Captain Malagigi, a *miles gloriosus*, whose rodomontades occupy much space in the play. Gostanzo is persuaded by the roguish servant of Cornelio that the lady will entertain his suit, but as she is most scrupulous in preserving appearances, he can only approach her in disguise and during her husband's absence. Gostanzo thereupon disguises himself as a locksmith and enters her house, only to be lured into a closet where he is locked up. Here he is discovered by the husband who returns unexpectedly, and subjected to rather harsh treatment. Escaping from the Captain's clutches Gostanzo runs home, where he is at first refused admission by his own porter, who pretends not to recognize him in his disguise, and on entering the house discovers his daughter in the arms of a stranger, as told above. The plot concludes with the reconciliation of Brigida and her angry husband, whom she persuades that the locksmith was not a lover but a burglar, and that the report of her visit in male attire to the house of Gostanzo rests upon a complete misunderstanding.

Finally we have as a sort of enveloping action the complicated and romantic story of Aloisio and Lucretia. Aloisio, the son of a Sicilian exile, has been for seven years disguised as a girl, and is living in the house of Cornelio's father as the supposed daughter of the latter's dead brother, under the name of Lampridia. As Lampridia she has resisted all her uncle's proposals to establish her in marriage as well as the suggestion of the bawd Nicoletta to take as a lover a certain Fortunio, for whom, however, she confesses a weakness due to his resemblance to a former friend. This friend was, in truth, a certain Lucretia, also the child of a Sicilian exile. So much we learn from Lampridia's soliloquy and conversation with the bawd in the first act. At the beginning of the second Fortunio in a long soliloquy informs us that he is this very Lucretia disguised as a boy, and that his pretended passion for Lampridia is due to her likeness to the lost Aloisio.

Nicoletta finally brings Fortunio to the chamber of Lampridia, where, as we learn later from a speech of the bawd's, he detects the true sex of the supposed girl. He lingers there until he is caught by Cornelio, who denounces him to his father, and condign punishment is threatened, whereupon Fortunio to save himself reveals the true sex of Lampridia. The solution then occurs by means of the conventional *anagnorisis*. A visiting Sicilian recognizes Lampridia as his son Aloisio, and a friend of the family recognizes Fortunio as his daughter Lucretia. The transformed [1] lovers are straightway betrothed and invited to celebrate their nuptials along with Cornelio and Lucilla.

Alessandro, who gives his name to the play, has a very subordinate part. He is a sage youth, the confidant of Cornelio. He rebukes him for his folly in yielding to love, but condescends to accompany him on his visit to Lucilla and testifies to her of Cornelio's modesty and good faith.

It is clear from what has just been said that *May-Day* cannot be regarded as an original work. Chapman took over practically the entire plot and most of the characters of the *Alessandro*. Yet *May-Day* is not a translation. Chapman not only renamed [2] the characters, but recast the whole, omitting and adding without the slightest regard for the great reputation of the original, and with a single eye to rendering the play more effective upon the English stage. In the first place he substituted for the passive figure of Alessandro the lively Lodovico, whose dramatic function it is to bind the threads of the intrigue more closely together. It is he who brings about the meeting of the lovers, who mocks the disguised Lorenzo (Gostanzo), and who discovers the true sex of Lucretia (Lampridia). Lodovico is, in short, the main intriguer, corresponding to Lemot and Rinaldo in Chapman's earlier comedies. It throws an interesting light upon Chapman's technic to see that he considered a figure of this sort so important that he actually departed from his source to introduce him.

It is in dealing with the Lampridia-Fortunio story that Chapman takes the greatest liberties and, to my mind, demonstrates most clearly his superiority as a practical playwright over Piccolomini. He cuts this story down to the quick, omitting not only the long accounts of Sicilian revolutions and foreign exile which encumber the first acts of the Italian play, but the very conventional recognition at its close. He suppresses the artificial soliloquies in which Lampridia and Fortunio in turn reveal their secret to the audience, and withholds this revelation till he can introduce it effectively in action. He expunges the whole business of Fortunio's pursuit of Lampridia with its lurking suggestion of unnatural passion, and provides the supposed girl with a male suitor. The rôle of Fortunio, so prominent in the Italian, is in this way reduced to a mere shred. Lionello, the corresponding figure in *May-Day*, might drop out of that play and never be missed. One is inclined to wonder at first why Chapman retained this story at all, since he omitted what was to Piccolomini its very *raison d'être*. A careful consideration of the play, however, shows that he retained this

---

[1] I have given the barest outline of this plot. The original introduces, a great amount of detail as to Sicilian politics, exile in France, and family relationships which I have omitted.

[2] Perhaps because he had already used some of them, Gostanzo, Cornelio and Fortunio in *All Fools*.

theme for the sake of a single situation. In the *Alessandro* the bawd reports Fortunio's discovery of Lampridia's sex. Chapman with his Elizabethan instinct for action on the stage saw that this discovery was, to use the technical term, a *scène à faire*. He therefore shows us Lodovico stealing gingerly into Lucretia's room in quest of amorous adventure, only to come flying out again fighting for his life against a figure whom the audience would at once recognize by dress as Lucretia, by bearing and speech as a youth. It is a *coup de théâtre*, one of the most effective [1] in Elizabethan comedy, and may well have furnished a hint for the much lauded exposure of Epicoene in Jonson's *Silent Woman*.

M. Schoell points out that Chapman's additions include a number of incidents which have analogues [2] in other Italian comedies. These may, perhaps, be borrowings, but they are not of any particular interest. More important are Chapman's original additions. These are almost without exception designed to heighten and develop the characters. To my mind the superiority of Chapman to Piccolomini in the matter of characterization is at least as great as in that of construction. The Italian is a slave to the conventions of his age. His characters are stock figures, types, not individuals. Chapman, like a true Elizabethan, has breathed life into the puppets. By the substitution of Lodovico for Alessandro, for example, *May-Day* gains as much in vivacity and lifelikeness as it does in concentration. Alessandro is a sort of personified chorus ; Lodovico is a highly individualized portrait. His part in the play is like that of Rinaldo in *All Fools*, but he is far from being a replica of that intriguer. He has not a trace, for example, of Rinaldo's contempt for the gulls on whom he plays. Lodovico is not only a fellow of infinite good humour, he is first of all a fountain of overflowing energies. ' Idleness is accounted with other men a sin ', he says ; ' to me 'tis a penance '. It is to satisfy his own itch for action that he aids Aurelio in his love-affairs, sets the mockers on the disguised Lorenzo, and in a moment of involuntary leisure follows with cheerful recklessness a well-known bawd to an appointment designed for another gallant. His tongue is a true index of his mind ; his speech pours out like a flood. He is, except for one embarrassing moment, always master of himself, and usually master of his company. In a word, instead of the colourless young Italian gentleman of *Alessandro*, Chapman presents a vivid picture of a harebrained Elizabethan cavalier.

It is in the figure of Quintiliano, however, that Chapman has been most successful. The corresponding figure in the *Alessandro*, Captain Malagigi, is the conventional *miles gloriosus* of Italian comedy. He is, of course, a braggart, boasting that his sword eats the hearts of captains only and disdains the flesh of lesser men. He is, equally of

---

[1] It must be confessed, however, that Chapman weakens the effect by the length of time he allows to elapse between Lodovico's exit and his reappearance. The retention of this story, moreover, involved him in the long and, to the modern reader, tedious explication of the last act. But the Elizabethans were rather partial to recapitulations at the close of a play, and the last act of *May-Day* would be enlivened at the Blackfriars with music and dancing.

[2] Such are Aemilia's sigh on first seeing her love, I, i, 195 ; Lodovico's comments on the supposed intoxication of Aurelio, I, i, 197-203 ; the putting of the *plaudite* into the captain's mouth, and so on.

course, a coward who blusters [1] before the door of Gostanzo, but runs away when the old man issues to join battle with him. His part in the play is limited to a few scenes, in all of which he is made more or less of a laughing-stock, and he is finally dismissed as the hopeless dupe of his quick-witted wife. Quintiliano, on the other hand, is a thoroughly English figure, a compound of the *miles gloriosus* and the sharking captain. The characteristics of the *miles gloriosus* are only lightly indicated, although enough remains to enable us to trace the connexion ; but the other side of his character is insisted on in great detail. New characters, the gull Innocentio, the silly scholar Giovanello, are invented, and new scenes are introduced to develop this aspect, and as a result our final impression of Quintiliano is that of a guller rather than a gull. The captain and his devices occupy a space in *May-Day* quite out of proportion to his importance in the development of the plot, but one never feels that they retard the action. Quintiliano is one of the most diverting of swaggerers, a near kinsman [2] of Valerio in *All Fools*, so like him, indeed, as to suggest the idea that the two parts were written, or perhaps one of them was revised, for the same actor. The rôle is, indeed, a capital ' character ' part for a lively actor who could hit off the swagger, the spouted ' tags ', and the cheating tricks which were familiar to every tavern-haunter and theatre-goer in Chapman's day. For Quintiliano is a portrait drawn from life of a figure common enough in London at the turn of the century, the false soldier whose boast of service abroad served as a cloak for his skeldering at home. The type had already appeared on the stage in the figures of Shift (*Every Man out of his Humour*) and Tucca (*Poetaster*). To Tucca, indeed, Quintiliano bears so plain a likeness that it seems probable that Jonson's captain suggested the lines along which Chapman worked in his transformation of the original stock figure. But Quintiliano is a far more agreeable rascal than the foul-mouthed, double-faced rogue of Jonson's play. Chapman had little of Jonson's indignant spirit of satire, and it is quite in keeping with his more genial mood that he carries Quintiliano triumphantly through to the end and puts the final *plaudite* into his mouth, whereas Tucca, like Shift and Bobadil, and the *miles gloriosus* in general, is put in the end to open shame.

I would repeat, in conclusion, that *May-Day* cannot be judged as an original and independent play. To call it with Ward (*English Dramatic Literature*, vol. ii, p. 440) ' a farrago of vulgar plots and counterplots ' is to show a complete misunderstanding of the task Chapman set himself. He took a much applauded comedy of the Italian school, so popular in cultivated English circles, and adapted it for the English stage. He eliminated the most offensive situations, simplified the action, bound the plot more closely together, introduced new and truly English characters, and rewrote the whole in the raciest and most idiomatic prose.[3] And to have done this is to have achieved no small measure of success. *May-Day* is not a good reading play, and it gives us little or nothing of what we expect to find in a work by Chapman. On the other hand, there is an abundance of action. The scenes in which

---

[1] This scene is imitated from *The Eunuch*.
[2] See note on p. 747.
[3] There is almost no verse in *May-Day*, only a few lines in III, iii, and two short passages in IV, ii. Chapman felt quite rightly that the tone of the whole play called for prose.

Lorenzo disguised as Snail is mocked by his friends or bullied by the Captain, the swagger of Quintiliano, and the lively chatter of Lodovico, must have been highly entertaining on the boards. There is no reason to think that the play was ever meant to be read. It is primarily a stage-play, and few of Chapman's comedies give us a better notion of his cleverness as a playwright than the neglected comedy of *May-Day*.

MAY-DAY

NOTES

I, i, 2. *Fit observance.* 'On the calends or first of May, commonly called May-day, the juvenile part of both sexes were wont to rise a little after midnight and walk to some neighbouring wood, accompanied with music and blowing of horns, where they break down branches from the trees, and adorn them with nosegays and crowns of flowers ; when this is done they return with their booty homewards about the rising of the sun, and make their doors and windows to triumph with their flowery spoils ; and the after part of the day is chiefly spent in dancing round a tall pole, which is called a May-pole '—Henry Bourne, *Antiquitates Vulgares*, quoted by Strutt, *Sports and Pastimes*, pp. 275–6. See also Ralph's May-morning speech in *The Knight of the Burning Pestle*, IV, i, 440 *ssq.*, and Dr. Murch's notes thereon in his edition of this play, *Yale Studies*, 1908. The *Chorus juvenum cantantes et saltantes* which precedes Lorenzo's speech was, of course, supposed to be engaged in the customary May-games.

I, i, 9–10. *Father January ... May's fragrant bosom:* probably a reminiscence of Chaucer's *Merchant's Tale* with its account of the marriage of hoar old January and fresh young May.

I, i, 32. *Oh hair, no hair.* Lorenzo's poem on his mistress appears to be one of the many parodies on a passage in *The Spanish Tragedy* beginning :

> *Oh eyes, no eyes, but fountains fraught with tears.*
> *Spanish Tragedy*, III, ii, 1.

See Boas's note on this line, in his edition of Kyd, p. 402. Koeppel (*loc. cit.*) notes the similarity between this scene and that in *Love's Labour's Lost*, IV, iii, 82 *ssq.*, in which Biron overhears and comments upon Dumaine's rhapsody on ' divine Kate '. A couple of Shakespeare's phrases in this scene, *as upright as the cedar*, l. 89, *as fair as day*, l. 90, have been taken over by Chapman and embodied, with slight changes, in the dialogue between Angelo and Lorenzo below, see ll. 123–4 and l. 119.

I, i, 38. Angelo intimates that her eyes do not match each other, i.e. that the lady squints. Cf. Chapman's phrase, *let but your eyes be matches*, in the address *To the Commune Reader*, prefixed to his translation of Musaeus, *Poems*, pp. 93–4.

I, i, 43. *Made out of wax:* finely fashioned, as though modelled in wax. Cf.

> *A sweet face, an exceeding daintie hand,*
> *A body, were it framed of wax*
> *By all the cunning artists in the world,*
> *It could not be better proportioned.*
> *Fair Em*, I, iii, 50–53.

The phrase was very common in Elizabethan English. See for further examples the note on *Romeo and Juliet*, I, iii, 76, in Furness's *Variorum*.

I, i, 47. *A deft dapper: deft* has here the sense of ' trim ', ' pretty '; Cotgrave renders *greslet* by ' little, pretty, deft, smallish '. Johnson's definition of *dapper* as applied to a person, ' little and active, lively without bulk ', exactly suits this passage. Lorenzo, of course, uses both adjectives in a commendatory sense.

I, i, 56. *She is discharged:* i.e. acquitted of blame as having done her full duty. See the *New English Dictionary* sub *discharge* 2b, and 4.

I, i, 88–9. *Just of my standing:* of my own position, or rank in society.

I, i, 93. *Ready to lie down:* cf. the phrase, *laugh and lie down, Gentleman Usher,* IV, ii, 83, and *Mother Bombie,* V, iii, 64.

I, i, 113–6. Lorenzo's speech is, I think, intentionally vague, but the sense seems to be that inasmuch as the unknown party is bountiful to his friends, Lorenzo will introduce Angelo to him to the latter's profit, provided that Angelo plays the part of a friend in bearing the message to Franceschina.

I, i, 123. *From the cushion:* wide of the mark ; cf. *New English Dictionary* sub *cushion,* where the parallel phrases ' beside, or wide of, the cushion ' are given. The phrase *from the cushion* is not given in the *Dictionary.* Heywood's *Proverbs,* pt. ii, chap. ix, has the phrase : ' Ye missed the cushion . . . and I may set you beside the cushion yet '.

I, i, 138. *I cannot do withal to die for't :* I can't help it if I were to die for it. For *do withal* see *Merchant of Venice,* III, iv, 72, and the notes *ad loc.* in Furness's *Variorum.*

I, i, 149. *Approved lowliness :* well-tried, or attested, modesty.

I, i, 151. *She's a woman* : cf.

> *She is a woman, therefore may be woo'd ;*
> *She is a woman, therefore may be won.*
> *Titus Andronicus,* II, i, 82–3.

This stock formula of Elizabethan literature appears to originate with Greene, in whose prose works it is, with slight variations, constantly repeated ; see Greene's *Works* (Grosart's edition), vol. iv, p. 288 ; vol. v, p. 567 ; vol. vii, p. 68 ; vol. viii, p. 88 ; vol. xi, p. 128 ; vol. xii, p. 78. Grosart (*Englische Studien,* vol. xxii, p. 402) asserts that the popularity of Greene's books put this saying ' into men's mouths and into proverbial speech ', and that it does not occur in Elizabethan literature prior to Greene.

I, i, 155. *This token shall be my gentleman usher :* these bracelets, cf. l. 98 above, shall go before to announce my visit to her.

I, i, 197–203. There is a certain similarity between this speech and Alessandro's rebuke of his friend, Cornelio, on their first meeting (*Alessandro,* I, iv). From the Italian *quanto grande aspettatione era venuta di te per tutta questa città : che non ci era giovano piu studioso,* Chapman gets his *man of good hope, a toward scholar.* There is no reference elsewhere in *May-Day* to the studies of Aurelio, but there are repeated allusions in *Alessandro* to the fact that Cornelio in the pursuit of his amour has abandoned his studies [1].

I, i, 208–9. Lodovico's stilted speech is, of course, a parody of the old tragic manner. It resembles somewhat a line spoken by Gloster :

> *If any spark of life be yet remaining.*
> 3 *King Henry VI,* V, vi, 66.

and still more closely one in the *The Spanish Tragedy,* II, v, 17.

I, i, 216. *Cuckoo :* used here simply as a term of reproach, equivalent to ' fool '. Cf. the corresponding use of *cuculus* (Asinaria, V, ii, 73), *Gowk,* and the German *Gauch.* The epithet, *Cupid's bird,* in this line is not, I think, directly connected with cuckoo, but denotes the sort of fool, i.e. a lovesick one, that Lodovico takes his friend to be.

I, i, 224. *An urchin :* a hedge-hog.

I, i, 233. *Shake her* [*ears*]. This phrase, common enough in Elizabethan literature, appears to have various meanings. The earliest instance that I know (Lyly, *Euphues and his England—Works,* Bond's edition, vol. ii, p. 35) evidently means ' to bestir oneself '. Bond in his note on this passage explains Chapman's use of the phrase in *Monsieur D'Olive,* II, ii, 234, in

---

[1] *Quanto è cambiato da quel ch'egli era ; egli prima non haveva i maggiori amici che i libri suoi : si stava la maggior parte del tempo in studio. . . . Adesso tutto'l contrario ; non vede mai libro, non sta mai in casa, nè notte, nè giorno. Alessandro I, i.*

the same sense. But it may also mean ' to show contempt or displeasure ', as in the example from Golding quoted in the *New English Dictionary*, and it is quite possible to take the phrase in *Monsieur D'Olive* in this sense. Perhaps its most usual meaning, however, is ' to endure a wrong or insult with forced patience ', as an ass shakes its ears when it receives a blow. This certainly is the sense in which it occurs in Shakespeare,[1] see *Julius Cæsar*, IV, i, 26, and *Twelfth Night*, II, iii, 134, and it is this sense which I attach to my emendation in the present passage.

I, i, 235. *Shake her heels :* no example of this phrase is given in the *New English Dictionary*, which gives, however, ' kick one's heels ' as equivalent to ' stand waiting idly, or impatiently '. Here I think the sense is stronger, equivalent perhaps to ' shake her heels in a halter ', ' be hanged,' possibly with a double entendre '.

I, i, 257-8. *A dog in a furmety-pot :* *furmety*, or frumenty, is a ' dish made of hulled wheat boiled in milk, and seasoned with cinnamon, sugar, etc.' —*New English Dictionary*. The phrase ' a dog in a furmety pot ' occurs with slight variations twice in Massinger, *The Bondman*, I, iii, and *The Maid of Honour*, V, i.

I, i, 262-3. *Touch her but with a kissed hand :* to kiss one's hand before touching one's mistress was a sign of the greatest respect. Thus when Suffolk has taken Margaret prisoner, and has fallen in love with his captive, he says :

> *O fairest beauty, do not fear nor fly !*
> *For I will touch thee but with reverent hands ;*
> *I kiss these fingers for eternal peace,*
> *And lay them gently on thy tender side.*
>
> 1 *King Henry VI*, V, iii, 46–9.

I, i, 266. *Tractable and tactable :* cf. Massinger's phrase :

> *They* [women] *being created*
> *To be both tractable and tactable.*
>
> *Parliament of Love*, II, i.

I, i, 276. *Wear in thy hat :* see note on *All Fools*, III, i, 363.

I, i, 277. *My skill in poultry :* my knowledge of women. Cf. below, II, i, 429.

I, i, 293. *Gossave :* a mincing pronunciation of ' God save ', repeatedly used by Innocentio, and no doubt meant to characterize him as a simpleton.

I, i, 296. *Puts finger i' th' eye :* a derisive phrase meaning ' to weep '. Cf. *Comedy of Errors*, II, ii, 206, and *Taming of the Shrew*, I, i, 79.

I, i, 298. *Tables :* the game of backgammon. Cf. *Love's Labour's Lost*, V, ii, 326.

I, i, 305-6. Among the stock jests of the clown which Hamlet cites is a reproach to his master for being slack in paying his wages. The passage was omitted when Shakespeare revised the play, but see Q_1, ll. 1212–13 (Furness's *Variorum—Hamlet*, vol. ii, p. 65).

I, i, 314-5. *With a wet finger :* with the greatest ease, as one wipes out a mark on a slate. The *New English Dictionary* cites an example from Udall's *Apophthegms*, 1542, and it is frequent in Elizabethan drama. Cf. *Sir Giles Goosecap*, II, i, 26–27, and the examples cited in Hazlitt's *English Proverbs*, p. 546.

I, i, 343. *Candle-rents :* rents derived from house-property which is constantly depreciating, as a lighted candle decreases in size. The phrase is used elsewhere by Chapman ; see *Poems*, p. 222 and p. 434.

I, i, 350-1. Destructive storms in Chapman's day were frequently attributed to witchcraft. Cf. *Macbeth*, IV, i, 52–60.

I, i, 357. *Twenty i' th' hundred for thy life.* As I understand the passage Quintiliano tells his dupe that he may invest the money derived from the sale of his houses in such a way as to receive 20 per cent. on the capital for the rest of his life. Quintiliano offers to take £200 himself on these terms.

---

[1] For other instances of this sense see the quotations given in the note in Furness's *Variorum* on *Twelfth Night*, II, iv, 134.

I, i, 372. *Red lattices :* cf. the note on *All Fools*, V, i, 69. There is, of course, a pun on *lattice* and *lettuce*.

I, i, 379. *Enter me at an ordinary :* introduce me at a tavern or eating-house where meals are provided at a fixed price. Such taverns were the resort of men of fashion in Chapman's day, and there are numerous directions, serious and satiric, for the instruction of the newcomer at such a resort. See, for example, *Every Man out of His Humour*, III, i, where Carlo Buffone instructs Sogliardo in the fashions at ordinaries. There are several points where Chapman seems to borrow directly from Jonson, cf. ll. 394–6 and 399–400 with Carlo's words : *When any stranger comes in amongst 'em, they all stand up and stare at him, as he were some unknown beast brought out of Africa,* and *you must be impudent enough, sit down and use no respect.* The most elaborate set of directions is found in Dekker's *Gull's Hornbook*, chap. v—*How a young Gallant should behave himself in an Ordinary.* Ll. 418–420 below resemble a passage in Dekker very closely : *When you are set down to dinner, you must eat as impudently as can be (for that's most gentlemanlike) when your Knight is upon his stewed mutton, be presently, though you be but a captain, in the bosom of your goose : and when your Justice of the Peace is knuckle-deep in goose, you may without disparagement to your blood, though you have a Lady to your mother, fall very manfully to your woodcocks.*

I, i, 414–15. There is a pun on *Warden* and *pear*—' a warden, or winter peare, a peare which may be kept verie long '—Cotgrave. There are frequent references in Elizabethan literature to the warden-pear, which seems to have been especially used for pies. See *Winter's Tale*, IV, iii, 48, and the note thereon in Furness's *Variorum*.

I, i, 425. *Bread's a binder :* apparently a familiar phrase of the time. I find it in *A Looking Glass for London*, I, ii, 249, and in Brathwait's *Barnabae Itinerarium*, pt. i, l. 5.

I, i, 430. *Carry no coals :* submit to no insults. Cf. below III, iii, 253, and *Romeo and Juliet*, I, i, 1. The guileless Innocentio, as appears from his answer, l. 431, is unacquainted with this bit of Elizabethan slang.

I, i, 433. *After dinner there will be play.* ' The dinner [at an ordinary] was usually followed by gambling '—*New English Dictionary* sub *ordinary*, b. See also *The Gull's Hornbook*, chap. v ; and the debate between Nigel and Lord Dalgarno as to whether an ordinary is a gaming-house in *The Fortunes of Nigel*, chap. xi.

I, i, 445, 448. A *mark* is two-thirds of the pound sterling. An *angel* is a gold piece, whose value in Chapman's day was about ten shillings.

II, i. The conversation between Lucretia and Temperance with which this scene opens is based upon a similar dialogue between Lampridia and Nicoletta in *Alessandro*, I, iii. Chapman has cut down the original and considerably softened the language of the bawd. There is little verbal similarity except in l. 41, where the phrase, *let's to the minster*, is taken direct from the Italian, *Eccoci al monastero*, i.e. the church whither Lampridia is going to pray.

II, i, 2. *Some inward news :* some private message.

II, i, 19. *The flower of Venice.* This phrase gives us the scene of the play ; see also IV, i, 14. The Italian original is laid at Pisa.

II, i, 26. *His Signiory:* his Lordship.

II, i, 29. *A brown dozen :* an obsolete phrase for a ' round ' or full dozen.

II, i, 44. *The priest have a penny :* i.e. get his wedding-fee.

II, i, 75. *Noverint universi :* the Latin words with which legal documents began—*Know all men by these presents*; cf. *Monsieur D'Olive*, V, ii. 85–9. The implication is that Gasparo has ruined many men by law-suits.

II, i, 77. *Disparage a gentlewoman :* drag a lady into a *mésalliance*. Cf. *All Fools*, I, i, 266, and the note *ad loc.*

II, i, 121. There is an allusion here to an old ballad, well known in Chapman's time, which appears in Percy's *Reliques* under the title of *Queen Dido*. There are further allusions to this ballad and to its tune in *Bonduca*, I, ii, and *The Captain*, III, i. See also *The Penniless Parliament of Thread-*

bare Poets, 1608, reprinted by the Percy Society, vol. vii. The copies of the ballad in the Pepys' collection, from which Percy printed, are headed *The Wandering Prince of Troy: to the tune of Queen Dido*. The first of these can hardly be dated before 1620, but both go back, no doubt, to a ballad entitled *The Wanderynge Prince*, which was entered in the Stationers' Registers as early as 1564–5. Lodovico parodies the first lines of the twelfth stanza of this ballad:

> When death had pierced the tender heart
> Of Dido Carthaginian queen;
> Whose bloody knife did end the smart
> Which she sustain'd in mournful teen.

II, i, 141. *Imbrue your hands with his liver:* become guilty of his death; the *liver* is here referred to as the seat of the affections, in particular of love.

II, i, 156. *These superfluous disgracings:* these insults you have wantonly heaped upon him.

II, i, 157. *Unhearty niceness:* unhearty may mean 'discouraging', 'disheartening'; cf.

> Yet, to bite his lip
> And hum at good Cominius, much unhearts me.
> *Coriolanus*, V, i, 48–9.

or, as the context seems to show, 'insincere'; *niceness* is, in either case, equivalent to 'coyness', 'over-scrupulousness'.

II, i, 211–17. So in *Alessandro*, I, v, Lucilla suggests in her letter the possibility of her lover entering her chamber by means of a ladder: *che con un poco di scala potrete accostarvi alla inferriata de la mia camera.*

II, i, 225–302. The interview between Temperance and Leonoro is based on that between Fortunio and Nicoletta, *Alessandro*, II, i. The verbal similarities which Stiefel tries to point out (*loc. cit.* p. 200) seem to me quite negligible. The only apparent analogy that his parallel columns of English and Italian contain is *an obstinate young thing* and *Ostinata, ostinatissima*, and even here *obstinate* is Stiefel's perversion of Chapman's text l. 244 which reads *an obstacle young thing*. One might almost fancy that Chapman placed this malapropism in the mouth of Temperance to avoid a verbal borrowing from his Italian source.

II, i, 240. *Broke with her.* 'To break with' means to disclose anything secretly to a person, but there is an undermeaning in the phrase equivalent to 'solicit', 'attempt to procure'; cf. Shakespeare's use of 'broker' as a synonym for 'bawd' or 'procurer' in *King John*, II, 582, and *Troilus and Cressida*, V, x, 33.

II, i, 316. *Lapwing.* 'Like the partridge and some other birds it [the lapwing] has a curious habit of trying to draw intruders away from its nest or young by fluttering along the ground in an opposite direction'—Harting, *Ornithology of Shakespeare*, quoted by Furness in his note on *Much Ado About Nothing*, III, i, 25.

II, i, 326–353. Stiefel's statement that this passage is only a free version of the latter part of *Alessandro*, I, v, seems to me too strong. Except that in both plays the servant promises his master to get his sweetheart's father out of the way, there is nothing in common between them.

II, i, 346–7. *Spy out:* the same phrase is used in *Monsieur D'Olive*, III, ii, 99: '*Discern and spy out*' is my motto.

II, i, 357–8. *With one trowel daub two walls:* apparently a proverb equivalent to 'kill two birds with one stone'. I have not, however, met with any analogous phrase in the old collections of proverbs.

II, i, 362. *D'ye lack, gentlewoman.* Angelo imitates the cry of the apprentice at his master's stall; cf. *Eastward Ho*, I, i, 65, and III, ii, 84.

II, i, 374–7. Angelo's speech sounds almost like a parody of Valerio's in *All Fools*, IV, i, 140–46. Cf. also *Antonio and Mellida*, II, i, 103–4.

II, i, 427. *An old colt:* the phrase seems, as Dilke says, a contradiction in terms, but *colt* has here the meaning of 'a wanton fellow'. Cf. the phrase, 'a colt's tooth', i.e. an inclination to wantonness, *Henry VIII*, I, iii, 48.

II, i, 434–512. Stiefel points out that this passage is in the main an adaptation of *Alessandro*, II, iii. It is a very free adaptation, and the parallel passages which Stiefel quotes contain no very close resemblances. Chapman, even when he is following his model closely, renders the simple and matter-of-fact Italian style in picturesque and figurative English Thus for *Voi sapete, Gostanzo, quant' honesta e da bene è questa vostra Brigida, e quanto è vaga del suo honore,* Chapman has : *And yet does this whirligig stand upon terms of honour, forsooth ; tenders her reputation as the apple of her eye.*

II, i, 449. *A very toy which runs in her head :* cf. *All Fools,* III, i, 78–9.

II, i, 455. *Mutton-monger.* See the note on *All Fools,* III, i, 396.

II, i, 464–5. *Tinkers, pedlars, etc.* In the Italian the servant remarks that certain sorts of people like[1] *acorespilli, spazzacamini, villetai, magnani, e simili* (i.e. pedlers, chimney-sweeps, locksmiths, and the like) can enter ladies' houses without suspicion, and so Gostanzo ought to disguise himself like one of them to visit Brigida. Gostanzo suggests disguising himself as a *villetaio* (cf. l. 473), but the servant says he would look too much like himself in that dress.

II, i, 475–6. *That disguise is worn threadbare upon every stage.* There is nothing in the Italian to correspond to this. It appears to be a gibe at the frequency with which English playwrights used the monk's gown as a disguise.

II, i, 505–10. In the Italian Gostanzo asks how he can kiss Brigida in his dirty disguise without soiling her, and the servant answers that when he is once in her house he may wash and clean himself at his pleasure. As usual where Chapman takes a passage directly from his original, he expands it and heightens the style.

II, i, 512. *Potatoes :* formerly thought to be aphrodisiacs. See *Byron's Conspiracy,* III, ii, 16, and my note *ad loc.*

II, i, 537–8. *Padua.* See *All Fools,* I, i, 316, and the note *ad loc.,* p. 714 above. Giovanello being *fresh* needs to be *powdered,* i.e. salted by being made acquainted with the knavish captain, who will then find him an appetiser for a carouse.

II, i, 540–543. With this speech cf. the scene in *Sir Giles Goosecap,* III, i, 185, *ssq.,* where the conversation turns on furnishing a lord with a good merry fool.

II, i, 555–6. *Meretriculated . . . colted.* The first of these words, according to the *New English Dictionary,* is a nonce-word of Chapman's invention, equivalent to ' deceived as by a harlot '. For *colted,* i.e. ' cheated ', cf. I *King Henry IV,* II, ii, 39.

II, i, 561. *Loath to break :* a pun on the implied sense, ' break my word ' and the common meaning of *break,* i.e ' go bankrupt ', as Quintiliano would do if he paid the bill.

II, i, 568. *Pose him :* question him.

II, i, 603–4. *Healths on our knees :* cf. *All Fools,* V, ii, 56, and the note *ad loc.*

II, i, 606. *How many miles to midsummer ?* There seems an implied allusion here to the ' midsummer moon ', ' the month in which lunacy is supposed to be prevalent '—*New English Dictionary.* The phrase ' midsummer moon ' occurs at least twice in Nash (*Works*—McKerrow's edition, vol. iii, p. 38 and p. 363) in the sense of ' madness '. See also Ray's *Proverbs,* p. 56, and the notes on *Twelfth Night,* III, iv, 61, in Furness's *Variorum.* Apparently Quintiliano asks derisively how near madness Giovanello is.

II, i, 607. *Tassel of a gander :* a *tassell,* or more properly a *tercel,* or *tiercel,* is the male hawk, so called as being one-third smaller than the female. See the notes on *tassel-gentle, Romeo and Juliet,* II, ii, 160, in Furness's *Variorum.* Since the goose is somewhat smaller than the gander we may, I suppose, take it that Quintiliano in a somewhat roundabout and fanciful fashion calls the student a goose.

---

[1] I cite the Italian *literatim* from the 1561 edition of *Alessandro.* It does not agree exactly with the text as quoted by Stiefel. The word *acorespilli* I have not been able to trace ; for *villetai,* we should read *velettai.* The two probably mean ' pedlers of pins and veils '.

II, i, 611. *The powdering-tub :* the sweating-tub used in Chapman's day in the treatment of venereal disease. It is constantly referred to in Elizabethan drama ; see especially *The Knight of the Burning Pestle*, III, iv, 133–144.

II, i, 634. *My Valentine :* a lady not elsewhere referred to in the play who is Quintiliano's *Valentine*, or sweetheart for the current year. Under the pretence of visiting their *nursed childs*, i.e. their children at nurse in the country, she and a neighbour or two are to accompany Quintiliano and his friends to the *carouse*. The form *childs*, l. 635, is a northern plural of which the *New English Dictionary* gives no example later than the *Towneley Mysteries* in the middle of the fifteenth century.

II, i, 642. *Barbary :* i.e. Barberland, the kingdom of the barbers. By a similar pun the barber who plays the part of the giant in *The Knight of the Burning Pestle* assumes the name of Barbarossa.

II, i, 648–9. *'Twill be the less perceived :* the visible token of married life, the horns, will not show so plainly if Cutbeard puts on his hat.

II, i, 650–1. *I'll maintain you both else :* I take it that Quintiliano asserts that if his barber and his tailor prolong their supposed quarrel, he will *maintain*, i.e. lend support and countenance to, both parties.

II, i, 680. *The Clarissimi :* Venetian grandees.

II, i, 687. *A squirting companion :* a paltry fellow, with reference to the syringe of the barber-surgeon.

II, i, 695. *Scrip or scroll :* any form of written receipt.
For a colour : as a mere pretence.

II, i, 696. *Lend it me simply :* lend it unconditionally, without qualification, such as might serve *for a colour*.

II, i, 704. *Burn'd i' th' hand :* i.e. burnt my fingers, suffered loss.

II, i, 718–9. *'Tis not this . . . my hands :* you'll not get this money back from me. Quintiliano's speech is purposely ambiguous, and his gull misunderstands it so far as to thank him, l. 720, for a promise not to repay the loan.

III, i, 5. *Presume of what thou wilt :* count upon anything you please.

III, i, 6. *Both ways :* i.e. ' drunk, as well as absent '—Dilke.

III, i, 24. *Holy water frog.* Dilke thinks there is an allusion to the game of leap-frog. Lean (*Collectanea*, vol. ii, p. 705) suggests that ' the practice of passing on the *eau bénite* from one to another on entering or leaving church to save going to the stoup itself is in view '. Perhaps both are right. Water passed on in this fashion from hand to hand might be said to be playing leap-frog, or be spoken of as *holy-water frog*.

III, i, 29–30. I understand Lodovico to say : I must keep faith with my uncle, and will tell you his secret only on condition that you do not repeat it.

III, i, 59–60. *Marcus Aurelius.* The reference is, in all probability, not to the original *Meditations* of the Roman Emperor, but to one of the most popular books of the sixteenth century, the *Reloj de Principes, o Marco Aurelio*, of the Spaniard Guevara, 1529. It was translated into French under the title of *Livre doré de Marc Aurèle* in 1531. This version served as a basis for the English translation of Lord Berners, *The Golden Book of Marcus Aurelius*, editions of which appeared in 1534, 1539, 1542, 1553, 1557, and 1559. Another translation by North appeared in 1557 entitled *The Diall of Princes ;* subsequent editions of which appeared in 1568, 1582 and 1619.

Gesta Romanorum, the famous Latin collection of anecdotes and tales compiled about the end of the thirteenth or beginning of the fourteenth century. It was one of the most popular works of the early Renaissance in England. The first English translation was printed by Wynkyn de Worde between 1510 and 1515 ; another translation by Robinson appeared in 1577, of which there are, according to Lowndes, six or seven impressions before 1601.

The Mirror of Magistrates : a famous collection of poems on the falls of princes by various authors, Ferrers, Baldwin, Phaer, Churchyard, Sackville, and others, which appeared in various forms and with constant

additions during the third quarter of the sixteenth century. From 1559
to 1587 at least seven editions were issued.

It is worth noting that all these works are of a highly moral, not to say
didactic tone.

III, i, 65–6. *Ring him . . . basons :* an allusion to the old custom of ' carting '
an infamous person. The mob which attended the cart beat basins and
other utensils to increase the uproar. There are frequent allusions to this
custom in Elizabethan drama ; see, for example, *The Silent Woman*, III,
v, 85 ; *The New Inn*, IV, iii, 99 ; and a stage-direction in *The Honest
Whore*, pt. ii, V, ii.

III, i, 66. *Besnowball him :* cf. the phrase *pebble 'em with snowballs, Eastward
Ho*, III, ii, 70–1.

III, i, 67. *Ashamed . . . seal it :* ' Ashamed of his guilty purpose before it
be effected '—Dilke.

III, i, 84–5. *Fortune de la [paix] :* a coined phrase after the analogy of ' fortune
of war '. Probably the French phrase was used for the sake of a pun with
Pax, immediately following. Dilke mistakenly identifies *the Pax* with
the Pyx, the box containing the consecrated wafer. *Pax* may mean either
the kiss of peace, or as here the tablet which was kissed by the celebrating
priest at Mass and passed to the other clergy and to the congregation to
be kissed, see Nares, *Glossary*, sub *Pax*.

III, i, 105. There is a pun on *natural* in the sense of ' foolish ', ' idiotic '.

III, i, 125–30. There is a close parallel to this song in one sung by Cocledemoy
disguised as a bell-man in *The Dutch Courtesan*, IV, v, and another in *Englishmen for my Money* (Hazlitt-Dodsley, vol. x, p. 530). Both are modelled
on the old street-cries, a collection of which is appended to Heywood's
Rape of Lucrece.

III, i, 132. Cf. the note on *The Blind Beggar*, i, 298.

III, i, 187–8. The word *rook*, now familiar as a term of reproach for a cheating
gambler, seems formerly to have meant, like so many birds' names, a fool,
specifically one easily cheated. See the quotations in the *New English
Dictionary* under *rook*, c. A *cheating-stock* on the analogy of ' laughing-
stock ' is a butt, or fool, made to be cheated. Cf. Jonson's phrase ' court-
ing-stock ' in *The New Inn*, I, vi, 154.

III, i, 249. *Shoeing-horns :* a slang expression, occurring as early as *Gammer
Gurton's Needle*, 1552–3, for an appetizer, a provocative to drink. Later
it came to be applied to people, of either sex, who provoked, or facilitated,
amorous interviews. Thus in *Monsieur D'Olive*, V, i, 170–199, Eurione
is charged with being a *shoeing-horn*, i.e. a pandress, to her sister. See also
the letter on ' shoeing-horns ' in the *Spectator*, no. 536. In the present
passage Lodovico uses the word in its first sense—the absence of Lorenzo
and Quintiliano is a means to facilitate the meeting of the lovers.

III, ii, 11. *Other men's stables :* see the passage in Ingleby, *Shakespeare Hermeneutics*, p. 77, ssq., already referred to in connexion with *All Fools*, IV,
i, 262–3.

III, ii, 12. *Rampant . . . passant.* There is a pun on the heraldic meaning
of the words. I take it that *passant* here has the obsolete meaning ' ex-
celling '.

III, ii, 17. *Past the pikes :* a phrase equivalent to ' run the gauntlet '. Cf.
Monsieur D'Olive, III, ii, 199. An instance of this usage occurs as late
as Cowper, 1785.

III, ii, 41. *The most slovenly case,* referring to Lorenzo's dirty dress as a
chimney-sweep.

III, iii, 10. *Undoing :* there is, I think, a double meaning here ; the word
carries with it a second sense, i.e. ' ensnaring ', ' tempting to ruin '.
To ' undo ' a woman meant specifically in Elizabethan English ' to ruin
her '. See *Titus Andronicus*, IV, ii, 75–76.

III, iii, 18. Probably Lodovico pronounced these words in a tragic tone that
would recall to the spectator one of the famous phrases of *The Spanish
Tragedy* (II, v, 4), *Who calls Hieronimo* ?

III, iii, 89. *Rope-ripe terms :* language fit for the gallows, with special allusion to Lodovico's use of *hemp, halter,* and *knot,* in the preceding speech. Cf. the use of *ropery* in *Romeo and Juliet,* II, iv, 154.

III, iii, 49. *A blue kitling.* I take it that *blue* here means ' frightened ', ' faint-hearted ', and that *kitling* means ' young thing '. See the *New English Dictionary* sub *kitling,* 3.

III, iii, 52. *His parting choler :* the anger in which he departed, cf. II, i, 113–130 above.

III, iii, 55. *Choose him :* let him choose, do as he chooses.

III, iii, 104. Mr. Crawford calls my attention to the fact that the first words of this line are borrowed from *Astrophel and Stella* (Fourth Song, stanza 5). Chapman's audience would no doubt be quick to recognize the loan.

III, iii, 142. *Ædificium cedit solo.* This appears to be a version of a passage from the *Institutes* of Justinian (II, i, 29) : *omne quod inædificatur, solo cedit,* everything built on the soil accedes to it. By a humorous confusion of Lodovico's this doctrine is made to bear upon the ownership of a calf. This was, however, settled on another ground, see *Institutes,* II, i, 19.

III, iii, 149. *A motion :* a puppet-show. The reference is to Madam Temperance, who has appeared on the terrace of Honorio's house, and whose gestures, as she peers about for Leonoro, remind Lodovico of a puppet's.

III, iii, 163–5. The mock citation from Pythagoras reminds one of *Twelfth Night,* IV, ii, 54–7.

III, iii, 196. A parody of *Hamlet,* I, ii, 114. The line parodied does not appear in the first version of Hamlet, the quarto of 1603. See above, p. 732.

III, iii, 202. *Ancient :* i.e. Giovanello, whom the Captain has promoted to be his ensign, or standard bearer.

III, iii, 209. *Scientia* is used in mediaeval Latin as an honorary title for a learned man, so that Giovanello's assertion is pedantic rather than ignorant.

III, iii, 217. *Balderdash :* a mixture of liquors, such as beer and milk (*The New Inn,* I, ii, 21–25), or, as here, wine and brandy (cf. the quotation from Bunyan under *fetch* 12, b in the *New English Dictionary*), whereas the Captain suspects the presence of salt water in the wine.

III, iii, 231–2. Quintiliano sings a snatch of some old ballad which has not yet been identified.

III, iii, 253. *Uncoal-carrying :* see the note on I, i, 430 above.

III, iii, 259, *ssq.* The incident of Innocentio's foolish letter of defiance is palpably adapted from *Twelfth Night,* III, iv, 156, *ssq.*

IV, i, 10. To *cast* is Elizabethan slang for ' to vomit ' ; cf. *Macbeth,* II, iii, 46. There are constant puns on this sense of the word.

IV, i, 15. Aristotle first defined continuity and distinguished between continuity and contiguity (*Metaphysics,* k, 1069). Quintiliano here refers scornfully to academic discussions of this distinction.

IV, i, 18–19. A garbled quotation from Marston's *Antonio's Revenge* (V, ii, 20–2) :

> *Fill red-cheek'd Bacchus, let Lyæus float*
> *In burnish'd goblets ! Force the plump-lipp'd god*
> *Skip light lavoltas in your full-sapp'd veins.*

The *lavolta* was a ' lively dance for two persons, consisting chiefly of high bounds '. It was introduced from Italy (*la volta,* the turn) and appears to have been very popular in Elizabethan England. Sir John Davies gives a description of it in his *Orchestra,* stanza 70.

IV, i, 24–27. Cf. the swaggering speech of Valerio in *All Fools,* II, i, 226–229, 300–304. The *shoulder-clappers* of l. 26 are, of course, the sergeants ; the term comes from their practice of clapping a man on the shoulder to signify his arrest ; the *pestles* are their staves, or batons.

IV, i, 31–2. *It stands a little.* Innocentio's phrase implies some depreciation of the sword, perhaps, as Dilke suggests, that it does not at once resume its position after having been bent, but *stands a little.* Quintiliano disposes of the criticism with the punning answer that the best *blades* (men of the sword) *stand* (put up a fight) *soonest.*

IV, i, 37. I cannot identify the old ballad from which this line is evidently quoted.

IV, i, 82. I can find no other instance of *hummerer*, but the meaning appears to be ' one who hums or buzzes about anything '. Dilke's alteration *humourer* seems to me to make the meaning less plain.

IV, ii, 18–20. ' Till by observing our fathers' tempers we find a fit time for proposing our marriage '. *Skill*, l. 20, is identical in meaning with *knowledge*.

IV, ii, 55. *Capricorn.* This constellation is mentioned here because of the supposed lascivious nature of the he-goat.

IV, ii, 83. *Betwixt the pales.* The phrase means, I think, ' within limits,' i.e. briefly.

IV, ii, 109. *Has the wind of :* catches scent of, is on the trail of.

IV, ii, 190. *Against the hair :* in spite of his natural inclination, or, in this case, aversion to love. Cf. *All Fools*, II, i, 380, and note *ad loc.*

IV, ii, 195. To ' *lay down the bucklers* ' is to own defeat ; cf. *Much Ado*, V. ii, 17, and the parallel passages cited by Steevens in the *Variorum* edition of this play.

IV, ii, 207. *Jump at three :* exactly at three ; cf. *Hamlet.* V, ii, 386.

IV, ii, 232. *The May-night show.* The masque at Honorio's on May-night closes the play as the *chorus juvenum* on May-morning opens it.

IV, ii, 242–3 *The tone . . . the tother :* forms arising from a misdivision of *thet* (that) *one, thet other. The tone* refers to *gifts* (l. 241), *the tother* to *courting* (l. 240).

IV, iii, 22–4. Chapman may have got the idea of comparing a feast with a battle from Latin comedy ; see *Captivi*, V, i, and *Menæchmi*, I, iii.

IV, iii, 46–7. *Culverins . . . minions :* names of various kinds of guns. *Culverins* are small hand-cannon ; the name is originally from *colubrinus,* snakelike ; *falcons* and *sakers* like muskets bear the names of birds ; a *minion* is literally ' a darling '. The comparison of flagons to ' Cannon, demi-cannon, saker, and basilisk ' reappears in *The Honest Whore*, pt. 2, IV, iii.

IV, iii, 66. *The dresser ;* the kitchen sideboard on which the cook knocked to indicate that dinner was ready ; cf. Massinger's phrase, *the dresser, the cook's drum* (*Unnatural Combat*, III, i).

IV, iii, 84–5. Cf. *An Humorous Day's Mirth*, sc. vi, l. 51.

IV, iii, 91. *Prisons.* It was a common practice in Chapman's day to send the broken victuals left over from a feast to feed poor prisoners. There are repeated references in the drama to the ' basket ' in which these victuals were carried. See *Eastward Ho*, V, iii, 55 ; *The City Madam*, I, i, etc.

IV, iii, 126. *By the meskin :* by the mass ; *meskin*, or *maskins* being a diminutive form.

IV, iv, 5. *Take in.* Angelo throws up the rope ladder for Æmilia to make fast.

IV, iv, 6. *Short-heel'd* : wanton ; cf. *The Blind Beggar*, vii, 21, and *The Widow's Tears*, III, i, 152.

IV, iv, 25. Since marriage takes away a man's faith, he is forced to rely on works for his salvation.

IV, iv, 37. *Hornstock :* stock on which to plant horns ; cf. *cheating-stock*, III, i, 187, above, and note *ad loc.*

IV, iv, 48. *Battle the pride :* feed fat, flatter, the pride.

IV, iv, 68. *Be here V with him.* It is possible that *V* was originally a marginal stage-direction, representing the sign of the horns which has slipped into the text.

IV, iv, 70–1. *Phtroh; ho, ptrough :* onomato-poeic words which Fannio imagines himself calling out to the horned beast, Quintiliano, and the ass, Innocentio.

V, i, 63. *For my love.* Lorenzo says that Franceschina has come to his house in disguise for love of him.

V, i, 66. *Hit it :* discover a token, cf. l. 68.

V, i, 93. *Lofty tricks :* high capers in the dance.

V, i, 113. *Branched gown :* ' gown adorned with sprigs or flowers in needle-work '—Dilke.

V, i, 143. *Woodcock :* here as elsewhere a synonym for a fool.

V, i, 196. *My waist :* a pun on ' waste ', dissipation ; cf. 2 *King Henry IV*, I, ii, 160–162.

V, i, 203. *Maw :* an old game of cards, spoken of in 1580 as having ' grown out of the country from the meanest into credit at court with the greatest '—*Popular Antiquities*, vol. ii, p. 450. Two people could play it.

V, i, 209. The *varlet* is the knave ; the *fivefinger* is the five of trumps. A *coat-card*, l. 216 below, is a court-card ; cf. Rowley's *When You See Me : I am a coat-card, indeed. Then thou must needs be a knave, for thou art neither king nor queen.* (Elze's edition, p. 28, where the original *coat-card* is emended to *court-card*.)

V, i, 267. To wipe any one's nose is to cheat one of something. Cf. a similar phrase in *The City Wit* (Brome, *Works*, vol. i, p. 356.) The first instance cited of this phrase in the *New English Dictionary* is under the date 1598, and it may have been borrowed from France. A similar idiom, *se torcher le nez de quelque chose*, occurs in the comedies of Larivey (*Six Comedies*, 1579).

V, i, 279. *New fireworks.* Quintiliano asks if this revelation of identity is part of the entertainment prepared for the feast.

V, i, 301. *Lead apes in hell.* There was an old saying that the girl who died unmarried was doomed to lead apes in hell. It occurs first, so far as I know, in Gascoigne, 1575 (*Works*, vol. i, p. 463) ; but is no doubt older. See the notes in the *Variorum on Much Ado*, II, i, 43.

V, i, 322. *Stand not too much upon goods :* do not insist upon too large a settlement on the young couple.

V, i, 326. *Ambo :* i.e. Æmilia and Aurelio.

V, i, 334. *Temperance* cannot only administer love potions, but treat venereal diseases.

V, i, 348. *Mutton and rabbit :* slang terms for loose women.

V, i, 351. *In authority wise :* as one of the officials charged with the preservation of public morals.

V, i, 354. Possibly a parody of a line of Marlowe's :

> *Whose hideous echoes make the welkin howl.*
>
> *Dido*, IV, ii, 9.

TEXT NOTES

May-Day was first published in 1611 in a quarto printed for John Browne. It is not particularly well printed, and the text needs correction at many points. The copies of Q. (two of which in the British Museum and two in the Bodleian I have consulted) agree fairly well among themselves. I have pointed out a few variations in the following notes.

The first reprint of this play appeared in *Old English Plays*, vol. iv, 1814. The editor of this collection is known to have been Charles Wentworth Dilke, and I refer to this edition in the following notes by the letter D. So far as I know *May-Day* has not been reprinted in any other collection of plays, nor has it been given the honour of a separate edition. It appears, of course, in the *Comedies and Tragedies of George Chapman* (P.), and in Shepherd's edition of Chapman's works, *Plays*, 1874 (S.).

Dramatis Personae. No such list appears in Q. The list here printed is based with a few changes and additions upon that printed by D.

The play is divided into acts, but not into scenes in Q. I have made the scene divisions and indicated the place of the action.

I, i, 26. Q. *wonder ;* D. and S. *wondered,* an unnecessary change.

29. Q. *trow we ;* following Brereton's suggestion (*Modern Language Review*, vol. iii, p. 61) I read *trow.*

39. Q. *cheeke ;* P. misprints *checke.*

43. Brereton (*loc. cit.*) stigmatizes the words *made out* as ' clearly an interpolation ', since they ' spoil Lorenzo's verse '. But it does not seem imperative that this line should be the exact complement of l. 41.

126. Q. *thy full ;* D. *the full.* Cf. l. 49.

131. Q. *parlesse ;* D. and S. *peerless.* I prefer to read *parlous*, the syncopated form of ' perilous '.

146. Q. has a question mark after *then,* which is followed by D. But here as often the question mark indicates an exclamation.

167. Q. *Godge you God morrow ;* D. *Godge you good morrow.* But *Godge* is evidently equivalent to *God gi'*, and *God morrow* appears elsewhere in this play ; cf. II, i, 225.

181. Q. *potion ;* D. corrects to *portion.*

233. Q. *shake her heels ;* D. corrects *heeles* to *ears*, citing *Twelfth Night*, II, iii, 134, for this phrase, which occurs also in *Monsieur D'Olive*, II, ii, 234. The Q. *heeles* was probably due to the presence of the same word in l. 235 below, which caught the printer's eye.

244. Q. *love stormes ;* so D. and S. I suggest *love scorns*, an emendation approved by Mr. Daniel.

255. P. misprints *how how deepe.* All the copies of Q. which I have seen have but one *how.*

257. Q. *sautring ;* D. *sauntering.*

278. The stage-direction *a purse, etc.*, is printed in Q., as here, in the margin. It is evidently an instruction to the stage-manager to provide Innocentio with the purse which he pulls out in l. 445 below. This seems to show conclusively that Q. was printed from a stage copy. Cf. a similar instruction in *Bussy D'Ambois*, I, i. 153 and Text Note *ad loc.*

372. P. followed by S. has *their hunger.* But all the copies of Q. that I have seen read *anger*, which is also the reading of D.

418. Q. *with ceremony,* followed by S. D. *without ceremony*, which is evidently required by the context. The corresponding passage in Dekker (see above, p. 742) reads *as impudently as can be.*

II, i, 9. D. inserts *you* after *say*, which does not seem necessary.

38–40. Q. and D. print as prose ;

but it is plainly verse, and was recognized as such by S.

94. Q. has the stage-direction *Enter Gasparo ;* but it is clear that he merely crosses the stage, and D. made the proper correction.

109. In Q. the stage-direction *Exit Aure.* follows the entrance of Lodovico.

156. One of the copies in the British Museum (C. 12. g. 5) reads *disgracing.* This is followed by P. ; but the other copies that I have seen read *disgracings.* Possibly we should read *disguisings ;* but as the passage is intelligible, see note p. 743, I have allowed the text to stand.

197. Q. *If doe not ;* D. inserts *I* after *If.*

214. P. misprints *Sod.* for Q. *Lod.*

222. Q. *Of my kindnesse from me*, so D. and S. ; but *my* is plainly a misprint for *any ;* cf. below III, i, 61, where the same misprint occurs.

264 Q. *ter dinner.* In Q. these words begin a line, and it is plain that *af* has simply dropped off. D. restores it.

353. Q. *enforce us ;* so D., but this makes nonsense. I read *inform us*, an emendation approved by Mr. Daniel.

354. P. omits *sir.*

357. Q. *ownes ;* D. and S. *own.*

364. Q. prints the stage-direction *Hold up, etc.*, in the margin to the right.

404. Q. *well may beauty ;* D. transposes *may* and *beauty*, which is no doubt correct.

427. Q. *colt ;* D. *cock*, a change which does not seem necessary ; cf. the note on this line, p. 743 above.

429. Here, as in I, i, 146, the question mark of Q. after *fethers* denotes an exclamation.

430–1. Q. *soon overcome ;* P. misprints *the sooner overcome.*

483. Q. *doe it earnest to carry it ;* D. *do in earnest carry it*, an emendation which I have adopted.

501. Q. *locks, fludgs ;* D. prints *fluds !* I have accepted Brereton's suggestion (*loc. cit.*) that *fludgs* is a misprint of a stage-direction, *sings.*

503. Q. *words ;* D. suggests *weeds,* a correction which Mr. Daniel had made independently, and I have adopted.

532–3. Q. *so make room ;* so D. and S. But the context seems to require *to make room.*

559. Q. *I finde ;* P. misprints *if finde.*

636. Q. *Enter Cuthbert Barber ;* D. *Cuthbert, a Barber.* But the name appears in the text, ll. 645, 654, *et al.* as *Cutbeard,* and I have altered the stage-direction to correspond.

657. Q. *doe they not both band themselves ;* D. substitutes *ye* and *yourselves,* but this seems unnecessary.

710. D. supplies the stage-direction, *aside to him,* in this line.

III, i, 14–15. There is a slight variation in the copies of Q. here. That in the Douce collection in the Bodleian places the parenthesis after *sweepers,* the Malone copy rightly after *beautifull.* The two copies in the British Museum agree with the latter. P. has followed a copy agreeing with the Douce Q.

25. I have followed Q. here, but would suggest the possibility of reading *better sport than at.* If *than* were written *thᵉ* in the MS., the mistake might easily have occurred.

29. D. arbitrarily alters *and* to *but will.* See note, p. 745 above.

61. Q. *Let my man ;* I accept the emendation of D. *let any man.* Cf. note on II, i, 222, above.

67. D. adds the *Exit* after this line.

78. P. misprints *Lon.* for *Hon.* in this line.

85. Q. *pace ;* D. emends *paix.* See note, p. 746 above.

102. Q. and D. read *sir ? ;* but the interrogation mark denotes an exclamation.

122. P. omits the question mark after *sir* which is found in Q.

153. D. alters *venery* to *Venice,* but this seems a mistake, for *venery* is again laid to Snail's charge below in l. 203.

196. Q. assigns this speech to *Lod.* ; D. gives it to *Lor.,* which is plainly correct.

227. D. supplies the *Exit* after this line.

III, ii. Stage-direction. Q. reads *Francisco above.* D. corrects.

ii, 6. P. misprints *foote* for *soote*

18. Q. *The Iayles of the love-god ;* D. suggests *joys,* which I have accepted. Brereton (*loc. cit.*) proposes *toyles,* but this does not seem to suit the context.

34. P. wrongly puts a period for the comma of Q. after *happinesse.*

III, iii, 9. Q. *houses ;* D. corrects *horses.*

61. Q. and D. *last ;* I emend *lasts.*

63. P. omits *does* before *so.*

68 and **102.** D. adds the stage-directions in these lines.

126. Q. *summe ;* D. corrects *sun.*

138. D. inserts *a* before *wench.*

157. D. inserts *Exit Temperance.*

204–5. Q. *desire you more ;* D. reads *I desire,* and states that Q. has *your,* but the copies I have seen all read *you.*

232. D. reads *he* for *she* in this line, urging that Quintiliano does not know that the page is really a woman, but I think *she* may well be used in jest of *a sweet-faced child,* l. 228.

253–4. Q. and D. have the first parenthesis before *he ;* but this is an evident mistake as *he* is the subject of *falls.*

287. Q. *seeing ;* I accept the emendation of S. *seeming*

IV, i, 7–8. Q. gives this speech to *Innoc.,* but it plainly belongs to *Lionello,* who is answering his master's remark in ll. 4–6. D. corrects.

20. D. adds the stage-direction.

56. Q. *and' cheare it ;* D. *an I hear it ;* Deighton (*Old Dramatists* p. 139) *and I hear it.* I follow the latter, for it is not likely that Chapman meant Quintiliano to use, in this place only, the rustic form of the pronoun, *Ich.*

61. Q. *Enter Quintil. and Lorenzo.* D. alters *and* to *dragging in.*

73. D. inserts the *aside.*

IV, ii, 49. Q. *berai'd ;* D. *betray'd ;* S. *bewrayed,* which is doubtless correct.

80. Q. *hast, &c.* D. *haste, haste.* The *&c.* of Q. may well be meant to indicate that Angelo is to improvise a series of ejaculations, while Aurelio bids farewell to Aemilia and descends. I have therefore allowed it to stand.

115. Q. *haud, hide ;* D. emends *hand,* and suggests that the passage might be otherwise altered. But the correction of this misprint makes the passage quite intelligible.

123–124. Q. *remnine . . . miads ;* D. corrects *remain . . . minds.*

135. Q. *In the more then temper,* which is unintelligible. I follow the emendation of D. Deighton (*loc. cit.*) proposes *I'll do thee more than temper,* but this involves the alteration of *your* to *you* in the next line, and seems to me inconsistent with the sense of the entire passage.

148. Q. *Use shall command ;* D. inserts *you* after *use.*

161. Q. *Gengerly, Gingerly ;* D. *Gingerly, Gingerly.*

196. Q. and D. *bald hewed ;* Deighton (*loc. cit.*) *bald haired*—whatever that may mean—Brereton (*loc. cit.*) *gall-dewed.* I emend *bold-hewed* in the sense of ' rough-hewn '.

198. P. misprints *no more,* and is followed by S. ; but all the copies of Q. that I have seen have *know more,* which makes perfectly good sense. D. follows Q.

202–3. Q., D. and S. assign this speech to *Lod.,* but it plainly belongs to *Aurelio,* who urges Lodovico to be patient.

206. Q. *perl's man ;* D. *perl'sman;* S. *pearl's man.* I accept the emendation of Brereton (*loc. cit.*) *per'lous man.*

214. Q. *mistesse ;* D. corrects. P. omits *with* before *him.*

IV, iii, 54. Q. *And more glorious shew ;* D. *a more.* I have preferred to retain *and* and insert the missing *a.*

75 Q. *as you ancient ;* but Innocentio, to whom the words are addressed, is not an *ancient,* but a *lieutenant.* I therefore accept the emendation of D., *your.*

77. Q. *Panbakez ;* D. *Pancakes ;* S. *Pancake.*

IV, iv, 2–3. Q. *Hist, hawe ;* D. *Hist ! ha !*

7. D. adds the stage-direction.

12. P. omits *Enter* in the stage direction after this line.

68. D. omits *V* and adds the stage-direction in this line. See note, p. 748 above.

V, i, 51–77. D. inserts the *asides* in this passage. In l. 63 he wrongly places the *aside* at the beginning of the speech. It is clear, however, that Lorenzo's first words are spoken to the company and not to Angelo. The *aside* begins with *For my love.*

84. D. inserts *dressed in Woman's Clothes* in the stage-direction after this line.

99. D. inserts the *aside.*

119. Q. *Omnes.* The speakers are, of course, only Aurelio, Leonoro, and Quintiliano, not the entire company.

127. Q. *Signor Lorenzo ;* a manifest blunder since *Lorenzo* is speaking. I emend *Honorio.* S. assigns the speech and l. 130 to *Le.* i.e. Leonoro.

159. D. inserts the stage-direction.

174. P. omits *only.*

222. P. omits *lay.*

242. D. adds *in his Male Dress* to the stage-direction after this line. I add the name of Temperance, who must enter with Lucretio (cf. ll. 229–30 above), and who is on the stage at the close, see ll. 333, *ssq.*

254. Q. *embarqu't us, and would have ;* D. omits *and,* which is necessary to restore the sense, for *following,* l. 252, is the subject of *would have.*

261. P. misprints *Leo.* for Q. *Lio*[*nello*].

269. Q. *more happy ;* D. suggests *not more happy,* which I accept.

275. Q. *being (as he supposed me).* This seems to me quite unintelligible, and I emend *I being as he supposed me,* i.e. a woman.

280. Q. *new sir ;* D. corrects *now, sir.*

302–314. D. inserts the stage-directions in these lines.

338–41. Q. and S. assign this speech to *Lod.*; D. assigns it to Quintiliano, which is plainly correct, since it is addressed to Innocentio who replies *Fore God, Captain.*

THE GENTLEMAN USHER

INTRODUCTION

The Gentleman Usher was entered, under the title of *Vincentio and Margaret*, in the Stationers' Registers, November 26, 1605, for Valentine Syms, the publisher of *An Humourous Day's Mirth*. It was published in 1606 with the following title-page :

The Gentleman Usher. By George Chapman. At London. Printed by V. S. for Thomas Thorppe, 1606.

Syms evidently had turned over his right of publication to Thorpe, the publisher of *All Fools* in 1605, on condition that he be allowed to print the play. This was the only edition published, and the play seems to have been almost forgotten [1] until its inclusion in the collected plays of Chapman in 1873.

It is impossible to fix with any certainty the precise date of *The Gentleman Usher*. Fleay (*Biographical Chronicle*, vol. i, p. 158) dates it in the Christmas season of 1601–2 ; Wallace (*Children of the Chapel*, p. 75) c. the summer of 1601. Professor Wallace has not yet published the evidence by which he determines this date, and so far as our present knowledge goes I should incline to fix it a year or so later, about the close of 1602.[2]

There is no reference on the title-page of the quarto to the company which produced this play, nor indeed does any record whatever exist of its performance. The stage-directions, however, are full enough to warrant the belief that the quarto was printed from a stage copy, and we may take it for granted that *The Gentleman Usher*, like Chapman's other plays of this period, was written for the Children of the Chapel and performed at Blackfriars. The frequent introduction of vocal and instrumental music, and the elaborate masques, mark it as a play composed for this company. Apparently it was never thought suitable for any other, for it does not seem to have been revived on any stage after the Children left Blackfriars.

No direct source of *The Gentleman Usher* has been discovered, and it is doubtful whether any exists. In my previous edition (*All Fooles and The Gentleman Usher*, p. 144) I suggested that the source of the main plot was probably some French or Italian story ; but I have since come to believe that the play as a whole may be regarded as an

---

[1] Langbaine, *English Dramatic Poets*, 1691, mentions it, but in such a way as to arouse the suspicion that he had merely glanced at a copy. There are several extracts and some commendatory remarks in an article on Chapman's comedies in *The Retrospective Review*, vol. v, 1822 ; and Lamb quotes a few lines from III, ii, without comment in *Extracts from the Garrick Plays*, 1827.

[2] *The Gentleman Usher* is certainly later than *Sir Giles Goosecap*, to which play there is a distinct allusion in our text, II, i, 81. The date of *Sir Giles* is also uncertain, but is supposed to fall after the visit of Biron to England in September, 1601. Wallace, however, dates it as early as 1600 (*op. cit.* p. 75).

original work of Chapman's, based upon incidents, scenes, and characters derived from various sources, and combined and adapted to suit his purposes.

The main theme, the rivalry of a father and a son for the affections of a young beauty, is a familiar subject of comedy. It occurs in the *Casina* of Plautus,[1] and in numerous later comedies. One of these, *The Wisdom of Doctor Dodypoll*, an anonymous play of the last decade of the sixteenth century, doubtfully ascribed to Peele,[2] has been suggested by Koeppel (*Quellen und Forschungen*, 1897, p. 221) as a possible source of *The Gentleman Usher*. This play presents the rivalry of Duke Alphonso and his son, Prince Alberdure, for the love of Hyanthe, daughter of Earl Cassimere. Apart from the familiar theme[3] and the fact that in each case the father is a Duke Alphonso, there is little likeness between the two plays.

The most striking incident in *The Gentleman Usher* is the mutilation of the heroine's face. This incident, appearing for the first time, I believe, in the *Heptameron* (Nov. 10), has a rather curious development. The original novel tells of the love of Amadour and the chaste Florinda. At one point in the story to protect her honour from her too eager lover Florinda bruises her face with a stone; but even this drastic measure does not lessen his passion. This tale appears in English in Painter,[4] *Palace of Pleasure* (Nov. 53), and is later referred to by Pettie, *A Pettie Palace* (Nov. 11). Another version of the mutilation theme appears in Sidney, *Arcadia*, book i. Here Parthenia, the betrothed of Argalus, is attacked by a discarded suitor, Demagoras, who smears her face with a poison ; ' the effect was such that never leper looked more ugly than she '. Argalus, none the less, insists upon marrying her ; she refuses to allow him to bind himself to a disfigured wife, and after a struggle in which each vies with the other in generosity, Parthenia flies away and sends word to Argalus that she is dead. Later on a veiled lady comes to him bearing a ring from Parthenia, with her last request that he marry this fair unknown. Argalus refuses, whereupon the lady unveils and reveals Parthenia herself, whose beauty has been restored by a physician, ' the most excellent man in the world ', and the marriage is at once solemnized.

This story is repeated in practically all its details in a crude but entertaining play, *The Trial of Chivalry*, printed 1605, of unknown authorship,

---

[1] See also the *Mercator* and the *Asinaria*.

[2] Schoell's suggestion that *Doctor Dodypoll* may be in part, at least, the work of Chapman, ' a romantic comedy of the same pattern as *The Gentleman Usher*, and Chapman's first work of this sort ', is interesting, but seems to me to demand more positive proof than has yet been offered.

[3] Plutarch in his life of Demetrius tells the story of the love of Antigonus for his father's young wife, Stratonice, and of the romantic generosity of the father, who, on discovering his son's unhappy passion, transferred the lady to him. This story, along with an incident drawn from Plutarch's *Pelopidas*, was admirably developed by Fletcher into the plot of *The Humorous Lieutenant*. Both in Plutarch and Fletcher the generosity of the father stands out in sharp contrast to the angry jealousy of Chapman's Alphonso, and I do not believe that any connexion can be traced between *The Gentleman Usher* and this story. I take this opportunity to recall the suggestion thrown out in my former edition of this play (*loc. cit.* p. 144) that a similar tale occurs in Lucian's *Toxaris*. The story of Zenothemes and Menecrates illustrates the classical ideals of friendship, and has no trace of the rivalry of father and son.

[4] See note on V, iii, 32–3, below.

possibly identical with the play, *Burbon*, mentioned by Henslowe, November 2, 1597. In this play Burbon, a rejected suitor of the heroine, smears poison on her face and disfigures her. Her lover, Philip of France, persists in his desire to marry her. She flies from court in disguise, is healed by a hermit-physician, and returns disguised to test the fidelity of her lover and to reward him with her hand. It is plain that the author of *The Trial of Chivalry* drew directly from the *Arcadia*. Koeppel (*op. cit.* p. 221) has called attention to the similarity of the incident and its treatment in this play and in Chapman's, and has suggested this play as a source of *The Gentleman Usher*. He has apparently overlooked the dependence of the older play on the *Arcadia*, and my own opinion would be that the likeness is due not to Chapman's borrowing from this play, but to their common source, Sidney's romance.[1]

Chapman, it is plain, was familiar [2] with both versions of the story, that in which the lady defaces her beauty to preserve her honour, and that in which she is mutilated by a rejected suitor. In the first instance she remains defaced, so far at least as we are told ; in the second she undergoes a semi-miraculous cure. Chapman deliberately combines the two versions, allowing Margaret to smear the ointment on her face in an agony of grief and fear, and introducing the contest in generosity and the wonder-working physician from the second, the *Arcadia* version. The gain in concentration and heightened dramatic effect obtained by this combination is patent to every reader.

Chapman seems also to have drawn upon an earlier play of his own for at least two scenes in *The Gentleman Usher*. I have shown elsewhere (*Modern Philology*, vol. v) the probability amounting to a practical certainty that *Sir Giles Goosecap* is a work of Chapman's. This comedy was never acknowledged by its author, and was still unprinted when he was at work on *The Gentleman Usher*. The entry in the Stationers' Registers, January 10, 1605-6, indicates that *Sir Giles* had been censored before publication, and internal evidence shows that a scene, or scenes, dealing with ' the drunken humour ' of Lady Furnifall, had been struck out. There can be little doubt that this excision was due to the personal satire contained in these scenes. But a ' drunken humour ' then, as now, was a sure theatrical device for provoking laughter, and it seems more than likely that Chapman transferred it from *Sir Giles* to his later play, evading the censor by the simple device of shifting the scene to Italy and rebaptizing Lady Furnifall Cortezza.

Another scene in *Sir Giles Goosecap* seems to have been somewhat more carefully worked over for *The Gentleman Usher*, that in which Momford brings a love-letter to Eugenia, and at her dictation writes an answer to it. This I take to be the original of *The Gentleman Usher*, III, ii, where Bassiolo performs the same office for Margaret. The

---

[1] In *Jack Drum's Entertainment*, a play acted in 1600, in large part, if not wholly, the work of Marston, we have another instance of a borrowing from the *Arcadia*. Here Mammon, a rejected suitor, rubs ' the oil of toads ' on Kathrine's face, and so destroys her beauty. The contest in generosity is wanting in this play, as Kathrine's lover goes mad at the sight of her disfigurement, and only recovers when she reappears cured by a skilful beldam.

[2] Chapman, like every one else in his time, had read the *Arcadia*, and he himself refers, though rather inaccurately, to the story of Florinda ; see note on V, iii, 32-3, below.

two scenes are by no means exact counterparts, yet it seems to me impossible to compare them without feeling that the second is a variant of the first, greatly surpassing it, by the way, in liveliness and comic force.

The titular hero of *Sir Giles* also reappears in *The Gentleman Usher* under the name of Poggio. There is nothing strikingly original about either figure; both represent a development of the Vice or Fool of earlier comedy, both, in accordance with the later practice of Shakespeare and Jonson, receive a higher social rank than that of the old comic figure, and both take part in the essential action of the play instead of merely furnishing incidental diversion. The special bond that connects Sir Giles and Poggio is the fluency and frequency with which each puts the cart before the horse in ordinary speech. It is worth noting also that this trick is in each play remarked [1] on by other characters, and thus impressed upon the audience. I fancy Chapman must have written the part of Poggio for the same actor who had made a hit as Sir Giles.

The character of [2] Sarpego, the pedant, is borrowed from Italian comedy in which the foolish pedant was a stock figure. The pedant had already appeared in English comedy, notably in the Pèdante of *Two Italian Gentlemen, c.* 1584, and Holofernes of *Love's Labour's Lost, c.* 1590. Chapman takes no special pains to elaborate or individualize the figure ; Sarpego appears only to furnish incidental amusement in the first two acts, and drops out of the play altogether when the real action begins.

It has been suggested by Koeppel (*op. cit.* pp. 8–9) that the character of Bassiolo owes his origin to Shakespeare's Malvolio. It seems to me not unlikely that, in a certain limited sense, this may be true. *Twelfth Night* (*c.* 1600) was already on the stage when Chapman began work on *The Gentleman Usher*, and it is quite possible that the success of Malvolio upon the stage should have given Chapman the idea of introducing a ridiculous major-domo as the chief comic character in his play. The rivalry that existed at this time between Shakespeare's company and the Chapel Children adds further plausibility to this suggestion. But I cannot regard Bassiolo as a mere imitation or replica of Malvolio. On the contrary, it seems to me that in this figure, one of the most elaborately portrayed of all Chapman's comic characters, we have an essentially new creation.[3]

In addition to these incidents, scenes and characters Chapman introduced with a liberal hand the elements of music, dancing and masque-like pageantry which at this time were regarded as special features in the performances of the Chapel Children. Indeed, he made so free a use of them as seriously to impair the interest of his play regarded as a piece of literature. The first two acts are largely taken up with preparation for and performance of the ' amorous device ' of the Duke, and the ' musical shew ' offered in return by Count Lasso. Both of

---

[1] *Sir Giles Goosecap*, III, i, 17–20 ; *The Gentleman Usher*, I, i, 26. For a fuller discussion of the relations of *Sir Giles* and *The Gentleman Usher*, see my article in *Modern Philology*, July, 1906, already referred to.

[2] The name is a form of serpigo, a kind of skin disease, cf. *Measure for Measure*, III, i. 31. It reappears as the name of a pedant in Brome's *City Wit*.

[3] For a comparison of the characters of Malvolio and Bassiolo, see my previous edition of *The Gentleman Usher*, p. xliii.

these, as is evident from the stage-directions, were performed with interludes of vocal and instrumental music. In the second of these there were at least two set dances, and a stage-direction at the beginning [1] of Act III points to a song by one or more of the Children between the acts.

Such were the sources from which Chapman drew, or rather one should say, the materials from which he composed, *The Gentleman Usher*. Taking the old theme of the rivalry of a father and son for a girl's love, familiar to him from Plautus and modern comedy, he shaped it into a romantic comedy, added the sensational incident of the heroine's self-disfigurement from the *Heptameron*, along with the contest in generosity and the miraculous cure from the *Arcadia*, and worked over some scenes of his own earlier play, *Sir Giles Goosecap*, to harmonize with their new setting. To heighten the comic side he introduced certain characters drawn from or suggested by earlier comedies, Italian or English, giving special attention to that of Bassiolo, from whom the play takes its name. And he embellished the whole with the music and dancing of the Chapel Children. If this analysis of the play be correct, it is plain that we need not look for a source of *The Gentleman Usher* in the sense in which one exists for *All Fools* or *May-Day*. It is, in the strict sense of the word, Chapman's own composition.

It is, perhaps, due to the lack of a source which might have served him as a model that we must attribute the uncertain and dragging workmanship of the first two acts. They are full to overflowing of incidental matter, the clownery of Poggio, the pedantry of Sarpego, the ' drunken humour ' of Cortezza, the songs, dances and 'shews'; but the main action with which we have become acquainted in the first scene practically stands still. It is not until the third act that the plot begins to evolve. From this point on, however, the movement is swift and easy, with sparkling interchange of mirth and high romance. These acts show Chapman at his best in the true Elizabethan field of poetic comedy. I should mark the sweet and passionate scene in which Vincentio and Margaret wed each other by vows of their own devising (IV, ii) as the highest flight of pure poetry in Chapman's comedies ; and no other scene in all his work seems to me to show so well his peculiar power of exploiting a comic situation as that in which Margaret's feigned reluctance yields to the importunity of the gulled usher the high favour of filling the post of go-between. Toward the close the story takes on a serious and almost tragic colour, only to have the impending cloud dispelled by the intervention of a *deus ex machina*. Such an ending is unique in Chapman's plays, and it speaks well for his judgment as an artist that he should have admitted it here, where alone in his work it would harmonize with the romantic tone of the preceding scenes. No other comedy of Chapman's has, I think, so

---

[1] I have pointed out in my previous edition of this play, p. 287, the fact that the short scene with which the third act opens belongs properly to the time covered by the second act, and is moreover a mere expansion of a couple of lines, III, ii, 303-4, which occur later on. I am inclined to believe that this scene was written after the play had been staged, in order to make quite clear to the audience the device by which Strozza was wounded. This supposition would not imply any revision of the play as a whole by its author, and, indeed, the scene in question may well have been the work of a theatre hack written for the purpose suggested and inserted at the most convenient place, the beginning of an act.

simple, straightforward, and well-managed a plot as these three acts, or so well-rounded and happy a conclusion. It is a if the author, after hesitating and fumbling, had at last caught fire and finished off his play in a burst of inspiration. I can only attribute the unwarranted neglect which has overtaken this delightful comedy to the impatience of the average reader with the dilatory action of the opening.

Considered from the point of view of the evolution of English comedy, *The Gentleman Usher* deserves more serious consideration than it has yet received. In many respects it is a distinct anticipation of the type which within a decade was to become dominant on the English stage and to hold its supremacy until the closing of the theatres. I refer, of course, to the tragi-comedy as it took shape in the hands of Beaumont and Fletcher, and was continued by Fletcher, Massinger, and Shirley. And when we remember the close relations existing between Beaumont and Fletcher and the Chapel Children, who brought out nearly all the early plays of these dramatists, it seems no unlikely supposition that they should, at least, have taken a hint or two from Chapman.

English tragi-comedy as defined by Fletcher [1] himself is ' not so called in respect of mirth and killing, but in respect it wants deaths which is enough to make it no tragedy, yet brings some near it, which is enough to make it no comedy . . . so that a god is as lawful in this as in a tragedy, and mean people as in a comedy '. In this definition it is plain that Fletcher attempted to differentiate *The Faithful Shepherdess*, and, doubtless, other plays already written or planned, from the traditional English type in which comic and tragic scenes, ' mirth and killing ' were merely juxtaposed. Fletcher's definition, however, by no means presents the essentials of English tragi-comedy. These may be stated as, first of all, a blending of serious and comic matter, the comic element not appearing as a sub-plot, but being more or less perfectly fused into the main action of the play. Secondly, the main action is of a romantic, but serious type. Tragic passions, lust, ambition, treachery, all play their part. The virtuous characters are constantly involved in tragic entanglements ; they are slandered, wounded, poisoned, condemned to death, but they invariably escape the impending tragic fate. The evil characters, on the other hand, seldom or never meet with their due reward, but are dismissed with full pardon, or, at worst, with disgrace or exile. In Fletcher's own words, ' it wants deaths '. The scene is laid in distant lands and times, sometimes in No-man's-land, often in an imaginary Italian court, and the atmosphere of the play lacks even the faintest semblance of realism. In fact, the tragi-comedy may be regarded as a revolt at once against the earlier tragedy of blood and the Jonsonian realistic comedy. The leading characters tend to become stock figures, the arbitrary sovereign, the virtuous hero, the chaste heroine, the plotting villain, and the blunt but faithful friend. The comic figures lack the sharp outlines of the Jonsonian ' humours ' ; the satiric note almost wholly disappears, and is replaced by a buoyant gaiety that ranges all the way from broad farce to high comedy. In general, both in serious and

---

[1] *Address to the Reader* prefixed to the first edition of *The Faithful Shepherdess*, 1609. Rustine, *English Tragi-comedy*, p. 107, has shown that this definition is taken bodily from the writings of Guarini, author of the *Pastor Fido*, the first true tragi-comedy of modern literature.

comic scenes stress is laid upon incident, and effective stage-situations
rather than upon character. Indeed, the chief defect of tragi-comedy,
regarded as a form of dramatic literature, is its reckless tendency to
sacrifice consistency of character to startling stage-effect. The technic
of these plays, on the other hand, represents a great advance over earlier
methods. By its ingenious employment of surprise, suspense, and
reverse it contrives not only to hold the interest, but to raise it to the
highest point immediately before the final solution of the complicated
plot. And the *dénouement* is brought about by some wholly unexpected turn of events so as to afford the double pleasure of a happy
surprise and a happy ending.

In nearly all points *The Gentleman Usher* corresponds to this conception of the typical tragi-comedy. The comic matter, if we disregard the futilities of the first acts, is admirably blended with the serious
—one cannot disentangle the gulling of Bassiolo from the romantic
courtship of Vincentio and Margaret. The scene is laid in an Italian
court, and the English atmosphere, with which Chapman surrounded
even such plays drawn from foreign sources as *All Fools* and *May-Day*,
is wholly wanting. Realism has vanished and we are in a land of pure
romance. The story progresses, after it has once fairly started, by a
series of surprises, and by suspense and reverse, until the final scene ;
and the *dénouement*, with its unexpected [1] turn, its happy reunion and
reconciliation, and its easy dismissal of the villain might almost stand
as a typical example of the tragi-comic solution of a tangled plot.

It would, of course, be idle to claim that Chapman anticipates in
this play the triumphs of Fletcher in his own peculiar field. *The Gentleman Usher* lacks Fletcher's easy flow and infectious gaiety, his
mastery of construction and of stage-effect. But it has merits that
amply atone for these defects. It has at its best a sweet seriousness
and elevation of tone that are seldom to be found in the work of the
younger dramatist. One trembles to think what Fletcher's ethical
looseness would have made of the scene in which Vincentio and Margaret interchange their vows ; and Strozza's fierce denunciation of
royal prerogative (V, iv, 56-66) strikes a stronger note than anything
in all the work of Fletcher. It sounds like a voice from ancient Rome
rather than the utterance of a courtly Jacobean dramatist. Chapman, in fact, even in this forerunner of Jacobean tragi-comedy, has
much of the old Elizabethan simplicity and seriousness. He takes
his situations seriously, and he believes in the characters he has himself
created.

It is for this reason, I suppose, that the characters of *The Gentleman
Usher*, although in a general way anticipating the usual *dramatis personae* of tragi-comedy—the amorous despot, the virtuous hero, the
chaste maid and so on—strike one as distinctly more real and more
individualized than the stock figures of Fletcher. Vincentio, although
not very elaborately drawn, is a very human prince and a very satisfactory lover. His mistress, Margaret, is one of the most delightful
girls in all the lovely garden of Elizabethan romance. Modest, merry,
passionate and self-sacrificing, she quite eclipses the romping hoydens
and sentimental ladies of Fletcher, and rises almost—one dare not risk

---

[1] The failure of Benevemus to cure the wounded Strozza is, no doubt,
meant to forestall the guess that his intervention is in the end to heal the
Prince and restore the beauty of Margaret.

the full assertion—to the sphere in which the heroines of Shakespearian comedy move. Cynanche is the matron, as Margaret the maiden, type of the loved and loving woman. Her character is less carefully developed than Margaret's, it is a study rather than a full-length portrait; but even this study of the perfect helpmate is enough to redeem Chapman from the charge of having been consistently cynical, not to say coarse, in his treatment of women.

The character of Strozza deserves, I think, some special notice as one of the most remarkable in Chapman's comedies. He appears at first merely as the friend and confidant of the hero, a frank, outspoken nobleman who detests his sovereign's unworthy favourite as much as he loves the neglected heir. If he were nothing more, Strozza would be a character indistinguishable from a host of figures in tragi-comedy. But as he develops in the last acts under the influence of suffering, he rises to a much higher plane and reveals more individual traits. Schoell remarks that ' the ground-note of his character is a mixture of Christian mysticism and pagan stoicism '. This would be no inapt characterization of Chapman himself, and, indeed, we feel more than once in the latter part of the play that Strozza is giving voice to the poet's own ideas, notably in his panegyric of the virtuous wife (IV, iii), in his apology for pilgrimages (V, ii), and in his outburst against royalty already cited. In these scenes Strozza shows a marked resemblance to certain characters in the tragedies in whom Chapman has embodied his own ideas and ideals, to Clermont in *The Revenge of Bussy*, and Cato in *Cæsar and Pompey*. But unlike these figures, Strozza remains in the framework of the picture. In tragedy Chapman never hesitated to stop the action in order to make room for long sententious and philosophical tirades, but in comedy he did not allow himself this licence. It is only for a brief space that Strozza is permitted to usurp the interest which properly belongs to the romantic action, and he is deftly brought back into the main current of the play in the last scene where he appears to administer a courageous rebuke to his misguided master and to expose and expel the favourite who misled him.

The Gentleman Usher is written almost entirely in blank verse. Prose occurs only in a few short speeches of Poggio and Cortezza, and at the close of the long scene between Bassiolo and Margaret; a few rhymed passages appear in the second masque. Chapman had by this time developed his mastery of blank verse to a point where it had become an almost perfect instrument for the expression of his ideas. It is interesting to note that he uses it not only for elevated passages, such as the wedding of the lovers (IV, ii, 125–200) and the speeches of Strozza to his wife (IV, iii, and V, ii), but also in passages of pure comedy such as the scenes in which the Prince and Margaret in turn play upon the credulity of Bassiolo (III, ii ; IV, ii ; IV, iv ; and V, i). The verse in these scenes is an admirable vehicle of fluent and familiar conversation. It has no trace of the gravity and sonority of Chapman's tragic style ; but it serves its purpose in lifting the comic action above the level of prosaic realism, and thus in blending it more perfectly with the romantic scenes. The last acts of *The Gentleman Usher* seem to me the most harmonious in Chapman's comedies. One has only to compare them with the sharply differentiated prose and verse scenes of *Monsieur D'Olive* to see how much Chapman gained in unity of effect by his employment of a metre flexible enough to rise to heights of impassioned poetry and to sink again to gay and lively dialogue. Here as elsewhere Chapman seems to me to anticipate the work of Fletcher. There is not, to be sure, the slightest trace of Fletcher's peculiar metrical characteristics in the verse of Chapman, but if a model for Fletcher's easy mastery of colloquial blank verse in comic scenes is to be sought, it is to Chapman rather than to Shakespeare or to Jonson that we must look.

THE GENTLEMAN USHER

NOTES

I, i, 23. *Brittle as a beetle.* A *beetle*, or paving-ram, was a type of slowness. The Latin phrase, *Celerius pariunt elephanti*, is rendered in Withals' *Dictionary*, 1634, ' quick as a beetle '. Poggio, of course, is talking nonsense.

I, i, 24–25. *Wehee . . . tehee.* Poggio, as usual, misuses words. *Wehee* represents the whinny of the horse, *tehee* the human laugh. Cf. Chaucer, *The Miller's Tale*, l. 554. A quotation in Nares, sub *tihy*, gives the proper use of the words :

> *But when the hobby-horse did wihy,*
> *Then all the wenches gave a tihy.*

I, i, 26. *Hysteron Proteron.* Strozza applies this term, which signifies the rhetorical figure of putting the last word first, to Poggio because of his habit of putting the cart before the horse, as above : cf. also ll. 47–8 below.

I, i, 29. *His late honour'd mistress :* the lady he has lately begun to honour as his mistress.

I, i, 47–8. *Heels about my hose :* cf. *Sir Giles Goosecap*, I, iv, 194–5.

I, i, 55–6. We have here several technical terms of falconry. A *cast* is a pair ; *daring* means frightening. Cf. *Henry VIII*, III, ii, 282, and the note *ad loc.* in the *Variorum*. *The stooped prey* is the prey on which the hawk is about to *stoop*, i.e. to pounce.

I, i, 57–9. The *hare or hind* is pursued as a musical theme is in a fugue. The *harmony* is the baying of the *well-mouth'd hounds*. Cf. *The Shadow of Night* (*Poems*, p. 13), where the cry of a pack is called *change of music*, and the famous passage in *Midsummer Night's Dream*, IV, i, 110–130.

I, i, 93. *Who* refers to *servant*, l. 92.

I, i, 94. *Are to begin :* have not yet begun, are only about to begin.

I, i, 108–109. *Fustian . . . buckram :* cheap stuffs. Strozza uses the words to denote his contempt for Medice, who as we see below, ll. 114–6, does not dress like a true courtier. With *map of baseness*, cf. *Monsieur D'Olive*, I, i, 393.

I, i, 110. *Unconstrued stuff.* Vincentio carries on the figure of Strozza's speech, calling Medice a bale of goods as yet *unconstrued*, i.e. unvalued.

I, i, 118. Use his livery as a licence for begging. Wearing the livery of a lord, they could not be arrested as masterless men.

I, i, 122. *Noble counterfeit :* counterfeit of nobility.

I, i, 152. *Hammer, hammer.* The yellow-hammer, like the woodcock, the gull, and other birds, was used as a nickname for a fool ; cf. *Monsieur D'Olive*, IV, ii, 153–4.

I, i, 159. *At the best :* in the best possible condition, spoken ironically.

I, i, 171. The induction, or introduction, to a masque.

I, i, 181. *Care not to proclaim :* do not mind proclaiming.

I, i, 199. *Padua:* see note on *All Fools*, I, i, 316.

I, i, 201. *His part :* the rôle of Curculio, the hungry parasite in the comedy of that name.

I, i, 206. *Take up :* strike up, trip.

I, i, 215–7. The quotation is from *Curculio*, II, iii. The lines are spoken by the parasite on his first entrance, and express his haste to reach his patron, tell of his success, and get to his dinner. Sarpego, of course, accompanies them with much absurd gesticulation.

I, i, 221. *Upon repletion :* after a full meal.

I, i, 222–3. Sarpego boasts that he has played the part of the hungry parasite with success (*drew it neat*) after having despatched the commons, or portions, of three scholars. This boast is an answer to Strozza's remark in ll. 220–1.

I, i, 242. *To pageant him :* to honour him, Medice, with a pageant or triumph.

I, i, 244. *Make us ready :* dress myself.

I, ii, 5. *At large :* fully, in every detail.

I, ii, 28. *Wagers.* It was common at this time to act a part for a wager. Thus Ralph, the stage-struck apprentice in *The Knight of the Burning Pestle,* ' *should have played Jeronimo with a shoemaker for a wager* '—*Induction,* ll. 94–5. See note *ad loc.* in Murch's edition of this play.

I, ii, 52. *Both your choice commands :* you may remain a lady, or become a princess by marriage, as you choose.

I, ii, 65–6. Medice's words contain a veiled threat against his tormentors, Strozza and the Prince.

I, ii, 94. *The English sign of great St. George :* the figure, or device, of the English St. George, referring to the common device of St. George on horse-back trampling on the dragon. Cf. *When he's mounted, he looks like the sign of the George—Every Man out of his Humour,* II, i.

I, ii, 99. *For soil.* ' To take soil ' is a technical expression in venery, used when the hunted beast, stag or boar, seeks refuge in a swamp or stream.

I, ii, 106. *The angry shadow :* the *figure* of l. 102 above.

I, ii, 112. ' The purpose of this action will be made clear in the report which the Enchanter is about to deliver '.

I, ii, 129. *Made you strange of this :* seemed to be shocked by this request. Cf. :

> *She makes it strange ; but she would best be pleased*
> *To be so anger'd with another letter.*
>
> > *Two Gentlemen of Verona,* I, ii, 102.

Cf. also *Sir Giles Goosecap,* IV, i, 92–3.

I, ii, 165. *Close stockings :* stockings fitting close to the legs. There is here and in the following lines a jest at the old-fashioned and formal costume of Bassiolo.

I, ii, 171–2. ' He has two mental characteristics (avarice and self-conceit, ll. 172–3) which will lead him to believe anything '. The *gudgeon,* a small fish often used for bait, was one of the many Elizabethan synonyms for a fool, a credulous person. The phrase *to swallow a gudgeon* meant to accept with credulity some false statement ; cf. *All Fools,* III, i, 94, and *Sir Giles Goosecap,* I, iii, 86.

I, ii, 176. ' Wave, or beckon, to him from a distance with your hat, and show him other signs of favour '.

II, i, 4. *In loving others :* by reason of her love for another.

II, i, 23. *Plied this gear :* took up this business, i.e. took to drinking.

II, i, 34. *Well seen in behaviour :* well versed in courtly manners.

II, i, 36. *The wind must blow at west.* The west wind is the lucky wind ; see Hazlitt, *English Proverbs,* p. 464, and Lean's *Collecteana,* vol. ii, pp. 102–3.

II, i, 51. *Huddle and kettle.* I take the phrase to refer to Cortezza's disordered speech and unfitting behaviour. Cf. *He speaks huddles,* III, ii, 218, and the phrase ' kettle of fish ' or simply ' kettle ', meaning a mess, a muddle.

II, i, 73. *His new-made Duchess for this night :* the lady who has been appointed to play the part of the Duchess during this night's festival ; cf. below, l. 181.

II, i, 81. *Sir Giles Goosecap.* The term *goosecap,* i.e. goose's head, is an Elizabethan synonym for booby, appearing first in *Martin's Months Mind,* 1589, and later in Nash, *Four Letters Confuted,* Dekker, *Gull's Hornbook,* and Ford, *Fancies Chaste and Noble.* In *Englishmen for my Money,* (1598) I find the phrase *Goodman Goosecap.* I am not aware, however, of any earlier case than the present in which the phrase *Sir Giles Goosecap* is used, and we may therefore consider it certain that we have here a direct allusion to the foolish hero of the play *Sir Giles Goosecap*, a figure who like the serving man rebuked by Bassiolo is 'of mere necessity an ass'.

II, i, 83. *In threaves :* a *threave*, or *thrave*, is a sheaf, a handful. The word reappears in Chapman's *Iliad*, p. 138.

II, i, 94. As I understand it, Vincentio remarks that Bassiolo's position as gentleman usher requires him to *be bare*, i.e. not to wear hat or cap. In l. 97 below Vincentio, after uncovering, remarks that he does so to do Bassiolo right, i.e. to return the usher's courtesy, as well as for his own ease.

II, i, 135. A *Broom-man* is not only a street sweeper, the one meaning given in the *New English Dictionary*, but also a seller of brooms. See *Club-Law*, l. 3, and note thereon in Moore Smith's edition. Poggio's words below, l. 231, show, I think, that he plays the part of a man bearing green brooms to sell.

II, i, 147–8. *Pluck his coat over his ears :* strip him of his livery, discharge him from his place.

II, i, 170. *Stand upon your tire :* make a great to-do about your costumes.

II, i, 173. *Hope* is used here in the sense of 'expect'.

II, i, 175. 'Accompanying your speeches with appropriate movements of your bodies'.

II, i, 184. The *state* is the 'chair of state' or *throne* of l. 181 above.

II, i, 186. 'Be gracious enough to remain in this throne', i.e. to occupy permanently, as the wife of Alphonso, the ducal throne which she is filling for the evening.

II, i, 189. 'I would hardly have presumed to take the high position, i.e. the throne, or chair of state, which I now fill for a moment'.

II, i, 191. *Sound, consort :* play up, musicians.

II, i, 195. If we take *moving* in this line as a participle agreeing with *silence*, it must mean 'powerful', 'effectual'. Dr. Bradley suggests that it is to be taken as a gerund governing *silence*, in which case the phrase would mean 'whose appeal for silence'. In either case the sense is about the same, i.e. 'Beauty needs no herald'.

II, i, 226. *A hall, a hall :* an exclamation used to make room in a crowded apartment for a dance or a masque. Cf. *Humourous Day's Mirth*, Sc. xiv, l. 181; *Widow's Tears*, III, ii, i,; and *Romeo and Juliet*, I, v, 28, and the note *ad loc.* in Furness's *Variorum*.

II, i, 230. The spots in the moon, according to a very old popular belief, represent a man with a bundle of sticks. Ritson in his note on an old ballad on the Man in the Moon (*Ancient Songs and Ballads*, vol. i, p. 68) suggests that the belief comes from the story in *Numbers*, XV, 32, of the Israelite who broke the Sabbath by gathering sticks and of his punishment. The connexion seems doubtful. Dante (*Paradiso*, II, 51) records the Italian superstition that the man in the moon is Cain bearing a fagot of thorns.

II, i, 251. 'To make the rush flaunt it in decasyllabic verse'.

II, i, 253. An ironical apology for trampling on the rushes.

II, i, 255. *That odd battle :* the allusion is to the *Batrachomyomachia*, a mock heroic poem attributed to Homer and translated by Chapman, *c.* 1624. In the war between the frogs and mice narrated in this poem the frogs used sharp bulrushes for spears.

II, i, 263. *Momus :* the god of mockery, here a scoffer. *Push*, an Elizabethan form of 'pish', 'pshaw'.

II, i, 266. *Bites them with his tongue :* mocks them.

II, i, 286. *Her [feral] friend :* the Sylvan, half man, half beast.

II, i, 318. 'What do you think of the young lady destined to be my step-mother'. It has been suggested that this speech should be addressed to Bassiolo, and that l. 319 should be assigned to that character. But such an abrupt address would not harmonize with the deliberate way in which the Prince introduces this topic in III, ii, 131, *ssq.*

II, i, 320. *Bugs' words :* words of a monster, terrifying words. Vincentio does not wish Cynanche even to hint in this public place at the possibility of a tie between him and Margaret.

III, i. The *song* mentioned in the stage-direction is the song set to music which filled up the interval between the acts. For the part played by music at the Blackfriars theatre, see Wallace, *Children of the Chapel*, chap. ix, especially the note on p. 114.

III, ii, 23. *You have me :* you understand me ; cf. *Hamlet*, II, i, 68–9.

III, ii, 37. *Brave beasts.* The allusion is to the heraldic beasts, *brave*, i.e. gorgeous in colour, that *support* numerous coats-of-arms.

III, ii, 61–2. 'With whom there is no foolish fastidiousness (*niceness*) nor regard for the common form of friendship'. With the sentiment in these and the following lines, cf. *Sir Giles Goosecap*, II, i, 181–4.

III, ii, 78. *Go[o]dly gudgeons :* proper baits, cf. the note on I, ii, 171–2.

III, ii, 84. *How are you :* how are you gulled ?

III, ii, 100. 'A palpably flattering figure of speech, mode of address, fit only for common men.'

III, ii, 110. *'Tis now in use.* Heywood in an often-quoted passage, *Hierarchy of the Blessed Angels*, book iv, mentions the Elizabethan fashion of abbreviating names :

> *Mellifluous Shakespeare, whose inchanting Quill*
> *Commanded Mirth or Passion, was but* Will.
> *And famous Jonson, though his learned pen*
> *Be apt in Castaly, is still but* Ben.

Heywood seems to approve of this fashion, for he adds :

> *I hold he loves me best that calls me* Tom.

Chapman, on the other hand, speaks of it (*Revenge of Bussy*, I, i, 260–61 as 'the corruption of names'.

III, ii, 194–5. *Hybla :* a district in Sicily famous for its honey. *Meander*, or Mæander, is a river in Asia Minor. Chapman gets the swans of Meander from Ovid, *Heroides*, vii, 1–2.

III, ii, 237. *A George :* St. George, see note on I, ii, 94, above.

III, ii, 244–5. *Set forth this gear :* take this business in hand, push your courtship.

III, ii, 246. *Be naughts.* The phrase, *be naught*, is familiar in Elizabethan English as a humorous imprecation. It had, however, at times a coarse significance as in the line quoted from *Swetnam* by Malone (*Variorum* note on *As You Like It*, I, i, 39), and in Burton (*Anatomy of Melancholy*, vol. iii, p. 33) where *are nought* translates the Latin *cum viris consuetudinem habemus*. This, I think, is the meaning here.

III, ii, 255. *Whittled her :* made her drunk. The phrase occurs also in Lodge *Wit's Misery*, p. 85, and in *Mother Bombie*, III, ii, 44.

III, ii, 290. 'By the unanimous consent of all my mental powers'.

III, ii, 297. *Solemn hunting :* formal hunting party, cf. *Titus Andronicus*, II, i, 112.

III, ii, 300. *My being :* my whereabouts.

III, ii, 304–5. *Till our sports . . . absence :* till the hunting party that we intend to give is ended by my withdrawal from the chase.

III, ii, 335–6. 'Was a woman ever so much mistaken in her opinion of a wise man's discretion ? ' Cf. *How are poor women overseen!—Hyde Park*, I, ii.

III, ii, 351. There is a double meaning in this line, either, ' I am so apt to follow your advice blindly ', or ' I am so dotingly fond of you '. Bassiolo takes it in the latter sense. Margaret's next speech is, I think, an aside.

III, ii, 370. *The liver :* in Elizabethan physiology the seat of love and other violent passions.

III, ii, 392. Cf. *Sir Giles Goosecap*, IV, i, 116.

III, ii, 395. ' Is this letter not worth your answering ? '

III, ii, 415. The word *endear* apparently enters the English language in Sidney's *Arcadia*, 1580. *Condole*, l. 418, appears for the first time in English literature in Daniel's *Complaint of Rosamond*, 1592. Shakespeare seems to have been amused by it, for he puts it into the mouths of Bottom (*Midsummer Night's Dream*, I, ii, 29) and Pistol (*Henry V*, II, i, 133). *Model* l. 423, is no older than Gascoigne's *Posies*, 1575. Bassiolo is trying to use ' fire-new words ' which he only partially understands.

III, ii, 432. 'Your objections fall away from the main point'.

III, ii, 479–80. Cf. the quibble in *Hamlet*, V, ii, 43.

III, ii, 507. *You may speed:* you may fare ill, i.e. he may win me for himself. For this sense of *speed*, cf. *The Ball*, IV, iii, 54, and *Taming of the Shrew*, V, ii, 185.

IV, i, 7. *A forked shaft:* a barbed arrow.

IV, i, 39. Strozza invokes the Furies as goddesses of madness to deprive him of sense and so conquer his intolerable suffering, *fury of my bane*.

IV, i, 41–2. 'Madness, which to human sense seems blind, sets free the soul immediately from hope and fear'.

IV, i, 57. *Th' Alcmenean conqueror:* Hercules, son of Alcmene.

IV, i, 60. 'Cries are hardly fitting even for beaten children'.

IV, i, 67–8. 'The soul's actions, conceived and performed *simply*, i.e. apart from physical admixture, remove the frailties of the body from our consideration'.

IV, i, 69–70. 'This balm of spoken words which is powerless to cure'.

IV, i, 73–5. This outburst, coming immediately after the self-restraint shown in l. 71, is due to a fresh spasm of pain.

IV, i, 77. *Religious noblesse:* pious nobility of mind, as shown in his promise of self-control, l. 71.

IV, ii, 2. *In respect of:* in comparison with.

IV, ii, 15. *Guevara's Golden Epistles.* For Guevara see note on *May-Day*, III, i, 59. His *Epistolas Familiares*, 1539–45, shared the popularity of his *Reloj de Principes* and was translated into English by Edward Hellowes in 1574. Another translation by Fenton, under the title of *Golden Epistles*, appeared in the following year. Fenton took his title from an early French translation, *Epistres Dorées*, 1556–60. Fenton's work was very popular in polite circles, and Bassiolo, as above III, ii, 415 *ssq.*, shows some acquaintance with courtly literature.

IV, ii, 68. *In his kind:* according to its nature.

IV, ii, 83. *Laugh and lie down:* the name of an old game of cards, often used, as here, with a double meaning; cf. *Mother Bombie*, V, iii, 64.

IV, ii, 93. 'The chink of his gold is like a peal of bells in honour of the highest merit'.

IV, ii, 138–40. A very characteristic thought of Chapman's. Cf. a similar expression in *Bussy*, II, i, 203–4.

IV, ii, 151–4. Cf. the marriage ceremony in *Hero and Leander*, V, 352–8, where the priest of Juno covers the bride's face with a veil, and ties the couple together with silk ribbons.

IV, ii, 191–2. 'Consider it well, for your decision shall be as unhampered as before your marriage'.

IV, ii, 200. *Custom's popular sects:* the conventional beliefs of the populace.

IV, ii, 212. *A Tantalus pig:* Poggio's mistake for a Tantony, i.e. St. Anthony pig. Stowe, *Survey of London*, gives the origin of the saying: 'I remember that the officers charged with the oversight of markets in this city, did divers times take from the market people pigs starved or otherwise unwholesome. . . . One of the proctors for St. Anthony's [the hospital of St. Anthony] tied a bell about the neck, and let it feed on the dunghills; no man would hurt or take them up, but if any gave to them bread or other feeding, such would they know, watch for, and daily follow, whining till they had somewhat given them; whereupon was raised a proverb " Such an one will follow such an one, and whine as it were an Anthony pig "'. (p. 190 edition of 1633). The expression 'to follow like a Tantony pig' was current till the middle of the eighteenth century.

IV, iii, 17. *The twins Hippocrates reports.* The twins of Hippocrates 'who were born together, laughed together, wept together, and died together', are mentioned by Lyly (*Works*, vol. ii, p 77). St. Augustine (*De Civitate Dei*, v, 2) says that Cicero reports Hippocrates to have pronounced a pair of brothers twins from the fact that both sickened at the same time and that the progress of the disease was similar and simultaneous in both cases. Cicero's reference is supposed to have occurred in his lost work, *De Fato*.

Chapman alludes to these twins in *The Masque of the Middle Temple* (ll. 320–327) and in his poem, *A Good Woman* (*Poems*, p. 152). This poem draws largely from Plutarch's *Conjugalia Praecepta*, but the twins of Hippocrates are not mentioned in that treatise.

IV, iii, 21. *His sweet ape.* The same phrase occurs in *Sir Giles Goosecap*, III, ii, 65–68.

IV, iii, 36–7. Cf. *All Fools*, III, i, 20–22.

IV, iii, 48. 'By virtue of which patience my mind extends the sway of her powers, which are by their nature incapable of suffering'.

IV, iii, 55–6. Cf. *Like frantic men that feel no wounds—Tears of Peace* (*Poems*, p. 120).

IV, iii, 62. *Sort of crystal globes :* a set of globes such as were used in divination by crystal-gazing.

IV, iii, 83. *His reasonable soul :* his soul which alone was capable of inspiring rational speech. For the notion that *idle talk* (l. 82) was a sign of approaching death, cf. *King John*, V, vii, 2–5.

IV, iv, 49. *Kind hands.* If the text is correct we must explain the phrase as equivalent to 'hands joined in sign of love'; but see Text Notes, p. 771.

IV, iv, 53. *At view :* by sight, rather than by scent, a phrase used when the pack sighted the chase.

IV, iv, 55. See note on IV, iii, 62.

IV, iv, 67–8. Lasso asserts that some passion (*fancy*) will be found to be the source (*forge*) whence these specious (*gay*) excuses proceed.

IV, iv, 101–2. 'If you mean to make an ass of me, you must get up early'.

V, i, 26. *Gosh hat .* probably a corruption of 'God's heart.' The pronunciation here and in l. 32, *shay*, combined with his behaviour in general in this scene, would seem to show that Bassiolo has fortified himself with Dutch courage.

V, i, 34. *Rufty tufty :* rough and tumble.

V, i, 48. *Go by :* slink off. The phrase was famous in Elizabethan English from its occurrence in *The Spanish Tragedy*, III, xii, 30. See Boas's note *ad loc.*

V, i, 52. *Belle piu, etc.:* evidently part of a song. The stage-direction, *Iterum cantat*, presumably means that Bassiolo sings a second song of which *Belle piu* is the title or refrain.

V, i, 56. *Bobadilla :* a reference to Bobadil, the braggart captain of *Every Man in his Humour.*

V, i, 103. *Wo ho :* the cry used by falconers to recall a hawk ; cf. *Hamlet*, I, v, 115.

V, i, 110. *Rule the roast :* have full power, a common idiom in the sixteenth century, as far back as Skelton.

V, i, 164–5. 'Thou (Nature) takest more harm in guiding the senses which are thus misled, than thou receivest bliss from submitting to the guidance of Reason'. So, at least, I understand this awkward passage. Perhaps we might construe *more bane* adverbially, and interpret *tak'st to guide sense*, as equivalent to 'tak'st the sense for thy guide'.

V, ii, 38. *Visibly resign'd to memory :* hung up as a visible memorial in the church.

V, ii, 40–42. 'In the practice of patience like mine, which patience, were it forgotten after my death, could not leave an example to the world'. A characteristic example of Chapman's involved style. Strozza means that by dedicating the arrowhead he will leave to posterity a profitable memorial of his patience.

V, iii, 23. 'Cleopatra in the meantime was very careful in gathering all sorts of poisons together to destroy men. Now to make proof of those poisons which made men die with least pain she tried it upon condemned men in prison'—Plutarch, *Lives—Antony.*

V, iii, 32–3. There are several curious mistakes in these lines. The true title of Pettie's collection of stories, 1576, is *A Pettie Palace of Pettie his Pleasure*, a title borrowed from the most famous Elizabethan collection of tales, Painter's *Palace of Pleasure*, 1566. Pettie does not tell the story of Adelasia (Painter, Nov. 44), and it is not Adelasia, but Florinda (Painter, Nov. 53) who defaces her features, and that with a stone, not a knife. Chapman seems to have had only a vague memory of the story. Possibly l. 33 is a marginal comment, giving a wrong source of the allusion, which has crept into the text.

V, iii, 72. [*Yet*] *in air :* still near the earth, cf. *Romeo and Juliet*, III, i, 131–2

V, iy, 16. *A poor maid's dower.* Schoell points out that Chapman is here borrowing a phrase from the *Arcadia* where Parthenia is spoken of as *disinherited of that goodly portion which nature had so liberally bequeathed unto her.*

V, iv, 20. ' Nor has it been made like unto any earthly form even the vilest ',

V, iv, 42. *Pagan Nero.* Nero murdered his mother ; Alphonsus, by consenting to his son's death, has slain not only his own posterity, but his parents, ll. 45–6. The point of the conceit lies in the Elizabethan commonplace that a man lived again in his children and descendants ; see Shakespeare, *Sonnets*, i–xvi, for an elaborate treatment of this idea.

V, iv, 54-5. An allusion to the myth of Saturn, who swallowed his newborn children.

V, iv, 56-62. With the sentiment of these lines cf. *Bussy*, II, i, 198–204.

V, iv, 85. The wounds are *unnatural* because inflicted upon a son by a father's connivance. I take *moaning right* to mean ' due lamentation ', see Text Notes, p. 772.

V, iv, 122. For the original punctuation of this line see Text Notes, p. 772. I take it that the words, *Give me your mask*, are addressed to one of the ladies present. The next phrase, *Open, etc.*, is addressed to the doctor's casket, from which he then takes the elixir.

V, iv, 125. *Medea's cauldron.* According to Ovid, *Metamorphoses*, vii, 251, *ssq.*, Medea by means of her magic cauldron restored youth to the aged father of Jason.

V, iv, 126. ' The most serious damage to a living being's constitution '.

V, iv, 138. *Renew recure :* be cured again.

V, iv, 194. *Set by your princely favour :* setting aside your favour shown to Medice, and judging him on his own merits.

V, iv, 211. *Your son :* dative of interest after *sought.*

V, iv, 248. *Scandal done to honour :* in that Mendice had usurped the noble name of the Medici.

V, iv, 251. *Zant :* Zante, or Zacynthus, one of the Ionian Islands.

V, iv, 281. *Fox, fox :* a Christmas game, called by Herrick *Fox i' th' Hole* (*Works*, vol. ii, p. 37, Grosart's edition) in which boys beat each other with gloves or bits of leather tied to strings.

TEXT NOTES

The Gentleman Usher first appeared in quarto form in 1606 (Q.). It was never reprinted, nor was it included in any collection of old plays, until 1873, when it appeared in the first volume of *The Comedies and Tragedies of George Chapman* (P.). In 1874 it was republished with modernized spelling and a few emendations in *The Works of Chapman—Plays* (S.). In 1907 it appeared, along with *All Fools*, in a volume of the *Belles Lettres Series* (Heath & Company), edited by T. M. Parrott (B.L.). For that edition the editor transcribed the copy of Q. in the Bodleian and collated it with copies in the British Museum, the Victoria and Albert Museum, and the Boston Public Library. The differences between these copies are very slight, merely an occasional variation in punctuation, or the restoration of a dropped letter.

In Q. the play is divided into acts but not into scenes. The divisions in the text are due to the present editor, who has also supplied the *Dramatis Personae* and added, in brackets, numerous stage-directions.

I, i, 54. Q. *facel : et ;* P. *face : let.*
60. Q. *rude Boares.* So S. Mr. Daniel suggested the punctuation of the text which was adopted in B.L.

64. Q. *vertuous.* Daniel suggests *venturous.*

113. Q. *nay of honest ;* S. emends.

114. Q. *she shames ;* S. emends.

163-4. Q. prints *Signieur Sarpego* in a separate line.

207-8. Q. prints Poggio's speech as two lines of prose.

215-7. Q.

> *Date viam mihi Noti, atq ; Ignoti.*
> *Dum ego, hîc, officium meum*
>   *facio.*
> *Fugite omnes atque abite, & de*
>   *via secedite, ne quem*
> *in cursu ; aut capite, aut cubito,*
>   *aut pectore offendam, aut genu.*

I have corrected the Latin by the Teubner edition of Plautus.

237. Q. *close ;* S. *clothes.*

248-50. Q. assigns the speeches here given to *Medice* to *Vincentio* and *vice versa.* I re-assigned them as in the present text in the B.L. edition, and although it has been suggested that the Q. arrangement might be defended by supposing a feigned quarrel between Strozza and Vincentio, I adhere to my alteration. For Strozza to tell the Prince that he is troublesome, and for the Prince to appeal to Medice against Strozza is quite out of keeping with the behaviour of these characters to each other and to Medice throughout the play. I take it that there has been a transposition of the names either by the transcriber of Chapman's MS. or by the printer. There are several other places in this play where speeches seem to be, or are certainly, wrongly assigned ; cf. notes on I, ii, 10, and IV, iv, 25 below.

I, ii. The stage-direction at the beginning of this scene reads in Q. *Enter Lasso, Corteza, Margaret, Bassiolo, Sarpego, two Pages, Bassiolo bare before.* S. follows this, but the proper entry of the ladies occurs after l. 36 below, where Q. reads *Enter Corte, Margarite, and Maids.* The first direction is merely a warning for the characters who took the ladies' parts to be in readiness.

I, ii, 10-15. I have followed Q. in assigning this speech to Bassiolo, but it has been suggested with much plausibility that he should only speak l. 10, after which Lasso should continue.

12. Q. *t'indure ;* Dr. Bradley suggests *t'induce*, i.e. ' to produce ', ' to perform '. Unless Chapman meant to make Bassiolo use a wrong word here, the suggestion would seem to deserve incorporating in the text. As there is some doubt, however, I have preferred not to alter the reading of Q.

29. Q. *your Lo ;* S. emends.

30. Q. *Snite ;* P. *Suite.*

43. In Q. the parenthesis includes only the words *as who should say.* This is evidently wrong, and I have extended it to take in the words governed by *say.*

59. Q. *Now cis . . . Peae.* The *c* in *Peace* has slipped into the line above in Q. ; P. corrects.

68. Q. *goddesle ;* P. *goddesse.*

70. Q. *Laugh your.* S. emends *you.*

114. Q. *chared ;* S. *chased.* I have followed a suggestion by Dr. Bradley and read *charged*, taking for granted that a letter has dropped out, and that *charged* is repeated from l. 97 above.

141. After this line Q. has simply *Exit*, which S. reproduces ; but it is plain that all but Vincentio and Strozza here leave the stage.

143-4. Q. prints as three lines ending *speech ?, fine,* and *all.*

154-5. Q. prints as three lines ending *farewell, that ?,* and *devise.*

II, i. To the stage-direction at the beginning of this act Q. adds the words *Strozza following close.* As the direction for Strozza's entrance is repeated in Q. after l. 27 below, I have treated this as a note to the actor playing Strozza to be in readiness (cf. I, ii, stage-direction and note), but it is possible that Strozza enters *close* at the beginning of the scene, and that the second direction marks the beginning of his taking part in the action.

II, i, 37. Q. *me thinke ;* I emend *methinks.*

44. Q. *do thy ;* I emend *do't thy.*

86. Q. puts the stage-direction after Strozza's speech, ll. 87-8.

124. After the stage-direction Q. has a question mark, probably representing the exclamation omitted in Q. after *yfaith.*

142–4. Q. prints Poggio's speech as two lines of prose, ending *I* and *it?*

195. Q. *moning;* S. *moving.*

216–7. Q. prints these lines as part of Strozza's speech; S. assigns them to Sarpego.

265. All copies of Q. that I have seen read *bring.* P. misprints *hung* and is followed by S.

286. Q. *female,* which is palpable nonsense. Following a suggestion by Dr. Bradley received too late to be incorporated in the text of B.L., I read *feral,* i.e. savage.

292. Q. *This;* but the Malone copy and that in the Boston Public Library have *Thus,* the better reading, as the catchword on the preceding page.

III, ii, 29–30. In Q. the parenthesis includes only the words from *though* to *gentleman.* L. 30 in Q. is printed as two lines ending *busines* and *nothing.*

33–4. Q. prints Bassiolo's speech as one line.

40. Q. *for your;* P. misprints *fory our.*

78. Q. *godly.* I follow the suggestion of Deighton (*Old Dramatists,* p. 130) and read *goodly.* I cannot, however, accept his suggestion that the next words should read: *whereas the deed's the perfect nobleman.*

89–90. Q. prints as three lines ending *words, too,* and *said.*

108. Q. *me Lordship;* B.L. *my lordship.*

134. Q. *too;* S. *two.*

137–8. Q. prints Vincentio's speech as one line.

154–5. Q. prints the words from *I cry* to *bitter* as one line.

199. Q. *Ler;* P. *Let.*

205. Q. places the *Exit* after l. 204.

212. Q. *iove;* P. *love.*

233. Two copies of those consulted drop the *s* in *attendants* in the stage-direction after this line. Two others print correctly *attendants.*

238. Q. *slabby;* P. *flabby.* I do not know whether P. follows a quarto with the correct reading or not, but I take *slabby* to be a mere misprint.

258. Q. *my Lord, all, and you; give;* S. *my lord, and all you give.* I suggest that an *s* has

dropped off the second word, and read *lords.*

275–6. Q. prints as one long line, ending *Duke,* and one short, ending *anone.*

343. S. inserts *stone* before *jug* on the authority of IV, iv, 120; but there is no need that the two lines should exactly correspond.

346. Q. *I common.* S. inserts *a* after *I.*

IV, ii, 13–16. Q. prints as prose.

20–22 Q. prints as prose.

46. Q. *be;* S. *by.*

59–61. Q. prints as two lines of prose ending *as* and *forepart.*

69–70. Q. prints as three lines ending *should, shall,* and *laugh.*

102. Q. prints the last words of Bassiolo's speech as prose continuously with the foregoing.

121. Perhaps we should read *love* for *loves.*

215–6. Q. prints as prose.

IV, iii. In the stage-direction Q. has *Benenemus* after *Cynanche,* but the doctor does not enter till l. 86. Cf. note on I, ii, above.

IV, iii, 22. Q. *alterations;* P. corrects.

72. Q. *Cares;* I emend *cures.* Cf. the misprint *carles* for *curles* in V, iii, 46.

78–9. Q. prints *Passing to Vincentio* as one line.

85–86. Q. prints as four lines ending *Physition, it, come,* and *lord?*

103–4. Q. prints as four lines ending *true, thinke, hurt,* and *well.*

IV, iv, 25–6. Q. gives this speech to Lasso, who does not enter till l. 57.

49. For *hands* we should perhaps read *hants,* i.e. haunts. Cf. *May-Day,* II, i, 179.

59. P. and B.L. read *the assured.* Three copies at least of Q. read *th' assured* which I have adopted in this text.

165. Q. *then I; faith;* S. *than i'faith.* Plainly the reading is *then I faith;* as I have punctuated.

170. Q. *the;* S. follows Q. I prefer to read *thy.* Cf. III, ii, 108, and IV, ii, 46.

V, i, 39–40. Q. prints as one line.

52. Q. *that ;* P. misprints *what*.

97. P. omits *your* in this line.

137. Q. *external,* perhaps influenced by *exile*. S. emends *eternal*.

V, ii, 37. Q. *this ;* P. misprints *thls*.

63–4 Q. prints Poggio's speech as two lines of prose, ending *uncle, my* and *uncle ?*

66–7. Q. prints Poggio's speech as one line of prose.

V, iii, 46. Q. *entring carles ;* P. misprints *entering*. S. emends *enticing curls*, which is no doubt correct.

70 Q. *The ever ;* S. emends *That ever*.

71. I am inclined to think that S.'s emendation *amazéd* for *amaz'd* is right.

72. Q. *it*, which S. follows ; but it is a palpable error for *yet*.

82. At the close of the scene Q. has *Exeunt*, but Margaret is alone on the stage, as Cortezza's exit is marked after l. 68.

V, iv, 20. Q. *resembled ;* S. *resembles*.

39. In the stage-direction Q. has the words *Strozza before* after *guard*.

85. Q. *moning right*. Mr. Daniel suggests *moving sight* (cf. II, i, 195) ; but I have preferred to read *moaning right*, i.e. with due lamentation.

120. Q. *affectious ;* P. corrects.

122. Q. Has commas after *Heaven, Art*, and *Maske*.

165. Q. prints *The* as the last word of l. 164.

208. Q. *Damne me my ;* P. *Damne me me my*.

223. Q. *of such ;* B.L. misprints *if such*.

255. Q. *that port ;* S. *the port*.

281. Q. *Fox, Fox ;* P. *Fo, Fox*.

295. Q. *ever ;* P. misprints *even*.

MONSIEUR D'OLIVE

INTRODUCTION

MONSIEUR D'OLIVE, perhaps the most entertaining of all Chapman's comedies, was published in 1606 in quarto form with the following title page:

> *Monsieur D'Olive. A Comedie, as it was sundrie times acted by her Maiesties children at the Blacke-Friers. By George Chapman. London. Printed by T. C. for William Holmes, and are to be sold at his Shop in Saint Dun-stons Church-yard in Fleete-streete, 1606.*

As usual the date of publication is some time later than that of the composition of the play. Wallace, indeed (*Children of the Chapel*, p. 75, *n*.) places it *c.* October–December, 1601, and claims to have 'solid' evidence for this date. The evidence on which he relies, however, has not yet been made public, and the general opinion tends to put the composition of *Monsieur D'Olive* some years later. Fleay (*Biographical Chronicle*, v. i, p. 59) holds that it cannot be earlier than January 30, 1604, when the Children of the Chapel received the title of the Children of the Queen's Revels, a name which is practically identical with that of the company mentioned on the title-page. The allusion to the prodigal [1] creation of knights by James I (I, i, 263–7), to the fact that knighthood had practically become purchasable (IV, ii, 77–80), and to the proclamation of 1603 calling in monopolies (I, i, 284–5) all seem to show that it belongs rather to the reign of James than to that of Elizabeth.

I believe it is possible to fix the date with comparative precision. In the first place if the play belongs, as seems probable, to the reign of James I, it can hardly have been put upon the stage before the spring of 1604, on account of the closing [2] of the theatres from May, 1603, till April, 1604, because of the plague. In the autumn and winter of that year three great lords accepted posts as ambassadors, Lenox to France, Hertford to the Archduke in the Low Countries, and Northampton to Spain. The town was all agog over the extraordinary preparations that were being made for these embassies. Specimens of the current gossip of the day are preserved in the letters printed in Winwood's *Memorials*. Thus we read (vol. ii, p. 39): ' My Lord Admiral [Northampton] prepareth against March to go with very great magnificence.

---

[1] Stoll, *Modern Language Notes*, vol. xx, p. 207, notes this allusion and adds the fact that James created 237 knights within six weeks after leaving Scotland. Stoll fixes the date of *Monsieur D'Olive* after the proclamation against monopolies and before Chapman's imprisonment in the spring of 1605 for *Eastward Ho*. Schelling (*Elizabethan Drama*, v. i, p. 398) agrees with Stoll.

[2] For the plague of 1603–4, see p. 702, *n*.

All his gentlemen shall have black velvet cloaks, and what else I know not ' ; later on (p. 41) : ' I hear he carries with him the title of Excellence and hath £15,000 allowed him for his expense, besides the charge of two of the King's best ships to transport him '.   In January, 1605, we hear (p. 45) : ' Our Lords Ambassadors begin now to prepare for the journeys, my Lord Admiral with great pomp ' ; in February (p. 50) :' The Lord Admiral makes great preparations for his journey.   He hath with him six lords . . . and fifty knights ' ; in March (p. 52) we learn of a misadventure that befel one of his attendants : ' Sir Adolphus Carey was robbed of £50 and three suits of clothes which were provided for the Spanish journey ', and in the same letter : ' Our great Ambassadors draw near their time, and you may think all will be in the best manner when the little Lord Hartford makes a rate of expense of £10,000 besides the King's allowance. . . .   My Lord Admiral's number is five hundred, and he swears five hundred oaths he will not admit [1] of one man more '.   The extravagant preparations and the long delay seem at last to have become a common jest ; ' Stone the jester ' we are told in the same letter ' was well whipped at Bridewell for a blasphemous speech that there went sixty fools into Spain besides my Lord Admiral and his two sons.   But he is now at liberty again, and gives his Lordship the praise of a very pitiful Lord '.   It was not until some time toward the end of the month that the much talked of embassy was actually dispatched.   On March 28, we learn that ' the Lord Admiral is now on his way toward Spain '.

Now in *Monsieur D'Olive* Chapman makes great play with the theme of an embassy.   A great part of the under-plot, singularly devoid of action by the way, is occupied by a satiric account of the preparations for D'Olive's famous embassy to the King of France, from which in after times ' men shall reckon their years, women their marriages ' (IV, ii, 114).   The satire is especially directed against the long delay in starting, the extravagant expense of the preparation, and the mad desire of gentlemen, and others, to take part in the embassy ; and these were, as we have seen from the letters quoted above, the very points which set tongues wagging in London in regard to the Admiral's embassy in the autumn and winter of 1604-5.   It seems to me more than a plausible supposition that Chapman looking about for matter with which to fill out the slight proportions of his under-plot hit happily enough upon the common gossip of the day.   It may perhaps serve as a bit of corroborative evidence that Northampton who was most likely to be vexed by such allusions was the mortal [2] enemy of Jonson, and that Jonson at this time was on the best of terms with Chapman.   I take it then that we may date the actual composition of *Monsieur D'Olive* some time in the autumn or early winter of 1604-5.   It must have been finished at latest before the spring, for by that time Chapman, along with Jonson and Marston, was busy on the composition of *Eastward Ho*.   As is known to all readers of Elizabethan drama, Jonson and Chapman were imprisoned for this play, and from prison Jonson wrote [3] to the Earl of Salisbury asking for his intercession.   Now the

---

[1] Cf. *Monsieur D'Olive*, III, ii, 47–50.

[2] See Jonson's *Conversations with Drummond*, published by the Shakespeare Society in 1842, p. 22.   It might be noted also that Northampton like Monsieur D'Olive (II, ii, 67–80) had lived apart from court in the preceding reign.

[3] A copy of the letter preserved among the Hatfield Papers was printed by

Earl of Salisbury was Robert Cecil, who received this title on May 4, 1605. This does not enable us to fix the date of *Eastward Ho* precisely, but it enables us to date the imprisonment, and we may therefore place the production of the play not earlier than the end of April. We may make a guess, therefore, that it was written in the early spring of the year, and in consequence that *Monsieur D'Olive* was on the stage in the winter of 1605.

Monsieur D'Olive was performed, probably for the first time, at Blackfriars. Fleay's conjecture (*loc. cit.*) that it is a revision of an older play called first *The Will of a Woman*,[1] and later *The Fountain of New Fashions*, written by Chapman for Henslowe in 1598 and presumably performed at the Rose has nothing to recommend it and has never been accepted. It is interesting to note that this play is quite lacking in the embellishments of music, dancing, and masque that are found in such abundance and variety in most of the plays produced at Blackfriars during Elizabeth's reign. Possibly after the death of the Queen the children no longer received the support they needed for such productions, and were obliged to rely wholly upon the excellence of their plays and their own acting. One would imagine that *Monsieur D'Olive* would have been a capital acting play, but we know nothing whatever of its stage history ; apparently it was never performed at any other theatre than Blackfriars.

No source, in the strict sense of the word, has yet been discovered for *Monsieur D'Olive*, although various suggestions have been made as to works from which Chapman may have taken hints. The play falls into two sharply differentiated parts, a romantic comedy and the ' humourous ' scenes which centre round the figure of Monsieur D'Olive himself. The first of these again falls into two parts, the story of Vandome's mistress, Marcellina, who has withdrawn from the world on account of the unjust suspicions of her husband, and the story of Vandome's brother-in-law, St. Anne, whose grief for his dead wife is such that he refuses her body burial, and devotes his life to a morbid worship of the embalmed corpse. Vandome, who serves as a link to connect these two actions, is the agent by whose means each is brought to a happy solution ; Marcellina is reunited to her husband, and St. Anne persuaded to bury his wife and marry Marcellina's sister. It seems to me unlikely that Chapman should have invented the first of these actions. It has distinct affiliations with the fashion of platonic love so popular in courtly circles in the early Renaissance, and I am inclined to believe that Chapman got at least a suggestion for it from some French or Italian story.

The second theme, that of St. Anne and his dead wife, has numerous prototypes. Josephus (*Antiquities*, xv, 7) records the story of Herod's passion for his murdered wife, Mariamne, and a later legend tells of his refusal for many years to consign her body to the grave. A somewhat similar tale is told of an Arabian[2] Caliph, of a King of Denmark, and

---

Gifford in the *Memoir* prefixed to his edition of Jonson, v. 1, p. 40, and by Schelling in his edition of *Eastward Ho*, p. 162.

[1] The true title of this play apparently is *The Isle of Women*, see above, p. 701, *n.*

[2] Pauls, *Der Ring der Fastrada*, 1896, from whom I take these references has collected a large number of similar tales. He seems, however, unacquainted with the appearance of this theme in Elizabethan drama.

of Harold Fairhair of Norway (*Heimskringla*—translated in the *Saga Library*, vol. iii, p. 120). The most famous predecessor of St. Anne, however, as Koeppel (*Quellen und Forschungen*, 1897, p. 222) was the first to point out, is no other than Charlemagne.

The story of Charlemagne's love for his dead wife is a late and apparently a local development in the cycle of legends that gathered round the name of the great Emperor. It is unknown in early French literature (Gaston Paris, *Histoire Poétique de Charlemagne*, p. 355) and appears for the first time in certain German [1] chronicles of the thirteenth and fourteenth centuries. According to this legend Charlemagne bestowed a magic ring upon his wife (or mistress), whom as a result he loved beyond all measure. On the approach of death she concealed the ring in her mouth, and in consequence the Emperor's love remained unaltered, and he refused to allow her body out of his sight. After many years a bishop [2] (or courtier) discovered the ring and possessed himself of it, whereupon Charlemagne's passion was transferred to the new holder of the charm. By chance, or design, the ring was dropped in the swamps surrounding Aix-la-Chapelle, upon which the Emperor became so attached to this neighbourhood that he declined to leave it, and built both a palace and a cathedral there, in the latter of which his body was by his order entombed.

This legend of Charlemagne's magic ring seems to have originated at Aix-la-Chapelle, where it remained a living tradition until comparatively recent times. Petrarch, who visited Aix in 1333, heard the tale from a priest and recorded it in a letter dated June 21, 1333 (*Epistolae de reb. fam.*, I, 3). From Petrarch the story spread through Western Europe. It is referred to by Skelton [3] (*Why Come ye not to Court*, 1522), retold by Tyndale (*Practyse of Prelates*, 1530), and Pasquier (*Recherches de la France*, 1596), and worked up into *novelle* by Doni,[4] 1513–74 and by Sebastiano Erizzo in *Lei Sei Giornati*, 1567. This latter novel was, perhaps, a source of an anonymous Elizabethan play preserved in manuscript until printed by Bullen (*Old Plays*, vol. iii) under the title of *The Distracted Emperor*,[5] but often referred to by the briefer title of *Charlemagne*.

[1] Enenkel's *Weltbuch*, thirteenth century, tells of Charlemagne's sinful passion for the body of his dead wife. A bishop, who learns of the sin by revelation removes the charm (*Zauberstein*) from her mouth. The body decays, and the King does penance. In *Karl Meinet*, a poem of the fourteenth century, the tale is told of a mistress of the King. A courtier who finds the charm, a ring, in the hair of the corpse wins the King's love, but later throws the ring in a brook near Aachen, whereupon the King loves this town and builds a minster there. Bränwald's *Chronicon* of the sixteenth century combines this story with that of a grateful serpent to which the King had rendered justice against a toad, and which in return bestowed on him a magic ring. Densusianu (*Romania*, vol. xxv, p. 612) contends that Bränwald presents a late and artificial combination of two quite independent tales.

[2] In some versions this bishop becomes the famous Bishop Turpin, of the Charlemagne cycle. Pasquier (*Recherches*, Book V, chap. 16, edition of 1596) gives this name which does not occur in his immediate source.

[3] Dyce prints Petrarch's letter in his edition of Skelton, who refers by name to Petrarch, vol. ii, pp. 364–6.

[4] Doni's novel which I have not seen is said by Pauls to be an almost literal translation of Petrarch. It is printed in *Tutte le Novelle di A. F. Doni*, Milano 1863.

[5] The MS. gives no title ; *The Distracted Emperor* was the not very happy designation of the editor, Mr. Bullen.

Mr. Bullen was struck with the similarity of this anonymous play to the acknowledged work of Chapman, and suggested (vol. iii, p. 161) that it might be the lost *French Tragedy*, which was entered in the Stationers' Register, June 29, 1660, as a work of that author, but never printed, and a manuscript of which was in the next century destroyed by Warburton's cook. His suggestion does not seem to have attracted much attention—Schelling, for example, does not even notice it—and it was left for M. Schoell in an appendix to his thesis and later in the *Revue Germanique* (Mars–Avril, 1912) to restate Chapman's claim with arguments of such plausibility as to establish at least a high degree of probability of his authorship. If this be actually the case we need, of course, look no further for the source of the Charlemagne motif [1] in *Monsieur D'Olive*. Chapman would simply have taken it over from his own work, modifying it to suit his purpose in the composition of a romantic comedy.

It must be admitted that the Charlemagne motif in *Monsieur D'Olive* has been reduced to its simplest form; the magic ring, the most striking feature of the old tale, does not appear in the play. If Chapman's claim to *Charlemagne* be not allowed, one might, in fact, hesitate to connect the St. Anne story with the Charlemagne legend, and find a sufficient source for it in the well-known story of Herod and Mariamne, the undoubted source of the same motif in Massinger's *Duke of Milan* and in the anonymous [2] *Second Maiden's Tragedy*. Yet, on the whole, it is more than likely that the Charlemagne story gave Chapman the suggestion for his St. Anne, since he can hardly have been ignorant of the Petrarch version and since he drew upon another work of Petrarch's for a scene (III, i), which is an integral part of the St. Anne story.

The work which Chapman used for this scene is Petrarch's *Colloquium de Contemptu Mundi*,[3] better known by its second title, *Secretum*. This work, an extraordinary piece of introspective psychological analysis, was written by Petrarch about 1342—possibly revised in the next decade—apparently for his own use rather than for publication. It is cast in the form of a dialogue between Petrarch and St. Augustine, introduced to the poet by Truth, who attempts to cure him of the disease, *accidia* (*acedia*), from which he is suffering. In a three days' debate St. Augustine, representing the medieval view of life, rebukes the pioneer of the Renaissance for his neglect of heavenly things and, especially in Book III, for his enthralment in the chains of Love and Fame. Petrarch represents himself as making a strong stand against the censure of the Saint, and although in the end he makes outward and formal submission, it is plain that he is by no means disposed to renounce the world and follow Augustine's injunction to devote himself wholly to the contemplation of death.

This work enjoyed a considerable popularity in the fifteenth and sixteenth centuries. It was printed by one of the early Germans, the

---

[1] M. Schoell notes, apart from this motif, two minor links between *Charlemagne* and *Monsieur D'Olive*, both of which are pointed out below in the notes on I, i, 145–8 and II, ii, 108, and calls attention to a certain similarity of situation between La Fue's offer to kiss Charlemagne and D'Olive's salute bestowed upon the Duchess. I do not think these details are of great importance, but they have some value as corroborative evidence.

[2] Possibly this story also lies behind Marlowe's account of Tamburlaine and Zenocrate.—2 *Tamburlaine*, II, iv.

[3] I owe this reference to M. Schoell.

' R printer ' of Strassburg, ca. 1475, again at Antwerp in 1489, and at Deventer in 1498. It was included in the Basel (1496) and the Venice (1501) editions of Petrarch's works, and published along with the *Seven Penitential Psalms* at Berne in 1600 and 1604. Since Chapman translated the *Seven Psalms* of Petrarch in 1612 it is possible that he became familiar with the *Secretum* in one of these Berne editions. The correspondences between Petrarch's Latin prose and the verse of Chapman pointed out below in the notes on III, i, 9–19, 20–35, and 36–40, are close enough to show that Chapman must have been working, so to speak, with the book open before him. St. Anne's description of his mental state, and Vandome's speech and St. Anne's reply, are no mere reminiscences of Petrarch, but a translation, free enough, indeed, selecting, suppressing, and enlarging in true Elizabethan fashion, but at times rendering the original almost word for word. Chapman uses his source to give to the figure of St. Anne something of the melancholy charm of Petrarch and to remove his passion, morbid as it is, from the realm of the fantastic or the barbarous.

In sharp contrast to the St. Anne story with its notes of old romance and Petrarchian melancholy stands the modern ' comedy of humours ' which forms the second and larger part of the play. In these scenes, Chapman discards all poetic and romantic elements, and reverts almost entirely to the prosaic comedy which he had already attempted in *An Humourous Day's Mirth* and in *Sir Giles Goosecap*. The influence of Jonson seems to me very marked in this part of the play. The chief figure is a character far more closely observed and precisely defined than any of the characters of Chapman's earlier plays. The scenes in which he takes part are singularly devoid of action, but we hardly feel the loss, so rich in entertainment is the character which reveals itself to us in a series of lively dialogues and monologues. So far as any action exists, it is patently introduced for the sake of the character ; situations are devised in which the character as the poet had preconceived it will be revealed in new lights and with fuller detail. Thus the business of the embassy is introduced, not for the sake of the plot, but in order that D'Olive may display his fluency and self-assurance before the Duke and his levity and careless cynicism in interviews with would-be followers. This, of course, is the earlier manner of Jonson, especially in that most typical ' comedy of humours ', *Every Man out of his Humour*. But here, as elsewhere, Chapman differs from Jonson in his greater spontaneity, ease, and geniality. We are less sensible of a studied composition, and we do not hear the somewhat strident voice of the moral satirist. Chapman is satisfied to give us a vivid presentation of a comic figure ; he has no desire to

> *Strip the naked follies of the time,*
> *. . . and with a whip of steel*
> *Print wounding lashes in their iron ribs.*

Jonson leaves the fop and would-be courtier, Fastidious Brisk, in hopeless imprisonment for debt ; Chapman dismisses D'Olive with the assurance of the Duke's favour and protection, and the assembled Court acclaims him, *Good Monsieur D'Olive*.

Several suggestions have been made as to the literary ancestry of D'Olive. Professor Koeppel (*loc. cit.*) sees in him an elaboration, enriched with various new traits, of the character sketch which Chapman had struck off in Bassiolo. M. Schoell notes certain resemblances to

Blurt in Middleton's comedy, *Blurt Master Constable*, to Balurdo in *Antonio and Mellida*, to Bilioso in *The Malcontent*, and to Malvolio. The resemblances, such as they are, lie on the surface. There is an undoubted likeness between the forged letter which exposes D'Olive to the ridicule of the Court and that which leads Malvolio to expose himself before his mistress. In fact, it is plain that we have to do here with an amusing bit of plagiarism. Having wound up the incident of the embassy, and lacking matter with which to fill out the last act and bring the leading figure of D'Olive on the stage again at the general assembly of the characters with which an Elizabethan comedy usually concludes, Chapman calmly lifted a well-known incident from *Twelfth Night* and adapted [1] it for his conclusion. But the plagiarism of an incident does not connote identity, or even similarity, of character, and few figures in Elizabethan comedy are more distinct in character than the self-conceited, stiff, and puritanic major-domo of *Twelfth Night* and the rattle-pated, witty, idle man-about-town of Chapman's play. Nor can I see that there is any such likeness between Bassiolo and D'Olive as to justify the assertion that the second character is an elaboration of the first. Bassiolo is primarily a slow-witted serving-man ; D'Olive a vivacious fop. Bassiolo falls completely into the trap and makes a most comic spectacle of himself, first in the airs he assumes in virtue of the supposed favour shown him, then in his frantic efforts to extricate himself on learning of the danger to which this favour has exposed him. On the other hand, it is hard to believe that D'Olive at heart takes the proposed embassy seriously. He presumes on it far enough, indeed, to risk a bit of foppish impertinence toward the Duchess, but his sole preparations for the charge assigned him consist apparently in making a face or two at Court, in allowing followers to attach themselves to him, at their own expense, and in gossiping with a pair of pages as to the world's opinion of his new honours.

As for the other suggested resemblances they seem to me even fainter. Blurt is a palpable imitation of Dogberry, and it can hardly be supposed that Shakespeare's sketch of a country constable gave rise to Chapman's picture of a witty man-about-town. Balurdo seems to me closer akin to the type of Sir Giles Goosecap than to that of D'Olive, and while there is an undoubted likeness between the embassy business of Bilioso in *The Malcontent* and that of Monsieur D'Olive, the two characters are totally different. Bilioso is described in the beginning as ' an old choleric marshall ', and dismissed at the close as ' a perfect old knave '. He is a bitterly satiric picture of the hardened courtier, a flatterer, a backbiter, and a turncoat, alternately insolent and fawning. It is not in such a character that the prototype of the light-hearted D'Olive can be found.

If a prototype must be established for D'Olive, I would suggest that Jonson's Fastidious Brisk may have given Chapman certain hints. Brisk is described as ' a neat, spruce, affecting courtier ' ; he is fond of dress, partial to tobacco, fluent in speech, a hanger-on of the Court, and something of a gull. ' His brain ', we are told, ' is lighter than his

---

[1] It may be noticed in passing that Chapman elaborates that part of the incident which Shakespeare left untouched, the actual preparation of the bait in the shape of a forged letter, and leaves untouched that part which Shakespeare had fully developed, the snaring of the victim through his vanity and gullibility.

feather '. In all these points his character approaches nearer to D'Olive's than do those of Malvolio or Bilioso, whatever external resemblances may connect these figures with Chapman's hero.

But at best it was only a hint or two that Chapman could have taken from Jonson's character, and, on the whole, I am inclined to agree with Ward (*English Dramatic Literature*, vol. ii, p. 437) that D'Olive is one of the most original figures in our comic drama. The essential features of his character are unruffled good-humour, unfailing self-assurance, a most ingenious and reckless wit, and an unquenchable flow of speech. ' A compound of a poet and a lawyer ' some one calls him, and the more one studies this character the deeper grows the conviction that it owes its origin not to books or to previous stage figures, but to Chapman's observation of life, and that it is, to all intents, a portrait—perhaps as easily recognized at that time as Jonson's Carlo Buffone—of some gay young member of one of the Inns of Court, possessed of a handsome fortune, some traces of a liberal education, some claim to the attention of the Court, and an unblushing self-confidence that stood him in better stead than all his other possessions.

In the matter of dramatic technic *Monsieur D'Olive* does not seem to me to take rank with the best Elizabethan comedies. There is a marked lack of unity in the construction ; the romantic and the comic plots are only artificially connected, and the scenes in which they are developed are merely juxtaposed. Throughout the play, until the last scene, where a belated effort is made to combine the two in a common *dénouement*, there is an almost mechanical method of construction. Each act contains two divisions, the first of which deals with the romantic story, the second with the comic underplot. The blending of romance and comedy, which Chapman effected so harmoniously in the last acts of *The Gentleman Usher*, is wholly wanting in *Monsieur D'Olive*. There is, moreover, as the play progresses, a marked decline in the interest of the romantic story. The opening scene, as Swinburne has pointed out (*George Chapman*, p. 63) is a most admirable bit of exposition ; it states the problem, if we may so call it, of the reconciliation of the Countess with her husband by the agency of her chivalric lover with such clearness and charm of style as to awaken expectations that are never fulfilled. Our disappointment is due, I think, to the lack of that character development which the first scene had given us a right to expect. The problem, as stated there, has its rise in the characters of Marcellina, Vaumont, and Vandome, and it is only by the development and interaction of these characters that a fit solution is to be obtained. But Marcellina remains, from first to last, a shadow, Vaumont, of whom so promising a sketch had been given at first, degenerates into a nullity, while Vandome, after the first part of Act II, falls completely out of his rôle and becomes the mere intriguer. For the problem that was stated in terms of character is solved in the end along the lines of a comedy of intrigue. If we are to take the seclusion of Marcellina seriously, as in the opening scene Chapman plainly means us to do, we can hardly accept the trick by which in the last act the lady is lured out of her house as a satisfactory solution. In Swinburne's words the romantic interest is at the close [1] fairly hustled into a corner.

[1] See V, ii, 21–4, for the actual close of this action. It is worth noting that neither the Countess nor her husband has a word to say, and that Vandome,

This lack of character development in the romantic plot is due, I fancy, to a shift of interest on the part of the author himself while actually at work upon the play. I have called attention elsewhere (p. 758) to the way in which Chapman seems to catch fire about the beginning of Act III in *The Gentleman Usher*, and dismissing the ' humours ' and farcical incidents with which he has been trifling, devotes himself with all his energy to the development of the romantic plot. The very opposite seems to have been the case in *Monsieur D'Olive*. Here Chapman made a prompt and promising start upon a true romantic theme. In order to afford the change and relief which the earlier comedy insisted upon, he introduced the ' humorous ' figure of D'Olive, and this character straightway proved so fresh and living that he took, so to speak, the management of the drama into his own hands, pushed the figures of the romantic plot aside, and claimed the playwright's interest and attention for himself. And since the interest of the sub-plot depends wholly upon the character [1] of D'Olive and not at all upon the action, it would seem that Chapman's faculty of characterization, never, I think, very affluent, was wholly given over to this new and entertaining personage, and as a natural result, the characters of the romantic plot sank more and more to the rank of puppets in a comedy of intrigue.

Roughly speaking, Chapman's use of verse and prose in *Monsieur D'Olive* corresponds to the division between the romantic and the ' humourous ' scenes. The correspondence is not exact, for an occasional bit of prose appears in the romantic scenes, and D'Olive occasionally expresses himself in graceful verse. The prose in which the greater part of his scenes are written seems to me perhaps the best that Chapman has to show. It is racy, vigorous, witty, fluent, and admirably clear. The wonder is that a master of such a perfect instrument should in his letters, prefaces, dedications, etc., have uttered his mind in such a clumsy, involved, and often almost unintelligible style. The probable explanation is that in his attempt to write like a scholar, Chapman only succeeded in expressing himself like a pedant. When, as here, he forgets the claims of scholarship and gives free course to his natural genius, he discloses a gift for prose style second, I think, only to Shakespeare's among Elizabethan dramatists.

The verse of *Monsieur D'Olive* covers a wide range from the grave beauty of the first scene, in which, to quote Swinburne (*loc. cit.*) ' every word is harmonious, appropriate and noble,' to the light fluency of the tobacco oration in the second act. In the dialogue between Vandome and Eurione in V, i, Chapman shifts at will from verse to prose and back again, and the verse is purposely pitched in so low a key that the change is hardly noticed.

All in all *Monsieur D'Olive*, while one of the most entertaining of

leaving them presumably in each others' arms, turns away to wind up the St. Anne action. It seems to me that this second action of the romantic plot escapes, on the whole, the charge that has been brought against the first. St. Anne's sudden passion for Eurione is not a mere stage device, but is motivated by his impressionable character and by her likeness, repeatedly insisted on, to his dead wife. Their marriage was, of course, a necessary convention of Elizabethan comedy.

[1] Schoell notes, for example, that the set speeches of D'Olive spring from his character and so have a living interest which is lacking in such set orations as those of the page and Valerio in *All Fools*.

Chapman's plays, cannot be said to denote any great advance in his art as a playwright. Nor has it the same interest in the history of Elizabethan comedy that attaches to *All Fools* and *The Gentleman Usher*. Its main interest lies in the intrusive and exuberant hero of the underplot. But Monsieur D'Olive is a character of such originality, vivacity, and genuine humour that he could redeem from oblivion a play with less claims to our attention than the romantic, witty, and amusing comedy which bears his name.

MONSIEUR D'OLIVE

NOTES

I, i, 1. *Your carriage:* the baggage which you are carrying; cf. the use of *carriage* in I, i, 33.

I, i, 15. *To that likeness:* in the circle to which love has been compared, the *ring* of I, i, 16.

I, i, 16. Dilke says *beat* is 'used in the language of sportsmen who are said to beat the ground in quest of game'. It seems better to take it in the sense of 'tread', see *New English Dictionary*, sub *tread*, 3.

I, i, 30. *It:* i.e. affection, see l. 29.

I, i, 31. *Attaint:* stain upon honour. Cf.:

> *Shore's wife is grac'd, and passes for a saint;*
> *Her legend justifies her foul attaint.*
> Daniel—*Complaint of Rosamond*, ll. 25-6.

I, i, 32. *Circular:* perfect. Cf. *Your wisdom is not circular.* Massinger, *Emperor of the East*, III, ii. Chapman uses the word elsewhere in the same sense, see the dedication of the *Georgics of Hesiod* (*Poems*, p. 209), and *The Hymn to Hermes* (*Poems*, p. 299).

I, i, 33. *Her even carriage:* her evenly balanced behaviour.

I, i, 39. *The centre:* i.e. the earth, then considered the centre of the universe; cf. *Bussy*, IV, ii, 182.

I, i, 72. *The corsie.* Dilke seems not to have understood this word as he suggests that it is connected either with 'curse' or 'corse'. It has nothing to do with either, but is a not uncommon Elizabethan form of 'coresive', i.e. corrosive, often used, as here, with the sense of 'cause of trouble', 'grievance'.

I, i, 97. 'With this one instance where her conduct might possibly be suspected of levity'.

I, i, 145-7. Schoell thinks these lines are based on a passage in Erizzo's tale, see above, p. 776: *come hai tu* [Death] *impoverito il mondo e questo regno di si bella e preziosa cosa? Forse per arricchire il cielo, o per farne di quella una stella.* The resemblance does not seem to me close enough to prove that Chapman made use of Erizzo, but it is at least worth noting.

I, i, 165. *An apoplexy:* with reference both to the suddenness of the attack and to the complete loss of the mental faculties incident to this disease.

I, i, 175. *Wracks me within my haven:* cf. *Bussy*, I, i, 33, and my note *ad loc.*

I, i, 183. *Curious:* fastidious, minutely exact, not 'ceremonious', as Dilke interprets it. Cf. a similar use in *Taming of the Shrew*, IV, iv, 36.

I, i, 209. *Fit stock to graff on.* Roderigue implies that Mugeron's credulity would make him an easy husband for a wife to graft horns on.

I, i, 211-2. *Saturn's time:* the golden age of innocency.

I, i, 214. *Luxury:* used here in its original sense, 'lasciviousness', the only sense in which Shakespeare uses it, see *Hamlet*, I, v, 83; *Merry Wives*, V, v, 98; *Lear*, IV, vi, 119. In Chapman's *Iliad*, XXI, 262, it appears to have the sense of 'superabundance', but, as a rule, this meaning appears much later.

I, i, 215. *Steal from a forbidden tree:* cf. *All Fools*, III, i, 305-6, and my note *ad loc.*

I, i, 230. *Puts it upon construction :* exposes it to criticism.

I, i, 238. *The stallion :* cf. *All Fools*, III, i, 275.

I, i, 247. *Turns Argus to Actaeon :* changes a jealous keeper to a cuckold, alluding to the hundred eyes of Argus and the horns of Actaeon.

I, i, 254. *Who :* in the objective case with a nominative form for emphasis ; cf. *All Fools*, I, i, 38.

I, i, 265-6. A sneer at King James's lavish creation of knights ; cf. *Bussy*, I, ii, 124, and my note *ad loc. Addition*, l. 265, means ' title '.

I, i, 269. *Beaver.* D'Olive's hat, which he was probably twirling about to attract attention to it, was not only *embroidered*, but gilded. Hence in l. 272, Roderigue compares it to the *parcel-gilt cover* of a cup or dish, i.e. to a cover gilded on the inside.

I, i, 275. *Satyrs to your sires :* because of your satirical disposition. It was an old notion that the word ' satire ', Latin *satira*, was derived from the Greek, σάτυρος, satyr, with reference to the chorus of satyrs in the Greek ' satyric ' drama. Thus Puttenham, *Art of English Poetry* (p. 6, Arber reprint) says : ' Ancient poets . . . used three kinds of poems reprehensive, to wit, the Satyre, the Comedy, and the Tragedy ; and the first and most bitter invective . . . was the Satyre ; which to th'intent their bitterness should breed none ill will . . . . they made wise as if the gods of the woods, whom they called Satyres or Silvanes, should appear and recite those verses of rebuke . . . as who should say these terrene and base gods being conversant with man's affairs and spiers out of all their secret faults, had some great care over man and desired . . . to bring the bad to amendment by those kind of preachings, whereupon the poets, inventors of the device, were called Satyristes '. Hence in the sixteenth and seventeenth centuries the Satyr was supposed to be of a censorious disposition. Greene, in his address *To the Gentlemen Readers*, prefixed to *Mamillia* (*Works*, vol. ii, p. 345) says : ' Let the savage Satyre himself, whose cynical censure is more severe than need, frown '. Cf. *The Ball*, V, i, where Barker, the cynic, appears disguised as a satyr, and especially Honoria's remarks, *The Ball*, V, i, 318–323.

I, i, 284. *Monopolies are now called in.* In Elizabeth's last Parliament, 1601, the question of the monopolies, which had grown to be a grievous burden on the people, was discussed with great vigour. The Queen yielded to the evident desire for reform, and in a proclamation, November 25, 1601, promised to revoke all vexatious monopolies. The promised reform was not, however, carried out, and the question arose again in the first year of her successor's reign. On May 7, 1603, James issued a proclamation bidding all persons to refrain from making use of their monopolies until they could satisfy the Council that they were not prejudicial to the interests of the nation. As a result the greater part of the existing monopolies were revoked. It is to this that Chapman alludes.

I, i, 301. *Wild-goose chase :* a race in which the leading rider chooses the course and obliges the others to follow him. Cf. *Romeo and Juliet*, II, iv, 75, and the note *ad loc.* in Furness's *Variorum*.

I, i, 307. *Sorbonne.* The professors of the Sorbonne, the theological faculty of the University of Paris, were constantly appealed to for decisions in dogma and in Canon Law by the whole Catholic world. Even the Papal Curia laid doubtful cases before them for decision.

I, i, 322-3. *This comet :* this phenomenon of the secluded Countess. *Admire* is used in the sense of ' wonder at '.

I, i, 338-9. *Valentines.* ' It is a ceremony ', says Bourne, ' never omitted among the vulgar to draw lots [cf. *draw cuts*, l. 339] which they term Valentines on the eve before Valentine's Day. The names of a select number of one sex are, by an equal number of the other, put into some vessel, and after that every one draws a name, which for the present is called their Valentine '—Brand, *Popular Antiquities*, vol. i, p. 47. Cf. also the device in *The Ball*, V, i, by which Honoria and Rosamond propose to decide which of them shall be Lord Rainbow's mistress.

I, i, 343. Cf. *fat and fulsome, Twelfth Night*, V, i, 112. I take *full* here to mean 'sated', although it might carry with it the idea of pregnancy, and *fulsome* to mean 'nauseating'.

I, i, 344. *A handbasket :* so that she might support herself by peddling.

I, i, 347-58. With this diatribe against marriage cf. Quicksilver's speech to Sir Petronel, *Eastward Ho*, II, iii, 61, ssq. With *shrewish if she be honest*, cf. *All Fools*, I, i, 69–72.

I, i, 358. *Liver.* Cf. my note on *The Gentleman Usher*, III, ii, 370.

I, i, 362. *O' th' order :* i.e. of married men. The *honour due to't* (ll. 364–5) is, of course, the horns, as appears from Roderigue's words, ll. 368–70.

I, i, 369-70. *Custom of the city.* Cf. in the same connexion *the courtesy of the City*, *All Fools*, V, ii, 325.

I, i, 376. *Lanthorn :* cf. the same pun in *Eastward Ho*, IV, i, 298, and 2 *King Henry IV*, I, ii, 51–5. The fact that lanterns were originally made almost always of horn gave rise to this common jest.

I, i, 382. *Frets.* A pun on *fret*, the ring or bar on the finger board of a lute or guitar, and *fret*, a sore spot.

I, i, 391. *Half a score birds in a cage :* gold pieces in a purse.

I, i, 393. *Map :* picture, embodiment.

II, i, 10. *Cast her water in her face :* diagnose her disease by her looks ; cf. *All Fools*, V, ii, 195. A common method of diagnosis in Chapman's time was by inspection of the urine, see 2 *King Henry IV*, I, ii, 1–6, and *Macbeth*, V, iii, 50–51.

II, i, 12. *Cardecu :* ' an old French silver coin worth ¼ of the gold *écu* (*quart d'écu*) '—*New English Dictionary*. It was equivalent in Chapman's time to about one shilling and sixpence.

II, i, 48. *Called her sister.* Cf. below, II, i, 90, where Vandome calls Eurione *sister*, and II, i, 130, where she calls him *brother*.

II, i, 111. *Cast :* used, I think, in the sense it has in venery. To *cast a hawk* is to throw her off at the prey ; dogs *cast* when they spread out and search for a lost scent. So *travellers* may be said to *cast far*.

II, i, 139. *My quarters :* suggested by *treason* in the preceding line. The punishment for high treason included quartering. There is, of course, a double entendre in the phrase.

II, i, 179. *The drunken froes :* the Bacchanals. The word seems to have come into literary use in English with Golding's translation of Ovid's *Metamorphoses*, where it appears in VII, 337, and XI, 21. See also my note on *An Humourous Day's Mirth*, sc. xiv, l. 19. *The Thracian Harper* is Orpheus who was torn to pieces by the Bacchanals, *Metamorphoses*, XI, 1–42.

II, i, 205-7. Dilke (see Text Notes, p. 793 below) misunderstands the passage. The melancholy of St. Anne might well be spoken of as *grounded on rational love* as opposed to sensual, and upon *philosophy* as opposed to emotion. Vandome means to recall him to the life of the senses.

II, i, 218. *Banquet :* a dessert of fruit, wine, and sweetmeats. Cf. *Romeo and Juliet*, I, v, 124, and the note *ad loc.* in Furness's *Variorum*. Eurione's *conserves* (l. 219) and *cordial still'd waters* (l. 221) would furnish a banquet.

II, i, 226. *In sadness :* seriously, in earnest.

II, ii. Stage-direction. Chapman seems fond of setting his ladies to work at sewing on the stage ; cf. the stage-directions after *All Fools*, II, i, 229, and *Sir Giles Goosecap*, II, i, 16.

II, ii, 10. *Wizard :* sorcerer, wise man, the word is used ironically ; see Text Notes, p. 794.

II, ii, 15. *Footcloth :* the large embroidered cloth thrown over the back of a horse or mule for a state procession. Here, I think, used for the ass, D'Olive.

II, ii, 21. *His mind is his kingdom.* Cf. the well known contemporary poem by Sir Edward Dyer, *My mind to me a Kingdom is*. The sentiment is a commonplace that goes back at least as far as Seneca : *Mens regnum bona possidet—Thyestes*, l. 380.

II, ii, 80. The precept ' Live unknown ', supposed to come from Epicurus, (Montaigne, II, xvi) is discussed by Plutarch in the essay—*De Latenter Vivendo*.

II, ii, 86. *King G[yges'] ring.* The story of the ring of Gyges which made him invisible is told by Plato, *Republic*, 359. It is again referred to below, V, ii, 7–8.

II, ii, 92-4. Cf. *Bussy*, III, i, 23–5 and my note *ad loc.*

II, ii, 95. *Burdello:* a variant of 'bordello', 'brothel'. The same form occurs in *Every Man in his Humour*, I, i, 245.

II, ii, 96. *Stammel:* a kind of cheap red woollen cloth.

II, ii, 101. *Predicables:* a term in Aristotelian logic. According to th: Schoolmen there were five *predicables :* genus, species (cf. l. 103), difference, property, and accident.

II, ii, 108. An almost exact parallel occurs in *The Distracted Emperor*, p. 233.

II, ii, 130. *In gross :* in a general way.

II, ii, 152-3. *An ancient subject, and yet newly call'd into question.* The subject of tobacco smoking had been *called into question*, i.e. made a matter of debate, with great vehemence shortly before the composition of this play. The controversy [1] began apparently with the publication of a tract entitled *Work for Chimney Sweepers*, 1602, the anonymous author of which alleges eight reasons against tobacco, the author and finder of which he declares to have been ' the Divell '. This provoked *A Defence of Tobacco*, 1602. Shortly after his accession to the English throne King James published, 1604, anonymously his well-known *Counterblast to Tobacco*, in which he took occasion to sneer at Raleigh, whose example, apparently, had done much to make smoking fashionable. In the same year James under cover of attacking an idle [2] luxury raised the import duty on tobacco from 2*d.* to six shillings and tenpence per pound. On the third day of King James's visit to Oxford in August, 1605, there was a public debate on the question : *Utrum frequens suffitus nicotianae exoticae sit sanis et salutaris.* Dr. Cheynell, of Corpus Christi, defended tobacco in a humorous speech, but the King naturally pronounced a verdict for the negative. In *The Queen's Arcadia*, a pastoral by Samuel Daniel, played before the Queen at Christ Church during the royal visit there is an amusing onslaught on tobacco, quite in the spirit of James. Alcon, a quacksalver, tells how he met a seaman who had brought from the island of Nicosia a certain weed :

> *And this in powder made and fir'd, he sucks*
> *Out of a little hollow instrument*
> *Of calcinated clay the smoke thereof ;*
> *Which either he conveys out of his nose,*
> *Or down into his stomach with a whiff.*
> *And this, he said, a wondrous virtue had*
> *To purge the head and cure the great catarrh,*
> *And to dry up all other meaner rheums.*

The quacksalver secured ' all this commodity ' and taught people how to use it, and he says,

> *Now do they nothing else but sit and suck,*
> *And spit and slaver all the time they sit.*

Then breaking into a moral vein he concludes :

> *But sure the time's to come when they look back*
> *On this, will wonder with themselves to think*
> *That men of sense could ever be so mad*
> *To suck so gross a vapour that consumes*
> *Their spirits, spends nature, dries up memory,*
> *Corrupts the blood, and is a vanity.*

The Queen's Arcadia, ll. 1119, *ssq.*

In opposition to the courtly Daniel, Chapman espouses the cause of tobacco.

---

[1] As early as 1598 Jonson introduced Bobadil and Cob praising and abusing tobacco in *Every Man in his Humour.*

[2] James remarked that some of the English gentry spent £200–400 a year ' upon this precious stink '.

The humour of the debate lies especially in the fact that he sets a **Puritan**, a sect most obnoxious to the King, arguing against smoking.

II, ii, 178. *Pushes :* pimples, or boils.

II, ii, 178-9. *His nose was like the ace of clubs.* Dilke thinks this may have suggested a similar comparison to Sterne, *Tristram Shandy*, III, 32 ; but it seems rather unlikely that Sterne knew this play, which in his time was only accessible in the old quartos.

II, ii, 184-5. *Being in drink :* probably a pun on the old phrase, ' drinking tobacco '. *His narrow passage* is the small nostrils of the weaver. It was the rule at that time to emit the smoke of a pipe through the nose ; cf. *Every Man out of his Humour*, IV, iii, where Sogliardo's nostrils are opened with a poking-stick ' to give the smoke a more free delivery '.

II, ii, 188. *A virginal jack.* A *virginal* was a kind of harpsichord ; the *jacks* were bits of wood inside the instrument which rose as the keys were pressed down.

II, ii, 191. *The Geneva print.* The reference is to the Genevan, or Breeches Bible of 1560, especially popular among the early Puritans.

II, ii, 191-2. *One ear shorter . . . for a difference.* The word *difference* is used here in the heraldic sense, a distinguishing mark upon a coat-of-arms. D'Olive insinuates that the weaver's loss of an ear at the hands of the hangman served to distinguish him from less zealous brethren.

II, ii, 214. *Sanctified :* by having a blessing pronounced over it.

II, ii, 227. *Noise :* a band of musicians. Cf. *The Blind Beggar*, sc. ii, l. 134, and *All Fools*, V, ii, 39. See also Text Notes, p. 794 below.

II, ii, 234. *Brake phlegm :* cleared my throat and blew my nose. *Shook mine ears :* cf. note on *May-Day*, I, i, 233.

II, ii, 238. *Amused :* puzzled, the etymological sense.

II, ii, 243. *The poet :* Virgil, see *Aeneid*, III, 39.

II, ii, 247. *True Trojans. Trojan* was a synonym for a boon companion, a good comrade. Cf. 1 *King Henry IV*, II, i, 77. The next words of the line, however, allude to the old belief, dating back to the middle of the seventh century, that the French were sprung from the old Trojans.

II, ii, 252. With D'Olive's eulogy of tobacco, cf. Falstaff's praise of sack, 2 *King Henry IV*, IV, iii, 92, *ssq.*

II, ii, 253. *Cannot want :* cannot be without.

II, ii, 273. *Johannes [Savonarola] :* Giovanni Michele Savonarola, 1384–1461, a grand-uncle of the famous monk of Florence, was himself a famous Italian doctor. His great work, *Practica Canonica de Febribus*, was no doubt known to Chapman, and an abbreviation used in one of its editions seems to have led to the mistake in the old text. See Text Notes, p. 794. below.

II, ii, 275. *Farts fire :* like the Devil in the old plays ; cf. *The Maid of Honour*, IV, iv.

II, ii, 280. *A sheep's head :* a fool. Cf. *All Fools*, II, i, 141.

II, ii, 293. *Murr . . . bone-ache.* The *murr* is a severe form of catarrh; the *bone-ache* is a venereal disease, for which tobacco was supposed to be a remedy. King James in his *Counterblast* asserts that tobacco ' was first found out by some of the barbarous Indians to be a preservative or anti-dote against the pox '.

II, ii, 297-8. ' You need not expect a written commission. The giving my hand to you to kiss will be a sufficient warrant '.

III, i. As pointed out in the *Introduction* to this play, p. 777 above, the first fifty lines of this scene are in the main an adaptation of Petrarch's *Secretum*, St. Anne taking the part of Petrarch in the dialogue, and Vandome that of St. Augustine.

III, i, 9-19. From the *Secretum : Fateor : et illud accidit quod omnibus ferme quibus angor aliquid falsi licet dulcoris immixtum est. In hac autem tristitia et aspera et misera et horrenda omnia ; apertaque semper ad desperationem via ; et quicquid infelices animas urget in interitum. Ad hoc et reliquarum passionum ut crebros sic breves et momentaneos experior insultus, Haec autem pestis tam tenaciter me arripit interdum ut integros dies noctesque*

illigatum torqueat, quod mihi tempus non lucis aut vitae sed tartareae noctis et acerbissimae mortis instar est.
Secretum, Basle edition, 1581, p. 347.

III, i, 20-35. From the *Secretum :* Saint Augustine is speaking : *Primum igitur, quod ait Cicero, nonulli veterem amorem novo amore tanquam clavum clavo excutiendum putant ; cui consilio et magister amoris Naso consentit, regulam afferens generalem :*

Quod, successore novo vincitur omnis amor.

Et procul dubio sic est : disgregatus enim et in multa distractus animus, segnior fertur ad singula. Sic Ganges (ut aiunt) a rege Persarum innumerabilibus alveis distinctus, atque ex uno alto metuendoque flumine in multos spernendosque rivulos sectus est. Sic sparsa acies penetrabilis hosti redditur : sic diffusum lentescit incendium. Denique omnis vis ut unita crescit sic dispersa minuitur.
Secretum, p. 358.

The reference to Cicero in the first lines of this passage is omitted by Chapman, who goes on at once to the quotation from Ovid, *Remedia Amoris*, l. 462.

III, i, 36-40. From the *Secretum*, Franciscus, i.e. Petrarch, is speaking : *Hoc igitur unum scito ' me aliud amare non posse. Assuevit animus illam adamare, assueverunt oculi illam intueri et quicquid non illa est inamoenum et tenebrosum dicunt.*
Secretum, p. 359.

III, i, 40-50. The first lines of this speech are original with Chapman and relate to the dramatic situation. With l. 44 the translation of the *Secretum* begins again. St. Augustine is talking : *Potesne igitur in animum inducere fugam exiliumve et notorum locorum caruisse conspectu ? . . . Quid ergo aliud dicam nisi Virgilianum versiculum paucis immutatis ?*

Heu fuge dilectas terras, fuge litus amatum.

Quomodo enim unquam his in locis tutus esse poteris, ubi tam multa vulnerum tuorum extant vestigia, ubi et presentium conspectu et preteritorum recordatione fatigaris ? Ut igitur idem ait Cicero, loci mutatione tanquam ægroti jam convalescentes curandus eris.
Secretum, p. 359.

The reference to Cicero is to the[1] *Tusculanae Disputationes*, IV, 35. The original of the *versiculum* adapted from Virgil is

Heu, fuge crudelis terras, fuge litus avarum.
Aeneid, III, 44.

A good but free translation of these passages may be found in W. H. Draper's version of the *Secretum*, 1911, on pp. 84, 138, and 139 respectively.

III, i, 72-4. Dilke refers to the *Colloquium Senile* of Erasmus in which the much married Polygamus declares that he never lived single above ten days, and that if his eighth wife died to-day he would marry a ninth to-morrow.

III, i, 78. *For a press :* for permission to impress followers.

III, i, 82-3. For a similar pun on *page* cf. *Sir Giles Goosecap*, II, i, 238-40.

III, i, 97. *Graceful :* used here in the sense of ' favourable ', cf. *Antony and Cleopatra*, II, ii, 60.

III, i, 120. *Dispair ;* see Text Notes, p. 795.

III, ii, 11. *Peagoose :* a fool, a ninny. The *New English Dicitonary* cites this passage.

III, ii, 17. *A tender place.* Dilke points out that there is a reference here to arrests for debt, usually made by tapping a man on the shoulder.

III, ii, 52. *Their income :* literally their entrance-fee, here a bribe to Mugeron to place them in D'Olive's service.

III, ii, 75. *A tub :* for the treatment of venereal disease, see note on *May-Day*, II, i, 611, and Warburton's note on *Timon of Athens*, IV, iii, 87.

III, ii, 82. *Frippery :* the selling of second-hand clothes ; cf. III, ii, 186, where it means the shop in which old clothes are sold.

---

[1] *Loci mutatione tanquam ægroti non convalescentes saepe curandus est.*

III, ii, 88. *Burn gold lace :* i.e. polish up the gold lace on old suits ; see the *New English Dictionary*, sub *burn* (v.) 2.

III, ii, 107. *Court cupboard :* a side-board, for the display of gold and silver plate ; cf. *Humourous Day's Mirth*, sc. viii, l. 2, and *Romeo and Juliet*, I, v, 8, with the note *ad loc.* in Furness's *Variorum*.

III, ii, 126. *A vice :* a vise, here in the sense of a cock, or tap.

III, ii, 131. *Helicon :* a mountain in Greece famous as the haunt of the Muses. The fountain Aganippe on Mount Helicon was believed to inspire him who drank of it. D'Olive proposes to tap this spring.

III, ii, 159. *A courser of Naples.* In the middle of the sixteenth century the most famous riding-school in the world was to be found at Naples. Hence *a courser of Naples* is a horse of the best school.

III, ii, 161. *By such a colour :* under the pretence of accompanying an ambassador.

III, ii, 167. *Whifflers :* the word means first a piper, then an usher or herald who cleared the way for his master. Cf. *The Widow's Tears*, II, iv, 104, where it is used to a gentleman usher, and Chapman's poem *To Master John Fletcher—Poems*, p. 255.

III, ii, 171. *Spurs :* the allusion is to the fashionable spurs of the day, for show rather than use, with large loose rowels which jingled as the wearer walked ; see Gifford's note on *Every Man out of his Humour*, II, i.

III, ii, 187. *A gambrel :* i.e. a cambrel, a piece of bent wood or iron used by butchers to hang carcases on. Brome in *The City Wit* (*Works*, vol. i, p. 335) uses *gambrel* as here in connexion with old clothes.

III, ii, 190. *Cases :* i.e. suits of clothes.

III, ii, 199. *Pikes :* cf. the note on *May-Day*, III, ii, 17. I have noted an earlier instance of the phrase in *Englishmen for my Money* (Hazlitt-Dodsley, vol. x, p. 533).

IV, i, 21. *Industrious :* designed, purposed. Cf. *The Revenge of Bussy*, II, ii, 104, and note *ad loc.*

IV, i, 48. *I am nearest to myself :* cf. *Heus, proxumus sum egomet mihi— Andria*, IV, i, 12.

IV, i, 98. *Our quick Hermes, our Alcides :* Hermes is here referred to as the god of persuasive eloquence ; *quick* is probably used in the sense of ' lively ', ' vigorous ' with reference to the speech of the god. *Alcides* is Hercules, and the reference, as the next line shows, is to the labours of that hero.

IV, ii, 6. *Begot i' th' Court :* cf. *The Widow's Tears*, V, iii, 330-31. A passage in Massinger throws light, if any is needed, upon this jest. A page remarks to an usher and a waiting-woman :

> *It may be you were both begot in Court,*
> *Though bred up in the City ; for your mothers,*
> *As I have heard, loved the lobby.*
>
> *Unnatural Combat*, III, ii.

IV, ii, 14. *The gourd, the fulham, and the stop-cater-trey :* various kinds of false dice. The *gourd* is defined by Grosart (Greene's *Works*, vol. x, p. 288) as a die ' scooped out on one side or more '. A *fulham* was a die loaded at one of the corners ; a high fulham would turn up 4, 5, or 6 ; a low fulham 1, 2, or 3. Hence the common term *high men* and *low men* for these dice, cf. *Merry Wives*, I, iii, 94–5. The name is said to be derived from Fulham, a London suburb, once a noted haunt of gamesters. See Gifford's note on the word in *Every Man out of his Humour*, III, i. A *stop-cater-trey* is a die loaded so as to stop at three or four. For further information on this topic see Malone's note on *The London Prodigal*, I, i, in *Supplement to Shakespeare*, vol. ii, p. 456. Dekker in the *Bellman of London* (Temple edition, p. 114) has a long list of the names of false dice among which he mentions *gourds*, *fulhams*, and *flat cater-treys*, perhaps the same as the *stop-cater-treys* of the text.

IV, ii, 25. *A Winchester goose* was a slang phrase for a venereal disease ; cf. 1 *King Henry VI*, I, iii, 53. The name came from the fact that the houses of ill-fame on the Bankside were licensed by the Bishop of Winchester, and the women inhabiting them were known as Winchester geese.

IV, ii, 26. *Petticoats.* William of Wykeham, the founder of the famous school at Winchester, ordered the scholars to be dressed in a gown of black cloth reaching to the feet.

IV, ii, 28. *Belfries :* that part of the floor of a church beneath the bell-tower. It was sometimes used as a school-room.

IV, ii, 29. *Proceed doctor :* the regular academic phrase for taking the degree of doctor in one of the faculties.

IV, ii, 44-5. *A setter and a verser :* a composer of music for songs, and a poet ; but Pacque puns on the cant meaning of these words. According to Greene's *Discourse of Cozening (Works*, vol. x, p. 15) ' the nature of the Setter is to draw any person familiarly to drink with him '. The *verser* was a second actor in the cony-catching scheme (see *ibid.*, p. 17). There is a further account of the tricks of the *setter* and *verser* in Dekker's *Bell-man of London* (Temple edition, p. 124) which is, however, based upon Greene.

IV, ii, 52-3. *Guarded coats . . . welted gowns :* the first were worn by serving-men, cf. *Merchant of Venice*, II, ii, 164 ; the second by lawyers, cf. *The Silent Woman*, IV, ii.

IV, ii, 54. *Horse you :* to *horse* a boy is to mount him on a man's back to be flogged, here simply ' to flog '.

IV, ii, 58. *Outrecuidance :* overweening insolence. The phrase *pride and outrecuidance* occurs in *Eastward Ho*, IV, ii, 279.

IV, ii, 78-80. In connexion with the purchase of knighthood under James I, Stoll (*Modern Language Notes*, vol. xx, p. 207) calls attention to two entries in the *Calendar of Domestic State Papers*, 1603-10 (pp. 60 and 110). The first of these is a petition from a certain William Bruce that he may have the profits of making four knights ; the second the signification of the King's pleasure that all persons having received knighthood should pay the accustomed fees. There was, of course, nothing new in requiring the payment of certain fees in connexion with the bestowing of knighthood ; but in the first years of James's reign knighthoods were so lavishly be-stowed and the fees so eagerly pocketed either by the King or some favoured courtier, that the notion arose that the title could be purchased by the payment of the customary fee. Cf. in this connexion *Eastward Ho*, IV, i, 179-83.

IV, ii, 96. *Achilles.* The reference is to the concealment of Achilles among the maidens at Scyros, where he was discovered by Ulysses ; see Statius, *Achilleid*, I, 242, ssq.

IV, ii, 103. *Bear a breadth :* the phrase occurs again in *The Widow's Tears*, V, iii, 334. Apparently it means here ' carry affairs of importance '. For a proposed emendation see Text Notes, p. 795.

IV, ii, 110. *The Seven Stars :* the constellation of the Great Bear.

IV, ii, 111-13. *Boulogne* was besieged and taken by Henry VIII in 1544. *St. James his field :* I suppose the reference is to the battle of St. Jacob on the Birs, where the French defeated the Swiss in 1444. *The loss of Calais* refers to the seizure of this town by the Duke of Guise in 1558 after it had been in English hands for over two centuries. *Cales*, or Cadiz, was sacked by Essex and Howard in 1596.

IV, ii, 121. St. Luke's day is October 18. The symbol of St. Luke, the horned ox, no doubt led to a comic association between St. Luke and cuckolds. See *Eastward Ho*, IV, i, 5 and note *ad loc.*

IV, ii, 137-140. A parody of Spenser's lament :

> *Dido, my dear, alas is dead,*
> *Dead and lyeth wrapt in lead :*
> *O heavie hearse,*
> *Let streaming teares be poured out in store :*
> *O carefull verse.*
> *Shepherds Kalendar—November,* ll. 58-62.

IV, ii, 153-55. *A hammer . . . a gudgeon :* cf. notes on *The Gentleman Usher*, I, i, 152, and *All Fools*, III, i, 94, for the significance of these names.

IV, ii, 156. *A Christmas Lord :* a Lord of Misrule, one chosen to lead the revels at Christmas.

IV, ii, 169. *Shift and hang :* note the pun in the double meaning of these words as applied first to the suits of clothes, then to the wearers.

IV, ii, 170. *Strike the Plaudite.* The comedies of Terence all conclude with the word *plaudite*, which came therefore in connexion with the drama to have the sense of ' Conclusion '. It is unfortunate that Chapman did not act upon this idea. The further trick played upon Monsieur D'Olive quite lacks the dash and comic force of the scenes connected with his embassy

IV, ii, 176. *Bough-pots :* vases for holding green branches, an old ornament of rooms ; see Pepys' *Diary*, September 13, 1665.

IV, ii, 180. *Retire :* used here in the sense of ' recall ' ; cf. :

> *All these retired not Hector,*
> Chapman's Iliad, XXII, 68

where it translates the Greek θυμὸν ἔπειθεν.

IV, ii, 251. *Vie it :* to ' vie ' is to ' heighten a wager ', ' raise a bet ' ; see the passage in Greene's *Discovery of Cony-Catching*, quoted above, p. 790, and my note on *Byron's Tragedy*, IV, ii, 107.

IV, ii, 258-9. Dilke notes that Jonson ridicules these affected subscriptions of letters in *Every Man out of his Humour*, III, ii, in the comments of Sordido upon his son's epistle.

V, i, 7. *Imaginous :* imaginative, full of fancies, cf. *Byron's Conspiracy*, III, i, 52.

V, i, 14. *Juno Lucina fer opem :* the prayer of a woman in travail, *Andria*, III, i, 15.

V, i, 24-5. *Women and parrots, etc. :* cf. Petruchio's method of dealing with Katharine, *Taming of the Shrew*, IV, i. See also *Othello*, III, iii, 23, and the note *ad loc.* in Furness's *Variorum*.

V, i, 33. *Dildo :* an old word, often with an obscene meaning, occurring in the refrain of ballads ; see *Alchemist*, V, v, 42, and *Winter's Tale*, IV, iv, 195. According to the *New English Dictionary* it was sometimes used contemptuously for a boy.

V, i, 42. *Watery meteors :* atmospheric phenomena were formerly classed as airy, watery, luminous, or fiery meteors. Watery meteors were rain, snow, etc. Here the allusion is to a bucket of water thrown from the window.

V, i, 50. *Hempstring :* like ' crackhemp ', ' crackhalter ', one who deserves to be hanged.

V, i, 59. *Unready :* undressed for the night.

V, i, 74. *At gaze :* a term of venery used of the deer when standing bewildered.

V, i, 95. *O' th' hair :* of his sort or kind ; cf. for this sense of the word 1 *King Henry IV*, IV, i, 61, and *Nice Valour*, I, i.

V, i, 161. See Text Notes, p. 796.

V, i, 175. See note on *May-Day*, III, i, 249.

V, i, 187. *Break betwixt :* act as a go-between. There is an offensive insinuation in the phrase (cf. *May-Day*, II, i, 245, and *broker*, i.e. pandar in *Troilus*, III, ii, 211) which Eurione at once fastens upon.

V, i, 191. *Petrarch :* cf. *All Fools*, II, i, 282-4.

V, i, 193. *Can your good :* know your business, know what is profitable for you. Dilke's note shows, I think, a misunderstanding of the passage.

V, i, 210. *A dry hand :* the sign of a cold, prudish disposition ; cf. the note on *Othello*, III, iv, 36 in Furness's *Variorum*.

V, i, 211. *Toward a husband :* about to marry.

V, i, 243. *Cut off the offending part :* cf. *Humourous Day's Mirth*, sc. xiii, ll. 85-6, and sc. xiv, ll. 52-3. The dialogue between Vandome and Eurione in the present scene seems to me like an elaboration, and a great improvement, of that between Lemot and the Queen in *Humourous Day's Mirth*, sc. xiii.

V, i, 250. *Set the house :* mark, point out the house, like a setter dog ; cf. 1 *King Henry IV*, II, ii, 53.

V, i, 261. *Hopeful spleen :* cf. *panegyric spleen, All Fools, Prologue,* l. 24, and note *ad loc.*

V, ii, 5. *Tressels.* Roderigue compares D'Olive's legs to the props of a puppet-show (*motion,* cf. *May-Day,* III, iii, 149). The comparison of legs protruding beneath a cloak to *tressels* occurs also in *The Alchemist,* IV, iii, 25 ; see also *The Widow's Tears,* V, iii, 332.

V, ii, 30-33. The situation, perhaps somewhat obscure to the reader, would be clear upon the stage. The Duke turns from Roderigue and Mugeron to Vandome, who has been whispering to Marcellina and her sister, and asks who is with him. The ladies were very likely wearing masks. Vandome does not reply at once, but turns to the ladies and calling them forward introduces them to the Duke.

V, ii, 64. *Could Achilles :* Roderigue refers to D'Olive's words, IV, ii, 96–7. Roderigue, to be sure, was not on the stage when D'Olive uttered them, but such a fact never troubled an Elizabethan dramatist.

V, ii, 70-1. *Habit . . . heart :* Mugeron pretends that D'Olive's disguise shows him to be a conspirator.

V, ii, 72-3. *Block . . . wits on :* cf. IV, ii, 158. The same phrase occurs in *Blurt Master Constable,* I, ii, 45–6.

V, ii, 76. *Earwigs :* parasites, flatterers ; cf. *The Broken Heart,* II, i, 13.

V, ii, 85-9. This jest seems to have been a current one. It occurs also in Bacon's *Apophthegms,* No. 28.

V, ii, 113. *Kibes :* ulcerated chilblains, especially on the heel ; cf. *Hamlet,* V, i, 153.

TEXT NOTES

Monsieur D'Olive was first printed, in quarto form, by T. C. [Thomas Creede] for William Holmes in 1606. Two copies of this quarto are found in the British Museum, two in the Dyce collection, and three, one of which (40, T. 39. Art.) is imperfect, at the Bodleian. It was printed as the elaborate stage-directions show from a stage copy, possibly a corrected copy of Chapman's manuscript, as indicated by such Latin directions as *Redit cum lumine* and *Stringit ensem* in V, i, 35 and 237. I have noted only one variation of any importance, III, i, 76, between the copies that I have examined. I refer therefore by Q. to a consensus of the quartos.

The play was next reprinted in *Old English Plays,* vol. iii, 1814, edited by C. W. Dilke. This edition deals somewhat arbitrarily with the text, but it often makes necessary corrections. I refer to it by the letter D.

It next appeared in *The Comedies and Tragedies of George Chapman* (Pearson, London, 1873, vol. i). This professed reprint silently corrects some blunders of Q., but introduces several misprints of its own. I have attempted to record all of these in the following notes where I refer to this edition as P.

The next and up to the present the latest edition is that of Shepherd, *Works of Chapman—Plays,* 1874. Like D. this presents a modernized edition, based mainly upon P. but making use also of D. I refer to it as before by S.

Dramatis Personae. Q. prints at the close of the play an imperfect list under the heading *Actors* as follows :

Monsieur D'Olive.	Gueaquin the Dutchess.
Philip the Duke.	Hieronime Ladie.
S. Anne Count.	Marcellina Countesse.
Vaumont Count.	Eurione her sister.
Vandome.	
Rhodoricke.	
Mugeron.	
Pacque } two pages.	
Dicque	

The list in the text is founded with a few slight changes on that of D.

The quarto is divided into acts only. *Scaena Prima* is prefixed to the head of each act, but there is never a *Scaena Secunda.* I have introduced scene divisions and added notes of locality where a change of scene seemed necessary.

I, i, 6. *Most.* D. states that this word is omitted in Q. It is found, however, in the Bodleian and British Museum copies.

14. Q. *abject*; D. corrects.

15. D. says Q. reads *in that*, but the copies I have seen all have *to that*. D. himself, probably by a slip, prints
Were worthy to employ us that likeness.

144. Q. omits *in*; D. supplies it.

175. D. omits *the*, probably to obtain a more exactly regular line. He has elsewhere altered the text for this reason, and I shall not hereafter notice such changes.

191. Q. *in*; P. misprints *iu*.

262. Q. *parcell*; D. *parcels*, probably because D'Olive is addressing two men. The change seems unnecessary.

279. Q. prints *Rho* as the name of the speaker; P. misprints *Rno*.

282. Q. *Good soothe*; D. *Good in sooth*; but the change is not needed if a comma is placed after *Good*.

292. Q. *doest*; D. *dos't*; S. *doest*; but it is plainly equivalent to *does't*.

293-4. Q. misprints *counttey*; D. corrects *country*.

311. Q. *for your stars*; D. alters *to your stars*; but the change is unnecessary, as *for* is equivalent to ' in respect of '.

329. Q. misprints *my turne*; D. corrects *by turn*.

375. Q. *it kind*; D. needlessly alters the old possessive to *its*.

408. Q. *mugrill*, which S. retains; but as D. noted it is a mere slip for *mungrill* (D. *mongrel*), the printer having failed to notice the dash over the *u* in mu͡grill in the MS.

II, i, 18. D. adds the stage-direction in this line.

23. Q. *but such a man as this was ever seen*; S. follows Q. D. alters to *was such a man, etc.* I think the true reading is *never* for *ever*, an emendation approved by Mr. Daniel.

50. Q. has no stage-direction after *Vand.* in this line; D. prints *Vandome heard within* before the line. Q. prints *an-other within* in the centre of the page above l. 50 , D. omits it and gives *Serv.* as the speaker's name for the last half of this line.

52. Q. prints *Sic.* as the speaker's name before *Whers my Lady ?*; D *Ser.* for *Servant.* So also in l. 53.

53-55. Q. prints the Servant's speech as prose ; D. follows Q. ; but it is plainly verse.

58. Q. prints 2 *Lec.* as the speaker's name ; D. emends 2 *Serv.*

61. Q. has *Sig.* as the speaker's name ; D. 1 *Serv.*; but it is evidently that the speaker is the Second Servant of l. 58.

63. Q. *night-walker'* ; D. emends *night-walker's.*

63-4. Q. prints as prose ; D. follows Q. ; but it is plainly verse.

66-7. Q. prints Eurione's speech as one line.

67-9. Q. prints as prose ; D. follows Q. ; but it is plainly verse.

71. Q. prints the stage-direction *Within* twice over. I insert *Voices.*

78. D. adds a stage-direction, *Lays his sword at her feet*, to this line.

89. Q. prints *Exit Mard:* in the margin after *word*, and *Exit Marc.* in the margin after *women*. It is plain that we have here a misprint and its correction in the original proof both embodied in the text. The Q. has made a sad botch of the stage-directions and speakers' names in this passage.

115-16. In the original l. 115 stands at the top of page C3 and the speaker's name does not appear, so that these lines seem to belong to the speech of Eurione. D. corrects by inserting *Vand.* as the speaker's name.

146. Q. *travaile*; D. emends *traveller.* Cf. l. 182, where Q. has *travailer.*

155. Q. *cast*; D. *casts*, a needless change.

205-7. On the ground that St. Anne's love ' was productive of *most irrational effects* ' D. alters *On* in l. 207 to *To* and puts the phrase *be it ne'er so grounded* in parenthesis. This quite changes the sense of the passage and seems to me an unwarrantable tampering with the text.

II, ii. Q. Enter *Philip.* I have inserted *Duke* and print *Duke* as the speaker's name throughout the play. Q. varies between *Phil.* and *Duke.*

II, ii, 10. Q. *wizzard.* Brereton (*Modern Language Review*, vol. iii, No. 1) suggests *buzzard*, ' a fellow blinded by his folly,' and cites in support *May-Day*, II, i, 398-400. This ingenious emendation was approved by Mr. Daniel, and may be right, but I have preferred to keep *wizard*, understanding it in a contemptuous sense.

20. Q. *sayes he ;* D. *he says,* a needless change.

26. Q. *this ;* D. *there,* a needless change.

38-40. Q. prints the speeches of the Duke and Mugeron each as one line.

61. Q. *spnrnd ;* P. silently corrects *spurnd.*

65. Q. *ere this ;* P. misprints *tere his.*

79. Q. *konow ;* D. *know.*

86. Q. *Giris ;* D. emends *Gyges'.*

100. Q. *Forty of fiftie ;* P. silently corrects *or fiftie.*

102. P. inserts *to* before *a higher,* and is followed by S. No Q. that I have seen has *to* in this line.

119. Q. *right ;* D. *rite,* which may be correct, but I have preferred to follow Q. The lady had a *right* to burial.

151. Q. prints as two short lines, assigning both to *Dol.* D. corrects.

162-3. Q. prints the Duke's speech as one line.

180-186. Q. prints the last lines of D'Olive's speech as prose. D. arranges as verse. In l. 184 D. transfers *stopp'd* to the following line after *passage,* and prints *as't* for Q. *as it.*

187. Q. *bricfely ;* P. silently corrects.

206. Q. *From ;* P. misprints *Erom.*

225. Q. *Or ;* D. emends *Our.*

227. Q. *noise ;* D. *nose.* This is a plausible emendation, for the reference is certainly to the nose,

but I think it not impossible that the weaver's nose may be here called a *noise,* or band of music. I prefer therefore to let the old reading stand.

243. P. *Poets sayes ;* but all quartos consulted have *Poet says.*

273. Q. *Johannes* (2 copies at the Bodleian *Jehannes*) *de savo et savo et.* P. points out in a note (vol. i, p. 342) that the reference is to a work, *Practica canonica,* by Johannes Savonarola. The contraction *Cano. Savo.* which appears at the foot of each folio of this work probably gave rise to Chapman's curious phrase, *de savo* (Qy. *cano ?*) *et savo.* The second *et* is probably a printer's error. I have ventured to place the true name in the text.

296. Q. abbreviates *Lord* to *Lo :* a contraction very common in Elizabethan printing.

299. Q. *Anbassador ;* D. corrects.

300. Q. *Present ;* P. misprints *Pesant.*

302. D. inserts a stage-direction, *Offers to salute her,* after this line.

III, i, 10. Q. includes only the words *and rotting sweetness* in parenthesis. This is palpably wrong. I have followed the arrangement of D.

39-40. Q. prints *Will tell* to *hatefull* as one line.

45. Q. *where ;* P. misprints *were.*

48-9. Deighton (*Old Dramatists,* p. 129) suggests ' *lips* for *steps* and perhaps *gape* for *gaspe'.* The discovery of the source of this passage in Petrarch's *Secretum* confirms the old reading, for the Latin has *multa vulnerum tuorum extant vestigia.*

50. D. adds the stage-direction, *They retire.*

55. Q. misprints *Gur* (for *Gue*) as the name of the speaker ; so also in l. 63.

76. There is a discrepancy between the copies of Q. here. Of five that I have consulted in the British Museum and the Bodleian, four read *thread,* which I have therefore adopted. One (Bodleian, 40 T. 39. Art.) has *throat,* which is followed by D. although in a note he says " It would be better to read *thread* "

In a parallel passage, *Widow's Tears*, II, i, 24–5, all the Qq. read *throat*, which might be taken as suggesting that this word is the true reading ; but I have preferred to retain the reading of the majority of copies consulted.

119-20. D. reads *wife* for *life* and *dispense* for *dispaire* in these lines. S. retains *life*, but reads *despair* which, I think, makes nonsense of the passage. Brereton (*loc. cit.*) points out that *dispair* means 'dissociate', a sense which fits the context perfectly and allows us to retain the old reading.

III, ii, 2-8. Q. prints these lines as verse, ending *upon you, hart, follow you, state, be, all I*. They are evidently prose and were so printed by D.

15. Q. *Scholares* ; D. *scholar*.

58. Q. *Your Lor. Steward ? ;* D. *your lordship's steward !* It seems to me plain that Mugeron is swearing at D'Olive, *a pox on your lordship !* and then repeating angrily the title which D'Olive had given him *Steward*, as if to say, Do you call me a *steward* ?

63. Q. *berayes ;* D. *betrays*. I think the true reading is *bewrays*, a word constantly confounded in spelling with *beray*.

83. Q. misprints *Prokery*. As the correct spelling *Broker* appears below in l. 94, I have not indicated in the text the correction, first made by D., *brokery*.

101. D. inserts the aside in this line.

101-2. Q. prints as two lines of verse ending *praier, bedd ;* D. follows Q. ; but it is evidently prose.

111-2. Q. prints as two lines of verse, ending *witts ?, drawne*. D. follows Q. ; but it is evidently prose.

115. Some copies of Q. misprint *Gourtly ;* Mal. 240 at the Bodleian and C. 12 g. 4 at the British Museum have *Courtly*.

148. Q. *Me ;* D. emends *We*. Q. places *Exeunt* after l. 146, and *Manet D'Olive* after l. 147.

IV, i, 33. Q. *any ;* D. emends *my*.

40. D. inserts *aside*.

62. Q. *deserns ;* S. *discerns ;* but I prefer the emendation of D. *deserves*.

86-7. Q. places *Exit S. Anne* after l. 86, and *Enter Vaumont* after *comes* in l. 87.

91-2. D. alters the reading of Q., preserved in the text, to make the lines read :

> has been held
> With all solemnity ; now must
> his nuptials

on the ground that Vandome has already (IV, i, 1–3) 'informed us that the exequies of his sister *had been* performed' and therefore 'either the poet forgot himself or the text was corrupt'. The former is much the more likely ; inconsistencies of this sort abound in Elizabethan drama, and it is not permissible for an editor to tamper with the text in order to obliterate them.

99. Q. *lobour ;* D. emends *labour*.

101. Q. *Braines-bould ;* D. emends *brain's bold*.

IV, ii, 14. Q. *goade ;* D. *goad*. The *New English Dictionary* gives this as a doubtful variant of *gourd*. I have preferred to use the more familiar form.

25. Q. sets only the words *I mean* in parenthesis. I follow D.'s arrangement.

90. Q. *now ;* P. misprints *how*.

103. Q. *beare a breadth*. Deighton (*loc. cit.*) proposes *bear a brain*, a common enough phrase, cf. *All Fools*, IV, i, 204, but one that hardly seems to suit the context. Mr. Daniel suggests as a possible reading *bear a wreath*, but this seems to me hardly admissible.

136. D. prints *you* and *buried* for Q. *your* and *beraid ;* the first of these, *you*, is probably a mere misprint ; but the change of *beraid (berayed)* to *buried* is quite unwarranted.

139. P. misprints *Diq.* for Q. *Pac.* as the speaker's name.

147. D. adds *and a Page* to the stage-direction to account for the presence of a page in l. 188. In l. 169 D. reads *Exit D'Olive with his two Pages* for the Q. *Exit cum suis.*

180. For Q. *retire* D. reads *re-trieve* probably grounding the change on the Q. *retrive* in l. 185 ; but *retire*, i.e. ' bring back ', makes quite good sense.

231. Q. *with with modestie.* Very possibly the second *with* is a misprint, but I have retained it, and followed D. in introducing a dash.

V, i, 54. There is no stage-direction in Q. D. prints *Euryone (Within)*; but it seems plain that she appears at this point upon the balcony. The same may be said of the stage-direction after l. 64 below.

76. Q. *bother ;* D. emends *brother.*

80. There is no stage-direction after this line in Q. That in the text is based, with a slight alteration, on D.

129-33. Q. prints the passage from *but my* to *hour* as prose. I follow D.'s arrangement as verse.

161. Q. *An't onward ;* D. *on't onward,* i.e. ' give us a specimen of it as we proceed ' ; but sug-gests as a preferable reading *on't!* *one word.* The proposed change does not seem advisable to me ; I take *onward* as an ejaculation equivalent to ' go on '.

170. D. inserts the *aside.*

210-11. D. places the words from *which* to *were* in parenthesis, but suggests that a part of the speech has been transposed, and that we should set *as he said you were* after *shrew.* The proposal is ingenious, but I do not think the change is necessary.

213. D. inserts the *aside.*

243. Q. gives *Pag.*; as the name of the speaker ; D. *Page.* I have preferred to print *Dic.* who may be still upon the balcony, see l. 50 above, or more likely has followed Marcellina and Eurione down to the main stage. Possibly his entrance should be indicated after l. 80.

V, ii, 43. Q. sets the stage-direction *To S. An.* in the margin after ll. 43-4.

THE WIDOW'S TEARS

INTRODUCTION

The Widow's Tears, probably the last of Chapman's comedies, was published [1] in 1612 with the following title-page:

The Widdowes Tears   A Comedie.   As it was often presented in the blacke and white Friers.   Written by Geor. Chap.   London, Printed for John Browne, and are to be sold at his shop in Fleet-street in St. Dunstanes Church-yard.   1612.

As the title-page shows it was acted at two theatres.   This does not imply, however, that it was acted by two different companies.   The Children of Her Majesties Revels, for whom Chapman wrote most of his plays, no doubt performed it at Blackfriars some time before they quitted that house toward the close of 1609, and again at Whitefriars, where they occupied ' a messuage or mansion house, being a parcel of the late dissolved monastery called White Friars '.   The company at this house is sometimes spoken of as the Second Company of the Queen's Revels, but it was essentially the same as the former company.   Nat. Field, whom Chapman called ' his loved son ' (*Poems*, p. 176) was the leading actor.   The *Revenge of Bussy* was written for this company at Whitefriars, *Bussy* was, I think, revised [2] for them, and they revived his comedy *The Widow's Tears*.   It seems a little strange that this should be the only one of Chapman's comedies that the company, so far as we know, thought worthy of a performance in their new theatre, but the play has always had a certain popularity, as is shown by Chapman's words in the Dedication—*of many desired to see printed*—by a performance at Court [3] on February 20, 1613, after the publication, and by its inclusion in the first great collection of Elizabethan plays, the Dodsley of 1744.

The exact date of the composition of *The Widow's Tears* is uncertain. Wallace (*Children of the Chapel*, p. 106) fixes it before September 18, 1602.   The evidence on which he relies is an entry in the journal of Philip Julius, [4] Duke of Stettin.   This journal, kept by his attendant

---

[1] It had been entered in the Stationers' Registers on April 17, 1612, along with *The Revenge of Bussy*, by Browne, the publisher in 1611 of *May-Day*. Browne subsequently transferred his rights in the tragedy to John Helme, who published *The Revenge of Bussy* in 1613.

[2] See my edition of Chapman's *Tragedies*, p. 541.

[3] See the accounts of Lord Harrington, Treasurer of the Chamber to James I; published in Shakespeare Society *Papers* (1845), vol. ii, p. 126.

[4] Philip Julius was at this time making an extended tour in England and other countries.   That part of his journal relating to England has been published in the *Transactions of the Royal Historical Society, New Series*, vol. vi. The passage in question appears on pp. 26–7.

tutor, Frederick Gerschow, later Professor of Law at Greifswald, contains under the date of September 18, 1602, an account of a visit to a performance by boy-actors—evidently at Blackfriars, since there is mention of the Queen's support of the company—where they saw a comedy, ' welche im Argument judiciret eine castam viduam, war eine historia einer königlichen Wittwe aus Engellandt'. Wallace assumes without hesitation that this comedy is to be identified with *The Widow's Tears*. I am, however, unable to see any grounds for this conclusion. It is only ironically that this play can be said to treat of a chaste widow—and the journal is notably matter of fact—and neither Eudora nor Cynthia can be described as a ' royal widow of England'. It is to me incredible that a scholar like Gerschow should not have recognized in Chapman's play, if it was this which he saw, the well-known story of the Ephesian matron, or that having recognized it he should have described [1] it in such misleading terms. Wallace's further arguments that Chapman's play, ' in the overcoming of feminine scruples is mindatory [sic] of *The Taming of the Shrew*', which he dates with some hesitation about 1602, and that the last act contains a satire on the injustice of a recent decision of the Star Chamber against Evans, the manager of the Chapel Children, seem to me to carry little or no weight. It is very doubtful whether Shakespeare's play should be dated so late as 1602, and I, personally, fail to see the slightest resemblance between the rollicking farce of Shakespeare and the satiric comedy of Chapman. As for the satire on ' one-sided justice',' in the last act, it seems to me rather to embody Chapman's personal resentment [2] for his imprisonment in the case of *Eastward Ho* than any dissatisfaction with a Star Chamber decision.

Apart from Wallace there is a fairly general consensus [3] of opinion that this play belongs to the year 1605 or thereabouts. There is no positive evidence for this date, but it fits in well with the general chronology of Chapman's plays so far as this has been fixed, and the general tone and technic of the play seem to me to indicate a late period in his career as a writer of comedies. If it follows *Eastward Ho*, as I believe, it must have been written some time after his release from prison, in May or June, 1605, and performed certainly before the closing of the theatres on account of the plague, July, 1608, presumably before the performance of the Byron plays at Blackfriars in the spring of that year. The approximate date of the autumn of 1605 or the spring of 1606 seems to me the most satisfactory.

The source of the main plot of *The Widow's Tears* is the story of the Ephesian matron as told by Petronius, *Satyricon*, 111, ssq. I append

---

[1] The description would apply better, I think, to *Sir Giles Goosecap*, in which the leading lady, Eugenia, is a chaste widow and of noble English birth, although strictly speaking the epithet *Königlich* could not be applied to her. It is possible that a study of the repertoire of the Chapel Children in 1602 might enable us to identify the play that Gerschow saw, but it seems plain that it has no connexion with *The Widow's Tears*.

[2] Cf. Jonson's words: *I am . . . unexamined and unheard committed to a most vile prison* in the letter to Salisbury, referred to above, p. 774, n.

[3] Fleay (*Biographical Chronicle*, vol. i, p. 61) dates it *c.* 1605 after Chapman's imprisonment; Stoll (*Modern Language Notes*, vol. xxii, p. 208) about the same time as *Monsieur D'Olive*, i.e. after the accession of James in 1603 and before the imprisonment of 1605; Schelling (*Elizabethan Drama*, vol. i, p. 462, *c.* 1605).

a version of the tale in eighteenth century English from the *Works of Petronius*, translated by Mr. Addison, 1736.

There was a lady at Ephesus, in such high repute for her chastity, that even the women of the neighbouring countries came out of curiosity to see her. When her husband was carry'd to the grave, she was not content with the vulgar form of following the funeral with dishevell'd hair, and beating her bosom thro' a crowd of spectators, but would attend him into the sepulchre itself ; where, according to the custom of the Greeks, she watch'd the corps and embalm'd it night and day with her tears. Nay, so violent was her grief, that she determin'd to destroy herself by hunger, neither could her nearest relations or friends prevail with her to desist from so fatal a resolution ; the magistrates themselves were the last repuls'd in the attempt ; and she was deplor'd by all as the most illustrious example of her sex, having now mourn'd five days without receiving any nourishment.

A faithful servant waited upon her sorrow, who mingled her tears with those of her mistress, and as oft as occasion requir'd, renew'd a lamp which burnt in the monument. Nothing else was talk'd off throughout the whole city, and all ranks of men confess'd there never was such a shining instance of chastity and affection.

It happen'd at this very time that the Governor of the province order'd certain robbers to be affix'd to crosses near the dismal cave where this virtuous lady bewail'd herself over her late-interr'd husband. The following night, the centinel who watch'd the crosses, lest the bodies should be stolen for burial, perceiving a light glimmering amongst the monuments, and hearing the groans of a person in distress, was led by a curiosity common to mankind, to see who, or what it might be. He descended therefore into the sepulchre, where seeing a very beautiful woman, he stood amaz'd at first, as at the sight of a spectre ; but viewing the corps which lay before her, and considering her tears and torn visage, he soon concluded, as it really was, that the lady could but ill support the loss of the deceas'd. Upon this he went back, and fetch'd his small supper into the monument, and began to exhort her to desist from her superfluous sorrow ; that to heave her lovely bosom with sighs would avail nothing ; that death was a necessary exit ; and that the grave was a home for all ; omitting no argument of use to cure a distemper'd mind. But she, starting with horror at so unlook'd-for a consolation began to beat her breast with double vehemence, and tearing off her hair, strow'd it upon the dead body.

The soldier is not at all discourag'd by this, but with the same exhortations endeavours to persuade her to take some nourishment ; till the maid, who was undoubtedly overcome by the grateful odour of the wine, reach'd out her hand to her obliging benefactor ; and having recruited her spirits by what she eat and drank, began herself to combat the obstinacy of her mistress. And what will it avail you, said she, to starve yourself in this manner, to bury yourself alive, and resign your breath before Heaven requires it ?

Think you the happy in the Shades below,
Or see your tears, or listen to your woe?

Will you revive your dead husband in spite of Fate ? Or won't you rather dismiss this female weakness, and enjoy the world whilst you may ? The very body that lies before you, might advise you to make a better use of your life.

None listen with regret when press'd to eat or live. The lady exhausted by so many days abstinence, suffer'd her obstinacy to be vanquish'd, and eat with the same greediness as her maid who had yielded before. You know what temptations usually follow a hearty meal ; the very same arguments the soldier had used to combat her despair, he now employ'd against her chastity ; and as the young fellow appear'd neither disagreeable, nor destitute of wit, the maid was not wanting on her part to do him all the good offices she could; saying to her mistress:

> Why thus unmindful of your past delight,
> Against a pleasing passion will you fight ?

But why should I keep you in suspense ? The lady observ'd the same abstinence, even as to this part of her body ; and the victorious soldier triumphed over both. Thus they continu'd together, not only the first night of their enjoyment, but the next day also, and the next after that: the doors of the monument being carefully shut, that whoever, whether friend or stranger, had come there, they would undoubtedly have imagin'd, this most virtuous of wives had expir'd on the body of her husband. Our soldier was so charm'd with his mistress's beauty, and the secret of his happiness, that what little stock he had he laid out for her entertainment, and as soon as night came on, convey'd it into the monument.

In the mean time, the relations of one of the malefactors, observing the remissness of the guard, carry'd off the body in the night, and bury'd it. The poor soldier, who was wrap'd up in his private pleasures when this trick was play'd him, finding on the morrow one of the crosses without a body, immediately repaired to his mistress in the greatest apprehensions of punishment, and acquainting her with what had happen'd, added that he was fully resolv'd not to wait his condemnation, but with his own sword to execute justice on his negligence ; that the only favour be begg'd of her was, to afford him a burial, and to make that fatal place at once the monument of a lover, and a husband.

At this our matron, as compassionate as chaste ; the gods forbid ! cry'd she, that I should at the same time, behold the funerals of two persons who are so dear to me. I had rather hang the deceas'd, than occasion the death of the living ; and accordingly ordered the corpse of her husband to be taken out of its coffin and fasten'd to the cross whence the body was stolen. The soldier immediately put in execution the advice of this discreet lady ; and next morning every one wonder'd, how a dead man should be able to find his way to the cross.

Certain resemblances in detail, especially in the second scene of act four are so close as to show that Chapman drew the story at first hand from Petronius. It does not follow, however, that he was unacquainted with some other version of the tale, and other versions are numerous. Langbaine (*An Account of the English Dramatic Poets*, 1691) names several of them, one in Latin verse by Romulus, one in ' French rhime by Hebertus',[1] a story in the *Ludus Septem Sapientium*, and another in the *Cento Novelle Antiche* (no. 59) by Gualteruzzi. A very full account of the origin, development and variants of the tale is given by Grisebach, *Die treulose Wittwe—eine Chinesische Novelle und ihre Wanderung in der Welt-litteratur*—Stuttgart, 1877. Grisebach makes it plain, not only that the story is far older than Petronius, but that originally it possessed certain distinct features which are wanting in the Latin version, and, apparently, in all succeeding forms except Chapman's. The essential difference is that in the oldest form it is the husband himself who tries the virtue of his supposed widow.

It is curious that Chapman, who certainly used Petronius, should have reverted to this form. Two explanations seem to me possible : either Chapman used[2] in addition some version which differed in this point from Petronius and approached the original, or else he swung back unconsciously to the old form in his attempt to work up the anecdote of Petronius, for it is little more, into a comic drama. Clearly there is nothing of the comic spirit in the story of Petronius. One of the original auditors expresses the natural[3] feeling of most succeeding readers when he declares that the widow should have been crucified beside her husband's body—hardly a comic solution. But if one should alter the story, make the husband himself the tempter in disguise, and allow the wife to discover his identity too late, a situation would arise of real comic value. The alteration seems so natural from the playwright's point of view that I think we may easily believe it to be Chapman's own.

Moreover if the incident so altered is to be cast into dramatic form, it is plain that a considerable amount of action must take place before the supposed death of the husband. The matron must be introduced protesting her abhorrence of widows' marriages, an occasion for these protestations must be given, and the husband's resolve to try her sincerity must be adequately motivated. So, at least, I conceive Chapman to have envisaged the problem that confronted him, and up to a certain point his handling of the theme shows a clear perception of its demands and a skilful treatment of its difficulties. He introduces the most natural cause imaginable for the matron's protestations, the somewhat scandalous marriage of a widow of her acquaintance ; he assigns the

---

[1] An error. The rhymed *Dolopathos* of Herbers (Herbertus) does not contain this story, but it is found in the French prose romance, *Les Sept Sages*. A long list of the versions, ancient and modern, of the story appears in Regnier's edition of La Fontaine, vol. VI, p. 63.

[2] Schoell holds that this explanation is the more likely, and that the shift of the scene from Ephesus to Cyprus also points to another source. But Chapman would not have hesitated at such an alteration. He shifts the scene of *May-Day*, for example, for no apparent reason except, perhaps, that Venice was more familiar to an English audience than the original Pisa. I would suggest that Ephesus was best known to the Elizabethans as the sacred city of Diana, a most inappropriate divinity for Chapman's theme, whereas Cyprus was closely associated with Venus, *our Cyprian goddess* (II, ii, 56).

[3] It is interesting to note an alteration of the Petronian version in the *novella* of Gualteruzzi which gives expression to this feeling. Here the cavalier who corresponds to the soldier of Petronius is so shocked by the widow's treatment of her husband's corpse—she knocks out a tooth to heighten its resemblance to the stolen body—that he reproves and leaves her in great disgrace. In the English version, in the *History of the Seven Wise Masters*, he cuts off her head.

most powerful motive for the husband's action, jealousy, not of an
actual, but of any possible rival; and at once economizes figures and
knits the main and the secondary portions of his plot together by making the suggester of this jealousy none other than the successful wooer
of the first widow.

This linking figure developed in the process of composition into a
character of extraordinary vigour and vitality; the whole first part
of the play was built up around him, and the story of his courtship
assumed an apparently independent value. We get thus the curious
phenomenon in Elizabethan comedy, which as a rule consists of a
major and a minor action running side by side through the play, of one
action evolving from another. A careful study of the plot as a whole
will show, however, that the first of these, that of Tharsalio's courtship,
is strictly subordinate to the second, the Ephesian matron story, that
its *raison d'être*, in fact, is at once to strike the keynote of the theme,
the frailty of woman's vows, and to prepare the way for the easy and
natural development of the main action. There is no need to search
for a source of the first acts of *The Widow's Tears*. They are patently
the creation of the playwright; and in their main outline they do
great credit to his inventive and constructive abilities. The one fault
to be found is that the introductory action occupies somewhat too
much space in them; Tharsalio rather overshadows Lysander and
Cynthia. But a nice sense of proportion is one of the rarest of dramatic
gifts; certainly outside of Shakespeare and Jonson it is infrequent
enough in Elizabethan drama.

If Chapman had worked out the conclusion with the same energy
and skill with which he led up to the central situation, *The Widow's
Tears* would have been the finest example of his skill in dramatic construction. But this is far from being the case. In the first place he
introduces at the point where the widow proposes the substitution of
her husband's corpse for the stolen body a stroke which at once throws
the whole carefully planned composition out of key. Lysander's
declaration that he murdered her husband is utterly unexpected, and
no doubt startled the audience as it was meant to do; but its effect
upon the character of Cynthia and the future conduct of the play is
simply disastrous. Cynthia's callous persistence in her proposal trans-
forms her from a frail woman into a monster wholly out of place in a
comedy. And the turn thus given to the plot rendered the natural
solution a matter of considerably greater difficulty than it was before.

The natural, one might almost say the only legitimate solution, of
the entanglement devised by Chapman was that the wife, once informed of the true situation, should declare that she had recognized
her husband from the first, upbraid him for his causeless jealousy, and
finally condescend to accept his penitent excuses. It is clear, I think,
that Chapman had this solution in mind. He prepares for it by Tharsalio's warning to Cynthia of the trap into which she has unconsciously
fallen, by her refusal to run away from the danger that threatens her
(V, ii, 182, *ssq.*) and by the sudden ' reversal ' when she snatches the
iron crow from Lysander's hand, reveals her knowledge of his identity,
and flies from the tomb. This is not bad for a beginning, but unfortunately this beginning is also the end. With Cynthia's flight from the
tomb the action proper practically ceases. The necessary scene in
which the wife should have convinced and reconciled her husband is
not so much as sketched, and the play comes to an abrupt and unsatis-

factory close with a farcical scene in which an ass in office shakes his long ears before a laughing and sneering world. The solution is simply burked.

It is somewhat difficult to account for this lame and impotent conclusion. It can hardly have been beyond Chapman's powers to have worked out in full a solution he had so clearly perceived. But it would have demanded time and a resolute grapple with a problem whose difficulty he had himself increased ; and it would have extended to an impracticable length a play already longer [1] than his average comedy. There are evident signs in the last act both of hasty composition and of ' cuts ' for acting purposes. It seems to me a probable explanation that Chapman, pressed for time and money and unwilling to undertake the careful revision which a proper and proportionate solution would have entailed, simply sat down to his desk, dashed off, *currente calamo*, the scene with the Governor to cover the collapse of his plot with a mantle of farce, and threw his manuscript to the impatient players. Poverty, haste, and a cynical contempt of his audience may well explain his action, though they can hardly excuse his failure.

Perhaps the most striking feature of *The Widow's Tears* is the pervading cynicism of its tone toward women. It is strange enough that a dramatist who a few years before had drawn the characters of Margaret and Cynanche should have turned, apparently with zest, to the portrayal of Eudora and Cynthia. And it is not in the characters alone, but in the whole tone of the play that this note of almost brutal cynicism makes itself heard. Apart from certain scenes in *The Blind Beggar* there is nothing in Chapman's earlier work to suggest this tone ; his comedies are as a whole sweet and sound. To a certain extent the note may be due to the theme itself. It would be difficult for the most optimistic of poets to present the Ephesian matron in an idealized form or to retell her story in the terms of romantic comedy. But how came Chapman to choose this theme ? The suggestion thrown out by Swinburne (*George Chapman*, p. 66) and elaborated by Dobell and Schoell in connexion with the Chapman [2] letters, that the play is Chapman's revenge for his refusal by a widow, seems to me a rather unsatisfactory explanation, even if the facts in the case were more definitely ascertained. A play in which widows are represented as only too ready to embrace a second husband would be a strange revenge upon a widow who was so far, at least, constant to her husband's memory that she repelled the poet's suit. Yet it seems to me certain that Chapman's own mood imparted to *The Widow's Tears* its peculiar tone, for the coarseness of this comedy is not inherent in the subject. Petronius in earlier and La Fontaine in later days have treated it with light and easy irony. But Chapman, more especially in the scenes of his own invention, displays a physical grossness almost unparalleled in Elizabethan comedy. Nothing, at least, that I can recall prior to the worst excesses of Fletcher and his imitators is comparable for sheer animalism to the

---

[1] At the point where Cynthia leaves the tomb *The Widow's Tears* has occupied 61 pages of this edition as compared with 52 for the whole of *Monsieur D'Olive*, 59 for *All Fools*, and 61 for *Sir Giles Goosecap*.

[2] Among the Chapman documents published by Dobell (*Athenaeum*, March 23, 30, April 6 and 13, 1901) are two letters (March 23) dealing with his courtship of a widow. Whether his suit was successful or not we have no knowledge, unless the silence of his first biographer, Antony à Wood, may be taken to show that he never married.

device by which Tharsalio, through the agency of the bawd Arsace, provokes the slumbering lust of his hitherto scornful mistress.

It is in the person of Tharsalio that this note of physical grossness is incarnated. And the character of Tharsalio, although repulsive enough to finer sensibilities, is a masterpiece of realistic portraiture. His rôle in the play is that of the arch-intriguer ; like Lemot and Rinaldo he holds all the threads of the action in his hands and moves the other characters about like puppets. It is he who first suggests to Lysander a suspicion of his wife's constancy, who discovers Cynthia in the embrace of the soldier, who removes the body from the cross, who realizes the identity of Lysander and the soldier and reveals his knowledge to Cynthia, and who, in the perfunctory conclusion, brings the husband and wife together again. But Tharsalio is more than the mere intriguer. His actions spring naturally from his character, a notable compound of unshameable impudence, malicious delight in others' troubles, and an unscrupulous ability in the attainment of his own desires. There is something hard and self-seeking in Tharsalio that we do not find even in the most reckless of Chapman's earlier figures, Lemot, Valerio, or Lodovico. The light-hearted buoyancy of youth, the dash of Elizabethan romance, which helped to atone for their wildest pranks is wanting in this character. We feel as we read *The Widow's Tears* the approach of a later brazen age. Tharsalio seems to me a plain anticipation of the roués and fortune-hunters of Restoration comedy. He would certainly be less out of place in a play of Wycherly's than in the work of such old-fashioned Elizabethans as Dekker and Heywood.

It is in his cynical wit, revealing as it does an utter disbelief in all womanly virtue, that Tharsalio approaches most nearly to the Restoration man-about-town. His scepticism, as Chapman makes plain, springs from his own unsavoury experiences. He is

> *A wild corrupted youth,*
> *Whom profane ruffians, squires to bawds and strumpets,*
>
> *Debauch'd perdus, have by their companies*
> *Turn'd devil like themselves and stuff'd his soul*
> *With damn'd opinions and unhallowed thoughts*
> *Of womanhood.*
>
> The Widow's Tears, II, i, 46–52.

Far from looking back with any sense of shame upon his past, Tharsalio regards it as having been a school of truth. It has taught him, he holds, to ' *see with clear eyes, and to judge of objects as they truly are, not as they seem* ' (I, i, 141–2). He is a thorough-going realist ; all ideals are in his eyes masks to conceal the gross truth, and the greatest of shams is woman's pretension to purity and constancy. Women are to him only mirrors that reflect whatever face is held before them, ' *weak paper walls thrust down with a finger* '. Below ' *certain moral disguises of coyness which the ignorant call modesty* ' there lurks in all women an appetite which once kindled boils quickly to ' *the full height of lust* ' ; and the secret of success with women is the ability to rouse this appetite. His courtship of Eudora is a marvel of cynical calculation. On his part there is only the desire to raise his fortunes ; on hers he reckons on the desire of a ' *young lady, gallant, vigorous, full of spirit and complexion* ', for a suitable husband. He offers himself to her frankly as the most sufficient male among her suitors, rouses her passions, and carries her by storm. Except for one bit of open mockery (II, iv, 243-9) he nevers stoops even to the pretence of love. To compare his wooing with Petruchio's, as has been done more than once, is to misread Shakespeare and to be blind to the plain meaning of Chapman.

Compared with the vigorous and masculine portrait of Tharsalio, the other characters in *The Widow's Tears* are pale and shadowy. As is too often the case with Chapman, the stage is crowded with figures—there are twenty-one characters in this play—that have no real part in the action and no particularly distinguishing feature. Even those who are essential to the plot have something of the air of puppets going through their appointed parts. Chapman makes no attempt, for example, to reveal the character of the Ephesian matron. Cynthia says but little in the play, and does what she has to do, no more, no less. The portrait of Lysander is drawn on a somewhat larger scale, but it is neither a convincing nor a finished figure. His sudden transition from rapturous eulogy to a fresh trial of his wife's virtue in IV, ii, is quite unmotivated and inconsistent.[1] Chapman lends full, if some hysterical expression to Lysander's agony of shame and rage after his wife's fall, but gives us no inkling whatever of his feelings at the equally important point of the plot where Cynthia declares her knowledge of his disguise, nor has he troubled to trace the mental process through which Lysander must pass before he can with any propriety, ethical or dramatic, be reunited to his wife. Something might be said of the character of Eudora, a hasty but vivid sketch of the great lady—perhaps drawn from a living model at the court of James I—whose professions of virtue and haughty bearing are but a thin veil, easily penetrated by such trained observers as Arsace, over her essential grossness and sensuality. But after all it is the figure of Tharsalio that dominates the play. He towers head and shoulders above all others like one of Nietzsche's supermen amid a decadent race. Nor is his superiority merely that of physical energy and the stronger will. Tharsalio is the intellectual superior of his environment. His judgments of the world in which he moves and of the individuals who people that world are proved right, and the conventional ideals of his fellows wrong, by the inexorable logic of events. And so far as Chapman shows us in this play, the world of Tharsalio is the world at large. There is no relief, no counterpoise, no hint even at a soul of goodness in things evil. It is this predominance of Tharsalio and all that he stands for which gives *The Widow's Tears* its unique position among the comedies of Chapman. It is only by a wide extension of the term that it can be called a comedy. The form remains, but humour, the true spring of comedy that flowed so freely through *All Fools, The Gentleman Usher,* and *Monsieur D'Olive,* has quite dried up. It is essentially a dramatic satire, harsh and unflinching and realistic. If *The Widow's Tears* be, as I incline to think, the latest in date of Chapman's comedies, there is little cause for surprise in his turning after this play wholly to the field of tragedy. His powers as a playwright were at their height, the faults of *The Widow's Tears* are those

---

[1] In this scene we can lay a finger on the cause of the inconsistency. The Lysander of the soliloquies at the beginning and end of the scene is the adoring, although capriciously jealous husband of Chapman's invention, the Lysander of the dialogue with Cynthia is the soldier of Petronius whose words Chapman does little more than expand and versify. The two characters are quite distinct.

of haste and recklessness rather than of incompetence ; but his attitude toward the world had changed.

The Widow's Tears seems to me the product of a mood of pessimism that had come over Chapman as he viewed the swift decadence of his age. The mood was not permanent, but it rendered him incapable henceforth of viewing the follies and vices of the world as a mere laughing matter, and prepared the way for the grave morality and the lofty idealism of his tragedies.

THE WIDOW'S TEARS

NOTES

Dedication. I have not been able to identify *Mr. Jo. Reed*. A John Reed, surgeon, from Gloucestershire, attained some distinction in London *c.* 1588; but I can hardly believe that he is the man to whom Chapman dedicates this play.

The dedication is of special interest as showing Chapman's acquaintance with Italian drama of the sixteenth century. *Gli Ingiusti Sdegni* by Bernardino Pino, printed in 1553, was dedicated to Cesare Panfilio; *Il Pentimento Amoroso*, a pastoral play by Luigi Groto known as Cieco di Hadria, the blind poet of Hadria, was performed in that town in 1575 and printed at Venice in 1576. It is dedicated to Vincenzo Naldi, Governor of Peschiera for the Signoria of Venice, and to Marina Dolce Naldi, his wife. *Calisto*, another pastoral by the same author, was performed as early as 1561, revised for another performance in 1582, and printed at Venice in 1583. It is dedicated to Alfonso II of Este, Grand Duke of Ferrara. The scene of both these plays is laid in Arcadia, and the characters are gods, nymphs, shepherds, and so on. *Il Pastor Fido*, the most famous of all Italian pastoral plays, by Battista Guarini, 1585, was dedicated to Vincenzo Gonzaga, Duke of Mantua. With Chapman's statement as to *Dukes and Princes*, cf. the *Dedication* to *The Revenge of Bussy* : ' Nor have the greatest Princes of Italy and other countries conceived it any least diminution to their greatness to have their names winged with these tragic plumes, etc.'. It is plain that Chapman, like Jonson, revolted against the low esteem in which the acted drama was held by scholarly and literary circles in his day, and by these references to aristocratic and courtly patronage in Italy hoped to rouse them to a juster estimate of the contemporary drama in England.

I, i, 12. *Confidence :* used here in the sense of ' presumption ', ' audacious assurance.'

I, i, 21-2. There is a pun on *grain*. In l. 21 it means ' quality ', ' nature '; in l. 22 *in grain* means ' fast dyed '.

I, i, 24. *Beaver :* not ' hat ' as in *Monsieur D'Olive*, I, i, 269 ; but the visor of a helmet, which concealed the face.

I, i, 35. *In written books, etc.* Collier's note that this phrase is in imitation of the formula of Italian Romance poets, *Come è scritto*, shows that he quite missed the point of the allusion. A parallel passage in *Humourous Day's Mirth*, sc. vii, l. 106 (see my note *ad loc.*) makes the reference to unpaid accounts in tailors' books quite clear.

I, i, 70. *Draw you up in a basket.* Fleay's idea that there is some personal allusion in this phrase is absurd. The reference is to the well-known story told of Virgil in the Middle Ages. According to this tale a lady whom the poet-magician was courting promised to draw him up to her room by night in a basket. She left him, however, suspended half-way to be mocked at in the morning by the passers by. In revenge Virgil extinguished all the fires in Rome, and prevented their being rekindled until the lady stooped to the disgrace of appearing in her smock in the Forum and allowing torches to be kindled by contact with her body. There is an allusion to this part of the story in I, iii, 136–8. The tale is told in full in Thoms, *Early Prose Romances*, vol. ii, p. 17, *ssq.* See also Comparetti,

Vergil in the Middle Ages, p. 326. In Haughton's comedy *Englishmen for my Money*, 1598, a similar trick is played upon Vandal, the Dutch suitor, by the three daughters of the merchant, Pisaro.

I, i, 84. *Stoop gallant:* dip the flag. *Gallant* was formerly used of all flags borne on the mizzen-mast. A similar phrase, *make her upstart humour stoop gallant*, occurs in Day's *Humour Out of Breath*, 1608 (Bullen's edition, p. 46). *She,* I take it, refers to *the blind goddess* (l. 81), i.e. Confidence.

I, i, 108-9. Cf. *All Fools*, II, i, 240.

I, i, 113. *His poisoner:* possibly a reference to *Hamlet*.

I, i, 125. *Monopolies:* see note on *Monsieur D'Olive*, I, i, 284.

I, i, 133. *Italian air.* It was a common charge that travel or sojourn in Italy corrupted the morals of Englishmen, see especially Ascham's *Schoolmaster* (Pt. I, p. 68, *ssq.*, Mayor's edition).

I, i, 144-5. *Weeping . . . mask.* Chapman applies to widows a saying of the comic writer Publius, preserved by Aulus Gellius, *Noctes*, XVII, xiv, 2 :

Haeredis fletus sub persona risus est.

The saying was a current one in Chapman's time. It is found in Montaigne's *Essays*, Book I, chap. 37.

I, i, 145. *Mourn in their gowns, etc.:* the same phrase occurs in Chapman's *Funeral Oration* (*Poems*, p. 261).

I, i, 157. *Acoast:* an old form of ' accost '.

I, ii, 14-5. *Ulysses.* According to Homer (*Odyssey*, XII, 39, 169) Ulysses stopped not his own ears but those of his comrades with wax, bidding them bind him to the mast so that he could hear the songs of the Sirens without danger. I do not know the origin of the version that represents Ulysses as stopping his own ears, but it was current in Chapman's day, as it appears in Ascham's *Schoolmaster* (Pt. I, p. 73, Mayor's edition).

I, ii, 20. *Spots in his train:* the same phrase occurs in *Byron's Conspiracy*, I, ii, 7–8, and III, ii, 234–5.

I, ii, 53. *Offered ware is not so sweet:* a more elegant version of the proverb : *proferred service stinketh*—Heywood's *Proverbs*, Pt. II, chap. 4.

I, ii, 70. *Fights:* used here, I suppose, in the sense of ' strives ', ' aspires '.

I, ii, 73. *Court-servant:* cf. *Monsieur D'Olive*, I, i, 236–9.

I, ii, 74–75. For a similar pun, see *Humourous Day's Mirth*, sc. iii, ll. 47–8.

I, ii, 113. *At window:* see note on *All Fools*, III, i, 422–3.

I, ii, 120. *Ouches:* sores on the skin. The play on *aches* and *ouches* was plainer in Chapman's day when the first word was a dissyllable (*aitches*). The first quotation given in the *New English Dictionary* for *ouch* = to cry out with pain is 1654, but I fancy from this passage that some such sense was current in Chapman's day.

I, ii, 146-9. Cf. I, iii, 34–5.

I, ii, 166. See Text Notes, p. 816.

I, iii, 10. *Saturnian peacock;* one of the peacocks that draw the chariot of Juno.

I, iii, 24. *Bisogno:* an early form of ' bezonian ', i.e. a needy fellow, a rascal ; cf. 2 *King Henry IV*, V, iii, 119.

I, iii, 28. *Engine:* used here in the sense of ' device,' or possibly ' artfulness ', ' cunning '.

I, iii, 83. *Not-headed:* close cropped, in distinction from the long-haired courtier ; cf. Chaucer's yeoman, *Canterbury Tales—Prologue*, l. 109.

I, iii, 98. *Juno:* referred to here as the protectress of marriage.

I, iii, 132-3. *Veney for veney:* thrust for thrust. *Veney*, also spelled venew, or venue, means either a fencing-bout, as in *Revenge of Bussy*, V, v, 90, or a thrust in such a bout, cf. *Love's Labour's Lost*, V, i, 62. The *speeding place* is a spot at which the body is capable of receiving a mortal wound.

I, iii, 143. *Make all split.* Dyce in a passage cited by Furness in his note on *Midsummer Night's Dream*, I, ii, 32, quotes from Greene's *Never too Late* (*Works*, vol. viii, p. 89) a passage which shows the nautical origin of this common phrase in Elizabethan drama : ' Such a sigh that as the mariners say a man would have thought all would have split again ' ; see also Grosart's note, vol. viii, p. 258, and cf. below, III, i, 195.

I, iii, 144. *Oyster-wives :* cf. *ripiers*, i.e. fish-pedlers, as retailers of gossip in II, i, 37.

I, iii, 148. *A beaten soldier :* an experienced soldier, cf. *Alphonsus, Emperor of Germany*, IV, i, 10.

I, iii, 156. *Was sped :* had been successful.

I, iii, 185. *Smockage :* according to the *New English Dictionary* a nonceword on the analogy of 'socage ', i.e. the tenure of land by the performance of a determinate service ; *smockage* would then be by smock-service.

II, i, 14. *Black shall take no other hue ;* cf. note on *Humourous Day's Mirth*, sc. viii, l. 223.

II, i, 22-3. *Aeneas :* with reference to the amour of Aeneas with the widowed Dido ; *reversion* has here its obsolete sense of ' that which is left ', i.e. the widow.

II, i, 23-4. *Turtle . . . withered branch :* one of the commonplaces of Elizabethan verse. It occurs in the sonnet of Montano in Lodge's *Rosalynde* (*Works*, vol. i, p. 46) ; in *The Distracted Emperor* (*Old Plays*, vol. iii, p. 223), and in *The Winter's Tale*, V, iii, 132–5. Malone in a note on this last passage quotes a line from the *Orpheus* of Johannes Secundus Nicolaius (1511–36, author of the famous *Basia*), which may have suggested the figure :

Sic gemit arenti viduatus ab arbore turtur.

II, i, 24-5. *Atropos . . . throat :* cf. *Monsieur D'Olive*, III, i, 75.

II, i, 40. *Tire on :* a term of falconry. A hawk is said to *tire* when she fastens greedily upon her prey. The word is often used figuratively ; cf. *Timon*, III, vi, 5, and *Cymbeline*, III, iv, 97. Other examples are given in Collier's edition of *Dodsley*, vol. ii, p. 299.

II, i, 50. *Perdus :* the word usually occurs only in the military sense, ' an outpost ', ' exposed sentinel ', see *Lear*, IV, vii, 35. The *New English Dictionary* gives only this instance of the word in the sense of ' roué '.

II, i, 63. *A buzz :* a false rumour, cf. *Hamlet*, IV, v, 90.

II, i, 66. *This isle :* Cyprus.

II, ii, 17. *Bear out :* support, back up.

II, ii, 30. *Without my privity :* a thing of which I have no private knowledge.

II, iii, 2. *Able it :* warrant it, cf. IV, iii, 14, and *Lear*, IV, vi, 172.

II, iii, 13. *Retrieve the game :* put up, or flush, the game a second time, the original sense.

II, iii, 21. *Titillation :* for this sense of the word cf. Marston, *Works*, vol. iii, p. 261.

II, iii, 28. *When they fly out :* when husbands transgress.

II, iii, 48. *Qualified :* moderated, cf. a similar use in *All Fools*, I, i, 395.

II, iii, 85. *Post-issue :* children by her second marriage.

II, iii, 93. *Listens after your speed :* inquires after your success.

II, iii, 106. *Calendars :* outward signs, here almost in the sense of ' omens '.

II, iv, 21. *Good-night to our good days ;* cf. *All Fools*, II, i, 212.

II, iv, 28-9. *Widows' marriages . . . like usury, permitted . . . not approved.* Bacon in his Essay on Usury speaks of it as '*concessum propter duritiem cordis* . . . usury must be permitted '. There is a rather curious parallel to this expression in *Northward Ho* (*c.* 1606), III ii : ' You were wont to say venery is like usury that it may be allowed though it be not lawful '. The *you* in this passage is Bellamont, who is by Stoll (*John Webster*, p. 65) supposed to be a satiric portrait of Chapman himself. In this case this passage might be regarded as an intentional wresting of Chapman's words.

II, iv, 50. *The two fortunate stars :* St. Elmo's fires, the electric phenomenon sometimes seen in storms at the mast-head or on the yard-arms of ships. In ancient days this phenomenon was regarded as a manifestation of the Twin Brethren, Castor and Pollux, stellified by Zeus, who were regarded as the protectors of travellers by sea, see the last speech of Castor in the *Electra* of Euripides.

II, iv, 62. *Penned the pegmas.* Properly a *pegma* is a stage used in a pageant, sometimes bearing an inscription, see Jonson's *Coronation Entertainment to King James.* Hence it comes to mean an inscription bearing upon, or indicating the character of, the masque or pageant.

II, iv, 97. *A widgeon :* a variety of duck, used here to denote a fool.

II, iv, 104. *Whiffler :* see note on *Monsieur D'Olive*, III, ii, 167.

II, iv, 149-50. *Cried cony skins :* peddled rabbits' skins, the fur of which was used for hats (cf. *Monsieur D'Olive*, I, i, 359–60) and other purposes.

II, iv, 170-1. *My foot my head :* cf. *Lear*, IV, ii, 28, where the reading of Q2 is *my foot usurps my head.* Goneril is speaking of a husband she despises as Eudora affects to despise Tharsalio.

II, iv, 191. *Lamb-skinned :* thrashed. The *New English Dictionary* cites three examples of this word between 1589 and 1635. The noun *lambskin* in the sense of a beating occurs in Heywood, 1546.

II, iv, 204-5. *Calydonian boar :* the pest sent by Diana upon the kingdom of Calydon. It is curious to note that Foxe (*Ecclesiastical History*, vol. ii, p. 450, edition of 1684) speaks of Gardiner, the persecuting bishop, as *Aper Calydonius.*

II, iv, 261. *Light huswives :* Eudora echoes Arsace's words in II, ii, 104.

III, i, 3-4. This seems to be an exaggerated form of the report preserved in Suetonius (*Nero*, 34) that Nero inspected the body of the mother he had murdered, handled it, praised and blamed her figure, and so on.

III, i, 6. *Tast :* an old form of 'taste' in the sense of 'touch', 'test'.

III, i, 38. *Wrapp'd in careless cloak :* cf. *Monsieur D'Olive*, V, ii, 6. Mr. Crawford notes that a similar phrase occurs in a poem of Surrey's (*Tottell's Miscellany*, p. 26, Arber's edition) : *Wrapt in my careless cloak.* Chapman in both cases uses the old and no doubt familiar phrase in a mocking way.

III, i, 39. *Outraging :* the *New English Dictionary* cites this passage as an instance of the sense 'furious', 'wild'.

III, i, 52. *Magnis tamen excidit ausis :* part of the epitaph of Phaeton—Ovid, *Metamorphoses*, II, 328.

III, i, 54. *Fortune . . . his foe :* a popular song of the day, cf. *Merry Wives*, III iii, 69. The air is printed in Chappell's *Popular Music*, vol. i, p. 162.

III, i, 95. *Busk points :* tagged laces which secured the ends of the *busk*, a strip of steel or wood used to stiffen the front of the corset. It is used here metaphorically for bosom.

III, i, 98. *Paper walls :* cf. Webster's phrase : *paper prisons boys use to keep flies in—Duchess of Malfi*, IV, ii, 130–1.

III, i, 127. *Paphos :* a city in Cyprus where the scene is laid.

III, i, 128. *Occurrents :* occurrences, cf. *Hamlet*, V, ii, 368.

III, i, 129. *Pretty and pathetical ;* the same phrase occurs in *Humourous Day's Mirth*, sc. i, l. 36.

III, i, 152-3. *Short-heeled . . . high i'th' instep :* cf. note on *May-Day*, IV, iv, 6. *High in the instep* means *proud ;* the *New English Dictionary* cites a number of instances of this meaning from Heywood's *Proverbs* to Fuller's *Holy War.* One of the 'lots' in the lottery by Lyly (see above, p. 694) combines both these phrases :

> You are high in the instep, short in the heel,
> Your head is giddy, your lot is a reel.

III, i, 159. Cf. *All Fools*, III, i, 62.

III, ii, 1. *A hall, a hall :* cf. note on *The Gentleman Usher*, II, i, 226.

III, ii, 13. See Text Notes, p. 817.

III, ii, 27-8. *Within me :* inside my guard, a phrase borrowed from fencing.

III, ii, 35. *Exchange that name :* give and take the name of sister reciprocally, cf. *change* in *Hamlet*, I, i, 163 ; *for stranger titles :* in the place of titles indicating a greater degree of distance and formality.

III, ii, 40. *To side :* to walk by the side of ; cf. *Masque of the Middle Temple*, p. 440, above.

III, ii, 77-8. For the original punctuation of these lines see Text Notes, p. 817. I take it that Tharsalio after calling Cynthia a *phoenix*, turns to Eudora and says : Let your wisdom show itself in your affection for your husband here present.

III, ii, 95. *Hays:* country dances, something like reels ; cf. *Bussy,* I, ii, 29.

III, ii, 99. *Past custom :* above convention ; *vulgar object :* popular, ordinary, objections.

III, ii, 109. ' Dance, and win his heart by showing your charms in the hands of another '.

IV, i. An interval of about a week elapses between Acts III and IV. Cynthia has been in the tomb for four days, see below, l. 119, and some time before her entrance must be allowed for the arrival of the news of Lysander's death, and the funeral obsequies.

IV, i, 2. Tharsalio tells Lycus that there is no need to stand bare before him when they are by themselves. He treats Lycus throughout as an equal, cf. l. 5, rather than as a servant.

IV, i, 23. *Dipolis :* there is no town of this name, so far as I know, in Cyprus. There is a Syrian town of this name mentioned by Pliny, *Nat. Hist.,* V, 79, and it is sometimes applied to Lemnos.   Fleay's attempt (*loc. cit.*) to find a contemporary allusion by rendering *Lysander of Dipolis* Freeman of Ditton, seems to me absurd.

IV, i, 28. *Strange knights :* the reference is to the *knights of the new edition* (*Bussy,* I, ii, 124) created in such numbers by James I.

IV, i, 104-5. One of the many paraphrases of the well-known line of Seneca :

Curae leves loquuntur ; ingentes stupent.

Hippolytus, l. 607.

Cf. the note in Furness's *Variorum* on *Macbeth,* IV, iii, 209-10.

IV, i, 125. *Muckinders :* a form of ' muckender ', a bib, or handkerchief.

IV, ii. The tomb which figures so largely in this and the succeeding scenes was no doubt placed in the recess, or alcove, of the stage beneath the balcony.   It must have had a practicable door, cf. stage-direction, l. 179 below, and the interior must have been visible to the audience since at times part of the action (see V, iii, 75, *ssq.*) takes place there.   I have supplied stage-directions in brackets throughout these scenes to make the action as clear as possible to the reader.

IV, ii, 42. *Huswifery :* house-keeping, with special reference to the table ; cf. Chapman's use of the word in his *Iliad,* xxiii, 242.

IV, ii, 57-8. Among the poems appended to the 1598 edition of the *Arcadia* there is a sonnet by Dyer on the theme of a satyr who kissed the fire he saw for the first time.   This is followed by a sonnet of Sidney's beginning :

A satyr once did run away for dread
With sound of horn which he himself did blow.

This sonnet was reprinted in *England's Helicon,* 1600 (Bullen's edition, p. 246) and was no doubt well known.   It appears to be the immediate source of Chapman's allusion.   Whether the idea was original with Sidney or not I am unable to state, but nothing of the kind appears in the collections of fables.   I owe this reference to Mr. Crawford.

IV, ii, 71. *Deucalion's race ;* according to Ovid, *Metamorphoses,* I, 371, *ssq.,* the human race is descended from the stones which Deucalion and his wife, the sole survivors of a universal flood, threw behind their backs.

IV, ii, 95-6. Cf. *Satyricon,* cxi : *Nemo invitus audit cum cogitur aut cibum sumere aut vivere.*

IV, ii, 128. *The rack'd value :* the value strained, or raised above the normal; cf. Chapman's use of *rack'd* in his *Georgics of Hesiod,* II (*Poems,* p. 224). See also *Merchant of Venice,* I, i, 181.

IV, ii, 130. *Proface.* Collier, who restored the reading *proface* from the Q., refers to 2 *King Henry IV,* V, iii, 30, where the same word appears.   It is the old French phrase *bon prou vous fasse,* contracted to *prou fasse,* may it do you good.

IV, ii, 137. *Do me right :* cf. note on *All Fools,* V, ii, 77, and see the notes in the *Variorum* on 2 *King Henry IV,* V, iii, 76.

IV, ii, 145. *Guaiacum :* a drug prepared from the resin of the guaiacum tree, *lignum vitae.* It is mentioned as a medicine in *Volpone,* II, i.

IV, ii, 147. *Limbo :* a slang phrase (from *Limbo Patrum,* the outer ward of Hell in which the righteous dead were confined till the Crucifixion), for any place of confinement, see *Comedy of Errors,* IV, ii, 32.

IV, ii, 151. *Aristotle . . . Posteriords :* Ero's mistake for Aristotle's *Analytica Posteriora.* With her citation cf. *Sir Giles Goosecap,* I, iv, 70–2.

IV, ii, 156. *Spinners :* an old name for spiders, cf. *Midsummer Night's Dream,* II, ii, 21, and *Romeo and Juliet,* I, iv, 59.

IV, ii, 182. *Concretion :* union with material substance.

IV, iii. An interval of twenty-four hours, more or less, separates this scene from the preceding ; cf. IV, ii, 177 and IV, iii, 42.

IV, iii, 20. *For an upshot :* to finish off.

IV, iii, 37. *Take it to thee :* speak for yourself. So, at least, I understand the phrase. Possibly, however, Ero is again offering the bottle to Cynthia, who declines it with these words.

IV, iii, 40. *Black Sanctus :* originally a burlesque parody of the ' angelic hymn ', *Sanctus, Sanctus, Sanctus.* A curious specimen of such a parody, *The Monks' Hymn to St. Satan,* is printed in *Nugae Antiquae* ', vol. iii, p. 304. ' To sing the black Sanctus ' was an Elizabethan phrase equivalent to 'lament one's case.'

IV, iii, 56-7. An adaptation of Chapman's own lines :

> *Then laid she wine on cares to make them sink ;*
> *Who fears the threats of Fortune, let him drink.*
> *Hero and Leander,* V., 59-60.

IV, iii, 74. *All of a piece :* all of the same kind, harmonious.

V, i. This scene is apparently continuous in time with IV, iii, for Tharsalio on his opening the tomb (l. 22) finds Lysander in Cynthia's arms.

V, i, 9. *Curious :* used here in the sense of ' exacting '.

V, i, 10. *Haunt :* resort, perhaps here in the sense of ' topic ', ' subject '.

V, i, 12. *Disposure :* disposition, cf. *Revenge of Bussy,* IV, iv, 37. Here it seems to have almost the sense of ' physical constitution '.

V, i, 24. *Lay :* wager. One would expect the past tense.

V, i, 26. *Drawing on :* there is a double meaning in the phrase, first ' drawing near death ', as Lycus evidently understands it, l. 27, then ' tempting ', 'enticing ', cf. *Monsieur D'Olive,* V, i, 171.

V, i, 45. *Eightpenny soldier :* a poor, worthless soldier, cf. 1 *King Henry IV,* III, iii, 119, and the phrase *Turk of tenpence—Jew of Malta,* IV, iv, 44.

V, i, 46. *Height of interjection :* loud exclamations, with reference either to Cynthia's laments for her husband, or her earlier emphatic protests against a widow's second marriage.

V, i, 94. *Complement :* formal ceremony ; in l. 107 *compliments* means ' conventional tributes '. The spelling is the same in both lines in Q., and should be so here.

V, i, 120. In Petronius the soldier triumphs over the widow's virtue.

V, i, 136. *Correspondent :* answerable ; the *New English Dictionary* cites this line.

V, i, 153-6. A fable, not found in the old *Aesop's Fables,* but included in L'Estrange's translation of *Aesop* (no. 487, edition of 1692), tells how an ass bearing a sacred image imagined that the reverence of the people was shown to him rather than to his burden.

V, ii, 20. *Cancro :* ' a curse that the Italians use to wish one '—Florio. Literally ' may you suffer from cancer '.

V, ii, 31. *Paunch'd him :* pierced his belly, cf. *Tempest,* III, ii, 98.

V, ii, 39. *Miching :* sneaking, literally hiding like a truant, cf. V, iii, 202, and *Hamlet,* III, ii, 147.

V, ii, 55-6. *Aid our hands to yours :* join our hands in aid to yours. So I understand the passage ; but Collier reads *add.*

V, ii, 61. *Antic ;* used here for a disguise, such as was worn in a pageant or masque, sometimes called ' an antic '.

V, ii, 71-6. A hopelessly corrupt passage; see Text Notes, p. 819. The *Acheloüs* was the largest river in Greece, and its river-god, of the same name, was regarded as the father of rivers. In a combat with Hercules one of this god's horns was torn off by the hero, and this horn, according to Ovid, *Metamorphoses*, ix, 87-8, was the horn of plenty. Lysander, with reference to the 'horn' which his wife's infidelity has bestowed on him, speaks of it as an *Acheloüs' horn*, not of good, but *of ill*. Hence also comes the following phrase *copie*, (an old form of 'copy' in the obsolete sense of 'plenty') *enough*. Something has probably been omitted by accident or design in l. 74. The name *Alizon* l. 75, is puzzling. No such river is known in classical geography; but Chapman may perhaps have meant the Halys, the largest river in Asia Minor; Homer (*Iliad*, II, 856) mentions a people *Alizones* of this region. I venture the suggestion, see Text Notes, p. 820, that we might read *Amazon*. Ida, the mountain near Troy, was famous for its forest; Hesiod, *Theog.*, l. 1010, uses the phrase Ἴδης ὑληέσσης, wooded Ida.

V, ii, 120. *Collections:* inferences.

V, ii, 136. Candia was the chief town in Crete in the Middle Ages; good wine was grown in the neighbourhood.

V, ii, 150. *Frubber:* literally 'furbisher', a term of contempt for the maid-servant.

V, iii, 26. *An old conclusion.* The fullest contemporary account of the old belief here referred to appears in the *Demonologie* of King James (p. 79, edition of 1603): 'As in a secret murder, if the dead carcass be at any time thereafter handled by the murtherer, it will gush out of blood, as if the blood were crying to the heaven for revenge of the murtherer, God having appointed that secret supernatural sign for trial of that secret un-natural crime'.

V, iii, 45-6. Cf. *Chabot*, III, i, 191, and *Caesar and Pompey*, III, i, 36.

V, iii, 62-5. The *disguise*, l. 62, is Cynthia's feigned devotion to her husband. For the corrupt passage that follows see Text Notes, p. 820.

V, iii, 66-8. These lines are far from clear, and the punctuation of the quarto (*lust, Note with . . . impiety. Her . . . corse l*) only makes them more con-fusing. I have adopted the punctuation suggested by Brereton (*loc. cit.*) and interpret them as addressed to his soldier's disguise which is to help him see Cynthia (*Act of lust*, I take as equivalent to the active principle of lust, i.e. the widow) and which is to look upon the supposed corpse taking part in an impious scene, i.e. that in which the widow assists in bearing it to the cross.

V, iii, 80. *Employments:* implements. The *New English Dictionary* cites this passage as the only instance where the word is used in this sense. The passage in *Twelfth Night*, II, v, 91, cited by the editor of the 1780 Dodsley does not seem a parallel case.

V, iii, 118. *Iron you:* catch you, put you in irons. The phrase is probably used for the sake of a word-play with *steel* in l. 117.

V, iii, 140. *Cross capers:* cf. *The Malcontent*, IV, ii, 11, *Cross capers! tricks!* and Brome's *City Wit* (*Works*, vol. i, p. 337), *Show you a cross caper*. The definition in the *New English Dictionary* is hardly satisfactory. The phrase means, as all these instances show, a *caper*, or unexpected start, which *crosses* another's plans.

V, iii, 146. On her exit here Cynthia presumably goes to put herself under the protection of Tharsalio and the Countess, with whom she reappears, l. 218 below. Lysander after his speech withdraws into the tomb and closes the doors. He is shortly after discovered there, stage-direction after l. 191.

V, iii, 150. *Braves:* in the sense of bravadoes, cf. Heywood, 1 *King Edward IV* (*Works*, vol. i, p. 54).

V, iii, 151. *Acquit:* in the obsolete sense of 'perform'.

V, iii, 206. *Blandation:* illusion. The *New English Dictionary* cites this passage.

V, iii, 212. *Colestaff:* a form of 'cowl staff', i.e. a staff used to run through the handles of a ' cowl ', a tub, or large basket so that it could be carried on the shoulders of two men ; see *Merry Wives*, III, iii, 156.

V, iii, 244. *Chop :* bandy words. See note on *All Fools*, I, ii, 51.

V, iii, 256. *Two parties.* One would expect *one party* ; but perhaps the *two* are the accuser and the judge himself, who does most of the talking. *Solon* is referred to in this connexion as famous for his wisdom in making and administering laws.

V, iii, 274. *Parrot :* cf. *terms, and tongues, and parroting of art—Tears of Peace* (*Poems*, p. 118).

V, iii, 275. *The Vice :* the buffoon-like character of the Vice in the moralities. The phrase *snap his authority at all he meets* perhaps refers to the Vice's ' business ' of beating his fellow actors with the wooden sword which was the badge of his part.

V, iii, 291. *Parboil :* with reference to the surgeon's tub, cf. note on *Monsieur D'Olive*, III, ii, 75.

V, iii, 294. *Pregnant :* ready, resourceful, cf. *Measure for Measure*, I, i, 12.

V, iii, 297-8. *No man shall do good but where there is no need :* a favourite phrase with Chapman, cf. *Bussy*, I, i, 97 ; *Eugenia* (*Poems*, p. 328), *A Great Man* (*Poems*, p. 149).

V, iii, 298-9. *Live at the head :* if a sense must be found in the Governor's foolish chatter I suggest ' live on the best '.

V, iii, 315. *Spaded :* apparently a form of ' spayed ', perhaps influenced by the Latin *spado*, a eunuch.

V, iii, 317-8. *Burnt :* cf. *They say in China when women are past child-bearing, they are all burnt to make gunpowder—The Fawn* (Marston, *Works*, vol. ii, p. 167).

V, iii, 334. *Bears a breadth :* see note on *Monsieur D'Olive*, IV, ii, 103.

V, iii, 342. *Given him :* apparently ' given in his name as worthy of punishment ' ; *uphold correspondence* means ' maintain good relations '.

V, iii, 348. *Take advertisement for us :* receive information on our part. Perhaps we should read *from us*, see Text Notes, p. 821.

V, iii, 367. *The ass :* a reference to the old fable of the Ass in the Lion's Skin (Avian, 4) printed by Caxton in the Appendix to his *Aesop*.

V, iii, 370. *Am at a non-plus :* cf. *hang and be at a non-plus—Pilgrimage to Parnassus*, ll. 684-5. It was a common phrase in Elizabethan English to denote a state of perplexity.

TEXT NOTES

The *Widow's Tears* was first published in 1612 by John Browne in quarto form. This is the only old edition. Two copies (644. d. 48 and C. 12. g. 5) are found in the British Museum, one in the Albert and Victoria Museum and four in the Bodleian, three of which are in the Malone collection and one in the Douce. A number of corrections seem to have been made while the play was going through the press, and there are an unusual number of variations in these copies, the most important of which I have recorded in these notes.

The *Widow's Tears* was first reprinted in Dodsley's *Select Collection of Old Plays*, 1744, vol. iv ; again in the 1780 edition of this collection, vol. vi, where the editor, Reed, asserts that he has collated the former edition with the quarto. Numerous corrections are made in this text, but a good many errors still remain in it. Collier included the play in his edition of Dodsley, 1825, vol. vi, making some further corrections. I denote these editions in the following notes by D1, D2, and Co. respectively.

There is a reprint, not always exact, of the quarto in *The Comedies and Tragedies of George Chapman*, 1873 (P.). I have attempted to record all the variations of this reprint from the quarto. The last edition up to the present is that of Shepherd, *Works of George Chapman—Plays* (S.). I have not attempted to make a collation of all the modern editions, and only occasionally record their variations from the original text, but I have tried to give each editor credit for those of his emendations which I have adopted.

The text of *The Widow's Tears* is far from satisfactory. It seems to have been printed from a stage copy, as is shown by the numerous and elaborate stage-directions (see I, ii, 37, that at the beginning of IV, ii, and V, ii, 145 for examples). Such directions in Latin as *Bibit Ancilla* (IV, ii, 135) and *Exit cum Ero* show that the manuscript was either Chapman's own, or a copy preserving his original directions. But the manuscript seems to have given the printers considerable trouble ; there are places (V, ii, 74, and V, iii, 133) where it was probably cut. It may have been more or less illegible, for the quarto abounds in errors of all sorts from ordinary misprints to grave corruptions. Many of these have been by the labours of successive editors and commentators corrected, but a number of doubtful cases remain, and a few passages are apparently hopelessly corrupt. The distinction between prose [1] and verse was not always observed by the original printers. Occasionally, indeed, it seems as it Chapman himself indulged in a curious mixture of verse and prose ; such a speech as the Captain's, V, i, 138–158, printed as prose in Q., contains some lines of unmistakeable verse, but some that are so lame as to suggest the conclusion that the passage was written in haste and never revised. I have tried in such cases to follow what I conceive to be Chapman's purpose, printing as verse passages that he meant as such, even when very far from being regular or harmonious. All emendations and stage-directions not included in the quarto are as usual printed in brackets.

Dedication. Collier, the first editor to reprint the Dedication, states that Reed, the editor of the previous edition, had printed the play from a copy lacking the dedication. I have shown below, p. 816, that Reed probably collated the text that lay before him with the Douce copy (Douce, C. 245). This copy as well as every other one that I have seen contains the Dedication. Collier's statement is therefore erroneous, and since he connects the absence of a Dedication in a copy of *The Widow's Tears* with a similar absence in the case of *All Fools*, to which he had already printed a forged Dedication (see above, p. 726), the chances are that his statement was wilfully made.

l. 4. Q. *Iniusti sdegnij.*
l. 5. Q. *Pentamento Amorose ; Calisthe.*
In all three cases I have printed the original Italian names.
l. 6. I have inserted *I* to complete the sense. It was probably dropped by accident.

Dramatis Personae. Q. prints the following list under the heading *The Actors :*

> *Tharsalio the wooer.*
> *Lysander his brother.*
> *Thir. Governour of Cyprus.*
> *Lycas ser. to the widdow Countesse.*
> *Argus, Gent. Usher.*
> *3. Lords suiters to Eudora the widdow Countesse.*
> *Hyl. nephew to Tharsalio, and Sonne to Lysander.*
> *Captaine of the watch.*
> *2. Souldiers.*
> *Eudora the widdow Countesse.*
> *Cynthia, wife to Lysander.*
> *Sthenio.*
> *Ianthe Gent. attending on Eudora.*
> *Ero, waiting woman to Cynthia.*

D_1, D_2 and Co. reprint the list as it stands in Q., only dropping *Thir.* (for which I read *The*) before *Governour*, and expanding *ser.* and *Gent.* after *Lycus* (Q. *Lycas* in the list, but always *Lycus* in the body of the text) and *Argus* to *servant* and *gentleman*, also *Gent.* after *Ianthe* to *gentlewoman*. D_1, D_2 print *Sthenia* ;

---

[1] Schoell notes that, in the main, prose is used in the 'Eudora', verse in the 'Cynthia plot'. The greater part of the first three acts are in prose with passages of verse here and there ; the last acts contain more verse, but such a 'Cynthia scene' as IV, iii, is entirely prose except for a rhymed couplet.

Co. *Sthenio*, remarking, p. 139, that the quartos print it uniformly *Sthenio*. I have noted the occurrence of the form in -*a* in the Douce copy in the stage-direction preceding II, ii, and in II, ii, 43. I have kept this form, apparently from σθένεια, an epithet of Athene in Lycophron. Collier notes that the names of *Laodice, Arsace, Thomasin* and *Clinias* are to be added, and that the names of the three suitors are *Rebus, Hiarbas*, and *Psorabeus* (see stage-direction after I, ii, 36). Properly speaking, only the first of these is a suitor, the other two are his attendant lords. The list of *Dramatis Personae* printed in the text is thus a full and, I think, a correct list.

Q. divides the play into acts, each of which contains but one scene. *Scæna Prima* is prefixed to each act in Q. Co. follows this arrangement. I have divided the acts for the first time into scenes and added the supposed place of the action.

I, i, 67. Co. in his note on this line implies that some Qq. have the reading *back*, which is that of D₂, for *beck*. The Bodleian and British Museum copies all have *becke*.

94-96. Q. includes all between *as perhaps* and *interred* in the parenthesis. Co. follows Q. I think the present arrangement brings out the construction of the passage more clearly.

I, ii, 111. Former editors put a question mark at the close of this line. There is none in Q., and Tharsalio's speech may better be taken as a command than as a question.

117. Q. *dub'd*, which is followed by all editors. Co. suggests *daubed*. There seems no sufficient reason for altering the text. There is probably a double pun on *dubb'd* and *daubed*, *lard* and *lord*, in the passage.

140-2. Q. prints as prose; Co. arranges as verse.

156-7. Q. prints as prose; D₂ and Co. as verse, but both erroneously insert *the* (from D₁) before *doors*, and in consequence place *shut* at the close of l. 156. S. follows Q.

165. Q. prints *Lurd* (Co. *Lord*; S. *Lu.*) as the speaker's name. The speech plainly belongs to Psorabeus.

166. Q. *begg'd*, which is followed by all editors. Brereton (*Modern Language Review*, vol. 3, p. 62) suggests *beg't*, i.e. beg it, that Tharsalio may be poisoned. This seems to me needless. Psorabeus suggests that Rebus *beg* Tharsalio, i.e. request of the Viceroy that he be put under guardianship as a fool or madman. Cf. *Sir Giles Goosecap*, IV, iii, 167-170, where Sir Giles misunderstands the term.

I, iii, 12. All copies of Q. that I have seen except one in the Bodleian (Douce, C. 245) read *lowe*; the Douce copy *loved*. This is the basis of the note in D₂ that the quarto reads *loved*; Co. speaks as if only one copy read *lowe*.

27. Q. sets this line in a parenthesis. I take this to indicate an aside and have so marked it.

73. One copy of Q. (Douce, C. 245), reads *mystical Adonis*, a variant which Reed, the editor of D₂, introduced into the text. Co. followed him, although stating, erroneously that *young* was the only reading of Q. I have preferred to keep the reading of all copies but one.

80. Q. *lease;* S. *leaf* which makes nonsense.

98. I have added *and Ero* to the stage-direction after this line to make it conform with the direction after l. 131, where the exit of Ero is marked in Q. She would naturally come upon the stage with Cynthia.

114. Q. *it but was*. This arrangement of words seems to have offended the editors. D₁ D₂ and Co. read *but it was:* S. *it was but*. There is no need of change.

II, i, 1. Co. follows D₂ in printing *are by ourselves*, but notes that one of the quartos omits *by*. I have not found *by* in any of the copies I have consulted.

25. Q. *throat*; editors *thread*. There seems to be no authority for this change. Cf., by the way, *Monsieur D'Olive*, III, i, 75–6, and the text note thereon.

II, ii, 13. P. misprints *Seth.* as the name of the speaker.

55. In the stage-direction after this line Q. reads *Enter Arsace*, and is followed by all previous editors; but Arsace has been on the stage since l. 20, and has had several speeches, ll. 40, 43–4, 49–50. Here, as elsewhere (cf. p. 696 above, note on sc. v, l. 165) an entrance in Q. merely indicates that a character advances from a place of retirement (cf. l. 24) to take part in the main action.

II, iv, 43. Q. *you*; P. misprints *your*.

56. Q. *my La*; D₁ *my lady*.

98. Q. *acknowledge : forecast is better*. Editors print *acknowledge forecast is better;* but I believe *acknowledge* means ' recognize me as your master ', and that *forecast* is the first word of a new clause. To me at least this seems to give a better sense than the former punctuation.

108. Q. *reformation;* P. misprints *eformation*.

194. One copy of Q. in the Bodleian (Malone, 216) reads *Atlas* for *outlaw*.

272. D₂ supplies the *exit* wanting in Q.

III, i, 6. Q. *tast;* all former editors *test;* but *tast* is a variant of *taste* in its obsolete meaning of ' touch '.

13–19. Q. and all editors as prose. I have arranged as verse.

53–4. Q. prints as prose. D₂ restores to verse.

112–18. Q. and all editors as prose. I have arranged as verse.

123. Q. *No wife.* D₂ *No, wife?*

146. Q. does not note the exit of Ero after this line, nor has the omission been supplied by previous editors.

151. D₁ reads *impression*. Co. restores *depression*, remarking that this, ' the true reading, is supported by the quarto Mr. Reed did not meet with '. This is one of Collier's flourishes with his only correct copy. The reading *depression* appears in all copies of Q. that I have seen ;

impression was probably an arbitrary change by D₁.

157. Q. *het ;* all editors *hot ;* but *het* is a form of ' heated '.

196–7. Q. prints as prose. I have arranged as verse.

227–9. It is not possible to determine whether Q. prints these lines as verse or prose. It divides them as in my text, but since l. 229 begins with a lower-case letter, *brother*, it is probable that the old printer took them for prose. They are so printed by all editors, but they seem to me plainly verse.

233–5. Q. prints *my wife* and *father* at the close of ll. 232 and 234 respectively. Co. transfers *my wife* to its present place ; I have transferred *father*.

III, ii, 6. I have supplied the entrance of Tharsalio after this line. As there is no division of scenes in Q. it is probable that he originally remained on the stage after the departure of Lysander and Lycus.

13. Q. *cornetting;* all previous editors *curvetting*. *Cornetting* would, it is true, be an easy misprint for *corvetting*, i.e. ' curvetting '; but I have preferred, with the *New English Dictionary*, to take this as a participle from ' cornet ', i.e. to play on the horn. Elsewhere in this play a satyr is described as winding a horn, see IV, ii, 57–8 and V, iii, 143–4.

25. Q. *my*, an evident misprint, which D₁ corrects to *may*.

39. P. omits *me*, which appears in all the copies of Q. that I have seen, and is retained by all editors.

41–4. Q. prints as prose ; D₂ arranges as verse.

43. Q. *suiting all ;* D₁ *unsuiting all*. Co. follows Q. and explains ' *suiting* means *clouding* or *covering* '. S. emends *ill*, a conjecture approved by Brereton and one which seems to me very happy,

77–8. The punctuation of these lines is very confusing in Q., which reads *cheere Love, with your husband be, your wisedome here*. D₁ punctuates *cheer ; Love with your husband be, your* and is followed by all editors.

I have punctuated to bring out the sense of the passage. See note above, p. 810.

110. Q. *Now, what the Power and my Torches influence.* The line seems to me plainly corrupt, but it has been followed by all editors. I fancy Chapman wrote *what ere Power my Torches,* that the printer set up *what the Power my Torches,* and that a proofreader, not the poet, in the attempt to correct this error, inserted *and* before *my.* I have emended the text accordingly. Another correction would be *What my Power and Torch's,* but this does not seem to me so good.

IV, i, 3. Q. *taken ;* P. misprints *take.*

104. Q. prints *These* as the last word of l. 103. D₁ corrects.

106. Q. *with Sepulcher ;* so D₁, D₂ and Co. ; S. *within a sepulchre.* The true reading is plainly *wi' th' sepulchre.*

134. Q. *braine of the West ;* so all editors. A note signed S.P. in D₂ suggests *wisest.* Co. explains the phrase as equivalent to ' parliamentary wisdom which is usually displayed at *Westminster* '. I follow the emendment of Deighton (*Old Dramatists,* p. 140), which receives some support from *breasts of the wise,* I, i, 52–3.

147–8. Q. prints as prose ; D₁ corrects.

IV, ii, 1. D₁ places the name *Lysander* before the first speech.

4. Q. prints as two short lines ending *condemn'd* and *Gods.* Co. corrects.

14. Q. prints as two short lines ending *Ho !* and *there ? ;* Co. corrects.

16. Q. *a Souldier ;* P. omits *a.*

22–33. Q. prints as prose ; Co. arranges ll. 30–3 as verse. I have printed the whole passage as verse, although the metre is often very ragged.

34–7. Q. prints as prose ; Co. arranges as verse.

46. Q. *Rape, and spoil'd of ;* D₁ corrects *spoil.* Probably *spoile* in the MS. was mis-read by the printer.

78. Q. *Good heare him ;* D₂ and Co. *Good ; hear him ;* S. *Good hear him.* Gilchrist in a note

printed by Co. suggests *good mistress,* which seems to me a certain emendation. Not only does it restore the metre, but it hits the trick of Ero's speech, cf. above, l. 22, *good soldier,* and below, l. 91, *good mistress.*

79–86. Q. prints this speech as prose ; D₂ corrects.

90. Q. prints as two short lines ending *husband* and *none ?* So all editors, but it seems to me plainly one line.

102–3. Q. prints as four lines ending *starve, to, first,* and *Ladie.* I have arranged as in the text.

108. Q. *Noble death ;* D₂ inserts *A* before *noble.*

110–12. Q. prints as three lines ending *husband, within* and *command.* I arrange as in the text.

123. Q. prints as two lines ending *enow* and *me ?* I arrange as in the text.

129. Q. *O know ;* D₁, D₂, Co., *O, I know ;* S. *I know.* I take it Ero's speech is addressed in a stage whisper to Lysander.

148. Q. *The spring ants, spoil'd me thinkes.* D₁, D₂, Co., *spring of't's.* S. reverts to Q. ; but his reading, *The spring ants spoiled,* has, as Brereton (*loc. cit.*) points out, a very comic look in a modern edition. *Ants,* of course, is equivalent to *on it is.*

155–7. Q. prints as prose ; D₂ arranges as verse.

166–8. I follow the arrangement of Q. Co. prints as two lines of verse ending *organ* and *element.* In l. 166 P. misprints *trurh* for Q. *truth.*

175. S. inserts *to* before *flesh.* This change is not necessary.

IV, iii, 3–4. Q. prints as prose ; Co. arranges as verse.

84–86. Q., D₂ and Co. print as four lines of verse, ending *edifie, Dido, hearke, hunters.* I follow S. in arranging as prose.

V, i, 30. Q. *Our sister.* So all editors ; but *Lycus* is not the brother or brother-in-law of Cynthia. I take *Our* to be a simple misprint for *Your.* Tharsalio has just spoken of *Cynthia* as *my sister,* l. 23 above.

43. Q. *windes ;* so all editors. It is, however, an evident misprint for *mindes.* P. misprints *constanly* for Q. *constantly* in this line.

74–6. Q. ends these lines with the words *bodies*, *fast* and *signe* respectively. So all editors, but I think the arrangement in the text preferable.

103. Q. puts the words *O that 'twere true* in parenthesis to indicate an aside.

113. Q. has no stage-direction after this line; D₂ *Exeunt Cynthia and Ero*; I add *into the tomb*.

127, 130, 135. In these lines Q. has *1*, *2*, and *1*, prefixed to the speeches; D₂ *First Soldier, Second Soldier, First Soldier.*

141. Q. *caresly*; D₁, *carelessly.*

142. Q. prints the captain's speech entirely as prose; so D₂ and Co. S. prints ll. 142–149 as verse. I believe the whole passage from l. 142 may be taken as the rough verse of which we have so much in this play.

V, ii, 8. Q. prints *I may* at the close of l. 7. P. silently corrects this.

13. Q. puts *Damnation* in parenthesis to indicate an aside. Former editors have not noticed this. I have thought best to take the whole speech as an aside, like l. 18, where neither Q. nor former editors note an aside.

19–20. Q. prints Cynthia's speech as one line. D₂ corrects.

20. Q. *Cancro.* P. misprints *Canero* and is followed by S. Deighton (*loc. cit.*) has a long note to show that *Cancro* is the right word, being apparently unaware that this was the reading of Q., D₁, D₂ and Co.

36. Q. *the Monster*, so S. D₂ *thee, monster*, which seems to me the correct reading.

40. Q. *tenant*; so S. D₁ *truant*, an emendation received by Co. and approved by Deighton and Brereton. It seems established by a passage below V, iii, 202, where *truant* and *mich't* occur together as *miching* and *truant* do here.

55. Q. *aide*; so S. D₂ and Co. *add*, but I believe the old text may stand, see note on p. 812.

67–8. Q. *Put women to the test; discover them; paint them, paint* *them ten parts more.* D₂ and Co. follow, with slight changes, the punctuation of Q. It seems to me, however, that the two main parts of this sentence are meant to stand in sharp contrast. Lysander says in effect : ' Shall men put women to the test, discover them, as I have done ? Nay, paint them more than they do themselves rather than see them as they really are '. I have punctuated to bring out this meaning. S. omits the second *paint them*, but the repetition adds emphasis.

71–2. Q. prints as prose; S. as verse. Deighton (*loc. cit.*) alters *store* to *stare*. Perhaps this is right, but I think *store* may be understood in the sense of ' heap up ', ' gather together '

73–6. Q.

> *There sticks an Achelons horne*
> *of all, Copie enough,*
> *As much as 'Alizon of streames*
> *receives*
> *Or lofty Ilea showes of shadie*
> *leaves.*

The passage is evidently corrupt, and has probably been cut after l. 73. No editor has succeeded in restoring it satisfactorily. D₁ emends *Achelons* to *Acheloüs*, and *Ilea* to *Ida*, both of which are, of course, correct ; but his further change, *of all copia enough*, is inadmissible. Deighton's emendation (*loc. cit.,* p. 141) *ill* for *all*, seems to me to suit the context perfectly. The words *Copie enough* have proved a stumblingblock. It has been suggested (P. *note*, vol. iii, p. 360) that they were originally a marginal comment which has crept into the text. Deighton takes them to be a marginal explanation of *Acheloüs horn*, often identified with the ' horn of plenty ', or ' cornucopia '. My own belief is that they are a fragment of a line, or more, which had been struck out of the stage version, from which this play was printed, and that the printer finding them still legible in the MS., included them in the text. I am not satisfied with *Alizon* in l. 75 (see note, p.

813 above), and would like to suggest *Amazon*, famous even in Chapman's day as a Father of Waters, but I have not ventured to embody this suggestion in the text.

140–46. Q. prints as prose, and is followed by all editors. I arrange as verse. The stage-direction on ll. 146–7 appears in Q. in the body of the text and in the same type.

162–3. Q. *plight indeede with him, the utmost pledge of Nuptiall love with him.* D₂ and Co. follow Q. D₁ drops the first *with him.* This seems to me correct ; the printer's eye probably caught the phrase too soon.

182–191. Q. prints as prose, and is followed by all editors. I arrange as verse.

V, iii. Throughout the scene Q. prints *1.* and *2.* for 1st *Soldier* and 2nd *Soldier.*

iii, 8–9. Q. includes the words from *though* to *dispenc'd* in the parenthesis. Co. corrects.

42. Q. *finde to be counterfait;* so all editors. I emend *found,* which the context seems to demand.

53. D₁ puts the question mark after *hearse.*

58. D₁ inserts *Lysander* before the speech.

64–5. Q.

Thou, false in show, hast been most true to me ;
The seeming true ; hath prov'd more false then her.

The passage is evidently corrupt. D₂ and Co. follow Q. only changing the semi-colon after *true,* l. 65, to a comma. S has no punctuation after *true.* Brereton (*loc. cit.*) proposes to read *she* for *The* and *thou* for *her.* This brings out the sense of the passage, which is the contrast between Lysander's disguise and his wife ; but it seems needless to alter *The* to *She* for *The seeming true* is, of course, Cynthia. In a note in Co. Gilchrist suggests *thee* for *her,* which I think is preferable to Brereton's *thou.*

81. Q. *prepares away;* so S. D₂

prepares a way, which is probably right, though if we take *prepare* in the sense of ' prepare to depart ', the old reading might be defended.

94. Q. *I bleede not;* D₁ emends *I* to *It.*

98. Q. prints *Gore* as the first word of l. 99.

117. Q. prints *Proofe* as the first word of l. 118, and puts *but I shall yron you* in parenthesis to denote an aside.

130. Q. *soft-r'ode;* D₁ *soft-toed,* probably a misprint, which Co. corrects to *soft-roed.*

133. The *etc.* in the Q. denotes that the speech was cut here, or perhaps that Chapman left it unfinished. This last act bears every mark of hasty composition.

137. Q. has a period after *most;* D₁ a dash.

146–7. Q. and editors print Lysander's speech as prose. I arrange as verse.

195–6. Q. *2. Come convay him to the Lord Governour.*
First afore the captaine Sir. Have the heavens, etc.
The arrangement of speeches is confusing. It is quite certain that the sentence beginning *Have the* belongs to Lysander, and S. gives him also the words *First . . . Sir.* D₂ and Co. take *First* as equivalent to *First Soldier,* and give him the entire line, beginning it *Afore the,* although C. in a note recognizes that the latter part appears to belong to Lysander. As Q. never prints *First* but always *1.* as the abbreviation of the speaker's name, I prefer to follow S.

204. Q. misprints *bur ;* P. silently corrects.

220. The *aside* in this line was inserted by Co. at the close of the speech.

238. Q. *creature Foole is ;* so all editors, although Co. suggests *a fool is.*

249. P. misprints *Lyb.* as the speaker's name.

255–6. Q. *but two ;* so all editors. Perhaps we should read *not two.*

274. Q. *Parrat ;* editors *parrot,*

which is no doubt correct. Deighton's emendation (*loc. cit.*) *prate* is unnecessary.

305. Q. *Doe heare ;* D_1 *Do you hear.*

348. Q. *for us ;* so all editors. Perhaps the original was *frõ,*

which might be easily misprinted *for*, if the dash over *o* were overlooked.

350. P. misprints *Lyc.* as the speaker's name.

362–4. Q. prints as prose ; S. as verse.

THE MASQUE OF THE MIDDLE TEMPLE
AND LINCOLN'S INN

INTRODUCTION

Ben Jonson told Drummond [1] that ' next himself only Fletcher and Chapman could make a masque. This judgment was perhaps influenced by Jonson's personal feelings, for Chapman and Fletcher were distinguished in his talks with Drummond as poets whom he loved. Yet Jonson's critical dicta always command respect, and since, apart from the masque-like shows and devices preserved in Chapman's plays,[2] the *Masque of the Middle Temple and Lincoln's Inn* is Chapman's only surviving work of this form, it deserves some special consideration.

It was composed, as the full title declares, to form part of the festivities accompanying the marriage of Elizabeth, daughter of James I. From 1610, when she was fourteen years old, Elizabeth's hand had been sought by various sovereigns.[3] Early in 1612 James concluded a treaty with the Protestant princes of Germany, and in May of that year signed a contract promising Elizabeth in marriage to Frederick V, the Elector Palatine, or Palsgrave, as he was commonly called in England, a nephew of the Protestant champion, Maurice of Orange, and the head of the league of Protestant princes in Germany. The proposed match was very popular in England as definitely committing the nation to the cause of militant Protestantism, and when the Palsgrave arrived in October, 1612, he received a royal welcome. A contemporary [4] account describes him as ' straight and well-shaped for his growing years. His complexion is brown, with a countenance promising both wit, courage and judgment. He becomes himself well and is very well liked of all '.

The young couple seem to have taken a genuine fancy for each other at their first meeting. It was reported of the Palsgrave that ' he plied his mistress hard, and took no delight in running at the ring nor tennis nor riding, but only in her conversation '. She invited him to a ' solemn supper ' and entertained him with a play by her own company of actors at the Cockpit. This happy period of courtship was, however, sharply interrupted by the sudden illness and tragic death

---

[1] *Jonson's Conversations with Drummond—Shakespeare Society Publications*, vol. viii, p. 4.
[2] In *The Gentleman Usher*, I, ii and II, i and in *The Widow's Tears*, III, ii.
[3] Gustavus Adolphus of Sweden and Philip III of Spain were both suggested as fit matches by the English partisans of the opposing Protestant and Catholic parties on the Continent.
[4] Nichols, *Progresses of King James*, vol. ii, p. 464.

of Henry Prince of Wales, November 6. A deep and sincere affection existed between Henry and Elizabeth. His last intelligible words were an inquiry for his dear sister, and during his illness Elizabeth more than once attempted to visit his sick-bed in disguise only to be turned back at the door of his chamber.

The death of the beloved Heir Apparent cast a gloom over the whole kingdom, but the policy which had determined the marriage of Elizabeth remained unaltered. On December 27 she and the Palsgrave were formally betrothed at Whitehall, and the marriage day was fixed for Shrove Sunday, February 14.

The six weeks between New Year's Day and the wedding must have been a period of feverish haste in the preparation of festivities. The marriage was to be celebrated with a magnificence unknown before in England. There were to be shows on water and land, fireworks, sham battles, processions, banquets, and, as a matter of course, masques. Jonson, the official masque-maker for the Court, was at this time in France [1] acting as tutor and travelling companion to a wild son of Walter Raleigh. In his absence Campion, the musician and poet, Beaumont, since Shakespeare's retirement, the chief playwright of the King's company, and Chapman [2] were entrusted with the task of composing three masques to be performed on three successive nights at Court.

The festivities opened on Thursday, February 11, with a great show of fireworks on the Thames, St. George and the Dragon, a hart hunted by fiery hounds, a sea-fight of Christians against Turks, and so on. On Saturday there was another show of fireworks ' in the manner of a sea-fight ', in which two Venetian ships were captured by galleys from Algiers and rescued by an English fleet. Further shows of a like nature were promised, but if a gossiping [3] letter-writer of the day can be trusted ' the King and all the Court took so little delight to see no other activity but shooting and potting of guns that it is quite given over, and the Navy unrigged and the Castle pulled down, the rather for that there were divers hurt . . . as one lost both his eyes, another both his hands, another one hand, with divers others maimed and hurt '. The cost of these somewhat unsatisfactory shows was reckoned at no less than £9,000.

The wedding itself was celebrated with great splendour in the Royal Chapel at Whitehall on Shrove Sunday morning, February 14. Bridegroom and bride were both in cloth of silver richly embroidered with silver, her train carried by thirteen young ladies, ' all in the same livery as the Bride '. The King appeared in a sumptuous suit of black, wearing jewels valued at £600,000 ; the Queen in white satin, ' most gloriously attired ', her jewels valued at £400,000. The Chapel was crowded with richly dressed courtiers ; Chamberlain noted that a Catholic lord, who had recently paid a heavy fine for recusancy, was yet able to spend £15,000 in apparel for his two daughters.

After the wedding ceremony a state banquet filled the afternoon

---

[1] The dates of this journey are uncertain, but it seems probable that Jonson left England very shortly after the Prince's death.

[2] Chapman had been ' Sewer-in-Ordinary ' to the deceased Prince Henry, but it is more probable that his position as chief playwright for the Children of the Revels led to his selection.

[3] Chamberlain, quoted by Nichols, *Progresses of King James*, vol. ii, p. 587.

and in the evening the lords of the Court presented Campion's masque [1] in the Banqueting Hall.

Inigo Jones assisted Campion in the preparation of this masque, which is remarkable rather for the splendour of its setting and the ingenuity of its transformation scenes than for its literary merit. The theme is drawn according to the usual convention from classic mythology. Orpheus acts as the presenter, and Prometheus and Entheus (poetic fury) assist him. The first anti-masque is a dance of ' frantics, six men and six women in sundry habits and humours ' ; the second a dance of sixteen pages ' like fiery spirits, bearing in either hand a torch of virgin wax '. Of the chief masquers the men appeared first as stars, then as courtiers ; the women first as statues, then as ladies brought to life. Campion's music, no doubt, appealed as much to the ear as the costumes and dances did to the eye, but the masque as a whole lacks any dominant idea. It is a splendid show rather than a true masque as Jonson conceived it.

On Monday there was a ceremonious running at the ring in the tilt-yard of the palace, in which the King, the Palsgrave and Prince Charles took part, while the Queen and the bride looked on from the galleries and windows of the Banqueting Hall. In the evening came the gorgeous procession, described in the Introduction to Chapman's *Masque*, from Chancery Lane along the Strand to Whitehall, and the perform-ance of the *Masque* in the great hall of the Palace.

On Tuesday, after much ' banqueting of foreign estates as well Princes' ambassadors as the peers and nobles attending upon the Pals-grave ', there was a splendid procession by water of the masquers from Gray's Inn and the Inner Temple. ' The barges were beautiful with many flags and streamers, lighted with a number of burning cressets and torches, attended on by drums and trumpets which sounded all the way most melodiously '.

The masque, however, could not be performed that evening. The great hall was so full of people that it could not be cleared for the performance ; many ladies of the Court who had gone into the galleries to see the boats land could not get back into the crowded hall ; and ' worst of all the King was so wearied and sleepy with sitting up almost two whole nights before that he had no edge to it '. When Bacon, who had spent much time and money in the preparation of this masque, pleaded with the King not to ' bury them quick with this disgrace ', James answered peevishly that they must then bury him quick for he could last no longer. By special arrangement the performance was postponed until Saturday night, when it was given before the Court in the Banqueting Hall.

This masque, the work of Beaumont,[2] assisted apparently by Bacon, was performed ' with great applause and approbation both from the King and all the company '. It is an interesting example of the new development of the masque along dramatic lines. The theme is the rivalry of Mercury and Iris as messengers of Jove and Juno sent to do honour to the marriage of the two rivers, Thames and Rhine.

---

[1] Published in quarto, 1613, and reprinted by Nichols, *op. cit.* and in Bullen's *Works of Campion*.

[2] It was published in quarto form, F. K. for George Norton, probably in 1613—the quarto has no date—and has been reprinted by Nichols, *op. cit.* vol. ii, p. 591, and in the various editions of Beaumont and Fletcher.

After a dialogue in blank verse Mercury summons the first anti-masque consisting first of Naides, to whom there are added in turn the Hyades, four hoodwinked Cupids and four statues.   To match this show Iris summons the second anti-masque, a rustic medley of a Pedant, a May Lord, a May Lady, a Serving-man and a Chambermaid, a Country Clown and Country Wench, a Host and Hostess, a He-baboon and She-baboon, a He-fool and a She-fool.   The comment in the old copy of the *Masque* states that the music to this device was 'extremely well-fitted, having such a spirit of country jollity as can hardly be imagined, but the perpetual laughter and applause was above the music. The Dance likewise was of the same strain ; and the dancers, or rather actors, expressed every one their part naturally and aptly '.   The phrase, the *dancers or rather actors*, indicates that this anti-masque was performed by professional players, doubtless members of the King's Company, and it seems likely that this part of the performance was not so much a dance as a comic pantomime.   It seems to have been carried back from the Court to the Globe and a version arranged for the public stage was incorporated in *The Two Noble Kinsmen* (Act III, sc. v).

The chief masquers were fifteen Olympian knights sent by Jove to renew the ancient games in honour of the nuptials of Frederick and Elizabeth.   They danced among themselves, led out the ladies of the Court to dance ' galliards, durets and corantos ' and then marched off to the sound of loud music, while the priests of Jove sang a hymeneal chant in honour of the bride and groom.

The crowded week of festivities closed on Sunday, February 21, with a solemn supper in the new Marriage Room of the palace, to which the King invited all the masquers and their assistants, according to each gentleman a special audience and the honour of kissing his hand.

I have given a somewhat detailed account of these festivities to show the nature of the occasion for which Chapman's *Masque* was written, and for purposes of comparison I have analysed the masques that preceded and followed his.   Campion's seems to me distinctly old-fashioned ; Beaumont's, on the other hand, marks the appearance of a new and more dramatic element ; Chapman's, I believe, is nearer than either to the true form of the masque as it had evolved in the first decade of the sixteenth century.

Chapman's work, first of all, springs from one central and dominating *motif*, a *motif*, moreover, which had, for a masque the unusual advantage of novelty.   The theme is Virginia, the first English colony beyond the seas.   From the beginning of his reign James had taken an interest in the projects of colonization in the New World.   Jamestown, named in his honour, was founded in 1607 by a London Company to which he had granted a charter, and there were repeated expeditions to Virginia and further settlements there in 1609, 1610 and 1611. It must be remembered that it was the lure of gold which drew the first English settlers to America.   Virginia was thought to be another Mexico or Peru, and the fabulous wealth of the Indies was to flow into England from this new land.   Chapman, always interested [1] in discovery and exploration, probably knew as little of the real resources of Virginia and the true nature of the aborigines as did the ordinary man in the street of his day.   To him as to most Englishmen of his

[1] See his *De Gutana* (*Poems*, p. 50) and *Eastward Ho*, III, iii.

day Virginia was a land of gold and its inhabitants sun-worshippers like the Aztecs. To bring the counterfeit presentments of these sun-worshippers to Court, clad in all the splendour of the monarch of El-dorado as Raleigh had pictured him, and cause them there to renounce their pagan rites and pay homage to the Sun of Britain, the Phœbus who had succeeded Cynthia upon the throne, was the idea that lay at the back of Chapman's mind when he set to work upon this masque.

The chief masquers would, as a matter of course, appear as Indian princes. The natural presenter of the masque would be Plutus, a fit representative of the riches of the Indies. But Plutus, according to the received mythology was a blind and heavy-witted deity ; some reason must be found to explain his presence at the Court and render his presentation of the masque acceptable. Chapman accordingly imagines him to have fallen in love with the Goddess Honour and to have come to seek her at her rich temple at the Court of James, where Fortune [1] had fixed her golden wings and rolling stone ' for sign she would never forsake this kingdom '. Through his love of Honour Plutus has recovered both his sight and wit, and so has become a proper presenter of this honourable masque.

According to the received convention each masque had to include an anti-masque,[2] a show which preceded the main masque and stood out in sharp contrast to it. This Chapman provided in a company of baboons, according to the belief of his day, inhabitants of the Indies East and West. A special presenter was needed for the anti-masque and for this purpose Chapman invented the figure of Capriccio, a needy, lively, fantastic, ' man of wit ', a poor kinsman, one might imagine of the magnificent Monsieur D'Olive.

Along these lines, then, and with these figures Chapman composed his *Masque*. The main presenter, Plutus, appears first, and drops some sarcastic remarks about the conventional scenery, the ' artificial rock ' described in the Introduction to the *Masque*. It splits open and Capriccio appears. After a prose dialogue between the two presenters Capriccio introduces the ' baboonerie ' from their hiding-place, ' a vast, withered and hollow tree '. After their dance, ' being antic and delightful,' they disappear, and Plutus, having dismissed Capriccio with a golden reward, proceeds to the main business of the performance. All that has passed so far has been but a ' low in-duction '.

Plutus now invokes Eunomia, the priestess of Honour, to summon her mistress. Honour descends from her temple and informs him that the Princes of the Virgin land are about to pay their homage to the setting sun. After a song by the Phœbades, the priests of the sun, comes the moment of greatest splendour in a masque, the ' discovery ' of the chief masquers. The upper part of the mount which filled the back of the scene, was now transformed into a cloud, which rose and revealed a mine of gold. Here were seated the chief masquers at-

---

[1] *Masque*, ll, 163-5.
[2] ' Anti-masque, " a foil or false masque " (Jonson's phrase) directly opposed to the principal masque. If this was lofty and serious that was light and ridiculous '—Gifford's note on Jonson's *Masque of Mercury Vindicated*. See also the anti-masque in *The Triumph of Neptune* where the Poet omits this feature in his work and it is supplied by the Cook, the figures of the anti-masque rising from the Cook's pot.

tended by their torch-bearers, all in the gorgeous costumes described in the Introduction (pp. 439–440).

The spectacle, arranged by Inigo Jones, must indeed have been magnificent.   It is followed by a lyrical interlude, songs of the Phœbades to the setting sun, songs of Honour's company in praise of the Phœbus of Britain, a song marking the conversion of the sun-worshippers to this new deity, and so on.

Then Eunomia calls on the chief masquers to do reverence to the King, but before they descend from their high seats, their attendant torch-bearers come down and present the second [1] anti-masque.   After this the chief masquers descended, danced two measures alone, and then invited ladies from the audience to join with them.   After this comes the speech of Honour in praise of Love and Beauty, i.e. Frederick and Elizabeth, and then, as a solo, sung to a single lute, the Hymn of Love and Beauty, each verse being followed by a chorus of voices. Then came another dance of the masquers with the ladies, then a choral hymeneal song, then the closing words of the presenter, Plutus, and the last dance of the masquers, after which Plutus and Honour led them up to the temple into which they disappeared and so ended [2] the performance.

I have been at some pains to give a full analysis of the *Masque*, for owing to the confused printing, the omissions, repetitions, and so on, the plan of the whole is by no means apparent at first sight.   It would be absurd to affirm that this masque is easy or entertaining reading ; but we must remember that the text of a masque was no more meant to be read than is the libretto of a modern opera.   Jonson's masques, indeed, are still amusing, partly because of their humorous satirical interludes, partly because of their lyrical beauty.   But Jonson stands alone as a writer of masques which are literature without ceasing— like *Comus*, for example—to be true masques.   The masque was primarily a spectacle, ' a lyric, scenic, and dramatic framework ' [3] for the dance of the chief masquers, which was not only its chief feature, but its very *raison d'être*.   The scenic effects were most elaborate, the music, instrumental and vocal, composed and performed by professional [4] musicians, was the best that England could afford at a time when English music was perhaps the best in the world.   The dances varied from the grotesque antics of baboons or country clowns and wenches to the elaborate and stately measures of the chief masquers.   The costumes were gorgeous beyond description

[1] The introduction of a second anti-masque seems to have been an innovation in the older form which appears for the first time in the three masques presented at this marriage.   We have seen the use Beaumont made of it ; Chapman, like Campion, introduced here the torch-bearers of the chief masquers, thus preparing the way for their ceremonious measures with a lively, but not a grotesque dance, much less a burlesque pantomime.   In Campion's masque sixteen pages appeared as fiery spirits, dancing a lively measure with a torch of wax in either hand.   Chapman's torch-bearers, dressed like their masters in Indian costumes, but 'more stravagant' (*vid.* p. 440), danced with wax torches lighted at both ends.

[2] The *Hymn to Hymen* which is appended to the *Masque* is not, properly speaking, a part of the performance, but Chapman's *L'Envoi* or *Epilogue*.

[3] Schelling, *Elizabethan Drama*, vol. ii, p. 93.

[4] The *Phoebades* in Chapman's *Masque* were ' the choice musicians of our kingdom ', see above p. 439.

and costly [1] to a degree. It was not the business of the masque-writer to compose a drama—any real action would have been overwhelmed and rendered unintelligible by the accessories of music, dancing and costumes—but to invent and elaborate a theme which would give unity and coherence to the separate parts of the masque, afford a fitting opportunity for the introduction of songs and dances, and, most important of all, have a direct bearing upon the occasion on which the masque was to be produced, and pay a flattering homage, couched in the somewhat pedantic mythological conventions of the late Renaissance, to the illustrious personages in whose honour it was performed. All these things, it seems to me, Chapman in the *Masque of the Middle Temple and Lincoln's Inn* has amply accomplished, and thus justified the praise of Jonson cited at the beginning of this Introduction.

[1] This masque is said to have cost the two Inns presenting it over £1,500, approximately £10,000 to-day.

THE MASQUE OF THE MIDDLE TEMPLE
AND LINCOLN'S INN

NOTES.

Dedication. Sir Henry Hobart, who is associated with Sir Edward Philips in this Dedication, was an old Lincoln's Inn man. He was knighted by James, July 23, 1603, appointed Attorney-General in 1607, and created a Baronet in 1611.

p. 439. *Cockle-demois.* The *New English Dictionary* gives this as the sole instance of the word and suggests the meaning ' shells representing money '.

p. 440. *Sided them :* walked beside them. The *New English Dictionary* cites this instance.

Watchet : a pale blue colour.

p. 441. *Pentacle.* Nichols takes this word to mean merely a tippet or mantle, but since it is used here as an adornment of a priest, it is probably to be taken as a garment cut in the shape of the sacred pentagram.

Clinquant : glittering, spangled. It seems to have been a common word at this time (cf. *Henry VIII*, I, i, 19). The Palsgrave, for example, said 'he would not see his mistress, but in clinquant' (Nichols, *Op. cit.*, vol. ii, p. 464). In l. 192 of the *Masque* it means ' illustrious ', ' distinguished.'

p. 442. *Greeces :* 'steps or stairs in a flight.'—*New English Dictionary.*

Coupolo or type : The *New English Dictionary* cites this passage, *sub* tipe or type. Both words mean the same thing, a dome-like lantern or skylight, *wie ein Lucern formieret in die Runde*, as it is described in a contemporary German account of this masque.—*Shakespeare Jahrbuch*, 1894.

These following : the following directions and explanations. Chapman and his printer seem to have been completely at odds. The next three paragraphs appear to have been written to supply the missing stage directions, but the printer seems to have received them in time to insert some sort of stage directions in the proper places, see for example pp. 447 and 452.

Never sending me a proof : a rather interesting phrase showing that, in spite of all that has been said to the contrary, the Elizabethan dramatist did occasionally read his proofs.

p. 444. *These of Menander.* Chapman found this quotation from Menander in Plutarch's *Morals—Amatorius* 763, b. For the original Greek see *Menandri Fragmenta*, No. xiv, p. 57 in *Scriptorum Graecorum Biblioteca*, edition Didot. Here the Latin translation appears as :

Morbus animi occasio est.
Haec si quem feriit intus, is vulnus trahit.

The next words in Chapman are an adaptation of the words of Plutarch immediately following the quotation : *Imo in causa est deus, alium tangens, alium praeteriens.*

p. 445. The Latin line is the latter half of a couplet by Ovid beginning :

Adde quod ingenuas didicisse fideliter artes.

Pontic Epistles, II, ix, 48.

p. 446. *Non est certa fides :* from Propertius, IV, vii (viii), 19. The half line following is from the same poet, IV, vi (vii), 36—Teubner edition.

p. 447, l. 30. *Land of Spruce.* ' Spruce ' is a variant form of ' Pruce ', Prussia. The ' land of Spruce ' apparently is equivalent to the land of Cockayne, where all good things abound. I know no other instance of this phrase.

l. 44. The Latin phrase is Chapman's alteration of the well-known Virgilian phrase :

Et penitus toto divisos orbe Britannos.

Eclog. I, 67.

p. 448, l. 65. *Miching.* See note on *Widow's Tears*, V, ii, 39.

p. 449, l. 107. *Shoemaker.* The reference is to Simon Eyre, the hero of Dekker's *Shoemaker's Holiday.* The historical Simon Eyre who built Leadenhall, Lord Mayor in 1445, was actually a draper, but the legend used by Deloney (*The Gentle Craft*) and Dekker made him a shoemaker.

l. 119. *Dizzards :* jesters, fools.

p. 450, l. 153. *A fetch of state :* a trick of state-craft.

p. 451, l. 182. *Complemental fardel :* bundle of accomplishments, referring to the dancing baboons.

p. 452, l. 234. *Strikes a plain :* Nichols, who prints *a-plaine*, compares the word to ' a-weary ', etc. I take it that *plain* here is used as a substantive from the adjective ' plain,' ' full ' and that the expression means ' strikes a full stroke '.

p. 453, l. 245. *His sea's repair :* his repairing to the sea, his setting in the sea.

l. 253. *Tethys*, the wife of Oceanus, used here for the sea.

p. 455, l. 320. *Those twins :* the twins of Hippocrates. See the note on *The Gentleman Usher*, IV, iii, 17.

p. 456. Stage-direction. *Single :* to the accompaniment of one lute only. The German account specifies *ein Laut allein.*

The Hymn, l. 2. *Parcae's tears :* referring to the tears shed for Prince Henry.

TEXT NOTES

There are two old editions of the *Masque*, both in quarto form. One, listed by Greg (*List of English Masques*, W. W. Greg) as the earlier [1] is represented by an apparently unique copy at the British Museum (C. 34. b. 61), It is imperfect lacking signatures D₂-E inclusive. The title-page is as follows : The Memorable Masque of the two Honourable Houses or Innes of Court ; the Middle Temple, and Lyncolnes Inne. As it was performed before the King, at White-hall on Shrove-Munday at night ; being the 15. of Febr. 1613. At the Princely Celebration of the most royal nuptials of the Palsgrave, and his thrice gratious Princesse Elizabeth, etc. With a description of their whole show, in the manner of their march on horse-backe to the Court, from the Master of the Rolls his house : with all their right noble consorts, and most showfull attendants. Invented, and fashioned, with the ground, and speciall structure of the whole worke : By our Kingdomes most Artfull and Ingenious Architect Innigo Jones. Supplied, Applied, Digested, and written, By Geo. Chapman. At London, Printed by F. K. for George Norton, and are to be sold at his shop neere Temple-barre.

The other edition has a title-page agreeing, apart from minute differences in spelling and punctuation (*maske* for *masque*, *Inns* for *Innes*, etc.) with this, except that the printer's name is given as G. Eld.

Apart from the F. K. quarto in the British Museum all the extant copies of

---

[1] There is some reason to believe that this copy is the sole remaining example of a second edition. Chapman seems to have been dissatisfied with the printing of the *Masque* (see his remarks on the unexpected haste of the printer, p. 442) and may have induced the publisher, Norton, to issue a second edition, the printing of which was entrusted to F. K. (Felix Kyngston, engaged in printing and publishing from 1597 to 1640). Norton had entered Chapman's *Masque* along with Beaumont's *Masque of Gray's Inn and the Inner Temple*, in the Stationers' Registers on February 27, 1613—the date is given in the Registers as *Januarii*, but this is an evident mistake. I imagine that to get the work done as quickly as possible he gave the printing of Chapman's *Masque* to George Eld, and Beaumont's to Kyngston. The omission of the *errata* in the F. K. edition, and some peculiarities of arrangement lead me to suspect that this is a second, not a first edition, an opinion which has the support of such authorities on Elizabethan printing as T. J. Wise and R. B. McKerrow. Owing to the mutilated condition of the unique copy, however, it is impossible to decide this matter positively and in the main we are forced to rely on Eld's edition.

the *Masque* with which I am acquainted belong to this edition ; there are three copies in the British Museum, three in the Bodleian, two in the Albert and Victoria Museum among Dyce's books, and one in the University Library, Cambridge. T. J. Wise also possesses a copy. There are a number of variations between these copies, of which I have tried to record the more important. One of those at the Bodleian (Malone 241) represents, I think, an earlier and less correct stage. Thus on A⁴ (p. 446 of this edition) it omits the words *all issuing* to *fidem* inclusive, and the list of *Errata*, probably furnished by Chapman after he had seen an early copy. Elsewhere also this copy differs from the others with which I have compared it, and always for the worse,

The *Masque* was reprinted for the first time by John Nichols—*The Progresses of King James*, vol. ii, pp. 566, *ssq.* Nichols seems to have printed from a copy of Eld's edition—he names Eld as the printer—which lacked the list of *Errata*, for he leaves unaltered several errors noted in this list. I refer to his edition as N.

The next reprint was that in the *Comedies and Tragedies of George Chapman*, 1873, (P.). This also is printed from a copy of Eld's edition—possibly from¹ C. 12. g. 6. It omits the *Errata*, but uses them to correct the text. This reprint, then, does not correspond exactly to any of the original copies. The last edition up to the present is that of Shepherd, *Works of George Chapman—Plays* (S.). As usual this is a modernized edition of P.

My own text rests upon a comparison of various copies. I have found that the unique copy is right in two² instances against all the others, but its imperfect condition has prevented me from using it throughout. I have reprinted the *Errata* in a footnote³ and corrected the text by them without indication of the changes so made. My own alterations are in brackets. In the following notes I refer to the text by page and line.

p. 437, l. 11. Q. *Hubberd*. So N. and P. I correct *Hobart*, see note p. 831 above.

P. prints the signature to the letter as follows : *By your free merits ever vowed honorer, and most unfainedly affectioned, Geo. Chapman*. This reading occurs, so far as I know, only in one copy C. 12. g. 6. in the British Museum. My text follows that of the other copies.

p. 440, last line. Q. misprints *Grotesea*. N. corrects.

p. 441, l. 17. S. inserts the word *car* which does not appear in Q.

p. 442, l. 19. *Scal'd*. So Q. and P. N. reads *seal'd*, i.e. *ceil'd*.

p. 443, l. 6. The Malone 241 Q. reads *in Orphean* ; all others *an Orphean*.

l. 13. *State*. All old copies that I have seen read *seate* ; but in one of the Dyce copies, originally in the Heber collection, there is an

MS. correction *state*. This seems to me the true reading, for the reference is to the *state*, or royal chair, of the King, and the misprint *seate* for *state* is very easy.

l. 15. *To set*. One copy (British Museum C. 12. g. 6) reads *to be set*, which is followed by P. ; all others that I have seen, and N., *to set*.

p. 444, l. 12. *Vain*. P. follows C. 12. g. 6. in reading *paine* ; all others that I have seen, and N. have *vaine*.

l. 26. Q. *cause of all mens :* so N., P., and S. But this is repugnant to the context ; *all* is an evident error for *some* which I have inserted in the text.

ll. 24, 26, 32. These lines show three instances where the Malone 241 copy stands alone in error. It has a period after *opportunitas*, reads *sleight* and *freedom* for *slight* and *Freedom*, and *writ* for *write*. I shall not hereafter note

¹ See the notes on Chapman's signature and on *Vain* p. 444, l. 12.
² See the notes on p. 449, l. 97, and l. 107.
³ *Errata* : In *Capri*. first speech for many, read maine [p. 447, l. 15], in c. i. for Pot. re. post [p. 449, l. 97], in c. 3. for answer, re. austerity, for purposes re. purses [p. 450, ll. 154–155], in c. 3 [an error for c. 4] for seemingly re. securely [p. 450, l. 172], in d. 2. for law, and vertue, re. love and beauty [p. 452, l. 222], in the first stance of the second song for this re. his [p. 453, l. 258], for sweet devotions, re. fit devotions [p. 455, l. 309]. This list does not appear in the F.K. quarto.

any of the peculiar errors of this copy.

p. 445, l. 8. *Ever.* N. misled perhaps by the old punctuation reads *never*, but this is an erroneous alteration. The sentence is to be construed : *But with no time, no study . . . will the chaste . . . beams of truth ever enter any arrogant, etc.*

p 447, l. 15. The unique copy reads *many*, all others *manie*. The true reading, *maine*, is given in the *Errata*, and followed by N. and P.

p. 449, l. 97. *Watering-post : post* is the reading of the unique copy ; all others *pot*, an error corrected in the *Errata* and by N. and P.

l. 107. *In a liberal.* So the unique copy ; all others *in in a liberal*, a misprint corrected in N.

p. 450, ll. 154–5. All copies, including the unique quarto, read *answer* and *purposes.* N. follows this reading in spite of the *Errata*, but P. corrects.

l. 158. *All is.* P. misprints *all this*.

l. 172. *Securely.* Q. *scmingly or seemingly*). N. follows this reading in spite of the *Errata*, but P. corrects. In the same line P. prints *the* for *thee* a false reading which occurs in Malone 241 and three British Museum Qq ; the unique quarto and two copies at the Bodleian have correctly *thee.*

l. 173. The unique quarto has *Antimasque* ; the others *Antemaske*. P. misprints *Autemaske*.

p. 451, l. 208. All the old copies, followed by N. and P. read *Love*,

but this is impossible. The words are addressed to *Eunomia or the sacred power of Law* (l. 202). That a confusion between *Lawe* and *Love* was possible is shown by the fact that in l. 222 all Qq have *Lawe* where the *Errata* corrects *Love*. I have therefore restored *Law* to the text.

p. 452, l. 216. All Qq, followed by P. and N., read *right* ; S. *rite*, which I take to be correct.

l. 219. P. omits *the* before *Briton*. I find no authority for this in any old copy.

l. 222. All Qq and N. read *Lawe and Vertue.* P. following the *Errata*, *Love and Beauty.*

p. 453, l. 258. All Qq read *this golden.* N. and P. following the *Errata*, *his golden.*

p. 454, Stage-direction after l. 293. All Qq, and N. P. and S. read *third stance* ; but the third stance has already been sung, ll. 280–291. This is the fourth, and I have made the necessary correction.

p. 455, l. 309. All Qq and N. read *sweet devotions* ; P. following the *Errata, fit devotions.*

l. 316. I have prefixed *Hon.* to this line ; cf. l. 306.

p. 458, l. 9. P. has a period after *heat*, but I find no authority for this punctuation in any old copy.

l. 31. N. thinks that the first *weeds* in this line is an error, and suggests *gems*, but the reading of the text is supported by all the old copies and is quite in Chapman's manner.

p. 459, l. 70. All Qq read *arts*, a mistake corrected by N.

EASTWARD HO

INTRODUCTION

Eastward Ho was entered in the Stationers' Registers, September 4, 1605, to William Aspley and Thomas Thorpe.[1] For some reason Thorpe, perhaps because he was about to publish *All Fools*, ceded his rights in *Eastward Ho* to Aspley, who issued this play later in the same year, 1605, with the following title-page :

> *Eastward Ho.* As It was playd in the Black-friers. By The Children of her Majesties Revels. Made by Geo: Chapman. Ben: Jonson. Joh: Marston. At London Printed for William Aspley. 1605.

There is a general consensus of opinion that *Eastward Ho* was composed not long before its publication, at earliest in the winter of 1604–5 (Fleay, *Biographical Chronicle*, vol. i, p. 60). If the date that I have suggested for *Monsieur D'Olive* (see above, p. 775) be correct, it would seem to follow that *Eastward Ho*, or at least Chapman's share in it, was composed early in 1605, possibly in the spring of that year. The play was, no doubt, put on the stage as soon as it was finished. It gave, as is well known, grave offence at Court. According to Jonson's report to [2] Drummond ' he was delated by Sir James Murray to the King for writing something against the Scots in a play, Eastward Ho, and voluntarily imprisoned himself with Chapman and Marston who had written it amongst them. The report was that they should then have had their ears cut and noses. After their delivery, he banqueted all his friends ; there was Camden, Selden, and and others ; at the midst of the feast his old mother drank to him and shew him a paper which she had (if the sentence had taken execution) to have mixed in the prison among his drink, which was full of lusty strong poison, and that she was no churl, she told, she minded first to have drunk of it herself '.

The authors seem to have escaped the threatened punishment through the intercession of powerful friends. A letter of Jonson's to Robert Cecil, Earl of Salisbury, preserved among the papers at Hatfield, has generally been accepted as referring to this imprisonment. It has been printed by Gifford (*Jonson's Works*, vol. i, p. 40) and Schelling (*Eastward Ho*, p. 162, *Belles-Lettres* edition). I cite here only the most important sentences. ' *I am here, my most honoured lord, unexamined and unheard, committed to a vile prison, and with me a gentleman (whose name may, perhaps, have come to your lord-*

---

[1] These two publishers evidently began about this time to take an interest in Chapman's work. Thorpe published *All Fools* in 1605, and *The Gentleman Usher* in 1606 ; Aspley *Eastward Ho* in 1605 and *Bussy* in 1607.

[2] *Ben Jonson's Conversations*, p. 20 (*Shakespeare Society Publications*, vol. viii).

*ship) one Mr. George Chapman, a learned and honest man. The cause
(would I could name some worthier, though I wish we had none worthy
our imprisonment) is . . . a play, my lord ; whereof we hope there is
no man can justly complain that hath the virtue to think but favourably of
himself, if our judge bring an equal ear : marry, if with prejudice we
be made guilty afore our time, we must embrace the asinine virtue, patience. . . . I beseech your most honourable lordship suffer not other
men's errors or faults past to be made my crimes ; but let me be examined
both by all my works past and this present ; and not trust to rumour but
my books . . . whether I have ever . . . given offence to a nation, to
a public order or state, or any person of honour or authority ; but have
equally laboured to keep their dignity as mine own person, safe. If
others have transgressed, let me not be entitled to their follies. But lest
in being too diligent for my excuse, I may incur the suspicion of being
guilty, I become a most humble suitor to your lordship that with the honourable lord Chamberlain . . . you will be pleased to be the grateful
means of our coming to answer ; or if in your wisdoms it shall be thought
necessary, that your lordship will be the most honoured cause of our liberty '.*

The letters communicated to the *Athenaeum*, March 30, 1901, by
Mr. Dobell also refer to an imprisonment of Jonson and Chapman,
presumably to the one imprisonment shared by the two poets of which
we have record. These letters are addressed to the King,[1] two to the
Lord Chamberlain, to the Earl of Pembroke, to an unknown lord, and
to ' the excellentest of ladies ' (the Countess of Rutland, or, perhaps,
the Countess of Bedford). With such defenders it was an easy matter
for the poets to obtain their release. The letter to Salisbury enables
us to date the imprisonment after May 4, 1605, when Robert Cecil
received the title of Earl of Salisbury. Since the letter, moreover,
appears to have been written immediately after the author's arrest
—note the opening words—we may suppose this to have taken place
about the first of the month, and, in consequence, that the play had
been produced in April, since it is unlikely that the play had been
on the stage any length of time before the authors were ' delated '
and arrested.

The scandal caused by the performance of *Eastward Ho* contributed

---

[1] Dobell ascribes the first three of these letters to Chapman, the others
to Jonson. M. Castelain in an appendix to his *Ben Jonson*, pp. 901 *ssq*.,
holds that these letters refer, not to the imprisonment connected with *Eastward Ho*, but to another imprisonment connected with some other comedy in
which the two poets had collaborated, probably, he thinks, *Sir Giles Goosecap*.
M. Castelain has little difficulty in pointing out certain discrepancies between
these letters and Jonson's statement to Drummond. There is, for example,
no mention in them of Marston's imprisonment, nor even of his collaboration
in the play in question. But to explain these discrepancies it is hardly necessary to imagine a second imprisonment of the two poets, shortly after the
Eastward Ho affair, for a second comedy in which they were again jointly
guilty of a similar offence. As a matter of fact no comedy except *Eastward
Ho* is known in which they collaborated, and M. Castelain's suggestion that
this second play might be *Sir Giles Goosecap* is ruled out of court, even if
Jonson's collaboration in this play were demonstrable, by the fact that there
is every reason to believe that *Sir Giles* antedates *Eastward Ho* by several
years—see below, p. 890. It seems likely, indeed, that shortly after the
appearance of *Eastward Ho*, Chapman ceased to write comedies. With the
possible exception of *The Widow's Tears*—see p. 798 above—not one of his
comedies can be referred to a period later than the spring of 1605.

no doubt to the withdrawal of royal favour from the children of the Queen's Revels,[1] but it does not seem to have brought about the suppression of the offending comedy. Not only did three editions of *Eastward Ho* appear in the same year, 1605, but the play remained in the hands of the company and was presumably acted from time to time. In 1613 we find Daborne suggesting to Henslowe[2] that *Eastward Ho* be billed for a certain day. This performance was to be by the Lady Elizabeth's Players, a company into which the Queen's Revels children had that year been absorbed. This company actually presented *Eastward Ho* at Court[3] before King James on January 25, 1614, probably in a form purged of offence. This is the last recorded performance before the closing of the theatres, but it is not unlikely that the play was revived from time to time during this period. A fresh revival after the Restoration was the probable cause of Tate's adaptation, *Cuckold's Haven or An Alderman No Conjuror,* 1685. This work of Tate's is one of the most outrageous of the many transformations of Elizabethan plays that occurred under the later Stuarts. It is a clumsy amalgamation of *Eastward Ho* and *The Devil is an Ass ;* the lively comedy of the original degenerates into gross farce ; the part of Touchstone, recast for the buffoon, Nokes, is degraded beneath contempt; and the sturdy bourgeois morality of the old play gives place to the conventional Restoration mockery of the intelligence and virtue of London citizens.

In 1751 Garrick substituted *Eastward Ho* in its original form for the customary performance of *London Cuckolds* on Lord Mayor's Day, October 29. It was, we are told,[4] driven from the stage and never repeated ; but Garrick had been struck with the possibilities of the old play and he later induced Mrs. Lennox to prepare a new version of it. This was produced under the title of *Old City Manners*[5] at Drury Lane, November 9, 1775, and favourably received. A comparison of *Old City Manners* with *Cuckold's Haven* would afford interesting testimony as to the change in theatrical taste between 1685 and 1775. The later work adheres on the whole fairly closely to its original, although, as a matter of course, it softens at times the Elizabethan frankness of speech. The most important change is in the character of Sir Petronel who appears as an affected coxcomb, but is in truth a runaway servant who has stolen his master's name as well as his money. The discovery of his previous marriage before his union with Gertrude sets that lady free, and the adventurer is not included in the jail delivery at the close of the play, but is dispatched to York, presumably to await the gallows for his earlier offences.

The sources of *Eastward Ho,* long unknown, have in recent years gradually become clearer. Koeppel (*Quellen-Studien zu den Dramen Jonsons—Münchner Beiträge*, vol. ii, pp. 31-2) believed that the plot was invented by the authors. Schelling (*Belles-Lettres* edition of *Eastward Ho*, p. 2) called attention to the early ' prodigal son dramas ',

[1] One of their masters, Kirkham, left them at this time, and took charge of their rivals, Paul's Boys, who in the following year, 1606, took their place at Court.

[2] Greg, *Henslowe Papers*, p. 71.

[3] Murray, *English Dramatic Companies*, vol. i, p. 263.

[4] Genest, vol. iv, p. 341. *Eastward Ho* in its original form was acted by Harvard undergraduates in 1902.

[5] Genest, vol. v, pp. 481-2.

Acolastus, The Nice Wanton, Misogonus, and *The Disobedient Child*
as embodying ' the underlying ideal ' of *Eastward Ho,* an ideal which
received its most elaborate form in Gascoigne's [1] *Glass of Government,*
1575. Curtis (*Modern Philology,* vol. v, 1906) pointed out a direct
source for the Petronel-Winifred plot in two tales (34 and 40) of the
Novellino of Masuccio, in 1476. He points out eleven details which
occur alike in these stories and in *Eastward Ho.* All but two of these
are found in No. 40, and these two—the deluded husband's uncon-
scious jesting at his own expense (cf. *Eastward Ho,* III, ii, 260–270)
and his uproar on the discovery of the trick that has been played him
(cf. *Eastward Ho,* III, iv)—are so slight and spring so naturally from
the situation that I do not see the necessity of insisting upon No. 34
as a source. The true source of the whole Petronel-Winifred plot is,
I think, the fortieth story of the *Novellino.*

A brief abstract of this tale will show the essential likeness and the
agreement in details between the *novella* and play. Genefra, a rich Catalan, falls in love with Adriana, the young wife of Cosmo, a silver-smith
of Amalfi. To obtain his end Genefra cultivates Cosmo's friendship
and so far wins over the unsuspecting husband that he is invited to
stand godfather to the first child of the marriage (cf. *Eastward Ho,*
III, i, 8–12). Forced to leave Amalfi, Genefra plots to carry off the
wife and enlists Cosmo as his accomplice by deluding him with a false
tale of his purpose to elope with a boatman's wife (cf. *Eastward Ho,*
III, ii, 205, *ssq.*). Cosmo gladly promises his aid (cf. *Eastward Ho,*
III, ii, 244, *ssq.*) forces his own wife to give a farewell kiss to Genefra
(cf. *Eastward Ho,* III, i, 20–22), and agrees to hire the boatman to
carry him to Genefra's ship in order that the latter may have free access
to the boatman's wife (cf. *Eastward Ho,* III, ii, 229, *ssq.*). Genefra
utilizes the absence of Cosmo from home to send a servant to bring
Adriana on board in disguise (cf. *Eastward Ho,* III, ii, 255, *ssq.*). She is
conveyed to the ship in the same boat with her husband, Cosmo, and
her supposed husband, the boatman (cf. the presence of both Security
and Bramble at the tavern, *Eastward Ho,* III, iii) and when she begins
to cry over her escapade, her deluded husband comforts her in much
the same manner as Security cheers up Winifred (*Eastward Ho,* III,
iii, 131–9). It is, perhaps, needless to say that the resemblance ends
here ; in the Italian tale the author's sympathies are wholly with the
lovers ; their trick succeeds and Cosmo returns home to discover too
late that it is his own wife and not a neighbour's that he has aided to
elope.

The Petronel-Winifred scenes of *Eastward Ho* constitute, as Curtis
noted, a fairly independent plot cleverly interwoven with the main
theme of the play, but by no means essential to it. They form an
organic and harmonious whole, contain, for this play, an unusual
amount of verse, and for the rest are written in a fluent prose that
shows marked differences from the prose of the other scenes. It is
plain, I think, that these scenes are the work, probably the unaided
work, of only one of the collaborators, and the bearing of this fact
upon the assignment to the three authors of their respective parts
will soon be made apparent.

---

[1] Gascoigne's play was probably not intended for the stage. An interesting account of its relations to earlier Latin plays by the German humanists
will be found in Herford, *Literary Relations,* p. 149, *ssq.*

It is probable that no source, in the strict sense of the word, exists for the main plot. The suggestion, that Quicksilver, the leading figure, had a prototype in Luke Hatton,[1] a notorious highwayman, executed at York in 1598, has nothing to recommend it beyond the fact that Luke, like Quicksilver, composed a 'Repentance' in prison. There is otherwise no recognizable likeness between the London apprentice who is led astray by his desire of aping gentility and the Northern gentleman—Hatton is said to have been a son or nephew of the Archbishop of York—who turns highwayman and ends on the gallows. If however, there is no source for the main plot, it is by no means impossible to determine the occasion which gave birth to this play. In fact this is pointed out in the *Prologue* itself of *Eastward Ho*. It was the performance, and apparently the success, of Dekker and Webster's *Westward Ho* by the rival company of Paul's Boys toward the close of 1604. Now this play, *Westward Ho*, does not stand alone. It is one of the first specimens of a new fashion in comedy which seems to have come into vogue shortly after the opening [2] of the theatres in the spring of 1604. This new fashion was the realistic comedy of London life. Certain fore-runners of this class had already appeared in *The Shoemakers' Holiday*, 1599, and *The Fair Maid of the Exchange*, 1602 ; but the new comedy is marked by a satiric note, a partiality for questionable scenes [3] and characters, and a general moral laxness, happily absent in the earlier plays. It seems probable that the first deviser of this fashion was Thomas Middleton, who after some years of experimental collaboration, opened in 1604, with *Michaelmas Term*, a vein that he continued to work for nearly a decade. Middleton has been well called [4] 'the most absolute realist' in Elizabethan drama. He paints life as it is, but without the sympathetic interest that marks such work as Dekker's best. He himself was a University and Gray's Inn man, and his attitude toward the life and manners of London citizens is characterized by a superior and somewhat cynical contempt. His bourgeois comedies are undoubtedly clever, entertaining, and valuable as pictures of contemporary life, but they are anything but edifying. He lacks Jonson's strong sense of morals as completely as he does Dekker's tenderness of heart. His influence upon his contemporaries, however, is undeniable, and it seems to have been particularly strong over Dekker.[5] These two playwrights had worked together for Henslowe on several plays [6] now lost. In *The Honest Whore*, 1604,

---

[1] *Athenaeum*, October 13, 1883 ; Fleay, *Biographical Chronicle*, vol. i, p, 346, accepts this suggestion.

[2] The plague closed the theatres on May 26, 1603, and it was not until April 9, 1604, that a royal licence permitted the opening of the Globe, the Fortune, and the Curtain. The private houses probably opened about the same time.

[3] Brothel scenes are not infrequent, the courtesan, or the deluded country wench, is a common character—she is often married off at the close of the play, and the affairs of citizens' wives with courtiers, affairs that hover on the very brink of adultery, furnish a stock theme.

[4] Schelling, *Elizabethan Drama*, vol. i, p. 516.

[5] Dekker's regard for Middleton is shown in the note he appended to the speech of Zeal in *The King's Entertainment*, 1604 (Dekker, *Dramatic Works*, v. i. p. 321).

[6] *Caesar's Fall* and *The Chester Tragedy*, apparently historical plays ; see Greg, *Henslowe's Diary*, pt. II. p. 222.

the first of their extant collaborations, the influence [1] of Middleton upon his fellow is plainly visible, and in *Westward Ho*, where he collaborated with Webster, Dekker swung over as far as his talent and temperament permitted to the manner of his former partner.   The scene is laid for the most part in the City, the theme is made up of the flirtations of a triplicity of citizens' wives with their gentlemen suitors, and the moral, so far as one can be found in the play, is that all things save the last step are permissible to merry wives in search of entertainment for their idle hours.   An even wider range is apparently permitted to their husbands who amuse themselves during the absence of their wives in a house of more than doubtful reputation.   To stigmatize this play with Schelling as marking the ' depth of gross and vicious realism to which the Comedy of Manners descended ' seems to me rather like breaking a butterfly upon a wheel.   Dekker's light touch and careless grace preserve even this play from the charge of deliberate viciousness.   But it would be absurd to deny that the picture it gives of London city life must have been then, as it is now, offensive to the moralist who took the comic drama seriously.

Eastward Ho, in its main outlines at least, seems to me a conscious protest [2] of such moralists against the new comedy of Middleton and Dekker.   It adopts their realistic treatment, excludes all trace of romance or sentiment, and presents a picture of city life completely convincing in its verisimilitude.   But in strong distinction from the work of Middleton and Dekker this picture is one of honesty, industry, and sobriety victorious over roguery, idleness, and dissipation.   Touchstone, the real hero of the play, a thorough-going citizen with all the citizen's limitations, is another guess figure than Quomodo or Justinian. There is no dallying with vice in his household, and if, against his will, one night is given up to wasteful prodigality, it is atoned for in the morning by the expulsion of the typical prodigal.   In other words instead of the laxness and confusion of morals which we have noted in *Westward Ho*, we have here a sharp differentiation between vice and virtue—the latter, to be sure, presented in a somewhat bourgeois form—an open conflict, and the final triumph of the good.

A play of this type was a novelty on the boards of Blackfriars.   A glance over the repertoire of that theatre from the beginning of the century shows us such plays as *Cynthia's Revels*, *Sir Giles Goosecap*, *The Poetaster*, *May-Day*, *All Fools*, *The Gentleman Usher*, *Monsieur D'Olive*, *The Malcontent*, and *Philotas*.   We find here the comedy of courtly life, enlivened by ' humours ' and personal satire, adaptations of Latin and Italian comedies, romantic comedy and tragi-comedy, and a single specimen of classical tragedy.   There is not a trace before *Eastward Ho* of the realistic comedy of manners and of London life. It is not surprising, therefore, that before attempting such a departure the three chief playwrights in this theatre should have laid their heads together and determined to produce in collaboration a work that might hold the field against the late success of their rivals at Paul's.

[1] Cf. *The Honest Whore*, II, i with *Michaelmas Term*, III, i, and the forced marriage of Mattheo to Bellafront with that of Lethe and the Country Wench.

[2] The statement of the *Prologue* that *Eastward Ho* was composed neither out of envy, imitation, nor rivalry with its immediate predecessor does not seem to me to alter the fact of such a protest.   The last thing to be expected of writers for the courtly audience of Blackfriars was a proclamation that they were taking up arms to maintain the good name of the City.

The initiative for this collaboration came, I fancy, from Marston. He had already been reconciled with Jonson [1] after the so-called War of the Theatres, and had joined the playwrights working for the children at Blackfriars. One of his first plays for this company, *The Dutch Courtesan*, 1604, shows him taking sharp issue with his former associate Dekker. *The Honest Whore* of Dekker and Middleton is mentioned in Henslowe's *Diary* at a date fixed by Greg before March 14, 1604. If so, the play was composed in anticipation of the opening of the theatres in April, and must certainly have been on the boards before *The Dutch Courtesan*. Now in *The Honest Whore* Dekker gives us a romantic, not to say a sentimental, treatment of the courtesan. His Bellafront, whether sinning or repenting, is a sympathetic and delightful figure. In *The Dutch Courtesan* [2] on the contrary the theme, as Marston himself tells us is ' the difference between the love of a courtesan and a wife', and the figure of Francesehina is a vigorous, realistic, and repulsive portrait of the harlot. Marston's indecency of language is so offensive to our modern ears that we are apt to consider him an immoral writer. He was nothing of the kind. Beginning as a satirist and ending as a preacher John Marston, like Swift whom he resembles in so many ways, was filled with a bitter indignation against the abuses and corruptions of his day. Not one of his works shows the blurring of moral issues or the sympathetic presentation of a vicious character which we have noted in Middleton and Dekker. It seems to me, then, no unlikely supposition that, as his unaided work, *The Dutch Courtesan*, is an intentional retort to *The Honest Whore*, so the idea of a joint reply to *Westward Ho* should have originated with him. It is quite unlikely to have been Chapman's, whose share in the play, as we shall see later on, was limited to the underplot, and Jonson's [3] attitude toward *Eastward Ho* can hardly be reconciled with the supposition that it was he who at once originated and dominated the work of collaboration.

The question of the collaboration of the three authors in *Eastward Ho* has often been touched upon, but never, I think, treated with the fullness and care that so interesting a problem deserves. The first

[1] See the *Dedication* of *The Malcontent*, published 1604.

[2] Even if it could be shown that *The Dutch Courtesan* preceded *The Honest Whore* on the stage there would be no need of renouncing the idea that Marston's play is a protest against Dekker's treatment of the courtesan. In the intimate association of playwrights and actors at that time, Marston might well have known of Dekker's work before it was actually produced and have hurried his opposition play through in advance as Jonson did with *The Poetaster*.

[3] Jonson never claimed *Eastward Ho* as his nor included it in his published works. Compare with this his treatment of *Sejanus*, also written in collaboration, which he published as his own, expunging the work of his associate, and substituting matter of his own. I have always thought that his words to Drummond that Chapman and Marston *had written it amongst them* referred to the play as a whole, and were intended to show Jonson's slight connexion with the work. Castelain (*op. cit.*, p. 905) takes the pronoun *it* to refer to the phrase *something against the Scots*. It seems to me unlikely that Jonson should have spoken of Chapman and Marston as having written *amongst them* the ' two clauses ', which according to Chapman's letter to the king, printed in the *Athenaeum*, March 30, 1901, were all that gave offence, for one would hardly speak of two authors collaborating to produce two clauses. Long and careful study of the play has convinced me, at least, that Jonson's share in *Eastward Ho* was rather that of an adviser and reviser than that of an originator.

attempt at an analysis occurs, so far as I know, in an article in *Blackwood's* for 1821 (vol. x, p. 136) where it is suggested that Jonson ' first sketched the plan which might be filled up by Chapman and receive a few witty and satirical touches from the pen of Marston. . . . The whole, it is likely, underwent the revisal of Jonson, traces of whom are discernible in the character of Touchstone and in the concluding scenes '. Swinburne (*George Chapman*, p. 55 *ssq.*) points out certain unmistakeable traces of Chapman in the third and fourth acts, suggests that Marston's hand is only visible in ' one or two momentary indecencies ' in the scenes in which Mistress Touchstone and Gertrude figure (I, ii, III, ii, IV, ii, and V, i) and concludes by saying that we may probably feel safe in assigning to each of the three ' as equal a share in the labour and credit as they bore in the peril ', a statement which hardly adds to our knowledge of the case. Bullen (*Marston's Works*, vol. i, p. xli) accepts Swinburne's suggestion as to Chapman's contributions, assigns the *Prologue* to Jonson, the first two acts to Jonson and Marston, a passage in the fourth act to Jonson (IV, i, 210–247) and declares that it would be of doubtful advantage to pursue the inquiry further. Fleay (*Biographical Chronicle*, vol. ii, p. 81) was the first to attempt anything like a complete analysis. He gives Marston the whole first part of the play (Acts I and II, i) Chapman the second as far as IV, ii, and Jonson the remainder. As usual with Fleay the assertion is unsupported by proof, but his acumen and wide reading in Elizabethan drama led him, I believe, to a conclusion not far from the truth. Ward (*History of English Dramatic Literature*, vol. ii, p. 441) inclines to attribute a greater part of the play to Chapman than to Marston, leaving only ' a few touches ' for Jonson. Schelling, the latest editor of the play (*Eastward Ho—Belles-Lettres Series*, p. xii) practically waives all attempt at any assignment, and intimates [1] pretty clearly that any such attempt is a waste of ingenuity. For my part I cannot accept the view that the problem of assignment is insoluble, or that its solution, if effected, would be valueless. We have in *Eastward Ho* the joint work of three of the most prominent dramatists of their day, each marked by his own peculiar traits of diction, dramatic method, and tone of mind. Such a work certainly affords a fair field for study and offers the prospect of arriving, if not at a mathematical certainty, at least at a generally acceptable conclusion. And if we can obtain this we certainly gain new light on the character and ability of the authors. If, for example, it could be shown that the greater part of *Eastward Ho* was indisputably Chapman's, we would be forced at once to revise our conception of that author's talent as a comic writer, particularly in the matter of dramatic construction.

It seems to me, moreover, that such an assignment is quite possible if we use the means that lie at our hands. External evidence, to be sure, is practically non-existent ; the three names appear on the title-page in alphabetical order, and Jonson's statement to Drummond is too terse and ambiguous to give us much aid. We are forced to rely on internal evidence and it may be frankly granted that the fact that

---

[1] He points out that Bullen finds ' a Jonsonian expression in a part of the play attributed by Fleay to Marston, and a favourite Marston word (*chuck*) in Fleay's Jonsonian part,' and goes on to say ' except where marked and distinctive qualities such as the versification of Fletcher . . . exist ascriptions of the precise limit of authorship cannot but be regarded askant '.

the greater part of the play is written in prose makes the analysis more difficult than that of a Fletcher-Massinger play. But to throw doubt upon the ascription of a scene to Jonson because of the presence in it of a so-called 'Marston word', and that work *chuck*, which occurs probably in most Elizabethan dramatists, is merely to bring contempt upon the resources of scholarship. It is by the evidence of the style as a whole in scene or act taken as a whole, by the accumulation of parallel passages, by noting similarities of method in the presentation of character and in the handling of situation, and not least by detecting the perhaps indefinable but unmistakeable tone and flavour peculiar to an author, that we are able to differentiate and determine the work of each contributor to a collaborated drama like *Eastward Ho*. Such an assignment need not exclude consultation among the authors before actually setting hand to pen, nor a certain amount of revision after the first draft of the play had been written; but no one familiar with the conditions under which the Elizabethan drama was produced can believe that three playwrights of that day worked together on a scene, mutually contributing, criticizing, and elaborating. So far as actual composition went we may safely believe that each author wrote for and by himself. Any scene, then, that we may find good reason for ascribing to one of our three writers may be considered as essentially his own composition.

As I have already said, I consider it likely that the conception of *Eastward Ho* originated with Marston; but it is hard not to see Jonson's hand in the careful planning and admirable adjustment of the whole. He was probably called into consultation before the work was begun, and gave his collaborators the benefit of that talent for dramatic construction which distinguished him above all his contemporaries. To Jonson, also, I would ascribe with Bullen the *Prologue*, written, no doubt, for the first performance.

The first scene [1] is unmistakeably the work of Marston. We have a characteristic example of his sentence structure in ll. 36–8, expressions that can be paralleled in his unaided plays in ll. 59–64, 119 and 124, and two of his favourite words in ll. 77 and 98. The rhymed moral tag with which the scene closes is the sort of thing that Marston produced in superabundance; handfuls of them may be culled from his works. More important than all these, however, is the treatment of character. Quicksilver here, and in all the Marston scenes in which he figures, is almost a replica of that impudent and entertaining knave Coccledemoy in *The Dutch Courtesan*. He is a little less foul-mouthed, to be sure, but the presence of such reverend seniors as Chapman and Jonson may have imposed some slight check upon Marston's easy flow in this kind. Touchstone, in turn, at once suggests the figure of Sim Eyre in *The Shoemaker's Holiday*, and it is tolerably certain that Marston alone of the three collaborators would have been willing, or indeed able, to have followed so closely in the footsteps of his former ally, Dekker. Finally the whole scene has a pungency of speech and a swiftness of movement that are found in Marston at his best, and

---

[1] For the full evidence of the points advanced in the following analysis the student is referred to the notes on the passages in question. I wish to take this opportunity of acknowledging my debt to the work of M. Schoell, whose analysis of this play is the most careful and complete that has yet been made. I have taken over many of his arguments and illustrations.

are in sharp contrast with the more deliberate and laboured manner of Jonson and the equable flow of Chapman's best prose.

The second scene of act one may also safely be assigned to Marston. The direct evidence is not so strong as in the first scene, but the general tone and manner of both is so much alike that it is almost certain that they are by the same hand. A situation occurs in this scene that has an interesting parallel in Chapman's first comedy ((see note on ll. 105-12) and toward the close Mr. Bullen notes 'a Jonsonian expression', but these isolated instances are not of sufficient importance to warrant our ascribing any essential part of this scene to either of these authors.

The first scene of act two is mainly, if not altogether, by Marston. Several close parallels are pointed out in the notes, and the drunken Quicksilver is even closer akin to Coccledemoy than in the first scene of the play. The only passage which appears doubtful is the dialogue between Golding and Mildred (ll. 53-83). At first sight the involved style of this passage seems so unlike the usual work of Marston as to suggest that we have here an interpolation by Jonson. But this passage is in designed contrast with what precedes and follows it, and that Marston was not incapable of such heavy and involved prose is shown by several passages in the more serious parts of his comedies—see especially *The Fawn*, I, i, 18-39.

The second scene of the second act presents some little difficulty. The opening soliloquy of Security is so unlike Marston that I was originally inclined to doubt his authorship of the scene. But closer study shows his hand visible throughout, in the stage-direction after l. 10, in the bit of blank verse beginning with l. 28, and in the parody of the old ballad that follows, in the rhymed moral tag (l. 53-4), and especially in the ironical apology for usury (ll. 107-126). The scene as a whole, I believe, may be assigned to Marston, although it is not impossible that it received some revision by Jonson. I should be inclined, for example, to assign to Jonson the opening soliloquy, possibly written to take the place of a less effective entrance for Security in the first draft, and, perhaps, also the closing lines of the scene.

Here, for the time at least, Marston's contribution ends and a new hand begins. The third scene of the second act shows unmistakeable traces of Chapman. A great part of the prose, particularly in the longer speeches (see ll. 61-88) is closer to the style of similar passages in *Monsieur D'Olive* than to anything in Marston or Jonson, and we find Chapman words and phrases in ll. 16, 89-90, and 138. The figure of Sir Petronel seems to me to lack the precision of outline peculiar to Jonson and the strong colours in which Marston would have painted the knight-adventurer. Quicksilver, too, is rather the witty intriguer of Chapman's comedies than the 'shameless varlet' of the preceding scenes. In this scene, moreover, we find the beginning of the Petronel-Winifred intrigue. After the entrance of Gertrude the dialogue becomes quicker and more pointed, and there is a possibility that the last part of this scene was revised, if not written, by Marston.

The short scene which opens act three is undoubtedly Chapman's. No one could mistake the prose of the opening speeches for the work of either Marston or Jonson, and characteristic words and phrases of Chapman's appear in ll. 19 and 37. This scene also belongs to the Petronel-Winifred intrigue and contains a couple of incidents from the Italian tale on which this plot is founded.

The second scene of act three seems to me to fall into two parts. From l. 205 to the close Chapman's hand is too apparent to admit of doubt. The verse is wholly in his manner—compare it for a moment with the only other blank verse passage in the preceding scenes, the Marston bit in II, ii, 29–37—and the likeness between Security's malicious delight in the proposed gulling of his neighbour and Gostanzo's similar attitude in *All Fools* (III, i) is unmistakeable. This part also is devoted to the further development of the Petronel-Winifred plot. The authorship of the first part of this scene (ll. 1–205) is at the first glance less certain. Much of the dialogue seems almost too vivacious and pointed for Chapman, and the parts of Gertrude and Touchstone are in such admirable accordance with the earlier scenes in which these characters appear that at first sight one is tempted to assign this part of the scene to Marston. But a careful examination shows numerous traces of Chapman's hand (see notes on ll. 7, 52, 70–1, 98–107, 113–5, 124, 127, 147) and nothing that is indisputably Marston's. We must conclude, I think, that Chapman wrote the whole scene, working at first along lines already laid down by Marston, and dropping back into his own manner when he came to deal with the Petronel-Winifred plot.

The third scene of the third act, the tavern scene, is clearly Chapman's. Its tone of lively revelry is exactly like that of the tavern scenes in *All Fools* (V, ii) and *May-Day* (III, iii). In all three cases Chapman departs from his sources to invent a tavern scene for which there is not the slightest hint in the original. I do not recall anything in the work of Marston or Jonson that resembles these scenes in frank realism and hearty good humour. One of Chapman's Latin stage-directions, *surgit*, appears in l. 123. The Petronel-Winifred plot is continued in this scene, and as before incidents from the *novella* are admirably recast in dramatic form.

There is, however, one difficulty as to this scene. In ll. 40–47 occurs the passage [1] which gave particular offence at court and which was deleted in the second edition of the play. Chapman's letter already referred to (see p. 841, *n.* above) appears to contain a direct reference to this passage. He begs the King to ' take merciful notice of two of his most humble subjects, George Chapman and Ben Jonson, whose chief offences are but two clauses, and *both of them not our own* '. If we take the last words as an exact and literal statement of the facts we are forced to believe that Marston wrote the lines in question, and however much we may dislike to think of Chapman shifting the blame from his own to his fellow's shoulders, I incline to think that this was the case. The two sentences beginning *But as* and *And for my part* occur in the midst of a paraphrase from More's *Utopia* (see note on III, iii, 27–34) which bears all the marks of Chapman's hand. They may be dropped from this passage, as they were in the second edition, with no injury to the sense. In fact they rather interrupt [2] the flow of the discourse and the passage as a whole reads more smoothly if we omit them. Perhaps the true solution is that Marston caught up Chapman's harmless fling at the ' industrious Scots ', elaborated it, and interpolated here the two offensive ' clauses '.

The little scene of five lines that follows (III, iv) does not contain

---

[1] See Text Notes, p. 865.
[2] I have to thank my colleague, Professor Kennedy, for having called my attention to this interruption.

enough material to make a definite assignment possible.   As an essential part of the Petronel-Winifred plot inserted here to account for
Security's presence on the river in the next scene, it would seem to
belong to Chapman, but the ejaculatory character of the style and
the parody of Shakespeare (see note on III, iv, 5) suggest a Marston
patch.

The first scene of the fourth act is almost entirely Chapman's.   The
prose of Slitgut's speeches at the beginning and end of the scene is
clearly his, and the blank verse put into the mouth of Quicksilver (ll.
120–139) is an admirable example of his graver moralizing vein.   The
satire on the Frenchified gentlemen of the court, and the broken French
of Sir Petronel find a close parallel elsewhere in Chapman (see note
on IV, [i, 155–6).   The gulling of Security by Winifred is quite in
Chapman's manner and represents his alteration of the source of this
plot.   The only passage which with any degree of probability may
be assigned to another hand is Quicksilver's proposal to retrieve
the fortunes of the shipwrecked band by various chemical operations
(ll. 210–240).   This passage savours strongly of the author of the
Alchemist, although we can hardly suppose Chapman to have been
ignorant of such tricks.   It is, perhaps, best to take it as one of Jonson's interpolations in the process of revision.

With this scene, I believe, Chapman's contribution to the play
closes.   I, at least, am unable to detect any convincing signs of his
hand in the remaining scenes.   I cannot, however, accept unreservedly
Fleay's ascription of the rest of the play to Jonson.   Marston, I feel
sure, had a hand in the next two scenes (IV, ii and V, i).   The interview between Gertrude and her father (IV, ii, 110–161) has a strong
flavour of Marston, and the last lines of this scene (IV, ii, 325–329)
show one of his characteristic tricks of style.   The reference to the
Spanish romances of chivalry (V, i, 29–31) has a parallel in Marston,
and Gertrude's song (V, i, 100–108) is very like one of Franceschina's.
Yet I cannot believe that these scenes are wholly Marston's like the
opening scenes of the play.   Either he worked here in close collaboration with Jonson, or, as seems to me more likely, Jonson here revised
and elaborated the fragmentary and half-sketched work of the younger
man.   Certainly the handling of the main characters and the general
temper of the scenes closely resembles the work of Marston at the
beginning of the play, but there are few stylistic evidences of his hand,
and the actual composition is, I incline to believe, mainly Jonson's.
One interesting feature of these scenes is the flood of proverbs that
streams through them.   Such a speech as that of Touchstone in IV,
ii, 150–158, for example, is little else than a mosaic of proverbs from
the collection of Heywood.   It seems at least a plausible hypothesis
that Jonson made use of these popular sayings to give his work an
air of colloquial verisimilitude.   No such use of proverbs occurs, I
feel sure, in Marston's work.

About the remaining scenes (V, ii, iii, iv and v) there can be, I think,
no question.   They are pure and unmixed Jonson.   I find in them
no trace whatever of the stylistic peculiarities of either Marston or
Chapman.   They lack Marston's raciness and pungency and Chapman's
easy humour, and they show a certain hardness and rigidity which
seems to me eminently characteristic of Jonson.   On the other hand,
they provide in a straightforward and business-like way what neither
Chapman nor Marston could have done so well, a coherent, consistent,

and well-motivated *dénouement.* Chapman's weakness in this respect
has been pointed out more than once, and a comparison of the last
scene of *The Dutch Courtesan* with that of any of Jonson's comedies
is enough to demonstrate Marston's inferiority in this point of dramatic
technic. The trick by which Touchstone is lured to the prison, the
way in which his change of heart is brought about, and the general
assembly of all the characters at the close, are as clear evidence of the
skilled and order-loving hand of Jonson as the simple straightforward
morality of these scenes is of his ethical sense.

If the above analysis of *Eastward Ho* is substantially correct, Marston wrote the entire first act and the first two scenes of the second,
and probably drafted the last scene of act four and the first of act five,
Chapman wrote the last scene of act two, practically all of act three,
and the first scene of act four, and Jonson's work is confined to insertions in the second and fourth acts, to the completion of Marston's
work in the fourth and fifth acts, and to the four last scenes of the play.
Such an assignment gives Marston the credit for the general conception
of the main plot and for the introduction and development of the chief
comic characters, Quicksilver, Touchstone, Gertrude, and her mother ;
Chapman was engaged mainly in the dramatization of the Italian tale
which furnished the underplot, while Jonson, in addition no doubt
to valuable advice as to the construction of the whole, did little more
than revise and finish the work of his collaborators.

Whatever the exact shares of the three authors may be, their collaboration brought forth one of the genuine masterpieces of Elizabethan
comedy. ' In no play of the time ', says Swinburne, ' do we get such
a true taste of the old city life, so often turned to mere ridicule and
caricature by playwrights of less good humour, or feel about us such
a familiar air of ancient London as blows through every scene '. Its
long success upon the boards, and the frequency with which it was
adapted after the Restoration testify to its effectiveness as an acting
play ; and its appeal to the student of Elizabethan drama is varied
and permanent. It is genuine comedy springing from real life ; but
it is no mere prosaic transcription of reality. On the contrary characters and incidents alike are shaped and grouped by the artists' hands
in accordance with a preconceived artistic purpose. The plot is well
conceived and carried out, the characters are interesting and lifelike,
and the dialogue is always vivacious and entertaining. The vindication
of the morals of the City against the attacks of the new comedy is
triumphantly successful. And finally the co-operation of the three
authors has produced a harmonious whole in which the best qualities
of each are blended, Marston's swiftness and pungency, Jonson's precision of touch and mastery of structure, and Chapman's genial humour
and grasp of situation.

Chapman's share of *Eastward Ho* is limited, as we have seen, to the
underplot, and while it is true that this portion contains neither the
most striking characters nor the most typically English city scenes, it
forms, none the less, no inconsiderable part of the whole. ' These
scenes ', Swinburne says, ' have in them enough of wit and humorous
invention to furnish forth the whole five acts of an ordinary comedy
of intrigue '. Since Chapman drew most of his incidents from the
Italian *novella,* it would be a mistake to insist too strongly upon his
' invention ' in these scenes ; but on the other hand it would be hard
to praise too highly the skill with which he has turned the *novella*

into a genuine little comedy, and has fitted it into its English setting. Sir Petronel's intrigue with Winifred is used to motivate his desertion of Gertrude, and the trick played upon Security comes as a fit punishment for his usury and malicious pleasure in over-reaching others. As usual in Chapman's comedy the characters are less important than the story ; Sir Petronel is but a slight sketch compared with the vigorous and life-like portraits of Quicksilver and Touchstone, and Winifred is a mere shadow beside the intensely human Gertrude. It is in the elaboration of single incidents, I think, that Chapman's comic genius, here as elsewhere, appears most clearly. The tavern scene, for example, in which the deluded Security exults over the supposed delusion of his neighbour and drinks to the health of all cuckolds, while unwittingly encouraging his own wife to bestow this title upon him, is an admirable example of Chapman's ability to expand a mere hint into a scene of vigorous comedy. Equally admirable is the scene upon the Thames in which, departing wholly from his source, Chapman depicts the fate that overtakes the runaways and introduces a sort of comic chorus in the person of Slitgut to narrate what cannot be presented. Finally I think Chapman's share in the play cannot be strictly limited to the scenes which he actually composed. His influence seems to be diffused throughout. Less bitter than Marston, less severe than Jonson, Chapman has a larger portion than either of the laughing spirit of true comedy, and the gaiety and kindliness of this rare old play, qualities that come out in high relief if we turn to compare it with Marston's *Dutch Courtesan* or Jonson's *Alchemist* are due, I think, in no small measure to the happy humour and broad humanity of Chapman.

ADDENDUM.—Since these pages were put into print another edition of *Eastward Ho* has appeared. It is included in the second volume of *Representative English Comedies*, 1913, and is the work of Professor Cunliffe of Columbia University. It is a reprint of Q₂. In the section of the introduction dealing with the 'division of authorship' the editor assigns to Marston Act I, III, iii, and V, i, giving all the rest to Chapman, and crediting Jonson only with devising the plot and supervising the execution. This analysis differs from mine mainly in assigning a larger share of the work to Chapman, the only exception being III, iii, which Cunliffe gives wholly to Marston, whereas I believe his share in it is limited to an interpolation. A careful study of this analysis has left my conclusions in the main unchanged. In particular I am quite unable to believe that Chapman wrote II, i, or IV, ii, or that any one but Jonson wrote the last three scenes of the play.

EASTWARD HO

NOTES

The Title. *Eastward Ho*, like the more familiar *Westward Ho*, was a call of the watermen plying on the Thames. The name is given to the play because the scene is laid in the City, east of Blackfriars Theatre.

Prologus. The complacent, not to say arrogant, tone of this address to the audience seems to mark it as the work of Jonson. Compare with this the prologues to Chapman's *All Fools* and Marston's *Dutch Courtesan*, both written for the same audience.

l. 3. *We*, i.e. the Queen's Revels Company playing in Blackfriars. There may be a reference in this line to the appropriation of *The Malcontent* by the King's Men at the Globe.

l. 5. *That . . . title :* a distinct reference to *Westward Ho*, entered in the Stationers' Registers, March 2, 1605 ; but probably staged shortly after the fall of Ostend, September 24, 1604—see the allusions to Ostend in that play (Dekker, *Dramatic Works*, vol. ii, pp. 284 and 339).

Dramatis Personae. Such significant names as *Touchstone, Quicksilver, Security*, etc. are in Jonson's manner, but the name *Sir Petronel Flash* appears in *Jack Drum*, an anonymous play, mainly, if not altogether, the work of Marston, produced *c.* 1600 by Paul's Boys. Compare also the significant names in *The Dutch Courtesan, Freevil, Malheureux, Burnish* (a goldsmith), *Mary Faugh* (a bawd).

I, i. The stage-direction at the beginning of this scene is interesting as it shows three entrances at the back of the stage. The central door before the alcove was hidden by a curtain or traverse, which Golding draws discovering the recess within fitted up as a goldsmith's shop.

I, i, 4. *Indeed, and in very good sober truth.* Marston elsewhere puts such asseverations into the mouth of a pretender to gentility ; cf. Balurdo's phrases : *forsooth in very good earnest, Antonio and Mellida*, I, i, 71 ; *In good sober sadness*, I, i, 81 ; *In sad good earnest*, I, i, 106, and *In very good truth, Antonio's Revenge*, IV, i, 4.

I, i, 12. *Work upon that now.* This catch phrase, so frequently put into the mouth of Touchstone, seems to me Marston's imitation of the catch phrases which adorn the speech of Sim Eyre in *The Shoemaker's Holiday*.

I, i, 17. *Ruffians'-hall :* a name given to West Smithfield where sword-and-buckler men met to fight out quarrels ; see Lean's *Collectanea*, vol. i, p. 143.

I, i, 23. *Of Quorum :* a phrase used to designate eminent Justices of Peace whose presence was necessary to constitute a bench. It is derived from the Latin wording of the commission by which they were appointed : *quorum unum A.B. esse volumus*; cf. *The Merry Wives of Windsor*, I, i. 6.

I, i, 26–8. These lines contain a characteristic example of a favourite trick of Marston's prose style ; cf. *Your love is to be married, true ; he does cast you off, right ; he will leave you to the world, what then ?—The Dutch Courtesan*, II, ii, 2–3 ; see also a passage in *The Fawn*, IV, i, 9–11, cited by Bullen, and another in the same play IV, i, 577–8, where the punctuation obscures the same trick ; see also *The Malcontent*, IV, i, 30–31.

I, i, 35. *Secondings.* Marston is partial to such participial substantives ; *secondings* occurs again in *Sophonisba*, II, iii, 67 ; *sufficings* in *The Fawn*, I, i, 30 ; *slidings* and *prolongings* in *The Dutch Courtesan*, II, i, 132, II, ii, 204.

I, i, 51–54. Schelling in his note on this passage refers to the description of a sixteenth century painting given in *Notes and Queries* (Series 7,vol. iv, p. 323). It represents a curved horn, the ends upwards. A man is being thrust into the butt-end, and emerging in a wretched state at the *buccal*, or mouth-piece. A previous victim stands by, wringing his hands. On the painting is the inscription :

> *This horn emblem here doth show*
> *Of suretyship what harm doth grow.*

Some such device is evidently alluded to in this passage. There seems also to have been a popular ballad on this subject, see *A Wife for a Month*, III, iii.

I, i, 59–64. Cf. a similar speech by Mrs. Mulligrub in *The Dutch Courtesan*, III, iii, 19–26.

I, i, 70. *Crackling bavins*. A *bavin* is a bundle of brushwood used for kindling fires, soon lighted and soon consumed. There is, perhaps, a reference here to the ' crackling of thorns under a pot ' to which the Preacher compares the fool's laughter (*Ecclesiastes*, vii, 6). Cf. also the *rash bavin wits* of 1 *King Henry IV*, III, ii, 61.

I, i, 77. *Dilling :* a Marston word, cf. *What You Will*, II, i, 25.

I, i, 84. *Court-cut and long-tail :* a variation of the old phrase ' come cut and long tail ', see the note above on *All Fools*, V, ii, 190. The allusion here is to the flowing dresses of ladies of the court.

I, i, 98. *Marry faugh*. Marston often uses this exclamation of disgust. It appears as the name of the bawd, *Mary Faugh* in *The Dutch Courtesan*. *Flat-cap :* a name given in derision to London citizens (cf. *The Dutch Courtesan*, II, ii, 35) from their flat headgear as contrasted with the beavers and pointed hats of the courtiers.

I, i, 99. *Give arms :* have the right, as a gentleman born, to display a coat of arms. Pock (*All Fools*, III, i, 380, *ssq.*) makes the same boast, but as Quicksilver has already (ll. 22–3) bragged of his gentility we need not ascribe this passage to Chapman.

I, i, 105. *Let the welkin roar*. Quicksilver is spouting scraps of Ancient Pistol's rant, see 2 *King Henry IV*, II, iv, 182. The words *Erebus* and *also* occur in Pistol's speech just before, see l. 171.

I, i, 111. *Satin belly and canvas-backed :* cf. the phrasing of a passage in *The Dutch Courtesan*, III, ii, 42.

I, i, 113. *Christ-church :* one of the parishes in the City of London.

I, i, 116. *Testons*. A *teston* was at first the name of the Henry VII shilling. Its original value, 12*d.*, declined until it was worth only from 2½*d.* to 4½*d.* Here, perhaps, it is equivalent to ' tester ', a slang word for sixpence.

I, i, 119. *A dropping nose :* cf. below IV, ii, 144–5. Marston uses a similar expression in *The Dutch Courtesan*, I, i, 3–4.
Pent-house : the projecting roof which partly covered the bench outside the shop on which the wares were displayed.

I, i, 120. *Bear tankards*. ' It was the general use and custom of all apprentices of London, mercers only excepted, to carry the water tankard to serve their masters from the Thames and the common conduits of London ', Stow, *Annals* (p. 1,040, edition of 1631) quoted in Collier's *Dodsley*, vol. vi, p. 404.

I, i, 122. *Who calls Jeronimo ? :* a quotation from a famous scene in *The Spanish Tragedy*, II, v, 4.

I, i, 124. *Golding of Golding Hall :* cf. *Frank o' Frank Hall*, and *Frail o' Frail Hall*—*The Dutch Courtesan*, IV, iii, i, and IV, v, 17.

I, i, 133. *Shot-clog :* a gull who pays the bill (*shot*) for the whole party at a tavern, cf. *Poetaster*, I, ii, 18, and *Every Man out of his Humour*, V, vi, 44.

I, i, 134. *Moorfields :* the fields lying to the north of the City, a favourite haunt of beggars, cf. *Every Man in his Humour*, IV, 3–4.

I, i, 145–8. This trick of ending a scene, not with a mere rhymed tag, but with a moral ' sentence ' marked as such by the rhyme, is common with Marston ; cf. *The Dutch Courtesan*, I, i, 169–170 ; I, ii, 271–2 ; II, i, 148–

9; III, i, 283–4; IV, ii, 47–8; IV, v, 103–4; V, i, 113–4; and V, ii, 140–1.

I, ii, Stage-direction. *A French fall* is an article of dress, perhaps a falling band. In *Westward Ho* (Dekker, vol. ii, p. 302) a lady is described as dressed in a *French gown and Scotch falls*.

Bettrice leading a monkey : Bettrice does not appear elsewhere in the play. She is introduced here with the monkey to ridicule Gertrude's affectation of Court manners, a monkey being a favourite pet of courtiers, see *Monsieur D'Olive*, III, ii, 123, and *Hyde Park*, I, ii, where a monkey is mentioned, along with a squirrel and a pair of Iceland dogs, as a lady's pet.

I, ii, 7. *In any hand :* for any sake ; cf. *All's Well*, III, vi, 45.

I, ii, 8–9. *Thus whilst she sleeps :* a line from a song in Dowland's *First Book of Songs* (1597), beginning *Sleep, wayward thoughts*.

I, ii, 15. *Licket :* this word does not appear in the *New English Dictionary*. The *Dialect Dictionary* gives *licket, lickut, ligget*, etc., with the meaning of ' rag ', ' shred '. It is probably Gertrude's contemptuous phrase for a ribbon on the *coif* worn by city women.

Stammel : see the note on *Monsieur D'Olive*, II, ii, 96.

I, ii, 16. *Buffin gown :* ' a gown of coarse cloth '—Bullen. Cf. *The City Madam*, IV, iv.

I, ii, 18–22. Cf. the construction here with that in I, i, 26–8 and see the note *ad loc.*

I, ii, 19. *Cherries only at an angel a pound.* This extravagance of city dames is alluded to by Dekker in *The Bachelor's Banquet*, 1603 (*Prose Works*, vol. i, p. 173) : ' She must have cherries, though for a pound he pay ten shillings.' An *angel* was a coin worth ten shillings. See also *Blurt Master Constable*, III, iii, 122.

I, ii, 24. *Taffata pipkins :* probably hats made of taffata, such as that in which Mildred was married, see below III, ii, 85. Dekker (*Dramatic Works*, vol. i, p. 157) also refers to a ' taffety hat.' The word pipkin does not appear in this sense in the *New English Dictionary*, but the *Dialect Dictionary* gives an example of *pipkin* in the sense of ' head.'

Durance : ' strong, buff-coloured stuff '—Bullen. Apparently a variant of ' durants ', plural of ' durant ' a woollen stuff ' by some called everlasting.'

I, ii, 31. *Bow-bell.* Gertrude calls Mildred a true cockney, one born within hearing of the bell of St. Mary-le-Bow in Cheapside, cf. l. 127 below.

I, ii, 37–9. I can find no such account of Ulysses. Hyginus (*Fab.* xcv) says that when he feigned madness he yoked a horse and an ox together and ploughed the sand.

I, ii, 49. *Profane ape.* I take this to refer to the monkey which was probably playing some trick at this point. The suggestion of Collier that the sentence in which these words occur should be assigned to Mildred, who is thus made to call her sister *a profane ape*, is not warranted by the text and is out of character with Mildred's usual manner.

I, ii, 50. *A right Scot :* referring to the Scotch farthingale of the stage-direction at the beginning of the scene. In *Westward Ho* (Dekker, vol. ii, p. 282) the wit of the city dames who rule their husbands is contrasted with the folly of the Court ladies in adopting the Scotch farthingale.

I, ii, 81. *Balloon.* Gervase Markham in *Country Contentments* (Book i, p. 109) describes *balloon* as ' a strong and moving sport in the open fields with a great ball of double leather, filled with wind, and driven to and fro with the strength of a man's arm armed in a bracer of wood.' See also my note on *Byron's Conspiracy*, V, ii, 157.

I, ii, 105–112. Gertrude's behaviour to her mother resembles that of Elimine to her sisters in *The Blind Beggar of Alexandria*, sc. v, ll. 1–33.

I, ii, 124. *Chittizens :* Gertrude's affected pronunciation of ' citizens ' ; cf. l. 126. For a similar affectation see *Blurt Master Constable*, III, iii, 41, 43, 94.

I, ii, 147–8. *Castle on his back.* The elephant was constantly depicted with a castle on his back. Golding expresses a fear that Sir Petronel's castle may have been sold to pay for the fine clothes he is wearing.

I, ii, 166. *Well-parted.* Bullen notes this as a 'Jonsonian expression'; the same epithet occurs in the description of Macilente prefixed to *Every Man out of his Humour.* But compare the analogous phrase *better meaned*, I. i, 68 above.

I, ii, 178. *Honest time's expense :* an honest, or profitable, expenditure of time.

II, i, 5. *Familiar addition :* title of familiarity, familiar mode of address.

II, i, 6. *Truss my points :* lace up the tags which attached the doublet to the hose.

II, i, 25-6. *Fulfil the scripture :* 'Woe unto them that rise up early in the morning that they may follow strong drink ; that continue until night till wine inflame them', *Isaiah*, v, 11.

II, i, 27. *O' their knees :* an allusion to the custom of drinking healths kneeling ; see below III, iii, 67, 79 and *All Fools*, V, ii, 56.

II, i, 87. *Holla, ye pampered jades of Asia :* one of the many jests in later comedy at the rant of Marlowe (2 *Tamburlaine*, IV, iv, 1) ; cf. also 2 *King Henry IV*, II, iv, 178.

II, i, 89. *Pull eo.* Collier suggests that Quicksilver is imitating the cry of the watermen on the-river.

Showse, quoth the caliver : ' bang went the gun '—Schelling.

II, i, 92. *Wa, ha, ho.* This cry of the falconer to recall the hawk occurs repeatedly in the mouth of Coccledemoy, see *The Dutch Courtesan*, I, ii, 24, 238, IV, v, 8, 72 and 75.

II, i, 107-8. *Hast thou not Hiren here:* a play-end also quoted by Pistol, 2 *King Henry IV*, II, iv, 173. It is supposed to be a line from Peele's lost play, *Mahomet and the Fair Greek Hiren*.

II, i, 110. *Who cries on murther, etc.* This is usually said to be a line from *The Spanish Tragedy*, but it does not occur in that play. It is found in Chapman's *Blind Beggar*, sc. ix, l. 49 ; see note *ad loc.*

II, i, 120. *Go Westward Ho :* westward from the city to Tyburn where the gallows stood, near the present Marble Arch. Cf. Greene's phrase (*Art of Coney Catching—Works*, vol. x, p. 155) : 'The end of such . . . will be sailing Westward in a cart to Tyburn.'

II, i, 127-8. *A duck in thy mouth.* The only other instance that I know of this phrase is a quotation from R. Capel (1656) in Spurgeon's *Treasury of David* (*Psalm* ix, 18) : 'Money, which lying long in the bank, comes home at last with a duck in its mouth', i.e. with interest. I take it that Quicksilver here bids farewell to his apprentice's wage and any interest or additions belonging to it.

II, i, 130, 133, 135-6. Lines from the long speech of Andrea which opens *The Spanish Tragedy*.

II, i, 131-2. *Change your gold-ends for your play-ends :* exchange your business as apprentice to a goldsmith—*gold-ends* are the bits of gold with which he works—for that of an actor. The word *gold-ends* occurs again IV, ii, 148.

II, i, 147-9. Marston is fond of such progressive enumerations ; cf. *The Fawn*, III, i, 82-5.

II, i, 157-8. Cf. *Hamlet*, I, ii, 180-1.

II, ii, 7. The reference to the *trunks* of apparel in this line, and the stage-direction below, after l. 10, in which Quicksilver enters half-dressed, and *gartering himself* recall the stage-direction at the beginning of Act II in *What You Will* : *Laverdure draws the curtains, sitting on his bed apparelling himself ; his trunk of apparel standing by him.*

II, ii, 16. *Ka me, Ka thee.* The word *Ka* is only found in this and similar phrases implying mutual help ; cf. Heywood's *Proverbs*, Pt. I, chap. xi : ' ka me, ka thee ' ; one good turn asketh another.' It occurs frequently in Elizabethan comedy, see the references collected by Nares *sub* Ka. *Ka*, like *Key*, was pronounced like the letter K, which is printed here in the original text. This explains the pun in l. 18 below.

II, ii, 25. *A scrap to the net of villany.* Schelling paraphrases : ' virtue is as nothing to the powerful and successful wiles of villany ' ; but I rather think the meaning of *scrap* in this passage is ' bait ', and that the sense of the whole is : ' If virtue is apparently practised, it is only as a bait to lure victims into the nets of villany.'

II, ii, 29–45. A bit of verse wholly in Marston's manner.

II, ii, 30. *Trunks.* Note the pun on *trunks*, i.e. ' chests ' and *trunks*, i.e. ' pea-shooters.' Nares cites examples of this latter obsolete sense from Howell's *Epistles* and Brome's *New Academy.*

II, ii, 33. *Via . . . Borgia.* The exclamation *Via* is frequent in Marston ; see *What You Will*, III, i, 264, 296 ; *The Dutch Courtesan*, I, ii, 233, II, iii, 76, and *The Fawn*, I, ii, 323, II, i, 97. The reference to Borgia is said to be to a scene in Mason's *Muleasses the Turk* in which Caesar Borgia appears ; but as this play was apparently not acted [1] until 1607, this explanation is impossible. The line is evidently one of Quicksilver's play-ends, probably from a lost play.

II, ii, 38–9. *When Sampson . . . than :* the first two lines of an old ballad entered in the Stationers' Registers, 1563 ; a later version appears in *Roxburghe Ballads*, vol. ii, p. 459. The verses which follow these in the text are, of course, Quicksilver's parody of the old song.

II, ii, 53–4. A characteristic Marstonian moral tag.

II, ii, 67. *Under the wide hazard.* The *hazard* in tennis is the court into which the ball is struck, also one of the winning openings into which the ball may be driven. Quicksilver here likens a ship sunk at sea to a ball driven into one of these openings.

II, ii, 69–76. Schelling sees in this and the next speech of Sindefy ' the moralizing vein of Jonson ' and compares them to two passages in Jonson's *Discoveries* (Schelling's edition, pp. 20 and 46). Personally I see only a vague general resemblance, nothing sufficiently definite to warrant our ascribing these speeches to Jonson.

II, ii, 82–3. *Rules the roast.* See the note on *The Gentleman Usher*, V, i, 110.

II, ii, 86. *A prentice, quoth you ?* Schelling's interpretation of this passage seems to me to miss the point. I take it that Sindefy refers to the scornful tone in which Quicksilver had spoken of his former condition as a prentice. ' Do you scorn that condition ? ' she asks. ' It is only a means of learning how to live.'

II, ii, 107–126. With this speech compare Freevil's ironical apology for the bawd's profession, *The Dutch Courtesan*, I, i, 105, *ssq.*

II, ii, 160–1. ' The design of this voyage is kept so close a secret.'

II, ii, 209. *Peterman :* fisherman, applied especially to Thames fishermen, perhaps from ' peter-boat ', a local name for a decked fishing-boat.

II, iii, 16. *Full butt.* Chapman uses this phrase in *May Day*, IV, iv, 33.

II, iii, 26. *Essex calves.* Ray (*Proverbs*, p. 203) quotes from Fuller's *Worthies :* ' This county produces calves of the fattest, fairest and finest flesh in England.' In *Northward Ho* (Dekker, *Dramatic Works*, vol. iii, p. 18) we have : ' The Essex man [loves] a calf.'

II, iii, 31. *Commodity :* a reference to an old and long continued practice of usurers by which part of the sum advanced to the borrower was not in money but in goods. ' If he borrow £100 he shall have forty in silver and three score in wares, as lute-strings, hobby horses, or brown paper '— Greene, *Quip for an Upstart Courtier.* See also Dekker's *Lanthorn and Candlelight* (*Prose Works*, vol. iii, p. 231) and *The Alchemist*, III, iv, 95–7.

II, iii, 35. *Frail :* a pun on the *frail*, i.e. basket, in which figs and raisins were packed.

II, iii, 46–47. *King's Bench :* a prison at Westminster, appropriated to debtors and criminals sent there by the supreme court of common law, the King's Bench.

The Fleet : a famous London prison taking its name from the Fleet stream, or ditch, near by.

The two Counters : debtors' prisons attached to the Mayor's or Sheriff's

---

[1] The title-page of *Muleasses the Turk* (Quarto of 1610) declares that it was ' divers times acted by the Children of H.M. Revels '. This was the boys' company that succeeded Paul's Boys at Whitefriars in 1607 and played there till 1609, after which it dispersed ; see Fleay, *Biographical Chronicle*, vol. i, p. 183, and Murray, *English Dramatic Companies*, vol. i, p. 353.

Court. The *Counter*, or *Compter*, in Southwark was the prison of the Borough of the City of London.

II, iii, 57. *There spake an angel :* a common phrase signifying approval of what has just been said, see *Sir Thomas More*, I, i, 176.

II, iii, 60. *Foisting hound :* stinking pet dog ; cf. *Lear*, I, iv, 125–6.

II, iii, 61–73, 75–88. With these passages cf. the diatribes against women and marriage in *All Fools*, I, i, 65 *ssq.* and *Monsieur D'Olive*, I, i, 347 *ssq.*

II, iii, 69. *Turnspit dog :* a breed of dog used to turn the great spits in kitchens by means of a tread-wheel.

II, iii, 84–5. *Never ha' married him :* perhaps a reflection on the laxness of Scotch marriage laws, a simple declaration before witnesses sufficing to make the union legal.

II, iii, 85 [*Panadas*] : a dish made by boiling bread to a pulp and flavouring it with sugar, currants, etc. ; cf. Massinger, *New Way to Pay Old Debts*, I, ii, where it is mentioned as a lady's dish.

II, iii, 89–90. *What a death is my life bound face to face to :* a characteristic Chapman phrase, cf. *Bussy*, V, i, 115–6 ; *Byron's Tragedy*, V, iv, 38, alluding apparently to the practice of Mezentius *Æneid*, viii., 484–7.

II, iii, 123–4. *Nun substantive . . . adjective.* In *What You Will*, II, ii, 9–11, a boy reciting his lesson says : ' Of nouns some be substantive and some be substantive ', whereupon the Pedant amends ' adjective.'

II, iii, 137. *Draw all my servants in my bow :* bend all my servants to my side. The *New English Dictionary* does not give this phrase, but examples of it occur in Foxe, *Book of Martyrs* (III, xii, 880–2, edition of 1631) : ' bend him unto their bow ', and in Dekker's *Northward Ho* (vol. iii, p. 17) : ' I now draw in your bow.'

II, iii, 138–9. *Read on a book . . . busy :* a close parallel to this phrase occurs in *All Fools*, II, i, 282–4, and again in *Monsieur D'Olive*, V, i, 185–194.

III, i, 19. *Wedlock :* wife, cf. *All Fools*, I, ii, 118. It occurs also in *The Fawn*, II, i, 197.

　　Make you strange : the same phrase occurs in *The Gentleman Usher*, I, ii, 129.

III, i, 37. *Foreright winds :* a Chapman phrase, occurring repeatedly in his translation of Homer, see *Iliad*, ii, 479, and *Odyssey*, iii, 182. It occurs again below III, iii, 58.

III, ii, 6. A jesting reference to Shakespeare's tragedy which had been on the stage for two or three years before the production of *Eastward Ho*.

III, ii, 7. *Brush up my old mistress :* cf. *Sir Giles Goosecap*, I, i, 75–6, where Foulweather is spoken of as able to brush up the silks of old Lady Kingcob.

III, ii, 9. *Blue coat :* the livery of a serving-man.

III, ii, 35. *Ancome :* a boil, a felon.

III, ii, 40–41. The refrain of a song in Campion's *Book of Airs* (1601) beginning : *Mistress, since you so much desire* (Bullen's *Campion*, p. 19). Another looser version in the fourth book seems more in accordance with Gertrude's character. This book was not published till 1617, but the song in question may easily have been current earlier, as Campion in the preface to this book speaks of reclaiming some of his verses which had been set to music by others.

III, ii, 44–5. *Gives no other milk :* is of no other use. To ' give ' or ' give down milk '—said of a person—is to yield assistance or profit, see Marmion's *Antiquary*, I, i.

III, ii, 52. *Honeysuckle :* a term of endearment, like the more familiar ' honey ' ; cf. *Humourous Day's Mirth*, sc. iii, l. 23.

III, ii, 60–61. Another reference to *Hamlet*, cf. note on II, i, 157–8 above.

III, ii, 70–71. *Pebble 'em with snow-balls :* cf. ' besnowball him with rotten eggs ', *May-Day*, III, i, 66.

III, ii, 77–9. A variant of one of Ophelia's songs, *Hamlet*, IV, v, 190, *ssq.* The music for this song is given in Chappell's *Popular Music*, vol. i, p. 237.

III, ii, 80. Stage-direction. For *rosemary* see the note on *The Blind Beggar*, sc. i, l. 308.

III, ii, 83–4. *Mistress What-lack-you.* Gertrude scornfully names her sister after the common cry of London shop-keepers ; cf. *Philaster*, V, iii, 131-2, where the courtier Dion speaks of the citizens as *dear countrymen What-ye-lacks*.

III, ii, 86. *A wanion t'ye :* a plague to you. The word *wanion* appears only in the phrase *with a wanion.* The *Century Dictionary* derives it from *waniand*, the waning of the moon, implying bad luck. Nares quotes instances from *Pericles*, II, i, 17, from Jonson, and Beaumont and Fletcher. An early example appears in Latimer's sermons.

III, ii, 98-107. Schoell notes this speech as a characteristic example of Chapman's prose ; cf. the first speeches of III, i, above.

III, ii, 113-5. A Chapman jest ; cf. *All Fools*, III, i, 384-6.

III, ii, 124-5. *A gentleman natural :* a pun on the double meaning of *natural ;* cf. *All Fools*, II, i, 408-9 and the note *ad loc.*

III, ii, 127. *Forth, I beseech thee.* With this phrase and its repetition slightly altered in l. 131, cf. *All Fools*, III, i, 202 : *Forth, boy, I warrant thee*, and l. 220 : *Forth, my brave Curio.*

III, ii, 133. *Gallantry.* Schelling takes this word as a collective noun equivalent to ' gallants ', and cites *Troilus and Cressida*, III, i, 149. It seems to me that the context demands the more familiar sense of ' fine appearance ', ' gay show ', referring to Quicksilver's dress.

III, ii, 145-6. A misquotation from a song in Dowland's *First Book of Airs* (1597) :

> *Now, O now, I needs must part,*
> *Parting though I absent mourn.*

III, ii, 147. *In capital letters :* cf. *All Fools*, IV, i, 250-2.

III, ii, 200. *The Blue Anchor :* a London tavern mentioned (1607) by Rowlands, *Diogenes' Lanthorn*, p. 7.

III, ii, 226. *To my best nerve :* to the best of my power ; cf. *Chabot*, I, i, 80.

III, ii, 245-6. *A point of neighbourhood :* a point in one's duty as a neighbour ; cf. the sense of *neighbourhood* in l. 230 above. *Point—device :* capital trick.

III, ii, 247. *Draco :* Francis Drake. Swinburne notes the simile in these lines as characteristic of Chapman.

III, ii, 262. Another of Chapman's many references to camels with horns ; see note on *The Revenge of Bussy*, II, i, 176-81.

III, ii, 268. *Quiblin.* This word occurs twice in Jonson, in *The Alchemist*, IV, vii, 110, where it means, as here, ' a trick ', and in *Bartholomew Fair*, I, i, 14, where it means ' a conceit.'

III, ii, 284. *Figent :* fidgetty. The *New English Dictionary* cites numerous instances from *Skialatheia*, 1598, to *The Little French Lawyer*, 1619.

III, ii, 289. *Mutton :* see the note on *All Fools*, III, i, 396.

III, ii, 292. *The best that ever.* Chapman is fond of this phrase in various modifications, cf. below l. 306, *Humourous Day's Mirth*, iii, 4, vi, 131-2, *The Gentleman Usher*, III, ii, 229-30, and *All Fools*, III, i, 93.

III, i, 316. *A toy runs in my head.* In a parallel situation in *All Fools*, III, i, 78-9, a very similar phrase occurs.

III, ii, 327. *Fetch you over :* gull you.

III, iii. There seems to be an allusion to this scene of Chapman's in *Northward Ho* (Dekker, *Dramatic Works*, vol. iii, p. 2) where Altamont, who is thought to be a satiric portrait of Chapman, is spoken of as ' drunk in the Ship-wrack Tavern.'

III, iii, 18. *Left there in '79.* Seagull is not accurate in the date. The first English colony in Virginia was that planted by Sir Richard Grenville in 1585. Possibly there is an allusion here to the second, or lost, colony of 1587.

III, iii, 27-34. Schelling notes that these lines are based upon a passage in More's *Utopia* (p. 98, edition of 1886) : ' Of gold and silver they make commonly chamber-pots and other like vessels. . . . Of the same metals they make great chains with fetters and gyves wherein they tie their bondmen. . . . They gather also pearls by the seaside and diamonds and carbuncles upon certain rocks . . . and therewith they deck their young infants.'

III, iii, 40–47. This is the passage which gave particular offence and was excised in all editions after Q_1.

III, iii, 53. At the close of this speech the later Qq insert a passage which I have relegated to the Text Notes, see p. 865.

III, iii, 67. *Cap and knee :* cf. the note on II, i, 27, above.

III, iii, 115. *Cuckold's Haven :* a point on the south shore of the Thames below London. It was marked by a high pole crowned with a pair of horns ; see below scene iv.

III, iii, 134. *Earns :* yearns, in the sense of grieves ; cf. *Julius Caesar*, II, ii, 129, and the impersonal use of the verb in *Bartholomew Fair*, IV, vi.

III, iii, 143. *A porcpisce even now seen at London Bridge.* The appearance of a porpoise so high up in the river was supposed to foretell a tempest. Stow (*Annals*, p. 880, edition of 1615) notes that on January 19, 1605, a great porpoise was taken alive at West Ham not far below the Bridge. In *Volpone*, I, ii, Jonson mentions as a prodigy the appearance of three porpoises above the Bridge.

III, iii, 147. *Blackwall :* a port for shipping on the Thames below London.

III, iii, 153. *Drake's ship :* the Golden Hind in which Drake sailed round the world. After his return it was laid up at Deptford in the Thames, some distance above Blackwall.

III, iii, 158. *Orgies :* ceremonies. Drayton (*Heroic Epistles*, v, 60) uses this word of the ceremonies of a bridal. Here it implies also a Bacchic revel.

III, iii, 180. *Cucullus non facit monachum :* a mediaeval proverb. The first known instance appears in the *De Contemptu Mundi* of Neckham, attributed to St. Anselm and printed among his works by Migne, *Pat. Curs*, 158 (*Anselm*, i, col. 689) :

> *Non tonsura facit monachum, non horrida vestis.*

In the *Roman de la Rose* (l. 11,546) 'it appears as : *La robe ne fait pas le moine.* In the *Colloquia* of Erasmus (p. 13 edition of 1698, Amsterdam) it takes the more familiar form : *cuculla non facit monachum.* The proverb was widely current in Elizabethan times ; see *Measure for Measure*, V, i, 263 ; *Twelfth Night*, I, v, 62 ; and McKerrow's note in his edition of Nash (vol. iv, p. 110).

III, iii, 194. *A proper taking :* cf. *The Gentleman Usher*, III, ii, 226, for this phrase applied to a state of intoxication ; see also the note on *The Blind Beggar*, sc. x, l. 101.

III, iv, 5. A parody on Richard's famous cry for a horse, *Richard III*, v, iv, 7. Similar parodies occur in *What You Will*, II, i, 126 and *The Fawn*, V, i, 43–4 ; but the phrase had already become a common catchword.

IV, i, Stage-direction. Slitgut probably appeared in the balcony at the back of the stage, drawing the curtains and disclosing the pole [1] decorated with horns which served as a landmark for Cuckold's Haven. From this point of vantage he is supposed to be able to see a long way up and down the Thames.

IV, i, 5. *Saint Luke.* A fair was held every year in Charlton near Greenwich beside the church of St. Luke on St. Luke's day, October 18. Tradition connected the founding of this fair with King John, who is said to have been caught in an intrigue with a miller's wife, and to have compensated the husband by giving him a large estate on condition that he walk around it every year on St. Luke's day with a pair of horns on his head. The fair commemorating this occurrence was held as late as 1832, and was not formally abolished until 1872. All sorts of articles made of horn were sold at it, and it seems to have been the occasion of much coarse revelry, including a procession of supposed cuckolds crowned with horns, who marched from Cuckold's Point to Charlton ; see Hasted, *History of Kent*, vol. i, p. 127, and Gorton, *Topographical Dictionary*, vol. i, p. 412.

---

[1] This pole, or tree, is mentioned by Dekker in *Northward Ho* (vol. iii, p. 41).

IV, i, 7. *This famous tree :* the pole at Cuckold's Haven.

IV, i, 18. *Full butt :* cf. II, iii, 16, above.

IV, i, 59. *St. Katherine's :* a hospital founded by Queen Matilda in 1148 on the north bank of the Thames near the Tower. It was used at this time as a reformatory for fallen women.

IV, i, 68. *The priest.* There is some local allusion here which I have not been able to trace.

IV, i, 73. Stage-direction. *The Tavern before :* the Blue Anchor, where the Drawer has appeared before, III, iii.

IV, i, 97. *More than good news :* a Chapman phrase.

IV, i, 112. *Wapping :* a district on the north shore of the Thames, just below London. A gallows, alluded to in *Northward Ho* (vol. iii, p. 22), stood here by the river-side, on which pirates and other criminals were hanged.

IV, i, 155-6. *Englishmen . . . Frenchified.* The aping of French manners by Englishmen was a common topic of Elizabethan satire. It occurs repeatedly in Chapman, see *Bussy*, I, ii, 39–45. In *Sir Giles Goosecap* Captain Foulweather, the *Frenchified* captain, is distinguished by his partiality for all things French. The word, *Frenchified*, occurs twice in *Goosecap* (I, i, 35 and I, ii, 42) ; it also appears in *Every Man out of his Humour*, II, i, which is the earliest instance cited in the *New English Dictionary*.

IV, i, 169-70. *A poor knight of Windsor.* These 'knights' were retired officers, pensioners of the King, who lived in the royal castle of Windsor. They are alluded to in *The Lady of Pleasure* (V, i) as disabled veterans.

IV, i, 174-5. *Isle of Dogs :* a low swampy peninsula projecting from the north bank of the Thames, almost opposite Greenwich.

IV, i, 179-80. A sneer at the cheapening of knighthood under James I ; cf. the note on *Monsieur D'Olive*, IV, ii, 78–80. It is not unlikely that the actor who spoke these words imitated the King's broad Scotch accent, and it seems strange that such a passage was allowed to remain in the text.

IV, i, 218. *Malleation :* hammering. The word occurs in *The Alchemist*, II, v, 28.

IV, i, 219. *Luna :* the alchemists' term for silver.

IV, i, 231. *Habebis magisterium :* you will have the philosopher's stone ; said, of course, ironically, for all that would be obtained by Quicksilver's method would be imitation silver.

IV, i, 233-5. Cf. the crime of which Face accuses Subtle (*The Alchemist*, I, i, 114), *laundring gold and barbing it*, ' To *launder* gold ', says Gifford in his note on this passage in *The Alchemist*, ' is probably to wash it in *aqua regia* ; barbing is clipping.'

IV, i, 243. *Sconces :* heads ; cf. this use of the word in IV, ii, 15 below.

IV, i, 249. *Your tavern :* the Blue Anchor. It is interesting to note the change of place within the limits of a scene. Winifred was washed ashore at St. Katherine's. Here, without any interruption of the action, we find her in Billingsgate above London Bridge. There is a similar change in *Bussy*, III, ii.

IV, i, 288-302. With this speech cf. the long oration by Valerio in praise of the horn, *All Fools*, V, ii, 236, *ssq.*

IV, i, 295-302. *Horn of hunger :* the dinner-horn. *Horn of abundance :* cf. *The Widow's Tears*, V, ii, 73, where also the cornucopia is connected with the cuckold's horn, and note the pun on *horn* and *adorn* here and in *The Widow's Tears*, I, i, 109, and *All Fools*, II, i, 240. Schelling sees another pun in *lanthorn* =land horn, sign-post. *Horn of destiny :* cf. *All Fools*, I, i, 40 and the note *ad loc. Horn tree :* the pole at Cuckold's Haven with its decoration of horns.

IV, ii, 5. *Cavallaria . . . Colonoria.* ' Latin law terms signifying the tenure of a knight and of an ordinary colonist '—Schelling. Ducange defines *Caballaria* as *praedium servitio militari obnoxium* and says of *ordo colonarius, id est ut coloni vivere solent.* Touchstone, of course, uses these terms in mockery of Sir Petronel's knighthood and of his plan of colonizing Virginia.

IV, ii, 8. *Monmouth caps :* sailors' caps.; cf. *Henry V*, IV, vii, 104.

IV, ii, 11. *A Gravesend toast.* Gravesend was the usual place of embarkation. I take it that a *Gravesend toast* is a parting cup, perhaps of sack with a toast in it.

IV, ii, 12–13. *Admiral and vice-admiral and rear-admiral :* names given to the ships bearing these officers in a fleet.

IV, ii, 14. *Remora :* not a barnacle, the meaning given by Bullen and Schelling, but the sucking-fish (*Echineis remora*) which was supposed to fasten upon the bottom of ships and arrest their progress ; see Pliny, *Hist. Nat.* IX, 41. It is twice mentioned by Jonson, *Poetaster*, III, ii, and *Magnetic Lady*, II, i.

IV, ii, 15. *Sconce :* a pun on the double meaning of the word, ' head ' and ' fort.'

IV, ii, 17. *Vie with you :* a term in card-playing, meaning to back one's hand against that of one's opponent ; see *Byron's Tragedy*, IV, ii, 107.

IV, ii, 23. *Weeping Cross.* ' To return by Weeping Cross ' was a common proverbial expression for repenting of an undertaking. Thus Florio, *Montaigne*, III, 5, has : ' Few men have wedded their sweethearts . . . but have come home by Weeping Cross and ere long repented them of their bargain.' See also Lyly (*Works*, edited by Bond, vol. ii, p. 28), and Davies of Hereford (*Works*, edited by Grosart, vol. ii, p. 42).

IV, ii, 24. *Madam and her malkin :* Gertrude and her maid. A *malkin* is a country wench, in which character Sindefy had been introduced to Gertrude.

IV, ii, 25. *Bite o' the bridle for William :* ' probably a hostler's proverb '— Schelling. To ' bite on the bridle ' is to chew the bit, and the sense of the proverb is plain. I have not found any other instance of it.

IV, ii, 38. *Commoners :* members of the Town or Common Council.

IV, ii, 39–40. *At presentation of the inquest :* ' on the report of the nominating committee '—Schelling. The *inquest* was the committee of the Council appointed to make legal inquiry into any matter.

IV, ii, 51. *Ta'en into the livery of his company :* made a freeman of the City and so entitled to wear the *livery*, distinctive dress of his company, the Goldsmiths'.

IV, ii, 68. *Will wear scarlet :* be an alderman, referring to the scarlet robes of these dignitaries.

IV, ii, 72. *Lady Ramsey :* the wife of Sir Thomas Ramsey, Lord Mayor of London, 1577. She was a benefactress of Christ's Hospital. See Stow, *Annals*, Book I, p. 278 (edition of 1722).

    Gresham : Sir Thomas Gresham, builder of the Royal Exchange, one of the most eminent of London citizens in the reign of Elizabeth.

IV, ii, 73. *Whittington :* four times Lord Mayor of London between 1397 and 1420. He bequeathed a large fortune to charitable and public purposes, and his executors founded conduits (see l. 75 below) at Cripplegate and Billingsgate. A play, now lost, bearing his name was entered in the Stationers' Registers in 1605. This play probably dealt with the *fable* of Whittington's cat which Stowe holds it beneath his dignity to mention.

IV, ii, 75–6. *Thy deeds played in thy life :* a reference to Heywood's play, *If You Know not me*, the second part of which treats at some length of the building of the Exchange by Gresham. It seems to have been produced by the Queen's Company in the very year of *Eastward Ho*, 1605.

IV, ii, 77. *Get-penny :* the word is used by Middleton in *Five Gallants* (*Works*, vol. iii, p. 134) of a harlot's face ; by Jonson, *Bartholomew Fair*, V, i, in connexion with a puppet-show.

IV, ii, 88. *A false brother :* an informer.

IV, ii, 96. *Under colour of a great press :* under pretence of impressing men for the army or navy. Thus in April, 1603, *a great press* took place in London by order of Cecil, acting in the King's name, and some eight hundred men, described as ' vagabonds ' were seized and sent to serve in the Dutch fleet, see *Pictorial History of England*, vol. iii, p. 3.

IV, ii, 102–3. *New officer . . . unreflected :* an official in his first term, not to be deflected from his duty ; cf. a line of Chapman's in his *Iliad*, xxi, 373 :

And prayed her that her son might be reflected

where *reflected*, i.e. turned away, translates the Greek παυέσθω, let him cease.

IV, ii, 114. *Fished fair and caught a frog :* from Heywood's *Proverbs*, pt. I, chap. 11. A passage from Bishop Latimer's *Letter to a Certain Gentleman* (Foxe's *Martyrs*, vol. iii, p. 483, edition of 1641) interprets the proverb : ' As the common saying is, Well have I fished and caught a frog, brought little to pass with much ado.'

IV, ii, 140. *Fist :* a common word with Marston whose hand seems visible in this colloquy between Gertrude and her father.

IV, ii, 141-2. *A fart from a dead man :* another phrase from Heywood's *Proverbs*, pt. I, chap. 11.

IV, ii, 144-5. *Hunger drops out at his nose :* also from Heywood, pt. I, chap. 11. Also in Heywood's *Epigrams upon Proverbs*, no. 192 :

> *Hunger droppeth out of his nose,*
> *That is the worst kind of the pose.*

IV, ii, 146. *Fair words never hurt the tongue :* cf. ' It hurteth not the tongue to give fair words ', Heywood, *Proverbs*, pt. I, chap. 9.

IV, ii, 150-1. *No man loves his fetters, be they made of gold :* from Heywood's *Proverbs*, pt. I, chap. 8.

IV, ii, 151-2. *My head fastened under my child's girdle :* cf. ' Then have ye his head fast under your girdle ', Heywood, *Proverbs*, pt. I, chap. 5.

IV, ii, 152. *As she has brewed, so let her drink :* cf. ' As I would needs brew, so must I needs drink ', Heywood, *Proverbs*, pt. I, chap. 8.

IV, ii, 153. *Witless to wedding :* cf. ' They went witless to wedding, whereby at last they both went a-begging ',Heywood, *Proverbs*, pt. I, chap. 11.

IV, ii, 164. *Good cow . . . ill calf :* cf. ' Many a good cow hath an evil calf ', Heywood, *Proverbs*, pt. I, chap. 10.

IV, ii, 171. *Melancholy :* used here in the sense of ' anger ', see *New English Dictionary* sub *melancholy*, 2.

IV, ii, 176. *Foil to set it off.* Touchstone borrows a metaphor from his own craft ; a foil is the thin leaf of metal put under a gem to heighten its lustre.

IV, ii, 182. *Trussed up :* hanged on the gallows.

IV, ii, 183. *In the island :* the Isle of Dogs, cf. IV, i, 174 and the note *ad loc.*

IV, ii, 185. *Carry an M. under your girdle :* be polite enough to use the term, Master. The phrase is not infrequent in Elizabethan drama ; see *The Blind Beggar of Bednal Green* (*Materialien zur Kunde des älteren Englischen Dramas*, vol. 1, p. 13, and note *ad loc*) and *Englishmen for my Money* (Hazlitt's *Dodsley*, vol. x, p. 531). Bullen also cites an instance in Heywood's *Maidenhead Well Lost*, III, ii.

IV, ii, 190. *Bridewell :* an ancient monastery used at this time as a house of correction for vagabonds and fallen women. Quicksilver and Sir Petronel were to have been detained there as ' masterless men ' until shipped to join the navy.

IV, ii, 230. *Gresco or primero :* games of cards. Nares gives a long account of *primero*.

IV, ii, 279. *Pride and outrecuidance :* the same phrase occurs in *Monsieur D'Olive*, IV, ii, 58. The word *outrecuidance* occurs also in *Cynthia's Revels*, V, ii.

IV, ii, 292. *Chop logic :* see note on *All Fools*, I, ii, 51.

IV, ii, 315. *Take security :* accept bail. Touchstone in the next line puns on the phrase and declares he will seize the person of Security.

IV, ii, 326-8. This seems a bit of Marston ; cf. the note on II, i, 147-9.

V, i, 7. *O hone, hone :* the refrain of an Irish lament, the Erse *ochoin*, oh, alas !

V, i, 15-23. With the repetition of *Sin.* in this speech, cf. that of *Win.* in *Bartholomew Fair*, I, i, in Littlewit's first speech to his wife. See also II, ii, 199-203 above.

V, i, 25-6. *Hunger breaks stone walls :* cf. ' Hunger pierceth stone wall ', Heywood, *Proverbs*, pt. I, chap. 12, and Shakespeare's use of the proverb, *Coriolanus*, I, i, 210.

V, i, 29–30. *Knight o' the Sun :* a character in *The Mirror of Knighthood* (published in seven parts, 1583–1601) a translation of the Spanish romance, *Cavallero del Phebo.* There is an allusion to this romance in *Antonio and Mellida,* II, i, 34. *Palmerin of England* is the hero of another Spanish romance, *Palmerin de Inglaterra* by L. Hurtado, 1547, translated by Antony Munday. This translation was entered in the Stationers' Registers as early as 1581, but the book seems to have been so eagerly devoured that the oldest extant copy dates from 1602.

V, i, 39. *Still prest :* always ready.

V, i, 44–5. *The Round Table at Winchester.* A large round table inscribed with the names of Arthur's knights was long preserved in the Sessions-hall at Winchester, see the long note on this passage in Collier's *Dodsley,* vol. iv, p. 259.

V, i, 46. *Hazard,* a game of dice, not unlike the American game of 'craps'.

V, i, 50–1. *By bread and salt :* a common sixteenth century oath. Thus in *Gammer Gurton's Needle,* sc. 2 Chat swears *by bread and salt.* To make the oath more binding bread and salt were sometimes eaten. Thus in Nash's *Lenten Stuff (Works,* vol. iii, p. 199) : ' Venus and Juno . . . took bread and salt and ate it that they would be smartly revenged'. See also *Honest Whore,* pt. I, I, 12.

V, i, 57. *Lay my ladyship in lavender :* pawn my title. To lay *in lavender* was a slang phrase meaning either to pawn or to imprison. See Shift's first bill in *Every Man out of his Humour,* III, i.

V, i, 60. *A peat :* a term of reproach. Jonson uses it in *Every Man out of his Humour,* in the description of the *Dramatis Personae,* of Fallace, *a proud mincing peat.*

V, i, 62. *Turn the lip and the alas :* cf. the phrases ' to fall a lip ', i.e. to show contempt, and ' to make up a lip ', i.e. to pout.

V, i, 81–3. For these superstitions see Bishop Corbett's *The Fairies' Farewell* (Chalmer's *English Poets,* vol. v, p. 582) mentioned in the note on *Humourous Day's Mirth,* sc. iv, l. 18.

V, i, 100–108. In metre, style, and tone this song seems to me closely akin to one in *The Dutch Courtesan,* I, ii, 220, ssq.

V, i, 121. *Blow at the coal :* cf. ' Let them that be a-cold blow at the coal ', Heywood, *Proverbs,* pt. I, chap. 10.

V, i, 122–3. *The hasty person never wants woe :* from Heywood, pt. I, chap. 2.

V, i, 125. *Did but my kind :* only acted according to my nature.

V, i, 131. *Gold-end man :* one who buys broken bits of gold. The phrase occurs in *The Alchemist,* II, iv, 21, see Gifford's note *ad loc.*

V, i, 140. *French wires :* wire frames for ruffs, see *Revenge of Bussy,* III, ii, 136.

     Cheat-bread : fine wheat bread ; *cheat* means ' wheat ' in Chapman's *Batrachomyomachia, Poems,* p. 272.

V, i, 150–1. *The leg of a lark is better than the body of a kite :* an old proverb, òccurring in Heywood, pt. I, chap. 4.

V, ii, 28. *Mortified :* used here in the almost obsolete religious sense, ' dead to sin ', perhaps an intentional mistake for ' edified.'

V, ii, 32. *Brownist :* a strict Puritan sect, taking this name from its founder, Robert Browne, 1550–1633.

     Millenary : a sect which believed in the Second Advent and the thousand years reign of Christ on the earth.

     Family o' Love : a sixteenth century sect of mystics, known also as Familists, founded by Hendrik Niclaes. Their doctrines were introduced into England where they spread widely, especially in the eastern counties. They were accused of teaching and practising free love, and Middleton attacks them on-this score in his comedy, *The Family of Love,* 1607. Marston also mentions them in *The Dutch Courtesan,* III, iii, 56–7.

V, ii, 42, 43, 47. *The Knight's Ward, the Hole, the two-penny ward :* names of different parts of the prison. ' The Counter had four divisions or wards, the Master's side being that in which the highest price was charged for accommodations [see *Westward Ho,* III, iii] ; then come the Knight's Ward, then the two-penny ward, and finally the Hole, a dungeon for the poorest prisoners', Gifford's note on *Every Man out of his Humour*, V, vii. In the prison scene in *Greene's Tu Quoque* (Collier's *Dodsley*, vol. vii, p. 71) Spendall, a moneyless prisoner, is advised to remove to the two-penny ward, or into the Hole where he may feed for nothing out of the alms-basket.

V, ii, 53.   *Cut his hair :* thus adopting the proper fashion of a citizen as contrasted with the long curls of the courtiers whom Quicksilver had formerly imitated. Cf. *Bartholomew Fair*, III, i, where Knockem promises to cut his hair as a sign of reformation.

V, ii, 55–6.   *The Sick Man's Salve :* a popular book of devotion by Thomas Becon published 1561. It is repeatedly mentioned in Elizabethan drama ; see *Silent Woman*, IV, ii and *Philaster*, IV, i. In *Sir John Oldcastle*, IV, iii, it is named, along with the Bible, the Testament, the Psalms in metre, and the *Treasure of Gladness*, 'all in English', as among the books found in Sir John's library and condemned to the fire as heretical by the Bishop.

V, ii, 63.   *An intelligencer :* an informer. There is a satirical implication that even this calling is respectable compared with that of a sergeant.

V, ii, 68–9.   *Fish is cast away that is cast in dry pools :* verbatim from Heywood's *Proverbs*, pt. I, chap. 11.

V, ii, 73–4.   *Lay mine ear to the ground :* cf. *Psalms* lviii, 4 : ' They are like the deaf adder that stoppeth her ear.' Calvin in his commentary on this passage refers to the common belief, reported by Bochart—*Hierozoicon*, pt. II, book 3, chap. 6—that the adder, on hearing the voice of the snake-charmer, lays one ear to the ground and stops the other with her tail.

V, iii, 29.   *Feast of her new moon :* alluding to the horns of the crescent, emblematic, to the jealous mind of Security, of the horns of Cuckoldry.

V, iii, 55.   *The basket :* containing the broken victuals collected for poor prisoners. There are repeated allusions to this practice in Elizabethan drama, see *May-Day*, IV, iii, 91 and note *ad loc.*, also Shirley's *Bird in a Cage*, III, iv. In *Greene's Tu Quoque* (Collier's *Dodsley*, vol. vii, pp. 73–4) there is a lively scene in which Gatherscrap appears in the prison with the basket and Spendall describes its disgusting contents.

V, iii, 60.   Collier sees here a direct allusion to Robert Greene's *Groatsworth of Wit* and *Farewell to Folly*. This seems unlikely considering that Greene had died over a decade before the appearance of *Eastward Ho*. The allusion is to the common practice of composing popular ballads on the last words and dying repentance of celebrated criminals.

V, iv, 17.   *Mandragora :* mandrake. Collier, in his note on this passage, quotes from an Elizabethan translation of Demosthenes to the effect that mandragora is ' of virtue to cast one into so heavy a sleep that being lanced or burned he shall not feel the grief.' See also the note on *Othello*, III, iii, 330 in Furness's *Variorum*.

V, iv, 32.   *The voice of the hyena :* cf. ' the Hyena when she speaketh like a man deviseth most mischief ', Lyly, *Euphues* (*Works*, vol. i, p. 250). Bond in his note on this passage of Lyly cites Pliny, *Hist. Nat.*, viii, 44, as authority for this trick of the hyena.

V, v, 24.   *White-Friars :* the district surrounding the old church of the Carmelites. It was at this time a sanctuary for debtors and minor criminals since an arrest could only be made within its limits under the writ of the Lord Chief Justice himself. See Scott's vivid picture of White-Friars, or Alsatia, in *The Fortunes of Nigel*.

V, v, 43–44.   *Mannington's:* ' *A woeful Ballad made by Mr. George Mannington, an houre before he suffered at Cambridge-castell* was entered on the Stationers' Register Nov. 7, 1576 '—Schelling. It was included in Robinson's *Handful of Pleasant Delights*, 1584, and has been reprinted in *The Gentleman's Magazine*, January, 1781, and in Ritson's *Ancient Songs*, vol. ii, p. 47.

V, v, 46.   This tune was that to which Mannington's ballad was sung, taking its name from the first line of that song.

V, v, 73.   *The ragged colt :* cf. Heywood's *Proverbs*, pt. I, chap. 11 : ' Of a ragged colt there cometh a good horse.' See also *The Widow's Tears*,

III, i, 58–9, where the same term is applied to a supposedly bankrupt scapegrace.

V, v, 79–80. With this rhyme, *daughter : after,* cf. *Lear,* I, iv, 341–4.

V, v, 81. *The black ox :* a symbol of trouble or old age. The phrase appears in a common proverb, found in Heywood, pt. I, chap. 7 : ' The black ox hath not trod on his (or her) foot.' Cf. also Lyly, *Euphues (Works,* vol. i, p. 203).

V, v, 124. *The Spital :* the hospital, with special reference here to the treatment of venereal disease.

V, v, 189. *Yellow :* the colour of Security's prison dress, and also emblematic of jealousy.

V, v, 196–7. The devils will take Security's horns as a sign that he is one of their number.

V, v, 199. *An innocent :* a pun on a common Elizabethan meaning of the word, i.e. ' idiot.'

Epilogus. Quicksilver, who spoke the Epilogue, evidently advanced to the front of the stage. He first takes, so to speak, the audience into the play, pretending that they are the crowd gathered in front of the Counter to see the release of Sir Petronel and his friends, a crowd as large as that on the *solemn day of the Pageant,* i.e. the Lord Mayor's Show, again referred to in the penultimate line. The *windows* of l. 4 are the ' rooms ', or boxes, of the theatre. In the two couplets which close the play he drops this pretence, and addressing the spectators directly begs their further patronage ; l. 9 contains an interesting hint as to the frequency, *once a week,* with which a successful play was likely to be given at an Elizabethan theatre.

TEXT NOTES

Three editions of *Eastward Ho,* all in quarto form, were printed for William Aspley in 1605. The first of these containing the offensive passage (III, iii, 40–47) seems to have been so promptly and effectually suppressed that no copies [1] of it remain. The second quarto apparently differs from the first only by the omission of the objectionable passage (79 words) and the addition of a passage of 31 words at the end of the speech in which the former occurs. These changes affected only two pages, and as these pages have been preserved and bound up in a copy of Q₂ in the Dyce collection at the Victoria and Albert Museum, it is possible to see exactly what took place when Aspley received the order to cease printing Q₁. The censored passage begins on E₃ *verso* two and a half lines from the bottom and extends to the middle of the fifth line in E₄. Thus seven lines or so were struck out. These two pages, of course, had to be reset, but in order to avoid resetting others, and to be able to use the unsold sheets of Q₁, Aspley induced one of the authors to write a new bit (printed in the present edition in the Text Notes, p. 865) which he added to the end of the speech and by printing fewer [2] lines than usual on these two pages, he managed to make the required alteration without disturbing the type for any pages but these two, E₃ *verso* and E₄. Q₁ and Q₂, then, are to all intents and purposes one and the same edition except on the two pages E₃ *verso* and E₄.

Q₃, on the contrary, has been entirely reset. It contains four pages less than Q₂, owing to abbreviations, closer setting of type, and a trick of printing verse from time to time in double columns. It corrects a number of trivial misprints in Q₂, but introduces a large number of new errors. On the whole, however, the text of *Eastward Ho* is fairly good, and there are few if any

---

[1] Schelling (*Belles-Letters* edition of *Eastward Ho,* p. xxxii) speaks of a copy in the South Kensington Museum. This is not strictly accurate, as no complete copy of Q₁ is to be found there, but only two pages of this edition (E 3 *verso* and E₄) inserted between E₃ and E₄ in a copy of Q₂.

[2] The difference in length between the cancelled passage and the new one was some 48 words, amounting to about four lines in Q₁. The new page E₃ *verso* contains only 37 lines instead of the usual 38 or 39, and the new E₄ only 35, so that the necessary space has been attained. See Schelling's remarks, *op. cit.,* pp. 145–6.

of the corrupt passages which appear so often in the earlier comedies of Chapman. Q₂ is, as a rule, to be followed ; its occasional misprints can often be corrected by Q₃, and the censored passage is preserved in the two pages of Q₁ already mentioned as bound up in a Dyce copy of Q₂.

Eastward Ho has often been reprinted ; first in Dodsley's *Old Plays*, 1744 and in the subsequent issues of that series, Reed's *Dodsley*, 1780, and Collier's *Dodsley*, 1825, in volume iv in all three. It was also reprinted in the Appendix of Chetwood's *Memoirs of the Life and Writings of Ben Jonson*, Dublin, 1756, and in *The Ancient British Drama* (vol. ii), 1810. It was included in Halliwell's edition of Marston, 1856, and in Bullen's edition of that dramatist, 1887, in each case in vol. iii. It does not appear in the Pearson reprint of the plays of Chapman, but is included in Shepherd's, *The Works of George Chapman, Plays*, 1874. Finally a careful reprint, based upon Q₂, was edited with notes and introduction by Professor Schelling for the *Belles-Lettres Series* (1904) where it appears bound up with Jonson's *Alchemist*.

The present edition, like Professor Schelling's, of which I have made constant use, is based upon Q₂. I have modernized the spelling, as well as the punctuation, except in a few cases where it seemed best to retain an old form. In preparing the text I have consulted copies in the British Museum, in the Dyce collection, and in the Bodleian where I have checked my proofs by comparison with a copy of Q₂ (Malone 765). In the following notes I have not attempted to record all the variations of all editions, especially as some of the earlier reprints are far from accurate, nor have I thought it necessary to note all the misprints of Q₃. Wherever I have departed from Q₂, except in the case of a palpable misprint, I have given my authority, and as usual all emendations, additions to the text and modern stage-directions, are inclosed in brackets. In these notes I use from time to time the following symbols : Qq to denote an agreement of Q₂ and Q₃, Co. Collier's *Dodsley* ; B. Bullen's *Marston*, and B.L. for Schelling's edition.

Dramatis Personae. There is no list of the characters in Qq. It was supplied by B. whose list is reprinted, with the addition of one name, *Toby*, in B.L. This addition seems to me idle, as *Toby*, a prisoner mentioned in V, v, 10, 33, has nothing to say unless, indeed, he is to be identified with Prisoner 2 of that scene. On the other hand both B. and B.L. omit the Messenger who appears in III, i, the Scrivener who appears in III, ii, and the Friend of the Prisoners who appears in V, v. I have added these to B.'s list and have corrected the misprint *Ford* for *Fond* which appears in B. and B.L.

The Qq divide the play into acts, but not into scenes. Each act has the heading *Actus Primi* (*Secundi*, etc.) *Scena Prima*, but there is no further division into scenes except in Act III, which marks *Scena Secunda* after l. 70, but contains no further division. I have followed the B.L. division into scenes, and the indications of place given, as a rule, in B.

Actus Primi : so Qq ; B.L. reads *Primus*, but the genitive form appears elsewhere in Chapman's work, see acts I, II and V of *All Fools*. I shall not note this alteration of B.L. in the other acts.

I, i, 12. *Work upon that now.* This phrase, and many of Touchstone's sayings, are printed in italics in Qq for the sake of emphasis. B.L. retains these italics, but I have not thought it necessary to do so, and shall not hereafter notice these cases.

71-74. *Master.* Qq *M.* I have filled out these contractions without marking them in the text, and shall not refer to them hereafter.

87. Q₂ *t'was* ; Q₃ *'twas.* I note this as the sort of correction that Q₃ often makes.

97. *Sirrah.* Qq *sra.*

99. Q₂ omits *and* before *my* and is followed by Co.

106. Qq *Don ;* B. emends *Dan.*

110-112. There is a good deal of difference as to the punctuation of these lines. B.L. following that of the Qq points thus : *Touchstone. Eastward, bully, this satin belly ! And canvas-backed Touchstone—slife, man !* This seems to me very awkward since *satin belly* must modify *Touchstone*. My punctuation is practically that of B.

I, ii. Stage-direction. Qq have *Girtred* for *Gertrude* and so throughout the play.

I, ii, 5. Q_2 *Medam ;* Q_3 *madam.*

16. Qq *Tuf-taffitie.*

27–28. Q_2 *Shoute ;* Q_3 *Shout.* Co. emends *Shoot*, which B. accepts.

49. Qq *Poldavis.* I follow B. in making the name agree with the form in the stage-direction.

58. B.L. and the other editors insert *a* before *thing.* But *thing* represents the old plural form, and the insertion is needless.

90. Qq, *A* 100 *li.*

179. *Moral.* Q_2 *morrall ;* Q_3 *mortall*, a mere misprint.

II, i, 52. Stage-directions. Qq have here only : *Enter Goulding.* It is evident, however, that Touchstone takes no further part in the action until l. 109, and that *Enter Goulding* denotes the advance to the front of *Mildred* as well as her lover.

79. Q_2 *ttade ;* Q_3 *trade.*

89. Q_2 (*Ump*) *pulldo, Pulldo ; showse quoth ;* Q_3 *Am pum pull eo, Pullo : showse quot.* B.L. here follows Q_3. My reading is made up from both. *Ump* best represents Quicksilver's *drunken hiccup*, as above in l. 3 ; *pull eo*, on the other hand, more nearly represents the cry of the watermen ; while *quoth* is preferable to *quot.*

135–6. Qq print as one line.

142. Q_2 *pisse ;* Q_3 *passe*

II, ii. Stage-direction. For *Securitie solus* of Q_2, Q_3 has *Ent. Secu.*

II, ii, 10. B.L. omits the words *Security following* in the stage-direction after this line. It seems to me they should be retained as they show that Security has retired after his speech to the back of the stage and comes forward again at the heels of Quicksilver. B. marks a new scene at this point, which does not seem necessary as there is no change of place.

14. Q_2 *thy usurous ;* Q_3 *my usurous.* Co. reads *cosenage* for *covetousness*, l. 15, for which I can find no authority.

25. Q_2 *but as a scrappe ;* Q_3 *but a*

scape. Co. and B. follow Q_3 in reading *scape*. In *Old City Manners* (see above, p. 837) we find *scape* in this place, which may show a stage tradition, but more likely follows the reading of the commoner Q_3. B.L. rightly reverts to the first reading. Personally I do not see what sense can be made here of *scape*, i.e. 'slip', 'fault'.

36. Qq *Dalida ;* B. emends *Dalila.*

42. Q_2 *wright ;* Q_3 *writ.*

55. Q_2 misprints *Hyn.* for *Syn.* as the speaker's name. Q_3 assigns the speech to *Secur.* and is followed by B. This is certainly wrong as the speech is in keeping with the following speeches of Sindefy, ll. 69 and 79.

142. Q_2 *hundered ;* Q_3 *hundred.*

202. After this line Qq have *Exeunt*, but it is plain that Quicksilver remains on the stage.

212. Quicksilver's *exit*, inserted in B.L., is not marked in Qq, and it is probable that he did not leave the stage here, but remained to greet *Sir Petronel.* B. runs these scenes together, but there is an evident change of place here.

II, iii. Stage-direction. Qq print *wan* for *wand.*

II, iii, 53. Q_2 *wise ;* Q_3 misprints *wife.*

85. Qq *Poynados.* I follow B.'s emendation *panadas.*

154. Qq *by lady.* B. emends *by'r.*

170. I follow Q_2 in reading *Thank.* All other editors prefer the reading of Q_3 *I thanke.*

III, i, 1. Q_2 *our ;* Q_3 *your.* B.L. follows Q_3, but there seems no need of this. With Co. and B. I read *our.*

9–10. Q_2 puts the words from *by* to *years* in parenthesis.

53, 63. Q_2 prefixes *Spoyl.* to the speeches beginning with these lines ; Q_3 *Spend*, which is followed by all editors. *Spoyl.* is, perhaps, a trace of a name altered in revision.

III, ii, 24. In the stage-direction after this line Q_2 misprints *Por. ;* Q_3 has *Pot.* for *Potkin.*

70. Q_2 *wee'd ;* Q_3 *Weele.*

92. Q_2 *call ;* Q_3 *cals*, which is evidently the better reading and is accepted by B.L.

101. Qq include the word *since* in parenthesis, but it seems to me that the construction is better, if it is placed outside and construed with *I am born*. This change is indicated in an old hand in a copy of Q_2 in the possession of Mr. Armour of Princeton.

113. Qq. misprint *Bridgegrome*. Co. corrects.

122. Qq have a question mark, equivalent to an exclamation, after *so* B.L. omits this, and the passage, perhaps, reads better without this break.

126. Q_2 *Touchstone;* Q_3 *Touch*. Co. and B.L. follow Q_3, but I take this to be one of the usual abbreviations of this edition. B. follows Q_2.

176. *God-b'w'y'.* Q_2 *God-boye;* Q_3 *God-boy*.

188. The word *the*, before *first*, wanting in Qq is supplied by Co.

258. Q_2 *his sterne;* Q_3 misprints *eyes sterne*, which Co. gives as the reading of Qq omitting to note the correct reading of Q_2.

262. All Qq that I have seen except the Armour Q_2 read *To find*. B.L. does not notice this so that the copies from which that text is constructed must have the true reading

306. Q_2 *shas;* Q_3 *was*.

310. After this line Qq have *Exit;* but from l. 314 it seems clear that Security has not left the stage. It seems to me better to read *Exiturus*, than with B.L. to read *Exit* and insert *Re-enter Security* before l. 314.

III, iii, 2. Q_2 misprints *bnt;* Q_3 corrects *but*.

40–47 *Only a few . . . do here.* This is the censored passage. I have supplied it from the pages of Q_1 bound up in a Dyce copy of Q_2, see above, p. 862. It was re-inserted in the text by Co.

50. *A nobleman*, the reading of Q_1. The later Qq read *any other officer*, a change which shows the censor's hand.

52. B.L. notes that Q_2 reads *furune* in this line. The Armour copy has *Forune* which shows that a *t* has dropped out.

53. At the end of this speech Q_2 and Q_3 insert a new passage : ' Besides, there we shall have no more Law then Conscience, and not too much of either ; serve God inough, eate and drinke inough, and *inough is as good as a Feast* '. Previous editors include these words in the text, but as they did not belong to the original play and were only written to fill up the gap left by the censor, I have preferred to relegate them to the Text Notes.

59. The phrase *with his followers* does not appear in the stage-direction Q_1. It is added in Q_2.

158. The Armour copy reads *O gies* showing the loss of a letter as in l. 52.

III, iv. Co. and B. do not mark a new scene here, but it is plain that Security does not return to the tavern, but is at his own house.

IV, i, 28–9. *In a.* B.L. notes here that Qq read *in an night-cappe*. This is not the reading of any copy that I have seen, and I think the B.L. note should refer to the stage-direction after l. 31 (l. 39 in the B.L. text) where Qq have *in an*.

53. Stage-direction. Qq *Exit creep*.

164. Qq *infortunes*. Co. emends.

181. *No no this*. So Q_2. Q_3 reads *Now this*, a variant not noted in B.L.

182. Qq *pound giving to a Page, all*. B.L. following Co. and B. reads *given to a page ; all*, but there is no need of altering the original. By placing the comma which in Qq follows *Page*, after *pound*, the original makes perfect sense.

251. Q_2 *stale;* Q_3 *stole*.

288. Co. supplies *Slit*, omitted in Qq, before this speech.

289. Q_2 *farthiest;* Q_3 *farthyest*.

293–5. I have followed here essentially the punctuation of Q_1, but I am not sure that it is not misleading. Certainly Slitgut does not bid *farewell* to *honest married men*. It would, I think, be a great improvement to read : *Farewell, thou dishonest satire to honest married men. Farewell*, etc., which would bring this clause into accord with the arrangement of the following lines, but I have not ventured to make this alteration.

IV, ii. Co. does not mark a scene here. I follow B.L.

IV, ii, 5. *Nor the Colonoria.* Q_2 has *not the Colonoria ;* Q_3 corrects.

47. Q_2 *let we,* corrected in some copies of Q_3.

83. Qq have a question mark after this line, which B.L. follows, but it is equivalent to an exclamation mark.

109. After this line Qq read, with some variations of spelling, *Touchstone, Mistresse Touchstone, Girtrude, Goulding, Mildred, Sindefy ;* but Touchstone and Goulding are already on the stage.

123. Some copies of Q_3 read *low cullion,* a variation not noted in B.L.

133. Co. B. and others read *nor put,* but there seems to be no authority for this. All copies of Qq that I have seen and B.L. read *not put.*

161. Stage-direction. Qq have only *Exit Gyrt.* B.L. adds *and Sindefy.*

167-8. All Qq that I have seen give this speech to Goulding, and are followed by Co. and B. B.L., without any comment, assigns it to the Constable who has just entered. This is a plausible alteration, but not, I think, necessary. In l. 168 two copies in the British Museum show a variety of misprints : *will hor broght* and *will them brought.*

227-8. Q_2 *Quicksilver ;* Q_3 *Quick.* This variation throws, I think, some light on III, ii, 126, where B.L. follows Q_3. In this case B. L. follows Q_2.

267. Qq put the words *God* to *thee* in parenthesis.

303. Q_2 *keepe ;* Q_3 *keepe it.*

304. *Master.* Qq *Mr,* an unusual agreement in abbreviation.

312. Q_2 misprints *yon ;* Q_3 correctly *you.*

320. Here Q_2 abbreviates *Lo. ;* Q_3 *Lord,* an unusual case.

V, i, 28. Q_2 *run ;* Q_3 *ran,* a variation not noted in B.L.

33. Q_2 misprints *Gry.* for *Gyr* before this speech ; Q_3 corrects, so also in III, ii, 110.

36. Q_2 *our ;* Q_3 correctly *ours.*

39. *Prest ;* B. *pressed,* which spoils the sense.

47. Q_2 *True ;* Q_3 *Trie.*

57. Q_2 *Il'd lay ;* Q_3 *Il'e lay.*

129. *Smell the Touchstone ;* so Qq. Co. *Smell o' the,* a correction which appears in an old hand in the Armour copy. It does not seem necessary. B. and B.L. follow Qq.

131. Before *a scurvy* B. inserts *to,* a correction made in the Armour copy in an old hand and accepted by B.L. It does not seem necessary. Co. follows Qq in omitting *to.*

V, ii, 14-15. *Sir Petronel . . . Francis Quicksilver ;* so Q_2 ; Q_3 *Sir Petro . . . Fra. Quick.,* an interesting instance of this edition's trick of abbreviation.

V, iii. B. inserts here and at scene v *The Compter.* I follow B.L. in using the old form *Counter* which occurs in the text, IV, ii, 254. I have added *apart* after *Security.* Previous editors strike out this name and insert *Enter Security* after l. 5. Qq have simply : *Holdfast, Bramble, Security.*

V, iii, 45. Qq have simply *Pri* or *Pris.* before this line. Evidently it belongs to the First Prisoner.

57-59. Qq give both these speeches to *Pris.* 2. I follow B.L. in assigning the first to the First Prisoner.

64. Qq. add *Woolfe* to the stage-direction after this line, but Wolf does not enter till line 80.

88. Q_2 *pat ;* Q_3 *part,* not *port* as B.L. says.

91. I have inserted *Exit* here as it is plain that *Quicksilver* is not on the stage at the close of the scene, and this seems a fit place for his departure. B.L. has here *Exit Bramble ;* which neglects to provide an *Exit* for *Quicksilver.* I would place this *exit* after l. 94, where Qq have only *Exeunt.* B. puts it after l. 102.

102. There is no stage-direction in the Qq after this line, but it is plain that Wolf sends Holdfast away here. To avoid multiplication of stage-directions, I send Sir Petronel off with him. B.L. marks Petronel's *exit* in l. 97.

V, iii, 109. Q_2 *make make,* Q_3 corrects.

V, iv. I follow B.L. in laying the scene at Touchstone's house.

V, iv, 8. Qq *our ;* Co. emends *your*.

V, v, 29–31. B.L. seems to me to give a wrong impression of this speech by pointing *Salute him.* and then inserting the stage-direction. Q_2 has *Salute him I pray, Sir, this ;* Q_3 *Salute him, I pray. Sir, this.* Both Qq have the stage-direction *Enter Quick. Pet. etc.* after the speech. I follow the punctuation of Q_3 and expand the stage-direction to include Security, Wolf, and Golding.

53. With Co. and B. I follow the Q_3 reading *bade* instead of Q_2 *bad.* Judging from the Malone copy Q_2 uses this form to save a space.

70–71. The name of the speaker is wanting before these lines in Qq but they are part of Quicksilver's song.

158. To the stage-direction after this line Qq add *etc.* It is hard to know who else appears here as all the chief characters except Bramble are now on the stage.

212. The Qq place an *Exeunt* after this line and not after the Epilogue, which is not assigned to any one of the *dramatis personae.* Possibly the Epilogue was an after thought, but it is evidently spoken by Quicksilver to whom Reed (*Dodsley,* 1784) assigns it, and the phrase *stay, sir,* shows that *Touchstone* at least is still on the stage. It seems best, with B.L. to place the *Exeunt* after the Epilogue.

THE BALL

INTRODUCTION

The Ball is first mentioned in the office-book of Sir Henry Herbert, Master of the Revels under Charles I. Under the date of November, 18, 1632, there occurs the following entry : *In the play of The Ball, written by Sherley, and acted by the Queens players, ther were divers. personated so naturally, both of lords and others of the court, that I took it ill, and would have forbidden the play, but that Biston* [1] *promiste many things which I found faulte withall, should be left out, and that he would not suffer it to be done by the poett any more, who deserves to be punisht ; and the first that offends in this kind, of poets or players, shall be sure of publique punishment—Variorum Shakespeare,* vol. iii, p. 231. There is an allusion to this intervention of Herbert's in a later play by Shirley, *The Lady of Pleasure* (I, i) 1635, which represents the matter in a somewhat different light. Referring to the ' meetings called the Ball to which repair . . . all your gallants and ladies ', the poet says :

> *There was a play on't,*
> *And had the poet not been bribed to a modest*
> *Expression of your antic gambols in't,*
> *Some darks had been discover'd, and the deeds too :*
> *In time he may repent and make some blush*
> *To see the second part* [2] *danced on the stage.*

During Shirley's stay in Ireland, which appears to have lasted with one brief interval from the spring of 1636 to that of 1640, his publishers,[3] Cooke and Crooke secured the manuscripts of a number of his plays. *The Example, The Gamester, The Duke's Mistress,* and others, which they proceeded to put into print. Apparently this was done without giving the poet an opportunity to supervise the publication, for these plays all lack the dedications which Shirley seems to have been accustomed to prefix to the works which he himself gáve to the press. *The Ball* was one of these plays, and was entered October 24, 1638, in the Stationers' Registers. The wording of the entry seems to me to have a distinct bearing upon the question of the authorship, and I give it here verbatim :

Master Crooke and William Cooke. Entred for their copie under the hands of Master Wykes and Master Rothwell warden a Booke called Phillip Chalbott *Admirall of Ffrance* and *the Ball* by James Shirley.

---

[1] Christopher Beeston, manager of the Queen's Company.
[2] This ' second part ', so far as we know, was never written.
[3] William Cooke was Shirley's regular publisher from 1632 on. After 1636 he usually associated Andrew Crooke with him in the publication of Shirley's plays.

In the following year these publishers issued *The Ball* in quarto form with the following title page :

> The Ball. A Comedy, As it was presented by Her Majesties Servants, at the private House in Drury Lane. Written by George Chapman, and James Shirley, London. Printed by Tho. Cotes, for Andrew Crooke and William Cooke. 1639.

The Ball, as the title-page shows, was produced by the Queen's Company, playing in the private theatre called the Cockpit, or the Phoenix, in Drury Lane. This was the company and the theatre with which Shirley had been connected since he began play-writing in 1625. With a single exception, *The Changes*, produced by the Revels' Company at Salisbury Court, all his plays were performed by this company at this theatre from 1625 till his departure for Ireland in 1636. Nothing further is known of the stage history of *The Ball*. There is no record of its being performed at Court, and it is not mentioned in the list of plays including many of Shirley's best, *The Traitor*, *The Example*, *Hyde Park*, etc., which in 1639 were confirmed by royal order, as the sole property of Beeston's [1] Boys. It is probable, therefore, that it was not taken over by this company. I find no mention of any revival of *The Ball* after the Restoration. It seems to me altogether likely that the play did not outlive its first season on the stage, and was dropped from the repertoire of the Queen's Company never to be revived.

The early disappearance of *The Ball* from the stage is not surprising, for the play has little real merit. Some of its scenes would, no doubt, be amusing enough if cleverly acted, but the play as a whole is a slight thing, inferior to many others of the same type which Shirley and his contemporaries turned out in superabundance. To the student of Elizabethan drama its main interest lies in the assertion of the title-page that it is the joint work of Shirley and Chapman. This statement has provoked numerous expressions of opinion, but with the single exception of Fleay, critics have confined themselves to a statement of their belief and have not attempted to analyse the play or to give any plausible account of the occasion, character, and extent of the supposed collaboration. Gifford, the first editor of Shirley, assigned the largest portion of this play to Chapman (Shirley, *Works*, vol. iii, p. 3), an opinion in which he stands alone, and which seems to me one of the most curious instances extant of editorial ineptitude. Dyce, on the other hand, who completed and published Gifford's work, declared that internal evidence showed *The Ball* to be almost entirely the work of Shirley (*Works*, vol. i, p. xix). Swinburne (*George Chapman*, p. 68) asserts that it is as difficult to discover any trace of Chapman in *The Ball* as of Shirley in *Chabot*. Taken by itself this would appear rather ambiguous, for, as I have shown elsewhere (*Chapman's Tragedies*, p. 633 sqq.) it is comparatively easy to detect in *Chabot* the revising hand of Shirley at work on Chapman's old play. But Swinburne believed *Chabot* to be wholly the work of the elder poet, and

---

[1] Beeston gave up the management of the Queen's Company in 1637 to organize and manage a children's company known as Beeston's Boys. He took over to this new company a number of the Queen's Company's plays. There seems to have been trouble about this and the matter was settled by an order of the King. See Murray, *English Dramatic Companies*, vol. i, p. 368. It is interesting to note that *Chabot* is in this list.

goes on to say : ' *The Ball* is thoroughly in the lightest style of Shirley, and not a bad example of his airily conventional manner '. This has been, in general, the received opinion. Koeppel (*Quellenstudien*, p. 69, *n.*) says that nothing in the play reminds him of Chapman ; Ward (*English Dramatic Literature*, vol. iii, p. 107) that if Chapman gave any assistance to Shirley, it must have been of the slightest description, and Schelling (*Elizabethan Drama*, vol. ii, p. 292) that it is difficult to discover anything of Chapman's in it.

Fleay, on the other hand, insists repeatedly that Chapman's hand is visible in *The Ball*. In his article on the Shirleys (*Anglia*, vol. viii, p. 406) he declares that it is clearly an old play of Chapman's, ' altered, or rather re-written by Shirley '. Referring to the statement in Herbert's Office-book, he goes on to declare his belief that the objectionable bits were expunged and replaced by bits taken from Chapman's play of a much earlier date, and that these insertions are still clearly perceptible in the duplication of names (Stephen, Lionel, and Loveall for Lamount, Travers, and Rainbow) in IV, iii, and V, i. ' In no other part of the play ', he continues, ' can I trace Chapman's hand ; but in the account of the lord's [1] travels in V, i, it is very marked '. These statements are repeated with little or no change in Fleay's *London Stage*, p. 336, and *Biographical Chronicle*, vol. ii, p. 238. It seems strange that so close a student of style and metre as Fleay should have believed it possible to detect Chapman's hand in IV, iii. It may safely be asserted that every metrical test would give the entire scene to Shirley. Fleay seems to me to have been quite misled by the duplication of names. This is an evidence of the revision which we know from Herbert took place, but not at all of collaboration. When Shirley altered the names, Stephen, Lionel, and Loveall, he simply neglected to make the necessary changes in the few cases where these occur in IV, iii, and V, i. As for Freshwater's account of his travels V, i), where the test of metre fails, since the passage is written in prose, I can assert without fear of contradiction that nothing in Chapman's work resembles it so closely as do two scenes of Shirley's, one in *The Gamester* (III, iv) where Young Barnacle reels off his ridiculous budget of news from the New Coranto, and one in *The Witty Fair One* (II, i) where the Tutor gives Sir Nicholas a mock lesson in geography.

The external evidence which connects Chapman's name with *The Ball* is limited to the publisher's statement on the title-page. This is, of course, entitled to a certain amount of consideration, but we must set over against it the statement of Herbert, who was probably quite as well informed as the publishers, that the play was written by Shirley. Moreover the publishers themselves seem to have been of two opinions in the matter, for their entry in the Stationers' Registers (see above, p. 869) ascribes this play as well as *Chabot* to Shirley without mention of Chapman. When we take into account the further fact that in the year following the publication of *The Ball* these same publishers issued one of Shirley's plays, *The Coronation*,[2] with Fletcher's

---

[1] This is a slip of the pen on Fleay's part. It is Freshwater, not Lord Rainbow, who gives an account of his travels in this scene.

[2] Shirley himself reclaimed this play in a list of his pieces appended to *The Cardinal* in *Six New Plays*, 1653, and his vexation at the publishers' mis-statement appears in his declaration that it had been ' falsely ascribed to Jo. Fletcher '. Swinburne speaks of this ascription as ' only exceeded in idiotic monstrosity of speculative impudence by the publisher's attribution of *The London Prodigal* to Shakespeare '.

name on the title-page, we are, I think, entitled to conclude that they were in general either very ill-informed or altogether unscrupulous.

I am inclined, however, to believe that in the case of *The Ball* the publishers were guilty of stupidity rather than of wilful error. It is to be noted that this play was entered in the Stationers' Registers along with *Chabot* as the work of Shirley only, but both *Chabot* and *The Ball* were published as the joint work of Shirley and Chapman. It seems to me that the simplest and most probable solution of the whole matter is that between the entry and the printing of these plays Cooke and Crooke were informed that *Chabot* was, in part, at least, the work of Chapman, and that he should receive credit for it on the title-page of the forthcoming edition. This information I believe they misunderstood as applying to both plays—the entry in the Stationers' Registers seems to show that they were both contained in one MS. volume—and accordingly they did Chapman more than justice by placing his name on the title-pages of both the editions which came out in 1639. All students of Elizabethan drama know that the statement of authorship on the title-page of a play is in itself by no means decisive evidence, and I have already shown that in Chapman's case his name appeared on the title-pages of two [1] plays with which he can in the nature of things have had no connexion whatever. In the case of *The Ball*, where the external evidence in two cases out of three speaks for Shirley to the exclusion of Chapman, and where an explanation for the appearance of Chapman's name on the title-page is so simple, it seems to me that the value of this statement is practically nil.

If we examine the internal evidence, the case against Chapman's collaboration with Shirley in *The Ball* becomes still stronger. In the first place the play closely resembles in theme, treatment, and general style a group of comedies written by Shirley between 1632 and 1635. These plays, *Hyde Park*, 1632, *The Gamester*, 1633, *The Example*, 1634, and *The Lady of Pleasure*, 1635, all deal with contemporary life in England; the scene is laid in London, and the society represented is that the circle immediately below the Court, the society of the well-to-do country gentleman, the rich citizen, and the gay man about town. They all contain a strong dash of topical satire and are full of local colour. *Hyde Park*, for instance, introduces the horse and foot races in that newly opened pleasure-ground of London, and *The Ball* deals with the dancing assemblies [2] which had recently come into fashion. They vary in interest as regards plot, situation, and characterization, but one and all present a vivid and realistic picture of the gay social life of London in the early days of Charles I. It is

---

[1] *Alphonsus Emperor of Germany* and *Revenge for Honour*. See my edition of Chapman's *Tragedies*, pp. 683 and 713.

[2] 'It would seem that there really was about this time a party of ladies and gentlemen who met in private at stated periods for the purpose of amusing themselves with masques, dances, and so forth. Scandalous reports of improper conduct at these assemblies were in circulation [cf. the passage from *The Lady of Pleasure* quoted above, p. 869] and evidently called forth this comedy, the object of which is to repel them. The gilded or golden *Ball*, from which the piece takes its name, was probably worn as an ornament and mark of authority by the presiding beauty. We have here the first rude specimen of what are now termed Subscription Balls'.—Gifford's note, prefixed to his edition of *The Ball* (Shirley, *Works*, vol. iii).

impossible to read *The Ball* in connexion with these plays without arriving at the firm conviction that it is the work of the same hand and of the same period, although, perhaps, the hastiest, slightest, and least memorable of the series.

The characters also are typical Shirley figures. Rainbow is the conventional lord who appears again and again in this group of plays, idle, witty, amorous, but not without a real sense of honour which is kindled into life by the events of the play. He is a blood relation of Lord Bonville in *Hyde Park*, of Lord Fitzavarice in *The Example*, and of Lord A. in *The Lady of Pleasure*. Lamount and Travers represent the pair of suitors who serve as foils and butts in several of Shirley's comedies, like Rider and Venture in *Hyde Park*, and Kickshaw and Scentlove in *The Lady of Pleasure*. Winfield is another character familiar to the reader of Shirley, the frank, hearty lover who endures the caprices of his mistress with good humour and wins her in the end in spite of them ; his nearest relative is, I think, Fairfield in *Hyde Park*. Lucina, among the ladies, is another characteristic Shirley figure, the merry mocking lady who teases half a dozen lovers only to succumb in the end to the one among them whom she really cares for. Like Celestina in *The Lady of Pleasure* she is a rich young widow ; in temper and behaviour she is closely akin to Carol in *Hyde Park*. Two of the minor figures of this play belong to the category of ' humours ', Freshwater, the supposed traveller, and Barker, the satirist. One can hardly avoid the conclusion that the author of *The Ball* had been reading *Every Man out of his Humour* just before he set to work on this play, for Freshwater is evidently suggested by Puntarvolo and Barker by Macilente. This palpable imitation speaks for Shirley rather than Chapman, especially when we note the way in which the ' humours ' are portrayed. In each case we find, instead of the severity and even bitterness of Jonson's satiric presentations, the light and almost playful touch which characterizes the satire of Shirley.

Certain incidents in *The Ball* also find close parallels in Shirley's plays. Thus the situation of Rainbow loved by two ladies and incapable of choosing between them is very like that of Gerard in *The Changes*, a comedy composed in the same year as *The Ball*. Lucina's relation to her suitors is not unlike that of Celestina in *The Lady of Pleasure*—note in each case that at a given signal the suitors rail at their mistress (*Lady of Pleasure*, III, i, and *The Ball*, III, iv). The trick that Carol plays upon her lovers in *Hyde Park* (I, i) in causing each of them to think himself the lucky man reminds one at once of the scene in *The Ball* where Lucina sends three suitors in turn posthaste for a marriage licence. Even in incidents of less importance to the plot a similarity to incidents in other plays of Shirley is often evident. Thus the exposure and kicking of the boastful coward Bostock (IV, i) resembles [1] that of the would-be swaggerer Young Barnacle in *The Gamester* (V, i).

As to the other evidences for which we are accustomed to look in determining the authorship of a doubtful play, similarities of words, phrases, allusions, etc., to the known works of an author, it is not too much to say that every scene of *The Ball* shows signs of Shirley's hand. A sufficient number of these are recorded in the notes that follow, and

---

[1] There is even a verbal similarity between these incidents ; see note on *The Ball*, IV, i, 59.

I have little doubt that they might be largely increased. In fact, it is almost impossible to read a comedy of Shirley's without finding a parallel of one sort or another to *The Ball*.

The versification also bears equally plain witness to Shirley's authorship. The frequency of light and weak endings, for example—see ll. 10, 18, 40, 47, 53 and 74 for a handful of instances in the opening scene —and the heavy enjambements which such endings involve, is a common trick of Shirley's. In general the verse has a lightness and irregularity, not to say licence, and a rhythm in passages of animated conversation which closely approaches that of ordinary speech and betrays only too plainly the approaching dissolution of Elizabethan blank verse. It is quite safe to say that there is not a passage in the whole play which for a moment recalls or suggests either the stately movement of Chapman's serious blank verse, or the easy yet comparatively regular rhythm of his best comic scenes.

There remains, then, not the shadow of a doubt of Shirley's authorship. If, however, we apply the same tests and look for any possible contributions of Chapman, we find, in my opinion, absolutely nothing. I have already shown in my study of *Chabot* that it is a comparatively easy matter to separate the Chapman and Shirley portions of a play in which their work is blended. Were it so blended here, we should have no difficulty in discovering Chapman's work. Chapman's manner is too unlike Shirley's to escape detection. He is, as we have had abundant evidence, fond of repeating himself, and it is in the main through such repetitions and parallels that the anonymous *Sir Giles Goosecap* has been determined as his work. But the scenes in *The Ball* that Fleay ascribes to Chapman (IV, iii and V, i) contain no such parallels. On the other hand, the rhythm alone proclaims them Shirley's—notice the heavy enjambements in IV, iii, 79, 107, 170 and V, i, 195, 203, 221 and 229.

Monsieur Schoell, who has submitted this play to a careful examination comes to the conclusion that situations, characters, and verse, seem to be Shirley's invention and workmanship. No single scene, on the other hand, he holds, can be entirely or even mainly Chapman's. He believes, however, that a few touches here and there betray the hand of the elder dramatist. Among these passages he notes a speech of Bostock's (I, i, 35–8) which reminds him of certain foolish utterances of Poggio and Sir Giles, the repetition of overheard words (I, ii, 89 *ssq.* and elsewhere) as a Chapman trick, the phrase *bury him in a baseviol* (III, i, 70) as a parallel to *May-Day* II, i, 485, and Rainbow's speech [1] IV. i, 169 as showing something of Chapman's spirit. I must confess that all these resemblances seem to me of the slightest, and I doubt whether they would ever have occurred to M. Schoell had he not set himself to discover something in *The Ball* that had at least a faint flavour of Chapman. Even were they more convincing, we would still have to account for the manner in which they came to be where they are. Had Shirley re-written an old Chapman play, as Fleay asserts, there would certainly be more of the original remaining than these few faint and uncertain traces. On the other hand the only possible explanation of Chapman touches in a Shirley play would

---

[1] The speech beginning IV, i, 194 would be an even better example, but ideas of this kind are by no means foreign to Shirley, cf. Julietta's words to Bonville, *Hyde Park*, V, i.

be that Chapman had revised the younger poet's work. And when one considers the disparity of their ages and positions in 1632 such a proceeding is most unlikely. That Chapman, shortly before his death and long years after he had renounced the practice of dramatic composition, should have been asked to revise the work of one of the most successful playwrights of the day is to me quite incredible.

The conclusion of the whole matter is, I think, plain. The external evidence speaks on the whole for Shirley alone rather than with Chapman's assistance. The internal evidence points directly and exclusively to Shirley, the weight of authority of students of Elizabethan drama is against Chapman's having any share in the play, and finally I believe that I have pointed out for the first time the way in which the original blunder of the publishers, which alone connects Chapman's name with this play, came to be made. We may then unhesitatingly dismiss *The Ball* from the Chapman canon, and consider it henceforth as the sole and unaided work of Shirley.

It may be thought that too much time has been devoted to the demonstration of a proposition which in its general outline, at least, is almost self-evident to the student of either Chapman or Shirley. But ascriptions of this sort once made are not easily shaken off. So late as the Mermaid edition of Shirley the editor, Mr. Gosse, remarks (p. xx) of *The Ball* that Shirley ' enjoyed some help in it from the aged Chapman ', and the article on Shirley in the *Dictionary of National Biography* makes the same statement. In my edition of Chapman's tragedies I took some pains to disprove his alleged authorship of *Revenge for Honour*, and, in part, for the same reason that has led me to give so much space to an examination of *The Ball*. If Chapman in his old age had been able to write tragedy in the manner of Beaumont and Fletcher, and comedy so like that of Shirley as to be quite indistinguishable from that poet's work, he would have possessed a versatility of talent, not to say an imitative faculty, which is quite at variance with anything that appears in his undoubted work. It seems to me a pious work once and for all to clear him from the charge of participation either in Glapthorne's sensational melodrama or Shirley's frivolous comedy of London manners.

THE BALL

NOTES

I, i, 10. *My.* Weak endings of this sort are not uncommon in Shirley ; cf II, ii, 73. I do not recall a single instance in Chapman's work.

I, i, 24. *Coats :* used here in the heraldic sense. Marmaduke in the following lines puns on *coat* = coat-card, i.e. one of the suited figures, king, queen, and knave.

I, i, 49. *Knight of the Sun :* cf. the note on *Eastward Ho*, V, i, 29. Shirley refers to the Donsel del Phebo as the flower of chivalry in *The Gamester*, III, ii ; cf. also *Bird in a Cage*, III, ii.

I, i, 118. *To have [five] for one :* cf. Puntarvolo's words : ' I do intend to travel . . . and because I will not altogether go upon expense, I am determined to put forth some five thousand pound to be paid me five for one upon the return of myself and my wife and my dog, from the Turk's court in Constantinople. If all or either of us miscarry in the journey, 'tis gone : if we be successful, why there will be five and twenty thousand pound to entertain time withal '—*Every Man out of his Humour*, II, i. On this passage Gifford has the following note : ' In this age when travelling was hazardous and insecure, it seems to have been no unusual practice to put out money at going abroad, on condition of receiving it back trebled, quadrupled, or, as here, quintupled, on the completion of the expedition. To this there are innumerable allusions in our old writers.' See *Tempest*, III, iii, 48.

In 1617 Moryson (*Itinerary*, p. 198) says that ' this custom of giving out money upon these adventures was first used in court and among noblemen ' and that some years before 1617 ' bankerouts, stage-players, and men ' of base condition had drawn it into contempt ' by undertaking journeys ' merely for gain upon their return.' The difference in social rank between Puntarvolo and Jack Freshwater marks the degradation of this practice.

I, i, 119. *Shotten herring :* a herring that has cast its roe, a worthless thing ; cf. 1 *King Henry IV*, II, iv, 142. Shirley applies this phrase in *The Gamester* (V, i) to the cowardly Young Barnacle.

I, i, 125. *Toothpick . . . statesman :* cf. Sir Politick's reference to the court-fool Stone's use of a tooth-pick, *Volpone*, II, i. See also Shirley's *Grateful Servant*, III, i, and *Constant Maid*, III, ii.

I, i, 126. *Is not his soul Italian ?* The allusion is to the Italian dress and deportment of Freshwater ; cf. below II, i, 100.

I, i, 132. *Salt-cellar.* ' The salt-cellars of our ancestors were both large and high. They were usually placed in the middle of the table, and the bowl which held the salt was supported by ornamented figures, whose awkward and extravagant attitudes are here ridiculed '—Dyce.

I, i, 141. *Chopinos :* more properly spelled ' chopines ' or ' chopins ' (see the *New English Dictionary*). They were shoes raised above the ground by means of a cork sole or the like. They seem to have been in special favour at Venice. Coryate (*Crudities*, p. 261) has a long account of the Venetian ' chopineys of a great height, even half a yard high.' The musical chopins of the text are, of course, an invention of Shirley's.

I, i, 154. *Pantalone :* the Venetian character (the name comes from St.

877

Pantaleone, once a favourite saint in Venice) in Italian comedy. He appears as a lean and foolish old man.

I, i, 174. *A complete gentleman :* cf. Shirley's use of this phrase in *Love in a Maze*, I, i. It is the title of a book on manners by Peacham which appeared in 1622.

I, i, 195. *Bethlem Gabor :* more properly Gabor (Gabriel) Bethlen, a famous Hungarian warrior, a Protestant, and the bitter enemy of the Hapsburgh Emperors. This, of course, gave him a special interest in England at this time. Shirley mentions him at least twice elsewhere, *Opportunity*, I, i, and *Bird in a Cage*, IV, i.

I, ii, 58. *Compositions :* used here in the sense of ' the combination of personal qualities that make any one what he is ' ; see the quotations in the *New English Dictionary*, sub *Composition*, 16 b.

I, ii, 67. *Hairy pent [house] :* the low fringe which concealed part of the lady's forehead.

II, i, 50. *Church-cloth :* the parish shroud.

II, i, 55-6. Cf. the note on *All Fools*, V, ii, 48-51.

II, i, 58. *Coryate :* Thomas Coryate, or Coryat, of Odcombe, Somerset, perhaps the most famous of English travellers in the early part of the seventeenth century. His journal was published in 1611 under the title of *Coryat's Crudities, hastily gobled up in Five Months' Travells in France, etc.* It is an interesting and valuable record, but Coryate's eccentricities brought much ridicule upon himself and his work.

II, i, 62. *Apple-John :* a kind of apple said to taste best when old and withered, but it was also a slang name for a pimp, see *Every Man out of his Humour*, III, i and *Bartholomew Fair*, I, ii.

II, i, 107. See Text Notes, p. 884. The only explanation that occurs to me is that *I ha'* = I have it, implying that the speaker has a plan to secure his money.

II, ii, 15. *Fiddling ladies.* Lucina purposely misunderstands *fiddling*, taking it as equivalent to ' trifling ', ' contemptible.'

Molecatcher : used elsewhere by Shirley as a term of abuse, *The Wedding*, III, ii.

II, ii, 23. *Passage :* a pun on *passage* = a pass, a thrust, and *passage*, a game of dice, in French *passe-dix*.

II, ii, 87. *The fens :* an allusion to the great work of draining the fens in the Eastern Counties, begun in 1630 by a company under the leadership of the Earl of Bedford.

II, ii, 170. *A head . . . of hair, I mean.* The same feeble jest appears in *The Gamester*, III, iii : ' He has a notable head. Of hair, thou mean'st.'

II, ii, 172-3. *Favours . . . bracelets.* It was a common custom at this time for ladies to present their lovers with a bracelet made of a lock of their hair ; see *Every Man out of his Humour*, IV, iv, where Fastidious Brisk boasts of such a gift. I know no other reference than this to a gentleman presenting his mistress with such a favour, and suspect that Lucina is hinting at the effeminacy of Sir Ambrose.

II, ii, 213. *Knights o' the post :* ' a knight of the post . . . a fellow that will swear you anything for twelvepence '—Nash, *Pierce Penniless* (*Works*, vol. i, p. 164) Shirley applies the phrase to informers in *Love Tricks*, I, i.

II, ii, 227. *Addition :* used here in the sense or ' title ', or perhaps ' social distinction.'

II, ii, 238-9. *Came in at the wicket . . . window.* See note on *All Fools*, III, i, 422-3.

II, ii, 244. *Lance-prisado :* ' the meanest officer in a foot-company '—Cotgrave. Lucina wilfully degrades Winfield from a colonel to a lance-prisado.

II, ii, 272. *Ostend.* The famous siege of Ostend lasted over three years from 1601 to 1604. There are innumerable references to it in Elizabethan drama.

II, ii, 278-9. *Siege . . . province.* There is a close parallel to this passage in *The Example*, II, i, where Fitzavarice says of an obdurate lady :

> *Would I had ne'er laid siege to her!*
> *The taking of her province will not be*
> *So much advantage to me as the bare*
> *Removing of my siege will lose me credit.*

II, ii, 296. The line as it stands seems to me almost unintelligible, unless one takes *to bring* in the sense of 'bring to pass', referring to the *something* of l. 295. This does not seem quite satisfactory. For Dyce's emen-· dation see Text Notes, p. 884 .

III, i, 71. *Jack-a-Lent :* the figure of a man set up to be pelted, an old sport during Lent, used figuratively as a butt. Cf.

> *Thou didst stand six weeks the Jack-o'-Lent*
> *For boys to hurl, three throws a penny, at thee.*
>
> *Tale of a Tub,* V, iii.

III, ii, 15. *Your nose is wip'd.* Cf. the note on *May-Day,* V, i, 267.

III, ii, 30. *By-smiles :* stray, accidental smiles.

III, ii, 61-2. *Tales . . . Greeks :* apparently a phrase to denote idle lying tales, like 'old wives' tales ', 'tale of a tub ', 'tale of Robin Hood ', etc.

III, iii, 11. *The breach o' the Bankside :* an allusion to the closing of the brothels in that district.

III, iii, 17–19. *Paul's . . . recover.* Throughout the reign of James I the old church of St. Paul's had been falling into a more and more ruinous condition—*she voids some stone every day.* When Laud became Bishop of London in 1628 he at once began to plan the restoration of his cathedral. The work was entrusted to Inigo Jones and the first stone was laid in 1633.

III, iii, 40–41. *We are famous for dejecting our own countrymen.* With these lines cf. the words of the Tutor to Sir Nicholas : ' It is not in fashion with gentlemen to study their own nation ; you will discover a dull easiness if you admire not, and with admiration prefer not, the weeds of other regions before the most pleasant flowers of your own gardens '—*The Witty Fair One,* II, i.

III, iii, 45. *Your faces with the Dutch.* Dutch portrait painters had long been popular in England. Mytens was appointed the King's painter in 1625, and was succeeded in 1632 by Van Dyck who came to England from Antwerp (see l. 56). Shirley refers to Van Dyck in *The Lady of Pleasure* (II, i) as ' the outlandish man of art . . . the Belgic gentleman.' The following passage in the text (ll. 50–57) refers, I think, to Van Dyck's luxurious habits and his susceptibility to ladies' charms.

III, iii, 53. *Regalos* or ' regalios ', a present, especially a treat of dainty food or drink. The word occurs in this sense in *The Lady of Pleasure,* V, i.

III, iii, 55. *Prunellas :* the finest kind of plums or prunes.

III, iii, 57. *Olla podridas :* a Spanish dish composed of small bits of many kinds of meat and vegetables boiled together.

III, iii, 120. *Box :* i.e. comb of yellow box-wood.

III, iv, 48. *Son o' th' earth :* a base person, *terrae filius.*

III, iv, 79. *Mirth :* in the sense of ' folly, as opposed to *brain.* The passage may well be corrupt. See Text Notes, p. 885.

III, iv, 145. *Tale of a tub :* an old phrase for a ridiculous story, occurring at least as early as More's *Confutation of Tyndale,* 1532. Fleay's idea that there is an allusion here to Jonson's play of this name is absurd.

IV, i, iv. *Carven knights.* I take this to mean knights carved out of wood, hence dull blocks. The word *carven* occurs as early as More's *Heresies,* 1528. Dyce prints *craven,* see Text Notes, p. 885.

IV, i, 30. *Gumm'd taffeta :* a silken stuff stiffened with gum. Such a stuff was very apt to rub or fret ; cf. ' I'll come among you . . . as gum into taffeta, to fret, to fret '—*The Malcontent,* I, i, 22–3, and ' There's no gum within your hearts ; you cannot fret '—*The Lady of Pleasure,* II, ii. The term is applied to Barker because of his fretful temper.

IV, i, 33. *Run o' the ticket :* run into debt ; cf. note on *Sir Giles Goosecap,* IV, ii, 130. Shirley uses the phrase elsewhere, *Bird in a Cage,* I, i, and II, i.

IV, i, 34. *Country-houses :* the garden houses in the suburbs so often denounced by Puritan moralists, see the note on *All Fools*, III, i, 215.

IV, i, 40. *Paddington :* at this time, and for a century or so afterwards, a pleasant little village an hour or two by coach from London.

IV, i, 59. *Let it go round :* the same phrase in the same connexion appears in *The Gamester*, V, i.

IV, i, 74. *Keep the [cornbin shutter]* : guard the shutter, or window, of the cornbin against birds.

IV, i, 77-9. *Shrovetide . . . cock :* alluding to the old Shrove Tuesday sport of setting up a cock for a mark to throw sticks at ; see Strutt, *Sports and Pastimes*, p. 227.

IV, i, 87. *Dorsers :* dossers, paniers carried on the back of a beast.

IV, i, 94. *Coddle :* parboil ; cf. ' Down with your noble blood or . . . I'll have you coddled '—*Philaster*, V, iv, 30.

IV, i, 116. *Otter :* a term of reproach, perhaps because the otter is ' neither fish nor flesh ', 1 *King Henry IV*, III, iii, 144.

IV, i, 131. *Eagles takes no flies : Aquila non capit muscas*, a Latin proverb occurring in Mich. Apostolius l. 144.

IV, i, 178-9. *Cullis thee with a bottom :* beat thee to a jelly with a skein of thread.

IV, i, 190. *Curse by Jack and Tom :* swear at them, using their familiar names of Jack and Tom.

IV, i, 191. *Fish-street :* famous for its taverns, the King's Head, The Boar's Head, the Swan, etc. Lobsters, oysters, and fish of all sorts were to be had here fresh from the sea. Pepys took the Pierces and Knipp to a tavern on Fish Street for a jole of salmon, *Diary*, August 6, 1666.

The Steel-yard, the old head-quarters of the Hansa merchants in London, had a Rhenish wine-house which seems to have been much frequented in Elizabethan times, and even later. It is mentioned by Nash in *Pierce Penniless :* ' Men when they are idle and know not what to do, saith one " Let us go to the Steel-yard and drink Rhenish wine " ', *Works*, vol. i, p. 208. The Writing-master in *Westward Ho* invites his fair scholars to meet him and some young gentlemen there to ' taste of a Dutch bun, and a keg of sturgeon ', Dekker, *Works*, vol. ii, p. 300. It is mentioned again by Shirley in *The Lady of Pleasure*, V, i.

IV, i, 230. *The blades :* the bullies, the predecessors of the Mohocks of later days. Cf. :

> *The list of those that are called blades, that roar*
> *In brothels and break windows, fright the street*
> *At midnight worse than constable, and sometimes*
> *Set upon innocent bell-men.*

> *The Gamester*, I, i.

IV, ii, 85. *Must figaries.* Le Frisk's broken English renders the exact meaning uncertain. *Figary* or *fegary*, a corruption of *vagary*, appears repeatedly in Shirley, *Love Tricks*, II, v, *Bird in a Cage*, III, ii, III, iii, *The Ball*, IV, iii, 112, and has sometimes the sense of ' hurry ' ' bustling about '. If it is a noun here, *must* is Le Frisk corruption of *much*. This is Dyce's understanding, see Text Notes, p. 885. I have allowed the old text to stand with the idea that Le Frisk has turned *figary* into a verb.

IV, iii, 41. *Severation :* i.e. separation, severance. The first quotation given for this word in the *New English Dictionary* occurs in 1649, but there is no reason why it should not have been used earlier. It applies here to the hypothetical separation of Bostock's presumably noble blood from his body.

IV, iii, 64-5. *Aristotle's Problems :* alluding to Book IV of the *Problemata* which deals with matters *quae ad rem Veneream pertinent*.

IV, iii, 119. *Hyde Park.* In the reign of Charles I Hyde Park, which had until that time been a strictly preserved deer-park was thrown open, and at once became a resort for the pleasure-loving public. Shirley's play, *Hyde Park*, speaks of the races that took place there and the crowds that gathered to see them.

Spring Garden : a garden, dating from the reign of James I, attached to the palace of Whitehall. It took its name from a concealed jet of water which sprung up with the pressure of the foot and wetted the unwary bystanders; see *London Past and Present*, vol. iii, p. 293. In 1629 a bowling-green and a new garden-house for the King were constructed here, and it became a very fashionable resort. It is mentioned as such in *Hyde Park*, II, iv.

IV, iii, 120. *The Ball :* see Gifford's note cited in the Introduction, p. 872 above.

V, i, 22. *All countries, etc. :* a paraphrase of the Latin proverb : *Omne solum forti patria est.*

V, i, 52. *Lutetia :* the old Latin name, *Lutetia Parisiorum*, for Paris.

V, i, 59. I have recorded the suggestions of Dyce and Fleay in the Text Notes, p. 886. Neither seems satisfactory, but I have nothing better to offer.

V, i, 62. *Women . . . actors.* No women, as is well known, appeared on the public stage as actors attached to the regular English companies until after the Restoration. The visit of a French company containing actresses to England in the autumn of 1629 provoked great excitement This company gave performances at Blackfriars, the Red Bull, and the Fortune ; see *Variorum Shakespeare*, vol. iii, p. 120 *n.* At the first of these theatres they were, according to a contemporary document (Collier, *English Dramatic Poetry*, vol. ii, p. 23) ' hissed, hooted, and pippin-pelted from the stage '. Prynne's abuse of these French actresses in his *Histriomastix* helped to draw upon him the wrath of the Court. It is not unlikely that the Court and its hangers-on—cf. ll. 63–4—desired to see the French practice established in England, and this wish seems to have been gratified in 1635 when a new theatre was opened in Drury Lane for a French company which, no doubt, contained actresses ; see *Variorum Shakespeare*, vol. ii, p. 122 *n.*

V, i, 80. *A cardinal :* possibly an allusion to Richelieu, a cardinal since 1622. Certainly the words *anger him and he sets all Christendom together by the ears* would have applied well enough to the great cardinal in 1632.

V, i, 94. *Mine host Banks :* probably identical with Banks, the owner of the famous dancing-horse Morocco. As late as 1637 he appears to have been a vintner in Cheapside ; see Halliwell-Phillips, *Memoranda on Love's Labour's Lost*, p. 52.

V, i, 107–8. *Florentines :* properly speaking ' meat-pies ', not *custards. Milan . . . haberdashers :* a play on ' milliners ', originally used to denote traffickers in Milan wares such as gloves, shirts, bands, etc.

V, i, 119. *Catazaners.* The *New English Dictionary* records this instance, but gives no meaning for the word. Dyce suggests ' a corruption of some term for revellers '. I suspect it is rather the corruption of some foreign name for a dance.

V, i, 124. *Piazza . . . Covent Garden :* a reference to Covent Garden Square, laid out from the designs of Inigo Jones *c.* 1631. An ' arcade or piazza ran along the north and east sides '—*London Past and Present*, vol. i, p. 461.

V, i, 144. *The Province :* i.e. the Spanish Netherlands. In September, 1632, the Prince of Orange issued a manifesto urging the Spanish province to declare itself independent and to form an alliance with the United Netherlands. This suggestion was regarded with suspicion in England as tending to an absorption of *The Province* in Holland, already a powerful rival of England in commerce and sea-power.

V, i, 173. *Province.* Dyce reads *problem*, which gives an easier sense, but I believe the text may be defended. ' This word *province* signifies a charge or care of business which he whose business it is committeth to another man '—Hobbes, *Leviathan*, xxii. This definition seems to me to fit the present case exactly, for Rainbow has committed to the ladies a business which was naturally his own, namely the decision as to which of them was *fairest, wisest, sweetest* (see above, I, ii, 154, *ssq.*) and so most fit to be his mistress.

TEXT NOTES

There is but one old edition of *The Ball*, the Quarto of 1639 (Q). Copies of this are found in the British Museum, in the Bodleian, and among Dyce's books at the Albert and Victoria Museum. I have had the advantage of comparing my proof sheets with a copy in the possession of Mr. George Armour of Princeton. So far as I have noted there is no important difference between these copies.

The play was first reprinted in *The Old English Drama*, 1824, where it appears in volume i. It was included in the Gifford-Dyce[1] edition of Shirley, 1833, vol. iii, a modernized edition, marked by many changes of the text, some of them sagacious emendations, others needless alterations introduced with no mark of change. I refer to this edition in the following notes as D.

The Ball was not included in the *Tragedies and Comedies of Chapman*, but appeared in *The Works of Chapman—Plays*. This edition, by R. H. Shepherd, is based upon D, although it occasionally departs from him. I cite it as usual by the symbol S.

The text of *The Ball* is in a most unsatisfactory condition. It abounds in misprints and corruptions, is deficient in stage-directions, and particularly unhappy in its omission of exits and entrances, and in its mis-assignment of speeches. There are also omissions and confusions due to the revision which the play underwent immediately upon its appearance. Notable among these is the substitution of the names Loveall, Stephen, and Lionell for Rainbow, Marmaduke and Ambrose in the last scene of Act IV, and in Act V.

The Quarto prints the whole play as verse. At least it begins every line with a capital letter, although some passages are clearly prose, Rainbow's letter in Act IV, sc. iii., for example. In such cases, I have paid no attention to the original arrangement ; elsewhere when I have altered it to show the metrical form, I have called attention to the fact in a text note.

The Quarto is divided into acts, but not into scenes. I have usually followed D in the scene division, although once or twice I have departed from him.

The text of the present edition is based upon the quarto. I have, as usual, modernized the spelling and punctuation.

All alterations and additions to the text, including stage-directions not found in the original, are included in brackets.

Dramatis Personae. The list of characters is printed under the heading *The Persons of the Comedy* on the reverse of the title-page of Q. The Confectioner mentioned in this list does not appear at all in the play as we now have it ; the character was probably dropped in the revision. The character of Cupid who appears in the Masque in Act V is not named in this list, possibly because it was acted by Le Frisk, see IV, ii, 105 *ssq.*

I, i, 2. D. suppresses the interrogation mark in Q. after *blood*.

17. Q. prints *deserve her ?* as a separate line, and is followed by D. and S. I think, making allowance for the loose versification of Shirley, that it may be scanned as part of the preceding line and have so printed it.

24. After *coats* Q. has a period. D. substitutes a dash. As the speech seems to be interrupted, I have followed D.

35. *Wo'not.* D. alters here and throughout in the play to *will*

not. I have retained the old form wherever it occurs and shall not notice D.'s change hereafter.

39. *Seen.* D. reads *been*, but the change, though plausible, does not seem necessary.

48. Q. *any.* D. emends *my*. The same misprint occurs in the Q. in III, iv, 74.

52. *Imp.* Q. *Nimph.* D. corrects.

55-6. Q. prints *Hast ? . . . commend* as one line, and *Thy judgement* as the next.

65. Q. prints *Your blood* as one line.

---

[1] As Gifford prepared this play for the press, see Dyce's preface in vol. i of the series, the changes for good or bad are probably his. But as I have in my edition of Chapman's *Tragedies* listed this edition of Shirley under Dyce, who prepared the text of Chabot, and who was finally responsible for the whole I use the same symbol, D, in this volume.

74–5. Q. prints *You . . . before* as one line.

78. D. silently transfers this speech to Bostock. Q. gives *Ma.* i.e. Marmaduke as the name of the speaker, and there seems no necessity of a change.

84–6. Q. prints Solomon's speech as two lines, ending *troubled* and *'em.*

89. D. silently transfers Marmaduke's speech to Lamount. This does not seem necessary.

93. *These.* Q. prints as the last word of l. 92.

95. Q. prints *me* as the last word. D. corrects.

96–7. Q. ends these lines with *surgeon* and *blood.*

105. Q. prints *Co.* i.e. *Coronell* as the name of the speaker, and so throughout the play. I follow D. in using *Win* as the prefix.

108–9. *A friend . . . travel.* Q. prints as one line.

110–12. Q. prints as three lines ending, *how I, Catalogue,* and *debts.* Like D. I print as prose.

117. D. inserts *then* after *and.* It does not seem worth while to alter the text merely to regularize the metre of this play.

118. D. inserts *five* after *have* Cf. II, i, 26.

119–20. *Jack . . . yet.* Q. prints as one line.

139. Q. prints *Mon.* i.e. *Monsieur* as the name of the speaker. I use *Le Frisk* throughout the play.

140. D. supplies *'em,* omitted in Q.

149–50. Q. prints as three lines ending *ly, Pia,* and *Strand.*

154. Q. *Platalone;* D. corrects.

168–9. Q. prints as one line. D. inserts *you* after *on,* but this is not necessary.

176–7. *A poor . . . tree.* Q. prints as one line.

187. Q. *Fling:* D. corrects.

197. Here and elsewhere D. alters the reading of the Q., *shanot,* to *shall not.* I keep the old form, and shall not note this change hereafter.

200. Q. prints as three lines, ending *Farewell, Countesse,* and *long.*

201. Q. prints this line as part of the preceding speech. D. assigns it to Lord Rainbow, but it evidently belongs to Bostock, to whom the Colonel has been speaking.

I, ii, 16. D. inserts *it,* wanting in Q.

18–19. *Yes . . . it.* Q. prints as one line.

27. D. inserts *be,* wanting in Q.

30. Q. *understand;* D. *understanding.* It is simpler to suppose that an *s* has dropped off.

58. Q. *composition;* D. corrects.

61–2. *It . . . them.* Q. prints as one line.

67. Q. *pentehrush;* D. corrects.

88. Q. prints as two lines, ending *too't* and *whom you,* and transfers *love* to the beginning of l. 89.

108. For Q. *it in,* D. reads *into* pronouncing the old reading absolutely unintelligible. But *it* refers to Rosamond's smiling upon Lord Rainbow.

132. Q. prints as two lines, ending *upon* and *forme.*

135–6. *This . . . inside.* Q. prints as one line.

144. Q. prints as two lines, ending *leave* and *love me.*

II, i, 28–9. Q. prints as one line. D. divides as here; but perhaps the old lining should be kept.

57. Q. *time,* a common misprint for *tune,* to which D. alters it.

66. D. alters the Q. *and* to *an.* If this is intentional, it seems to me a mistake, as it changes the sense of a perfectly intelligible passage.

67–8. *Fine . . . think.* Q. prints as one line.

69. I have accepted D.'s insertion of *a* before *railing*; but I am not sure that it is necessary.

75–6. *Was . . . you.* Q. prints as one line.

88. Q. prints *Hum, tis he* as a separate line.

93. Q. *A wy, Je ne pas parlee Anglois.* The French in this play is very corrupt. As a rule I follow D.'s corrections; here, however, I reject his change of *pas* to *puis,* and *parlee* to *parler.*

94. D. supplies *Fresh.* as the name of the speaker, which is omitted in Q.

95. Q. *Je ne parle Anglois.* I insert *pas* after *parle.*

97–99. Q. prints Freshwater's speech as four lines, ending *peeces, he?, fashion,* and *morning?*

100–101. Q. omits the name of

Gudgeon as the speaker. D. supplies it.

107. D. omits this line which he thinks has been 'shuffled out of its place'. It certainly seems misplaced here, but I have preferred not to drop it altogether. See my note above, p. 878.

II, ii. I have followed D. in printing the first forty-one lines of this scene as prose. In Q. each line begins with a capital as in verse, but it is impossible to arrange the passage so as to obtain even a broken metrical effect.

D. begins a new scene after l. 7; but this seems wrong, as Scutilla remains on the stage, cf. l. 33.

8. Q. *an* : D. *ah*.

9. Q. *fout*; D. *f—*; S. *foutre*.

11. Q. *Pla it ill*; D. corrects.

31. Q. *deu allei moy moselle*; D. omits the first word and reads *allez, mademoiselle*. S. corrects *deu* to *Dieu*.

32. Q. *for boon*; D. *fort bon*. In Q. the stage-direction *Dance* is printed as if in the speech of Le Frisk.

41. Q. *for boone*; D. *fort bon*.

49. Q. *All a murdu France, fit, fit adiew*; D. *A la mode de France. Vite! vite! vite! adieu*.

51. D. assigns this speech to Lucina; in Q. it is printed as part of Le Frisk's speech.

55. Q. prints as two lines, ending *service* and *it*.

66. D. adds a stage-direction *Retires*; I prefer *Exit* in view of Winfield's re-entry in l. 259.

77. Q. prints *and* as the last word in l. 76.

112. Q. *a mine*, which is followed by D. and S.; but it seems clear that *a* is an abbreviation for *of*.

123-4. Q. ends these lines with *word* and *gone* respectively.

131-3. Q. prints as three lines ending *none, Lamount*, and *for?*

134. Q. omits *Ambrose*; D. restores it.

136-9. I insert the stage-directions in these lines. D. puts *Exit Sol.* after l. 135.

140-2. Q. prints Lucina's speech as two lines, ending *Batchellor* and *sir*.

150. Q. *exceedingly*; D. silently alters to *exceeding*.

172. Q. *looke*, which D. follows,

but it is unintelligible to me. I suggest *lock*, i.e. *lock up*.

178. D. inserts *aside*; I prefer *within*, as Winfield is behind the traverse.

182-7. I follow D. in printing this passage as prose.

242. Q. prints *Travers* as the first word of l. 243.

243. D. inserts *you* after *say*; but it does not seem necessary.

253-9. Q. prints as 9 lines ending *fall, ha, wonder, up, now and, taske, over, play* and *Coronell*.

281-2. Q. prints as one line; I follow D.'s arrangement.

291. Q. *venge*; D. *vengeance*.

296. Q. *to bring*; D. *again*, suggesting that something may have dropped out after *bring*. Cf. note, p. 879.

III, i, 6-7. *And . . . modesty*. Q. prints as one line.

8-9. *You . . . believ'd*. Q. prints as one line.

24-92. With D. I print the rest of this scene as prose.

35. Q. *alkey*; D. *allez*.

43. Q. *plait ill*; D. *plait-il*.

48. Q. *not pardonne moy*; D. *no pardonnez moi*. D.'s change of *not* to *no* is unnecessary.

53. Q. *an*; D. *ah!*

62. Q. *beene*; D. *bien!*

92. Q. *Allei hah boone*; D. *Allez hah! bon!*

III, ii, 8. D. inserts *me* after *pardon*.

23-4. *What . . . my*. Q. prints as one line.

29. D. inserts *I* after *not*.

30. Q. *by smiles*; D. *bye-smiles*.

31-4. I take Winfield's speech as prose. Q. arranges as five lines of verse, ending *to-day, get, dayes, service*, and *morning*.

43. Q. *Patent*; D. corrects.

48-9. *Hum . . . me*. Q. prints as one line.

65. *You coxcombs*. Q. prints as a separate line.

85-6. *'Tis . . . gentlemen*. Q. prints as one line.

87. *Discovery*. Q. prints as first word of l. 88.

93. *And if*. Q. prints as the last words of l. 92.

94. *With language*. Q. prints as the last words of l. 93.

III, iii, 7. Q. *and*; D. *are*. Perhaps we should read *stand*.

8-32. With D. I take this passage as prose.

34. Q. misprints *So,* for *Ro[salind]* as the speaker of the last half of this line ; D. corrects.

35. *Your picture.* Q. prints as the first words of l. 36.

40. *We are famous.* Q. prints as the first words of l. 41.

46. Q. *faces,* an evident misprint, due to *faces* in l. 45. D. corrects.

65. Q. *my* ; D. needlessly alters to *your.*

75. Q. prints *Sol.* as the name of the speaker ; D. corrects.

77–9. D. prints this speech as prose. I follow Q.

81–2. *He's . . . is't.* Q. prints as one line.

90. D. inserts *you* after *love.*

114. Q. prints *Co.,* i.e. *Coronel,* as the name of the speaker. D. corrects.

125. Something has dropped out after this line.

III, iv, 3. Q. *other* ; D. corrects.

4. *Earlier.* Q. prints as the first word of l. 5.

8–9. *They've . . . access.* Q. prints as one line.

10. Q. prints *Bo.,* i.e. *Bostock,* as the name of the speaker of the passage beginning *So, so.* D. alters to *Luc.* Perhaps Bostock was meant to utter the ejaculation, and Q. omitted to print *Luc.* as the speaker of l. 11, which is plainly hers.

23. Q. *shat* ; D. *shoot.* Perhaps we should read *shot.*

31. Q. *she feind* ; D. corrects.

44. Q. *Prorsepnie* ; D. corrects.

53. Q. *Gentlemen,* which D. accepts ; but the speech is plainly addressed to Winfield.

56. Q. *part* ; D. corrects.

70. Q. *shall* ; D. silently alters to *should.*

71. Q. *could* ; D. *should.* I follow Q.

74. Q. *any* ; D. corrects.

79. D. inserts *of which* before *you,* and alters *mirth* to *mouth.* I believe the old reading may be kept ; see note, p. 879.

85. D. inserts *Have e'er* before *done. Have* seems necessary, but *e'er* is only inserted to normalize the metre.

90. Q. *impudent* ; D. *O, impudence.* Another attempt to normalize the metre.

94. Q. *her manners* ; D. *your manners.* The Q. reading is a misprint due to the following *her.*

120. Q. *if* ; D. corrects.

149. Q. *he* ; D. corrects.

153–7. Q. prints as four lines, ending *possible, my, ever,* and *fashion.*

IV, i, 4. Q. *carven* ; D. prints *craven,* although admitting that *carven,* i.e. ' wooden ' may be right.

22. Q. *tis* ; D. *'twas.*

26. Q. separates *myself* into two words, printing *my* as the last word of l. 25.

28. Q. *satinist* ; D. corrects.

29–34. Q. prints as eight lines ending *cause ?, now, taffata, weare, keepe, with, debts,* and *houses.*

57. *So.* Q. prints as the first word of l. 58.

66. *Ay, ay.* Q. prints as part of Barker's speech. D. assigns to *Bos.*

74. *To.* Q. prints as the last word of l. 73.

Q. *corne, beane shatter* ; D. prints *corn, bean shatter,* but owns that he does not understand the passage. My emendation at least makes sense of the passage. Cf. the misprint *shadder* for *shudder* in *Chabot,* I, i, 220, a play printed by the same printer and in the same year as *The Ball.*

117. Q. *minde* ; D. corrects.

131. Q. *Eagles* ; D. silently alters to *eagle.*

135. Q. *taking* ; D. *talking.* I accept this, although possibly the old reading might be defended.

149. D. inserts *For* before *which.*

155–6. Q. prints as three lines, ending *in, affront,* and *blow.* I follow D.'s arrangement.

162–3. *We . . . lord.* Q. prints as one line.

IV, ii, 11–13. Q. ends these lines with the words *tormented, cause* and *power* respectively.

20. Q. *mention* ; D. *invention.*

61–2. *To conquer . . . wishes.* Q. prints as one line.

62–3. *I love . . . mistaken.* Q. prints as one line.

65. Q. *my* ; D. *any.*

72. D. inserts *not* after *does.*

85. Q. *must* ; D. *mush,* for ' much.'

89, 99. Q. *Aller* ; D. *Allez.*

98. Q. *all a more* ; D. corrects.

100. Q. *For boone*; D. *Fort bon!*

101. Q. *mofoy*; D. *ma foi!*

111. Q. *Moun.* D. *mounsieur?*

123-4. Q. *de ban eur*; D. *de bonheur*; S. *de bonne heure.*

133. Q. *gallowne*; D. *gallon.*

IV, iii, 2. Q. *Loveall*; D. *Rainbow.*

6-7. Q. prints as verse ending *thou* and *to.* I follow D. and print as prose.

24. *But friends.* Q. prints as the first words of l. 25.

28-9. Q. prints Lucina's speech as one line.

31. Q. *blood*; D. corrects.

36. Perhaps *strange* should be reckoned as part of l. 35.

41. Q. *severation*; D. *generation.* See note, p. 880.

45-6. *And he . . . company.* Q. prints as one line, transferring *Sweet lady* to the beginning of l. 47.

47. D. inserts *you.*

53. Q. *Loveall*; D. corrects.

54-5. Q. prints Lucina's speech as one line.

56. Q. prints *in fashion* as a separate line.

77. Q. *and*; D. *had.*

79-80. Q. *I wod not buy This flesh now, etc.* D.'s emendation seems to me very happy.

83-4. Q. prints Winfield's speech as one line.

95-6. Q. puts *so* at the beginning of line 96 with no punctuation mark following, Q. likewise sets *soldier,* l. 96, at the beginning of l. 97.

101-2. Q. prints Lucina's speech as one line.

111-2. Q. prints *Yes . . . fagaries* as one line.

116. Q. *Pasties*; D. *Parlies.*

126. Q. *no more wit.* This does not seem to make sense, and I follow D. in deleting *no.*

135. Q. *Christian ? widdow.* The misplaced question mark is equivalent to an exclamation.

148-9. Q. prints Winfield's speech as one line.

159-60. Q. prints Lucina's speech as one line.

169. Q. *But*; D. silently alters to *Out,* which seems unnecessary.

187. D. inserts *Not* before *worse.* This seems unnecessary, as the speech may be an aside.

190. Q. prints *resolution* as the first word of l. 191.

193. Q. *for's*; D. *for us.* A copy in the Bodleian has *for.* In l.ᵗ214 below the same copy has *we as* for *well as.*

200-1. Q. prints Lucina's speech as one line.

201. Q. *gintracke*; D. corrects.

V, i, 1. Q. *Bone forbone.* D. corrects.

6. Q. *Madam*; D. *mesdames.*

14. Q. *servire*; D. corrects.

22. Q. *lost*; D. *to a.*

41. Here and in the following lines Q. has *civill* for *Seville.* This old spelling permits the pun in l. 45.

59. *Martheme.* D. suggests this may be 'a designed blunder for a tragedy on the Massacre of St. *Bartheme* (or Bartholomew) '. This does not seem plausible. Fleay (*Biographical Chronicle,* vol. ii, p. 239) would read *Bartleme* and identifies the play with Jonson's *Bartholomew Fair.* I find these emendations so unsatisfactory that I have preferred to let the old text stand.

89-90. The dashes after *w* and *that* occur in Q., and probably mark omissions due to the revision. So also after *a* in l. 94.

98. Q. *pilgrim*; D. *pilgrimage,* which is unnecessary.

101. Q. *driuk*; D. *drank.*

108. Q. *Permount*; D. *Piemont.*

122. Q. *Pialto*; D. corrects.

125. Q. has a dash after *the.* So also in l. 152.

126. Q. omits *one,* supplied by D., who also inserts *that* before *fell,* l. 127, which seems needless.

133. Q. *Madrill*; D. corrects.

148. Q. *charme*; D. *churn.*

155. Q. *Queene Hive*; D. corrects.

165. Q. *excuser moy*; D. corrects.

173. Possibly we should read *problem* for *province*; but I prefer to let the old text stand, as Shirley often uses *province* in a metaphorical sense. See note, p. 881.

173-5. Q. prints as four lines ending *not, if, devis'd* and *happy.*

179. Q. *notary*; D. corrects.

181. Q. *divide*; D. *decide.*

186. Q. prints as two lines, ending *Lord,* and *favour ?*

190-1. Q. prints as one line.

197. Q. *both these, is*; D. *both : this is.* Perhaps we should read **both these, 'tis.**

209. Q. prints as two lines, ending *solv'd* and *confident*.

217–18. *Say . . . perceive.* Q. prints as one line.

231. Q. *Jewell*; D. *jewels*.

232. In the stage-direction Q. has *Enter Rainebow*, who is already on the stage, and omits the name of *Lucina* who must enter here. D. corrects.

233. Q. *cruells . . . full set*; D. *revels . . . full yet*.

237. *Are.* Q. prints at the end of l. 236.

244. The dash after *my* occurs in Q.

257. Q. *to*; D. *on*.

273. Q. *Envying one*; D. *Endymion*.

282. Q. *Brand*, which D. accepts, but it is a plain misprint for *Brav'd*.

283 and 291. *Moder*, which D. retains. It may have been written to denote Le Frisk's pronunciation, but there is no sign of his jargon elsewhere in Cupid's speeches. S. corrects.

307. For Q. *that* D. needlessly reads *not*.

311. Q. assigns the latter part of this line to *Ro.* i.e. *Rosamund*. But it must be to *Honoria* that Barker speaks. Cf. III, iii, 138–46. D. corrects here and in ll. 314, 318.

318–9. *Ha . . . satyr*, Q. prints as one line.

323–4. Q. prints as three lines ending *beast, pension*, and *ha*. Q. omits *Do*, supplied by D. in l. 323.

337. Q. has *Sir Stephen* and *Sir Lionell* in the stage-direction. Also *Ste.* before ll. 338, 340, and 353. D. corrects.

343. *So desperate.* Q. puts at the close of l. 342.

347. Q. *May it concerne*; D. corrects.

364–8. Q. prints Freshwater's speech as verse, the lines ending *now, mony, night, morning, Ile*, and *reveng'd*. I follow D. in taking it as prose.

369. Q. prints this line as part of Freshwater's speech. D. inserts *Lord R.* as the speaker's name.

370–71. Q. prints Winfield's speech as one line.

SIR GILES GOOSECAP

INTRODUCTION

The anonymous play, *Sir Giles Goosecap*, was entered in the Stationers' Registers, January 10, 1605–6, as follows:

Edward Blounte. Entred for his Copie . . . an Comedie called *Sir Gyles Goosecap* provided that yt be printed accordinge to the Copie whereunto Master Wilson's hand ys at.

It was published in quarto form in 1606 with the following title-page:

Sir Gyles Goosecappe Knight. A Comedie presented by the Chil: of the Chapell. At London: Printed by John Windet for Edward Blunt.

A second quarto [1] appeared in 1636 with the following title-page:

Sir Gyles Goosecappe Knight. a Comedy lately Acted with great applause at the private House in Salisbury Court. Printed for Hugh Perry, and are to be sold by Roger Ball, at the golden Anchor, in the Strand neere Temple barre. 1636.

Neither quarto, it will be noticed, gives the author's name. It is not unlikely that in 1606 there was good reason [2] for this omission. The second publisher, Perry, states in his dedication that the author was dead. This would seem to imply that he knew the author's name, but the statement may rest upon mere hearsay. It seems unlikely that if Perry had really known the dead author's name he would have omitted it from the title-page. It must be frankly confessed that the omission of a name so well known as Chapman's from the title-page of a play published at a time when there seems to have been a considerable demand [3] for his work establishes a presumption against his authorship, but this presumption will not, I believe, hold good in face of the strong internal evidence.

The date of composition can, I believe, be fixed for *Sir Giles Goosecap* within comparatively narrow limits. As it was acted by the

---

[1] To this edition Perry prefixed an elaborate dedication, reprinted in the Text Notes, p. 907 below.

[2] The entry in the Stationers' Registers shows that objection had been raised to the publication of this play, which is only to be permitted if the printer follow a specified, no doubt a censored, copy. The printed play shows plain traces of omissions, but it is possible that the prescribed copy was not exactly followed and the publisher may have wished to preserve the author from any possible unpleasant consequences. Castelain's suggestion that the publication of *Sir Giles* led to a second imprisonment of Chapman and Jonson seems to me quite untenable, see above, p. 836 *n.*

[3] Four of Chapman's comedies appeared in two successive years: *Eastward Ho* and *All Fools* in 1605, *Monsieur D'Olive* and *The Gentleman Usher* in 1606.

Children of the Chapel, it must have been produced before that company took the name of the Children of Her Majesty's Revels (January 30, 1604), probably before the closing of the theatres on account of the plague in May, 1603. The patent reference to Queen Elizabeth in I, i, 140, points to a date before her death, March 24, 1603. On the other hand the reference to the late presence at Court of the ' greatest gallants in France ' (III, i, 48) seems a plain allusion to the famous embassy headed by Biron, September 5–14, 1601. This would fix the *terminus a quo* in the autumn of 1601, so that the play [1] must have been written between that time and the early spring of 1603. Professor Wallace, it is true, asserts positively (*Children of the Chapel*, p. 75 *n*) that it was produced ' *c.* the autumn of 1600 ', but as he has not yet offered any proof of this statement, it seems best for the present to hold to the above dates.

Nothing is known of the stage history of this play beyond the facts furnished by the title-pages of the quartos that it was first produced at Blackfriars by the Children of the Chapel, and revived many years later at Salisbury Court, a theatre opened in 1629. Various companies performed at this theatre. I take it that *Sir Giles Goosecap* was probably produced there by the King's Revels ' Company who occupied this house from 1629 to 1632 and again from 1633 (or 1635, the date is uncertain) to 1636. Shirley wrote *The Changes* for this company in 1632 and it is possible that the revival of a comedy so antiquated as *Sir Giles* must have seemed at that time was due to Shirley's suggestion and ‾to his friendly interest in the older poet. It may be that he brought about a revival [2] of this play in, or about, 1632, as a means of assisting Chapman in the poverty of his later years. The revival, if we can trust the statement of the title-page of Q2, was very successful, but after this date we hear nothing more of the play. It was apparently dropped from the boards and completely forgotten. There is nothing to show that it was revived after the Restoration, and I find no reference to it between Langbaine's brief mention (*English Dramatic Poets*, p. 549) 1691, and Lamb's quotation of a passage from Act I in *Extracts from the Garrick Plays*, 1827. It was not reprinted until 1884, when it was included by Mr. Bullen in the third volume of his *Old English Plays*.

The question of the authorship of *Sir Giles Goosecap* may now, I think, be regarded as definitely settled. Bullen in his Introduction to the reprint, while stating that ' there is no known dramatic writer of that date (1606) to whom it could be assigned with any great degree of probability, was none the less struck with the similarity of certain passages in the serious scenes to the work of Chapman, and attributed this likeness to the study by the unknown author of Chapman's work.

---

[1] If the reference in Dekker's *Satiromastix*, to Lady Furnifall refers to the character in *Sir Giles*, we can fix the date of our play within a few months. *Satiromastix* was registered November 11, 1601, and it would follow that *Sir Giles* was written and staged between September 14 and November 11. But this is not a necessary conclusion since both plays may refer to the same character in real life. See below, p. 893. Dekker's distinct allusion to the chief comic character of this play in his *Wonderful Year* (*Prose Works*, vol. i, p. 116) shows that the play was in existence in the year in which his pamphlet appeared, 1603, but does not help us to fix the date more precisely.

[2] Fleay (*London Stage*, p. 342) dates this revival in the period 1633–36, but he gives no proof of this.

Fleay, who saw the proof-sheets of Bullen's edition, wrote to the *Athenaeum* (June 9, 1883) to suggest that Chapman was himself the author. Bullen reprinted the substance of this letter in a note appended to the play (*Old English Plays*, vol. iii, p. 93) in which he admitted the resemblance between the style of Chapman and parts of *Sir Giles*, but urged that this was more apparent in the serious than in the comic scenes. Apparently he was reluctant to admit Chapman's authorship of the play as a whole. In his *Biographical Chronicle* (vol. ii, p. 322–3) Fleay repeated his assertion of Chapman's authorship ; Ward (*English Dramatic Literature*, vol. ii, p. 412 *n*) noted the views of Bullen and Fleay without venturing on an opinion of his own ; and Kittredge in an article in *The Journal of Germanic Philology* (vol. ii, p. 10 *n*) accepted without discussion the ascription of the play to Chapman.

While preparing an edition of *The Gentleman Usher* for the *Belles-Lettres Series* in 1906, I was struck by several points of close resemblance between this play and *Sir Giles Goosecap*. A careful study of the anonymous comedy convinced me that Chapman was certainly the author of the comic as well as the serious parts, and I published my conclusions in *Modern Philology* (July, 1906) in an article entitled *The Authorship of Sir Giles Goosecap*. The arguments there advanced have never been controverted, and since the appearance of this article Schelling (*Elizabethan Drama*, vol. i, p. 463) and Castelain (*Ben Jonson*, p. 901) have accepted Chapman's authorship without question. M. Schoell in his thesis, *Chapman as Comic Writer*, accepted my conclusions and was able to add further bits of internal evidence. There seems no reason, then, to doubt the authorship of the play, and it will be sufficient to sum up briefly here the evidence upon which Chapman's claim rests.

The evidence which Fleay brought forward was mainly external. The only known authors writing for the Chapel Children *c.* 1601 and dead in 1636 were Marston, Middleton, and Chapman. This play does not in the least resemble anything in the work of either Marston or Middleton, whereas the strong Jonsonian influence which it betrays is readily explained by Chapman's close relations with that author. The internal evidence, says Fleay, is even more decisive ; but this evidence he does not produce except to affirm Chapman's undoubted authorship of such a passage as the speech of Clarence at the beginning of Act II, and to point out the likeness between the scene in which Momford writes a love-letter for Eugenia and a scene in *The Gentleman Usher* (III, ii) and another in *Monsieur D'Olive* (IV, ii).

This evidence, as I have said elsewhere, seems to me suggestive rather than decisive. The real proof of Chapman's authorship lies in the large number of parallels, repetitions, similarities of expression, and analogous situations to his undoubted works which occur in this play. I pointed out enough of these to settle the case in my article in *Modern Philology*. Since then I have noted a few more and M. Schoell has pointed out others. All of these are recorded in the following notes. Here I would only call attention to such striking parallels as those to *All Fools* in the notes on I, iii, 86 and II, i, 302–4, and to *The Gentleman Usher* in I, iv, 190–5 and III, ii, 67. If we bear in mind the fact that neither *All Fools* nor *The Gentleman Usher* was in print when *Sir Giles Goosecap* was written and that they were both written before this play was in print, the hypothesis of imitation becomes impossible, and it seems certain that we have to do with repetitions by one and the same author. And as every reader of Chapman knows, his plays and poems abound, even above what we may expect in an Elizabethan dramatist, with repetitions of words, phrases, similes, ideas, and situations. The character of Sir Giles himself seems to me the elaboration of a ' humour ' that Chapman had already sketched in the figure of La Besha in *An Humourous Day's Mirth*, and was to take up again in Poggio in *The Gentleman Usher*. A common characteristic of Sir Giles and Poggio is the ingenious faculty of misplacing [1] words so as to talk pure non-sense, and it is worth noting that their fellows in each play comment upon this trait. Strozza calls Poggio *Cousin Hysteron Proteron* (*Gentleman Usher*, I, i, 26) and Rudesby remarks to Sir Giles : *I lay my life some crab-fish has bitten thee by the tongue, thou speakest so backward still* (*Sir Giles Goosecap*, III, i, 18–20). In each case the dramatist evidently desired to call attention to this ' humour '.

Probably if we possessed *Sir Giles Goosecap* in its original form we would find a still more striking parallel to *The Gentleman Usher* in the figure of Lady Furnifall. In the first scene of the third act the three knights resolve to attend a supper at Lord Furnifall's to divert them-selves with ' the drinking humour ' of his lady, who, we hear, ' is never in any sociable vein till she be tipsy ' (III, i, 174–5). Now no Lady Furnifall appears in the list of characters prefixed to the play or in the play itself, and at the supper at Lord Furnifall's house (IV, ii) no such ' drinking humour ' is displayed. The scene, on the other hand, is padded out with such an unusual amount of idle talk as to suggest revision. The inference is forced upon us that the character of Lady Furnifall gave such offence at Court that the poet was forced to strike out her part before the publication of the play was permitted. In *The Gentleman Usher*, on the contrary, this ' drinking humour ' is embodied in the person of Cortezza, whose ' humour of the cup ' (III, ii, 280) is portrayed in two scenes (II, i and III, ii). Like Lady Furni-fall Cortezza is affable only in her cups ; in sober moments she is a malignant shrew like her prototype, of whom it is said ' in her sobriety she is mad (i.e. bad-tempered) and fears (i.e. frightens) my good little old Lord out of all proportion '. Further, Lord Furnifall is said to ' make his wife drunk and then dote on her humour most profanely,' (III, i, 178–9) exactly as Poggio boasts that he has made Cortezza ' so drunk that she does nothing but kiss my lord Medice ' and then calls her behaviour ' the best sport that ever was ' (*The Gentleman Usher*, III, ii, 228–31). It seems to me practically certain that this character and a scene or two, which in the first performances of *Sir Giles Goosecap* had tickled the groundlings, were simply transplanted into *The Gentleman Usher*.

Another scene [2] in *Sir Giles Goosecap*, that in which Momford writes a love-letter at Eugenia's dictation (IV, i), seems also to have been worked over for *The Gentleman Usher*.

The line of cleavage between the two parts which compose this play is very distinct. The first, which gives the play its name, deals with the sayings and doings—especially the sayings—of Sir Giles himself, his companions, Rudesby and Foulweather, their kinsmen, Sir Clement

---

[1] Cf. Poggio's speech in *The Gentleman Usher*, V, ii, 71–5, with that of Sir Giles in this play, III, i, 7–12, and 96–106.
[2] See above, p. 755.

Kingcob and Lord Decem Tales, the ladies whom they honour with their attentions, and a trio of pages. We are here in the world of the Comedy of Humours as it had been developed by Jonson. The very names of the characters, Goosecap, Rudesby, and Foulweather, are ',humourous ', a trait wanting in *An Humourous Day's Mirth*, Chapman's first effort in this line, and due, no doubt, to the influence of Jonson. Jonsonian, too, is the stress laid upon dialogue instead of action as a means of revealing character. In *An Humourous Day's Mirth*, the action, although not especially interesting, is elaborate and complicated. In the comic scenes of *Sir Giles* there is nothing that can be called a plot, and a curious absence even of incidents. What little incident appears, as, for example, the luring of the knights on a fool's errand to Barnet, is evidently invented to display character rather than to advance a plot. This is the manner of Jonson as developed to its fullest extent in *Cynthia's Revels*, a play brought out only a year earlier at the same theatre where *Sir Giles Goosecap* was produced. The preliminary description [1] of the chief characters in this part of the play which appears in the pages' dialogue in the first scene is another characteristic device of Jonson's. To Jonson's influence, also, we may attribute whatever of personal satire appears in this play. In one character, that of Lady Furnifall, this element was so noticeable as to call for the intervention of the censor, and I am inclined to agree with Fleay (*Biographical Chronicle*, vol. ii, p. 323) that in the figures of Sir Giles, Rudesby and Foulweather, Chapman is satirizing contemporary personages, well known at the time although undiscoverable [2] now. Little or nothing of this sort appears in Chapman's other plays. As a rule he appears to have shaken off all feeling of personal animosity when he engaged in dramatic composition. The 'ancient [3] comic vein of Eupolis and Cratinus . . . subject to personal application ' was not his chosen field. But in the composition of *Sir Giles Goosecap* he seems to have been more than at any other time of his life under the influence of Jonson, and in the three ' comical satires ' which Jonson produced about this time [4] personal satire is rampant.

This temporary subjection of Chapman to Jonson's influence is, I think, easily accounted for. Chapman had left the Admiral's Company, for whom he had hitherto been writing, some time in 1599 or 1600, and if *Sir Giles* was his first play for the Chapel Children, as seems to be the case, he may well have felt the need of following Jonson's guidance in the preparation of a play for the more refined and critical audience of a private theatre. The coarse buffoonery of *The Blind Beggar* which had delighted the gross public of the Rose was not likely to suit the taste of the gentlemen and courtiers who frequented Blackfriars.

Another influence than that of Jonson's is also perceptible in the comic scenes of this play. The witty mocking pages, Will and Jack, trace their descent from the pages of Lyly's *Endimion*; and the de-

---

[1] Cf. the elaborate descriptions of Hedon, Anaides, etc., in *Cynthia's Revels*, II, i.

[2] Fleay's notion that Drayton is attacked in the person of Sir Giles seems to me altogether unlikely.

[3] *All Fools*, Prologus, ll. 13-15.

[4] *Every Man out of his Humour*, 1599 ; *Cynthia's Revels*, 1600, *The Poetaster*, 1601.

light in word-play, in conceits, in wit-combats, which appears in *Sir Giles*, is also in the last resort traceable to the courtly comedy of Lyly. But little or nothing of Lyly's characteristic style is visible in *Sir Giles*, and I should rather attribute the traces of Lylian influence to the tradition which he established for children's companies than to direct imitation on Chapman's part. The three children, for example, who appear in such entertaining fashion in the *Induction* to *Cynthia's Revels*, show Jonson's acceptance of this tradition, and, indeed, the whole elaborate allegory of that satire of courtly conditions is very plainly a continuation of the work of Lyly. Chapman, it seems to me, followed the first writer of courtly comedy only at a distance and, so to speak, at second hand,[1] His immediate master and guide was Jonson.

The serious scenes of *Sir Giles Goosecap*, on the other hand, show Chapman striking out for himself into a field where he was later to achieve his most striking success as a comic writer. Connected only in the slightest way with the 'humourous' scenes, they constitute a little romantic comedy which, however faintly and falteringly executed, foreshadows in its happy union of sweet seriousness and easy mirth the best scenes of *The Gentleman Usher* and of *Monsieur D'Olive*. In *An Humourous Day's Mirth* Chapman just hinted at the theme of a scholar turned lover. Here he uses it as the leading *motif* of his first attempt at romantic comedy.

As Kittredge [2] has shown, the story of Clarence, Eugenia, and Momford is based upon that of Troilus and Criseide as contained in the first three books of Chaucer's poem of that name. The chief incidents of the play correspond, up to a certain point, almost exactly with those of the old poem : the silent and hopeless love of Clarence, the confession wrung from him by his friend, Momford's offer to intercede with the lady, who here as in Chaucer is the niece of the friendly go-between, his bearing a letter to her, the device by which he forces it upon her, her first reluctance to hear of a lover, her hesitating response to his passion, even the feigned sickness which finally brings her to his arms, all these are found in their due order in *Troilus and Criseide*, and if it were possible for so close a correspondence to be accidental, this possibility disappears when we note the frequency with which Chapman borrows hints for his dialogue from the work of Chaucer. Full proof of this borrowing is contained in Kittredge's article. I need only say here that the dialogue of *Sir Giles Goosecap*, II, i, and IV, i,[3] contains words, phrases, and sometimes whole lines, lifted from Chaucer and skilfully interwoven 'into the fashion of Elizabethan comedy conversation '.

---

[1] Since this Introduction was in type M. Schoell has pointed out to me a source for the comic scenes of *Sir Giles* in *Les Apophtegmes du Sieur Gaulard*, a series of jests added to Etienne Tabourot's *Les Bigarrures du Seigneur des Accords*, 1583-4 ; cf. *Sir Giles*, I, ii, 7 with *Gaulard*, p. 9; I, ii, 33-4 with p. 16; I, iii, 51-5 with pp. 9, 25-6, and so on. Poggio's tale of the 'curtal' (*Gentleman Usher* I, i, 5-10) also occurs here, p. 16. I cite from the Rouen edition of 1640.

[2] *Journal of Germanic Philology*, vol. ii, p. 10.

[3] With these scenes cf. *Troilus and Criseide*, II, 78, *ssq.* and II, 1104 *ssq.* Cf. also *T. and C.* II, 1002, and 1023, *ssq.* for the original of the scene in which Clarence writes to Eugenia. See further Ballman's article *Der Einfluss Chaucers (Anglia*, vol. xxv) for one or two points omitted by Kittredge.

Chapman handles his source even in this early play with the same easy freedom he shows when adapting Terence or Piccolomini to the Elizabethan stage. Naturally he modifies the tragic catastrophe of Chaucer's poem and leaves the lovers united in holy wedlock. This was demanded by the convention of Elizabethan comedy. But he does more than this. He changes the whole tone and temper of the scene in which the lovers are united. His heroine is not trapped into surrender, but stoops of her own will to lift her lover to her. It is interesting, moreover, to note how Chapman catches a hint from his source and expands it into a situation. In *Troilus and Criseide* (II, 1162) Pandarus offers to write at Criseide's dictation a reply to the first love-letter of Troilus. Nothing comes of his proposal; Criseide writes the letter herself and by herself and only gives it him to carry. From this slight hint Chapman has built up a situation which approaches more nearly the realm of genuine high comedy than anything else in the play, the scene (IV, i) in which Momford offers himself as secretary to Eugenia, coolly adds to her dictation words which give quite another sense to the letter, and then half bullies, half wheedles her into signing it. It is a scene instinct with Chaucer's own humour, skilfully transferred from an epic to a dramatic setting.

The greatest liberty, however, which Chapman has taken with his source is in the characterization. Troilus in Chaucer's poem is hardly so much an individual as a type. He is the courtly lover par excellence, young, noble, brave, modest, devoted, generous, and secret. The lover in Chapman's play departs widely from this type. So far as Clarence approaches a type at all, it is the Renaissance ideal of the gentleman that he resembles. Although poor and of mean estate, he is gently bred and 'wealthily furnished with true knowledge' (II, i, 182). He is a scholar, in particular a Platonist (III, ii, 2), a lover of music, and a poet. He does not, like Troilus, fall an easy victim to love, but for a time struggles against it as a passion only too likely to divert him from the true aim of his life, the pursuit of celestial knowledge. It is only when he convinces himself that 'divine Eugenia bears the ocular form of music and of Reason' (III,ii, 7–8) and that his union with her will further rather than retard his progress, that he gives rein to his desires and permits his friend to play the go-between. Chapman's alteration is extremely characteristic of his age; but it is hardly one to provoke much sympathy in ours. We are more apt to be interested in the lover as such than in the scholar turned lover, and while Chapman has avoided the sentimentalities and lacrimose effusions which at times make Troilus an almost repulsive figure to our modern taste, he has fallen into the other extreme. His Clarence is a singularly cold-blooded and ratiocinative lover. If Troilus is at times little better than a morbid sentimentalist, Clarence is too often little short of a scholarly prig.

This alteration in the character of the hero necessarily involved a change in the characters of the heroine and the go-between, Eugenia and Momford. Since the love of Clarence was a sober and temperate passion there was no place in Chapman's scheme for the strong contrast between the high-flown sentiments of Troilus and the frank materialism of his friend and counsellor. As a result the figure of the go-between has been so toned down that, except for his part in the action, Momford would hardly be recognizable as the counterpart of Pandarus. He is a frank and friendly figure, disinterested, high-spirited, and somewhat domineering, but he quite lacks the rich humour, the homely mother-wit, and the ingratiating wiles of his prototype.

The character of Criseide has suffered a still greater change in Chapman's hands. It is not too much to say that Chaucer's heroine is the subtlest, fullest, and most masterly piece of characterization in English literature before Shakespeare. Even Shakespeare's Cressid, that ' sluttish spoil of opportunity ', seems a mere sketch struck off with a few swift, hard strokes, when compared with the full-length portrait, worked up with a thousand delicate and loving touches, of Chaucer's Criseide. In Chapman's hands the figure has undergone a complete transformation. Instead of the gentle medieval lady, living wholly in her emotions and yielding step by step with sweet reluctant amorous delay to the solicitations of her lover, we have an Elizabethan *grande dame*, ' a good learned scholar '—a bit of a blue-stocking, in fact—wholly mistress of herself and her emotions. There is no trace in Chapman of that gradual awakening of passion which makes Chaucer's heroine one of the most interesting of all psychological studies of a woman's heart. On the contrary we see Eugenia at one time scornfully disdaining the proposed match because of the loss of reputation which marriage with a poor gentleman would, in the world's censure, bring upon her, and then, with almost no visible transition, accepting this same poor gentleman as husband on the ground that ' knowledge is the bond, the seal, and crown of their united minds ' (V, ii, 215–6). Eugenia is not without fine and even charming qualities, but one feels that Chapman has rather sought to construct a suitable figure for the plot he had in hand, than to create and embody an ideal of womanhood, or to reproduce to the life a very woman like Criseide.

The reclamation of *Sir Giles Goosecap* for Chapman does not, I think, add greatly to his reputation as a dramatist. Neither in plot nor in characterization does this play approach the level of his best work. The prose dialogue seems to me for the most part notably deficient in his characteristic raciness and vivacity, and the verse, although at times full and high is too often inflated and heavy. But this play has a special interest for all students of Chapman in the picture it presents of the poet himself. Fleay (*Biographical Chronicle*, vol. ii, p. 323) long ago suggested that Clarence probably stood for the poet himself, and this suggestion has been worked out in detail by M. Schoell. There seems to be evidence [1] that at some time in his life Chapman paid suit to a wealthy widow. We know so little of the events of Chapman's life or of the order of their succession that it would be a fruitless task to attempt to connect *Sir Giles Goosecap* with this suit. But quite apart from this no student of Chapman can fail to see in Clarence many characteristic traits of the poet himself. We have only to compare the speeches of Clarence with the poems in which Chapman is speaking *in propria persona* to realize the closeness of this correspondence. In the first long speech of Clarence to Momford, for example (I, iv, 36 *ssq.*) we find a complaint against envy and detraction and a dissatisfaction with the awards of Fortune, notes that constantly recur in Chapman's poems. His first speech in Act II is a little epitome of the philosophic studies of Chapman, and the opening

---

[1] See the Chapman letters in the *Athenaeum*, March 23, 1901.

lines of Act III scene ii show Chapman's special interest in Plato. Chapman's scorn of the world and ' all the pomp she hugs ' is revealed in more than one speech by Clarence—see, for example, III, ii, 40, *ssq.* and V, ii, 124, *ssq.* Chapman's love of paradox shows itself in Clarence's defence of the feminine fashion of painting the face (IV, iii, 41 *ssq.*). Chapman's dualism, his strict separation of mind and matter, and his exaltation of the things of the soul above those of sense appear again and again in Clarence—see, for example, IV, iii, 6–7 and V, ii, 43–50. M. Schoell does not go too far, I think, in saying that the philosophy of Clarence contains in the germ, at least, almost all the tenets of Chapman's later philosophy. And there are other more general characteristics common to the poet and the hero of this play, a sincere love of learning, not untouched at times by the pedantry of the Renaissance, an eager desire to pierce through appearances to abiding reality, and a profound melancholy due in the last resort to a keen sense of the discord between the ideals of a poet-philosopher and the actualities of life. Clarence may not be a conscious portrait of the poet by himself, but no attempt to estimate the character of Chapman can be successful which does not take this figure into account. Along with Chapman's ideal portrait of the Stoic hero in Clermont (*The Revenge of Bussy*) and his personal confession of faith through the mouth of Cato (*Caesar and Pompey*), it constitutes the chief contribution of his plays to our knowledge of the personality that lies behind them.

Such, then, are the claims of *Sir Giles Goosecap* to our consideration. Taken by itself as a comedy the play is a poor thing, certainly unworthy of a place among Elizabethan masterpieces ; but it has a real historical value as connecting Chapman at any earlier date than is commonly supposed with the company for which his best comedies were written, it shows us his failure as a recorder of ' humours ' and the dawn of his success in the higher field of poetic and romantic comedy, and most important of all, it gives us the fullest and truest revelation of the poet himself that is to be found in all his dramatic work. For these reasons, if no others, *Sir Giles Goosecap* seems to me to deserve more careful consideration and sympathetic study than it has yet received from students of Elizabethan drama.

SIR GILES GOOSECAP

NOTES

Title : *Goosecap*, i.e. a booby, a fool. The word seems to have appeared during the Marprelate controversy, and was perhaps coined by Nash. The first quotation given in the *New English Dictionary* is from *Martin's Month's Mind*, 1589. This pamphlet is not certainly the work of Nash, but it belongs to his school, and Nash himself uses the word in *Four Letters Confuted* (*Works*, vol. i, p. 281). It promptly became domesticated in Elizabethan comedy ; I find it in *Englishmen for my Money* (1598), in *Michaelmas Term* (1604), in *The Honest Whore* (1604), and as late as Ford's *Fancies Chaste and Noble*, 1638. Chapman seems to have coined the apt alliteration *Sir Giles Goosecap* which appears elsewhere in his work (*The Gentleman Usher*, II, i, 81). The only other instance of this phrase of which I am aware appears in Dekker's *Wonderful Year*, 1603 (*Prose Works*, vol. i, p. 116), and probably refers to the hero of this play.

I, i, 24. *Provant :* provender, the food which the pages are carrying.

I, i, 34. *Moped monkies.* This is the earliest quotation given in the *New English Dictionary* for *moped* in the sense of ' bewildered '.

I, i, 35. *Frenchified :* see note on *Eastward Ho*, IV, i, 155–6.

I, i, 59–60. *Shower into the laps of ladies :* cf. :

> That the Augean stable
> Of his foul sin would empty in my lap.
> *Bussy D'Ambois*, IV, i, 187–8.

I, i, 60. *Captinado.* This word does not appear in the *New English Dictionary*. It is an anglicized form of the Spanish *capitinazo*, i.e. great captain.

I, i, 64. *Make the cold stones sweat :* cf. :

> I'll make th' inspired thresholds of his court
> Sweat with the weather of my horrid steps.
> *Bussy D'Ambois*, IV, ii, 184–5.

I, i, 66. *Domineer, and reign :* cf. *The Gentleman Usher*, V, i, 110.

I, i, 70. *Lie like a lapwing.* The same phrase is used in *The Revenge of Bussy*, V, v, 41, and there, as here, it is applied to a coward.

I, i, 75–76. *Brush up her silks :* cf. *Eastward Ho*, III, ii, 7.

I, i, 122. *At rovers :* at random. The phrase is from archery ; ' to shoot at rovers ' is to shoot at any chance mark, not at the butt. Cf. *Let not your tongue run at rover*—Heywood, *Proverbs*. pt. II, chap. 5.

I, i, 123. *A Switzer :* a mercenary soldier ; see note on *Revenge of Bussy*, I, i, 277.

I, i, 137. *Noddy :* a game of cards, frequently mentioned in Elizabethan drama. See *A Woman Killed with Kindness*, III, ii, *Hyde Park*, IV, iii and elsewhere.

I, i, 140. *Best scholar of any woman, but one :* the exception, of course, is Queen Elizabeth.

I, i, 154. *Assumpsit :* a legal term denoting a promise to perform some specified action, used here mockingly of Jack's implied promise to prove the lady ' half a maid, half a wife, and half a widow '.

I, i, 180–1. ' Measure the neck with a ribbon, then double the length, and bringing the two ends together, place the middle of it between the teeth. If we find that it is sufficiently long to be carried from the mouth over

the head without difficulty, it is a sign that the person is still a virgin',
an Italian superstition cited by Ellis, *Commentary on Catullus*, p. 339.

I, ii, 33.   *Indite.*   The word occurs twice in Shakespeare, *Romeo and Juliet*,
II, iv, 135 and 2 *King Henry IV*, II, i, 30.   In both these cases, as in the
present instance, it seems an intentional mistake for ' invite '.

I, ii, 80.   *Subtle, as the Pomonian Serpent :*   probably with reference to the
serpent which induced Eve to eat the apple ; ' now the serpent was more
subtle than any beast of the field '—*Genesis*, iii, 1.

I, ii, 118–9.   *In nova, etc.* :   the first line of Ovid's *Metamorphoses*.

I, ii, 120.   *Minceatives :*   mincing, affected people ;   cf. *Poetaster*, IV, i, 40.

I, ii, 121.   *Bisogno :*   cf. the note on *The Widow's Tears*, I, iii, 24.

I, ii, 123.   *Dutch skipper.*   For the behaviour of a Dutch skipper in courtship, see Hans Van Belch in *Northward Ho*.

I, iii, 3–4.   *Frost . . . nipped :*   cf. ' In frost, they say, 'tis good bad blood
be nipped ', John Taylor (*Works*, Spenser Society, p. 247).   This was
apparently an old medical superstition.

I, iii, 16–17.   *Made a lane . . . shot :*   cf. *Bussy D'Ambois*, III, ii, 469
and Chapman's *Iliad*, V, 96.

I, iii, 20.   *Knight o' the post :*   cf. *The Ball*, II, ii, 213, and note *ad loc.*

I, iii, 60.   *Moucheron :*   literally a fly, a gnat, used also for a boy.

I, iii, 82.   *After my hearty commendations :*   a phrase commonly used at the
beginning of a letter (cf. ll. 84–5) ;   see the speech in the form of a letter
in *Soliman and Perseda*, II, ii, 4–5.

I, iii, 86.   *Gudgeon swallowed :*   cf. a similar phrase in *All Fools*, III, i, .94,
and the note *ad loc.*

I, iii, 90.   *Vaunt-couriering device :*   a trick running on in advance, like a van-
or vaunt-courier.

I, iv, 1–55.   The poetry with which this scene opens is eminently characteristic of Chapman in its union of obscurity with real depth of thought.

I, iv, 11.   *Estimative power.*   Chapman is fond of using a phrase of this sort
to denote the human reason ;   cf. *apprehensive powers*, *Poems*, p. 293
and *impassive powers*, *The Gentleman Usher*, IV, iii, 48.

I, iv, 13.   *My whole man :*   cf. *this whole man*, *Bussy D'Ambois*, V, ii, 41
and *his whole man*, *Poems*, p. 148.

I, iv, 14–15.   *Soul . . . infusion :*   cf. *The soul's infusion, immortality,
Poems*, p. 127.

I, iv, 28.   *My bed-fellow.*   It was common at this time for intimate friends
to share one bed, see below III, i, 99–100, and *All Fools*, I, i, 27.   Thus
in *King Henry V*, II, ii, 8, Scroop is spoken of as the King's bed-fellow,
and Aubrey (*Lives*, vol. i, p. 96, edition of 1898) reports that Beaumont
and Fletcher, ' both bachelors, lay together '.

I, iv, 39.   *Resolv'd misdooms :*   obstinate misjudgments.   This is the only
instance of *misdooms* given in the *New English Dictionary*.

I, iv, 43.   *Ill-lunged.*   The same epithet occurs in Chapman's translation
of Hesiod's *Georgics* (*Poems*, p. 216) where he has a foot-note to say that
it renders δυσκέλαδος, *male seu graviter sonans*.

I, iv, 60–64.   Marston seems to have imitated this passage in *The Fawn*,
II, i, 178–9.

I, iv, 67–8.   *Division . . . plain song.*   ' *Division* was a technical term in
music for the running of a simple strain into a great variety of shorter
notes to the same modulation.   The *plain song* was the simple air without
variations '—Bullen.

I, iv, 70–2.   Cf. *The Widow's Tears*, IV, ii, 153–4.

I, iv, 87.   *Leap out of my skin :*   cf. :

> *Never were men so weary of their skins,
> And apt to leap out of themselves.*
> Bussy D'Ambois, I, ii, 42–3.

I, iv, 123.   *Above probability :*   above what could probably be expected.
With the sentiment cf. *Monsieur D'Olive*, III, ii, 11, 23.

I, iv, 126–8.   With this sentiment cf. the Friar's words to Bussy, *Bussy
D'Ambois*, II, ii, 187–9.

I, iv, 127. *Aspire :* in the sense of 'attain', the usual meaning in Chapman; cf. *All Fools*, I, i, 6 ; *Revenge of Bussy*, I, i, 296 ; *Byron's Tragedy*, I, i, 28, and elsewhere.

I, iv, 138. *Upper hands :* higher social position, such as gave ' the upper hand ' or precedence.

Brave men of dirt : men who make a brave show by reason of their landed property, cf. *All Fools*, I, i, 67.

I, iv, 143. *Turn her, and wind her :* cf. *The Gentleman Usher*, III, ii, 372–3.

I, iv, 190–95. With this jesting about *points, hose,* and *heels* cf. *The Gentleman Usher*, I, i, 41–8.

II, i, 1–16. With this speech cf. the opening lines of Chapman's address to M. Harriotts (i.e. George Heriot) *Poems*, p. 53.

II, i, 9. *Eternesse :* a word apparently coined by Chapman. It occurs also in *Byron's Tragedy*, V, iii, 191.

II, i, 11. *The world's soul :* cf. *God, the soul of all the world—The Gentleman Usher*, IV, ii, 143.

II, i, 16. With the stage-direction after this line cf. that after *All Fools*, II, i, 221, also *Mildred sewing* at the beginning of *Eastward Ho*, I, ii.

II, i, 26–7. *With a wet finger :* see the note on *May-Day*, I, i, 314–5, and cf.

> *With a wet finger ye can fet*
> *As much as may easily all this matter ease.*
>
> Heywood, *Proverbs*, pt. II, chap. 9.

II, i, 33. *Sentences :* maxims, cf. *All Fools*, V, ii, 98, and note *ad loc.*

II, i, 38. *Mankindly :* cruelly. The *New English Dictionary* cites only this one instance ; but *mankind,* i.e. cruel, appears in *All Fools*, IV, i, 235 and *The Gentleman Usher*, IV, i, 49.

II, i, 51. *Learning in a woman :* cf. Chapman's praise of female scholarship in *A Good Woman, Poems*, p. 151.

II, i, 75. The stage-direction after this line resembles several others in Chapman. Thus in *All Fools*, II, i, 397 we have *He untrusses and capers* and in *The Widow's Tears*, V, i, 31 *He dances and sings.*

In *May-Day*, IV, i, 18–20, although a stage-direction is wanting in the quarto, it is plain that Quintiliano dances and sings. It seems to me not unlikely that the same actor took the parts of Valerio, Tharsalio, Quintiliano, and Momford, and that in each play an opportunity was given him to do a dancing ' turn '.

II, i, 80. *Dancitive.* The *New English Dictionary* gives this as a nonce-word with the meaning ' inclined to dancing '.

II, i, 82. *Duncitive.* This word does not appear in the *New English Dictionary*. It was probably coined for this occasion to furnish a play on words with *dancitive.*

II, i, 83. *Christmas block :* the Yule log.

II, i, 120. *The crises :* the tokens, the signs, used here of the facial features as appears from the following lines.

II, i, 137–8. *With your virtues . . . in love :* cf. :

> *Methinks my blood*
> *Is taken up to all love with thy virtues.*
>
> *Revenge of Bussy*, V, i, 189–90.

II, i, 141–2. These lines are from Ovid, *Metamorphoses*, I, 322–3, where they are said of Deucalion and Pyrrha. For the text see Text Notes, p. 909.

II, i, 160. *Sensual powers :* the senses, with special reference to their cognizance of earthly things, cf. the same phrase in *Byron's Tragedy*, V, iv, 25, and in *A Hymn to Christ (Poems,* p. 144).

II, i, 161. *Thrust her soul quite from her tribunal :* cf. :

> *We are toss'd out of our human throne*
> *By pied and Protean opinion.*
>
> *Hymn to Christ (Poems,* p. 146).

II, i, 162. *Sedes vacans :* interregnum. *Sedes* is used especially of an episcopal see.

II, i, 165. *Doubled in her singular happiness :* cf. :

> *If once she weds, she's two for one before ;*
> *Single again, she never doubles more.*
>
> *A Good Woman (Poems,* p. 152).

II, i, 170. *A fool's bolt :* part of an old saying going back at least as far as the *Proverbs of Hendyng, c.* 1300. It appears in Heywood : A fool's bolt's soon shot, *Proverbs,* pt. II, chap. 3.

II, i, 181 4. A sentiment that appears frequently in Chapman ; cf. *The Gentleman Usher,* III, ii, 57–65 and *Bussy D'Ambois,* III, ii, 76–8.

II, i, 186. *Coats of honour :* coats of arms, the heraldic insignia of a gentleman, an *armiger.*

II, i, 194. *This circle.* Momford, I fancy, holds up here a piece of gold. If this, he says, is held too close to the eye it obscures the sun from our vision. Were it possible to remove the coin to a distance halfway between us and the sun (*sustain it indifferently betwixt us and it*), it would no longer hide the sun, which would then appear *without check of one beam.*

II, i, 201. *More than done.* Chapman is extremely addicted to the phrase *more than* in connexion with an adjective to express the highest degree of comparison. Numberless instances occur in his work. I cite only *Revenge of Bussy,* IV, i, 101, V, i, 124 ; *Byron's Conspiracy,* I, i, 177, II, i, 60–1 ; and *Monsieur D'Olive,* II, i, 170.

II, i, 211. *Thus low :* i.e. at your feet. Momford bows low as he speaks.

II, i, 215. An adaptation of a line from Horace :

> *Falsus honor juvat et mendax infamia terret.*
>
> *Epistles,* I, xvi, 39.

II, i, 216. Here Momford retires to the back of the stage where Clarence has been waiting since l. 16.

II, i, 236. *A cooling card :* apparently a term from some unknown game of cards. It is applied to anything which checks or cools a person's desire. Thus Euphues ' to the intent that he might bridle the overlashing affections of Philautus, conveyed into his study a certain pamphlet which he termed a cooling card for Philautus, yet generally to be applied to all lovers ', Lyly, *Works,* vol. i, p. 246.

The phrase was very common in the sixteenth and seventeenth centuries. The *New English Dictionary* quotes examples from Holinshed, 1577, down to Dryden, 1678.

II, i, 238–9. *Pages . . . leaves :* cf. a similar pun in *All Fools,* V, ii, 42.

II, i, 241. *Their great pagical index :* the overgrown page, Bullaker.

II, i, 263. *The Family of Love :* see note on *Eastward Ho,* V, ii, 32.

II, i, 284. *Cornish :* referring to the phrase *strike up men's heels,* l. 282. Cornishmen were famous as wrestlers.

II, i, 291. *Put up for concealment :* indicted for the suppression of facts.

II, i, 302–4. A very close parallel to these lines appears in *All Fools,* V, ii, 14–21, where the same talent is attributed to Dariotto.

II, i, 307. *Spanish titillation.* This seems to have been the fashionable scent. Jonson (*Alchemist,* IV, iv) declares :

> *Your Spanish titillation in a glove*
> *The best perfume.*

II, i, 314. *French purls :* The pleats or folds of a ruff or band of the French fashion.

III, i, 48. *Greatest gallants . . . in France :* probably a reference to the embassy of Biron to Queen Elizabeth, September 5–14, 1601. It might possibly refer to a later visit of French noblemen in April, 1602, for which see Nichols, *Progresses of Queen Elizabeth,* vol. iii, p. 577, but the former is the more likely.

III, i, 54–5. *Hold . . . tack :* are a match for.

III, i, 61. *Left-handed François :* spurious Frenchman.

III, i, 62. *Monsieur L'Ambois.* No name resembling this appears in the list of Biron's company given by Stow (*Annals,* p. 795). Perhaps there is a reference to Bussy D'Ambois dead long before this embassy.

III, i, 68. *Pickt-hatch :* a cant word in the time of Elizabeth for a part of London, Turnmill Street, Clerkenwell, inhabited by strumpets. See the note on *Merry Wives of Windsor,* II, ii, 19, in the *Variorum Shakespeare.* The word was derived from the *hatch,* or half-door, in the houses of ill fame being guarded with *picks,* or spikes. Here the word is used figuratively ; a *pickt-hatch compliment* is one proper to such a locality. A close parallel is given in the *New English Dictionary's* quotation from Walkington's *Optic Glass,* 1607 : ' These be your picke-hatch courtesan wits '.

III, i, 71. *Vie it :* see notes on *Monsieur D'Olive,* IV, ii, 251 and *Eastward Ho,* IV, ii, 17.

III, i, 88. A somewnat similar phrase appears in *Monsieur D'Olive,* IV, ii, 249. See also *Englishmen for my Money* (Hazlitt, *Dodsley,* vol. x, p. 550).

III, i, 90. *Sleight.* Note the pun, involved in the old pronunciation, on *sleight* and *slate.*

III, i, 97. *Mastie :* a dialect torm of mastiff. The *New English Dictionary* quotes instances of this form from the middle of the sixtenth century to Wycherly's *Plain Dealer,* 1676.

By commission : cf. *The Gentleman Usher,* I, i, 5–6.

III, i, 101. *Sackerson :* the name of a bear famous in sporting circles *c.* 1600. He is mentioned by Sir John Davies, *Epigrams,* no. 43, and in *Merry Wives of Windsor,* I, i, 307.

III, i, 102. *Loaves.* I do not understand this allusion. Probably Sir Giles is talking nonsense as usual.

III, i, 154. *Viliacos :* from the Italian *vigliacco,* defined by Florio as ' a rascal ', ' a base varlet '. The word occurs repeatedly in Elizabethan drama ; see *2 King Henry VI,* IV, viii, 48, *Every Man out of his Humour,* V, iii, 61, and *Satiromastix,* I, i.

III, i, 169. *Decem Tales :* a legal term. When a full jury did not appear a writ was issued to the sheriff *opponere decem tales,* i.e. to summon ten such jurors as had already been summoned, in order to make up the deficiency.

III, i, 227. *Bacon.* Bullen notes that the reference is probably to a work of Roger Bacon : *Libellus de retardandis senectutis accidentibus, etc.,* published at Oxford, 1590.

III, i, 234. *Elixirs :* used here in the sense of ' quintessences '. This is an earlier instance of this sense than any given in the *New English Dictionary.*

III, i, 260. *Finsbury :* a swampy district to the north of the City of London. Stow (*Survey,* pp. 123, 159) mentions the windmills and ditches ' of which Sir Giles speaks.

III, i, 268. *A pearl in her eye :* see the note on *Humourous Day's Mirth,* sc. viii, l. 225.

III, ii, 4–6. Cf. Chapman's footnote in *Ovid's Banquet* (*Poems,* p. 27).

III, ii, 7. *Ocular :* visible. Cf. a like use in Chapman's *Homer* :

> The scar
> That still remained a mark too ocular.
> *Odyssey,* XXIII, 349.

III, ii, 9. With this line cf. the praise of patience in *The Gentleman Usher,* V, ii, 8–13. In each case we have the conception of a soul present in the body, yet exempt from the ills of the flesh.

III, ii, 14. *In floods of ink.* The same phrase occurs in Chapman's continuation of *Hero and Leander,* VI, 139.

III, ii, 15–17. With these lines cf. the four stanzas headed *Olfactus* in *Ovid's Banquet* (*Poems,* p. 26). In both cases there is the same conception of love as an odorous flame ; cf. also *All Fools,* IV, i, 143–6.

III, ii, 20. *Digested life :* well ordered, harmonious life. Cf. Chapman's use of 'digest' and ' digestion ' elsewhere, *Humourous Day's Mirth,* sc. vii, ll. 210–11 ; *Bussy,* IV, i, 164 ; *Revenge of Bussy,* V, i, 2 ; and *Caesar and Pompey,* II, v, 9. The word is usually contrasted with *Chaos,* here with *Embryon.*

III, ii, 21. *A lifeless Embryon :* cf. *an Embryon that saw never light—Hero and Leander,* III, 302.

III, ii, 27. *Merit clad in ink :* cf. :

Ink
Of which thou mak'st weeds for thy soul to wear.
                Tears of Peace (Poems, p. 115).

III, ii, 35. *A r[e]deless veil :* a very puzzling phrase. The reading of the quarto is *rudeless ;* but no such word is known. Bullen's suggestion *thridless* does not seem acceptable. No such word is known, and ' thread-less ', according to the *New English Dictionary,* does not appear before 1822. I prefer *redeless* in the sense of ' indecipherable ', ' impossible to pierce through '. Dr. Bradley suggests that the word might be *rende-lesse,* i.e. not to be rent, but this too is a word unknown elsewhere.

III, ii, 38. *Stance :* stanza. The same form occurs in Chapman's *Masque,* stage-direction after l. 251.

III, ii, 40. *Bid states :* invite people of high estate.

III, ii, 49. *On the right, perhaps :* in case his wife has the upper hand of him, and so takes the right side instead of the left.

III, ii, 63. *Anti-dame.* No other instance of this word is known. Apparently it was coined by Chapman on the analogy of ' anti-hero ', ' anti-wit ', etc.

III, ii, 67. *Sweet apes :* cf. *In all things his sweet ape—The Gentleman Usher,* IV, iii, 21. This is one of the most evident Chapman repetitions in the play.

III, ii, 89. *At midnight :* at the last hour, in allusion to Clarence's tardy confession of his love.

III, ii, 95-7. With these lines cf. *Troilus* and *Criseide,* II, 1275.

III, ii, 102-3. *Pine . . . box-trees.* A very similar figure to this appears in *Byron's Tragedy,* V, iii, 13-14 ; cf. also *Bussy D'Ambois,* IV, i, 91.

III, ii, 104-6. With the conception and diction of these lines, cf. :

Learning, the soul's actual frame,
Without which 'tis a blank, a smoke-hid flame.
                Tears of Peace (Poems, p. 116).

III, ii, 106. *Elemental smoke :* the smoke, or fog, rising from the earthly element in man, cf. :

Earth's gross and elemental fire.
                Tears of Peace (Poems, p. 123).

III, ii, 107. *Daphnean flower :* the laurel, cf. *the Daphnean laurel—Poems,* p. 12.

III, ii, 113. *Just Deucalion :* cf. II, i, 141-2 above and the note *ad loc.*

IV, i, 1. *Chests :* an old form of ' chess ', used here for the sake of the pun in l. 5.

IV, i, 13. *White son :* cf. *All Fools,* IV, i, 29, and the note *ad. loc.*

IV, i, 16. *Wisest of fifteen :* a proverbial phrase ; *fifteen* is used for a large indefinite number ; cf. *Hickscorner* (p. 6, Farmer's reprint) : ' That is the least thought that they have of fifteen '.

IV, i, 31. *Spanish needle.* Spanish needles were of peculiar excellence and are often referred to in Elizabethan literature, see Nash (*Works,* vol. i, p. 18), Lyly, *Galathea,* III, iii, 12 ; Middleton, *Blurt Master Constable,* II, i, 7, and elsewhere.

IV, i, 44-6. With this sentiment cf. *Bussy D'Ambois,* II, ii, 179-190 and *Ovid's Banquet (Poems,* p. 28).

IV, i, 49. *Tear one's ruffs :* cf. Pistol's threat to Doll Tearsheet, *2 King Henry IV,* II, iv, 144 and Doll's words below, II, iv, 156.

IV, i, 62. *Eat not your meat, etc.* I do not understand the bearing of this *principle.* From the context one would imagine it should read : *Eat your meat, etc.* Bullen suggests reading *hot* for *not,* but this does not seem idiomatic. Possibly the stress should be laid upon *your,* so that the sense would be : Send not your own meat to other men's tables to feed upon it there.

IV, i, 65. *Feres :* companions ; the obsolescent word is used for the sake of the pun with *fares* and *fair.* It occurs elsewhere in Chapman, *Iliad,* XVIII, 383.

IV, i, 70–74. With this incident cf. *Troilus and Criseide* II, 1,154–7.

IV, i, 80. *Bear you on my back* : i.e. as an oppressive burden. The phrase is used for the sake of the pun with *bear it back*, l. 79.

IV, i, 82. *Rooks :* a pun on *rook*, a chess-man, and *rook*, a gull, or fool.

IV, i, 154–5. With Eugenia's answer cf. the reply of Corinna to Ovid, *Ovid's Banquet*, the stanza beginning *Pure love* (*Poems*, p. 34).

IV, i, 205. *Cydippe.* There is another reference to Cydippe in *The Shadow of Night* (*Poems*, p. 16).

IV, ii, 7–11. There is a fairly close parallel to these lines in *Monsieur D'Olive*, III, ii, 2–4.

IV, ii, 24. 'O very rarely do they drop into our familiar tongue.' I take it that Furnifall is repeating the exclamation of the *accomplished gentleman* (l. 21) expressing his surprise at being addressed at the French Court in his own tongue.

IV, ii, 26. *Set me forth :* exhibit, extol, me.

IV, ii, 39. *Good accost :* polite salutation.

IV, ii, 65. *A botts o' that stinking word :* cf. ' a plague on that phrase ', *Monsieur D'Olive*, V, ii, 103.

IV, ii, 77–8. *The bravery of a St. George's day.* The festival of St. George, April 23, was for many years celebrated with great splendour at Windsor and elsewhere, see 1 *King Henry VI*, I, i, 153–4.

IV, ii, 129. *Concatical :* apparently a word of Sir Giles's invention.

IV, ii, 130. *Upon ticket :* on credit, or in the common phrase ' on tick.' The phrase occurs in *The Gull's Hornbook* (Dekker, *Prose Works*, vol. ii, p. 252).

IV, ii, 141. *Cast of Merlins.* A *cast* is a pair ; Chapman uses it of vultures (*Iliad*, XVI, 428) and of eagles (*Odyssey*, XXII, 302). *Merlins* are falcons ; the word is used here for the sake of the pun on Merlin the wizard.

IV, ii, 164. *Beggar knows his dish.* Sir Giles perverts the old proverb : ' I know him as well as the beggar knoweth his bag '—Heywood, *Three Hundred Epigrams*, no. 295. See also *Blind Beggar of Bednal Green*, ll. 748–9.

IV, ii, 167. *Beg me.* Sir Giles misunderstands the phrase and takes offence at the meaning he imputes to it, for which see note on *Widow's Tears*, I, ii, 166.

IV, ii, 168. *In Paul's.* The middle aisle of old St. Paul's was at this time a common resort and meeting-place for idle gentlemen, tradesmen, servants out of place, bullies, etc. This is admirably brought out in *Every Man out of his Humour*, III, i.

IV, ii, 185. *Novations :* apparently used here affectedly in the sense of ' novelties ' or, perhaps ' news-bearers.' Elsewhere in Chapman (*Revenge of Bussy*, III, ii, 68) it has the usual Elizabethan sense of ' revolutions.'

IV, ii, 192. *O' the last :* on the form, cf. *Byron's Conspiracy*, III, ii, 258. *O' the tainters :* on the rack. *Tainter* is an obsolete form for ' tenter ', ' tenter-hook ', cf. *Byron's Tragedy*, V, iii, 57.

IV, ii, 204. *Tits :* young things, used of girls or boys ; cf. *Cynthia's Revels*, *Induction*, l. 116.

IV, ii, 215. *Hold, belly, hold.* This exclamation appears in the mouth of the clown Robin in the later version of *Dr. Faustus* (Brooke's edition, p. 197).

IV, iii, 2. *Common sense :* this term is used by Chapman to denote the inner intelligence as opposed to the five external senses ; see *Revenge of Bussy*, V, i, 43 and *Ovid's Banquet* (*Poems*, p. 26).

IV, iii, 10. *Expansure.* According to the *New English Dictionary* this word is peculiar to Chapman. It occurs in *The Shadow of Night* (*Poems*, p. 5), in *Hero and Leander*, v. 470 and in the *Iliad*, XVII, 317.

IV, iii, 22–3. With the sentiment and diction cf. :

> *Rich fruitful love, that doubling self-estates,*
> *Elixir-like contracts, though separates.*
> *Hero and Leander*, III, 416–7.

IV, iii, 24. *Said like my friend :* a common phrase in Chapman ; cf. *Revenge of Bussy*, V, v, 109 ; *Byron's Conspiracy*, V, i, 46 ; *Gentleman Usher*, IV, iv, 170 ; and *Monsieur D'Olive*, I, i, 184.

IV, iii, 32. *An answerable nice affect :* a scrupulous sentiment, corresponding to, etc. ; *answerable* is construed with l. 33.

IV, iii, 36. *Tromperies :* an obsolete form of ' trumpery ', used here in its original sense of ' deceit ', ' fraud ' ; cf. *King Henry V*, v, ii, 119.

IV, iii, 45. *To shun motion :* to avoid arousing men's passions.

IV, iii, 58–60. The reference is to Samuel Daniel whose acquaintance included nearly all the most cultured noblemen of the day. In his *Complaint of Rosamond*, ll. 148–150, *abator* rhymes with *Nature*.

IV, iii, 63. *Inchastity.* This uncommon form appears again in *The Shadow of Night* (*Poems*, p. 15).

V, i, 13–16. With this conceit cf. Savoy's words, *Byron's Conspiracy*, I, i, 165–9.

V, i, 31. *Cacus :* mentioned elsewhere by Chapman, *Revenge of Bussy*, IV, iv, 51.

V, i, 37–8. *Camel . . . horns :* a familiar reference in Chapman ; see note on *Eastward Ho*, III, ii, 262.

V, i, 42. *Bobbed :* mocked ; *bob*, l. 43 means ' flout ', ' mocking jest.'

V, i, 52–3, 58–59. Phrases like these *the best that ever I saw, heard,* etc., are very common in Chapman ; cf. *All Fools*, III, i, 93, *The Gentleman Usher*, III, ii, 19, *Eastward Ho*, III, ii, 292, and elsewhere.

V, i, 55. *Pantables :* an old form of ' pantofles ', i.e. slippers. It occurs in *All Fools*, V, ii, 224.

V, i, 88. *Strain . . . courtesy*, i.e. act with less than due courtesy, said to excuse his hasty departure ; cf. a like sense in *Romeo and Juliet*, II, iv, 55.

V, i, 98. [*Shepherd's*] *holland :* possibly a reference to the shepherd's smock of *holland* linen.

V, i, 112. *Excellent courtship of all hands :* cf. ' a spirit of courtship of all hands ', *Bussy D'Ambois*, III, ii, 187.

V, i, 138. The idea that the man who is able to rule himself is master of the world is a favourite one with Chapman. It is developed in the figure of Clermont in the *Revenge of Bussy*.

V, i, 150. *Standing lake :* a favourite phrase with Chapman ; cf. *standing lakes* (*Poems*, p. 432), *standing plash* (*Poems*, p. 145), *that toad-pool that stands* (*Bussy D'Ambois*, III, ii, 452), *a dull and standing lake* (*Chabot*, I, i, 196).

V, i, 152. *Prostituted light :* cf. ' the whoredom of this painted light ' (*Poems*, p. 7) and ' the shameless light ' (*Poems*, p. 123).

V, i, 161. *A cipher :* cf. *Bussy D'Ambois*, I, i, 35. In each case the word is used to designate a man of no importance.

V, i, 185. *Implements :* i.e. ' furnishings ', the original sense.

V, ii, 25. The line is from *Ovid, Metamorphoses*, i, 523 ; *medicabilis* is a variant reading of the usual *sanabilis*.

V, ii, 40. *The rational soul :* cf. ' *his reasonable soul* '—*The Gentleman Usher*, IV, iii, 83.

V, ii, 49. *Empress of Reason :* cf. the phrases *Prince of Sense, King of the King of senses, the senses' Emperor*, in *Ovid's Banquet* (*Poems*, pp. 33, 35, 36).

V, ii, 51. *Divinely spoken :* cf. ' *spake most divinely* ', *Byron's Conspiracy*, IV, i, 4.

V, ii, 78–81. *The Queen of P[h]asiaca ;* possibly Tomyris, the name seems to come from the river Phasis, once held to be the boundary between Europe and Asia. I have failed after long search to find the source of the Latin couplet.

V, ii, 95. *A latten candlestick : latten* was a mixed metal resembling brass. The pun on *latten* and *Latin*, seems to have been common, see Dyce's note in his edition of Webster, p. 136.

V, ii, 98. *A reason of the sun :* punning on a ' raisin of the sun ', i.e. a sun-dried grape. For a similar pun see I *King Henry IV*, II, iv, 264–5.

V, ii, 100–102. Cf. above III, ii, 9 and note. For this use of *rarefied* cf. *Poems*, pp. 34 and 146. Cf. also :

> You patrician spirits that refine
> Your flesh to fire.

De Guiana (Poems, p. 57).

For the idea in general of turning flesh to spirit or sense to soul, see *Humourous Day's Mirth*, sc. vii, ll. 213–4 and *The Gentleman Usher*, IV, i, 66

V, ii, 166–7. *Here . . . here:* pointing presumably to her heart and her feet.

V, ii, 194. *Rap:* ravish. Chapman uses the word elsewhere; see *Revenge of Bussy*, II, i, 89; IV. v. 28.

V, ii, 197. Cf. *Troilus and Criseide* iii, 69–70.

V, ii, 207. *Impoisoned form:* cf. the phrase 'empoison'd spring', *Byron's Conspiracy*, Prologue, l. 20, and 'impoison their desires', *Poems*, p. 16.

V, ii, 223. *Give . . . the slip:* evade, slip away from. A like use of the phrase occurs in *Romeo and Juliet*, II, iv, 51.

V, ii, 234–5. *Pass their guard:* 'the teeth being that rampire or pale given us by Nature in that part for restraint and compression of our speech', Chapman's note on ἕρκος ὀδόντων, *Odyssey*, I, 64.

V, ii, 256. *Aspen humours:* cf. 'aspen fear', *Ovid's Banquet—Poems*, p. 28; 'aspen pleasures', *Fragment of Tears of Peace—Poems*, p. 154; and 'aspen soul', *Caesar and Pompey*, I, i, 71.

V, ii, 261. *An artificial cobweb:* cf. 'an artificial web', *Justification of Perseus—Poems*, p. 195.

V, ii, 270–1. *A mote . . . only seen:* cf. 'gilt atoms in the sun appear', *Ovid's Banquet—Poems*, p. 25, and see also *Bussy D'Ambois*, I, i, 55–6.

V, ii, 273. *Passion of death.* The same exclamation occurs in *The Gentleman Usher*, IV, iv, 32 and *Bussy D'Ambois*, I, ii, 150.

V, ii, 277. *A dor:* a scoff, a mocking jest. It usually occurs in such phrases as 'to give (or endure) the dor.' See *Cynthia's Revels*, V, i, for a good illustration of its use.

V, ii, 355. *Pom'roy:* a variety of apple.

V, ii, 387. *Rosemary:* see my note on *The Blind Beggar*, sc. i, l. 308, and Bullen's note on *Blurt Master Constable*, I, i, 110.

TEXT NOTES

Sir Giles Goosecap was first printed, in quarto form, in 1606 by John Windet for Edward Blunt. A second quarto appeared in 1636, published by Hugh Perry who prefixed to it the following dedication:

To the worshipfull Richard Young of Wooley-farme in the County of Berks, Esquire. Worthy Sir. *The many favours, and courtesies, that I have received from you, and your much honor'd father, have put such an obligation upon me, as I have bin long cogitateing how to expresse myselfe by the requitall of some part of them; Now this Play having diverse yeeres since beene thrust into the world to seeke its owne entertainment, without so much as an epistle, or under the shelter of any generous spirit is now almost become worne out of memory: and comming to be press'd to the publique view againe, it having none to speake for it (the Author being dead) I am bold to recommend the same to your Worships protection, I know your studies are more propense to more serious subjects, yet vouchsafe, I beseech you, to recreate yourselfe with this at some vacant time when your leasure will permit you to peruse it, and daigne mee to bee,*

Your Worships bounden Servant,

Hugh Perry.

There are copies of both these quartos in the British Museum, in the Bodleian, in the Boston Public Library and in the Albert and Victoria Museum. This play is not included in *The Comedies and Tragedies of George Chapman*, 1873, nor in Shepherd's edition of Chapman's works. It was not, in fact, reprinted in any form between 1636 and 1884 when Mr. Bullen included it in the third volume of *Old English Plays*. This text is based in the main upon Q_1, but was apparently corrected by Q_2 as it adopts many readings of the later quarto and often agrees with it rather than with the first in spelling. In 1909 Professor Brotanek reprinted in volume xxvi of *Materialien zur Kunde des älteren Englischen Dramas* a copy of Q_1 which is found in the K. and K. Hof-Bibliothek at Vienna. The Introduction and Notes to this play by Professor Brotanek have not yet (June, 1913) appeared. A reprint of the British Museum Q_1 appeared in *Tudor Facsimile Texts*, 1912.

The present edition is founded upon a copy of Q_1 in the Bodleian (Malone 207). I have, however, collated it with a copy of Q_1 in the British Museum and introduced into the text the corrections of the latter. Brotanek's reprint agrees at times with the Bodleian; at times with the Museum. The variations of the quartos are recorded in the following notes; I have not, however, recorded the mere misprints of Q_2. I have, as usual, modernized the spelling and punctuation throughout, and have divided[1] the play into scenes. All modern emendations and stage-directions are included in brackets.

In these notes I have used Qq to denote an agreement of Q_1 and Q_2, B. for Bullen's edition and Bro. for that of Brotanek.

Dramatis Personae. This list appears, without heading, and with certain omissions at the beginning of the play in Qq. The names of the added characters are included in brackets.

---

[1] In Qq no act except the first contains more than one scene. In this act there is no second scene, but *Scaena Tertia* and *Scaena Quarta* appear in their proper places in the text.

I, i, 13. Q_1 *gods*; Q_2 *Cods.* So also in II, i, 36, 41, and 94.

30. Q_1 *your sir*; Q_2 *you sir.*

70. Q_1 *a will*; Q_2 *will.* B. follows Q_2; but there seems no reason for departing from Q_1.

96. Q_1 *comes*; Q_2 *come.* B. follows Q_2.

127. Qq *preprative*, apparently a misprint for *preparative* which B. prints in the text.

134. Q_1 *ye*; Q_2 and B. *you.*

151. Qq place the words *True* to *Parenthesis* in a parenthesis.

187. Q_1 *suppers*; Q_2 and B. *supper.*

I, ii, 33. Qq *La :* I shall not hereafter record this or similar (*Lo :* for *Lord* or *Lordship*) abbreviations.

77–8. Qq *this plaine*; I amend to read *this is plain.*

94. Qq *verb stand*; I follow B. in reading *adverb stand.*

97. Q_1 *construe*; Q_2 and B. *conster.*

125. Qq *Lacquay ? allume le torche.* I emend as in the text.

I, iii, 39. Q_1 *mile*; Q_2 and B. *miles.*

60. Qq *Buffonly Mouchroun.*

85. Qq *Alloun.* B. prints as if this word were a stage-direction.

90. Q_1 *vaunt - Curriing*; Q_2 *vaunt-currying.* I emend *vaunt-couriering.*

I, iv, 2. Qq *spring*; B. misprints *soring.*

17. Before this line Qq repeat *Cla.*

97. Q_1 *world ? Love I*; Q_2 and B. *world, Love ? I*, which is, of course, correct.

112–3. Q_1 *frends sets*; Q_2 and B. *friend sets*, which is the true reading.

113. Q_2 omits *What.* Qq *and nephews.*

115. Qq place the words *as to doe* in parenthesis.

129. Q_1 *buildes*; Q_2 and B. *binds.* The Bodleian Q_1 has *bindes.*

136–7. *Hope well, if she.* This is the reading of Qq B., and Bro. and I have not ventured to change it. Perhaps we might punctuate *hope. Well, if she,* and take the clause *Well* to *dirt* (l. 138) as a conditional one, lacking an expressed conclusion.

141. Q_1 *hortetur*; Q_2 and B. *hortatur*, which is, of course, correct.

142. The Bodleian Qq and B. *rightest*; I follow the Museum Q_1 and Bro. in reading *richest.*

144. Q_1 *through*; Q_2 and B. *thorough.*

148. The Bodleian Q_1 *Where is*; the Museum Q_1 Bro., Q_2 and B. *here is*, which is, of course, correct.

Both Bodleian Qq *for*; the Museum Q_1, Bro., and B. read *from*, which is correct.

159. Both Bodleian Qq and B. *deare*; I follow the Museum Q_1 and Bro. in reading *sweet.*

171. Both Bodleian Qq and B. print *then* after *are.* I follow the reading of the Museum Q_1 and Bro.

194. Qq *Ladies*; B. emends *Ladie.*

205. After this line Q_1 has *Finis. Actus Primis*; Q_2 *Primi.*

II, i, 9. Qq *Eternesses*; B. emends.

13. Q_1 *what is*; Q_2 and B. *what's.*

49. Qq *Inimico*; I emend *inimicos.*

75. The stage-direction after this

line is wanting in the Bodleian Qq, but appears in the Museum Q1, Bro. and B.

78. Both Bodleian Qq *be well*; I follow the Museum Q1 and Bro. in reading *do well*. The repetition of the phrase seems to me to be called for.

79. Both Bodleian Q *tro yee*; the Museum Q1 and Bro. read *tro*.

80. Qq *Lo*; which B. expands to *Lord*, but *lordship* is plainly the word required.

104. Q1 *above*; Q2 *about*.

120. Q1 *Creses*; Q2 corrects *Crises*.

142. Q1 *Dearum*; Q2 and B. *Deorum*. *Dearum* occurs in certain *MSS.* of the *Metamorphoses*, and it is possible that Chapman used a text which contained this reading, as it did the reading *reverentior* instead of the accepted *metuentior*.

148. Qq place the words *how to trial* in parenthesis.

171. Q1 *viritate*; Q2 and B. *veritate*.

197. Q2 and B. omit the second *it* before *would*, reading *us, and it would* which destroys the syntax of the sentence.

200. Q1 *of*; Q2 *so*.

204. Q1 *one*; Q2 *on*. I follow B.'s emendation *on't*.

214. After this line Qq have *exit*, but, as is plain from ll. 216-8, Momford only retires to join Clarence at the back of the stage. They go out together after l. 218.

213-14. Bro. reads *meus* and *meutem* for *mens* and *mentem*. I have not noticed this misprint in any copy of Q1.

255. Here and elsewhere in this scene (ll. 262, 269, 284) Qq read *Cutberd* or *Kutberd* for *Clement*, which I have restored from the *Dramatis Personae*.

297. I have substituted a question mark for the period of Qq after this line. It appears from the next speech that Penelope has asked a question.

III, i, 2-4. I have inserted *Within* before Bullaker's speeches, as he does not appear on the stage in this scene.

15. Here and in l. 60 I have altered the *Sir Moyle* (or *Moile*) of Qq to *Sir Cut*. This is one of the various confusions of names

that appear in this play, due, perhaps, to a revision.

34. Q1 *Gods pretious*; Q2 *Cods precious*.

61. Qq erroneously assign this speech to Foulweather. I follow B.'s emendation.

65-67. Q1 repeats the words from *in* to *your* at the top of the page (sig. E) following that on which they first appear.

68. Q1 *pick-thacht*; Q2 *pickt-hatch*.

74. Bro. reads *ptesence*, a misprint which I have not noted in Q1; Q2 *presence*.

92. Qq omit *would*, which B. supplies.

96. Qq *Wood*. I emend *would't*.

96-7. Qq and B. repeat the words *I'll be sworn*. I omit them as a mere typographical error like that noted ll. 65-7 above.

100. Qq and B. *be*; I emend *by*.

101. Q1 *oremost*; Q2. *foremost*.

117. Q2, followed by B., omits *not*.

131. Qq omit *Cut.*, which is restored by B. In both Qq the preceding word, *Sir*, comes at the end of a line, and *Cut* has evidently dropped out by mistake.

158. Qq and B. read *Cutbert* for *Clement*. See note on II, i, 255 above.

177-9. Qq assign this speech to *King.*, i.e. *Kingcob*, who is not present. I follow Bullen's emendation.

182. Q1 *exceedinly*; Q2 corrects.

186. Q2 omits *if*.

197. Q1 *Bear with*; Q2 *Bear off with*. B. follows Q2, but there seems no reason for departing from Q1.

210. Q1 *not*; Q2 *no I*.

214. Q1 *something*; Q2 and B. *sometimes*.

230. Qq *Remercy*.

257. Q1 *What*; Q2 *Why*.

III, ii. In the stage - direction at the beginning of this scene Qq read *Enter Lorde Momford and Clarence* and then, in a line below, *Clarence Horatio*. Momford probably enters after the other two and remains at the back, as Clarence seems to speak of him as absent, ll. 11-15, 29, 37, etc. He does not take part in the action till l. 62.

III, ii, 9. *Inflam'd;* so Qq. Fleay suggests *infram'd,* but see note, p. 903 above.

11. Q₁ *starre*; Q₂ *state.*

27-8. Q₁ *merrit . . . mourner*; Q₂ distorts into *merry* and *manner.*

29. After *write* Q₂ inserts *our.* This seems to be an alternate reading for *my,* which crept from the margin into the text of Q₂.

35. Qq *rudelesse.* See note, p. 904 above.

38. Q₁ *stauce*; Q₂ *stance.*

53. Q₁ *sit*; Q₂ and B. *est.*

55. Q₁ *objects*; Q₂ and B. *object.*

62. Q₁ *two rule to*; Q₂ *to rule two.*

63. Q₁ *antedame*; Q₂ *antheame.*

IV, i, 52. Here, as in II, i, *Kingcob* is called *Cutbeard* (Q₂ *Cutberd*). See also below, ll. 81, 88, where Q₁ has *Cuthbert.*

75. B. omits *if.*

101-2. Qq print as prose; B. as verse.

140. Q₁ places the stage-direction after this line in the margin opposite ll. 143-4.

165. The Bodleian and Museum Q₁ *marriarge*; Bro. and Q₂ *marriage.*

186. Q₁ *it, but*; Q₂ and B. *in, but,* which seems preferable.

192. Qq *me*; I emend *my.*

234-8. Qq print this speech as prose; B. as verse.

IV, ii, 93. Q₁ *Tha'st*; Q₂ and B. *Tha's.*

100. The Bodleian Q₁ and Bro. *meane haint*; the Museum Q₁ and Q₂ *meane paint.*

112. Q₁ *me*; Q₂ *my.*

118. Qq *S. Cut.* B. *Sir Cut.*

122. Qq and B. misprint *Cud.* for *Rud.* as the speaker's name. I emend.

137. Qq *gray mercy.*

141. Q₁ *cast of*; Q₂ and B. *cast-of.*

157. Qq *cheates*; I emend *cheat's,* for *cheat us.*

163. Qq print *Giles* or *Gyles,* instead of the usual *Goos.* as the speaker's name.

181. Q₁ *ont*; Q₂ and B. correctly *ant,* for *an it.*

220. Qq *porte vous.*

IV, iii. In the stage-direction at the beginning Bro. reads *Enier.* The Museum Q₁ and Q₂ have plainly *Enter.*

IV, iii, 5. Qq and B. print *Mom.*

before this line as the speaker's name, a palpable mistake for *Clar.* I emend.

45. Q₁ *He*; Q₂ correctly *Her.*

46. Q₁ *defect*; Q₂ and B. *defects.*

48. Qq place the words from *which* to *nature* in parenthesis.

53. Qq. *lame*; I emend *lamer,* as the context requires.

58. Qq *poets*; I emend *poet,* as the reference is to one man only, see note, p. 906 above.

73-76. Qq place the question after *errs,* l. 76. B. shifts it to the end of l. 73.

80. Qq *all*; I follow B.'s emendation *add.*

94. Bro. and the Bodleian Q₁ *speske*; the Museum Q₁ and Q₂ *speake.*

V, i, 19. Bro. and the Bodleian Q₁ *uinsmans*; the Museum Q₁ and Q₂ *kinsmans.*

62. Qq. *him*; I emend *'em.*

89. Q₁ *Gods*; Q₂ *Cods.*

98. Qq *shippards*; I emend, with some hesitation *shepherd's.* See note, p. 906. above.

163. Bro. and the Bodleian Q₁ *yon*; the Museum Q₁ and Q₂ *you.*

166. Bro. and the Bodleian Q₁ *konwe*; the Museum Q₁ and Q₂ *know.*

V, ii, 7. Q₁ *ye not*; Q₂ and B. *you not.*

25. Q₁ *nullus*; Q₂ and B. *nullis.*

53. Qq. omit the name of the speaker before this line; B. prints [*Fur. ?*] for *Furnifall,* but the speaker is evidently a servant replying to Momford's call (l. 52). I have emended accordingly, and indicated the entrance of this servant in the stage-direction above.

73. Q₁ *udgment*; Q₂ *judgment.*

79. Qq and B. *Pasiaca.* I emend *Phasiaca,* see note, p. 906 above.

80. Q₁ *Antevenit sortem moribus*; Q₂ and B. *Moribus Antevenit sortem.*

91. Q₁ *marre*; Q₂ correctly *marry.*

92. Q₁ *sine*; Q₂ correctly *fine.*

117. I follow the reading of Qq, but perhaps *yourself* should be repeated before *uphold.*

159. Qq *weend*; B. *weeud,* for *weav'd.*

209. Qq *Clest*; B. suggests *Cleft,* which I have accepted.

224. Q$_1$ *villayne ?*; Q$_2$ and B. *villaynes ?*

249. Qq print *out* as the first word of l. 250; B. corrects.

250. Q$_1$ *nad*; Q$_2$ correctly *and*.

277. Bro. prints *dott*. The word

is blurred in both Qq, but I think in both it is *dorr*.

280-2. Qq print as prose; B. arranges as verse, as in the text.

321. For *Clement* Q$_1$ has *Cutberd*; Q$_2$ *Cuthberd*.

ADDENDUM.—V, ii., 78-81.   Professor Cook of Yale, who has kindly furnished me with a note on this passage, holds that the reference is to Medea whom Ovid calls *Phasias* and *Phasis*.   The distich itself he takes to be a Renaissance production.   In this latter opinion I concur, but I cannot believe that a Renaissance writer would either describe Medea as *most chaste* or speak of her in the eulogistic terms of the distich.   The source and reference of these lines seem to me still an unsolved problem.